INTERNATIONAL HANDBOOK
OF CHILD CARE POLICIES
AND PROGRAMS

International Handbook of Child Care Policies and Programs

EDITED BY

Moncrieff Cochran

GREENWOOD
PRESS

Westport, Connecticut
London

Library of Congress Cataloging-in-Publication Data

International handbook of child care policies and programs / edited by
  Moncrieff Cochran.
    p. cm.
  Includes bibliographical references (p.   ) and index.
  ISBN 0–313–26866–5 (alk. paper)
    1. Child care—Government policy. 2. Child care services—
Government policy. I. Cochran, Moncrieff.
HQ778.5.I58   1993
362.7—dc20   92–25746

British Library Cataloguing in Publication Data is available.

Library of Congress Catalog Card Number: 92–25746
ISBN: 0–313–26866–5

First published in 1993

Greenwood Press, 88 Post Road West, Westport, CT 06881
An imprint of Greenwood Publishing Group, Inc.

Printed in the United States of America

The paper used in this book complies with the
Permanent Paper Standard issued by the National
Information Standards Organization (Z39.48–1984).

10 9 8 7 6 5 4 3 2 1

To Eva

whose love for child care across cultures—both public and private—has inspired my work on this book.

CONTENTS

ACKNOWLEDGMENTS

Pulling this handbook together was turned into a labor of love by a wonderful group of contributing authors. Thank you for your colleagueship and your kindness. Lars Gunnarsson played a special role: recommending contributors, reading proposal drafts and chapter guidelines, and maintaining a sense of proportion. Tack så hemskt mycket, min vän. Alan Pence and Cassie Landers were also very helpful. Willem van der Eycken and his colleagues at the Bernard van Leer Foundation, at The Hague in the Netherlands, provided a good deal of assistance in the process of identifying potential contributors. The Consultative Group on Early Childhood Care and Development was also very helpful in that regard and assisted in the initial effort to develop a conceptual framework for the case studies.

Primary support for this book was provided by the Ford Foundation, where Shelby Miller was more than "just a Program Officer." The Swedish Ministry of Health and Welfare and the Swedish National Board of Health and Welfare provided much needed additional funding. The following organizations at Göteborgs Universitet were generous with their support and assistance: the Department of Education and Educational Research, the Early Childhood Research and Development Center, and the Study Program Committee for Nursery and Infant Education. Appreciation is also expressed to the Child Care Initiatives Fund of the Department of Health and Welfare, Canada, for its financial contribution.

Generous financial assistance has also been received from the following organizations at Cornell University: the Center for International Studies, the Institute for African Studies, the South Asia Program, the Latin American Studies Program, the Western Societies Program, and the College of Human Ecology. Appreciation is also expressed to regional offices of Unicef and to those organizations in participating countries that assisted with author expenses.

In the end it was Sandy Rightmyer who sent the facsimiles and cables, word processed the entire manuscript at least three times, and picked me up when I was down. For that she deserves an honorary doctorate. Thank you, Dr. Rightmyer.

INTERNATIONAL HANDBOOK
OF CHILD CARE POLICIES
AND PROGRAMS

---- **1** ----

INTRODUCTION

Moncrieff Cochran

The second half of the 20th century has been marked by a world-wide transformation in child care practices, a change brought about by forces ranging from labor shortages and falling birth rates to poverty, liberation movements, and externally imposed ideologies. These forces have led to profound alterations in family form and in the roles of women. With these changes have come new definitions of the relationship between the private and the public, between family and state. These definitions are often translated into public policies, which are expressed in local communities as child care programs. The primary purpose of this handbook is to provide the reader with easy access to reference material related to these policies and programs, and to the social changes that they reflect. The most useful way to learn more about the public face of child care is in the context of a particular country. That way child care practices can be understood as evolving processes, intimately tied to that unique combination of broader cultural, historical, political, economic, and social dynamics that defines the given society. This handbook is organized to reflect these cultural realities: chapters on 29 countries are included and are almost always written by natives of those lands. For the first time readers have available in a single volume comprehensive overviews of public policies and programs in Africa, Asia, Latin America, and Oceania, as well as in Europe and North America. Each chapter contains a description of existing policies and programs, presented against a particular historical, cultural, and ideological backdrop. The authors relate child care policies to other work and family policies in each country, showing how public involvement in child care is linked to more comprehensive policy goals. In this way, and through the use of "strengths and shortcomings" critiques, the writers are able to convey the processes of change that give life to their societies.

Although its primary purpose is to serve as a library resource, *The International Handbook of Child Care Policies and Programs* was conceived to provide a research-based cross national comparison. In developing a conceptual framework for the case studies from which the chapters derive, I began three years ago with an interest in those differences in patterns of thought, speech, and action that distinguish cultures, assuming based on my earlier crosscultural child care research that such cultural differences would make an important contribution to the shape of policies and programs in every society. The few previous international efforts to provide systematic documentation of public child care policies and programs had done little to illuminate the cultural dimension. These efforts, while ground breaking in their time, contained several limitations we have sought to avoid. For example, the International Study Group for Early Child Care, established in 1969, produced extensive monographs during the 1970s addressing child care policies and programs in nine Western, industrialized countries, providing rich cultural and political context but no crossnational comparison.[1] This lack of comparative perspective was addressed by the work of Sheila Kamerman and Alfred Kahn, first in 1979 with an introductory examination of family policy in 14 societies, and then in 1981 with a much more intensive comparative analysis of policies and programs in six countries, again all Western and highly industrialized.[2] In this more in-depth comparison the authors stressed that policies and programs in a particular country are the result of a unique combination of traditions, history, politics, and economic and demographic circumstances, and that they develop and change. But Kamerman and Kahn were most interested in convergent patterns of relationships between the imperatives of birth rate and labor supply as stimuli and public child care as a response. The significance of culturally prescribed beliefs as explanations for policy and program choices went unaddressed, perhaps because such beliefs result in divergent rather than convergent trends.

The possibility of divergence is also enhanced when the societies studied are built on clearly different cultural traditions. The Kamerman and Kahn choices all derived from a European base. This reduced the range of possible differences in cultural value system, and thus the potential for documenting the impacts of those differences. Two volumes have been published recently that begin to broaden the cultural base. One, edited by Patricia Olmstead and David Weikart (1989), presents 14 national profiles, six of which are Asian (4) or African (2). These profiles are the first step in Phase One of a very ambitious project aimed at assessing the quality of children's experiences in the different national settings and the effects of those experiences on child development. Very little crosscultural comparison is attempted in this initial compendium of profiles.

The second recent treatment (1992) of crossnational child care is a collection of 12 analytical case studies, which are drawn from five of the six continents and which have been carried out during the same time period as those forming the basis for the present volume. Edited by a pair of Americans (Michael Lamb and Kathleen Sternberg) and a pair of Swedes (Philip Hwang and Anders Broberg), this too is a book designed to guide the conduct of and analysis carried out in a larger study, the Study of Early Child Care, sponsored by the U.S. National Institute of Child Health and Human Development (NICHD). The national chapters and associated commentaries are designed to place non-parental child care in a social and cultural context, and to make "cautious and informed" comparisons. The volume begins to fill the "cultural gap" in the Kamerman and Kahn work noted earlier, providing refreshing insights from several sociocultural perspectives, in part by giving heavier weight to traditional child care practices than have earlier authors. This understanding of culture is manifested in the identification of four dimensions of crosscultural variation that accord nicely with some of those introduced at the conclusion of this chapter and elaborated on in Chapter 31.

OTHER WAYS TO USE THE REFERENCE MATERIALS

The alphabetical presentation of countries in the handbook does not clearly show the overriding crossnational themes. Although the alphabetical system was chosen for ease of reference, the reader is also encouraged to consider the chapters by geographic region (Asia, Eastern Europe, Latin America, North America, Scandinavia, Western Europe) for an appreciation of the similarities in policy and program that have resulted from commonalities in cultural history, language, and physical proximity.

Some readers will be especially interested in questions of child care policy or programs that transcend national and regional boundaries. For example, how do the child care needs of rural families differ from those of families living in urban areas? Are there ways that child care policies can be designed to combat severe poverty? Has day care provision been used as a strategy for job creation? What sorts of administrative structures work best for national day care or early childhood service systems, and to what extent should such structures be decentralized? What role has religion played in public child care? How is child care related to primary schooling? What impact has Friedrich Froebel, Maria Montessori, or Jean Piaget had on the international child care arena? Are there cost-effective ways of providing field-based training of high quality to caregivers? Do home-based day care models exist, and what are their advantages and disadvantages? These questions address just nine of the more than 60 crossnational themes uncovered by my analysis of the 29 national chapters contained in this handbook. In order to provide ease of access to interested readers I have organized the book's index around the subjects to which such questions are addressed. For instance, under "decentralization" are page numbers for more than a dozen discussions of issues related to the decentralization of decisions about program content and delivery; "Froebel" provides all the references to his pervasive influence on preschool pedagogy; and under "home-based care" the reader can find where most of the different authors have described day care programs that are designed with residential family dwellings as the starting point. The reader is urged to spend some time examining the index in order to get a picture of the range of child care related themes addressed by the volume as a whole.

Two other sets of reference materials complement what is provided in individual chapters. Maternity and parental leave policies are of particular interest because of their impact on the need for extra-familial infant care. Those policies are summarized for each country in Appendix 1. Certain kinds of demographic information are particularly helpful for understanding the social and economic context within which child care policies and programs are developed. Appendix 2 provides information for each country about the number of children under age five, the infant mortality rate, the total fertility rate, the urban/rural distribution of children, and the total percentage of women with young children in the work force. Although some of these data are also presented in individual chapters, crossnational comparison is facilitated considerably by bringing them together in a single location.

THE PARAMETERS OF CHILD CARE POLICIES AND PROGRAMS

One major consideration is how to define "child care policies and programs" for the purposes of comparison. My original idea had been to focus on those public policies and child care programs that exist as supplements or complements to the child-rearing activities of parents in order to make it possible for parents to be employed or for children to develop according to standards approved by society. The term "public" simply distinguished this care from that provided by parents in the privacy of their own homes. But public care is not necessarily provided by government; it includes day care delivered by non-governmental agencies, and in the private sector in both centers and family day care homes, as long as that care is regulated in any way by the public sector. However, it soon became clear from case study materials that this "public child care" must also encompass more than simply "day care"; it needed to include those early childhood education and comprehensive child development programs that are designed to reduce poverty by keeping children healthy and preparing them for school. Also significant was the question of whether to include in the definition that growing number of programs in many countries aimed at educating parents about ways of rearing children, and how to use community resources on the child's behalf. I decided to expand the definition to include such programs and the policies guiding their provision because of their direct link to child-rearing practices and to the broader demographic and social factors effecting changes in those practices. So the child care policies and programs addressed in this handbook are public and involve the provision of (a) day care while parents are employed (formal and informal work sectors), (b) child development and early education experiences to preschool-aged children, and/or (c) child development related information to the parents of those children.

DAY CARE TERMINOLOGY

The terminology used to label basic day care program components can be confusing. For instance, the term "creche" refers to center care for newborn to three year olds in France, Germany, Hungary, and Vietnam, but in India to care for newborn to six year olds. The creches in those countries become nurseries in China, day nurseries in Denmark and the former U.S.S.R., and day care centers in Israel. This confusion has been reduced for the handbook reader by providing a simple glossary containing the labels used for basic program types by each author, the age range covered by that program, and some indication of program duration (part or full day). This glossary provides the reader with an introduction to terms used in the 29 national chapters. It can also serve as a reference during the reading of later chapters when there is a need to understand the terms used by one author in relation to those utilized by others.[3] All of the terms in the glossary refer to center-based provision except those with "family," "home," or "minder" in their titles.

The glossary contains only the most common forms of care in each country, presented in simplified form for comparative purposes. Descriptions of a wide variety of other program types are provided in each national chapter.

A CONCEPTUAL FRAMEWORK

The results of my crossnational thematic analyses are outlined in chapter 31. There I present and discuss a framework for understanding particular child care programs in the context of the macro-level forces that stimulate policy formation and the influences mediating how societal needs are translated into policy and programmatic form. A schematic representation is provided below for that purpose.

The left-hand box in the framework contains those factors identified by our national experts as stimulating public child care policies in their countries. No factor shown in the "causal" box played a primary causal role in all 29 countries, but every factor shown occurred in more than a single case.

Table 1.1
Glossary of Terms

Country	Type of Care	Age Range	Duration (day)
Australia	center-based care	preschool	full day
	family day care	0 - 12	full day
Brazil	day care services	young preschool	full day
	preschool services	older preschool	part day
Canada	day care centre	0 - 5 or 6	full day
	family day care	0 - 5	full day
China	kindergarten	3 - 7	full/part day
	nursery	0 - 3	variable
C.I.S.(former U.S.S.R.)	day nursery	0 - 3	full day
	kindergarten	3 - 7	full day
Colombia	child welfare home	0 - 7	variable
	preschool center	0 - 7	variable
Denmark	day nursery	0 - 3	full day
	family-based care	0 - 4	full day
	kindergarten	3 - 6	full day
Finland	day care center	1 - 6	full day
	family day care	1 - 6	full day
France	day care center/creche	0 - 3	full day
	family day care	0 - 3	full day
	nursery school	3 - 6	full day
Germany	childminder	0 - 3	full day
	creche	0 - 3	full day
	kindergarten	3 - 6	part day
Hungary	creche	5 mo. - 3 yr.	full day
	kindergarten	3 - 6	full day
India	creche	0 - 6	part/full day
	family day care	0 - 6	variable
	nursery/kindergarten	2 1/2 - 5	part day
Israel	day care center	0 - 3	full day
	kindergarten	2 - 5	part day
Italy	day care center	9 mos. - 3 yr.	full day
	preschool	3 - 5	full day
Japan	hoikuen (nursery)	0 - 6	part/full day
	yochien (kindergarten)	3 - 6	part day

Table 1.1 (continued)

Country	Type of Care	Age Range	Duration(day)
Kenya	day care center day nursery kindergarten nursery school	all 3 - 6	all variable
Mexico	center-based care family day care	0 - 5 0 - 5	full day full day
Nicaragua	child development center	0 - 6	full day
Norway	day care center family day care	0 - 7 0 - 7	full day full day
Peru	center-based care family day care	0 - 6 0 - 6	variable variable
Philippines	center-based care home-based care	2 - 6 0 - 6	2 - 3 hours home visits/ parent groups
Poland	kindergarten nursery	4 - 6 1 - 3	part/full day part/full day
Sweden	day care center family day care preschool	0 - 6 0 - 6 4 - 6	full day full day part day
South Africa	childminder creche educare center nursery school	0 - 6 0 - 6 0 - 6 4 - 6	full day full day full day part day
U.K.	childminding day nursery nursery school	3 - 4 0 - 4 0 - 4	full day full day part day
U.S.	day care center family day care kindergarten nursery school	0 - 5 0 - 5 5 3 - 5	full day full day part day part day
Venezuela	day care home preschool center	3 - 6 3 - 6	full/part day full/part day
Vietnam	creche day care home nursery school	0 - 3 3 - 5 3 - 5	full/part day full/part day full/part day
Zimbabwe	early childhood center	0 - 6	variable

Notes: 1) Duration shown is maximum available. Some children attend fewer hours. 2) many programs serve older children after school. 3) In some countries parental leaves result in little public child care in 1st year.

Figure 1.1
A Framework Linking Macro-level Causes and Mediating Influences
with Policy and Program Outcomes

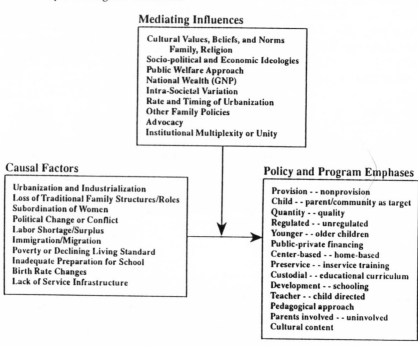

Mediating Influences

Cultural Values, Beliefs, and Norms
Family, Religion
Socio-political and Economic Ideologies
Public Welfare Approach
National Wealth (GNP)
Intra-Societal Variation
Rate and Timing of Urbanization
Other Family Policies
Advocacy
Institutional Multiplexity or Unity

Causal Factors

Urbanization and Industrialization
Loss of Traditional Family Structures/Roles
Subordination of Women
Political Change or Conflict
Labor Shortage/Surplus
Immigration/Migration
Poverty or Declining Living Standard
Inadequate Preparation for School
Birth Rate Changes
Lack of Service Infrastructure

Policy and Program Emphases

Provision - - nonprovision
Child - - parent/community as target
Quantity - - quality
Regulated - - unregulated
Younger - - older children
Public-private financing
Center-based - - home-based
Preservice - - inservice training
Custodial - - educational curriculum
Development - - schooling
Teacher - - child directed
Pedagogical approach
Parents involved - - uninvolved
Cultural content

The box in the center contains a number of influences that our case studies indicate operate to *mediate the nature of the policy responses and the shape of the programs developed to implement those policies.* Shown in the box on the right is a set of dimensions and categories distinguishing national approaches to public child care.

Child care policies and programs in a given country have been developed in response to some particular combination of the demographic, economic, cultural, and social factors shown to the left in the framework as causes, and differing causes contribute to differences in policies and programs along the lines indicated on the right-hand side of the figure. However, the data provided in this handbook show that even when the factors stimulating policies and programs are similar in two societies, outcomes will differ if the economic, political, cultural, and social contexts surrounding those objectives—the mediating influences—are dissimilar. Perhaps the greatest danger in presenting a framework in schematic form is that readers will focus only on individual elements in the scheme, without being able to appreciate how those elements interrelate and how that interrelated whole changes over time. Also lost are the dynamic tensions that give energy to the processes of policy and program development in a given society, like the struggle between family and state as responsible for child rearing, the centralized versus decentralized provision of services, and day care as focused on development versus schooling. The great strength of the case study approach used by the chapter authors is that each country provides an illustration of how these various elements and tensions are synthesized. The 29 national presentations that make up the heart of this volume provide evidence for the variety of ways that this synthesis can occur. In the concluding chapter I elaborate on aspects of the conceptual framework introduced above and describe a number of the thematic tensions that accompany the development of public child care in all of the countries profiled.

NOTES

1. These country studies, coordinated by Halbert and Nancy Robinson of the United States, were published both as special issues of the journal *Early Child Development and Care* and as volumes by Gordon and Breach.

2. The Federal Republic of Germany, France, the German Democratic Republic, Hungary, Sweden, and the United States. More recently (1990) Edward Melhuish and Peter Moss have edited a volume comparing the United Kingdom, the United States, France, Sweden, and East Germany that gives special emphasis to the day care research conducted in each country. The contributors focus on the child's environment as a central theme and highlight the influence of social context on day care.

3. I refer to terminology as used by authors rather than by societies because often the term is simply an English translation from the first language of that society.

REFERENCES

Barker, W. (1987). "Early childhood care and education: The challenge." *Occasional Paper No. 1*, The Hague, Holland: Bernard van Leer Foundation.

Berfenstam R. and William-Olsson, I. (1973). Early child care in Sweden. *Early Child Development and Care*, Vol. 2, No. 2, pp. 97–249.

Cochran, M. (1977). "A comparison of group day care and family childrearing patterns in Sweden." *Child Development*, 48, pp. 702–707.

Cochran, M. and Gunnarsson, L. (1980). "Samma könsskillnader på dagis som hemma." (Sex differences among day care and home-reared children). *Forskning och Framsteg*, 5, pp. 22–27.

Cochran, M. and Gunnarsson, L. (1985). "A follow-up study of group day care and family-based childrearing patterns." *Journal of Marriage and Family*, Vol. 47, No. 2, pp. 297–310.

Cochran, M., Larner, M., Riley, D., Gunnarsson, L. and Henderson, C., Jr. (1990). *Extending Families: The Social Networks of Parents and Their Children.* Cambridge, Eng./New York: Cambridge University Press.

Cochran, M. and Robinson, J. (1983). "Day care, family circumstances, and sex differences in children." In S. Kilmer (Ed.), *Advances in Early Education and Child Care*, Vol. 3. Greenwich, CT: J.A.I., pp. 47–67.

David, M. and Lezine, I. (1974). "Early child care in France." *Early Child Development and Care*, Vol. 4, No. 1, pp. 1–148.

Hermann, A. and Komlos, S. (1972). "Early child care in Hungary." *Early Child Development and Care*, Vol. 1, No. 4, pp. 337–459.

Kahn, A. and Kamerman, S. (1987). *Child Care: Facing the Hard Choices*. Dover, Mass: Auburn House.

Kamerman, S. and Kahn, A. (1981). *Child Care, Family Benefits, and Working Parents*. New York: Columbia University Press.

Kamerman, S. and Kahn, A. (Eds.) (1978). *Family Policy: Government and Families in 14 Countries*. New York: Columbia University Press.

Kellmer-Pringle, M. and Naidoo, S. (1974). Early child care in Britain. *Early Child Development and Care*, Vol. 3, No. 4, pp. 299–473.

Khalakdina, M. (1979). "Early child care in India." *Early Child Development and Care*, Vol. 5, No. 3/4, pp. 149–360.

Luscher K., Ritter, V. and Gross, P. (1973). "Early child care in Switzerland." *Early Child Development and Care*, Vol. 3, No. 2, pp. 89–210.

Lamb, M., Sternberg, K., Hwang, C.-P., and Broberg, A. (Eds.) (1992). *Child Care in Context: Cross-Cultural Perspectives*. Hillsdale, N.J.: Lawrence Erlbaum.

Melhuish, E. and Moss, P. (Eds.) (1990). *Day Care for Young Children: International Perspectives*. London: Routledge.

Myers, R. and Indriso, C. (1987). "Women's work and child care: Supporting the integration of women's productive and reproductive roles in resource-poor households in developing countries." Paper prepared for the workshop in Issues Related to Gender, Technology, and Development, The Rockefeller Foundation, New York, N.Y.

Nimnicht, G. and Arango, M. (1987). "Meeting the needs of young children: Policy alternatives." *Occasional Paper No. 2*, The Hague, Holland: Bernard van Leer Foundation.

Omstead, P. and Weikart, D. (1989). *How Nations Serve Young Children: Profiles of Child Care and Education in 14 Countries*. Ypsilanti, Michigan: High/Scope Press.

Pence. A. (1979). "Child care in two developing countries: Kenya and the United States." *Young Children*, May 1979, pp. 49–53.

Rapaport et al. (1976). "Early child care in Israel." *Early Child Development and Care*, Vol. 4, No. 2/3, pp. 149–345.

Robinson, H., Robinson, N., Wolins, M., Bronfenbrenner, U. & Richmond, J. (1973). "Early child care in the United States of America." *Early Child Development and Care*, Vol. 2, No. 4, pp. 359–582.

UNESCO. (1988). "The learning environments of early childhood in Asia: Research perspectives and changing programmes." Bangkok: UNESCO Principal Regional Office for Asia and the Pacific.

Ziemska, M. (1978). "Early child care in Poland." *Early Child Development and Care*, Vol. 5, No. 1/2, pp. 1–148.

2

AUSTRALIA

Deborah Brennan

In the last two decades, child care has become a highly political topic in Australia. Aspects of child care policy and funding are widely debated in the media, in parliament, in trade unions, and in the general community. The major political parties (the Australian Labor Party, the Liberal Party, and the National Party) have quite distinct policies on child care and, since the mid-1970s, promises concerning child care have routinely featured in federal election campaigns as the parties have vied to capture the "women's vote."

The child care debate in Australia is not so much about the existence of publicly funded children's services, although this has been controversial in previous decades. Rather, it tends to be about more practical issues such as the form such services should take, the appropriate level of government funding, whether all families should benefit from public subsidies or only selected types of families (the poor, employed parents, etc.) and, most particularly, whether the government should subsidize services directly or should provide tax concessions to individuals and allow them to find their own services in the private market. One of the most notable features of the contemporary child care scene in Australia is the range of interest groups that seek to impact government policy in the area. Historically, child care has been of interest mainly to charitable organizations and, more recently, feminists. Now, however, in addition to those groups, trade unions, professional early childhood educators, employers, providers of commercial services, political parties, and child care lobby groups all seek to have a say.

BACKGROUND TO CHILD CARE PROGRAMS
IN AUSTRALIA

The term "child care" and "children's services" are used here mainly to refer to services for children under school age. The age at which children start school in Australia is determined by the states and thus varies across the country; generally, most Australian children start school at between five and six years of age. Services for young primary school children are also discussed. Since the focus is on services that complement (rather than substitute for) parental care, other forms of child care such as residential institutions and foster placement are outside the scope of this analysis.

In June 1987, 864,000 children under six used some form of child care, as did 506,000 children aged between six and eleven years. Of the children under six, 421,000 were provided with "formal" care, while this form of care was received by only 34,000 six to eleven year olds.

Aborigines and Child Care

A special note on the subject of Australian aborigines and children's services is warranted. Aborigines are under-represented in every service type funded by the Australian government. There are a number of reasons for this. Without doubt, the existence of racist behavior and discriminatory practices on the part of whites is a considerable problem, particularly in rural areas. Another factor is the structure of some children's services and their general lack of consonance with the needs and practices of aboriginal families. Examples of such structural features are the set hours of attendance insisted upon by some services, often regarded as rigid and undesirable by aboriginal families, and the policies that give preference to the children of parents in full-time employment (aborigines have disastrously high levels of unemployment—in many areas three quarters of the adult population is without work). Moreover, many aboriginal mothers did not wish to be separated from their young children for the hours of care involved in early childhood services (especially day care) and are especially reluctant to part with their children if this involves handing them into the care of white teachers. Australia has a shameful history in relation to black people, particularly children. Over a period of decades thousands of black children were forcibly taken from their own families and either raised in institutions or handed over to white families who brought them up with no knowledge of their own heritage. Many aborigines have "bitter memories of attempts by white people to 'assimilate' them, and of the use of white child welfare laws to take their children away" (Chisolm, 1985, p. 1).[1] Overall, there can be no doubt that aboriginal families are extremely under-resourced in terms of children's services. The solution to this problem, however, does not lie solely within the child care arena—it is part of a broader and extremely far-reaching struggle for political and economic equality.

HISTORICAL DEVELOPMENT OF CHILDREN'S SERVICES

Publicly funded child care services in Australia have a relatively short history. The Commonwealth government became involved in this area only in 1972 with the introduction of the Child Care Act. Before that, child care provision was left largely to state governments, private interests, and the voluntary sector. The program has developed rapidly. In 1970 it was estimated that only about 2,000 children in all of Australia had access to non-profit, subsidized child care programs. These were mainly services run by philanthropic organizations such as the Victorian Association of Creches and the Sydney Day Nursery and Nursery Schools Association. Currently, some 160,000 children are catered to in Commonwealth supported services. Under the Commonwealth's Children's Service Program, subsidies may be provided toward both the capital costs and the recurrent costs of non-profit child care services. In addition, families whose children attend these community based centers and whose joint income is below a certain level are eligible for 'fee relief,' which means, in effect, that the Commonwealth picks up the tab for part of their fees.

The role of the Commonwealth government in regard to the provision of children's services has varied considerably depending largely upon which party is in power. The Whitlam Labor government (1972–1975), which oversaw the initial years of funding under the Child Care Act, saw the Commonwealth's role as that of the major catalyst and the major provider of funds for all types of children's services. In keeping with its social democratic philosophy, this government was committed to the provision of services for all children, not just those designated to be in some way "needy." Unfortunately, the government's administrative and funding mechanisms did not always match its philosophical goals. The most obvious instance of this was that although Labor was committed in principle to providing higher levels of funding and greater assistance to the most needy parts of the community, it did not develop ways of ensuring that this actually occurred. In determining where new services were to be located, for example, the Whitlam government relied on submissions from community groups. No central planning was undertaken. As a result, most funding went to relatively well-off areas where there were people with the skills and know-how to write persuasive submissions. Areas with high proportions of working mothers, single parents, and migrant families did not fare nearly so well. Nevertheless, the hallmark of the Whitlam period was commonwealth government commitment to universal provision of government subsidized services.

The Liberal-Country Party Government led by Malcolm Fraser (1975–1983) had a quite different philosophy. In line with its general efforts to minimize the role of government in the provision of community services and to emphasize the role of families and private enterprise in the provision of community welfare services, attempts were made to restrict access to subsidized child care and to define it as a service for families designated by officials as "needy." The everyday demands of life—such as the need to go to work, to study, or to have a break from one's children—were not regarded as sufficiently pressing in themselves to warrant access to child care. Families were increasingly required to demonstrate that they were "needy" (with all the associated connotations of inadequacy) in order to gain a place in a child care center or family day care scheme. By the end of the Fraser government's period in office children's services in Australia had reached a low point. Total funding had been reduced by more than a third in real terms, submissions for hundreds of new projects had been rejected, and there were plans to move away from a publicly funded child care system toward one that relied on subsidies to users of private, profit-making services. With the election of the Hawke Labor government in 1983, the priorities of the government in children's services changed yet again.

RELATION OF CHILD CARE POLICIES TO OTHER WORK/FAMILY POLICIES

Under the Hawke government child care policy has been developed in relation to the broader policies and concerns of the government, particularly its labor market and social security policies. This represents a remarkable change. No longer is child care an isolated policy issue of interest mainly to feminists on the one hand and traditional early childhood organizations on the other—as it was during the two previous administrations. Child care policy is now integral to a number of the government's social and economic policies and of interest to a far broader range of community groups, trade unions, policy makers, and government ministers than ever before.

Women's Employment

The expansion of job opportunities for both men and women has been one of the major achievements of the Hawke government. Between 1983 and 1989 more than 1.5 million new jobs were created and 56 percent of these were filled by women. Slightly more than half of the new jobs occupied by women have been full-time positions: women accounted for 46 percent of full-time employment growth and 77 percent of part-time employment growth over the period. Other indicators also suggest a strengthening of women's employment situation. During the period under consideration the total number of women employed rose by over 600,000 or 27 percent, and women's rate of work force participation rose from 42 to 51 percent. (Men's participation rate actually declined over this period from 78 to 75 percent, largely because of the reduction in participation by men aged 55–64). Women were also recorded as having declining levels of unemployment (from 10 to 7 percent), and the number of women classified as hidden unemployed or discouraged job seekers was also substantially reduced.

Women have thus been the "star performers" in the Australian labor market (Maas, 1989: p. 16). Within the broad category of "women," moreover, the highest rates of growth, both in labor force participation and numbers employed, have been experienced by married women with children under school age. Between 1984 and 1988 the participation rate for this group grew by 32 percent, compared with 19 percent for all married women with dependent children and 10 percent for those with no dependents. By 1988, 45 percent of women with children aged four years or under were in the labor force. Twenty percent of all married women in the labor force had children under four years. In the majority of couple families with dependent children, both parents are now in the paid labor force; the so-called traditional family with a breadwinning male and homemaking female now comprises less than 40 percent of all such families.

Such figures, however, tell only part of the story of women's employment. Despite the significant growth in women's participation rate, the structural characteristics of the female labor force have not changed significantly. Women are still overwhelmingly concentrated in low-paid work in a limited number of occupations and industries. Indeed, some studies have suggested that gender segregation in the Australian labor market has actually increased slightly over the last two decades. Women still earn considerably less than men. In August 1988 women's average total weekly earnings were 66 percent of those for men—not significantly different to the ratio in 1972, when "equal pay" was won. The present ratio can partly be explained by women's location in the labor force, particularly their heavy dependence on part-time work. However, even when full-time workers are considered and overtime payments excluded, adult women still receive only 83 percent of male earnings. There are differences, too, in the impact of age and experience on male and female earnings. As men get older and gain more experience in the labor force their earnings tend to increase; a 40-year-old, full-time male employee earns, on average, 20 percent more than a 25-year-old male. In contrast, as women get older their earnings tend to decrease; a 40-year-old female employee earns, on average, 10 percent less than her 25-year-old female counterpart.

The fact that women continue to carry the major responsibility for child care is one of the primary reasons for their disadvantaged position in the labor market and lower earnings. Women with children are far more likely than other women (or men) to work part time, particularly if their youngest child is under school age. Statistics on hidden unemployment also show that the absence of affordable child care is one of the major constraints to women actively seeking work.

The labor government has introduced a number of legislative measures designed to improve the position of women in the labor market. In 1986 it passed the Affirmative Action (Equal Opportunity for Women) Act requiring private sector employers with more than 100 employees and all higher education institutions to introduce equal employment and affirmative action policies for women. This complemented the Public Service Reform Act of 1984, which introduced equal employment policies into the Commonwealth public service and the various state acts concerning equal employment in the public sector.

The Commonwealth government's affirmative action programs do not, however, directly address the issue of child care provision. Although it has exhorted private employers to provide child care services for their staffs, and has introduced tax concessions and other measures to encourage them to do so, the Commonwealth has not set an example by providing such services in the public sector—despite considerable union pressure to do so. The government has, however, introduced new guidelines governing priority of access to day care and family day care services provided through the Children's Services Program. Since 1986 priority of access to these services has been given to working parents and those studying or training in order to enter the labor market. Low income families have priority within these categories.

An interesting sidelight on the relationship between employment issues and child care provision is that in recent years there has been explicit recognition of the direct job creation potential of child care services. New services create short-term jobs in the building and construction industries and long-term jobs for teachers, child care certificate workers, cooks, cleaners, and clerical assistants. The Labor government in Victoria, under John Cain, placed particular emphasis on the employment creation aspect of child care. The announcement of the first round of new services under the planning model in Victoria stressed that, in addition to increasing the number of subsidized child care places by 25 percent, the new services would create 250 permanent full-time jobs in child care centers, 100 part-time jobs in after-school care centers, and hundreds of construction jobs in the building and renovation of centers.

An intensive review of social security initiated by the Minister for Social Security Brian Howe in 1986 and carried out under the leadership of feminist sociologist and policy analyst Bettina Cass has also contributed to the focus on child care provision. The review stimulated debate and policy change in a number of areas, including the crucial one of facilitating the entry of welfare recipients—especially sole parents—into the labor force.

From the mid-1970s to the mid-1980s Australia's sole parent population increased by 73 percent, from 183,000 to 316,400, while the number of two-parent families with dependent children rose by only 4 percent to 1,884,400. Over the same period there was a sharp increase in the proportion of sole parents reliant on Commonwealth income support. Not surprisingly, this growth in dependence on government support was paralleled by a decline in the labor force participation rates of both male and female sole parents. From 1975 to 1983 the proportion of female sole parents in the labor force declined from 48 percent to 39 percent; for male sole parents the decline was from 93 percent to 80 percent. Since the low point of 1983 (the year in which the Hawke Labor government was elected) there has been a steady increase in the work force participation of sole parents, arguably as a result of increased child care provision and strong job growth. Forty-seven percent of female sole parents and 83 percent of male sole parents were labor force participants in 1988.

Studies have shown that a high proportion of sole parents would like to have a job. The barriers to their work force participation range from low self-esteem and lack of self-confidence to the costs of working, including the poverty traps that reduce the overall benefit of undertaking paid work. Research has also shown that the lack of appropriate, affordable child care is one of the most important work force barriers confronting sole parents. According to Australian Bureau of Statistics data, 56 percent of sole mothers who wanted work and could start within four weeks were not actively seeking jobs because their children were too young or they could not find suitable child care. A study commissioned by the Department of Social Security also showed that more than half of those not currently working saw child care as the main factor inhibiting them from seeking employment. A small study carried out for the Social Security Review showed that 60 percent of sole parents saw child care as the major barrier to work force participation. According to the author of this report, child care was unequivocally "the most commonly cited workforce barrier" (Frey, 1986).

During its period in office the Hawke government has initiated some important changes in policies that affect the labor force participation of sole parents and widows. The government has made it clear that it does not accept any obligation to provide indefinite financial support to these groups. Nor does it accept that it is in the interests of the client groups to be maintained for lengthy periods outside the labor market. A number of research reports had demonstrated the strong desire of women, including those with young children, to undertake paid work in preference to long-term dependence on welfare. The policies of the Hawke government do not attempt to compel sole parent pensioners with young children to join the work force (as has been done in some parts of the United States of America), but to encourage and facilitate work force participation where this is desired by sole parents themselves. In general, the policies have been designed to smooth the transition between dependence on benefits and work force participation and to remove the "poverty traps" and other factors that previously discouraged this move. In 1988 the government introduced Job, Education, and Training (JET), a scheme aimed at providing education, training, and other forms of assistance to enable single parents to enter the work force. Child care provision is an important component of JET.

Policies for Workers with Family Responsibilities

Another change in the context of child care policy under the Hawke government has been the move toward ratification of International Labor Organization (ILO) Convention 156 "Equal Opportunities and Equal Treatment for Men and Women Workers: Workers with Family Responsibilities." Ratification of this convention commits a country to promoting and encouraging the sharing of domestic responsibilities between men and women. It also implies a commitment to developing services that enable workers (and prospective workers) with family responsibilities to undertake training and educational programs as well as to take part in employment. Countries that ratify the convention commit themselves to working toward the provision of parental leave, to introducing laws that prohibit direct or indirect discrimination on the basis of marital status or family responsibilities and to providing a range of community services such as home help and child care. Convention 156 was adopted by the ILO in 1981. At a conference of Commonwealth and State Labor Ministers held at the end of 1984, it was agreed that the convention should be ratified by the Australian government. The Australian Council of Trades Union (ACTU) has actively promoted the ratification of the convention, most notably by its support for work-based child care and its successful test case on parental leave for all workers.

An Aging Population

Finally, over the next 30 years Australia is likely to see an increase of almost 50 percent in the number of its citizens who are in the over-65 age group and a drop of 22 percent in the number of those under 15 years. As the oldest group in the population is also the one that makes the heaviest demands on the public sector (notably through pensions and health services), this trend has significant social and economic implications, not least for child care. In order to finance the necessary services and supports for our aging population, it will be necessary to encourage labor force participation and high productivity from the younger age groups. Providing child care so that women do not need to have long career interruptions is one way of doing this.

All the contextual issues mentioned so far—economic policies, moves to encourage and facilitate the labor force participation of women (including single mothers), the review of social security, trade union pressures for work-based child care, and other measures to secure the equal treatment of workers with family responsibilities and the aging of the population—have contributed to an intensive focus under the Hawke Labor government on child care in relation to employment. The government's overall goal has been to expand services and ensure that services funded by the Commonwealth are primarily used by work force participants. The provision of child care for reasons other than parents' work force participation—to enhance the social development of children or to provide respite for home-based mothers, for example—has received much lower priority. The language of the debate about child care has also changed. Child care is now about "facilitating work force participation," "enhancing productivity," and "assisting the welfare-to-work transition." The rhetoric of the 1970s feminist movement—which promoted child care as enhancing women's autonomy, providing alternatives to traditional nuclear family care arrangements, and encouraging independence and sociability among young children—has all but disappeared from public debates about child care.

THE ECONOMICS OF PUBLICLY FUNDED CHILD CARE

Toward the end of 1987 the Minister for Community Services and Health, Neal Blewett, commissioned a study from the Centre for Economic Policy Research at the Australian National University on the economic issues surrounding publicly funded child care. The terms of reference for this study were (1) to review and comment on the data used to evaluate the economic benefits of the Children's Services Program; (2) to identify additional data sources and to provide additional arguments on the fiscal impact of the program; (3) to provide qualitative arguments on the labor market effects of the program; and (4) to construct models that could be applied to measure the economic benefit of the program.

The Centre's report was published by the Department of Community Services and Health in May 1988. It argued that publicly funded child care resulted in major economic and social benefits and that society as a whole (not just individual parents) had an interest in the upbringing of children. According to the authors of the report, the non-taxation of child care (and other domestic services) provided in the home, plus the high costs of purchasing child care outside the home, combined to create strong disincentives to women's participation in the work force and thus distorted their choice. This had consequences for the economic well-being of families, since women's participation in the labor force was one of the chief ways for low-income families to avoid poverty. It also had implications for the economy as a whole, as high employment rates for able-bodied adults contributed to economic and industrial development and aided governments in providing for those outside the labor force because of age, poor health, or disability.

Another argument addressed by the report concerned the return from public investment in women's education. Government subsidization of child care, the report argued, would help avoid the depreciation of "human capital" associated with women's lengthy withdrawals from the labor force for child-rearing purposes.

The greater the fraction of education and training paid for by the government the greater the community interest in the decision to leave and return to the workforce. The child care subsidies should be seen as part of the contribution that government makes to the development and maintenance of the stock of human capital embodied in the labor force. (Anstie et al., 1988, p. 12)

It was also argued that society as a whole has an interest in how children are raised and that therefore high quality services that help children to develop their full potential are socially desirable. Further, such programs are important elements in the campaign against poverty, especially child poverty.

The child of competent, happy and well-off parents has a flying start in life, whereas the child of parents with the opposite characteristics begins with a handicap. In a variety of ways, Australian governments do much to improve the prospects of the less advantaged child, by providing free or subsidized schooling, medical attention, and so on. Increasingly, because of community expectations, there is a need to do more to assist the child in the pre-school ages. Funded childcare is an integral part of that increased effort on behalf of children. (Anstie et al., 1988, p. 28)

According to this study, publicly funded child care (particularly schemes such as the Children's Services Program where the major beneficiaries are low and middle income families) contributes to social equity and income redistribution. In the absence of public subsidies, the cost of child care creates a significant work force disincentive for women with low-income earning potential. The existence of such a program, therefore, by helping to facilitate entry into the labor market by single parents and second earners in low-income families, contributed to a fairer distribution of jobs and income.

Probably the most influential and widely quoted aspect of the report was its assessment of the net fiscal impact of publicly funded child care. Against direct expenditure on the Children's Services Program, it set the gains to the Commonwealth that accrued from increased taxation revenue, savings on the dependent spouse rebate, and savings on social security pensions and benefits. The report estimated that gains from the program could have been as high as $296 million in 1987 and 1988, compared with the expenditure of $190 million. Hence, publicly funded child care may have resulted in a net addition to the budget of as high as $106 million. The sources of that additional revenue are shown in Table 2.1.

Table 2.1
Possible Fiscal Gain to the Commonwealth from Working Mothers with Birth to
Four Year Old Children in Commonwealth Funded Services

	Married Women ($m)	Sole Parents ($m)	Total ($m)
Tax Revenue and Medicare Levy	121.9	21.0	142.9
Dependent Spouse Rebate	63.3	-	63.3
Marginal Tax Rate on Unearned Income	6.3	-	6.3
Family Allowance Supplement	28.1	-	28.1
Supporting Parents Benefit and Rent Assistance	-	55.8	55.8
TOTAL	219.6	76.8	296.4

Source: Derived from Anstie et al., 1988
Government Spending on Work-Related Child Care

COMMONWEALTH GOVERNMENT POLICY
AND PROVISION

The major program through which the Commonwealth government in Australia funds child care is the Children's Services Program, administered by the Department of Community Services and Health. The Commonwealth does not directly operate any child care services itself. Instead, it provides capital and recurrent funding to non-profit organizations to run "community-based" child care services. The state and territory governments also contribute funding for these services.

The Commonwealth's stated policy objectives for the Children's Services Program are as follows:

Accessibility—to improve the supply of child care places in areas of greatest need and to ensure access to child care by children whose parents are in the work force and by children with special needs (e.g., children from non-English speaking backgrounds).

Affordability—to assist low and middle income families to pay their child care fees through an income-related fee relief system; and

Quality—to ensure that child care services offer consistent standards of care and positive outcomes for children and parents.

State-based planning committees provide advice to the Minister for Community Services and Health on high need areas, taking into account the number of children in the targeted age group, parents' labor force status, the existing supply of government funded and commercial child care places, journey to work factors, and the results of community consultations.

In funding child care services, the government's priority is work-related care and over 80 percent of Children's Services Program expenditure goes to services that assist working parents. Under priority of access guidelines that Commonwealth funded services must apply, children whose parents are working or training to enter the work force are given top priority. Within this category, special consideration is given to families on low incomes, single parents, and other special needs groups.

The main types of services funded under the Children's Services Program and the subsidy systems that apply to each are as follows:

Center-Based Day Care provides full-time care (8 hours per day, 5 days per week, 48 weeks of the year) for children under school age. The Commonwealth government subsidizes this form of care in three ways. First, *capital* subsidies are negotiated with the sponsoring agency, the relevant state government, and possibly local government. The value of such subsidies varies. It may cover the full cost of land acquisition, building, and equipment or it may contribute to coverage of these costs. Second, there is an operational subsidy paid at a flat rate of $12.50 per week for each child over three and $18.70 for each child under three. Finally, there is fee relief, which enables services to reduce charges to low income families. Centers that open for more than ten hours per day receive a small additional subsidy. To be eligible for these subsidies, centers must have their budgets approved by the Department of Community Services and Health and must demonstrate that the fees they charge users will enable the center to break even. Centers must also abide by Commonwealth guidelines, which require them to give first priority to children with both parents or a sole parent working, training for work, or seeking work.

Family Day Care is a system of child care provided in the homes of individual caregivers who are organized into a network on a locality basis. Children from 0–12 are catered to in family day care. The Commonwealth provides a capital grant to each scheme to enable it to purchase toys, office furniture, and such equipment as strollers and car restraints. An operational subsidy of $14.50 per week is paid by the Commonwealth for each full-time place in the network, or its equivalent. Low-income users are eligible for fee relief on the same basis as users of center-based services. Family day care schemes are subject to the same priority of access guidelines as center-based services.

Outside School Hours Care and *Vacation Care* programs operate before and after school hours and during holiday periods and cater to children from 5 to 12 years. These programs are often located at schools or community centers. The Commonwealth government provides limited operational assistance to out-of-school hours services. Some states also provide these services.

Occasional Care centers provide a service where parents can leave young children for short periods when they require care for personal reasons, for example, to keep medical appointments or to undertake recreational activities. Limited capital assistance is available for occasional care services. Operational subsidies are paid at the rate of $17.40 per week per child. Fee relief is available only to holders of Social Security benefit cards—a very restrictive provision.

Users of Services Under the Children's Services Program

Services funded under the Children's Services Program appear to be effectively targeted to sole parents, low- and moderate-income families in which both parents are employed, and children with special needs. It is not the intention of the Commonwealth to provide access to these groups exclusively; rather, the Commonwealth's purpose is to ensure that they have priority.

About 28 percent of the families who use these services for work-related reasons are sole-parent families. Since only 7 percent of working parent families are headed by sole parents, this figure represents very effective targeting. Low-income couples are also well represented. In 1988, an estimated 12 percent of families using Commonwealth funded child care had incomes below $14,000 and 70 percent had incomes below $32,000. The corresponding proportions for the whole community were 15 percent and 55 percent. Of the 35 percent of children who attend publicly funded child care for reasons other than their parents' employment, many represent other "special need" groups that the Commonwealth is attempting to target. For example, about 15 percent of children attending center-based care are migrant or Aboriginal children, children with disabilities (or who have disabled parents), and children deemed to be at risk of abuse.

In addition to the Department of Community Services and Health (which administers the Children's Services Program), a number of other Commonwealth government departments contribute to child care provision. The Department of Employment, Education, and Training grants capital subsidies for child care services provided in some universities and technical colleges. It also pays the fees of some sole parents who are undertaking study programs or training programs. The Department of Immigration, Local Government, and Ethnic Affairs assists with the costs of child care for recent migrants undertaking English language courses, and the Department of Social Security meets the child care costs of some sole parents undertaking training under the JET program.

PROVISION BY STATE/TERRITORY GOVERNMENTS

For historical reasons, preschool services in Australia (as distinct from child care) are the responsibility of state governments. Preschools are generally available only to children in the year before school entry. Most preschools provide several half-day sessions per week to each child; they are closed during school holidays. In most states and territories (Queensland, Western Australia, Tasmania, South Australia, the Northern Territory, and the Australian Capital Territory) preschool is almost universally available to children in the year before they start school. In all these states (except South Australia) preschools are run by the State Education Department. In Victoria and New South Wales, where preschool is provided by non-profit organizations that receive some financial assistance from the states, the service is not nearly as widely available.

LOCAL GOVERNMENT INVOLVEMENT

Local government authorities play a major, if somewhat variable, role in children's services throughout Australia. Many of them act as sponsors of Commonwealth funded services such as center-based day care, family day care, and out-of-school-hours services. Some local authorities provide additional subsidies to these services, either by meeting administrative costs or by providing services in kind (such as maintenance of buildings, gardening, cleaning). Some local councils pick up the deficits incurred by inadequately funded services.

COMMERCIAL CHILD CARE SERVICES

Commercial services play a significant role in the overall provision of child care in Australia. Approximately 25 percent of care is provided through such centers. Since the beginning of 1991 users of approved commercial child care centers have been eligible for Commonwealth fee relief on the same basis as users of publicly funded child care services.

Despite some obvious similarities, private and community-based child care centers provide different services and cater to different groups. For example, most private centers do not provide care for young babies and toddlers—they tend to cater to children in the three to five years age group. Community-based centers look after children from a few weeks of age. Another difference between the two is that private centers tend to operate for shorter hours than those that are community based.

RECENT TRENDS IN SERVICE PROVISION

The number of child care places funded by the Commonwealth has grown from 46,000 in 1983 to 122,000 in 1990. In 1988 the Commonwealth initiated a National Child Care Strategy under which, in conjunction with the State/Territory governments, it will fund another 30,000 places comprising 20,000 outside-school-hours care, 4,000 center-based care, 4,000 family day care, and 2,000 occasional care places. During the 1990 election campaign, the government promised to expand the National Child Care Strategy to provide an additional 50,000 places in non-profit services by 1995 and 1996 (30,000 outside school hours, 10,000 center-based, and 10,000 family day care).

The Commonwealth also anticipates a growth of some 28,000 commercial/employer child care places by 1995 and 1996, as a result of a decision extending Commonwealth fee relief to the private sector for the first time in January 1991.

REGULATORY MECHANISMS

The power to license and regulate children's services in Australia—state funded, Commonwealth funded, and commercial—rests with the state governments. The states vary significantly in the content of their regulations and in the range of services covered. There are no *national* standards governing children's services in Australia. Hence factors widely deemed to be crucial to determining the quality of services, such as staff qualifications, group sizes, staff-child ratios, and indoor and outdoor space requirements all vary between states. In addition to these regulations, child care services in some states are governed by health, fire, and building code regulations.

ROLE OF CHILD CARE AT THE WORKPLACE

Until the 1980s, employer-supported child care had not played a major role in the overall provision of services in Australia. Australian companies have shown little interest in supporting child care, and some organizations within the community have been quite suspicious of and hostile toward work-related services. However, there are signs that this situation is changing. In June 1988 the ACTU released a proposal for the government to contribute to work-related child care.

Much of the impetus for change has come from trade unionists within the public sector. Nurses, transport workers, Australian Broadcasting Corporation employees, students, and staffs in higher education institutions are some of the groups who have raised the issue of child care provision at the workplace. Workers within the private sector have not been nearly as active on this issue, probably because they are less unionized than their public sector counterparts and also because many of them work in very small workplaces where the idea of an employer-supported child care center would not be feasible. Recently, however, some large private employers have begun to show an interest in supporting child care. In some cases this has been motivated by the need to retain highly skilled executive staff members; in others it is seen as an aspect of more broadly conceived equal employment opportunity and affirmative action programs. The Hawke government is keen to encourage this trend—at least as far as the private sector is concerned. In its 1988–1989 budget Commonwealth government commenced an "industry initiative" in relation to child care. Under this initiative 1,000 of the 4,000 day care places to be established over the next four years are to be set up in conjunction with private employers.

Two distinct models of work-related child care have emerged in Australia. In the first, the service is essentially a community-based center located either at or near a particular workplace. Such services may have received Commonwealth funds for capital construction, fee relief subsidies, and operational grants. Management committees include parents as well as staff. In this type of service the Commonwealth's priority of access guidelines must be followed. Hence low-income households with parents in the labor force are likely to benefit. Centers of this type usually build in some safeguards in order to protect the places of children whose parents leave a particular workplace (no matter what the reason). In some cases the child's place is guaranteed for as long as the parent's wish to retain it; in others, the child is allowed to remain for a fixed period, say six months, after the parent leaves the workplace. Guidelines such as this represent an attempt to make the child and not just the parent the focus of the service.

In the second model, an employer takes responsibility for the capital costs of establishing a center for his/her employees. This may be done as a "joint venture" in conjunction with another employer, either public or private. Centers established in this way must meet the relevant state or territory regulations regarding staff: child-caregiver ratios, qualifications of workers, and other matters relating to the actual service. Fee relief (targeted to low-income families) is provided by the Commonwealth government. The rights of the child to continuity of care if parents leave the workplace are, in general, not assured. Furthermore, an employer may decide to admit only children whose parents are employed by the enterprise or corporation, excluding others who live in the area or work for other employers.

It is clear that the present government's preferred direction is to encourage employer-subsidized child care. This raises a number of problems. First, if child care comes to be seen more and more as a means to facilitate work force participation, then families needing to use it for other reasons are likely to be disadvantaged. Second, the needs of children in some types of work-related care may be forgotten as managers focus almost entirely on such gains to the company as productivity increases, reduced employee absenteeism, and so on. For example, what happens to a child cared for in a company-owned center when his or her parents change jobs? Does the child automatically have to lose his or her friends, caregivers, and familiar environment? Publicly funded, community-based centers (including those that are work related) can overcome this problem by allowing a child to retain his or her place in the center. However, those run purely for the benefit of the employer will have no incentive to do this—indeed, it would be directly counter to their interests. Hence, the strong attachments that children form in day care will be extremely vulnerable to changes in their parents' employment. Likewise, in this type of model there is unlikely to be any meaningful parental involvement in the running of the service. Third, there are many workers whose needs are not addressed in the current model of work-related care. Commonwealth government employees and staff and students in higher education institutions are two groups that are specifically excluded from benefiting from the "industry initiative" and that will find it virtually impossible to gain funds through state planning committees.

THE WORKING CONDITIONS OF
CHILD CARE PERSONNEL

The industrial conditions of child care workers are a significant issue in debates about children's services in Australia. Child care staffs work under highly stressful conditions. They are usually required to work rotating shifts (i.e., starting and finishing work at different times each week); many of the children they care for have been referred by state welfare agencies either because they are the victims of abuse or because they are considered "at risk" of abuse; and they suffer from a high level of infectious illnesses. Yet child care workers are one of the lowest paid groups in the community.

In the view of many groups, such as the National Association of Community Based Children's Services (the major lobbying group for non-profit child care services), poor working conditions constitute a threat to the quality of services. For example, there is mounting evidence of extremely high staff turnover rates in children's services, and this appears to be directly related to industrial issues within the center. A study of publicly funded long day care centers conducted in 1988 by Community Child Care (Sydney) found a turnover rate among staff of 58 percent over a two-year period. Poor working conditions, low wages, and limited career prospects were the main reason for this disturbing pattern. The Federated Miscellaneous Workers Union and the ACTU have lodged a case in the Industrial Relations Commission arguing that child care workers' rates of pay do not take sufficient account of the value and complexity of the work. The case seeks to establish an employment structure for the child care industry, with each step linked to appropriate levels of training and experience. The aim of the case is to link this structure to the new minimum wage rate sought by the ACTU for all low paid workers. If successful, this case will eventually result in a significant increase in wages throughout the child care industry. Since it is highly desirable (in the interests of the workers, the children, and the families concerned) that the case is won by the union, some clear thinking needs to be done in advance concerning how the costs of achieving wage justice for child care workers should be borne throughout the community.

Women who work in their own homes as family day care workers are also becoming more industrially conscious and active. These workers face even worse working conditions than their center-based counterparts. They do not receive sick pay, holiday pay, workers compensation, or any of the other normal benefits enjoyed by employees. Their wages are abysmal, sometimes as low as $1 per hour per child, with overtime rates (derisory as these are) coming into effect only after an 11-hour day has been worked. The Commonwealth government regards these women as self-employed and thus claims to have no responsibility toward them as employees. Recently, as result of a test case brought by Municipal Employees Union of Victoria, the Industrial Relations Commission has ruled that family day care workers who work in council-sponsored family day care schemes are in fact employees of those councils. The decision is likely to be appealed, and so it is not possible as yet to assess the consequences of this decision for the future of family day care.

PAYING THE COST OF CARE

Good quality child care is expensive to provide. A family with one child in care and not in receipt of fee relief is likely to pay nearly $115 to $130 per week (or $5,000 to $6,000 per year) in child care fees. As discussed above, the Commonwealth government provides assistance to users of the child care centers and family day care schemes that are part of its Children's Services Program. This assistance takes several forms. Users benefit from the capital expenditure that goes into building and equipping services, ongoing operational assistance is another source of benefit, and many users also receive fee relief.

For a parent who is not receiving fee relief and who may be paying $130 per week for child care, this represents a significant outlay. Recently, the government has come under increasing pressure to make child care affordable for ordinary families. In past years there has been a good deal of interest (especially from groups representing professional women such as the Business and Professional Women's Association, the Women Lawyers Association, and the Women Members Group of the Australian Society of Accountants) in some form of tax concession (whether deduction or rebate) for child care expenses incurred in earning one's living. The ACTU, the Australian Council of Social Service, and the National Association of Community Based Children's Services have all opposed tax concessions on the grounds that they deliver the greatest benefits to high income earners and are of no value to those whose income is below the tax threshold. An alternative way of dealing with the crisis in affordability of child care would be to increase operational subsidies, thereby lowering fees for all users. While some might object that in times of financial stringency it is unfair to benefit all users, flat-rate increases in the operational subsidy level are fairer than tax concessions that give the greatest benefit to those paying the highest marginal tax rate. It appears that pressure for some kind of tax relief for child care is beginning to build up again and this issue is likely to become an important one in the coming decade.

TRAINING

The training of early childhood workers across Australia presents a complex and often confusing picture. Training colleges for preschool teachers were originally established by the kindergarten unions and reflected the desire of these pioneers to have their work recognized as a profession—not just a job that could be done by any warmhearted woman. The colleges remained private, fee-charged institutions until the early 1970s when they became government funded colleges of advanced education. More recently, a fundamental restructuring of tertiary education has resulted in virtually all of these colleges becoming amalgamated with universities. These changes have resulted in early childhood teachers being far more socially representative than was previously the case. On the negative side, the pressure for the training of early childhood educators to be subsumed under the preparation of school teachers has become very strong in some parts of the country.

University trained teachers are only one group—and indeed they represent a distinct minority of the trained workers in the field. In the early 1970s, as the variety and type of children's services expanded, so too did training programs. A range of new training programs principally offered through Technical and Further Education (TAFE) colleges have been initiated since then. The most significant of these are the diplomas and associate diplomas in child care.

New South Wales is the only Australian state in which university or college trained teachers are employed in long day care centers. In the other states, staff members who have acquired a diploma or associate diploma from a TAFE college, as well as nurses, are the norm. Preschools, however, continue to employ fully qualified teachers in all states.

Early childhood training has traditionally stressed child development, the importance of play, parental involvement in programs, and the like. Philosophically, this is quite different from the focus of school education. Regrettably, the pressures resulting from the restructuring of higher education in Australia have pushed many university-based early childhood courses more toward the primary school model. At the same time, academics have come under increasing pressure to be researchers, rather than practice-oriented teachers. This, too, has pushed many vocational forms of education toward a more theoretical orientation.

This lack of an adequate supply of trained staff members is a serious problem in many areas of Australia. Governments have at times undertaken major programs of services expansion without paying adequate attention to the lead time required to prepare adequate trained staff.

STRENGTHS AND SHORTCOMINGS OF THE
CHILD CARE SYSTEM

The Australian child care system has many strengths. It is growing rapidly, services are being planned in accordance with specified criteria—not left merely to the chance operations of the market—and it has wide public support. The system appears to be successful in targeting benefits to specific groups; it does this, however, without stigmatizing or in any way segregating those who benefit in a major way from the funding system and those who do not. The program is increasingly able to offer parents a choice of the type of care they would prefer to use—center based, family based, at the workplace, or in the local neighborhood.

The Australian child care system also has some striking weaknesses—in particular, the shortage of places, the lack of focus on the child, and the poor industrial conditions of staff.

While the level of child care provision has expanded rapidly in recent years, uncertainty still remains on key issues dealing with the philosophy of child care and the actual day-to-day delivery of services. In this chapter I have identified and discussed several issues that are likely to be at the forefront of debate in the coming decade: the role of commercial child care, the expansion of work-related services, industrial issues for child care workers, and the quality of care. Beneath each of these issues lies the question of how much we, as a society, value children and their careers and how much of our national resources we are prepared to devote to them. Also at the core of each of these debates is the issue of gender: accessible, affordable child care is a prerequisite for a more just distribution of society's goods between men and women as well as between generations. Struggles over child care—the extent of its availability, its funding mechanisms, its distribution in terms of race and class, and worker compensation and benefits—are struggles that connect with the most fundamental issues of justice and equality in our society.

NOTE

1. Since the early 1970s, a number of initiatives have been taken to establish services based on the principles of Aboriginal self-determination. One example is the Aboriginal Child Care Agencies that have been established in Melbourne, Brisbane, Adelaide, and Perth. These concern themselves very broadly with the care of Aboriginal children and do not confine themselves to the types of services described above as "child care." Aboriginal Child Care Agencies are mainly concerned with children who have come under the notice of state welfare authorities and who are considered to be at risk of being sent to child welfare institutions. The agencies organize emergency foster placements and temporary child care for such children and attempt wherever possible to avert the need for institutional care. Another example of Aboriginal self-help and autonomy in relation to children's services is

Murawina, a Sydney-based organization that runs two preschools in which Aboriginal children are "taught to be proud of their Aboriginality whilst learning the basics they will need when they begin school" (McConnochie and Russell, 1985).

REFERENCES

Anstie, R., et al. (1988). *Government Spending on Work-Related Child Care: Some Economic Issues*, Center for Economic Policy Research. Australian National University, Canberra.

Australian Bureau of Statistics (1989). *Persons Not in the Labor Force, Australia, September, 1989*, Cat. No. 6220.0.

Australian Council of Social Service (1988). *Child Care: A Background Paper*, (ACOSS Paper No. 16), Sydney.

Belsky, Jay (1984). "Two Waves of Day Care Research: Developmental Effects and Conditions of Quality." In R. Ainslie (Ed.), *The Child and the Day Care Setting*. New York: Praeger.

Brennan, Deborah (1982). *Children's Services in Australia: The State of Play, A Review of Commonwealth and State Policies, 1972–1982*, Family and Children's Services Agency.

Brennan, Deborah (1983). *Toward a National Child Care Policy*, IFS, Melbourne.

Brennan, Deborah and O'Donnell, Carol (1986). *Caring for Australia's Children: Political and Industrial Issues in Child Care*. Sydney: Allen & Unwin.

Cass, Bettina (1990). "Reforming Family Income Support; Reforming Labor Markets; Pursuing Social Justice in Australia in the 1980s." In Nick Manning and Clare Ungerson (Eds.), *Social Policy Review, 1989–1990*. Cheshire, London.

Chisolm, Richard (1985). *Black Children: White Welfare?* Social Welfare Research Center Reports and Proceedings No. 52, University of New South Wales.

Cox, Eva (1983). " 'Pater-patria': Child-rearing and the state." In Cora V. Baldock and Bettina Cass (Eds.), *Women, Social Welfare and the State*, Sydney: George Allen & Unwin, pp. 188–200.

Davis, Lynne (1983). "Now you see it, now you don't: The Restructuring of Commonwealth government child care policy." *Australia and New Zealand Journal of Sociology*, Vol. 19, No. 1, March, pp. 79–95.

Department of Community Services and Health (1989). *Children's Services Program Long Day Center-Based Child Care, Australia*.

Dowse, Sara (1988). "The women's movement's fandango with the state: The movement's role in public policy since 1972." In Cora V. Baldock and Bettina Cass (Eds.), *Women, Social Welfare and the State* (2nd ed.), Sydney, pp. 205–226.

Frey, Dianne (1986). *Survey of Sole Parent Pensioners' Workforce Barriers*, (Background/Discussion Paper No. 12), Social Security Review, Canberra.

Huntsman, L. (1989). *A Guide to Regulations Covering Children's Services in Australia*. Sydney: Community Child Care.

Jones, A. (1988). "Child care policy—Where to now?" *Current Affairs Bulletin*, Vol. 65, No. 6, November, pp. 4–9.

Karmel, T., and MacLachlan, M. (1986). *Sex Segregation—Increasing or Decreasing?* Canberra: Bureau of Labor Market Research.

Lyons, M. (1989). *Funding Options for Child Care and Their Relationship to Social Justice*, Sponsored by the Child Accident Prevention Foundation and the Australian Early Childhood Association.

Maas, F. (1989). Demographic trends affecting the workforce. In *Corporate Child Care: The Bottom Line*, Papers from a National Conference on Employer Supported Child Care, Sydney, November.

McConnochie, K. R., and Russell, A. (1982). *Early Childhood Services for Aboriginal Children*, Australian Government Publishing Service.

Montague, Meg, and Stephens, Jenny (1985). *Paying the Price for Sugar and Spice, A Study of Women's Pathways into Social Security Recipiency*, Canberra: AGPS.

Panckhurst, F. (1984). *Workplace Child Care and Migrant Parents*, Canberra, AGPS.

Raymond, Judy (1987). *Bringing Up Child Alone: Policies for Sole Parents.* (Issues Paper No. 3.) Canberra: Social Security Review.

Ryan, P. (1988). *Staff Turnover in Long Day Care: A Survey of New South Wales Long Day Care Centers.* Sydney: Community Child Care.

Spearritt, P. (1970). "Child care and kindergartens in Australia, 1890–1975." In Peter Lansford and Patricia Sebastian (Eds.), *Early Childhood Education and Care in Australia.* Kew, Victoria: Australia International.

Stonehouse, Anne (1988). "Nice ladies who love children: The status of the early childhood professional in society." Australian Early Childhood Association, *Conference Proceedings* (18th National Conference, Canberra, 1988). Canberra: AECA.

Sweeney, Tania (1982). *An Analysis of Federal Funding of Children's Services: A Sourcebook.* Social Welfare Research Center (University of South Wales), Reports and Proceedings, No. 22, Kensington: SWRC.

Sweeney, Tania (1983). "Child welfare and child care policies." In Adam Graycar (Ed.), *Retreat from the Welfare State: Australian Social Policy in the 1980s.* George Allen & Unwin, pp. 35–54.

Sweeney, Tania and Jamrozik, Adam (1982). *Services for Young Children: Welfare Service or Social Parenthood?* Social Welfare Research Center (University of New South Wales), Reports and Proceedings, No. 19. Kensington: SWRC.

Women's Bureau (1970). Department of Labor and National Service, *Child Care Centers* (Women in the Workforce Series No. 7), Melbourne.

3

BRAZIL

Fulvia Rosemberg

1974—Upon my return to Brazil with my baby son after having lived
for a long period in France, I enrolled him in one of the three private
day care centers that existed in the city of São Paulo (population approximately 9 million in 1972). One of the many comments that I heard
at the time, especially from my mother, who was a woman committed
to the importance of women with careers, was "Poor André, so young
and already in a day care!" (He was nine months old and crawling.)

1975—The first public demonstration in São Paulo at the opening of
the UN "Women's Decade." We had been living for a long period under
a dictatorship, and the opportunities for public demonstrations were
rare. A woman in the audience spoke out in favor of handicraft programs
for women as a means to increase family income. She argued that such
programs would allow women to work at home without having to leave
their children in the hands of "day care mercenaries."

1987—Prime time on television. The channel with the highest audience rating shows a soap opera, in which one of the main characters is
a woman who gets involved in a complicated plot, leading a movement
of female workers who are fighting for the right to have day care for
their children.

1988—Election campaign for the first president to be directly elected
since 1960. Debates among the candidates receive very high audience
ratings on the major TV networks. The candidate from a large political
party asks an opponent about his day care plans for the large number
of women with jobs outside the home. The matter-of-fact response is
that according to the constitutional rights of 1988, "the education of
small children in day care centers and pre-schools is a right of every
child, as well as a duty of the State and of society."

In fifteen years a taboo based on the belief that day care centers were inadequate institutions for the development of small children, acceptable only for inadequate or socially anomic families, had become a constitutional right and a platform for political candidates of various persuasions. While concretely—in terms of administration, budget, quality, and extent of service—the education of preschool children in Brazil is still inadequate and may be criticized, there has been a remarkable change regarding its acceptance within various segments of the population. Nowadays to enroll a small child in day care may still be a reason for a mother to feel guilty, but it is a more and more accepted alternative for families with young children.

The contemporary history of day care in Brazil starts during the second half of the 1970s, with the advent of social movements, especially those of women, and with the macro-structural transformations of the Brazilian society, which were related to greater female participation in the work force and to the economic crisis of the early 1980s. Although the agitations and transformations that have characterized the last fifteen years are certainly evident, not everything has changed. We live in a transition period, where new and old ideas interact. As a result, the education of small children in Brazil presents a rather complex profile.

The objective of this chapter is to describe and analyze this complexity, highlighting innovations and barriers, and situating early education in the context of social politics.

THE COUNTRY AND ITS PEOPLE

Cut by the equator and the Tropic of Capricorn, Brazil occupies a vast territory of 3.3 million square miles. The large distance between its geographic extremes includes four time zones and temperatures that range from -2 degrees Celsius in the South to over 40 degrees Celsius in the Northeast.

Colonized by the Portuguese in the 16th century (who gave us their language and the Catholic religion), the country became independent in 1822, abolished slavery in 1888, and became a Republic in 1889. Presently, Brazil is a Federal Republic composed of states, territories, and a Federal District containing the capital city of Brasilia. The population projection for 1990 was 150 million, predominantly urban and young.

Brazil can be divided into many smaller "Brazils." The more urban, affluent, and populous southeastern region contrasts with the more rural and poorer northeastern region, which contains concentrations of the black and mestizo populations. This regional counterpoint is not absolute. Due to an intense within-country migration toward the metropolitan areas, there are extremely poor segments of the population mingled with extremely wealthy ones. This leads to the process where the former are pushed to the city outskirts. For example, while the rate of infant mortality in 1986 was 53 per 1,000 births for the entire country and 48 per 1,000 for the city of São Paulo as a whole, that rate was 125 per 1,000 for Ferraz de Vasconcelos, a small town within the São Paulo metropolitan area, a rate nearly double that of the northeast region (75 per 1,000).

Economic and Social Changes

Brazil has lived through major changes during the past two decades. In the 1970s Brazilian society became industrialized and urbanized, due in large measure to enormous loans from developed nations. This period is referred to as the "Economic Miracle." On the political level, these alterations occurred in the context of a dictatorship installed in 1964.

Changes in values were also observed during this period and were clearly reflected in family life. Although the Brazilian family could be characterized as "traditional" (large in size, composed of a couple and their children, and having the husband as the head of the family), patterns observed during the last two decades indicate considerable transformation. These include a smaller size, due among other things to a decreasing fertility rate, and the significant increase in families headed by a single woman. Individualistic values and a concern for privacy not only reinforce the tendencies mentioned above, but also are reflected in another recent phenomenon—the increase in number of people living alone, which tends to reinforce the urban and "nuclear" way of life of the Brazilian family.

Brazilian society has also gone through changes in social politics during the past 20 years. Ours is by no means a welfare state. Many rights have been accomplished only on paper. For example, compulsory, public, and free education for 7- to 14-year-old children was legislated in 1971. However, this right is not yet a reality: in 1986, 16 percent of the Brazilian children in this age group were not attending school. The highly regarded public system of higher education, which is of very good quality and is very costly to the state, serves almost exclusively students from the middle and higher economic strata, who do not have to pay for it. This is an example of "mis-targeting" in the country's social expenditures. Although these investments represent a significant portion of the gross national product (20%), they do not give priority to those with fewer resources. When one combines social welfare, education and health, employment, housing, and urban infrastructure, one finds that the 41 percent of Brazilians occupying the lower economic strata receive only 20 percent of these social benefits, while 34 percent are received by those in the upper strata.

The "Economic Miracle" slowly came to an end during the 1980s, and the country began to live through a major economic crisis, a recessionary period caused by the low influx of external financial resources and the intensification of international interest on the foreign debt accumulated during the years of dictatorship. The crisis combines negative growth in the gross national product with increased unemployment (primarily in metropolitan areas), decreases in wages, dramatic increases in inflation and in the cost of food, a greater disparity in income distribution, a decrease in the per capita production of food, a decline in social spending, the transfer of resources out of the country as payment of the foreign debt, and an internal debt that has led to an increased concentration of resources in financial sectors.

These elements have led to an increase in the labor participation of mothers, especially in the informal sector, and of children and youth, in order to compensate for the loss of income and for increasing inflation. Important impacts on the quality of children's lives have also been observed, especially in rates of mortality and morbidity and in school performance.

Children under the Age of Seven

There are approximately 24 million children under seven years of age in Brazil, and they make up about 17 percent of its population. These children are concentrated predominantly in the southeastern and northeastern regions of the country. They are more highly concentrated in urban (69 percent) than in rural areas, but again there are regional variations (82 percent urban in the southeast, only 50 percent urban in the northeast).

Within the newborn to six age group there is a uniform distribution into subgroups: 14 percent are under one year old; 42 percent are between one and three; and 44 percent are between four and six. Thus, the potential clientele for day care programs could be estimated to be 13.2 million children (newborn to age three), and for preschools approximately 10.5 million children (aged four to six).

Recent studies have shown that Brazilian children tend to come from families with very low incomes. Data gathered in 1986 show that 43 percent of newborn to six-year-old children live in households with monthly per capita income of less than half the minimum wage,[1] which can be characterized as living under needy conditions. Of these, approximately 20 percent live in households with monthly per capita incomes of only one-fourth of the minimum wage, a situation characterized as of "absolute poverty." The figures above consider only those children living in households, omitting an unknown number of children living in orphanages or foster care institutions, whose families most probably have the lowest incomes of all.

Most socio-demographic indicators show that children in the rural areas of the northeast constitute the majority of children living in very poor households. Within the metropolitan areas 24 percent of newborn to six-year-old children live under conditions of absolute poverty. In these areas the poorest families, which are those with the largest numbers of small children, are expelled into neighborhoods with urban infrastructure of the worst quality, where there is little community organization and not enough mobilization to influence public policies.

Female participation in the work force reflects the intricate association between family poverty, the incidence of small children, and working mothers. The presence of children greatly interferes with female participation in the economically active population: the activity of women declines when they become mothers and declines even more when they have more than one child. These patterns change with increases in mothers' educational levels because educated women have fewer children and can afford to rely on purchased services (i.e., maids, day care centers).

The basic sanitary conditions of homes of small children are a valuable indicator of their life quality and serve as important factors in determining their health situation. The energy spent to raise children is heavily influenced by whether or not the household has running water. This influence is even greater for children under a year old because these children are more biologically vulnerable to problems caused by the inaccessibility or poor quality of water and are a greater demand on motherly attention and time. In 1986, 60 percent of all children under age one, 92 percent of those children in families earning less than one fourth of the minimum wage, 85 percent of those living in the northeastern area, and 96 percent of children living in rural areas lived in homes with inadequate sanitation.

Adequate sanitation infrastructure is especially important in day care center and preschool projects as new programs are established in Brazil because aggregations of small children easily become focal points of contagious disease.[2] Some of the sanitary programs already established in Brazil have been particularly careful in this regard. However, those day care programs using the so-called free spaces available in the community provide no better sanitary conditions than do the poor households themselves.

Given the poverty associated with the Brazilian infant population, the high infant mortality rates and their differentiated distribution reported earlier in this chapter are hardly surprising. These rates have improved somewhat since 1980, but this improvement has not been continuous. During 1983 and 1984, at the peak of the economic crisis, the mortality rate returned to the 1980 level in the northeastern and northern regions of the country.

Again it is important to emphasize that the public policy response to the economic crisis in Brazil has been inequitable. A World Bank document (1988) shows that Brazilian children under five years of age, who make up 13 percent of the population, receive only 7 percent of the total social benefits. Families living in absolute poverty with children under five, who represent 19 percent of the total population, receive only 6 percent of those benefits. Concrete evidence of this inequity in Brazilian social policies can be found in the analysis of day care and preschool policies and programs provided in the next section of this chapter.

DAY CARE AND PRESCHOOL PROVISION IN BRAZIL

There is no administrative organization in Brazil, public or private, with sole responsibility for day care centers and preschools. The responsibility for such matters has been divided among different ministries and administrative departments at the federal, state, and municipal levels, diluting and dispersing actions and resources and preventing proper monitoring of those programs that have been established. Moreover, nowhere in the country is there a clear delineation of the concepts of day care and preschool, either in terms of child groupings by age or regarding the time (full or part) spent in the institution. In general, day care centers and preschools must accept only children under seven, which is theoretically the age when elementary school begins.[3]

While not specified formally, traditions have led to differentiation between day care and preschool. Day care services tend to be under the responsibility of welfare agencies, to offer a more custodial program, to accept younger children, and to operate full time. Preschools are more likely to be administered by the educational system, to function with more qualified personnel (professional teachers), to operate part time, and to serve children from more well-to-do families.

Day care centers and preschools may be public or private. The public programs may be under the supervision of federal, state, or local municipal administrative bodies. Lately, there has been a tendency to consider the local agency the most satisfactory form of administration. The public programs are usually free, with the family contributing for school supplies and to the Parents and Teachers Association. Among private programs the preschool generally differs from the day care center in that the former is paid for and serves a richer segment of the population, while the latter may be managed by private charitable, philanthropic, or community agencies and is nonprofit. When the day care program is free and depends totally or partially on public money, it serves low resource families. However, there are also private day care centers, which are paid for with parent fees and so serve the children of richer families.

Both day care and preschool programs offer free meals, the quality and quantity of which varies by program. In the city of São Paulo, for example, there are day care programs that supply 100 percent of the children's daily caloric and protein needs.[4]

Family day care is rare in Brazil. Center-based day care and preschools predominate. Family-based day care does not seem to have found a place in Brazilian tradition, perhaps because poorer families, who do not use day care centers or preschools, prefer to raise children at home (see Table 3.1).

QUALITY OF CARE

The present situation with Brazilian day care services reflects a transition period, in which old and new orders interact to bring about a rapid ex-

Table 3.1
Age Groups of Children and Number of Educators

AGE	Number of Children	Number of Educators			Ratio Educator/Children
		Mornings	Afternoons	Total	
0 to 11 months	15	3	3	6	1/5
from 1 yr to 1 yr 11 months	15	3	3	6	1/5
from 2 yrs to 2 yrs 11 months	20	2	2	4	1/10
from 3 yrs to 3 yrs 11 months	20	2	2	4	1/10
from 4 yrs to 4 yrs 11 months	20	2	2	4	1/10
from 5 yrs to 5 yrs 11 months	20	1＞1	1＜1	6	1/13.5
from 6 yrs to 6 yrs 11 months	20	1	1		

São Paulo Department of Childhood and Youth

pansion and a clear image of these services. No consensus has developed to provide a nationwide definition of the minimum requirements concerning program quality. There are lots of debates, many proposals, and some experimental alternatives, but as yet nothing has been settled. Thus it is impossible to describe the patterns of activities in "typical" Brazilian day care centers because there are neither standard norms at any level (national, state, or local) nor any agency responsible for their registration and inspection. Anyone can start a day care center, defining her/his own criteria concerning staff size and qualifications, space, equipment, time schedule, quantity and quality of food, teaching material, and curriculum.

In this context the quality of service varies as much as the income distribution of Brazil; that is, the quality of services varies according to the available resources and the clientele. The poorer the population the less "per child investment" in day care. This means more children per adult, caretakers with less education, and consequently an exclusively custodial type of service.

Questions related to type of day care curriculum and professional qualification of caretakers are raised in debates, and the majority demands that day care have an educational—not just custodial—role, that is, that the day care system be under the jurisdiction of the educational system and that day care personnel should have at least secondary education and receive specific training.

This demand is being met in some counties and in some public day care networks. However, at the present time anyone can be a caretaker, just as anyone can start a day care center. Nowhere in Brazil is there a caretaker career path, with established criteria for training or for salaries. No formalized curriculum exists for training day care workers. Day care programs serving poor families try to save money precisely in terms of the number and qualifications of caretakers, whose education is usually elementary and whose social-educational profile (including salary) is very similar to that of domestic workers. When caretakers are trained at all, this occurs on the job or in sporadic workshops.

Thus the current quality of day care centers in Brazil is extremely varied, be they center based, home based, or in the workplace. The best way to appreciate this diversity is with concrete cases. I will describe two examples drawn from the public sector: a small network of day care centers (20 centers, each serving 130 children) under the jurisdiction of the São Paulo Department of Childhood and Youth and a more extensive network in the Northeast called "Ceará Community Day Care."

The São Paulo Network

Although this system was defined as giving priority to children whose family wages equal three times the minimum wage (US $171) or less, its program can be considered a model that many people would like to see implemented for all Brazilian children. The service is free, totally subsidized by the state. The building housing the program was designed specially for day care: it is ample, colorful, and equipped with furniture and equipment carefully chosen to facilitate the staff's work and to offer a stimulating, warm, and safe space to the children. The program offers rich and varied food (five meals a day), based on a nutritionist-prepared menu that satisfies all the dietary needs of the children.

The children are organized in small groups according to age. Based on Vigotsky's and Wallon's theories of socio-interactionism, the daily activities of the children (although not yet systematized in a curriculum) are organized to offer learning possibilities through interactions with the people and objects in the day care setting. A split between education and care is carefully avoided, so that children will not have the common Brazilian day care experience of spending their day waiting—to be changed, to take a bath, to eat, to sleep, and finally, for their mothers to pick them up.

In order to fully meet the goal of supporting the well-rounded development and learning of children, the caretakers in this day care center are required to have at least a secondary school degree and to complete a specific training program before they are hired. They receive systematic supervision for the six hours each day that they work directly with the children. Adult-child ratios meet international standards (see Table 3.1). Thus, this is a public day care program that can be compared to good day care in developed countries, where any middle class Brazilian family would feel comfortable placing its children.

The Ceará Community Care System

This system differs greatly from that described above. It is much larger (147 programs), serving 11,000 children in the age range from 0 to 6 years and 11 months (an average of 78 children per day care center). As in São Paulo, the buildings were built as day care centers, but due to local poverty and scarce resources the majority of them are simply of cement construction with no running water, sanitation, or garbage collection. More than half of these day care centers use no pedagogical approach and are without sufficient teaching material. Caretakers have only elementary educations and no specific day care training. Each one is responsible for 20 children. The result is a service that provides only custodial care, a standard that is typical of day care centers that serve poor populations.

The differences between the care provided in these two types of centers can really only be appreciated by spending time in each setting. Because the São Paulo system provides a standard representative of Brazil's long-term goals, an overview of staffing, staff training, and caregiver-child ratios in that system is provided in Tables 3.1 to 3.3.

Table 3.2
Center Staffing Pattern (Enrollment: 130 Children)

Position	Number	Educational Level
Director	1	University with training in education
Pedagogical Coordinator	1	University (psychology or pedagogy)
Assistant Director	1	University with training in education
Administrative Assistant	1	Technical school (secretary)
Nurse	2	Middle, technical school (nursery)
Educator	30	Middle, preferably teaching, with specialization in pre-school
Chef	1	Elementary (4th grade)
Cook	5	Elementary (4th grade)
General Services	5	Literate
Janitor	1	Elementary (8th grade)
Guard	2	Literate

Day Care at the Workplace

Since 1942 there has been a law in Brazil that requires private establishments with more than 30 women of reproductive age to "provide adequate place for nursing their children." This is extremely restrictive legislation, which excludes smaller enterprises and rural and domestic workers. It has never been very effective and has resulted in day care at only a few establishments. This lack of effectiveness can be explained by the absence of state inspection, extremely low penalties for non-compliance, and lack of commitment by the unions.

In the 1980s the public sector demanded an extension of this law to workers at federal, state, and municipal work sites, and such legislation was established in some states and counties. In the state of São Paulo, for example, the following amendment to the State Constitution was approved: "The State will maintain, in the prescribed legal form, in public establishments with more than 30 women workers, appropriate place where their children under seven years of age will receive assistance and supervision while their mothers are working."

This obligation was met effectively only where women mobilized to make it effective. Nonetheless, São Paulo now has 180 day care centers for its workers' children. The majority of university day care centers may be included in this group because most of them are public and operate to serve the children of professors, workers, and students rather than as experimental

Table 3.3
Content of Staff Training: Day Care Centers

Content of general training:

- Training presentation.
- Presentation of day care/pre-school of the Department: architectural project; food, health and psychopedagogic outlines; integration among areas.
- Conceptions of day care, children, education, and family.
- Development of small children.
- Economic, social, and cultural characteristics of intended users.
- Health: outlines, conceptions, and actions in promoting health.
- Food: outlines; food in day care/pre-school and at home; meaning of the kitchen and the lactary place.
- Hygiene: basic principles of environmental and clothes hygiene; notions of contamination and roles of professionals in contamination prevention; procedures for environmental hygiene.
- Work at day care/pre-school; routine, evaluation, and norms.

Content of educator training:

- Child development from 0-6 years old.
- Working with 0 to 3 year-old children: food, health, psychological, and pedagogical aspects.
- Sexuality.
- Developing knowledge of 0 to 6 year-old children.
- Researching pedagogical material.
- Educator's methodological working tools: observation, report, reflection, synthesis, evaluation, planning, routine, and meetings.
- Educator's role in work with children.

centers for faculties of education or psychology. Many of these day care centers are excellent. They have introduced innovations and can be considered the best in public day care. One example of such innovation is the acceptance of men as caretakers by the day care program at the University of São Paulo (the most important university in the country), a practice rarely accepted in Brazil.

The new Brazilian Constitution, promulgated in 1988, extended the chapter on social rights (free assistance to children and dependents from birth to six years of age in day care and preschool) to include the right to day care and preschool for all children under 6 years and 11 months of age of women and men working in the private sector. However, ironically this right was not applied to workers in the public sector.

In Brazil legal guarantees are not necessarily translated into practice. Presently the country is going through a process of adjusting implemented laws—including labor legislation—to the new constitutional rights. We do not know yet which mechanisms in the local legislation will be used to ensure the fulfillment of this new right. It is very possible that in addition to building workplace day care centers, use will be made of day care coupons and salary payments. Day care coupons, a little used practice, involve complementing the worker's salary in order to pay (totally or partially) for the day care or preschool used by the family. Salary payments, a mechanism that has been in use in the country for a number of years, involve having the private sector transfer funds to the public sector for the purpose of building and maintaining schools.

These are welcome ways of fulfilling constitutional rights since they are flexible and they respect the employee's freedom of choice. However, they can be a hindrance to mothers who work outside the home and want to nurse their babies.

Preschool Services

The situation for preschools is somewhat different from that of day care because theoretically they are under the jurisdiction of an educational administration. This is "theoretical" because in fact there are "clandestine" preschools operating without being registered or inspected by any such educational body. This is made possible by calling them day care, little hotel, nursery, or any other name with which one associates children and physical space (e.g., Center for Children's Acquaintanceship).

No national guidelines or requirements for preschool curricula exist, and as a result great variation in curricular practices is found. The main theoretical orientations guiding educational practice derive from Montessori, Piaget, Wallon, and Freinet. The following overview of the curriculum in the São Paulo county preschool network (containing 401 programs, serving 169,000 four- to six-year-old children) provides an example:

• Language: body, oral, plastic, music, writing.
• Knowledge of physical and social environment: family, community, school, means of transportation and communication, natural phenomena, animals, vegetables, and minerals, other themes of interest to children.
• Mathematical (logical reasoning): classification, seriation, sequence, time, space, measurement, numbers.
• Perceptual-motor development: ample motor coordination, visual-motor coordination, visual discrimination, auditive discrimination.
• Socio-emotional development: self-concept, socialization.

Preschools under the jurisdiction of an educational administration theoretically serve four- to six-year-old children. Like all educational institutions in Brazil, their teachers (usually women) have secondary level teacher training, many of them with specialization in preschool.

Preschool specialization takes one year beyond the secondary level teacher training. There is no nationwide curriculum for the training of preschool teachers. In the State of São Paulo this training consists of the following disciplines: fundamentals of preschool children's education (considering historical, legal, philosophical, and sociological aspects); preschool children's development, emphasizing its biological and psychological aspects; didactics of preschool education; practice of preschool education, which includes supervised work; physical education, with emphasis on recreation and games; artistic education (especially the plastic arts); health programs, especially in terms of preschoolers' nutrition and hygiene; and moral and civic training. Although preschool teachers are required to have training, a number of them in fact are not so qualified. Ten percent have only an elementary school education.

There are no nationwide norms establishing the number of children per preschool class or teacher. Existing ratios, levels of teacher training, and age distribution of preschool enrollees are shown for Brazil as a whole in Table 3.4.

Literacy Classes

In addition to day care and preschool programs, some Brazilian states have recently created so-called literacy classes, which are mainly located in state elementary schools. Without an official conceptualization, these classes are neither part of the mandatory elementary school nor are they preschools because they receive children who are both younger and older than seven years (seven years being the legal age for mandatory elementary schooling). In 1987, 1.4 million Brazilian children were registered in these classes. Forty-eight percent of these children lived in rural areas, and 35 percent were less than seven years old. In these classes there is one teacher per 23 children. The proportion of teachers without educational qualifications is high: 54 percent do not have magisterial training. The large majority of these classes are in the Northeast area of Brazil (72%), and they are not found in the richer states like São Paulo. Some of them parallel the first elementary grade. They receive children whom school directors maintain are likely to have literacy problems in regular schools. This parallel educational track has high potential for becoming a form of economic and racial segregation.

Types of Child Care in Urban Metropolitan Areas

Since both program and administration responsibilities are so dispersed and decentralized in Brazil, the total amount invested in day care and preschool services is unknown. Although the day care and preschool statistics are rare, sparse, and not always reliable, there has been some effort lately to improve them. The best evidence of this effort is the 1985 Household Survey, which included a supplement about the population under the age of 17. This supplement included six different questions about the attendance rate at day care centers and preschools in the ten major metropolitan regions

Table 3.4
Registered Preschools in Brazil (1987)

Teacher Training	Teachers in Preschool (N = 137,702)
1st grade	10.4%
2nd grade	69.2%
Superior	
Students	**Students in Preschool (N=2,172,082)**
Public network	66.0%
Private network	34.0%
- 4 years	9.8%
4 years	18.6%
5 years	32.3%
6 years	33.3%
+ 6 years	6.0%
Urban area	90.6%
Rural area	11.4%
Teacher/Student Ratio	
National average	1/24
Public network average	1/25
Private network average	1/22

of Brazil. The most significant information from this survey is included in Table 3.5. Notice first, that although rather insufficient, use of day care/ preschool service seems to have grown considerably in the last few years. While not entirely reliable, earlier studies suggested that in the early 1980s less than 10 percent of children under seven years of age were attending day care centers or preschools. Table 3.5 indicates that in metropolitan areas this number had increased to 23 percent in 1985.

The variations among regions were not very significant. However, Table 3.5 shows that the percentage of children attending private institutions was high. This figure must be understood in the context of the ambiguity of the concepts of public and private when applied to day care or preschools. Unlike the private school, private day care centers are usually publicly supported but administered by private institutions (see earlier).

The high percentage of people who pay for attendance at day care centers and preschools (87%) deserves comment. It indicates that most institutions, including the public ones, charge parents something for their services, even if indirectly through the Parents and Teachers Association.

The fact that most children (80%) attend day care centers/preschools part

Table 3.5
The Care of Children Age Birth to Six in Ten Metropolitan Areas of Brazil
(1985)

Question	Percentage of children
Attend Day Care/Pre-School	23.2
Type of Facility	
private	56.8
public	34.2
company-owned	0.4
Pay to Attend Facility	87.4
Hours/Day	
up to 4 hrs	80.2
more than 4 hrs	9.4
8 or more hrs	6.8
Age Started Attending	
less than 1	4.3
1-2 years	18.6
3-5 years	66.7
6 years	6.9
Why Not Attend	
not necessary	70.0
lack of financial resources	15.1
far from home	5.0
Who Cares for Child When Not in Day Care	
mother	72.4
sibling over 13 years	1.8
alone or with sibling under 14	2.5
on the streets	0.0
Who Cares for Children Majority of Time	
mother	78.4
siblings over 13 years	1.9
alone or with sibling under 14	2.7
on the streets	0.0

*The total of the above percentages is not 100% due to a large percentage of unanswered questionnaires.

time (up to four hours) is not surprising, considering that part-time services are especially available, in both the public and the private sectors. One of the most interesting findings shown in Table 3.5 relates to the age at which children start attending these institutions. Two thirds start between the ages of three and five, and nearly one fourth start under the age of three, which indicates real change in family attitudes toward the value of these facilities. The fact that very few children (4%) started attending day care centers at less than one year of age is understandable, given the lack of availability of nurseries in workplaces (only 0.4%) and the reduced number of vacancies for babies in both public day care centers and those provided by companies.

Finally, it is important to comment on the data at the bottom of Table 3.5. When not attending day care centers or preschools, the majority of newborn to six-year-old children are at home with their mothers, and very few are left alone, with young siblings, or in the street. It is possible that self-imposed censorship played a role in these answers, due to the still prevalent social expectation that the mother should be providing full-time care for her small child. However, these percentages may also represent the first evidence that the "abandoned child" phenomenon is not as extensive as the national and international media would like us to believe. I do not want to minimize the hardships of the poor families that make up the majority of the Brazilian population. But it is important to point out that building arguments for the expansion of day care and preschool facilities based on large numbers of abandoned children may be mistaken, either in terms of concrete reality, or in terms of the political-philosophical stance this represents, and the message it sends about the organizational abilities of poor families. Based on ethnographic observations, Claudia Fonseca (1987) has shown how common it is for mothers in the slums of the southern region to leave their children with relatives or friends while they work and to continue to feel very bonded with them. The separation of the child from the mother that usually occurs in times of crisis, when minimum living conditions are under serious strain, is considered by group members not as abandonment, but as the mother meeting her responsibility for working to support her child.[5]

What is needed are public services intended for the general population that are planned in such a way as to reach as first priority the poorest families, which have life styles different from those of the middle class. The recognition of the need to expand day care and preschool facilities to all families that would benefit from them has now been formalized in the new 1988 Constitution as a right acquired by all Brazilians. The processes leading to this latest legal development provide some insight into the future of day care in Brazil and thus are the subject of the final section of this chapter.

FORCES AFFECTING FUTURE DIRECTIONS IN DAY CARE POLICY

A new discourse and new practices related to day care were generated in the city of São Paulo during the latter half of the 1970s. These new developments involved the interaction of three social protagonists, whose agendas were often conflicting; the State, neighborhood organizations, and the feminist movement.

The State

The State, represented in the city of São Paulo by the city government, had been formulating political and administrative programs to address social problems since the 1950s. A social climate demanding public services (transportation, schools, health facilities) pressured the city to create a social work agency, which traditionally has been responsible for the welfare of young children.

Prior to the 1970s, the ideological orientation of this social work agency was the result of a confluence of three paths: the social doctrine of the Catholic Church, Marxism, and community work strategies stimulated by international agencies (The United Nations, UNICEF). The result of this confluence was an emphasis on a normative conception of the family: the goal to be pursued by the social work organization was to support or to recover the integrity of poor families, in the sense of avoiding adjustment problems in children and adolescents. Day care centers were introduced from this perspective, as a support service to the family in its functional role as provider of human capital for the work force. Besides having this preventive character, day care was also seen as an institution capable of overcoming deficiencies in the development of poor children. This was the beginning of the spread of theories of "cultural deprivation" in Brazil that would underlie and shape the proposals for day care centers in public agencies until the end of the 1970s.

This compensatory and prophylactic view of the role of day care—as agencies destined to avoid or compensate for family deficiencies—was also introduced on an administrative level in social work organizations. Because they were characterized as assistance programs rather than as a right, as is the case of basic education, the State did not assume total responsibility for their implementation, but instead appealed to partnerships with private institutions.

Thus both on the local and on the national levels, the customary Brazilian practice until the late 1970s was indirect action on the part of the State in the care of small children, through the channeling of public funds to private institutions (first philanthropic and assistance organizations and later community-based agencies). This practice was stimulated during the 1960s by the proposals of international organizations aimed at massive participation through the so-called alternative programs, which were installed on "free spaces" in the community and developed with "community participation" through the collection of funds to maintain services and volunteer work.[6]

The Neighborhood Organizations and Feminist Involvement

In 1964 a military coup produced a dictatorship that severely restricted freedom of expression and the freedom to organize. Political parties, unions, and other organizations ceased to operate or remained under the direction of intermediaries. The media were censored. People who opposed the regime were imprisoned, tortured, exiled, or assassinated, or they simply disappeared.

Despite this authoritarian presence, beginning in the 1970s there was evidence of organized citizens' groups in the larger cities that revolved around neighborhoods. Singer and Brandt (1979) point out that "the obstruction of institutional channels for public representation...stimulated basic ties of solidarity for the daily survival of the population; neighborhood relations, kinship, friendship and camaraderie, provided protection for individuals in a social climate of fear. To a great degree, it was the development of these direct ties between people who could trust one another which led to various grassroots movements" (p. 13).

Women were active participants in these movements. Starting in 1975, feminist organizations began to spring up in Brazil, whose participants were drawn mainly from the middle class and from clandestine leftist parties. At about this same time, both in the women's movements and in the community movements, the demand for day care was initiated. Public protests began to occur (prohibited to a certain point by the military regime), as well as initiatives to demand or to expand day care centers. Organizations of both public and private employees struggled for day care, documenting the need with data. They developed projects, evaluated costs, formed committees, and accomplished the establishment of day care centers. Organized groups at the neighborhood level, composed mainly of women, mobilized themselves, organized and built day care centers using community volunteer labor, centers designed to be eligible to receive financial support from the city government. Groups of women from the neighborhoods traveled long distances by bus to demonstrate the need for day care to municipal officials, and to the mayor himself.

Separate groups came together to form a coalition movement in 1979 called the Movement to Fight for Day Care (O Movimento de Luta por Creches). Within this movement feminists redefined women's identity by revising the concept of day care: day care became something women fight for not as mother looking for aid, but as women demanding the right to work. Through exchanges with community-based groups, a model was developed by the Movement to Fight for Day Care containing the following characteristics: day care should be public, free, non-custodial, and include parents' participation.

The beginning of the 1980s brought a pre-electoral period at the end of the dictatorship. The elections affected legislative assemblies, the Senate, and the city and state governments. Political parties, both those in power and the opposition, included expanding the network of day care centers in their platforms. The mayor of São Paulo, representing the party controlling the national government, wooed voters in the communities.

During this period the Movement to Fight for Day Care obtained promises from São Paulo city government: 830 day care centers would be established in three years. The movement did not merely demand more facilities; it also pushed for improvement in the quality of care. Certain construction standards were requested, and special attention was paid to staff selection, including the centers' management. One hundred twenty new centers were built in the city of São Paulo, the majority of which were directly managed by the municipal administration. For the first time in Brazil, a rather large network of public day care centers was available, with plans for expansion, operating guidelines, and a commitment to something more than custodial child care.

In 1983, the Municipal Chamber of São Paulo (now controlled by the opposition party) installed a Special Committee of Inquiry on Day Care because the network of public day care centers was having serious problems. This committee argued that construction was very expensive and that maintenance costs were high. They suggested the provision of incentives to motivate participation of the private sector (church, charity organizations, community groups), arguing that the State should contribute only indirectly through affiliated organizations. The Movement to Fight for Day Care ceased to operate as a political force, as a unified movement. Its members were drawn instead into reorganized political parties.

Differences in Feminist Perspective

Why did the movement disband? A close analysis of the events of that time shows that beyond the collective and objective demands for day care there were shades of disagreement. It is as though the issue of day care had been used temporarily to cover up fundamental political differences among the women's groups, allowing the development of a common strategy for the moment: the mobilization of women.

What were these differences? On the one hand, the feminists, considered radical and stigmatized as "bourgeois revisionists" for focusing on gender discrimination, took on the fight for day care because the issue permitted criticism of the traditional role of the mother—it fit feminist ideology. On the other hand, groups that had recently been converted to feminism, rising out of political movements that gave priority to class struggles, found in the demand for day care the possibility to mobilize and organize women and so were able to ally themselves with the "radical feminists" without confronting the divisive questions of sexuality, family planning, decriminalization of abortion, and women's control over their own bodies.

Participation by organized feminist groups in the Movement to Fight for Day Care was episodic and ended quickly. While the issue of day care continued to be raised in meetings of feminists, feminist groups gave higher priority to other issues, such as violence, health, decriminalization of abortion, and family planning. The reorganization of political parties, with the strengthening of the opposition, corresponded to the so-called political opening (the weakening of the military dictatorship), which undid established alliances among feminists. Once again these new political parties were able to serve as galvanizers and mobilizers and in this context differences between protagonists became explicit.

Day Care and Mainstream Politics

In keeping with the proposal to enlist community participation in the actual running of the centers, a significant portion of the leadership from the Movement to Fight for Day Care was absorbed by city institutions as public employees of the municipal day care network. In addition to losing part of its staff, this absorption by the State created a crisis of loyalty in the movement: the question became for whom is this woman fighting? Part of the moral dilemma stemmed from the fact that while the city was providing an insufficient number of available spaces in day care, at the same time it had perhaps the largest and most complex administrative bureaucracy and staff in the world. This made this day care model expensive to operate (although not necessarily of high quality), which became the fundamental argument used by the city government to limit expanding the day care network and to propose instead emergency programs (like family day care) as essentially temporary solutions.

Despite all this, São Paulo's experience in mobilizing for day care has spread throughout the country. For the first time there was the established experience of a rather large public network of working day care centers, which were rather adequate and very different from earlier efforts that stressed emergency aid and assistance. There was a practice that permitted the criticism of proposals for emergency "alternative" programs with imposed "community participation." Thus, despite the weakening of the Movement to Fight for Day Care, the issue did not disappear from the social agenda. It was incorporated by the Women's Councils (Conselhos de Mulher), administrative organizations that attempted to mediate between the State and the women's movement following the political "opening" provided by the return to an elected government.

Since its installation in the state of São Paulo, the Council on Women's Condition has served as an umbrella organization for a number of committees, including one on day care that provides outreach, seminars, and lectures, offers advice, and develops proposals for creating day care centers. In 1985 the National Council on Women's Rights (CNDM) was created. It also housed a day care committee and participated like other political and civic associations in a key task that had been made possible by the democratization of the country: the elaboration of a new constitution. At that time, in a nationwide seminar, the CNDM day care committee planned and discussed a new day care proposal: "That day care be understood as an extension of the universal right to education of the citizen-child in the age range from 0 to 6 years."

This proposal, which also reflected the ideas of other segments of society, was based on evaluations from and the experience of these programs that had been installed in Brazil. Critics of the emergency programs, which had proliferated in the years of economic crisis as a means of fighting poverty, focused mainly on three aspects: the ambiguity of the concept of community participation, the eminently custodial (especially nutritional) nature of the programs (with little or no educational focus), and the concern that these programs supported and reinforced gender discrimination.[7]

In its day care proposal to the constituents, CNDM showed its concern for both women and children, as can be seen in the statement of principles released in 1985, where day care was considered both an educational service complementing the family and a part of a child's right to an education. In this sense, the statement criticized the custodial model of day care and proposed the following: administrative support, an integrated national policy that takes into account regional differences, legal definition of administrative competency, specification of to whom funds should be distributed, and acknowledgement of caretakers as professionals with adequate training and adequate salaries. The statement also emphasized the need to consider the rights of both children and women in the implementation of any day care policy.

Along with diverse segments of society, CNDM organized the Children for Constitution Movement, which in turn proposed a new charter for children's rights, including the right to day care. Lobbying was organized to put pressure on deputies and senators. The result of this effort is that the new constitution, enacted in 1988, contains an article in the education section specifying that "the duty of the state concerning education will be carried out by means of (among others) a guarantee to enroll in day care and pre-school children from 0–6 years of age."[8]

The fact that the right to day care and preschool is in the education section of the Constitution represents, at least at the constitutional level, a step forward in the direction of overcoming the protectionist, welfare-based character predominant in programs aimed at this age group. It also opens up new possibilities for administering the multiple organizations that finance and manage day care centers and preschools. It is expected that through complementary legislation the distinction between day care and preschool will be based only on age: doing away with the idea that day care centers are for the poor, emphasizing care, and preschool for the richer, focusing on education.

The Fundacao Carlos Chagas research group participated in this political process of reformulating the Brazilian conception of attention to small children. We developed a proposal for creation of a National PreSchool Educational System (to include both day care centers and preschools), that would be responsible for the development and establishment of a "unified and decentralized" policy, with the local municipality as the agency that would carry out educational programs for young children.

At the time this chapter was written the new president, the first one to be democratically elected since 1960, had begun a recessive economic policy as a way to fight inflation. The 1988 Constitution was said to be inflationary and in need of revision. It is likely that the budget cuts are going to affect the social rights of young children, although I hope this prediction does not become reality.

NOTES

This chapter was written as part of the Ford Foundation project "Service of Documentation on Day Care" (Grant Number 870–0887).

1. The monthly minimum wage salary was equivalent to US $57.00 at the official exchange rate.

2. The most common cause of infant illness and death is the malnutrition connected with infectious/contagious diseases of the digestive and respiratory tracts.

3. Recent data shows that preschool has been used as an alternative form of elementary school, especially for seven- to nine-year-old black children. Thirty-four percent of black children in preschool in Brazil are seven to nine year olds. In northeastern Brazil this proportion is 43 percent.

4. The day care network in the city of São Paulo serves approximately 70,000 children.

5. Inflation of the number of abandoned children in the country has been used as a manipulative tactic, either to show that poverty is so immense as to be beyond solution or to get more money allocated to so-called special population segments (children who, hypothetically, are abandoned by their families).

6. The quotation marks in the text have a double meaning: they indicate material borrowed from other texts and also a distancing on the part of the author. Criticism of "community participation" and of the "alternative" character of these programs is offered at other points in the chapter. It is important to realize that there is no "free space" in the community. Every free space is a political space and, as such, is a space in dispute, the use of which must be negotiated.

7. In an attempt to greatly reduce costs and to maximize coverage, these emergency programs depended on volunteer or semi-volunteer work of community members. They used labor that was underqualified (or unqualified) as a means to lower costs, which compromised the development of educational programs. By employing almost exclusively women with low salaries, without the professional training necessary to work with groups of children, they locked day care into a domestic and familial paradigm. Criticism of these programs addressed not only the exploitation of women's labor and its non-professional character, but also pointed out the psychosocial risks of this abusive generalization of the maternal experience.

8. The 1988 Constitution contains a series of other clauses that regulate the rights of children and the family. The following are outstanding instances: maternity leave extended to 120 days; recognition of paternity leave; the right of female prisoners to nurse their children; and acknowledgement of children's legitimacy irrespective of the type of bond between their parents.

REFERENCES

Barbosa, E. M, (1990). *O financiamento de política social para a infância: situacão atual, tendências e perspectivas* (The financing of childhood social policies:

Present situation, tendencies and perspectives). Brasilia: Instituto de Plane-jamento Econômico e Social.

Becker, R. A. (1988). "Brasil: principais causas de mortalidade infantil" (Brazil: Principal causes of infant mortality). In J.P.Z. Chadad and R. Cervini (Eds.). *Crise e infância no Brasil: o impacto das políticas de ajustamento econômico* (Infancy and crisis in Brazil: The impact of economic adjustment policies), pp. 269–280. São Paulo: JPE/USP/UNICEF.

Branco, H.A.C. (1988). *Família: indicadores socias* (Family: Social indicators). Rio de Janeiro: Instituto Brasileiro de Geografia e Estatístiá.

Bruschini, C. (1989). *Tendências da força de trabalho feminina brasileira nos anos setenta e oitenta* (Tendencies of the female work force in Brazil in the seventies and eighties). São Paulo: Fundacão Carlos Chagas. (Textos FCC, 3.)

Campos, M. M., Rosemberg, F., Ferreira, J. M. (1989). *Diagnóstico sobre a edu-cacão pré-escolar na Região Metropolitana de São Paulo* (Diagnosis of the condition of preschool education in the São Paulo metropolitan area). São Paulo: Fundacão Carlos Chagas/Secretaria de Educação.

Chahad, J.P.Z. and Cervini, R. (Eds.) (1988). *Crise e infância no Brasil: o impacto das políticas de ajustamento econômico* (Infancy and crisis in Brazil: The impact of economic adjustment policies). São Paulo: IPE/USP/UNICEF.

Conselho Nacional dos Direitos da Mulher (1986). *Criança: compromisso social, carta de princípios* (Child: Social obligation, statement of principles). Brasília, DF: CNFM.

Draibe, S. (1989). "Por uma nova política social: questões de princípio gestões e administracão" (Toward a new social policy: Issues of priorities, management and administration of basic social programs). *São Paulo em Perspectiva, 3,* 7–12.

Fonseca, C. (1987). "O internato do pobre: FEBEM e a organizacão doméstica em um grupo portoalegrense de baixa renda" (The poor person's orphanage: FEBEM and domestic organization in a low income group in Porto Alegre). *Temas IMESC, Sociedade, Direito, Saúde, 4,* 21–39.

Franco, M.A.C. (1989). "Lidando pobremente com a pobreza" (Dealing poorly with poverty). In F. Rosemberg (Ed.) *Creche* (Day care), pp. 179–216. São Paulo, Cortez.

Haddad, L., & Oliveira, E. C. (1990). "A Secretaria do Bem Estar Social e a creche: dos primórdios a 1979" (The Social Welfare Ministry and the Fight for Day Care). *Serviço Social e Sociedade, 34*(ii), 90–110.

Hammoud, T. (1984). *A participacão popular no movimento de luta por creche* (Popular participation in the Fight for Day Care Movement). Deposition given at Special Inquiry Commission on Day Care at Municipal Chamber of São Paulo.

Jaguaribe, H. (1987). *Brasil, 2000: para um novo pacto social* (Brazil 2000: Toward a new social agreement). Rio de Janeiro: Paz e Terra.

Mattioli, O. (1989). "No reino da ambiguidade" (In the Kingdom of ambiguity). Unpublished master's thesis, São Paulo, SP: Pontifícia Universidade Católica.

Rosemberg, F. (Ed.). (1989). *Creche* (Day care). São Paulo: Cortez.

Rosemberg, F. (1989). O a 6 anos: desencontro de estatísticas e atendimento (0 to 6 years: disagreement between statistics and services). *Cadernos de Pesquisa, 71,* 36–48.

Rosemberg, F., Campos, M. M., Haddad, L. (1991). *A rede de creches no municipio de São Paulo* (Day care networks in São Paulo Town). São Paulo: Fundacão Carlos Chagas. (Textos FCC, 6.)

Rosemberg, F., Campos, M. M., Pinto, R. P. (1985). *Creches e pré-escolas* (Day care and preschools). São Paulo: Nobel/CECF.

Singer, P., and Brandt, V. C. (1979). *São Paulo: o povo em movimento* (People's movements in São Paul). São Paulo: Vozes.

Vieira, L. (1988). "Mal necessário: creches no Departamento Nacional da Crianca" (Necessary evil: Day care in the National Department for the Child). *Cadernos de Pesquisa*, 65, 3–16.

Vieira, L., and Melo, R.L.C. (1988). "A creche comunitária Casinha da Vovó: prática de manutenção/prática de educação" (Grandma's House, Community Day Care Center: Maintenance, practices and education). In F. Rosemberg (Ed.), *Creche* (Day care), pp. 153–178. São Paulo: Cortez.

World Bank (1988). *Creche* (Day care). (Report No. 7086–88.) Washington, D.C.

4

CANADA

Alan R. Pence

Canadian day care has no face; it has only facets, like the many surfaces of a gemstone. Some of these facets are the result of social and political forces as old as Europeans' first contact with Indigenous Peoples and settlement by English and French immigrants, while others are as recent as the result of the latest provincial election. These forces, old and new, interact with changing social conditions to produce a diversity of responses, a faceted array of policies across the country.

The enduring strength of the forces that shape Canadian policies in child care and influence most other aspects of Canadian life were recently evidenced by events associated with the 1990 constitutional discussions generally referred to as the Meech Lake Accord. On the surface the issues addressed by the Meech Lake Accord seemed calm and clear enough, but beneath the surface, complex currents of beliefs and values, most of which well up from deep in the political and social history of Canada, have sunk not only the accord (June 1990) but threaten the present government and potentially the country itself. The accord is a doorway of the present that leads both into Canada's past and into her future. The events that will ultimately shape the resolution of the Meech Lake crisis will also play a powerful role in shaping the multi-faceted face of child care in Canada in the future.

THE MEECH LAKE ACCORD

On first impression, the rationale for the creation of the Meech Lake Accord seems clear: to bring the province of Quebec into the Constitutional Act of 1982. Quebec alone among the ten provinces was not a signator to

the Constitution brought home to Canada from England in 1982 by the
Liberal government of Pierre Trudeau. The Conservative government of
Brian Mulroney, elected in 1984, noted its intent to bring Quebec into the
Constitution. Quebec's premier Robert Bourassa set out five conditions for
that entry:

1. Recognition of Quebec as a distinct society
2. A provincial role in appointments to the Supreme Court
3. A greater provincial role in immigration
4. Limits on federal power in federal-provincial shared-cost programs
5. A veto for Quebec on constitutional amendments.

At a meeting of the First Ministers at Meech Lake (a lodge north of Ottawa,
the nation's capital) in 1987 and a further meeting a month later in Ottawa
all ten premiers and the Prime Minister agreed to seven principles. In addition to the five identified by Quebec, the following two were added:

6. The right of provincial governments to make nominations for the Senate.
7. The entrenchment of annual "First Ministers' Conferences" to initiate further
   constitutional change.

The next step in the constitutional process called for each of the premiers
in attendance to gain the approval of their legislative assemblies by June
1990. By the summer of 1989 eight of the ten premiers had gained the
provincial legislative approval, but two governments were voted out before
the approval had been gained. In March 1990 a third provincial government,
also under a different party's leadership than the one that had initially
approved the accord, reversed its position and rescinded its approval. As
the deadline for approval rushed forward only seven of the ten provinces
had ratified the accord and the submerged tensions of a country some argue
was forged more out of convenience than conviction a little more than 120
years earlier (1867) surfaced to threaten the future of the federation.

The issues and concerns that boiled to the surface of Meech Lake stem
from two interrelated socio-cultural and political-jurisdictional issues. The
first is the question of what constitutes a "distinct society" and the legal
ramifications of that designation. The second, and related, issue is the relative power and responsibility of a central, federal government versus decentralized, provincial governments. The central question at the heart of
both issues is: "Is Canada one or is Canada many?" and a corollary to that
question is: "If it is many, then who are the many and what are their
distinctive rights?"

Quebec's first point, the designation of Quebec as a "distinct society," is
at one level generally accepted within Canada—French-speaking Quebec *is*

different than English-speaking Ontario, for example. But that point then raises the question, "Are there not many 'distinct societies' within Canada?" For example, the many aboriginal peoples present a clear case in point, and certainly East-Indian and Chinese immigrants are very different than Polish or Ukrainian immigrants to Canada. As a follow-up to the issues of "distinct society," a concern has been raised regarding the legal implications of such a statement. Does such a constitutional designation enhance the ability of Quebec to accept or reject conditions, programs, or laws that would be binding on other provinces, or on other distinct groups within Canada?

The question of federalism is a second critical question raised by the Meech Lake Accord. Does acceptance of the accord carry with it the "dismantling of federalism" as former Prime Minister Pierre Trudeau argues? Does Canada, under the accord, become a nation of unequals?

These two concerns lie at the center of the currents of controversy that now boil up from the depths of the Canadian experience. Both the resolution and the manner in which these concerns are resolved will be the primary determinantes of the future of Canadian child care and many other features of Canadian life during this last decade of the twentieth century.

In addition to the dynamics associated with the Meech Lake Accord, several other aspects of Canadian life will influence the future of Canadian child care. Those other forces include (1) the broader social history of Canada, (2) the dramatic transformation of the Canadian labor force in the post–World War II period, and (3) the history of child care in Canada. The following sections will briefly explore these forces as part of a necessary context for an understanding of child care in Canada.

THE DEEPER CONTEXT: A SOCIO-HISTORICAL OVERVIEW OF CANADA

The First Peoples of Canada may have arrived from across the Bering Sea land bridge as early as 80,000 years ago. By the time European contact was established (probably first by Norse Vikings around the year 1,000 A.D.) Aboriginal Peoples had evolved well-developed societies with established trading relations among various tribal groups. Norse settlements did not prosper in North America and ultimately died out; it was not until the 17th century that earlier European voyages by Cabot (British: 1497), Cartier (French: 1534, 1541), and finally by Champlain (French: 1605, 1608) resulted in the creation of enduring European settlements.

From its earliest 15th- and 16th-century contacts with Europe, the land that was to become Canada felt the competition of European interests for its resources. The aboriginal peoples of the maritime regions were decimated by European aggression and diseases and were pushed back from the more desirable lands. One tribe, the Beothuk, became extinct. The politically stronger and larger tribal groups of the St. Lawrence River and Great Lakes areas were pulled into European-initiated conflicts, with tribes such as the Iroquois, Mohawk, Algonquin, and Huron aligning with either the French or the English in those countries' battles for control of the vast land mass.

As the French voyageurs and the British and Scottish traders and trappers pushed ever further into the interior regions, the indigenous peoples were recruited as partners in the fur trade. In many cases, native women became partners as well in the formation of mixed race families living on the frontier. In the case of French and Indian families a new ethnic population, the Métis, became established in certain settlement areas. The history of European and indigenous peoples' contact in Canada was often not as militarily pitched as it was south of the border in the United States, but the legacies of widespread death (largely through disease) and cultural destruction (largely through the decimation of the traditional economic bases of the Native peoples and through the policies of government and church groups) were no less severe.

Although France claimed most of Canada as New France, based on Cartier's discoveries, the French met with only limited success in attracting settlers to the colony. Settlement was thinly established except near and within what became the principal cities of New France, Montreal, and Quebec, with a strip of settlement along the St. Lawrence River. The city of Quebec was lost to the British in 1629 and restored in 1633, the Iroquois threatened the French settlers through much of the latter half of the 1600s, and in 1763 the British completed the occupation of New France following military victories at Louisburg (1758), the city of Quebec (1759), and Montreal (1760).

Under the Quebec Act of 1774 certain traditions of the French in British North America were allowed, such as the continuation of the French system of civil law, and Catholics were allowed appointment to a governing council (reversing an earlier ban intent on full Anglicization). Soon the British colonizers were involved in a war with their American colonies to the south (the United States' War of Independence). Tensions spilled over into Canada, with Americans taking Montreal in 1775. Despite some sympathies with the Americans in both Quebec and Nova Scotia, neither colony joined the revolution to the south. Indeed, the Maritime and Quebec provinces became the recipients of approximately 30,000 British loyalists from the newly proclaimed United States of America during and immediately following the American Revolution.

Tensions remained between British North America (Canada) and the United States following the Peace Treaty of 1783. The War of 1812 between Britain and the United States saw U.S. attacks on Canadian soil at York (now Toronto) and Montreal, while Britain successfully attacked Detroit, controlled much of Maine, and in their most effective campaign drove south from Halifax in 1814 to burn the U.S. capital of Washington, D.C. The Treaty of Ghent in 1814 ended the war and established the forty-ninth parallel as the international boundary extending from Lake of the Woods to the Rocky Mountains. Both sides agreed to jointly occupy the huge Oregon Territory west of the Rocky Mountains for a period of ten years. A distrust of her neighbor to the south has continued to characterize the Canadian attitude toward the United States to the present day.

Much of Canada's history and economic development is regional in nature. The Atlantic provinces split over entering the Confederation largely due to mistrust of Upper and Lower Canada; the interests of neither Upper Canada (Ontario) nor Lower Canada (Quebec) were seen as necessarily compatible with those of the provinces along the Atlantic. On the west coast many in British Columbia advocated for joining the United States. In the Prairie provinces one of Canada's most bitter national conflicts took place when a Métis organization under the leadership of Louis Riel established a provisional government with the intent to negotiate entry into Canada with guarantees for Métis' land and protection of French-speaking rights. The "Rebellion" was ultimately put down and Riel hung, but not without creating further tensions between French Quebec and the rest of English-speaking Canada.

Throughout its history the land that is Canada has felt regional, linguistic, intergovernmental, and cultural tensions. Never resolved, only temporarily appeased, Canada pulsates under the competing and continuing pressures of centripetal and centrifugal forces. That historical context and its contemporary manifestations is central to an understanding of the forces that have in the past and will in the future shape the many facets of child care in Canada. Various historical aspects of Canada play a major role in this overview of Canadian day care precisely because their influence is not just "then," but "now." A second necessary context for an understanding of the forces that shape Canadian day care is the socio-demographic and economic transformation that Canada has experienced in the period since the Second World War.

THE SOCIO-DEMOGRAPHIC TRANSFORMATION OF CANADA IN THE POST–WORLD WAR II PERIOD

Prior to the Second World War Canada was not a major figure among the world's economic and political powers. However, in the aftermath of the war Canada found itself among a small number of industrialized western powers that had not been devastated by the conflict. With its industrial, economic, and population base intact, the post-war period was a period of economic growth, expansion, and optimism about the future of the country.

For many young adults forming families in the late 1940s and early 1950s, the post-war period represented the first period of economic and social stability that they had known following the depression of the 1930s and the war years of the 1940s. By comparison to these two earlier decades, the

1950s was an era of peace and prosperity. The labor force demands of post-war Canada (unlike those in some parts of Europe) did not require the participation of both men and women—mothers and fathers—in equal numbers in the out-of-home paid labor force. What Strickland (1983) refers to as the Victorian family model, with its strongly differentiated roles for fathers as breadwinners and mothers as home-makers, was tailor-made for the economic structure of the time. Not since the 1800s had support for this "separate spheres" model of the family been so strong, and never in Canada's history, with its growing, affluent urban population, had conditions been so ideal for its realization by so many families.

The 1950s were not years for the development of child day care; it was *the* decade of mother care in Canada. Support for the mother–care ethic was solicited from sources as divergent as misplaced research (e.g., the use of R. A. Spitz's work, [1945], based on residential care, rather than day care studies), religious leaders and the Bible, and business as well as labor groups. For most families the "ideal" had become achievable, and popular culture in the form of television shows of the era (produced in the United States but popular in Canada as well) reflected that growing urban and suburban reality.

The quiet certainty of Dad at work and Mom at home that characterized the great majority of Canadian families in the 1950s and early 1960s experienced a gradual transition in the mid- to late 1960s. A similar transformation in the United States was described by Ralph Smith as "The Subtle Revolution" in his 1979 book by that title. Smith's terminology captures well both the significance of the transition and its failure to capture the attention of policy makers and the public at large during the period of the 1960s and 1970s. At the heart of Canada's subtle revolution was a dramatic increase in the percentage of women, more specifically mothers, entering the out-of-home labor force (see Figure 4.1). Other dramatic changes affecting Canadian family life during this period include a decline in the fertility rate from 3.7 in 1961 to 1.7 in 1986; an approximate two-fold increase in divorce rates from .6 per 100,000 in 1971 to 1.2 per 100,000 in 1986, and an increase in single-parent families from 9 percent in 1971 to 13 percent in 1986. (If not noted otherwise, all demographic statistics are based on data from Statistics Canada, Canada's central bureau of statistics.)

Taken individually, such changes are at variance with the Victorian family model of the 1950s; taken collectively, their effect was to create a diversity of family forms where one form had been predominant before. Within all families, two-parent and one-parent, full parental employment outside of the home became ever more commonplace, commencing in the late 1960s and continuing through the 1980s. By the early 1980s approximately one-half of the mothers with children under the age of six were employed outside of the home. The welfare oriented child care system of the 1960s (described

Figure 4.1
Percent of Women in the Labor Force and Percent of Mothers with Children
Under the Age of Six in the Labor Force

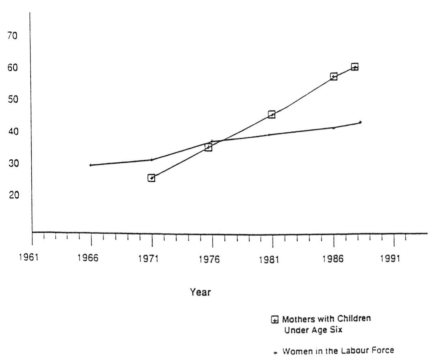

Year

⊞ Mothers with Children
Under Age Six

+ Women in the Labour Force

SOURCE: Pence, A., and Church, M. (1989). Figure based on Statistics Canada
Census Data and Status of Day Care Reports.

in the following section) was not able to keep up with the greatly increased
demand for child care spaces. The unmet need for formal, licensed services
spilled over into the informal, unlicensed sector of child care, swelling the
cottage industry of informal caregiving, and ultimately accounting for up
to 85 percent of all day care provided in the country. Such statistics, and
the findings of a Toronto-based child care study in the late 1970s (Project
Child Care, Johnson, 1977, 1978), led to the description of a mounting
"day care crisis in Canada." Prior to the late 1970s day care in Canada
had never been termed a "national crisis," and prior to that period few
Canadians would have believed, or chosen to use, such a charged statement.
The history of child care in Canada, a history developed in what Pence
(1989) has called the "shadow of mother-care," will be briefly examined
as a "third context" for understanding contemporary Canadian child care.

A BRIEF HISTORY OF CHILD CARE IN CANADA

For most of Canada's history child care has not been an issue. The care of children was resolved within the context of typical familial roles, which in turn operated within a social context that tended to integrate various age groups into the collective society to a greater degree than is the case in the latter part of 20th-century Canada. Given this lack of age separation and institutionalization for specific age groups, it is somewhat surprising to note that Canada's first programs for young children, the Infant Schools, developed in the early part of the 19th century. By the mid-1820s it is known that Infant Schools could be found in at least three Canadian cities: Montreal, Halifax, and Charlottetown. It is very possible that additional programs existed in other parts of seaboard Canada, but the full history of Infant Schools in Canada has yet to be written.

Based on the development of Infant Schools in the United States and Great Britain, it can be assumed that the Canadian programs also arose largely as a result of the impact of growing industrialization and urbanization, with the concomitant impacts of these forces upon family life and the economic structure of families. As was the case in the United States, the Infant Schools of Canada had largely disappeared by 1840 as Canada entered a century and a half of family life and values predicated on what the Victorian family model, with its support of an ethic of mother care.

Child care in Canada during the period of the late 1830s to the late 1970s can be seen as existing within the shadow of a mother-care ethic. During this period, and persisting to the present, a stigma was attached to those families that did not realize the ethic of mother care. Child care programs that arose during this period (including creches of the mid-19th-century day nurseries and settlement kindergartens in the late 1800s and early 1900s and day care programs of the mid-20th century) were all predicated on a welfare model of service for those "few" needy families that could not meet the social norm of mother care. Those programs, initiated largely by church groups in the mid-19th century, settlement workers in the late 19th century, and professionals first from private agencies in the early 1900s and then by public auspices in the mid-1900s, all shared a welfare service orientation that stigmatized not only the families and children in need of care, but the entire concept of day care as well. The century-long history of day care as welfare care established a legacy of opposition to such care even when the demographics of the need for care shifted from the "unfortunate few" to the normative many.

The furthest evolution of federal government support to child care as a welfare service took place in 1966 with the introduction of the Canada Assistance Plan (CAP), designed to provide financial support to those families "in need or likely to become in need" of assistance. The Canada Assistance Plan allows for a sharing of welfare related expenses between the federal government and participating provincial governments. The only other time that the federal government of Canada supported child care, and again it was through a cost-sharing plan with provincial governments, was from 1942 to 1945 (in Quebec) and from 1942 to 1946 (in Ontario), the period of the Second World War when women were needed to work in essential war industries. Only Ontario and Quebec took part in that short-lived Dominion-Provincial agreement, although several other provinces considered participation. While the experience of the war years did not establish a continuing role for the federal government in support of child care, it did help to establish a base for later child care developments, particularly in the province of Ontario.

It was not until 1970 that the federal government officially evidenced an awareness of the shifting demography of child care need across Canada. The report of the Royal Commission on Women, released in 1970, noted: "The time is past when society can refuse to provide community child care services in the hope of dissuading mothers from leaving their children and going to work." A few of the recommendations of the report were considered by the federal government, but in general the profile of child care rose only slowly in the 1970s, awaiting the 1980s for more dramatic actions and activities. Key Canadian day care events in the period 1970 to 1990 include the following:

1970   The Royal Commission on Women Report is released. For the first time a major government document noted the shifting structure and economic base of families and called for enhanced government involvement in the provision of child care.

1971   The Federal Department of Health and Welfare, in cooperation with the Canadian Council on Social Development (CCSD), co-sponsored the First National Child Care Conference in Winnipeg, Manitoba. Recommendations from the Winnipeg conference called for the establishment of a Federal Day Care Information Office.

1972   The Federal Day Care Information Office is established within the Department of Health and Welfare, and in 1973 the first annual *Status of Day Care in Canada* report is issued. The report marked the earliest effort on the part of the federal government to document the status of day care services across the provinces and territories.

1982   It was ten years before the Federal Government agreed to co-sponsor a second National Day Care Conference. Again the co-sponsor was CCSD and again the conference site was Winnipeg. Many (including this author) see "Winnipeg II" as a key catalyst for bringing the issue of childcare to the fore in Canada. The origins of two national day care organizations can be traced to events that took place at the second Winnipeg Conference in 1982: the Canadian Day Care Advocacy Association (CDCAA), an active day care lobbying association committed to a comprehensive system of "universally" accessible, publicly funded, high quality child care services; and the Canadian Child Day Care Federation (CCDCF), an organization committed to improving the quality of child care services by providing information and support services to the child care community.

1984   Within two years of the second Winnipeg conference the national Liberal government of John Turner appointed a four-person Task Force on Child Care. The task force, led by Dr. Katie Cooke, a sociologist and researcher who had served as Canada's first president of the National Status of Women Office, undertook an extensive research and review process that culminated in the 1986 release of the task force's final report. The report recommended the development of "complementary systems of child care and parental leave that are as comprehensive, accessible, and competent as our systems of health care and education" (Task Force on Child Care, 1986, p. 281).

1986   The short-lived Liberal government of John Turner was defeated in the fall 1984 elections and Brian Mulroney and the Progressive Conservative party took office that same year. With the report of the Task Force due out early in 1986, the Mulroney government took action on their own child day care initiative, noting late in 1985 their intent to establish a Special Parliamentary Committee on Child Care. The Parliamentary Committee report, a less research oriented document than the Cooke Report, was released in 1987 and provided the government with a statement upon which its own proposed legislation could rest.

1988   The Conservative government introduced child care legislation, Bill C–144, in 1988. Debate on the bill extended throughout the 1988 sitting of Parliament, but it died in Senate when the government called an election in the fall of 1988. With the re-election of the Progressive Conservatives that fall, the new government issued a commitment to address the day care issue within its second mandate to govern.

1990   On several occasions in 1989 and 1990 the Prime Minister and other cabinet ministers reiterated their intent to introduce child care legislation before the end of their current term in office.

The dates noted above provide a very brief overview of key recent events in the history of child day care in Canada, one of three key contexts necessary for an appreciation of the dynamics that shape the evolving facets of Canadian day care.

CANADIAN DAY CARE: A CONTEMPORARY SNAPSHOT

The preceding sections have painted elements of the social, political, and historical "backdrops" necessary for an understanding of the current drama of child care in Canada. Without that context the current provision of care could be described, for comparative or other purposes, but the uniqueness of the road that Canada has followed to arrive at its current position(s) would not be understood, nor would one's ability to anticipate future developments be informed. It is important to bear in mind as one considers the following picture of day care in Canada (largely based on 1988 data), that there currently does not exist any federal legislation in Canada directly addressing the issue of child day care. The abortive Bill C–144 (1988) was not passed by Parliament and the welfare oriented CAP legislation (1966) remains the primary vehicle for the cost-share funding of day care in Canada. Furthermore, it is important to remember that the regulation of child care in Canada is a provincial/territorial responsibility, a fact that is clearly evident in the great range of regulations, service providers, and funding arrangements that will be considered later in this section.

Children and Families in Contemporary Canada: A Demographic Overview

Children in Canada form a diminishing proportion of the overall population. The percentage of the population made up of children 14 years and younger has continuously decreased from a post–World War II high of 34 percent in 1961, to 21.3 percent in 1986. The ratio between those over 65 years and those 14 and under has shifted dramatically over the past century and a half, with future projections indicating even more dramatic transitions toward an aging society.

Although the proportion of children in the overall population is declining, the actual number of children six years old and younger has been relatively stable throughout the 1980s. The above stability suggests an expanding Canadian population despite the fact that Canada's fertility rate has been below the replacement level of 2.1 since 1972. Clearly, immigration is a major factor in Canadian population dynamics. Canada's population growth of approximately 1 percent per year throughout the 1980s is largely due to immigration (150,000 to 160,000 individuals per year in the late 1980s). As Figure 4.2 indicates, for much of Canada well over 25 percent of the population has neither French nor British ethnic origins. In some population centers such as Vancouver, British Columbia, approximately one half of the children in the elementary grades speak neither English nor French in their homes. Canada is increasingly a non-European ancestry, multi-cultural, urban society (over 50 percent of all Canadians live in cities with populations over 50,000).

Canadian home life has changed a great deal in the past several decades. Not only has the uni-modal distribution of families shifted from the Victorian out-of-home employed father with mothers and children at home to a broader variety of family forms, but also characteristics such as the composition of those families have changed a great deal as well. For example,

Figure 4.2

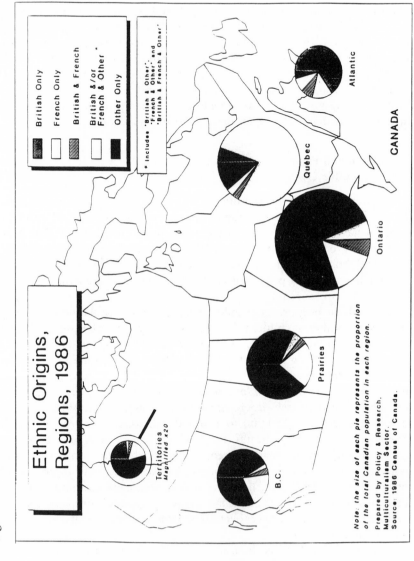

Ethnic Origins,
Regions, 1986

British Only

French Only

British & French

British &/or
French & Other *

Other Only

* Includes "British & Other",
"French & Other", and
"British & French & Other".

Territories
Magnified x20

B.C.

Prairies

Ontario

Québec

Atlantic

CANADA

Note: the size of each pie represents the proportion
of the total Canadian population in each region.

Prepared by Policy & Research.
Multiculturalism Sector.
Source: 1986 Census of Canada.

in 1966 approximately 30 percent of all two-parent families had three or more children; in 1986 that figure was less than 15 percent—middle children are becoming increasingly rare within Canadian families.

As increasing numbers of mothers enter the out-of-home labor force, increasing numbers of children receive non-parental care. As noted earlier, the number of children requiring care has soared since the mid-1970s, while the provision of licensed care has grown slowly. For child care advocates and for a growing number of parents this discrepancy represents a crisis in child care, and both the federal and provincial governments are under pressure to respond to the increasingly obvious and critical needs of parents and children.

The Regulation and Provision of Care in Contemporary Canada

In the case of Canada, the paradoxical assertion of the permanence of change is central to an understanding of child care. The specific regulations, funding mechanisms, and numbers served vary enormously from province to province, and from year to year. What is more permanent, in the Canadian context, are the forces that influence change.

Figure 4.3 provides a quick reference to the rapidly increasing number of children presumed to be in need of child care services and the much less dramatic increase in the number of licensed spaces available. This ratio of licensed spaces to child care need is perhaps the most significant statistic available concerning the Canadian child care system. It underlines the fact that Canada does not have what could be properly termed a regulated child care system. The majority of child care in Canada is provided through informal arrangements operating beyond the scrutiny of government. The current provision of care bears witness to Canada's orientation toward child care as a service for welfare eligible parents. Just as welfare services are designed for the few, so too is licensed child care in Canada available only for the few.

The Federal Day Care Information Office includes in the annual *Status of Day Care Report* a glossary of child day care program types typically considered in their annual surveys. This glossary provides a quick reference to the various forms of care typically considered as part of "child care" in Canada.

As with all other facets of Canadian child day care the caregiving picture varies greatly across Canada's ten provinces and two territories. Table 4.1, taken from Health and Welfare Canada's annual report *Status of Day Care in Canada, 1988*, notes the variability in the number of licensed family day care spaces versus licensed center care spaces across the 12 jurisdictions.

Two terms from the glossary warranted a special table in the 1988 Report: "Non-profit" and "Commercial." The inclusion of Table 4.2 highlights the current interest in issues of program ownership/sponsorship and reflects a

Glossary

Day Care Facility

For the purposes of this report, a day care facility refers to a licensed or provincially approved center or private home which provides care for children outside of their own home for eight to ten hours a day.

Center Care

Care that is given to groups of children in licensed day care center.

Commercial Center

A licensed day care center that is set up as a proprietary operation. It includes the large franchise operations, as well as the small singularly owned center.

Community Board Center

A licensed day care center that is established as a non-profit organization and is governed by a community board of directors.

Non-Profit Day Care

For the purposes of this report, non-profit day care includes both the Community Board Centers and the Cooperative Day Care programs.

Public Day Care

A licensed day care center owned and operated by a municipal or provincial government.

Family Day Care

Family day care is defined as a program involving the selection and supervision by a government or authorized private agency of private families who give care to children during the day.

Private or Casual Day Care Arrangements

This involves the use of babysitters or other similar types of arrangements made between the parent and the provider and which are not under the supervision of a licensing authority or day care agency.

Infant Day Care

Care provided by a day care center or a family day care home for children under the age of two.

Preschool Day Care

Care provided by a day care center or a family care home for children aged to two to six.

School-Aged Day Care

Supervision of young school-age children before school begins, during the noon hour, after class, and on days when school is not in session.

Latch Key Child

This term originated from the observation that many young school-age children of working parents were carrying house keys to gain entrance to their homes between the hours that school closed and their parents returned to work.

Figure 4.3
Estimated Number of Children in Need of Day Care per Year versus Estimated Number of Licensed Spaces per Year

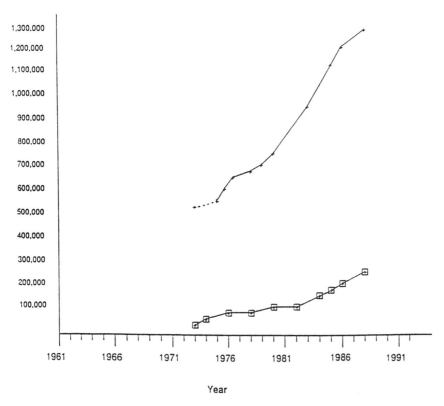

Year

+ Children in Need of Day Care

⊞ Licensed Spaces

SOURCE: Pence, A., and Church, M. (1989). Figure based on Statistics Canada
Census Data and Status of Day Care Reports.

shift, much desired and promoted by day care advocates across the country, toward more non-profit sponsorship.

The issue of private/for profit versus non-profit sponsorship is typical of the many different facets of child care found across Canada. Non-profit center sponsorship ranges from a high of 98 percent in Saskatchewan to a low of 22 percent in Alberta. For some provinces, such as Ontario, program sponsorship has generated intense advocacy efforts to move more fully toward a non-profit service system, while in provinces such as Alberta, the for-profit commercial sector has been politically effective in blocking efforts to promote greater non-profit sector.

Table 4.1
Interprovincial Comparison of Licensed Day Care Spaces

Province	Center Spaces	Family Day Care Spaces
Newfoundland	1,640	-
Prince Edward Island	1,584	49
Nova Scotia	5,508	145
New Brunswick	5,175	33
Quebec	59,892*	4,850
Ontario	86,361	10,115
Manitoba	9,172	2,057
Saskatchewan	3,700	1,900
Alberta	41,161**	6,157
British Columbia	17,816	5,494
Northwest Territories	403	-
Yukon	375	72
National Totals	232,787	30,839

*20,898 of Quebec spaces are operated under the auspices of the Department of Education

**Alberta provided data for preschool spaces and municipal officials provided estimates for school-aged spaces.

SOURCE: Canada. Department of Health and Welfare. (1988). Status of Day Care Reports. Ottawa, Ontario: Government of Canada.

Child care advocacy and lobbying mix with regional and provincial politics to produce different results in various parts of the country. It is interesting to note the differences in regulations, financial support, and types of services available between Alberta and Ontario and realize that both, through the mid-1980s, had long histories of Progressive Conservative governments. As another example, the territory of the Yukon was, until 1988 and 1989, far back in the development of its provincial regulations. However, with the election of a New Democratic Party government in the mid-1980s, the Yukon has instituted one of the most progressive pieces of child care legislation in the country. Two measures of a province's/territory's commitment to quality in licensed center care are staff-child ratios and staff training requirements. Again, as can be seen in the table below, Canada is

Table 4.2
Sponsorship of Center Space, 1987 and 1988

Type of Sponsorship	1987 Spaces	1988 Spaces	Increase No.	Percent
Non-Profit	126,229	143,875	17,576	13.9*
Commercial	90,386	88,912	-1,4748	-1.63*
Total	216,685	232,787	16,102	7.43

SOURCE: Canada. Department of Health and Welfare. (1988). Status of Day Care Reports. Ottawa, Ontario: Government of Canada.

seen to extend from quite progressive legislation to relatively traditional welfare positions.

From the 1988 center ratios and training requirements reported in Table 4.3, one can see that even within some provinces, ratios and group size restrictions may be of a high standard, while training requirements may be quite low. Alberta, for example, had one of the strongest staff-child ratios (1:3) and group size (6 children) requirements for infants 0 to 19 months, but it was also one of the least progressive provinces for staff training requirements, requiring only a "first aid certificate" (as of 1988). A further anomaly in the Alberta situation is the presence and strength of several well-regarded two-year early childhood education programs in a province requiring only minimal training for employment. The Northwest Territories, New Brunswick, and the Yukon Territory present similar staff training versus child ratio and group size dichotomies.

A second dichotomy for some provinces is a discrepancy between regulations governing family day care and regulations governing centers (Tables 4.3 and 4.4). A province such as Manitoba, with relatively strong center ratios, has one of the poorest (highest) family day care ratios in the country (1:8). Again, unique and complex mixes of progressive and regressive forces have interacted over time to create a complex and multi-faceted image of child care in Canada.

Yet another point of variability across the provinces and territories is the funding system employed within each jurisdiction. Table 4.5 shows the ratio of federal to provincial expenditures of public funds for child care in 1987. This ratio varies from 27 percent federal to 73 percent provincial in Alberta to 72 percent federal and 28 percent provincial in the Northwest Territories.

A constant across the provinces and territories is the relatively low wages and low status afforded child care workers. As was noted on Tables 4.3 and 4.4, training requirements in many provinces/territories are minimal, requiring no specific early childhood education and care (ECEC) training. Largely as a result of such minimal standards, and the implicit projection

Table 4.3
Child Care Centers: Standards and Regulations (1988)

Province	Maximum Center Size	Child Age Groupings	Staff/ Child Ratio	Maximum Group Size	Standards for Staff Training
British Columbia	75	*<18 mos. 18 mos.-3 yrs. 3-6 yrs. 5-6 yrs. 7-12 yrs.	1:4 1:8 1:10 1:15	12 25 20	E.C.E. Certificate issued upon completion of Level 1 Basic Requirements (approx. 10 mos. training). Certificates for <3 and Special Needs upon completion of Post Basic Requirements. No training required for Out of School Programs.

*B.C. Regulations (1988) do not specify standards for infant-18 mos. programs; those existing care centers were licensed on an individual basis by the Provincial Child Care Facilities.

Province	Maximum Center Size	Child Age Groupings	Staff/ Child Ratio	Maximum Group Size	Standards for Staff Training
Alberta	80	0-19 mos. 19-35 mos. 3 - 5 yrs. 5 yrs. 6 - 12 yrs.	1:3 1:5 1:8 1:10 unregulated	6 10 16 20 n/a	First Aid Certificate
Saskat- chewan	60	*<18 mos. 18-30 mos. 31 mos.-6 yrs 5 - 12 yrs.	1:5 1:10 1:15	n/a	40 hour E.C.E. training program

* Saskatchewan Regulations (1988) do not specify standards for children <18 mos.

Province	Maximum Center Size	Child Age Groupings	Staff/ Child Ratio	Maximum Group Size	Standards for Staff Training
Manitoba	70	12 wks.-1 yr. 1-2 yrs. 2-3 yrs. 3-4 yrs. 4-5 yrs. 5-6 yrs. 6-12 yrs.	1:3 1:4 1:6 1:8 1:9 1:10 1:15	6 8 12 16 18 2 30	Child Care Worker I Basic Requirement is to begin child care training (of approx. 600 hrs.). Child Care Worker II & III completed child care training. 2/3 of staff must be I or II.
Ontario	n/a	<18 mos. 18-30 mos. 31 mo.-5 yrs. 6-12 yrs.	3:10 1:5 1:8 1:15	10 15 24 30	One program staff required to have equivalent to 2 yr. Diploma in Child Studies & 2 yrs. experience. No formal training for other staff members.
Quebec	n/a	<18 mos. >18 mos. 5-12 yrs.	1:5 1:8 1:15	15 30 u/a	1/3 of all staff must have diploma in E.C.E. or a related field & 3 yrs. relevant work experience.
New Brunswick	n/a	<2 yrs. 2 yrs. 3 yrs. 4 yrs. 5 yrs. 6-12 yrs.	1:3 1:5 1:7 1:10 1:12 1:15	9 10 14 20 24 30	No training required. Staff must be willing to take training as required.
Nova Scotia	50	0-2 yrs. 2-3 yrs. 3-5 yrs.	1:3 1:5 1:10 1:12	6	One person must have E.C.E. training and experience. Have to undertake some upgrading every 2 years

Table 4.3 (continued)

Province	Maximum Center Size	Child Age Groupings	Staff/ Child Ratio	Maximum Group Size	Standards for Staff Training
New-foundland	50	*<2 yrs. 2-3 yrs. 3-5 yrs. 6-12 yrs.	1:6 1:8 1:15	n/a	New staff required to have one year supervised work experience or suitable E.C.E. or related training

*Newfoundland Regulations (1988) do not specify standards for children under 2 years.

Province	Maximum Center Size	Child Age Groupings	Staff/ Child Ratio	Maximum Group Size	Standards for Staff Training
North-West Territori es	n/a	0-18 mos. 19-35 mos. 35 mos.-5 yrs 6-12 yrs.	1:3 1:6 1:8 1:10	6 12 16 20	None required, no training programs available. Children's cultural background to be reflected in background of staff.
Yukon	n/a	<18 mos. 19 mos. -3 yrs. 3-5 yrs.	1:4 1:6 1:8	n/a	None required. Minimum 18 years old.

Key:
  n/a - not applicable
  u/a - information difficult/impossible to collect

SOURCE: Canadian National Child Care Study. (1992). <u>Provincial and Territorial</u>
           <u>Reports</u>. Ottawa, Ontario: Statistics Canada.

that "any woman can provide care," the wages and working conditions of most child care workers are less than that found for "zookeepers" (a popular statement found in many Canadian media reports in the mid-1980s). As part of the *Task Force on Child Care Report* (1986) a study was commissioned titled "The Wages and Working Conditions of Workers in the Formal Day Care Market" (Schom, 1985). Some of the findings of that study are noted in Table 4.6 below.

Given the minimal requirements and low salaries associated with employment in child day care, it is somewhat surprising to find in most provinces and territories relatively strong ECEC programs in the post-secondary college system. These colleges generally offer between nine-month and two-year education and training programs specific to child day care and pre-school employment (an increasing number offer family day care course work as well). Instructors, by and large, are B.A. and M.A. level individuals who serve as visible leaders in their provincial and territorial child care and ECEC professional and advocacy associations.

Strengths and Shortcomings

The theme of this report on day care in Canada has been diversity. Within the range of day care options one finds both greater and lesser training opportunities, funding supports, and regulations. Choosing selectively, one could make a case that Canada has significant strength within its child care system, or alternatively, one could argue that Canada's system is woefully

Table 4.4

Family Day Care Homes: Standards and Regulations (1988)

Province	Child Age Groups	Maximum # by Age Group	Maximum # of children in Care	Staff Training
British Columbia	<12 mos. 13-14 mos. 24 mos.-5 yrs. 3-5 yrs. Out of School	*1 *2 5 2	7	n/a n/a n/a n/a

*BC Regulations (1988) state that only 2 children under age 24 months can be on premises at one time.

| Alberta | <2 yrs.
*<3 yrs. | *2
*3 | 6 | n/a
n/a |

*Alberta Regulations (1988) state that only 2 children under age 2 or 3 children under age 3 may be on premises at one time.

| Manitoba | <2 yrs.
3-5 yrs. | 3
5 | 8 | First Aid Certificate |
| Saskatchewan | 6 wks.-30 mos.
6 wks.-6 yrs. | *3
5 | 8 | n/a
n/a |

*No other preschool children allowed.

| Ontario | <2 yrs.
<3 yrs.
Handicapped | *2
*3
2 | 5 | |

*Ontario Regulations (1988) state that only two children under age 2 or 3 children under age 3 may be on premises at one time.

In Ontario, the Private Home Day Care Agency must hire one Home Visitor for every 25 homes, who has completed an approved post-secondary program of studies plus 2 years experience working with age groups enrolled in the day care homes.

| Quebec | n/a | | *4 | n/a |

*Unlicensed family day care permitted up to 9 children with 2 caregivers. Unlicensed family day care are those that do not belong to a family day care agency.

| New Brunswick | <2 yrs.
2-5 yrs.
>6 yrs.
Mixed ages | 3
5
9
6 | *9 | n/a
n/a
n/a
n/a |

*Community day care home figures

| | **<2 yrs.
**2-5 yrs.
**>6 yrs.
Mixed ages | **2
**4
**5
**4 | **5 | n/a
n/a
n/a
n/a |

**Family day care home figures

| Nova Scotia | nsr | nsr | nsr | nsr |
| P.E.I. | <2
3 yrs.to school-age | 6
7 | 7 | 1 unit continuing Education, personal references. |

76

Table 4.4 (continued)

Province	Child Age Groups	Maximum # by Age Group	Maximum # of children in Care	Staff Training
Newfoundland	n/a	n/a	8	n/a
N.W.T.	<2 yrs. <3 yrs. <6 yrs.	2 3 6	8	n/a n/a n/a
Yukon	n/a	n/a	6	n/a

SOURCE: Canadian National Child Care Study. (1992). Provincial and Territorial Reports. Ottawa, Ontario: Statistics Canada.

Key: n/a not applicable
      nsr not specified in the standards and regulations

Table 4.5
Government Expenditures for Child Care (1987)

Province	Federal	Provincial
British Columbia	48%	52%
Alberta	27%	73%
Saskatchewan	54%	46%
Manitoba	43%	57%
Ontario	52%	48%
Quebec	39%	61%
New Brunswick	57%	43%
Nova Scotia	58%	42%
Prince Edward Island	61%	39%
Newfoundland	60%	40%
Northwest Territories	72%	28%
Yukon	54%	46%

SOURCE: Canada. Department of Health and Welfare. (1988). Status of Day Care Reports. Ottawa, Ontario: Government of Canada.

Table 4.6

Wages and Working Conditions in the Formal Day Care Market

Length of Career

	B.C.	Prairies	Ontario	Quebec	Atlantic	Total
Less than 1 year	11.1% 3	5.9& 3	14.3% 17	0.0% 0	12.5% 1	10.2% 24
1 to 3 years	31.5% 6	22.2% 24	47.1% 31	26.1% 11	36.7% 2	25.0% 74
3 to 5 years	20.9% 5	18.5% 10	19.6% 20	16.8% 12	40.0% 2	25.0% 49
More than 10 years	12.8% 5	18.5% 3	5.9% 22	18.5% 0	0.0% 0	0.0% 30
Total Sample	235	27	51	119	30	8

Turnover of Day Care Workers

Length of Career

Length of Employment in Present Job	Less than One Year	1 to 3 Years	3 to 5 Years	5 to 10 Years	More than 10 Years	Total Sample
Less than 1 Year	39.0% 23	37.3% 22	6.8% 4	13.6% 8	3.4% 2	59
1 to 3 years	1.2% 1	60.2% 50	20.5% 17	12.0% 10	6.0% 5	83
3 to 5 years	0.0% 0	0.0% 0	53.7% 29	31.5% 17	13.09& 7	54
5 to 10 years	0.0% 0	6.5% 2	0.0% 0	74.2% 23	16.1% 5	31
More than 10 years	0.0% 0	0.0% 0	0.0% 0	0.0% 0	100.0% 11	11

Average Hourly Wage of Workers, by Region

Region	B.C.	Prairies	Ontario	Quebec	Atlantic	Total
# in sample	27	49	123	31	7	237
Maximum Wage	$13.00	$18.05	$14.00	$11.25	$10.00	$18.00
Minimum Wage	$4.00	$4.25	$4.00	$6.25	$3.00	$3.00
Mean Wage	$7.00	$7.61	$7.12	$7.86	$5.05	$7.29

Source: Schom, Moffatt, P. (1985). The bottom line: Wages and working conditions of workers in the formal day care market. Report to the Task Force on Child Care. Ottawa, Ontario: Supply and Service Canada.

weak. The problem with either statement is that Canada does not have a "system" of day care; it has only a collection of dissimilar policies and programs. This lack of a system of day care services and supports to families that fully recognizes the normative nature of care needed in Canada today, as opposed to a welfare orientation of care for the few "needy," is the single greatest weakness, the most significant shortcoming, in Canadian day care.

If political decisions were to be made that Canada should have a "system" in place to support children and families in their need for day care services, a number of somewhat latent strengths within Canadian day care could be brought to the fore to inform and strengthen such a system. These not yet fully realized strengths include the following:

1. As noted earlier, in the majority of provinces and territories reasonably strong college-level early childhood education programs have been established. In many provinces college instructors form the dedicated backbone of efforts to improve the quality of care in Canada.

2. Over the past five to ten years, Canada has made major strides in developing its own credible research base. In a number of significant areas of research it is no longer necessary for Canadians to look "south of the border" or to Europe for their research information and expertise. Increasingly Canadian day care research is being recognized internationally as well as nationally.

3. Canadian child care associations have experienced tremendous growth and increasing sophistication during the 1980s. Once a more or less negligible force for change, provincial and national associations are beginning to come of age politically and professionally. Many of the provincial associations have begun to network effectively with their provincial counterparts and with two important national organizations: the Canadian Child Day Care Federation (a federation of professional associations) and the Canadian Day Care Advocacy Association (a national lobby group).

As Canada enters the 1990s it is clear that child day care will not be easily erased from the political agenda. The number and percentage of women and mothers entering the out-of-home labor force continues to rise, as does the number of children requiring care and not finding it in the licensed sector. Child care has become a national issue in Canada and one that is not limited to the concern of families alone. Increasingly, employers, as well as government and families, are seeing the need to take action in support of more and better child care options for children and their families. Despite the recession of the early 1990s, it appears that child care will remain a key issue on the political agenda of Canada, at both the federal and provincial/territorial levels.

REFERENCES

Brown, C. (1987). *History of Canada.* Toronto: Lester and Orpen Dennys.

Calgary. Social Services Department. (1977). *Status of day care in Calgary.* Calgary: Author.

Canada. (1988). *The Canada child care act.* (Bill C–144.) Ottawa: Government of Canada.

Canadian National Child Care Study (Pence, Lero, Goelman and Brockman). (1992). Canadian Child Care on Context: Perspectives from the Provinces and Territories. Ottawa, Ontario: Statistics Canada.

Careless, J.M.S. (1970). *Canada: A story of challenge.* Toronto: Macmillan.

Childcare Resource and Research Unit. (1987). Provincial expeditions on child care. Toronto, Ontario: Author.

Doyle, A. and Somers, R. (1978). "The effects of group and family daycare on infant attachment behaviors." *Canadian Journal of Behavioral Sciences, 10*(1), 38–45.

Fowler, W. (1978). *Day care and its effect on early development.* Toronto: Ontario Institute for Studies in Education.

Goelman, H. and Pence, A. R. (1983). Proposal for a national child care research workshop. Submission to Health and Welfare Canada.

Johnson, L. C. (1977). *Who cares: A report of the project child care survey of parents and their child care arrangements.* Toronto: Toronto Social Planning Council.

Johnson, L. C. (1978). *Taking care: A report of the project child care caregiver survey.* Toronto: Toronto Social Planning Council.

Johnson, L. C. and Dineen, J. (1981). *The kin trade: The day care crisis in Canada.* Toronto: McGraw-Hill.

Lero, D. S., Pence, A. R., Goelman, H., and Brockman, L. (1987). *Canadian families and their child care arrangements: A proposal for a national child care survey.* Proposal submitted to Department of Supply and Services, Ottawa.

May, D. L. and Vinovskis, M. A. (1976). "A ray of millennial light: Early education and social reform in the infant school movement in Massachusetts, 1826–1840." In T. Harevan (Ed.), *Family and kin in urban communities.* New York: Watts.

Pence, A. R. (1986). "A favorable change: Infant schools in North America, 1825–1840." In S. Kilmer (Ed.), *Advances in research in early education and day care.* Greenwich, Conn.: JAI Press.

Pence, A. R. (1989). "In the shadow of mother-care: Contexts for an understanding of child day care in Canada." *Canadian Psychology, 30*(2), 140–147.

Ross, K. G. (Ed.) (1978). *Good day care.* Toronto: The Women's Press.

Royal Commission on the Status of Women. (1970). *Report.* Ottawa: Government of Canada.

Saskatchewan Social Services. (1977). *Report on the day care users survey.* Regina: Author.

Schom–Moffat, P. (1985). *The bottom line: Wages and working conditions of workers in the formal day care market.* Report to the Task Force on Child Care. Ottawa, Ontario: Supply and Services Canada.

Schulz, P. V. (1978). "Day care in Canada: 1850–1962." In K. G. Ross (Ed.), *Good day care*. Toronto: The Women's Press, pp. 137–158.

Smith, R. (Ed.) (1979). *The subtle revolution*. Washington, D.C.: The Urban Institute.

Special Committee on Child Care (S. Martin, Chairperson). (1987). *Sharing the responsibility: Report of the special committee on child care*. Ottawa: Government of Canada.

Spitz, R. A. (1945). "Hospitalism: An inquiry into the genesis of psychiatric conditions in early childhood." *Psychoanalytic study of the child*, 1, 53–74.

Statistics Canada (1988–1990). A number of different publications from Statistics Canada were utilized in preparing the report. Most are derived from the 1986 census and the on-going labor force survey.

Strickland, C. (1983). *Victorian domesticity*. Unpublished manuscript, Emory University, Atlanta, Ga.

Task Force on Child Care (K. Cooke, Chairperson). (1986). *Report of the task force on child care*. Ottawa: Status of Women Office, Government of Canada.

Woodcock, G. (1970). *Canada and the Canadians*. Toronto: Oxford University Press.

5

CHINA

Wei Zhengao

During the latter half of the 19th century, after the outbreak of the Opium War in 1840, China evolved from feudalism into a semi-feudal and semi-colonial society. The advent of the "foreign matters" movement and the reform movement of 1898 in the late Qing Dynasty, and the missionary activities of the imperialist powers, stimulated efforts to modernize China's cultural and educational institutions. This included the initial effort to reform the early childhood education of three- to seven-year-old children, which for several thousand years had been confined to family education processes characteristic of the feudal tradition, into a more public socialization process. The first regulations regarding preschool education were formulated and promulgated in 1903, and the first group of preschool educational institutions was born at that time. According to available statistics, 4,893 children were enrolled in kindergartens in 1907. The total number of children newly admitted to these programs in 1908 was 2,610 and in 1909 was 2,664, indicating a very slow rate of growth.

Practice in preschool education in the early years was profoundly influenced by Japanese institutions,[1] so much so that the approach could be referred to as Japanese-style preschool education. The first regulations on kindergartens were drawn up based on Japanese models. Japanese teachers or students returning from study in Japan were employed in the few kindergarten teacher training centers established in the 1900s. Teaching materials and methods were largely borrowed from Japanese institutions.

With the victory of the 1911 revolution, a bourgeois democratic republic was established, without bringing about a fundamental change in the semi-feudal and semi-colonial nature of Chinese society. Influenced by the New

Cultural Movement and the May 4 Movement, China shifted from Japanese to European-American style preschool education.

Curricular patterns, teaching materials, and methods were largely borrowed from European countries and the United States. The theory of education was deeply influenced by John Dewey's progressivism. The prevailing curricular items included music, storytelling, children's songs, play, talk about society and nature, and like topics.

In 1922 the Beijing warlord government promulgated a new educational system. Although preschool education was made an integral part of the new system, its development was very slow and extremely uneven throughout the country. By 1946, when the enrollment rate in kindergartens reached its pre-liberation peak, there were only 1,301 kindergartens in the whole country, with a total enrollment of 130,000 children, served by 2,100 teachers.

Several educationalists imbued with democratic values and patriotic ideas, including Tao Xingzhi, Chen Heqin, and Zhang Xuemen, criticized the feudalistic view of the child, the blind following of Western practices, and the aristocratic styles in preschool education. These leading thinkers initiated kindergartens catering to the needs of workers, peasants, and the populace, set up kindergarten teacher training schools, and conducted experimental studies in their pioneering efforts to find a way for preschool education to fit China's needs. Their theoretical work and practices are rich intellectual resources to be drawn upon by their successors. Noteworthy educational regulations promulgated by the Chinese government in the 1930s and 1940s included "Norms and Standards of Kindergarten and Primary School Curriculum" (1932), "Kindergarten Regulations" (1939), and "Procedure for the Establishment of Kindergartens" (1943).

It should be pointed out that in the late Qing Dynasty and the early Republican years, kindergartens and kindergarten teacher training courses run by missionaries preceded those run by Chinese nationals or public authorities. According to a report released by the Chinese Christian Education Investigation Group in 1921, there were 138 kindergartens set up by Christian churches with a total enrollment of 4,324 children. During the Republican era, there were four kindergarten teacher training schools run by churches.

The Communist party of China has always shown great interest in the needs of children and concern for the development of preschool education. Nurseries were established by the revolutionary cadres as early as 1927, when the first revolutionary bases were set up. This marked the beginning of day care in rural areas. Regulations concerning preschool education were also formulated and promulgated in those days. In the Labor Law of the Chinese Soviet Republic formulated in 1931 were explicit provisions for fixed breast-feeding time for mothers and the establishment of nursing rooms and child care centers in factories. In 1932, the Hunan-Hubei-Jiangxi Provincial Government promulgated a transitional education system, of which kindergartens serving three- to seven-year-old children were an integral part. In 1934, the Central People's Commissariat of Internal Affairs promulgated regulations for nurseries serving one-month to five-year-old children.

In March 1938, during the Sino-Japanese War, the Chinese Wartime Child Care Society was established in Wuhan. More than 20 local chapters of the society were established in various provinces and regions, including the Shaanxi-Gansu-Ningxia Border Region, and in Hong Kong and the South Sea Islands. Under the auspices of the society, 53 child care centers were established during the War of Resistance against Japanese Aggression, accommodating more than 30,000 war-stricken children.

During the difficult times of the 1940s, the Shaanxi-Gansu-Ningxia Border Region government promulgated a number of regulations to protect expectant mothers and women in labor, and promote child care. Child care in the Border Region was conducted in accordance with three fundamental principles: (1) the institution of a system of public child care—all the children of front line soldiers and party and government functionaries would be taken care of by the government; (2) the promotion of child care in a systematic way throughout the Border Region; (3) the effort to improve child care in the Border Region in a comprehensive way, for the well-being of all children. A Division for Child Care was set up within the Department of Public Health of the Border Region government, to be in charge of all affairs related to the survey, registration, and statistics related to expectant mothers, women in labor, and children, and the awarding of prizes to meritorious workers and units. A Child Health Care Section was set up within the only hospital in the Border Region, to serve the needs of children. By 1945, a system of public child care had taken shape, including a network of nursery schools, public creches, and kindergartens, accommodating 1,180 children. Other smaller nurseries or creches, accommodating at least 930 children, were also in operation. These child care institutions were operated in various modes, including boarding programs, day nurseries run by the children's mothers through labor exchange, breast-feeding rooms, and preschool classes attached to primary schools.

During the times of the Third Revolutionary Civil War, the task of caring for the offspring of revolutionary cadres became all the more arduous. In November 1946, the Second Nursery School in Yan'an had to be evacuated due to war contingencies. All its workers, caring for 136 children ranging in age from a few months to seven years old, succeeded in traversing 800 kilometers in three months, surviving the threats of enemy bombing and strafing and the rigors of mountain and river crossings, to reach the Taihang Liberated Area. With the gradual expansion of the Liberated Areas, a number of nurseries, kindergartens, and nursery schools were set up in various liberated areas to meet the needs of waging the war and reconstructing the rear areas. These wartime institutions laid a sound basis for the development of child care and early childhood education in the People's Republic of China.

SOCIAL AND ECONOMIC FACTORS SUPPORTING DAY CARE POLICIES

A number of factors, some originating in mid-century and others more recent, have converged to create appreciation for the value to society of national policies related to early child care and education. Five of these themes are discussed briefly below.

The Women's Liberation Movement in China

The founding of the People's Republic of China in 1949 and the establishment of the socialist economic system provided great impetus to the liberation of Chinese women. Women's extensive participation in various spheres of social life, and the realization of the socialist principle "from each according to his ability, to each according to his work," liberated women from the confines of the household and made them equal partners with men in the employment arena. The equal rights women enjoy in all spheres of life—political, economic, cultural, social, and family—were written into the Constitution. Promulgation of the first Marriage Law of the People's Republic in 1950 and the second Marriage Law in 1980, as well as a number of other legal instruments used on constitutional provisions, also protect the rights and interests of women and permit the healthy development of the women's liberation movement.

Both the Communist party and the government have emphasized alleviating women of the burden of household chores, partly by "socializing" aspects of housework (with non-profit cafeterias and ready-to-eat foods), and partly by promoting the sharing of household chores among members of the family. These efforts, along with the gradual development of child care institutions and the diffusion of household appliances, all serve to emancipate women from the demands of the household.

Level of Economic Development

The success of the socialist system is a fundamental prerequisite to the development of preschool education in China. The development of preschool programs is heavily dependent on the availability of needed resources, which in turn depends on the level of productivity of the national economy. Therefore, the development of the national child care program must be at a pace that is synchronized with the pace of economic development. During the "Great Leap Forward" initiated in 1958, preschool education expanded

Table 5.1
The Development of Kindergartens between 1957–62

Year	Number of Programs	Enrollment (in thousands)	Number of Staff
1957	16,420	1,088	101,400
1958	695,297	29,501	1,553,000
1959	532,043	21,722	1,131,100
1960	784,905	29,331	1,584,400
1961	60,307	2,896	294,800
1962	17,564	1,446	161,400

very rapidly, despite real economic constraints. The result was an inevitable subsequent decline in preschool programming. Table 5.1 shows the development of kindergartens during the 1957–1962 period.

There was an over 40-fold increase in kindergarten care in a single year (1958), but by 1962 the number of programs had declined nearly to the point at which it had been five years earlier. During the last decade the steady development of preschool education has resulted from care in making a good match between the need for those services and the resources available to provide them.

Family Planning and Changes in Family Structure

Family planning has been a fundamental policy of the People's Republic in its efforts to exercise control over increases in population. The proportion of married couples resorting to some method of family planning or birth control has been steadily increasing. According to the Bulletin of the 1989 National Family Planning Sample Survey, the percentage of couples employing family planning methods increased from 51 percent in 1980 to 58 percent in early 1988.[2] Inferring from this survey, there were about 28 million couples receiving certificates as single-child families in 1988, accounting for about 14 percent of married fertile couples.

In order to facilitate enforcement of the one child policy, various rewards and disciplinary sanctions have been instituted. Among the rewards are the following: (1) parents of an only child shall be awarded an "honorary certificate of single-child parents" upon application; (2) holders of the above-mentioned certificate are entitled to receive a monthly monetary reward until the child reaches 14 years of age; (3) full expenses of medical care and part of the expenses of early childhood education shall be borne or reimbursed by the working units of the parents in accordance with relevant regulations; (4) the maternity leave of the mother may be extended from three to six months, subject to the approval of the working unit (those practicing late marriage and late birth shall be given even more liberal extensions of the maternity leave); (5) preferential treatment in the allocation of a plot for building living quarters are given to the parents of a single child living in the countryside. Parents in disadvantaged families may have their contribution to voluntary labor in public projects reduced or even exempted, and preferential treatment is to be given them in finding employment in village and township enterprises.

In concert with social transformations and economic growth taking place in the country, the average size of families has been shrinking, giving rise to changes in the structure of families. The data revealed by the 1987 National 1 percent Sample Population Survey document the following changes in the Chinese family:

1. *Decrease in the average size of families.* The average size of the Chinese family was 4.2 persons in 1987, a reduction of 0.2 compared with data gathered in 1982. In the economically more developed provinces, the average family size has fallen below four persons. From a long-term perspective, family size tends to decrease with increases in economic growth.

2. *Increase in the number of nuclear families.* Two-generation or nuclear families have become the dominant family pattern, accounting for two thirds of all households nationwide.

3. *Three-generation families are on the rise.* Even as the average size of families is becoming smaller, the proportion of three-generation lineal families is slightly increasing. According to the 1987 sample survey, the percentage of three or more generation lineal families among the total number of households increased from 17 percent in 1982 to 19 percent in 1987. This indicates that lineal families still have their legitimate place in Chinese society and are likely to continue to exist in the years to come. This is because lineal families are usually of medium size, with a relatively low cost of living, and are well adapted to the needs of caring for children and the aged. Lineal families are also more advantageous than nuclear families in the countryside, where households continue to function as productive units and shoulder the responsibilities of organizing and managing production, and of rational allocation of the labor force within a family.

As more and more married couples are practicing planned parenthood and the percentage of single-child families is increasing, "striving for better pregnancy outcome, and better care and education for children" have increasingly become the concerns of the whole society, providing strong impetus for the development of early childhood health, day care, and education programs.

Implementation of the Nine-Year Compulsory Education Policy

In 1986 a law was passed mandating nine years of compulsory education for all children in China.[3] This requirement has enhanced the development of preschool education by drawing the attention of educational authorities, especially in the countryside, to the need for primary school preparation. In order to better prepare young children for primary schooling and raise its initial standards, a number of governmental bodies at provincial, municipal, and county levels have adopted measures to speed up the development of pre-primary classes, and even made their attendance compulsory, in order to help children adapt more quickly to school life. Consequently, the one-year pre-primary classes have recently made great strides. According to statistics for 1989, of the 611,668 kindergarten classes existing nationwide, 46 percent were attached to primary schools. Of the total enrollment in kindergartens (18,476,559), 47 percent of the children were in pre-primary classes attached to primary schools.

Growing Demand for Highly Skilled Workers

The successful realization of the goals of socialist modernization of the country ultimately depends on the quality of the work force. This requires the successful completion by all citizens of a sound basic education. The new demands placed on worker skills by the drive to modernize in China have aroused widespread concern about education in early childhood from all quarters of society, and this is providing further impetus for their development.

Day Care and Preschool Policies and Programs

China encompasses a vast territory, populated by more than 1.1 billion people. As a developing country its industrial and technical capabilities are not yet highly advanced, and its development is uneven. Under these conditions it is absolutely impossible to develop a system of preschool education reliant solely on state financing. Forty years of experience have taught us that the only feasible way to develop preschool education is based on a policy of starting from the realities of local economic and social development and mobilizing the resources of society.

In a joint notice promulgated by the Ministry of Education, the Ministry of Public Health, and the Ministry of Internal Affairs in February 1956, the following policy guidelines were given:

With the progressive development of economic and cultural construction of the country, there will be more and more women joining productive and social work. In order to help working mothers take care of and educate their children, nurseries and kindergartens should be developed accordingly. In cities they should be sponsored and run by factories and mines, enterprises, institutions, social organizations, and the communities. In the countryside, agricultural production cooperatives should be encouraged to run their own nurseries and kindergartens (mainly seasonal ones for the time being). The public health and educational departments should strive to run well a small number of nurseries and kindergartens, serving as demonstration models.

This community development approach involves drawing financial support from three main sources: the state, the collective enterprises, and parents. Nurseries and kindergartens are also run under three different auspices: public agencies, collective enterprises, and individual service providers. Within this general framework, the implementation is somewhat different in urban and rural areas. In the cities a few kindergartens run by public educational departments serve as demonstration models for the majority of the other programs, which consist of kindergartens run by industrial and commercial enterprises, public institutions (hospitals, museums, etc.), governmental bodies, the armed forces, public schools, and local neighborhoods. These programs are supplemented by those run by individuals (most often in their own homes). In rural areas, kindergartens and nurseries run by the township (*xiang*) government serve as models, with the majority of programs run by villages.

Management of the Preschool Education System

In 1956, the Ministry of Education, the Ministry of Public Health, and the Ministry of Internal Affairs jointly promulgated a "Joint Notice Concerning Several Questions Related to Nurseries and Kindergartens," which stipulated that various types of nurseries and kindergartens should be, as a matter of principle, managed at different levels under unified guidance. At the local level, all matters concerning financing, personnel, buildings or housing, equipment, and routine administrative work of various types of nurseries and kindergartens were to be handled by the bodies sponsoring local programs: public agencies, work enterprises, collective farms, and local neighborhoods. Guiding principles, policies, regulations, legal provisions, educational plans, educational curricula, methods of teaching, and the health care of children were to be developed at the national level by departments of public health with respect to nurseries, and by educational departments with respect to kindergartens. Those nurseries and kindergartens set up by civil administration units as a relief measure (for orphans, abandoned babies, and handicapped children) were to remain under the jurisdiction of these agencies, but matters concerning health care and education were to be under the guidance of departments of public health and departments of education respectively.

Between 1966 and 1976, during the Ten Years of Turmoil (or Cultural Revolution) the administrative bodies supervising preschool education at the various levels were either abolished or seriously weakened, resulting in the neglect or weakening of effective guidance.

The year 1979 was pivotal in the development of the Chinese preschool system. In that summer a National Working Conference on Nurseries and Kindergartens was convened jointly by the Ministry of Education, the Ministry of Public Health, the State Labor Administration, the All China Federation of Trade unions, and the All China Women's Federation. The summary of the Deliberations of the Conference was approved and transmitted to all departments concerned by the Central Committee of the Chinese Communist party (CPC) and the State Council. This resulted in the establishment of a national Steering Committee of Nurseries and Kindergartens and an administrative office responsible for formulating and implementing guiding principles, policies, and instructions concerning the development of nurseries and kindergartens, and for drawing up development plans. Division of labor among the various departments was also clarified.

In 1982, in the course of streamlining the governmental bureaucracy, the above-mentioned steering committee and administrative office were abolished, without clarification of which governmental bodies should carry on their responsibilities. This gave rise to an unclear division of labor and demarcation of responsibilities, and adversely affected the development of preschool education. In order to solve these problems, a number of central ministries and agencies submitted a report to the State Council with concrete suggestions, and in October 1987, the General Administration Office of the State Council transmitted this report to all concerned government bodies. The report stated that preschool education is, on the one hand, an important component of socialist education and a preparatory stage for school education, and on the other, a social and public welfare undertaking. The report urged governments at all levels to pay due attention to its reform and development, and to implement a system of "being administered by local authorities with a multiple-tier management system and proper division of labor among the departments concerned," as follows:

The educational departments should be responsible for:

a. Implementing the guiding principles, policies, and instructions formulated by the CPC Central Committee and the State Council, and formulating administrative decrees and other important regulations;
b. Studying and formulating the policies of preschool educational development, and synthesizing and compiling those development plans;
c. Providing guidance to the operation of a variety of kinds of kindergartens, instituting a system of inspection and evaluation;
d. Organizing the initial and in-service training of kindergarten heads and teachers, and instituting a system of certifying and appraising the qualifications of kindergarten heads and teachers;
e. Running a few exemplary kindergartens as demonstration models;
f. Providing guidance to the conduct of research in preschool education.

The responsibility for formulating decrees and regulations concerning health care in kindergartens, and providing guidance for sanitation, hygiene, and health protection work in kindergartens should be in the hands of the public health departments.

The planning departments should be responsible for incorporating the development and construction plans related to preschool education buildings into the plans drawn up by planning bodies at various levels.

The finance departments should be responsible for studying and formulating, in consultation with relevant departments, the institutional arrangements and provisions concerning the financing of preschool education. In the same way the labor and personnel departments should be responsible for arrangements and provisions concerning the size of staff, labor protection, and fringe benefits.

The urban and rural construction and environmental protection departments take responsibility for ensuring that kindergarten facilities are provided in conformity with the size of communities under unified planning and take steps to urge relevant departments and units to build these facilities.

The departments of light industry, textile industry, and commerce should, in accordance with their proper division of labor, be responsible for the research and development, production, and supply of foods intended for infants and preschool children; apparel; footwear; cultural and educational (school) supplies; tools and utensils used for sanitation, hygiene, and living; teaching aids; and toys.

Administration of kindergartens shall be carried out by their sponsoring agencies or organizations.

Since 1979 much work has been done by the State Education Commission and other central ministries to formulate and promulgate decrees and regulations concerning early childhood or kindergarten education, so as to create a legal basis for the operation of preschool education and to promote its healthy development and scientific management. Some of the more important decrees and instructions related to preschool education promulgated in recent years include regulations on work in urban kindergartens (1979), opinions on the development of early childhood education in the countryside (1983), sanitation and health regime in nurseries and kindergartens (1985), a catalog of teaching aids and toys for equipping kindergartens (1986), norms for calculating the staff size for full day care and boarding kindergartens (1987), specifications for the architectural and building design of nurseries and kindergartens (1987), and regulations on management of kindergartens (1989).

The formulation and promulgation of these regulations have greatly facilitated the work of provincial and lower echelon education departments in handling matters related to early childhood or kindergarten education, enabling the provincial authorities to formulate more detailed regulations, rules, and measures in light of local conditions.

After the convening of the National Conference on Early Childhood Education in 1987, a number of provinces and municipalities directly under the central government started re-registration of various kinds of kindergartens under their jurisdiction. These authorities have drawn up criteria for the categorization of program quality in kindergartens on the basis of regulations promulgated by national and provincial authorities. It is incumbent upon each district or county authority to set up its own ad hoc team to carry out the work of categorization in its own area. For those kindergartens that fail to meet minimum quality standards set for that program category, their certification will be suspended for the time being, so as to stimulate improvement of their work and facilities. Thus through those processes of categorization and evaluation, an element of competition has been introduced into management, and guidance to kindergartens will be provided in light of the specific conditions identified through this process. Currently only urban kindergartens have been evaluated and categorized in this way.

Program Types

Nurseries in China serve children under three years of age. Kindergartens provide day care and preschool services to children from three to seven years old. Pre-primary classes serve children six or seven years old.

Nurseries. The agency responsible for administering nursery care differs from province to province. In some provinces routine administration is handled by the relevant education department, providing unified guidance to both nurseries and kindergartens. Some provincial authorities set up an independent body to handle early childhood education, either as a department of the government or a division of the Women's Federation. However, limits on their jurisdiction seldom allow them to provide effective unified guidance.

During the past four decades the development of nurseries has taken place mainly in large and medium-sized cities. The minimum age of children admitted to these urban nurseries usually starts at about two, when children can walk independently. In nurseries run by large factories and mines, public agencies, and educational institutions, where female employees are in high demand and very numerous, the minimum age may be six months. According to the 1 percent sample population survey conducted in 1987, the national enrollment rate of the newborn to age three group was 6.4, involving about 4 million children. But enrollment patterns were very different in the cities and in the countryside, with 24 percent in the urban and 2 percent in the rural areas. Two or three year olds were also much more likely to be enrolled than were children under age two; the enrollment rate of the urban age two and three group reached 40 percent in 1987.

It is also important to note that female workers in China receive a ma-

Table 5.2
Group Sizes and Staff/Child Ratios: Nurseries in Beijing

Group Sizes		Staff/Child Ratios	
2-3 year-olds	25	day care	1:4 - 1:5
1.5-2 year-olds	20	24 hour care	1:3 - 1:4
under 18 months	15		

Table 5.3
Group Sizes and Staff/Child Ratios: Kindergartens in China

Group Sizes		Staff/Child Ratios	
3-4 year-olds	20-25	full-day	1:6 - 1:7
4-5 year-olds	26-30	24 hour care	1:4 - 1:5
5-6 year-olds	31-35		

ternity leave of 90 days with full pay, 15 days of which are to be taken before the child's birth. In addition, some jobs permit mothers to take up to one year of leave with 70 percent of the working wage paid. These leave policies help explain why most of the children in Chinese nursery programs are at least a year old.

There are no national norms for the group size and staff-to-child ratios applicable to nurseries in China. These regulations are determined by local authorities. Table 5.2 shows the regulations applied by the relevant authorities in the capital city of Beijing.

Kindergarten. These programs are regulated by local education departments, although many of them are not attached to primary schools. A flexible policy is adhered to with regard to the forms of kindergarten, designed to meet the needs of economic production and the living conditions of the workers. Children are enrolled for three, two, or one year. Most kindergartens are conducted as full-day programs (from 8:00 A.M. to 6:00 P.M.), and a few are boarding schools (children arrive Monday morning and leave Saturday afternoon). In addition, there are half-day kindergarten programs and flexible part-time programs to suit the needs of parents. In the countryside there are seasonal (temporary) kindergartens and nurseries during harvest or other busy seasons. Table 5.3 provides nationwide statistics for children served by kindergartens in 1989.

Table 5.3 provides the group size and staff-child ratio requirements for kindergartens, as established by current national regulations (promulgated in 1987).

Pre-primary Classes. One year pre-primary classes are usually attached to ordinary primary schools. They are quite popular in the countryside and in less developed urban areas. Their main goal is to help children prepare for primary schooling. In order to avoid premature use of first grade text-books, a number of provincial education departments have prepared special materials for the children in these classes (mother tongue, calculation, common knowledge, and artistic activities).

Only 27 percent of these kindergarten and pre-primary programs served four- and five-year-old children. Nearly half the children served were in the last kindergarten year. Seventy percent of the programs were located in rural areas. Less than 10 percent of them were run by education departments; worker collectives ran more than three quarters of the kindergartens.

The enrollment rate of the kindergarten age group reached 26 percent countrywide in 1987, with a much higher rate (80%) in large and medium-sized cities. Almost all children in the economically more developed regions now attend one-year pre-primary classes as preparation for primary school.

The Training of Caregivers and Teachers

In pre-liberation days, there were very few institutions providing training for kindergarten teachers. Since the founding of the People's Republic, because of the rapid expansion of preschool education, the supply of qualified kindergarten teachers has always fallen far behind the demand. Therefore, with regard to the training of teachers, we have adhered to a policy of using diverse training channels, and different models have worked successfully under various circumstances.

There are now 22 college-level teacher training institutions in China offering programs in preschool education. A few of these institutions offer masters degree level preparation. There are also 63 kindergarten teacher training programs at the secondary school level. Some training is also provided by regular teacher's colleges and by vocational schools at the secondary level. Some of these vocational schools specialize in offering such programs.

Over 100,000 students are currently enrolled in kindergarten teacher training programs at the secondary school level. The total output of graduates from these programs has been nearly 100,000 teachers over the past decade.

During the period from 1983 to 1989, multi-lateral aid in the field of preschool education, provided mostly by UNICEF, was available to the Chinese government. These resources were used primarily to improve the school buildings and equipment of eight of the college-level teacher training institutions and 17 secondary level kindergarten teacher training schools, and for the upgrading of the instruction in these programs. This effort has contributed a great deal to the establishment and improvement of educational standards and enhanced the role of these institutions as the mainstay of kindergarten teacher training. As a continuation of this program, UNICEF will provide additional aid in the 1990–1994 period to help four more colleges add programs in preschool education and to strengthen the development of 16 more secondary school level kindergarten teacher training schools. When this cooperative program is completed, each province will have at least one kindergarten teacher training school with adequate facilities and qualified staff, and there will be better provision for the college-level training of teachers.

A lot of work has been done in curriculum development and the publication of suitable textbooks for kindergarten teacher training schools in the past decade under the auspices of the Ministry of Education and the State Education Commission (SEDC), which replaced the Ministry of Education in 1986. The typical teaching plan for the kindergarten teacher training school was revised and promulgated in 1985. The People's Education Press has been entrusted with the task of organizing the compilation and publication of a full set of 46 textbooks for these schools, including textbooks on general educational subjects, pedagogical theories, practices, and skills. This project was completed in 1989 and constituted the first attempt to comprehensively and systematically provide textbooks.

In order to disseminate professional knowledge and skills to rural kindergarten teachers, in 1984 the Ministry of Education organized experienced educators in a joint effort to write a set of 12 popular texts. In addition, a number of provincial bureaus of education have taken steps to provide texts for local kindergarten teacher training schools.

In 1986 the State Education Commission promulgated provisional regulations on the awarding of professional titles to school teachers, including kindergarten teachers, and provisional measures for the examination and certification of school and kindergarten teachers. This has expanded the need for in-service training of kindergarten teachers. In response to this demand the educational authorities at various levels have organized teacher training colleges, in-service teacher training schools, and kindergarten teacher training schools to provide training or refresher courses through diverse modes of delivery, offered at different levels to suit the demands of the trainees. These include full-time, part-time, and spare-time programs. A number of long-distance self-instructional programs, delivered by radio and television programs as well as by correspondence, have been offered in addition to state-administered examinations. Trainees who have successfully passed qualifying examinations at a certain level will be awarded a certificate corresponding to the completion of first-degree programs, short-cycle higher education programs, secondary teacher training programs, or competency certificates of more limited scope (testifying to the ability to teach a certain subject). Such in-service training programs have contributed significantly to raising the qualifications of kindergarten teachers. Between 1981 and 1989 the proportion of kindergarten teachers (including heads of kindergartens) having received at least one year of professional preschool education training increased from 8 to 30 percent.

The training of nursery staffs is undertaken by the public health departments of various localities, and is usually limited to short-term training at the junior level. Although these training programs are of crucial importance to upgrading staffs and improving performance of nurseries, they suffer from inadequate provision and uneven development. A good example of these efforts is the programs undertaken by the Shanghai Municipal Bureau of Public Health for the initial training and upgrading of nursery staffs. The Shanghai effort has the following features:

1. Full use of the existing maternal and child health (MCH) network in organizing training courses offered by various levels of MCH institutions.

2. Systematic development of teaching plans and teaching programs to ensure the quality of training and the provision of a core of qualified personnel.

3. Encouragement of the development of exemplary nurseries as bases to train child care workers through professional practice. According to the stipulations of the Shanghai Bureau of Public Health, the MCH Center of each urban district is required to help run a community-supported nursery and a key factory-supported nursery to serve as models.

4. Formulation of standards for the qualifications of child care workers to provide the legal basis for the certification and promotion of child care workers. The Shanghai Municipal Government promulgated "Standards on Grading the Professional Proficiency of Child Care and Health Workers" (for trial implementation) in early 1983, and organized unified examination and certification of applicants on a trial basis. These efforts succeeded to a certain extent in providing an incentive to encourage individual child care workers to strive to raise their qualifications and boosted the morale of these workers.

PRESCHOOL EXPERIENCES IN CHINESE NURSERIES AND KINDERGARTENS

Because the Ministry of Public Health has overseen the development of day care for children under three, the content of the day care experience for those children has placed particular emphasis on physical health and has begun to systematically promote early cognitive and social development only in the past decade. Care of the older preschool children traditionally has had a more educational content because of its sponsorship by the Education Ministry. Increasingly, the effort is to reduce the distinctions between care for the younger and older children, and to bring a strong developmental emphasis to the experiences provided for children in both age groups.

The Scientific Management of Nurseries

Nursery management is based on the principle: "Take health care as the key link, and strive to integrate education with health care." As mentioned earlier, the years 1979 and 1980 formed a turning point in the development of a comprehensive approach to nursery as well as kindergarten care. The Ministry of Public Health released a series of regulations and requirements during that period that strengthened the scientific management of nurseries accommodating newborns and children to age three, and in October 1980, it joined with the Ministry of Education to promulgate the "Regime of Health Care in Nurseries and Kindergartens" in draft form. After six years of trial implementation this document was revised and officially promulgated in 1986. The departments of public health in Shanghai, Beijing, Tianjin, and Harbin have done a commendable job of strengthening health care in nurseries by training health care personnel, implementing the health care regime, and evaluating the physical development of different age groups of children enrolled in preschool institutions, thereby significantly enhancing the health of all groups of children.

In May 1986, the Ministry of Public Health promulgated a "Program for Prevention of Four Common Childhood Diseases," setting forth prophylactic requirements for rickets, iron-deficiency anemia, pneumonia, and diarrhea among children. This document was partially based on previous experiences of various localities. For example, in the early 1980s, the public health authorities of Heilongjiang Province, aware of the high incidence of rickets among the local population, took steps to investigate the incidence of rickets among the children enrolled in the nurseries and kindergartens located in the prefectures of Suihua and Heihe, and the appropriate ways to prevent and treat the disease. Through three years of publicity and guidance, systematic observation, prophylatics and medical treatment, the average incidence of rickets among children of these two prefectures decreased from 61.7 percent in 1981 to 28.8 percent in 1984, testifying to the success of the measures taken.

At the same time, the practice of emphasizing health care to the neglect of education is now seen as a widespread drawback of nursery operations. In order to overcome this inadequacy, in 1981 MOPH formulated and promulgated "Guidelines on Nurturing Infants Under 3," aimed at more conscientious implementation of the principle "take health care as the key link, and strive to integrate education with health care," so as to promote the healthy physical and mental growth of infants. These guidelines provide information about the primary indicators of physical and mental growth for children ages newborn to three years, and child-rearing principles related to children of that age. Child-rearing tasks are specified in such areas as good habit formation, verbal language development, sensory motor experience, cognitive ability, and interpersonal affection. Individualized methods are emphasized for children in this age group, provided through daily living experiences and play. For the two- to three-year-old children there are also five-to-ten-minute group activities, aimed at language development, physical exercise, singing, calculating, and artistic development.

Concepts of Kindergarten Education

For a long time teaching practice in kindergartens was profoundly influenced by traditional pedagogical thinking, focusing on the pivotal role of the teacher and the importance of textbooks and classroom activities (usually expressed as teacher centered, textbook centered, and classroom centered in Chinese literature). This approach gave rise to a high level of uniformity in curricular patterns. The regulations and guidelines promulgated by the Ministry of Education in the 1950s were all based on similar documents drawn up by Soviet educators.

In 1981 MOE promulgated "Regulations on Work in Urban Kindergartens," which were drawn up based on a summary of the experiences of the past 30 years and a revolution in pedagogical thinking. In response to the disruptions in kindergarten education caused by the Cultural Revolution (also called the "Ten Years of Turmoil"), and in view of the fact that a large number of teachers had not had any pedagogical training in preschool education, the Ministry of Education sponsored the production of a set of kindergarten textbooks (teacher's manuals) with seven titles and nine volumes in 1982, for the benefit of in-service teachers. A number of provincial authorities followed suit in producing similar materials in light of local conditions. While these efforts contributed to the restoration of normal operations in kindergartens, they still bore the imprint of past educational theories and practices and so contributed little to breaking the constraints of old curricular patterns.

With more recent reforms, and the increased opening of China to the outside world, there has been more and more international cooperation and exchange in the preschool field, which together with the advance of science and technology is enlarging the field of vision of many educators. In recent years, the belief that "education should be oriented to modernization, to the world (having an international perspective), and to the future" has become the order of the day. A large number of theoretical and practical workers in the field of preschool education, under the general guidance of dialectical materialism, have strived to discover new ways to reform kindergarten curricula. They have been dissecting the weaknesses of traditional pedagogical thinking, acquiring modern concepts of education and of children, and assimilating new advances in educational theories and practices at home and abroad, all in the light of China's realities. In the past few years, these endeavors have yielded results, and diverse curricular patterns have emerged. The main characteristics of these curricular patterns are as follows:

1. Promotion of the all-round development of children physically, intellectually, morally, and aesthetically as the goal of developing curricula for kindergartens;
2. Emphasis on creating a good environment for education, on fostering interaction between teachers and children, between children and children, between children and adults, and between children and environment, and on fostering friendship, mutual respect, mutual trust, and democratic and equal relationships between teachers and pupils;
3. Children are to be the main actors in teaching and learning activities, under the general guidance of teachers, so that children may fully display their enthusiasm, initiative, and creativity in various activities, and have their individuality better cultivated.

There have also been efforts to design new curricula with specific emphasis on particular subjects: mathematics education, science education, physical education, integrated fine arts (combining features aiming at sensitizing music perception, and enhancing cognitive and emotional development).

Despite the successes of these preliminary endeavors at curricular development and reform, much theoretical and experimental work remains to be done to scale the heights of educational reform. Nevertheless, these efforts are praiseworthy, as they have succeeded in changing the heretofore uniformity prevailing in curricular matters. In October 1989, an International Symposium on the Reform of Kindergarten Curriculum provided testimony to the fact to that curricular reform in China during the past decade is tending to advance along the same lines as reforms in other countries.

INTEGRATING THE EFFORTS OF SCHOOLS, FAMILIES, AND SOCIETY

The development and growth of children are conditioned by a multitude of factors. Modernized concepts of education stress that only by better coordinating the efforts of schools, families, and society can we expect to achieve better educational results.

The education of children is the inherent responsibility of the family. According to Karl Marx, "The vocation of parents is to educate their children." China, as a country with a long recorded history, has had the tradition of promoting proper "family tradition" or "parental precepts." There is a rich heritage of family education in China, which can be usefully adapted to the needs of modern society.

With the progress of economic reform and the implementation of family planning as a fundamental policy of the nation, the traditional multi-generational and large families have been replaced by nuclear families, and even single-child families. This has far-reaching implications for the organization of Chinese society and family relations, giving rise to a number of new challenges to be tackled through family education.

In response to these needs, a large number of parent schools, family education consultation stations, and family education research associations have popped up all over China. At present, there are over 130,000 parent schools nationwide, mostly sponsored by kindergartens and primary and secondary schools. There are some 6,000 family education consultation stations.

The parent schools deliver their educational programs through a number of educational modes, including face-to-face instruction, correspondence, instruction through periodicals, and radio and television broadcasts, trying in these ways to impart systematic knowledge of family education. Lectures for lay audiences on specific themes and seminars on specific topics have been organized as well.

The forms of family education consultation are also varied and very flexible: consultation arranged on festival or red-letter days, periodic consultations; consultation provided by mobile vans. These consultation services are usually provided by experienced specialists and teachers.

The National Family Education Society was established on September 10, 1989. Closely following its steps, family education research associations or promotion societies have been set up in 28 provinces, autonomous regions, and municipalities directly under the central government, as well as in 13 major cities listed as independent planning entities. The mission of the National Society of Family Education is to promote the scientific study of family education, to organize theoretical studies of family education, and strive to develop a scientific system of family education. The society also provides services to the nation through the dissemination and popularization of scientific knowledge of family education, so as to raise the quality of parenting and elevate the level of family education.

STRENGTHS AND SHORTCOMINGS OF PRESCHOOL CARE IN CHINA

Great strides have been made in the last 40 years by the child care and early education system in China. Services have expanded, care and education have become more scientific, and there has been increased understanding of how families, schools, and the community must work together on behalf of the growth and development of the child. At the same time, there is much still to be done. More children need access to preschool programs, the training of caregivers and teachers must be improved, curricula need further reform, non-formal preschool educational facilities must be developed, and the overall management of preschool education needs to be reorganized and streamlined.

The Availability of Preschools

Although the number of kindergartens in China has increased a hundredfold during the past 40 years, when compared with what existed in pre-liberation days, they are still far from being able to satisfy parental needs. According to the data given in the Bulletin on the 1987 sampling Survey of Chinese Children (conducted with UNICEF aid), 70 percent of the children in the three to six age bracket were not able to be accommodated in existing programs. Although access to kindergartens has been eased a great deal in large and medium-sized cities, the issue of having access to kindergartens of adequate quality remains acute. Sometimes people say "it is even more difficult to have access to a good kindergarten than access to a university."

The Qualifications of Kindergarten Teachers

During the past decade the quality of the corps of kindergarten teachers has improved a great deal through a process of adjustment and training. However, 40 percent of the existing work force of teachers still falls short of the completion of upper secondary education, and only 30 percent of teachers have received pedagogical training for more than one year. These unqualified teachers are mainly employed in kindergartens run by non-educational departments, which account for about 90 percent of the total number of kindergartens in the country. Therefore, it is imperative to initiate reforms in the recruitment of students and in the placement of graduates, so that kindergarten teacher education may be better adapted to supply teachers to kindergartens run by non-educational departments, without sacrificing the needs of kindergartens run by the educational departments.

As preschool education continues to develop, it seems advisable and feasible to gradually raise the level of kindergarten teacher training to two years beyond the completion of upper secondary school, starting in economically and culturally more advanced provinces and municipalities. It also seems reasonable to initiate new educational programs of a broader profile, catering to the needs of both preschool education (including both nurseries and kindergartens) and the early stage of primary education, thereby producing a better articulation of preschool with primary education and extending the scope of placement of graduates. The recruitment of students by teacher training schools should not be limited to female students; males should be encouraged to enter this field. In order to promote the further advancement of teacher training for preschool education, teacher training institutions of various levels, especially those entrusted with the in-service training, should make an intensive effort to conduct diverse training programs through different modes of delivery, to satisfy the needs of various categories of trainees. Often training is not available in a given locality, or is too far away to be accessible, reflecting an inadequately thought through distribution and location of training resources.

The Study and Reform of Theory and Practice

Looking back at the history of the development of preschool education in China, one finds that our society has absorbed the ideas and practices of Japan, Europe and the USA, and the U.S.S.R. successively. In the future it will continue to be important to learn from other countries all that is valuable in theory and practice for advancing China's education. Yet the utmost attention must be paid to the development of scientific research in the field of preschool education specific to China's own realities, to build a system of preschool education concepts and practices with Chinese characteristics that gives due attention to China's cultural heritage.

During the past decades preschool education reform in China was well begun, but this is only the first step in a long and arduous process. The renewal of educational concepts and the diversification of curricular patterns cannot be realized in a day. The popularization of successful practices can only be achieved step by step. A good demonstration model is the surest way to diffuse good practices in an area.

In response to the call "education should be oriented to modernization, to the world, and to the future," it is imperative to step up efforts in reforming teacher training related to preschool education at all levels, to prepare qualified teachers and managerial and research personnel. It is also essential that an assessment system be established to evaluate the work of various organizations concerned with or engaged in early childhood education (including administrative bodies, educational and research institutions, and the inspectorate), so as to raise the level of scientific management and promote the healthy development of early childhood education.

The Development of Non-formal Preschool Education

Currently more than 70 percent of children in the three to six age bracket do not have access to a preschool education. If the children of the newborn to three age range are added, then the number increases to over 80 percent. In light of current realities in China, it is impractical to think in the near term of enrolling all children in formal nurseries and kindergartens. Therefore, in the coming decades, along with the energetic development of formal preschool education institutions, more effort should be directed to developing less expensive non-formal preschool education facilities. Such programs include children's playgrounds, simple children's libraries or reading rooms, toy rooms, common recreation rooms shared by grandparents and grandchildren, Sunday nurseries, and kindergartens serviced by voluntary parents, all set up and maintained by local communities and scattered throughout them. More radio and television programs should be developed to cater to the needs of preschool education, aimed at both children and their parents, and popular books for children should be published. This kind of non-formal preschool education may be easily combined with family education, and therefore these facilities may properly be operated and managed by women's organizations. In order to promote the development of non-formal preschool education, it is suggested that the state encourage toy manufacturers, publishers of children's books, and other related businesses to donate some of their products or supply them at reduced prices to these facilities, supported by tax incentives. The handling of the proposed donations and supplies at reduced rates could be facilitated with the participation of women's organizations at various levels, under the general guidance of the All China Women's Federation. It is feasible and advisable to mobilize the resources of various quarters of society and the communities and individuals to contribute money or services to the establishment of these facilities.

Ways to Improve the Current Management System

In October 1987 the State Education Commission, in its effort to streamline the management system of basic education, reiterated that preschool education catering to children three to six years old is an integral part of the socialist education undertaking, emphasized that educational departments should strengthen leadership of preschool education, and clarified their responsibilities in this respect. This was a marked improvement. But the commission failed to give adequate consideration to the prevailing reality, which is that many kindergartens and nurseries are housed under the same roof, and that it is not appropriate to separate them in the management system simply because of financial constraints.

As noted earlier in the chapter, when the Steering Committee of Nurseries and Kindergartens and its office were set up in 1979, nurseries and kindergartens were under unified leadership. In 1982, when the Steering Committee was abolished, this was done to streamline and simplify administration, and not because of a belief that providing unified leadership to nurseries and kindergartens was inappropriate. Even at that time many local authorities maintained their Office of Nurseries and Kindergartens, or abolished it for a short while and soon re-instituted it, reflecting the fact that the existence of such coordination is responsive to objective needs. In reality, when kindergartens are separated from nurseries, this is usually because they are maintained by education departments. The majority of nurseries and kindergartens of various descriptions sponsored by other bodies exist side by side and cannot be easily separated.

Even after October 1987, when the document on the division of labor was issued, the majority of provincial authorities have maintained the old management system, or at least retained the Office of Nurseries and Kindergartens to facilitate the provision of unified guidance. From a developmental standpoint, improvements in the rearing and nurturing of babies and infants has to be given greater attention. Currently in China, the departments of public health are responsible for sanitation, hygiene, and health care in nurseries, but educational matters, the training of child care workers, and the management of nurseries are all interwoven with early childhood education. Therefore, the issue of providing unified leadership to the early childhood education of the children in the entire newborn to age six range must be addressed sooner or later.

NOTES

1. The first Japanese kindergartens were inspired by F. W. Froebel's educational thought and practice.

2. These percentages and amounts of change between 1980 and 1988 differ considerably in cities (84% to 94%), towns (52% to 57%), and rural areas (46% to 52%).

3. The adoption of such a law does not mean that it can be enforced at once throughout the country. In large urban centers it is already realized, while in the poorer regions the first step is to universalize five or six years of primary schooling. Full implementation is of necessity a protracted process.

REFERENCES

Chen Xuexun. (1981). *Zhongguo jindai jiaoyu dashiji* (A Chronology of Major Educational Events in Modern China). Shanghai: Shanghai Education Press.

Department of Basic Education. (1989). SEDC, *Youeryuan guanli gongzuo fagui xuanbian.* (Selected Decrees and Regulations Concerning the Management of Kindergartens). Changsha: Hunan Normal University Press.

Department of Planning and Construction. (1985). Ministry of Education, *Achievement of Education in China, Statistics 1949–1983.* Beijing: People's Education Press.

Department of Planning and Construction. (1989). SEDC, *Zhongguo jiaoyu tongji nianjian 1988* (Educational Statistics Yearbook of China 1988). Beijing: Beijing Polytechnic University Press.

Department of Planning and Construction. (1990). SEDC, *Educational Statistics Yearbook of China 1989* (Bilingual edition). Beijing: People's Education Press.

Department of Population Statistics. (1989). State Statistical Bureau, *Zhongguo renkou tongji nianjian 1989* (China Population Statistics Yearbook 1989). Beijing: Kexue jishu wenxian chubanshe.

Department of Social Statistics. (1990). State Statistical Bureau, *Statistics of Children in China* (Chinese-English bilingual edition). Beijing: China Statistics Publishing House.

Ding Gaiping. (1933). *Zhongguo jin qishinian lai jiaoyu jishi* (Chronicles of Education During the Past Seventy Years). Nanjing: Guoli bianyiguan.

The Editorial Board of China Education Yearbook (1984). *Zhongguo jiaoyu nianjian 1949–1981* (China Education Yearbook 1949–1981). Beijing: Zhongguo dabaike quanshu chubanshe.

Editorial Group of a History of China's Preschool Education. (1989). *Zhongguo xueqian jiaoyu ziliao xuanbian.* (Collected Articles and Documents on the History of China's Preschool Education). Beijing: People's Education Press.

He Xiaoxia (ed.). (1990). *Jianming zhongguo xueqian jiaoyushi.* (A Brief History of China's Preschool Education).

Li Xiuzhen (ed.). (1990). *Xin zhongguo yufang yixue lishi jingyan disijuan* (The Historical Experiences of Preventive Medicine in New China). Beijing: People's Health Press.

Ministry of Education (ed.) (1934). *Diyici zhongguo jiaoyu nianjian* (The First Yearbook of Education in China). Shanghai: Kaiming Book Publishing Company.

Ministry of Education (ed.) (1948). *Dierci zhongguo jiaoyu nianjian* (The Second Yearbook of Education in China). Shanghai: The Commercial Press.

Office of the Leading Group of Early Childhood Education of Tianjin Municipality. (1986). *Tuoyou gongzuo huibian* (Collected Documents and Articles on Early Childhood Education), Tianjin.

Office of Survey on the Situation of Children in China and Department of Social Statistics. (1989). State Statistical Bureau, *Zhongguo ertong qingkuang diaocha tongji ziliao* (Statistics on 1987 Survey on the Situation of Children in China). Beijing: China Statistics Publishing House.

People's Education Press. (1986). *Jiaoyu gaige zhongyao wenxian xuanbian.* (Selected Important Documents Concerning Educational Reform). Beijing: People's Educational Press.

Zhongguo ertong zhuangkuang de diaocha yu yanjiu. (1990). (Survey and Research on the Situation of Children in China: Findings of a Survey Conducted with UNICEF Support). Beijing: China Statistics Publishing House.

Zhongguo jidu jiaohui nianjian. (1914). (Yearbook of Chinese Christian Churches). Shanghai: The Commercial Press.

6

Colombia

Marta Arango

The healthy development of young children is crucial to the development of a nation. By promoting the welfare of the people, which includes their healthy physical and psychological development from the moment of conception, a country promotes its growth and strength. When such positive development does not occur, as is the case today in many parts of the world, then the insidious effects of prolonged malnutrition, untreated sickness, and related psychological problems rob the people of much of their mental and physical capacities. The consequences in terms of lost human potential are as tragic for the nation as for the people themselves. Any country that wants to prevent the devastating effects of malnourishment and psychological impairment must necessarily formulate and implement comprehensive national policies for integrated child care and development.

In the last two decades a great deal of scientific and practical knowledge has been generated that can guide the formulation and analysis of national policies for child care and development (Myers, in press). I will look at the policies for child care and development in Colombia from the perspective of this new knowledge and experience. The chapter begins with a brief description of the general characteristics of Colombia, to help the reader put the existing policies and programs in the appropriate context. Then a brief retrospective view of policies of child care and development serves as an introduction to existing programs, which are described in more detail based on some guidelines for policy formulation and implementation. An analysis of these existing policies and programs and related issues is then carried out. The chapter concludes with a summary of perceived strengths and shortcomings.

THE CONTEXT

Colombia is a country located in the northwestern part of South America with a population of approximately 30 million people, of which 70 percent live in urban areas. Colombia has experienced significant economic growth and social progress in the last 25 years. However, between 1964 and 1985, the average population growth rate dropped from 3.7 percent to 1.8 percent. Maternal and infant mortality declined appreciably over the period (from 254 to 107 deaths per 100,000 births, and from 81 to 61 per 1,000 births respectively).

These improvements are explained in part by rapid urbanization (the urban population increased from 30 percent to 70 percent from 1950 to 1985) and by increasing participation of women in the education system and the labor force. About 80 percent of the population, approximately 50 percent females, attended primary schools in 1987, representing a doubling of the enrollment since 1960, and women's participation in employment rose from 20 percent to 30 percent between 1965 and 1985, although about 60 percent are still in informal sector occupations. Despite these advances, economic and social benefits are greatly imbalanced, and severe poverty affects 40 percent of the population.

These economic and social inequalities have a tremendously negative effect on children under seven years of age. About 40 percent of the population, 13 million people, live in absolute poverty. Of this group 2.3 million are under the age of six. The incidence of poverty is worst in urban slums. The quality and coverage of basic services are limited or lacking in these densely populated areas. Infants, young children, and pregnant and lactating mothers are at particularly high risk of illness and malnutrition. Living conditions in low-income urban areas are generally unsanitary due to inadequate water supply, sanitary facilities, sewerage, and health services.

Low income among the poorest groups increases the risk of malnutrition among children and adults. The prevalence of malnutrition in children under five is 12 percent. Only 75 percent of the population has access to health services, and only 30 percent of the people in rural areas have access to pure water.

Among those living in conditions of absolute poverty, an especially heavy burden is placed on women. About 26 percent of poor households are headed by women reporting incomes substantially below the minimum wage, and within these households fertility and maternal and infant morbidity are also higher than among the population at large. Children in these families tend to suffer greatly from lack of protection, accidents, violence, abuse, and neglect. Information provided by the National Institute of Family Welfare (ICBF) indicates that an average of 13 out of every 1,000 children are abandoned each year by their parents, primarily because of poverty and other family disintegration factors.

Low educational level is also associated with poverty. In 1985, about one third of Colombia's poorest 40 percent of the population was classified as illiterate, compared with only 12 percent of the population at large; 44 percent of children from poor households did not attend elementary school, compared with 20 percent of the total population.

This brief description of some of the existing conditions in Colombia points to the fact that unless an integrated strategy to attend to the needs of the poorest families and children is implemented, the development of the country as a whole will suffer severely.

A RETROSPECTIVE VIEW

Policies and Programs for Child Care and Development in Colombia

For the past two decades Colombia has been greatly concerned about the welfare of its children. However, it has taken a long time to develop approaches that tackle the problem in socially significant ways while at the same time contributing to the economic development of the country.

At present in Colombia the care and development of children are the legal responsibility of the National Institute of Family Welfare (ICBF), in coordination with the National Planning Office and the Ministries of Health and Education. These agencies are gradually working toward an integrated policy of child and family welfare. This has been a very slow process. Invariably policies have existed several years before their implementation has become a reality.

The Institute, established in 1968, supports programs in school feeding, day care (including feeding), legal assistance, family education, and other community development activities with a focus on children from birth to seven years of age. At present, it serves over 2 million children and their families directly or in cooperation with other government or private agencies. Other ICBF programs include those that serve the homeless and orphans, the physically and mentally handicapped, teenagers and juveniles with legal problems, and those providing legal services to families and their children.

The Ministry of Health provides maternal, neonatal, and infant care in cooperation with non-governmental and private volunteering organizations (NGOs and PVOs), and it complements ICBF's nutrition and day care programs. The program "Supervivir" (the Survival Program) implements the four basic strategies advocated by UNICEF: vaccination, breast feeding, oral rehydration, and pure water. In addition the Ministry of Health coordinates programs of environmental sanitation, garbage disposal, and sewage systems, all of which benefit the community at large.

The Ministry of Education provides three forms of support for young children and their families. One is the conventional preschool program. These preschools enrolled about 40,000 children in 1989. Another is PE-FADI, a program for the education of the family, which promotes the adequate care and education of young children mainly in the rural population. This program is the result of a coordinated effort by the different institutions that have a presence in the rural area. Without increasing their personnel or resources these organizations have redefined their functions and reoriented the use of those resources to focus on the healthy development of young children, becoming a very inexpensive and effective way to reach isolated and dispersed populations while also increasing their self-reliance. PEFADI served about 800,000 children and their families in 1990. A third form is the program of Hogares Comunitarios (Community Homes) for the care and education of children, again mainly in the rural areas. This is an ambitious project aimed at training community leaders to foster the education of young children, with the cooperation of many institutions. This is the rural equivalent of the Hogares de Bienestar Infantil (Homes of Child Welfare) that are serving children in the urban areas.

In addition, through the program of Basic Education for All, the Ministry of Education is cooperating with ICBF and other institutions to improve the educational component of the Hogares de Bienestar Infantil (HBIs), which constitute the main program of ICBF. These agencies indirectly serve an additional million children through the program "Vigias de la Salud" (Health Vigilantes), a system of family health training carried out with the help of high school students (see Table 6.1).

Several programs used during the last 15 years played an important role in the development of a better understanding of the types of strategies required to implement a national integrated policy of child care and development. Different innovative experiences in child care and development, supported by the Bernard van Leer Foundation, UNICEF, and other international agencies in cooperation with national public and private organizations, have been implemented on a small scale. Furthermore, an analysis of culturally relevant strategies for child care and development was carried out by UNICEF and other groups. An effort was made by several groups, especially NGOs, to strengthen and expand some of those culturally relevant strategies. Also various national and international meetings were organized to analyze the implications of these experiences for national policy. These were attended by policy makers, program implementors, and representatives of institutions in charge of preparing personnel.

Table 6.1 provides an overview of the entire program serving almost 5 million Colombian children. "Direct Attention" refers to programs organized to work directly with children. "Indirect Attention" involves programs designed to attend to children through parent and community education oriented strategies. "Supplementary Support" includes programs organized to reach children as part of other efforts like nutrition programs.

Table 6.1

Early Childhood Care and Development Programs (Thousands of Children, 1989)

	Direct Attention	Indirect Attention	Supplemental Support
National Health System			
Institutional maternal child Care			500
Community Programs		320	
Subtotal		320	500
National Institute of Family Welfare			
Integral Preschool Centers (CAIPs)	280		
National Nutrition Program	68		
Child Welfare Homes (HBI)	830		
Family Education			
Program for maternal/infant nutrition			694
			738
Neighborhood Homes	3		
Subtotal	1,181		1,432
Education Sector			
Public preschools	136		
Private preschools	200		
Private day care	20		
Community open preschools	40		
Subtotal	396		
Family Health Programs		900	
Child Development Programs		240	
Subtotal		1,140	
TOTAL	1,577	1,140	1,932
GRAND TOTAL	4,969		

Source: Ministry of Education, 1989.

The National Institute of Family Welfare (ICBF)

A more in-depth description of ICBF programs will provide insight into the evolution of policies and strategies for child care and development in Colombia. The Colombia Institute of Family Welfare was founded in 1968, mandated by Law 27. Since 1972 it has had economic resources specifically to provide nutrition, legal assistance, social protection, and preschool care programs through its national, regional, and local offices.

The institute began providing care for children under the age of seven in 1972, at the Centros Comunitarios para la Infancia (CCI). About 100 of these centers were organized in different parts of the country. Even though special emphasis was to be given to prevention programs and community participation, at that time those two concepts were still not well understood in Colombia. As a result the strategies used to implement them were not the most appropriate, and the outcomes of the program were not very significant in either qualitative or quantitative terms.

Law 75 of 1974 entitled the ICBF to specific financial resources equivalent to 2 percent of the payroll of all public and private institutions. These funds were designed to guarantee care for children from birth to seven years of age. Because this law was considered a victory for working women, their children had priority. The Centros de Atencion Integral al Preescolar (CAIPs) were developed, which continue to provide center-based day care in well-equipped physical facilities staffed by trained professionals, including health workers, nutritionists, social workers, and educators. The CAIPs now provide services free of charge in about 1,100 centers for about 280,000 children.

From early on in their development the CAIPs have been criticized for being too costly, for providing services largely to a middle rather than low-income population, and for not allowing community participation. With 2 percent of the payroll from all companies going to only 3 percent of the population—and not even serving the families in most need—it became increasingly obvious that this alternative was not well suited to the overall conditions in the country.

Parallel to the growth and development of the CAIPs, several NGOs and private institutions sponsored by the Bernard van Leer Foundation, UNICEF, and other groups were developing alternative home-based and community-based, low-cost, culturally relevant child care approaches and parent education programs implemented by the mothers themselves or by community leaders. These approaches, which included day care homes, community-based child centers, and programs administered by the parents, had a number of key features. In order to provide child care and education based on the socio-cultural conditions of the families and the communities, programs were planned, administered, and evaluated with the participation of local parents and organizations, leading to growth in self-reliance. They were implemented using existing human, physical, and material resources, taken from the local environment, and their main implementation strategies were based on some variations of those natural systems used by the diverse cultures and communities to solve their child care problems. Those areas where there was need for improvement are strengthened, especially those dealing with the training and enabling of the family and the community to solve the problems related to the healthy development of their young children. The results of these innovations were disseminated through a variety of means, including publications of different levels of complexity addressed to different local, national, and international audiences; seminars; demonstrations; and training programs.

Law 75 of 1974 was reformed by Law 07 of 1979, with the purpose of broadening the access to ICBF services to all children up to 18 years of age, which meant that children of women who were not working had legal access to child care services. During 1979, which was the International Year of the Child, the national government for the first time included a "National Policy of Child Care" within its national development plan. The main objectives of this policy were to decrease infant mortality and morbidity, reduce the conditions of child abandonment, and increase coverage of child care services.

This document constituted an important advance in the development of awareness and acquisition of knowledge about specific needs and conditions of children in Colombia. In it guidelines were formulated for child care and education, especially involving aspects of health and socialization, that went beyond the concept of "day care services" for children to the concept of "preschool education" as a means to develop the physical and psychological capacities of children and guarantee their normal development in "readiness" for life and formal schooling.

In 1983, as a result of an analytical study "The Colombian Family," conducted by the Department of National Planning, a "National Policy of Integral Care to the Family" was formulated as part of the national plan "Development with Equity." This plan underlined the importance of the family and the community as the fundamental objective of social policy. Furthermore, it framed the child care and education process within a set of broader actions in the areas of employment, recreation, housing, and health, designed to improve the quality of life of families and communities. Also emphasized was the need to provide child care and education services, taking into account the socio-cultural conditions of the child's family and community. As a consequence, this new policy made it possible to use some of the available financial resources for parent education programs. Until then all resources had been used only in conventional programs addressed directly to children.

In 1984 the Ministry of Education, through the Decree 1002 of April 24, introduced the policy of providing integral child care and education with the participation of the family and the community in the Ministry-sponsored institutions. By the mid-1980s the socio-economic conditions of the country and the evidence accumulated by the experimental programs had led the decision makers at ICBF and National Planning to look in detail at the emerging child care and development initiatives, and in particular to look for cost-effective, high-coverage alternatives to the CAIPs. These concerns and priorities led to the establishment of the Neighborhood Homes (Las Casas Vecinales del Niño) and the Child Care Homes (Los Hogares Infantiles). The neighborhood homes were designed and equipped to serve 30 children in a community facility run by community educators and administered by the parents and the community. The Hogares Infantiles were designed to function in community homes, providing care to from six to ten children.

A number of factors converged to generate a profound analysis of how to establish cost-effective, high-coverage, and socially, culturally, and politically relevant child care alternatives. These factors included the problems of the very low coverage (10 percent of children from birth to age seven), the high cost of the conventional alternatives (together with the fragmented way of providing these services), the scarcity of human, technical, and financial resources, their lack of adaptability to the diverse cultural and family conditions (especially to the conditions of working women), and the role played by the mass media in the value and attitude formation of children and adults.

This analysis led in 1987 to the establishment of the Hogares de Bienestar Infantil (Homes for Child Welfare). In 1988 Law 89 increased the contribution made by Colombian companies to ICBF from 2 percent to 3 percent, with the purpose of using the extra funds exclusively to develop and administer the Hogares de Bienestar to serve the neediest children of the country, especially those in the urban marginal areas.

In 1989, a new Case for the Minor (Codigo del Menor) was issued, which provides a comprehensive legal base for the protection and care of children and youth in all aspects of their development and life.

THE HOMES FOR CHILD WELFARE

The Homes for Child Welfare (HBIs) program, initiated in 1987, is one of the basic strategies within the national plan that was based on the concept of "social economy." The HBI is an innovative approach, aimed at tackling several aspects of poverty simultaneously. It combines community administered day care with nutrition and health services for children between two and six. In addition, child development services as preparation for school readiness are provided with the cooperation of many NGOs and PVOs. The goal is to serve the 1,500,000 neediest children from urban marginal areas, in 100,000 homes, by 1995.

The establishment of HBIs has been based on community interest and need, but promoted by personnel from ICBF. The target neighborhoods are identified using income, population, local service standards, and willingness of the community to participate in the establishment and management of the program as criteria, with priority being given to the poorest urban neighborhoods. Groups of interested parents organized by ICBF select a "community mother" to care for 15 children in her home. The main qualifications that must be met by the community mother are her willingness to work with the community, her openness to learning, and her availability of time and space to attend the children. An initial training session on nutrition, hygiene, protection, and child care provided by ICBF helps the parents identify the most suitable mother for the job.

The ICBF pays a small monthly bonus, equivalent to about half of the minimum legal salary (about $40) and provides loans, so the community mothers can improve their homes to meet minimum standards for the provision of day care. Extending roofs, upgrading floors, and installing toilets are the most common improvements. The loans have been provided through the Low-Income Housing Institute, a government sponsored financial institution. ICBF provides equipment and materials for each home, including a stove, kitchen equipment, and water filters, and finances food to cover more than half of the nutritional needs of the children. ICBF also produces and distributes "Bienestarina," a nutritional supplement made with cereal flour (60%), soybean flour (30%), and milk (10%), and supports the purchase of local fresh foods.

The HBIs are administered by the community. The parents of children from ten to fifteen homes form an association. The parents from each home elect two or three representatives to join a local assembly made up of from 30 to 45 members. The assembly elects five representatives to serve as its board of directors. Through these boards, the parents' associations administer the ICBF funds and the parents' contributions. A large number of institutions, including NGOs, universities, and high schools, cooperate in the implementation of the program, particularly in providing training, technical assistance, and support to the mothers and the community.

This program has shown significant results in just three years. By July 1990, approximately 49,784 HBIs were operating, serving about 926,130 children. The program has been very successful, and the demand is high.

An evaluation of costs and impact, carried out by consultants to ICBF in 1989, verified the HBIs as a viable, low-cost, high-coverage program reaching the poorest urban children. The turnover of the community mothers is minimal. The program is benefiting several groups. The children are benefiting from day care and feeding. The community mothers are benefiting from educational opportunities and new acquired skills, home improvements, improved incomes, and new meaningful roles within the community. The mothers of the children, many of them heads of household, have the opportunity to obtain employment outside the home. The community in general is benefiting and generating many other programs as a result of their participation and the support provided by other institutions. For example, the feeding program, the home improvement program, and the need for equipment and materials are generating many cooperative and organized forms of production and income-gathering activities in the communities. Many innovative strategies for interinstitutional cooperation and complementarity have evolved in the process of program implementation, which are contributing to the more efficient use of existing resources.

BASIC ISSUES IN ANALYSIS OF CHILD CARE AND DEVELOPMENT POLICIES AND PROGRAMS

General guidelines, in a question and answer format, are presented below as a basis for the analysis of existing child care and development policies and related issues in Colombia.

1. Are the policies for child care and development an integrated part of the national policies for social and economic development and are the strategies for implementation coherent with those national policies? The present policies for child care and development in Colombia are framed within a broader set of social and national policies aimed at developing a social economy, which assumes openly that economic development depends on social development. This model of social economy implies that government investments be directed toward the less privileged groups of society to improve their quality of life and increase their capacity to demand goods and services. The Homes for Child Welfare (HBIs) have been one of the most important dimensions of this social economy program. This new development model has two main objectives:

a. To create an organic relationship between economic and social development, which implies a change in the form by which the government intervenes in social programs, redefining social responsibilities as responsibilities of both the government and the population. To accomplish this requires moving toward the use of political processes, municipal decentralization, participatory democracy, local autonomy, the development and strengthening of local institutions, and the guarantee of individual freedoms.

b. To fight against absolute poverty, because it is openly recognized that absolute poverty impedes the exercise of political freedom, breeds social violence, and limits economic expansion.

So far, it looks like the strategies used to implement the policies are producing the desired results. Forty-six thousand jobs have been created directly in the communities, and the indirect potential for new jobs is greater because the provision of services for the program is being carried out by local groups, and the mothers of the children attending the HBIs acquire the capacity to look for new jobs. In the next phase, it is very important to analyze the economic impact of this program at the local level. There is great potential for added economic benefits once the communities achieve a more sophisticated degree of organization and understanding of the program.

2. Are the policies fostering children's integrated development, and do they include mechanisms and strategies to guarantee that the institutions and programs that serve the different dimensions of child development can work in an articulated and complementary way? Existing policies are designed to provide integrated care through an interinstitutional approach. Great progress has been achieved in terms of obtaining intersectorial and interinstitutional cooperation and complementarity. ICBF, the Ministries of Education and Health, and National Planning are working as a team and are creating innovative mechanisms to facilitate the articulation of services at the regional and local levels. Many institutions in the social and productive

sector are jointly contributing training, community promotion and organization, and technical assistance.

However, even though the policies are aimed at serving the needs of children in an integrated way, the strategies for meeting the nutritional and psycho-social needs of children from birth to age two are not clearly defined, with the exception of some health factors. Strategies to attend to the integrated needs of children from the moment they are born, including socio-affective and cognitive development aspects, and strategies to identify and treat children at risk and children with special needs must be designed. Also, there is need to formulate strategies to ease the transition between home and school and to strengthen the articulation of early childhood education programs with primary school.

Are the priorities within the program defined to respond to the changing needs of the children and their families at their different stages of development? Each program (HBIs, the Survival Program, PEFADI) tries to respond to the different types of needs of families and children as well as their institutional capacity and functions will allow. They are finding ways to cooperate among themselves and with other institutions, so that services are provided according to the needs of families and children, not from the perspective of the institution.

3. Are the programs implemented using strategies that strengthen the ability of families or the communities to attend to their needs and those of their children, and that foster self-reliance, community participation, and community organization? One of the strengths of existing policies and programs is that they are designed to be implemented by the communities, in this way promoting self-reliance. Their successful implementation requires community and family participation at several levels. The community mothers must participate in training, planning, and evaluating to develop the appropriate competencies to run the HBIs. The mothers of the children need to participate in parent education and child involvement activities to achieve the competencies required to profit from the program and develop self-reliance. The community at large needs to participate in the administration of the HBIs and in the generation of complementary actions to enhance the program.

Women in urban areas, many of whom are heads of household, work up to 20 hours a day, frequently seven days a week and quite often outside their homes. These conditions obviously limit their capacity to participate systematically in the parent education programs and other community activities that would benefit them and their children. New and innovative strategies to involve the mothers of participating children in the program need to be developed because their involvement is crucial to the success of the program. The community mothers and the community at large are participating in the different dimensions of program administration and implementation, but the training and preparation for these new activities in the first phases of the program has not been adequate. Self-study groups have been organized at different levels, but more systematic training needs to be provided.

4. Are the policies designed to serve first the most needy children and families of the urban and rural areas? Even though the new policies and programs focus on serving the neediest population, especially in the urban areas, at present the program does not reach all of those in need, and the demand for expansion is high.

Also, the services and programs for children and families of the rural areas are not of the same quality and are not reaching the same proportion of the population as the urban ones. The challenge of organizing articulated programs in the rural areas is great. The population is very dispersed, and the existing facilities, human resources, and services are not of the same quality and quantity as in the urban areas. The family education program PEFADI, which functions as an interinstitutional program administered by the Ministry of Education and has access to all infrastructure and resources in the rural areas, is attempting to reach isolated populations in very informal ways with the existing human and institutional resources of the education and health systems, using training, decentralization, community participation and interinstitutional cooperation as its main strategies.

5. Are the policies being implemented with all the human, financial and institutional resources of the country? As mentioned earlier, Colombia assigns 3 percent of the payroll of all companies to ICBF. New ways of financing the expansion of HBI services need to be found. The 3 percent allocated to ICBF is insufficient, in part because the institute has many other priorities and responsibilities. Since the conditions of children are a reflection of the socio-economic conditions of society in general, which in Colombia are characterized by great imbalances, there is need for political determination to continue this social economy program on a long-term basis. This will require finding new ways of financing the expansion, as well as retooling the institutions for its implementation.

The CAIP program, which is still functioning, costs about three times more per child than the HBI program and is not serving the neediest children. ICBF has the great challenge, during this new phase, of finding creative ways of expanding coverage and of using the existing human and institutional resources from the CAIPs to benefit the new programs. Of prime importance at this time are decreasing the cost per child and finding partners to share the cost, including the families that are benefiting from the program.

A very significant step to be taken by ICBF involves preparing the additional human resources needed and strengthening its institutional capacity to administer the program, especially in the areas of management, training, research, and evaluation. Emphasis will be given to the legal and administrative requirements for decentralized, participatory, and interinstitutional programs. There is a possibility of financing some of these actions initially through a loan from the World Bank, but in the next phase they will need to be financed by ICBF's budget, or other national resources.

6. Are the policies designed to respond and be adapted to the diverse and changing cultural values, socialization patterns, and socio-economic needs of different groups? The fact that existing programs are designed to be implemented with a great degree of participation from the family and the community, and that the HBIs are designed to serve 15 children per home, allows for flexibility and cultural relevance. In reality what is happening is that within each community the "model" has been gradually adapted to fit specific needs, and many interesting variations are emerging. However, the aspects related to socialization patterns and child-rearing habits need to be addressed systematically to guarantee the quality of the care and development services.

Most families in urban areas have rural backgrounds and come from extended families, but have lost all their support systems and find themselves in completely different cultural settings. Parents are bombarded by information and mass media messages that create a great deal of conflict and confusion as to how to approach the education and care of their children. So the programs must systematically address themselves to these issues and involve the parents and communities in a process of reflection and analysis of their child-rearing practices and socialization practices. Also, some research into the socialization patterns of special groups is needed, for example, ethnic (Indians, Blacks), regional (coast, valley, mountains), children with special needs (handicapped, blind), in order to organize programs in ways that best respond to these different needs and cultural frames of reference.

7. Do the policies make provisions for strengthening the institutions that serve children and preparing the personnel needed as the strategies change? Since policy implementation is a process requiring many changes in the system, it is very important that every policy formulation be accompanied by an implementation plan in phases. This plan must deal with strengthening the capacity of the institutions that implement the programs to deal with the new policies, and to bringing about the appropriate attitudinal and behavioral changes in the implementors, the community, and the participants or beneficiaries of the program. Perhaps the greatest weakness of the new program was to have started it without a careful plan for the reorienting of the existing institutions and their internal and external management structures. The National Institute of Family Welfare (ICBF) and the other participating institutions were faced with the task of implementing the new policies on a national scale before the appropriate political, technical, and administrative conditions had been created at the national, regional, and local levels. These new policies require the implementation of a large-scale program with a very high dimension of participation and decision making

by the people at the local level, a high degree of decentralization, and a totally different financial and administrative management style and philosophy from the previous ones.

The emphasis during the first phase was to get started, set the program in place, and increase the coverage. The emphasis in the second phase is being placed on strengthening the institutional capacity of the institute to administer a large-scale program and to improve the quality of the services. This includes strengthening the management of the program, including its evaluative and information systems, and developing appropriate training for all personnel participating in the program at all levels. Although not all of the people at ICBF, the Ministries of Education and Health, and the National Planning Office have developed the desired attitudes and understanding for the adequate implementation of the new policies and programs, something has been generated that is remarkable from the point of view of the process of change. Most of the changes taking place within these institutions are being implemented by people who have been there for a long time and have themselves experienced great change. This has been especially obvious with the personnel from the technical divisions of ICBF. The greatest internal resistance to change has come from the administrative and financial divisions, where many changes in procedures and attitudes still need to take place.

8. Are the policies designed to make child care and development a concern for society at all levels? This guideline is necessary in all societies but acquires special meaning in developing countries. Since children are the future of any country, and in developing countries a great percentage of them live in conditions of extreme poverty that jeopardize their normal physical and psychological development, it is of extreme importance to devise strategies that involve society as a whole in the development and care of their children. Moreover, this task cannot be left to one institution.

In Colombia, under the influence of existing policies and the pressure created by the extremely difficult social, economic, and political conditions, most of the institutions of the social and productive sector contribute to the implementation of the policies. However, there are large segments of society, including many upper and upper middle class people, that do not see the problem of the poor children and their families as their own, and they are thus not doing their best to guarantee the healthy physical and psychological development of their own children.

9. Is policy formulation accompanied by political will? Political will is a necessary condition for implementing national policies. However, unless these policies are supported by adequate monetary and institutional resources, and massive advocacy and training programs, they will remain as dead words on a piece of paper. Also, it is very important to recognize that new policies require so many changes at the personal and institutional level

that the process of implementation is very slow, even when great effort is made to achieve needed goals. This has been the case in Colombia.

PERCEIVED STRENGTHS AND SHORTCOMINGS

In Colombia the child care and development policies and programs have evolved slowly, yet in constructive directions. Conventional preschool programs, reaching only very few children and not the most needy, are becoming family- and community-based programs fostering participation and self-reliance and reaching the neediest children. The shift has been from programs focusing mainly on psychosocial aspects of child development to programs with a multi-faceted, integrated approach. What was a single program implemented in all of the regions is now diverse alternatives that are attempting to respond to the different socio-cultural characteristics of the different groups and to the economic needs of the country. Programs that were only serving children in urban areas are now reaching many children and families in both urban and rural areas. Previously the responsibility of only one institution, the programs are now based on interinstitutional coordination and complementarity involving the families, communities, and a diversity of institutions interested in working with children.

There has been a shift from a focus exclusively on children to an emphasis on improving the conditions under which children grow and develop at the family and community levels and on strengthening the institutions that serve them. Whereas programs had previously been implemented only by professionals in expensive physical facilities, they are now implemented with the cooperation of the natural educational agents (the families and the communities), which make effective use of the communities' resources and physical facilities. This has been accompanied by a shift away from high-cost programs serving only a small number of children to low-cost, more effective programs, attempting to serve a great number of children. Finally, there is a transition from centralized programs to decentralized ones, administered with the participation of local groups.

Even though great progress has been made in Colombia toward the formulation and implementation of integrated policies for child care and development, a number of areas require special attention in the next phase. Strategies that guarantee the integrated care and development of children from birth to 20 years must be formulated. Since institutionalized care for children under age two is both expensive and quite often not culturally relevant, it is desirable to design strategies that provide support networks for the mothers within the community, including income-generating activities. This will enable mothers to work closer to their children, so that they can spend their time and psychological energy attending to some of their needs. Obviously, strategies of this kind need to be designed with the most needy mothers in mind, since it would not be possible to provide them for every mother.

Also, it is important to analyze what kinds of alternatives need to be designed to guarantee that parents and other family members participate in parent and family education programs. There is ample evidence to suggest that programs that involve parents in meaningful ways in the education of their children yield the best results on a long-term basis. The strategies need to be designed to gradually increase the individual and collective self-confidence of the parents, so that they acquire renewed energy to solve their problems and interact with their children in more positive and meaningful ways.

Because the new programs require a very different type of personnel from previous programs at all levels, it is necessary to develop new integrated policies for worker preparation that are coherent with the existing policies. This process should take place in two phases. On a short-term basis innovative programs using the most advanced open strategies should be designed to be implemented in cooperation with different institutions. On a long-term basis, an integrated policy of personnel preparation for these types of programs should be developed. These should include curricular reforms of existing programs at the university and high school levels in the areas of preschool education, social work, medicine, nursing, and social promotion. Some new careers that focus on administering and evaluating social development programs need to be established.

Because so much has been achieved within the first phase of development of the program, in this new phase there is need to consolidate actions, strengthen the weak aspects, improve the quality of the program in specific areas, and strengthen the capacity of the ICBF and other institutions to manage the program and provide the support the communities need. Special efforts should be made to develop alliances with NGOs and PVOs which have proven effective in the last decade in implementing innovative programs for child care and development.

By making a national commitment to the implementation of policies and programs for early childhood education and development, Colombia is moving toward a better future not only for its children but for the whole society. However, this commitment needs to be expanded and maintained on a long-term basis and accompanied by a continuous search for appropriate strategies for addressing the ever-changing social, cultural, political, and economic conditions of the country.

REFERENCES

Acousta, Alejandro (1988). El programa de Economí Social en Colombia. Manuscrito. CINCE, Bogotá.

Arango, Marta. (1984). Preparación de Personal para Programas de Atención a la Niñez en la Década del 80. Medellin, CINDE.

(1982). Implementing Alternative Programs for the Healthy Development of Young Children: A Challenge for Social and Economic Development. CINDE, Medellin.

Bernard van Leer Foundation, UNESCO. (1984). Taller sobre Alternatives de Atendión a la Niñez en América Latina y el Caribe. Síntesis y Conclusíones. CINDE, Medellin.

DNP-UNICEF-ICBF. (1988). Pobreza y Desarrollo en Colombia. Su Impacto sore la Infancia y la Mujer. Bogotá.

Instituto Colombiano de Bienestar Familiar. (1988). Report Prepared for the World Bank Visit on October 18–28, Bogotá.

(1991). *Marco de Política y Plan de Acción del Sistema Nacional de Bienestar Familiar.* 1990–1994. Bogotá Ministerio de Educación Nacional

(1989). "Programa de Educación Familiar para el Desarrollo Infantil (PEFADI)" Informe de Avance. Bogotá.

(1989). "Programa de Educadión para el Desarrollo Infantil. Lineamientos Básicos." Bogotá.

Myers, Robert G. (in press). The Twelve Who Survive. Paris: UNESCO, and New York: The Consultative Group on Early Childhood Care and Development.

Nimnicht, Glen and Arango, Marta. (1990). Highlights of Programa PROMESA. CINDE, Fort Lauderdale, Fla.

(1989). Código del Menor. Bogotá, Colombia.

Presidencia de la República de Colombia. (1989). Plan de Lucha contra la Pobreza. Informe de Avance 1988–1989. Bogotá.

Sanz de Sanatamaría, Anita. (1989). "Programa Social Hogares Comunitarios de Bienestar." A paper prepared for the Innocenti Global Seminar on Early Childhood Care and Development. Florence, Italy.

Uribe, Fanny. (1988). El Instituto Colombiano de Bienestar Familiar: Del Asistencialismo a la Participación Comunitaria. Master's Thesis. Nova University–CINDE, Medellin.

7

THE COMMONWEALTH OF INDEPENDENT STATES

Yekaterina V. Foteeva

The day care system in the former U.S.S.R. is unique in many respects and is a continuation of ongoing historical processes. The first child-rearing centers in Russia were opened as early as the middle of the 19th century. They were mostly instituted as private or charitable organizations. The so-called public child rearing centers, supported by state funds, were few in number. The first free kindergarten for the children of lower class families was opened in St. Petersburg in 1866. Such programs appeared in other industrial centers of Russia as well during that period. However, in general it was still early to speak of a developing network of day care centers. In 1913 there were less than 300 day care centers, found only in large cities. These centers served only about 4,500 children.

Rapid development of the day care system was triggered by the Socialist Revolution of 1917. From the beginning this system was created to attain specific ideological, political, and economic goals. The first of these aims was to realize the ideals of public preschool child rearing. Soviet theoreticians and practitioners of preschool child rearing had for some time been arguing the necessity of rationally balancing public and home-based forms of child rearing, of optimizing the unique and specific nature of each. Early in the post-revolution period, however, preference was given to center rearing. This emphasis emanated directly from the goals related to socialization of a new generation: the need to rear members of a new socialist society, collectivist by nature, who would put public interests over personal ones, and would see the aim of life as working for the sake of the state. Individual interests were not neglected, but it was assumed that they should be subject to public interests. It is quite understandable that home rearing—individualized and emotionally rich, and aimed at raising a unique person—must fail to meet such a challenge. Over time, life conditions led to shifts in goals and expectations regarding the proper balance of home and public rearing, and the goals for socialization of a new generation dramatically changed.

The second primary purpose for developing a national day care system was associated with the interest in the emancipation of women. This aim was to be attained through higher levels of female employment in public production and to result in increased economic independence and in the provision of greater opportunity for women to participate in the public, political, and cultural life of the country. The emancipation of women, their social equality with men, and their active participation in all spheres of public life was believed to be the most important condition for the social progress of society. This idea has continued to be a central theme in Soviet ideology.

Changing Relationships among the Individual, the Family, and the State

This brings us to the ideological question of the relationship between care policy and the striving of women for self-realization and self-development. Specific historical developments in the U.S.S.R. (emphasis on the equality of women with men; great losses in the male population during the Second World War, with a resulting shortage of male workers) have for many decades led to an emphasis on the professional and public functions of women. The importance of this sphere of the woman's life was heavily stressed by the mass media (cinema, literature, etc.) during the half-century following the revolution. The place of the woman within the family and her role as a mother, while not forgotten, received much less public attention than her professional achievements.

The 1970s brought a distinct reaction to this emphasis, which has led to an enhanced pro-family orientation in Soviet society. At the official government level there was acknowledgement that work and family are equally important to a modern woman. By early in the 1980s a state family assistance policy was under way. The goal of this policy was to establish an appropriate balance between communal and home upbringing, to ease the situation for employed mothers, and to level out differences in the living standards of families with different numbers of children.

From the women's perspective, a return to family values should not be considered an attempt to revive traditional family relations—to return to the closed family world. Studies have shown that only 5 to 7 percent of women questioned would like to completely stop working. The majority still wish to combine professional and family roles. It is not that we are seeing an increase in the number of women who want to confine themselves to the role of mother and a housekeeper, but rather that there are growing numbers of employed women not planning to abandon professional activities, for whom the family and family values have taken on greater importance than work.

Thus, three shifting images of a woman can be identified in the history of the Soviet woman since the Revolution of 1917. The first image is woman as a labor force. This image was replaced by the employed mother for whom professional activities and family were equally important. Now we see the emergence of the woman as a self-realizing person, corresponding to a new social reality.

Changing Attitudes toward the Socialization of Children

It is important not to lose sight of the child in this discussion of labor economics and demography. As mentioned earlier, it is important also to understand current child care directions in the context of the historical evolution of child socialization in the Soviet Union. The first Soviet children's programs were influenced by pre-revolutionary child-rearing attitudes and practices. In the 19th century, Russia adopted the idea that the personality of the adult is molded in the preschool years and believed in the importance of consciously and purposively guiding the child-rearing process. Even before the turn of the century progressive Russian teachers considered child rearing a single process extending from early childhood to maturity.

In the second half of the 19th century preschool pedagogy became an established field of knowledge through the work of Fredrich Froebel (1792–1852), a German educational theoretician. Beginning in the 1870s the so-called Froebel societies appeared in Russia. These societies united intellectuals seeking to improve family-based care through the organization of group care arrangements. It was for this purpose that they opened kindergartens, published pedagogical literature, and organized teacher training courses. The principles of preschool education were developed by distinguished Soviet scientists based on fundamental principles of classical Russian pedagogy—the idea of unity and continuity in child rearing among the family, care center, and school; the importance of respecting the child's personality; the value of developing his creative potential; and inspiring his activity and independence. The first institutions of higher education for training preschool workers and training specialists were established in Russia during this time.

Post-revolutionary changes. The achievements of Soviet preschool pedagogy became increasingly visible during the 1920s. Beginning in the early 1930s the idea of a unified system of day care centers as a purposeful means of child rearing came to the fore. A common core of directive documents played an important role in the practice of child rearing during this period.

However, the prevalence of authoritarian leadership methods and the widespread repressions of the 1930s impeded the long-term development of the theory and practice of preschool child rearing. The scientists providing

Table 7.1
Changes in Female Employment in the U.S.S.R. Between 1922–1988

Year	Female employees (in thousands)	Women as % of entire work force
1922	1,560	25.0
1940	13,190	38.9
1960	29,250	47.2
1970	45,800	50.8
1980	57,569	51.2
1988	59,273	50.6

the most important directions in scientific studies were killed, which made it impossible to realize a differentiated approach to rearing preschoolers. As recently as the mid-1950s children in day care centers were brought up according to "a standard program of rearing and education." The objectives set out in this document were noble—fostering development, molding the child's activity and independence, and developing his creative abilities. But in practice this program turned into a dogmatic interference with the initiative of the teacher. A single authorized teaching style and the excessive organization of children's life turned day care centers into "bureaucratic establishments," introducing the school lesson method into the centers and completely orienting preschoolers to preparation for school. The 1960s and 1970s was a period of stagnation, with the development of no really new theories or concepts of child rearing. Not until the 1980s did progressive scholars and practitioners articulate the need for radical changes in the whole system of preschool child care.

CHANGES IN THE LEVEL OF FEMALE EMPLOYMENT

The U.S.S.R. had the highest level of female employment in the world. Table 7.1 shows how that rate has changed since 1922, and the numbers of female workers involved at each time point. Beginning in the mid-1970s the growth rate stabilized, with women making up somewhat over 50 percent of the work force.

The Soviet Union was made up of various ethnic groups, cultures, and religions. These general indices level important regional differences caused by ethnic, cultural, and religious differences. Among the states that formerly made up the Soviet Union there are two groups that differ sharply on these dimensions. Russia, Byelorussia, the Ukraine, Lithuania, Latvia, and Estonia are characterized by high levels of female employment, egalitarian family relations, and low birth rates. Here women make up over 50 percent of the total work force. The other group—made up of the Central Asian States (Uzbekistan, Tadjikistan, Kirgizstan, Turkmenia, and Azerbaidjan)—is characterized by traditional, patriarchal relations in the family, the strong influence of the Moslem religion in everyday life, and a high birth rate (five to eight children per family). Here only 39 percent to 48 percent of the work force is female. The other states (Moldavia, Georgia, Armenia, and Kazakhstan) fall between the two extremes on these dimensions.

Even taking the Central Asian states into account, the involvement of women in the labor force has been high. During the past two decades, 90 percent of able-bodied females between the ages of 16 and 55 were either working or studying. Clearly, the "employed mother" has become a dominant life pattern for adult women in much of the world formerly known as the U.S.S.R.

Day Care in the Context of Family Policy

Increases in the indicators of marital and family strain and disruption witnessed during the past decade have stimulated the development of family policy and increased state aid to families. At the time of dissolution five elements in Soviet family policy had emerged:

1. Legal actions concerning marital and family relations.
2. Economic measures aimed at helping families.
3. Informational and educational measures.
4. Family therapy and assistance in the search for a marital partner for those wishing to start a family.
5. Measures enabling parents, especially women, to successfully combine family with extra-family activities.

This fifth set of policies is central to the child care theme of this chapter. They include maternity leave, leaves for looking after a sick child, the right to additional paid and unpaid leaves for mothers with two or more children under age 12, the right to a shorter working day and a flexible working schedule (recently introduced in the Soviet Union), and extended day care for school-aged children.

The development of a network of day care centers has a prominent place among these policies. In this context a child care policy emerges as part of a larger family policy. This policy has appeared both as a result of increases in female employment and as a means of generating the enhanced economic activity of women.

Family needs in day care centers are dependent, among others, on legislation determining the maternity leave period. In the U.S.S.R. employed mothers were given a fully paid leave—70 days prior to a childbirth and 56 days after birth (in case of grave complications and multi-fortus birth— 70 days). After this, mothers had a right to a partially paid leave until a child became one and a half years old. In most regions the payment was 80 rubles a month. After a partially paid leave a mother could still take care of a child for another one and a half years, until the child reached age three. Payments were not provided in this period, but the continuous service life (which is important for determining the size of a future pension) was guaranteed and the working place was reserved.

At present children under a year and a half old are most often reared at home. But a family with older children faces the problem of day care if the material circumstances of the family prevent the parent from taking an unpaid leave.

The different elements of a family policy may serve a variety of purposes, and this is the case for day care. Apart from its main aim—caring for children while their mothers are at work—day care contributes to a purely demographic goal: increasing the birth rate, or at least preventing its decline. In the U.S.S.R. the optimization of a reproductive family function was thought of by specialists as a most important feature of family policy.

Research conducted in various regions of the Soviet Union has revealed that difficulties with the placement of children in day care centers and inadequate care of them in those settings were conditions contributing to the unwillingness of couples to have larger families. When making the decision about having a second or third child, parents consider the demands of caring after them in their second and subsequent years of life. Z. Zh. Goscha (1986), having studied the reproductive behavior of families and forms of day care, noted that the development of a day care system prevents the mother from having to choose professional activities to the detriment of caring for a child, or full devotion to housekeeping and child rearing at the expense of self-realization outside the home.

THE PROVISION OF DAY CARE

In 1919 the First All-Russia Congress on preschool child rearing adopted the resolution "On the basic type of preschool day care center." This document contained the most important principles for the organization and functioning of preschool centers.

About 5,000 day care centers had been established in Russia by 1920, serving nearly 250,000 children. A network of such centers was developing not only in the central parts of the union, but in the republics as well, where they had been virtually nonexistent prior to the Revolution. For instance, in 1921, 115 kindergartens were opened in Kazakhstan, one of the southern republics.

During the 1920s a system of day care centers continued to develop quite quickly. Initially centers were opened at factories and plants, especially those employing large numbers of women. Day care centers of various types, different from the state-run model and primarily on a cooperative basis,

Table 7.2
Development of a Day Care System in the U.S.S.R. (in Thousands)

	1940	1960	1970	1980	1988
Number of day care centers					
total	46.0	70.6	102.7	127.7	147.1
urban	23.6	43.4	61.5	69.1	75.6
rural	22.4	27.2	41.2	58.6	71.8
Number of children attending centers					
total	1,953.0	4,428.0	9,281.0	14,337.0	17,354.0
urban	1,442.0	3,565.0	7,380.0	10,887.0	12,599.0
rural	531.0	863.0	1,901.0	3,450.0	4,381.0

started to appear during the period of the new economic policy (1921 to the late 1920s). However, after the shift from the new economic policy to the totalitarian management methods of the Stalinist bureaucratic apparatus, the alternative forms of day care center philosophy and organization disappeared quite quickly.

But the number of state day care centers continued to grow, as these were years of intensive industrial development, with women increasingly involved in production. Along with this industrial growth, the introduction of compulsory primary education introduced a special need for the organized preparation of children for school. In 1932 there were 19,111 kindergartens in the U.S.S.R. attended by 1,061,172 children. By 1937 the number of programs had increased to 24,533. This increase was especially apparent in the republics. Table 7.2 provides data related to growth of the Soviet day care system between 1940 and 1988, distinguishing between urban and rural parts of the country.

Types of Day Care

The main types of state-run day care centers in the states that were formerly the U.S.S.R. are day nurseries (for children under age three), kindergartens (for children ages three to seven) and programs combining the nursery and kindergarten. Most of these centers operate 12 hours a day, from 7:30 A.M. to 7:30 P.M., five days a week. However, there are some day-and-night centers as well (for children more than a year old).

Children in these programs are grouped by age. The number of children in a group, as stipulated by the Ministries of Education and Health, ranges from 10 to 12 children under age two, 15 children ages three to four, and 20 children ages five to seven. However, these group size standards have been raised to 18 children (under two), 20 to 22 children (three to four), and 25 children (five to seven), to accommodate the severe shortage of centers and service personnel.

Groups of infants under 20 months old are given one trained nurse with a special medical education and one nurse assistant. Other age groups receive one teacher with a secondary pedagogical education and one nurse.

Financing. The national government has provided primary funding for these day care centers. Parents have paid about 20 percent of the cost, on the average, with this amount dependent on the average per capita income of the family. Low-income families have paid nothing. This category includes one-parent families and those with many children. In general, having a child in a day care center provides a financial incentive to a family, as it is less costly than providing full-time support at home.

The Typical Urban Day Care Center

Most of the day care centers in large cities and towns are housed in standard two-story buildings especially designed and built for this purpose. In city centers, where land is scarce, centers are located in the first floors of large apartment complexes.

As a rule the center has at its disposal a rather large, fenced play area around the building for the outdoor activities of the children. Each age group occupies a particular part of this area, with its own arbor, large sand box, swings, jungle gyms, and so on.

Inside the building the groups also have separate spaces, with entrances from one joint corridor. If there is enough room, each group has a bedroom, with a permanent bed for each child, including his own pillow and blanket. The other large space for the group is a playroom. In day care centers too small to provide separate bedrooms, the children rest on "lay-out" beds in the playroom. Each group also has a small kitchen area, toilet, and bathroom, and an entry room complete with wardrobes for each child, each marked with a special picture for easy identification, where the children take off and put on their outdoor clothing.

Each of the playrooms is divided into several play and learning areas. The contents of these areas depend on the ages of the children in the group. Usually there is a doll play area (with toy furniture, stove, plates and dishes, and the like), a toy cars area, a Lego toys area, and a reading area with bookshelves. Some of the centers also have a zoo area, where the children look after squirrels, birds, or fishes.

The children have structured group activities and meals sitting at small tables, with two children per table. Each child has his or her own special seat. In the table's drawer the children keep their own pencils, sketchbook, colored paper, and other craft materials.

The center also has a large hall for use by all the children, where the groups take turns in music/dance and gym lessons. It is here that the children celebrate the New Year, Mother's Day, and other holidays, with parents always invited to participate.

All day care centers have a first aid station, with a medically trained person who looks after the general health of the children and cares for a sick child until a parent can take him or her home. The daily routines are quite similar from center to center, with variation primarily due to differences in the ages of the children. Here is an example based on the group of five year olds in the center next to my house in Moscow.

> The center opens at 7 A.M., but most of the children arrive at 8. Two or three boys and girls, whose turn it is for meal-time duty, help the nurse set the tables. At 8:30 A.M. everyone has breakfast.
>
> For the next 90 minutes the children play indoors. Fifteen to thirty minutes of this time is devoted to structured group activities in the form of lessons. During this time, the children either go to the big hall for music and gym, or remain in their own play room to follow a fixed educational curriculum specified by the Education Ministry, aimed at the development of language and speech, arts and crafts, and the like.
>
> If the weather permits the children dress in their outdoor clothes and spend the next two hours outside. Playing in the outdoor air is considered very good for the children, and so the teachers try to spend as much time as possible outside.
>
> Lunch begins during the noon hour. After lunch all of the children put on their pajamas and go into the bedroom for two hours of sleep. Although many of them say that they hate these hours, most of the children fall asleep and are awakened at about 3:30 P.M. for a snack.
>
> During the last two or three hours the children play inside or outdoors. At this time of the day there is normally no structured group activity, and the children themselves choose the games they would like to play. Often children who were not enthusiastic about going to the center in the morning do not want to part with friends when their parents come to pick them up in the evening.

Shortages in Center Care

Despite obvious achievements by the U.S.S.R. in the development of a national day care system, the establishment of a family policy that provides families with free choice in the most appropriate and desired form of child care now faces serious difficulties. First and foremost, the choice is restricted by a shortage of centers. This problem is aggravated by geographic inconsistency in the provision of centers. Thus, studies show that if on the average 58 percent of children of a given age are cared for in day care centers, then that translates into 39 percent in rural areas and 70 percent in cities and towns.

Substantial differences in the percentages of children attending care centers are also found from one region to another.[1] The situation in Russia is adequate, except in the rural areas. However, the circumstances in the Central Asian States and in Azerbaijan are highly unfavorable. Only 13 percent of the children in the village of Turkmenia attend care centers, and the percentages are still lower in Azerbaijan (7%) and in Tadjikistan (4%). While this may be partially attributed to the historical traditions of lifestyle and household in this region referred to earlier in the chapter, which to some extent affect the relationship of families to public forms of child rearing, the primary reason for the situation is a shortage of child care facilities. Table 7.3 provides the official statistics for the years 1980 and 1988 on the number of unmet parental requests for places in day care centers by republic. While the number of unmet requests dropped between 1980 and 1988 in the U.S.S.R. as a whole and in many republics of the European part of the country, in the Central Asian republics these requests increased considerably.

Quality and Quantity

This shortage of centers has led almost everywhere to group sizes much larger than those specified by official regulations. In some centers groups containing 30 to 40 children have become not the disappointing exception, but the rule. Therefore, the most important need is to reduce group sizes to those designated by state regulations.

No less important, but apparently more difficult to solve, is the problem of enhancing the quality of the care provided in these day care centers. This level of quality currently meets the standards of neither the public requirements nor the parents. In 1982 researchers questioning parents in Vilnius and Kaunas, Lithuania, cities with relatively good day care systems, found that 52 percent of mothers with children in day nurseries and 29 percent of those with kindergarten children evaluated the programs negatively. Causes of concern were child rearing practices, diet, hygiene, and daily routines.

Specialists in the child care field also assess the quality of center care very negatively. They attribute these conditions to several factors. One factor has already been discussed—groups that are too large. Other reasons cited are poorly trained caregivers, low pay, and a lack of child care specialists. At present nearly 27 percent of teachers have no special pedagogical background, and of those with training more than half are not strongly motivated to engage in truly pedagogical activities. Day care teaching, and to an even larger extent nursing, are considered low-prestige professions. Furthermore,

Table 7.3
Number of Unmet Requests for Day Care Center Places in the Soviet Union
(in Thousands)

	1980	1988
U.S.S.R. (Total)	2254	1845
Russia	1300	910
The Ukraine	333	205
Byelorussia	153	112
Uzbekistan	60	204
Kazakhsfan	180	184
Georgia	9	2
Azerbaijan	--	3
Lithuania	17	17
Moldavia	48	38
Latvia	39	41
Kirghiztan	40	49
Tadjikstan	21	54
Armenia	17	2
Turkmenia	17	50
Estonia	20	4

there is a staff shortage in many centers. For example, only 60 percent of kindergartens are staffed with the required number of children's nurses, even with groups so much larger than they should be. It should be remembered that for high-quality child care the number of nurses per group should be at least doubled. These shortages are also found in kindergartens. In September 1988 there were 700 vacant places for kindergarten teachers in Moscow, while 50,000 children were on center waiting lists. At times the directors of centers have had to employ people without specialized education, who do not love children and are not suited to working with them. Such people are discharged as soon as better personnel can be found. As a result, in 1987 personnel changes in the day care system were 9 percent of the average center staff.

The Issue of Choice

By now it should be clear that until recently the choice of care arrangements by parents has been virtually absent. The existing day care system was formed as a highly unified system of state or work site establishments with a unified working regime, a standard child rearing program, standard buildings, and so forth. Parents had nothing from which to choose. At the same time, the need for more differentiated forms of child care is obvious. A study carried out in Moscow in 1984 among parents waiting for a place in a kindergarten showed that 45 percent of respondents would not send their children to a state kindergarten if they had the opportunity to place them in an alternative type of program.

Choice of location has also been an issue. Usually a child is able to attend the center closest to home, and centers prefer to serve children from nearby neighborhoods. Work site centers are usually located close to the enterprise to which the working parents belong, or in an area where many of the employees live. On-site care is less convenient because many people live far from their places of employment. Thus the basic idea has been to place centers close to living areas, for the convenience of the families they serve.

Developing Alternatives

Starting in the mid-1980s alternative forms of child care arrangements began to appear quite randomly in various regions of the country, as a result of a thriving demand by various types of families. These alternative forms can be grouped into three basic types.

The first type is a center functioning within the framework of a traditional kindergarten, occupying the same building and following the same basic program as a state kindergarten. The change is in the quality of caring. The number of children in a group is reduced, and supplementary studies of music, foreign languages, sports (usually, figure skating and swimming) and other subjects are provided. These supplements are offered by agreement with the parents, and for additional payment. Thus the salaries of teachers and nurses are increased along with the quality of care. The center director develops the overall program in coordination with a parents' committee, which is never the case in state kindergartens.

A variation on this type of center is the short-term group, where parents can leave their children for several hours in the daytime, evening, and on days off from the regular program.

The second type of alternative care arrangement is a small home kindergarten (mini-kindergarten), where a professional teacher works with two to five children in her own home. These are usually retired teachers living on a pension, or young teachers having small children who do not want to send them to state-run centers. Such teachers usually have good living conditions. While dependent on the scope of services provided and the number of children in a group, the payment for one child in such an arrangement is five times higher than the average salary in a state center.

The third alternative is a cooperative association made up of parents themselves, where several families agree to take turns in caring for their children, or a mother on maternity leave receives payment to care for several children in addition to her own.

A group of scientists and practitioners participating in the "Kindergarten in the Year 2000" seminar offered their concept of how to organize a day care system that would bring both the forms of care and the care routines into harmony with the needs of both children and parents, and to stop orienting so strongly to meaningless statistical averages. In this concept a new caring organization would be created to function for the community in a new role: serving children and families with child care in various forms by coordinating work at all care centers. Current state nurseries and kindergartens should be supplemented with part-time nurseries or kindergartens (for two to four hours), strolling groups, groups for aesthetic studies, evening groups, sporting groups, and the like. This would require changes in the financing of child care centers. At present every center gets funds from the state and has strict controls over how to spend them. The "Kindergarten in the Year 2000" scientists and practitioners propose that centers be given the right to dispose of their earned money as they see fit.

Attitudes toward Child Care

General speculations about the advantages of center-based or home care have a long history in the Soviet Union. In the first years of the Soviet power, and in the years immediately following, the idea that day care should be given an absolute preference over home care was very popular. This viewpoint is still shared by some people. However, most scientists believe that private and public forms of upbringing should not be mutually exclusive. The belief is that they supplement each other and may compensate for each other to a certain extent.

Several studies provide insight into the attitudes of parents. Carried out in various regions of this country, these studies indicate that parents have had to place children in centers at a younger age than they would prefer.

Child care preferences also vary considerably by family type. Research indicates—not surprisingly—that the proportion of children attending day care centers increases with a child's age. This percentage is also higher in one-parent families than in those with two parents, and higher in nuclear families than in families with several generations living together.

The three-generation family deserves additional comment. In the U.S.S.R. there has been a strong tradition of grandchildren being reared by their grandparents. However, in recent decades this situation has changed considerably, due to a number of factors—the increased social activity of women, the larger number of retired people willing to work, and the fact that grandparents are now still relatively young when their grandchildren are of preschool age (and so still actively involved in professional activities).

EVOLVING DAY CARE PEDAGOGIES

A training-disciplinary approach to child rearing prevails at the present time in most care centers. Its main objective is to provide children with knowledge and skills. Teachers communicate with children through directions, explanations, prohibition, demands, threats, reprimands, punishments, and orders. The general approach is to prescribe or guide. A teacher's motive is primarily to meet the requirements of the director and central supervising bodies. Principles of child rearing include group obedience, the subordination of individuality and creativity, and passive reception of information. The results are mutual estrangement of grown-ups and children, prevalence of reactivity over activity, neurosis and even psychopathologic manifestations, and loss of initiative. In the absence of a teacher the children's behavior changes drastically, suggesting that they have already learned to live with a double standard—"for themselves" and "for grown-ups."

Obviously, the situation is not so extreme at all day care centers. There are many good centers and excellent teachers, which have anticipated official changes in concepts of child socialization in their pedagogical approach to children. But most teachers still follow the outmoded principles.

A new teacher is needed, one who loves and understands children, who is open to cooperating with them and with their parents, who has the desire and the skills to work creatively with children.

Both specialists in preschool child rearing and the public as a whole feel the sharp discrepancy between the current style of child rearing at most centers and the present requirements of social life—a time of humanization in the relations between society and the individual. Several teams of specialists have taken the initiative to develop new concepts of public preschool child rearing. While the proposals differ in their details, the models are united by basic principles and aims. The basic postulate underlying them is the humanization of the rearing process through orientation to a child's personality. Thus the main objective becomes to assist in the process of molding a child as an individual person. With this goal in mind, methods of communication become understanding, acknowledgement, and recognition of each child's unique personality. The approach is a cooperative one. The teacher thus proceeds from the interests of the child and perspectives of his or her development. The child and the grownup are partners. The principles guiding the teacher from this new perspective would include, first, a belief by the adult in a child's abilities and in the need to avoid inflicting a "soul wound" on a child. A second principle involves the teacher's responsibility to change herself or himself to meet the special needs of each child, rather than the reverse. A third principle is to avoid directives—to use indirect influence rather than orders when working with a child.

Public preschool rearing in the U.S.S.R. was a constituent part of the whole system of public education, and so preschool rearing has been oriented to preparation for school. If we take the level of this preparation as a criterion, then evidence indicates that center care is more effective than exclusive rearing at home. A study of 2,500 children six to seven years of age ranked them as follows, based on an intellectual index and on preparedness for school: first, urban children attending centers; second, rural children attending centers; third, urban children brought up at home, and finally, children in rural areas without preschool center experience.

However, if we do not compare day care centers with the "home" alternative, but instead try to evaluate the absolute quality of public preschool rearing, then the results are disappointing. One researcher taking this approach found that half of the children involved had not learned all that was being taught in the program. The first reason given for this situation was the outdated methods of teaching—training for order, regime, and obedience, but not for creativity and for problem solving.

If a pedagogical approach oriented to the development of a child's personality is to be adopted, then fundamental changes in the activities of day care centers will be required. First of all, it will be necessary to limit the organization of a child's life, where the observance of a regime takes on a life of its own. Each child must have free time to pursue his or her own personal interests. It will be very important to not only change group size, but the ways groups are organized. A child needs to communicate with different kinds of children as well as adults. Parents, who from the teacher's viewpoint are intrusive outsiders, will need to be encouraged to become truly involved in the activities of a center. This will mean breaking down the barriers between the center and the family, and a new "openness" of centers to the involvement of parents.

Realization of these new concepts of preschool child rearing will require serious changes in the whole system of training teachers. A clear incompatibility currently exists between the typical approach to "producing" teachers and the emergence of their individual and creative natures.

STRENGTHS AND SHORTCOMINGS

The present state of day care in the Commonwealth of Independent States is contradictory. It is characterized both by obvious achievements and acute problems. Among the achievements are the creation of a diversified system of state day care centers, which are accessible to all categories of families. At the same time, the number of centers is insufficient, with especially acute shortages in rural areas, "new" towns, and the Central Asian States. For this reason the day care center development program has set as its most immediate objective an increase in the number of centers.

However, the most serious and difficult problem facing child care in the commonwealth is the need for a sharp qualitative improvement in the care provided by the centers. The inability of existing centers to meet the current needs of both society and the family underscores the need to reform pre-school child-rearing goals and methods. The main feature of this reform must be democratization of the whole system of rearing and education, and a rejection of the concept "man—cog on a wheel" in favor of the concept of man as the highest value of society. This involves the departure from uniformity in day care center form, scope, methods, and means of working with children, and a shift to variety, flexibility, and harmony. The first step toward democratization involves overcoming the stereotype of a center as limited to the state model, with a highly programmed routine and system of relations. This will mean emancipating teacher-child relations, changing their essence, and transforming a system of subjugation or opposition into one of cooperation.

Thus the reform of preschool rearing in the Commonwealth of Independent States should be realized in combination with other measures, ranging from the theoretical development of new concepts to new ways of training pedagogical personnel and the further development of the material base of day care centers. A minimization of regimentation and regulations and a maximization of initiative and social dynamics will be needed to accomplish these reforms.

In this context the changed objectives of the policy in the field of day care may be formulated as follows. Earlier the major aim was to make it possible for mothers to work outside home within the image "woman—a labor force." Then the aim was to create conditions for combining family and professional roles that corresponded to the image "employed mother." At present we witness the transition to a new formulation of the policy objective with respect to day care centers, which consists of ensuring self-realization for a woman and a free choice of a life-style by a mother, combined with the development of uniqueness in individual children and the recognition of their differing needs.

NOTES

Editor's note: A transition from one country (The Soviet Union) to many (The Commonwealth of Independent States) occurred in the time between the writing of this chapter and publication of the handbook. The chapter has been edited in a manner that reflects the changes in national boundaries, using national designations to replace what were previously republics. The tables refer to the U.S.S.R. because the data reported there were compiled prior to formation of the Commonwealth.

1. The day care system is well developed in the three Baltic countries (Lithuania, Latvia, and Estonia), where 90 percent of the children attend.

REFERENCES

Aigistov, R. O. (1985). "O gosudarstvennoi pomoshchi molodoi semie" (On the state aid to the young family). In D. I. Valentey (Ed.), *Molodozhony*. (The newly marrieds), pp. 43–49. Moscow: Mysl.

Bahmetova, G. and Nauduzhas, V. (1984). "Zanyatost zhenshchin v ocshchestven-nom proizvodstve i razvitie sistemy detskih doshkolnyh uchrezhdeniy" (Women's employment in public production and the development of the system of day care centers). In D. I. Valentey (Ed.), *Chelovek v aktivnom vozraste*. (A person in an active age), pp. 48–55. Moscow: Finansi i Statistika.

Chumakova, T. E. (1978). *Trud i byt zhenshchin* (Work and everyday life of women). Minsk: Nauka i Tekhnika.

Eglite, P. A., Gosha, Z. Zh., Zarinsch, I. V., et al. (Eds.) (1984). *Faktory i motivy demograficheskogo povedeniya* (Factors and motives of demographic behavior). Riga: Zinatne.

Eliseyeva, I. I. (Ed.) (1983). *Trud, byt, otdyh* (Work, everyday life, leisure time). Moscow: Finansy i Statistika.

Gosha, Z. Zh. (1986). "Zanyatost i semiya" (Occupation and family). In A. G. Novitskii (Ed.), *Trudovaya aktivnost naseleniya* (The working activity of population), pp. 87–101. Moscow: Mysl.

Grishayeva, N. P. (1988). "Kooperativnye doshkolnye uchrezhdeniya v krupnom gorode" (Cooperative preschool centers in a city). *Sotsiologicheskiye issle-dovaniya, 1*, pp. 67–68.

Grishayeva, N. P. (1983). "Sotsialnye aspekty podgotovki detei k shkole: Opyt provedeniya ekspertizy" (Social aspects of children's preparation for school: The experience of conducting an expertise). *Sotsiologicheskiy issledovaniya, 4*, pp. 112–115.

Kink, K. A. (1987). "Ob obespechenii detei doshkolnym vospitaniyem v Estonskoi SSR" (On the preschool care supply of children in Estonian SSR). In *Sot-siologicheskiye issledovaniya voprosov demografii, semyi i zdravookhrane-niya* (Sociological research of demographic family and health care issues). Proceedings of the Fourth Symposium of Sociologists of Baltic Republics (pp. 119–121). Vilnius: Institute of Philosophy, Sociology and Law, Lithu-anian Academy of Sciences.

Kuzin, N. P., et al. (Eds.) (1980). *Ocherki istorii shkoly i pedagogicheskoi mysli narodov SSSR: 1917–1941* (Essays on the history of school and pedagogical science of the peoples of the U.S.S.R. 1917–1941). Moscow: Pedagogika.

Mashika, T. A. (1989). *Zanyatost zhenshchin i materinstvo* (Women's occupation and motherhood). Moscow: Mysl.

Mishle, A. P. (1989). "Doshkolnaya sistema: problemy i faktory razvitiya" (Pre-school system: problems and factors of development). *Sovetskaya Pedago-gika, 9*, pp. 75–78.

Narodnoye khozyaistvo SSSR. 1922–1982: Statisticheskii sbornik (National econ-omy of the U.S.S.R. 1922–1982: Statistical abstract). (1982). Moscow: Fin-ansy i Statistika.

Narodnoye khozyaistvo SSSR. 1988: Statisticheskii sbornik (National economy of the U.S.S.R. 1988: Statistical abstract). (1989). Moscow: Finansy i Statistika.

Novikova, E. E. (1985). *Zhenshchina v razvitom sotsialisticheskom obshchestve* (Women in a developed socialist society). Moscow: Nauka.

Ryabushkin, T. V., et al. (Eds.) (1985). *Netrudosposobnoye naseleniye: sotsialno-demograficheskiye aspekty* (Population incapable for work: socio-demographic aspects). Moscow: Nauka.

Shapiro, V. D. (1981). "Vzaimootnosheniya starshgo i srednego pokolenii semii" (The relationships of the older and middle generations in the family). *Sotsiologicheskiye issledovaniya*, *1*, pp. 127–133.

Shcherbakova, E. I. (1987). "Podgotovka starshih doshkolnikov k ovladeniyu obshcheuchebnymi umeniyami" (Preparation of senior preschoolers to master school skills). *Sovetskaya pedagogika*, *6*, pp. 58–61.

SSSR v tsifrah v 1959: Kratkii statisticheskii sbornik (U.S.S.R. in figures in 1959: Statistical abstract). (1960). Moscow: Gosstatizdat.

Zaikina, G. A. (1986). "O ponyatii i objekte sotsialnoi politiki v sfere brachno-semeinyh otnoshenii" (On the notion and object of social policy in the sphere of marriage and family relations). In M. G. Pankratova (ed.), *Semiya kak objekt sotsialnoi politiki* (Family as an object of family policy), pp. 8–18. Moscow: Institut Sotsiologicheskih issledovanii.

Zhenshchiny v SSSR, 1990: Statisticheskiye materialy (Women in U.S.S.R. 1990: Statistical materials). (1990). Moscow: Finansi i Statistika.

8

DENMARK

Ole Langsted and Dion Sommer

BACKGROUND FOR PRESENT POLICY AND PROGRAMS

To be a child in contemporary Denmark is not what it used to be. Changing socialization patterns, work arrangements, life-styles, family structures, and conceptions of the child translate into a childhood that is substantially different from that experienced by the parents of today's children.

Changing Socialization Patterns

Throughout the 20th century Denmark has undergone a change from being a country with agriculturally based production to becoming an industrialized country. This transformation process continues, and Denmark is well on its way to becoming a post-industrial, information oriented society.

These profound and rapid changes have had a decisive impact on living conditions. Larger groups of the Danish population have acquired higher education and a better standard of living. There has been a major shift from rural areas to suburbs, and the city and its life have become the physical and social environments for an increasing number of small children. The vast majority now spend their childhood and adolescence in suburban or urban environments. The parents of these children have developed "urban attitudes," including the idea that caring for children takes place outside as well as within the family unit.

Institutional experience has become a distinctive feature of modern childhood in Denmark. During the past 25 years young Danish children have spent a considerable amount of time within the public socialization sphere, and this pattern will continue into the foreseeable future. As a consequence, childhood is now shaped by two major divergent systems of social norms and child-rearing practices. On the one hand, there are the norms and traditions of the family, and on the other those of professional educators. The result is a complex web of influencing forces. Adults play a decisive mediating role in this process, such that one might argue that childhood is created not *by* children, but *for* children. Thus one factor of great importance to the transformation of young children's daily life has been those societal changes that intervene in and affect the dispositions and choices of parents. This means that a closer look at the relations existing between society and parents with young children is of vital importance.

In order to grasp this new context of societal integration and development we conceptualize it as a "dual-socialization" situation. This implies that the child acquires important and often qualitatively different social knowledge from the dual contexts of family and day care. The daily life of young Danish children is increasingly characterized by having their experiences and actions contrasted and heterogeneously responded to in these two different socializing contexts. Because of differences in norm systems, the number of interaction partners and the logic of social interactions are markedly different in two environments. The modern Danish child is in a situation where he or she transfers experience gained in one environment to the other and vice versa. What actually is experienced by the child in each of the settings assumes meaning dependent on how the actual elements of experience are integrated into the total configuration of social knowledge of the child in the dual socialization process. In order to grasp the developmentally new consequences of this new complexity it is not sufficient just to add the varied influences and elements from each of the socializing contexts. There must be recognition that through the metamorphosis of the psychological processing of the child a new gestalt will be constructed as a result of the dual-socialization situation.

Very early the child must learn that the adults in the family context cannot be expected to respond in the same way to the behavior of the child as do the adults in the day care institution. Divergent and often confusing attitudes about upbringing occur in the everyday life of the child and contribute both to complicate and to expand the child's norm-integration process. This requires orientation toward developing skills that make the child able to cope with different demands and expectations, which place great adjustment demands on contemporary Danish children.

In the light of these new demands it has been expected that today's children generally should have become more restless, less able to adjust and concentrate, and generally are more aggressive than children of earlier eras. But these behaviors have not been documented by research. What has been overlooked is that it is the context in which the children are growing up, rather than the children themselves, that has changed. In fact, the explanatory power of many traditional conceptions of and assumptions about the development and socialization of children seems inadequate in the reality of today. On the contrary, what deserves highlighting is the surprising flexibility in children's responsiveness, which transcends commonly held beliefs about the capacities of the young child.

Labor Market Participation and Work-Family Attitudes of Parents

Between 1960 and the present time an increasing number of mothers have become active in the work force. In summarizing the situation, the following pattern illustrates the most distinct secular trends in the mother's relation to employment and children in Denmark.

1950s Mothers stayed at home and cared for their children.

1960s Mothers began working outside the home, but stopped during their children's preschool years.

1970s Still more mothers were employed, but stopped or worked part time while their children were small.

1980s Not only are most mothers with children ages newborn to six years in the labor market, but more are working full time and are keeping their jobs even while their children are small. Furthermore, a new trend is that the smaller the children, the more hours per day Danish mothers work.

At the present time 95 percent of mothers of newborn to six year olds are enrolled in the work force, while twenty years ago two thirds of all mothers were housewives. Even within the Nordic and European contexts this process in Denmark has been particularly marked, such that the traditional type of family, with a woman caring exclusively for children, has become an exception to the ordinary life pattern. Married couples with a youngest child in the newborn to six-year-old range work outside the home for an average of 76 hours each week, with fathers working 42 hours and mothers 34 hours.

Thus, within this relatively short period of time there has been a revolution in the everyday life of small children. Changes in mothers' attachment to the work force have been one decisive element in this transformation. These changes have led to the development not only of new social and political initiatives but also of new child-caring options for use when the parents are absent. The societal expansion of the required day care programs took place so quickly during this period that there was insufficient time to wait for research results or professional evaluation of these options.

Changing Parental Attitudes toward Work and Family

Are there indications of secular changes in the social beliefs of parents that reflect some of the distinct transformations in the lives of families? When mothers of small children are asked to consider whether they will maintain or drop their involvement in the labor market, only 2 percent of a representative sample answer that they want to leave work. On the other hand, half of them state on behalf of both themselves and their husbands that they would prefer a reduction in their daily working hours, and 80 percent of mothers employed full time with small children want such a reduction. Only very few want more hours at work. In addition, more than half of these women feel that their husbands work too much. This reflects the desire of today's women for more involvement in the family by their spouses than is the case currently.

If one looks closely at parental cultural beliefs concerning the ideal family arrangement as it relates to job/home/day care, one finds that a large majority of mothers think that a combination part-time arrangement, with both parents and their children involved part time in work/day care arrangements and part time together as a family is the ideal. This "part-time model" for all members of the family has been a recent development in maternal attitudes, growing in strength during the 1980s. This ideal does not approach reality as practiced in Denmark today. Remarkably few women express acceptance of the arrangement in which mother and father are employed full time, with children in extended day care provision, despite the evidence that an increasing number of families are actually living under these conditions. Thus, the following paradox arises: the way that many families with small children are actually living today is acceptable to only very few, and the way that mothers of young children wish to live is experienced by hardly anyone.

Behind these attitudes are some general, widely accepted cultural beliefs that are deeply rooted in Danish society. Scarcity of family time is seen as the universal explanation for children's problems in contemporary society, and greater amounts of time for parent-child contact is also seen as the universal solution of these problems. These beliefs underlie the new cultural ideal: that when the children are small, the modern family in Denmark is a "part-time family." Working outside the home is considered an equal right for both parents, and caring for the child outside the home has become widely accepted (with the important reservation that the time of external care should not be too extended). At the same time, there is a growing consensus that all members of the family should be spending more time together during the day than is actually the case for most people.

Population Shifts and Changes in Life-style and Family Structure

The emergence of the Danish welfare society has been accompanied by the growing need for personal development and for the creation of meaning in the life of the individual. When daily life is no longer devoted to simple material survival, people are free to strive for an existence based on individual decisions about the affairs of life. Having a child is an important part of parents' efforts to give their lives meaning. Whether a child should be born or not and how many children are thought to be appropriate in a family are more than ever subjected to calculation and control. This has resulted in considerable alterations in family structure in Denmark over the last decades. Such changes are not only an expression of a private decision by the individual couple. They also can be attributed to developments in the fundamental economic welfare of Danish society. Specific consequences include the following:

Fewer children. There are currently approximately 404,000 children aged newborn to six years in Denmark, and that number has dropped by more than 100,000 in the past decade. Denmark scores lowest of the five Nordic countries regarding small children as a percentage of the total population (7.9%). Since 1980 only a relatively high immigration rate has prevented a decrease in the overall population.

Smaller families and fewer siblings. The typical contemporary Danish child grows up in a small family, with 70 to 75 percent living together with only one sibling.

Changed cohabitation styles. The proportion of children born outside of wedlock has risen sharply through the last decades, and this trend reflects a rapidly growing cultural skepticism about marriage as the only "natural" and morally decent frame in which children should be born. In 1965, 9 percent of Danish children were born out of wedlock, while 20 years later this figure had risen to 45 percent. Marriage as such has not been abandoned by most parents, but today's Danish culture reflects a more relaxed attitude toward having babies within or outside of marriage. Central to understanding these changes are the sentiments that tie the adult couple together, and thus function as prerequisites for the unity of the modern family. The emotional obligation and contract between the cohabiting partners is seen as constituting and securing the continuation of the modern family. From this perspective it is less important whether life together is within a traditional marriage or a more informal relationship.

Increases in divorce. There has been a threefold increase in the Danish divorce rate between 1960 and 1990. However, this has been a rise from a rather low starting point, and the fact is 86 percent of newborn to six year olds in Denmark still are living in a nuclear family together with their biological mother and father.

The View of the Child as Distinct from the Family

In many countries children's needs and interests are often seen as identical to those of the family, with no contradictions between the parents' desires and demands for their child and the legitimate interests of that child. The mother and the father, as representatives of the family, are seen as legitimate protectors of the child, with the obvious right to make decisions on behalf of the child.

As one of the world's oldest democracies, Denmark has recognized with increasing strength of conviction the rights of minority groups to live personally fulfilling lives protected from oppression by more powerful groups in society. As part of this process, the child has become more visible as part of a minority group with special rights of its own. Today the Danish child has a legal status as an independent subject with its own interests and needs.

In the part of the Danish law that regulates the relationships between parents and children, the family is still underlined as the distinctive, social entity, seen as the major contributor to the child's physical and psychological well-being and protection. The law states that the parents must take care of the child. They have the right to make decisions on behalf of the child and the freedom to raise the child according to their own social, cultural, and class beliefs. But those parental rights are modified such that their upbringing must be accomplished "according to the interests and needs of the child" (Myndighedsloven). This ideological statement underlies the autonomy of the child in relation to the power and rights of parents. As a result, situations can be identified in which the interests and needs of the child are not always necessarily identical to those of the mother and father.

The Nordic countries, including Denmark, have a rather unique role in the international community regarding the protection of children's rights when their interests differ from those of their parents. The Nordic countries are almost alone in claiming this type of right for children. The cultural belief that children should not be abused or even physically disciplined by the parents and that they should be heard and consulted in matters that concern them directly (e.g., deciding with whom they want to live in the case of divorce) is much less accepted in other parts of the world.

DANISH DAY CARE POLICY

In spite of rather similar general developments related to expanding levels of industrialization, decreases in the birthrate, and the increased participation of women in the work force, problems involving the care of children and socialization outside the home have been solved in very divergent ways in the different European countries. Even within the Scandinavian model of welfare, where material and demographic developments have been rather the same, differences exist in how and to what degree public authorities are involved in the establishment of day care facilities, as well as in the proportion of children who are cared for in these public arrangements. Ideological, cultural, and political aspects thus play a decisive role in explaining the actual developments of day care programs and policies in the specific country under investigation.

The Danish Welfare State

The Danish welfare state is clearly of the institutional type, as opposed to the residual model, which is built on the assumption of sovereignty of the market and in which the public sector plays only a minimal role. The institutional welfare state is based on the belief that it is the responsibility of the state to take care of the social needs of the individual and to intervene if the individual has social problems. The ability of the "free" market and the individual to secure welfare are seen as inadequate. At the same time the institutional welfare state rests on a strong egalitarian principle. The limits of state involvement are not set; this involvement can include many areas and spread widely.

The Danish welfare state is thus characterized as having:

- A large public sector
- High social benefits and public services
- Extensive public intervention

But what makes the Danish (and Scandinavian) model unique and special are the following characteristics:

- A public sector at all levels (national, regional, and local)
- The social principle that every citizen has a basic right to have a satisfying standard of living
- Universal rather than categorical access to services: available to all people rather than to certain categories of people
- Services and benefits financed through taxes, with many of them free

Child Care Policy

The child care system has been developed in line with these general aims. Before 1960 the elaboration and coverage of child care institutions were very low, but beginning at about that time the national day care policy changed from being primarily a residual one into a component of the institutional welfare state. A new child care law passed through Parliament with almost unanimous support in 1964. This law broke away from the historical tradition of Danish public day care institutions, in which the preventive and the caring functions had been given priority over the developmental or pedagogical function.[1] It also removed the rule requiring that a grant from the state to a locality be conditioned on the fact that two thirds of the children served in the locality come from low-income families. Now, at least in principle, all children can be enrolled in public day care. Two thirds of this service is financed by taxes; the rest of the cost is paid for by parents.

Despite the fact that credit for these changes in day care policies and programs was claimed by the Social Democratic party, from the beginning there was broad political support for the legislation. This support came even from right wing parties, which traditionally were skeptical about or even antagonistic toward interference by the State in what was considered private family matters and concerned about the growing professionalization of child care. But the non-socialist parties more or less hesitantly supported the child care policy primarily because of the need to gain easier access to (wo)manpower in an expanding economy. Both the employers' association and the labor unions exerted their influence on the shaping of the policy. In spite of the fact that women's work outside the home was at that time mainly part time, the rather low priority given to part-time day care can be attributed partly to the unions' resistance to part-time jobs. Unlike in the other Scandinavian countries, the women's unions and organizations had very little influence on the new developments in child care policy and programs, failing in their attempt to incorporate their "combination" approach, that is, part-time employment for mothers and part-time institutions for children.

Between the mid-1960s and the present the coverage provided by public day care has expanded greatly, until Denmark is now one of the countries in the world with the highest distribution and accessibility of public day care for infants and young children. Even among the Scandinavian welfare states Denmark has the highest level of provision. Compared to many other Western European countries it is remarkable not only for the high general percentage of coverage, but also for the high degree of coverage involving very small children (newborn to age two) and school-aged children (from six or seven years and older).

According to the latest statistics, 70 percent of Danish children one to five years old are cared for in public settings. Relatively few infants under one year are in day care because of parental leaves that allow mothers (and for a shorter period fathers) to take care of their child themselves. Danish children begin school at age seven, and in the year before starting school nearly all are enrolled in a kind of "preschool" preparatory arrangement, which combines kindergarten and school educating tasks. This is done in order to make the transition from the day care context to the demands of school smoother for the children. During this period many parents find other caring arrangements for their children, but as Figure 8.1 illustrates,

Figure 8.1
Percentage of Children in Public Day Care

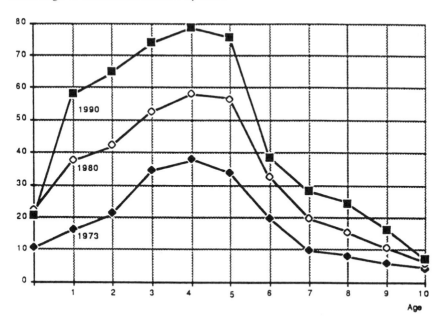

Source: Den sociale ressourceopgorelse

even in the early school years nearly one third of Danish children are in a public arrangement.

Other Policies Affecting Children and Families

It is important to note that Danish day care policy has not been planned as a part of a more general family policy. In fact, there has never been such a broad family policy in this country. At the national level there is no single ministry responsible for affairs affecting families (e.g., a family ministry). Although there have recently been steps taken to coordinate new legislation that has consequences for families and children, this legislation is diffused among and administered by a host of different ministries. The administration of day care is the responsibility of the Ministry of Social Affairs, other children's affairs are under the domain of the Ministry of Health, and other matters with considerable consequences for parents and children are addressed in other parts of the national bureaucracy.

The most important legislation with direct implications for families with infants and young children includes:

Maternity and parental leave. Until 1985 Danish maternity leave was quite short: 14 weeks and limited to the mother. Today this benefit has grown into 4 weeks before birth and 24 weeks after the birth of the child. Ten of the last 24 weeks can be split between mother and father at their own discretion. Furthermore, fathers have a right to "paternal leave" for two weeks after the birth of the child. Each parent is given some economic compensation, which can vary from a full wage for the entire period to about a 50 percent reduction, with many possible combinations between those extremes.

Economic support for child/family. This is given as a payment per child that is approximately equivalent to 3 percent of a person's average yearly gross income, or around 5 percent of yearly income after tax. This economic support is given to all families with children. Furthermore, single parents are given a supplementary subsidy, and families with very small children receive somewhat more economic support. However, there is no tax legislation favoring families with children, and it is not possible to take a tax deduction for children, as in some other countries.

Parental care legislation. This is not found in Denmark, except as maternity and parental leave. But all parents employed by state and local public authorities have a right, based on collective bargaining, to be absent from work on the first day of illness of their children. After that, it is assumed that the parents have found a provisional care arrangement for the sick child because the child must not attend day care while ill. This situation puts both parents and children in a very stressful situation, and at this moment new legislation is being discussed that would ensure the rights of parents to stay home a certain number of days each year to care for their ill children and perform other related tasks.

The provision of preventive health. Within this system the health visitor may be judged to be the most important element. This program, which is based on the belief that society has a duty to be active in securing the health and well-being of every new citizen, offers regular preventive visits, free of charge, to all Danish families with young children. The Danish health visitor, who is a specially educated nurse, will most typically visit the family quite frequently in the home until the child is 12 or 18 months old, and after that only in relation to special needs. Her responsibilities are to offer advice and help concerning care to the family and to check on the physical and psychological well-being of the child.

Public day care subsidy. Although two thirds of the cost of day care is covered by public authorities, the amount paid by the parents can be a considerable economic strain. For example, an average couple with two children between birth and six years might pay 10 percent or more of their income after tax for child care. In order to protect families of relatively low income, they pay on a sliding scale according to income.

In summary, it can be argued that rules and legislation concerning children and their families are not developed in Denmark as an integrated and coordinated family policy, but rather as separate pieces of legislation, passed when rapid innovations in society have demanded changes and when public opinion and pressure have demanded reforms as an indispensable part of the Danish democratic process.[2]

DANISH CHILD CARE ROUTINES AND PROGRAMS

One way to get a feel for how day care programs in Denmark intersect with the care provided by parents is through a case example.[3] Sofie is four years old. It is 7 A.M. and she is waking up in her parents' bed. Sofie has her own room in the new detached house in which the family lives, and the previous evening she went to sleep in her own bed, but in the night she moved in with her parents. Mother wakes up one-year-old Peter while father uses the bathroom. Subsequently father moves to the kitchen and prepares breakfast while mother goes to the bathroom to wash together with the children. She concentrates on washing and dressing Peter, while Sofie manages most tasks by herself.

The family gathers in the kitchen for breakfast. The parents believe in the importance of being together in the morning. Regardless of how much work Mother has to do today, she takes the time to listen to Sofie telling about what happened yesterday in the day care center. Mother is a registered nurse who is employed each day from 8 A.M. until 2 P.M. with a few extra night appointments.

At 7:45 Mother bicycles to work, while Daddy and the children stand in the window waving good-bye. The children then have time to play a little before heading for their day care programs, while father puts the dishes in the dishwasher and the milk in the refrigerator. At 8:15 they are in the hall putting on their hats and coats. Father dresses Peter and helps Sofie with one or two obstinate buttons. He is a school teacher who does not have to start work before 9 o'clock. This year he has been able to arrange a time schedule that requires him to be at his job at 8 A.M. only one day a week, but on that day he must be up at 6 o'clock in the morning in order to get everything done.

The family car is used first to drop Peter off at the day nursery. Sofie goes into the day nursery with her father and little brother, to visit the place where she herself stayed until she was three years old. Peter's section of the center consists of a social milieu with 10 children newborn to two years old, two trained female caregiver/teachers (pedagogues), and two untrained female assistants. When father has helped Peter take off his coat, they join the other children and the staff in their group. Father gives himself time to play a bit, building blocks with Peter, while Sofie is telling one of the pedagogues about her new doll and that the family is going to visit Grandmother on the weekend. After playing some time with Peter and facilitating his contact with the other children, father gets up and tells Sofie that it is time to leave. When they are in the car, a pedagogue comes to the window with Peter in her arms and waves good-bye.

When father and Sofie arrive at the kindergarten, Sofie runs into the building. Some children have arrived, a few of them a couple of hours earlier, but many are coming at the same time as or a little later than Sofie. She immediately joins a group of children who are playing in a playhouse, on the way over saying a quick "hello" to the pedagogue. Soon she is absorbed in play with the other children, whom she knows well, and so is hardly aware that her father comes in and converses briefly with one of the pedagogues. He says good-bye, and she responds with a smile and a wave as she continues to play.

In Sofie's section of the kindergarten the social context consists of 20 children aged from three to six years, two trained pedagogues, and one untrained assistant. Each such group has a room of approximately 40 square meters, filled with a variety of play things, a small passageway, and a bathroom. The center as a whole shares a major combined hall/playing room, an office, a central kitchen, and a room for the staff. Outside there is a shared playground.

Sofie plays with the other children until the caregiver tells them that they must prepare themselves for the tour. Today they are visiting the woods; on other days they have visited the creamery, exhibitions, and so on. More typically the children spend the day in the play group and on the playground. In both of these settings they are allowed a high proportion of free play, alternating with more structured activities initiated by the pedagogues. The staff stresses the provision of a variety of experiences for the children, including visits and activities outside the institution. Within the day care setting there is a reasonable amount of room and space to develop more elaborated playing sessions among the children without direct interference by the adults.

When the group returns from the tour in the woods it is time for lunch. While they have been away the cook has prepared a warm meal, which some of the children are now fetching in the kitchen. The children sit around three small tables adjusted to their size, at each of which also sits an adult. While eating, they are talking about the tour and about what spontaneous suggestions the children have for their afternoon activities. As soon as the children are finished eating, they leave their seats to put their plates on a small trolley, go into the bathroom to brush their teeth, and then go outside on the playground. This is the only period of the day when the children must be outside because the staff is having a half-hour break. But this is a negotiable rule for the children, and if one or two prefer to stay inside they may be given permission. Almost all the children from the separate groups in the center are playing on the playground, with only one or two adults outside to supervise them. The children are spontaneously playing in small groups, scattered all over the playground. If a child is in need of comfort or asks for help, the adults are ready to respond. Furthermore they make sure that the activities of the children do not get out of control. Once in a while, the adults participate in the children's play.

Around 2 o'clock in the afternoon the group of children and adults gather again in the main room. They have fruit and talk together about when Mom or Dad will be coming today to take them home, and what they want to do until then. Sofie says that she prefers to continue playing with the two girls from another group whom she had been playing with earlier on the playground. She is allowed to mingle with these children in another section of the center as long as she tells the pedagogue where she can be found. Finishing her fruit, Sofie walks off to join the other two girls.

Mother fetches Sofie at 3:30 in the afternoon. Having been shopping beforehand, she wants to hurry home. But Sofie is in the middle of an unfinished game with the other two children and so negotiates to be allowed to finish her activity. Mother will not promise but tells Sofie that she can play for ten more minutes. Sofie's mother goes off to have a chat with the pedagogue, and when she returns Sofie is still not ready. Sofie argues that the three girls can continue to play together at home. The children get mother to telephone the parents of the two other girls in order to get their approval for them to go home with Sofie.

At Sofie's place the three children play together until supper. Mother and Father are preparing a rather early supper in order not to interfere with a television program for children. The other two girls are picked up by their parents before the meal. After having eaten, Sofie, little Peter, and Mother watch television, while Father does the dishes. After that, Mother reads a story to Peter and Father reads to Sofie. The two children play for some time in the living room while the parents watch the television news. Then the children are washed and put to bed, where they get a good night story. At 8 P.M. Father and Mother kiss them good-night, and Sofie falls asleep in her own bed.

Child Care Settings in Denmark

Sofie's day represents a rather *typical* day in the life of a three- to six-year-old Danish child—a day that is very common for many contemporary children. But of course this pattern varies for many other children. For example, everyday life is quite different in some respects if the parents are not middle-class, like Sofie's, but instead are manual laborers, or if the mother is alone with the child, or if the child is taken care of in another type of caring arrangement. What kinds of caring arrangements are actually found in Denmark? Table 8.1 provides a picture of the variation in those arrangements.

Table 8.1

Day Care for Danish Children from Birth to Six Years (1989)

	Percentage of 0-2 year olds	Percentage of 3-6 year olds	Percentage of 0-6 year olds
Public day care	47	71	60
Day care center	18	61	42
Public family based care	29	10	18
Private day care	22	9	15
Private family based care	12	4	8
Grandparents or other relatives	8	3	5
Nannies	2	2	2
Only by parents	29	17	23
Parents on maternity/ parental leave	9	1	5
Parents not on maternity/parental leave	20	16	18
Other	1	3	2
	99%	100%	100%

Source: Glavind (1989a).

Public Day Care

As seen in Table 8.1, many more than half of Danish preschool-aged children are in a public day care arrangement, and there are different types of public day care. Within each of these arrangements legislation ensures certain minimum standards concerning, for example, the adult-child ratio, the amount of space per child, and so on. Such standards ensure that each type of arrangement will be relatively homogeneous from locale to locale, despite the fact that a number of other important decisions regarding the care of children—reflecting cultural beliefs about local autonomy—are made by local authorities, and even at the level of the specific setting.

The distribution of children among the various public day care arrangements in Denmark is shown in Table 8.2.

Sofie's little brother, Peter, is in a *day nursery*. Day nurseries are for children from six months to three years of age. The children are separated

Table 8.2
Public Day Care Arrangements for Danish Children from Birth to Six Years
(1989)

	Percentage of 0-2 year olds	Percentage of 3-6 year olds	Percentage of 0-6 year olds
Day nursery	28	1	11
Kindergarten	5	61	40
Age-integrated institution	8	17	14
Recreation center	0	4	3
School-recreation arrangement	0	5	3
Public family based child care	60	12	29
Total	101	100	100

Source: Den Sociale Ressourceopgørelse (1990) and calculations by the
           authors.

into smaller groups of 10 to 12 children each, and the institution itself
decides whether age segregation or mixed age groups are preferred. For
every three children there is a full-time adult, and somewhat more than half
of these adults have a three-year pedagogical education degree. The day
nursery is open 11 hours a day on weekdays and is closed on weekends.

Sofie is in a *kindergarten*. As seen in Table 8.2, this is the dominant type
of caring arrangement for children three to six years of age. Kindergartens
are meant for children between two and seven years. The children are most
often separated into groups of 18 to 24 and usually they have their social
contacts in mixed age groups. For every six children there is a full-time
adult, and two thirds of the adults have a degree in pedagogical education.
The kindergarten is open for ten hours on weekdays and is closed on weekends.

Both Sofie and Peter might have been in an *age-integrated center* rather
than one specializing in a specific age range. Although there is less emphasis
on age segregation in Danish day nurseries and kindergartens than in facilities in many other countries, there has been criticism of the restricted
social milieu of the child in these rather age-homogeneous institutions. In
the light of this concern experiments with new age-integrated institutions
were initiated 20 years ago, and since then the proportion of this type of
program has increased markedly. These centers have tended to serve children
ranging in age from birth or three years to 14, but more recently a new

type of institution with children from birth to six years old has been developed. This will probably become the model institution of the future for infants and young children in Denmark. Group size, adult-child ratio, and hours of operation are much the same as in the kindergarten.

The remaining types of day care institutions, *recreation centers*, and *school-recreation arrangements*, are directed toward school-aged children but also serve those six-year-old children who have left the kindergarten and are now in a nursery class in school. It is expected that in the years to come the school-recreation arrangements, as a part of the school setting but run by kindergarten pedagogues rather than school teachers, will improve and become the preferred arrangement for all six year olds. This would help to relieve what, in spite of the heavy investment in public day care in Denmark, has become an acute shortage of public care for newborn to six-year-old children. Thus the latest developments in the day care structure in Denmark suggest that the future will bring more age-integrated institutions for children from birth to five years of age, and school-recreation arrangements for the six to ten or eleven year olds.

Little Peter might well have been cared for in a *public family-based child care* arrangement, which is in fact the typical pattern for a one-year old child (Table 8.2). Such care is private in the sense that it takes place in the private home of the caregiver but public in the sense that local authorities pay her salary and most of the expenditures associated with provision of care. The caregiver must be approved and licensed by the local municipality. Usually she has been through a two to three week educational course and is supervised by representatives of the municipality, who provide advice about how to provide pedagogically sound care. In contrast to unofficial and unauthorized private family-based care, this licensed caregiver averages only three children in her care, not including her own children. The age span of the children could range from birth to 14 years old, but this is nearly always an arrangement for children from birth to three or four years of age.

Two main factors explain the significant proportion of parents using a family-based arrangement for their children, as shown in Tables 8.1 and 8.2:

1. A large group of parents desire that their very small child be raised within the framework of a more "family-like" setting than is the case in center care. They prefer what they expect to be closer personal contact provided by a woman in her own home, and because the child is still quite young, do not rank so highly the more varied social relations that their child might experience in a day nursery.

2. Another large group of parents does not have any other choice. Either they are living in a local community, often rural, where few day nurseries are to be found, or there will be a long waiting list at the available centers, making it unrealistic to expect a place in the day nursery even if it is the preferred type of arrangement.

Private Family-Based Child Care

Earlier mention was made of the parents of the 10 percent of Danish children who have an acute need for a public day care arrangement but who are forced to wait. The solution for these families is usually a private, family-based arrangement. This private arrangement for the caring of infants and young children has diminished during recent years, and in 1989 it constituted 15 percent of all care arrangements for children (Table 8.1). Many parents are concerned about the fact that this care is provided without the supervision or control of local authorities that typifies the public system. This type of arrangement is usually of relatively short duration, as is the case provided by grandparents and nannies, indicating that these more private arrangements are mainly provisional solutions used while waiting for a place in the public day care system.

As seen in Tables 8.1 and 8.2, there is a major divergence in the care arrangements for the newborn to two year olds and the three to six year olds, with the younger age group much more frequently in family-like arrangements. This is largely a function of the social beliefs of many parents of young children in Denmark, where the family-like arrangement is preferred by many for the very young children, while the more elaborate world of playmates in the institution is thought more appropriate for the older child.

PEDAGOGY AND EDUCATION

The objectives of the national government and of local authorities concerning socialization and upbringing in Denmark are few in number, very general, and offered only for guidance. There are no centralized instructions concerning goals, means, or content of socialization as it should be administered or practiced in public institutions. This is in accordance with the widely held belief in decentralization, in which such matters are seen as best developed in the specific institutions in cooperation with the actual people involved in the process.

The interest of the State in the regulation of public care has been restricted to the following rather global and open formulation:

Public day care institutions have the task, in cooperation with the parents, of creating a milieu for the children that can supplement the upbringing in the home. The aim should be that particular children develop as open and independent human beings with the willingness to be cooperative, and try to employ their knowledge to improve their own and other people's living conditions. Public day care institutions, therefore, have to offer the children security and protection, and furthermore maintain the possibilities for experiences that stimulate their need for exploring the environment in such a way that their field of knowledge is developed and their activity enhanced.

This task has to be pursued with consideration of the different age and developmental levels of the children. (Daginstitutionscirkulæret 1976)

Interesting ideological assumptions are reflected in this statement. First, there is a marked acceptance of the fundamental upbringing role of the family in comparison with the public care system and no indication of a society that would encourage the State to take over the socialization of the child or replace the family. Instead there is a moderate "cooperative" and "supplemental" view of public day care, and no indication of antagonistic relations between socialization objectives in family and day care.

Another important ideological content in the public objective is its conceptual jargon as formulated by experts. The psychological and pedagogical expressions concerning the needs and interests of the child indicate a changing society, with changing demands for new competencies and skills, which even within the very ideologically loaded arena of child rearing are increasingly inclined to be based upon the judgments and formulations of experts.

It is widely believed that there should be great latitude in how socialization should actually take place in a particular institution. The Danish public day care system is known for its great diversity when it comes to the pedagogic content and the planning and administration of the concrete child-rearing process. These specific aspects of the day care provision are, to a large degree, handed over to the pedagogues of individual institutions, in cooperation with the parents.

The Education of Caregiver/Teachers

One important reason for such decentralization is attributed to the rather high educational level among the day care staff. Sixty percent of these workers have three years of education in pedagogy (from 1992 extended to 3.5 years), comprising theoretical knowledge in sociology, psychology, and pedagogy, art subjects like music and drama, and a number of practical skills (e.g., clay modeling and woodworking). Included in the education are several periods of supervised practice in the field. These education and training programs are most often centered around the projects and activities of the students, with relatively little concentration on acquiring formalized knowledge. It is important that the student develop as a person as well as acquire certain knowledge and skills. Such development should make the individual more capable of acting independently in both routine and unanticipated situations occurring in the daily contacts with colleagues, children, and parents. One result of this socialization is that few Danish pedagogues are willing to accept ready-made "programs" developed by people higher up in the hierarchy. Instead they are oriented to implement the socialization process themselves, according to the situation at the institution in which they are working, on the basis of their knowledge about the theory and practice of pedagogy acquired through their educational experience.

It is important to involve the parents when developing the pedagogical plan. A parent council is attached to most centers, which in cooperation with the staff makes decisions about pedagogical, economic, and practical matters concerning the institution.

Given the relatively late age at which children start school in Denmark, it is remarkable that the public day care system is completely separated from the school system. Public day care pedagogues hold beliefs that are quite different from those of school teachers. Where the teacher is supposed to educate the children, and to teach them rather specific information and skills in different subjects, the pedagogue holds a broader developmental perspective with regard to the personality and the social development of the child. Through play, creative activities, and social encounters the pedagogue tries to develop versatile competencies in the child.

The public day care system is more closely connected to the *social service system*. This is partly because public day care is placed under the Ministry of Social Affairs, and partly because the pedagogue, through her daily work, is in touch with children and parents with diverse social problems, the solutions to which often require cooperation among people from different social services.

PERCEIVED STRENGTHS AND SHORTCOMINGS

The accelerated participation of women and mothers in the work force beginning in the 1960s produced a major change in Danish day care policy, which as a consequence started a marked expansion of the public day care system. This process has continued into the present, although somewhat more slowly during the past several years (see Figure 8.1). But despite this expansion, the need for places in the public day care system has not been fully met, resulting during the whole 30-year period in long waiting lists. These shortages have been highly criticized as one of the shortcomings of Danish day care policy. Because the directive role of central government is only modest, the local authorities themselves have the power to decide how quickly and completely to meet the need for places in public day care, and this has resulted in major differences in coverage in different municipalities. Even in the municipalities where the policy has been to obtain full coverage, this goal has not been reached. Paradoxically, when new institutions are built and more places are available, the waiting lists expand instead of decreasing. This is attributed to "latent need": as soon as there is a realistic possibility for parents to get their child into a public day care institution, they join the waiting list.

Recently many municipalities have been having economic difficulty. The consequence for public day care has been continued expansion, but combined with cost-saving reductions in the adult-child ratio. This has triggered harsh criticism from parents, pedagogues, and other experts. But despite what in the Danish context is seen as a deterioration of quality, by international standards, Danish public child care institutions still have some of the most favorable adult-child ratios in the world.

The shortage of day care places has to do in part with parental beliefs. Danish parents today have generally accepted public day care as it currently exists. When parents are asked to outline why they prefer public day care, they emphasize:

a. The continuity and stability of the arrangement.
b. The fact that any differences with the professional pedagogue can be solved without too much emotion.
c. The pedagogical substance provided by public day care.

At the same time, parents have two important reservations about the present system. The first involves the length of time spent in external care, and the second involves the differing social/emotional needs of children from birth to two years and from three to six years old.

As shown earlier the modern ideal for parents on behalf of all family members is to live in a "part-time" arrangement, that is, with parents in the work force and with children in day care, the concern has been that time outside the family not be too extended for any family members. A widely held belief, shared by parents, professionals, and experts, is that day care extending beyond approximately six hours per day is not beneficial to the child. An average Danish child spends about seven hours in public day care per day. Any negative effects of this length of time have not been confirmed by research. On the contrary, a new representative study of children with many years of day care experience (included rather extended care) shows that Danish children living in what might be called the "new normality"—with both parents working full time, or one part time—have the fewest physical and mental problems when they start school.

Regarding the different social/emotional needs of younger and older preschool children: a majority of parents desire that their very small child be raised within the frame of a more "family-like" setting than is the case in the day care center. They prefer the closer contact they expect to find in the family-like setting. At the same time, most parents with children three to six years old prefer public day care centers because they offer greater possibilities for peer contact.

During the 1980s the professional pedagogues, through their union, have become increasingly active in the implementation of a more open-minded pedagogical debate. While the fundamental belief is still that public day care is a necessary and positive aspect of children's socialization, it is accepted that the structure and content of day care can be improved. There is a general feeling among pedagogues that the very long day at the center is not beneficial for the child.

Increasingly pedagogues have been paying more attention to the ideas and information provided by independent researchers and experts on children, and there is more appraisal of and concern for the knowledge and results stemming from research. Experimental and developmental innovations in day care institutions are receiving both moral and financial support by the child care worker's union.

When the perceived strengths and shortcomings of day care as seen by experts in Denmark are summarized, the following conclusion may be drawn:

1. Experts are seldom speaking on the basis of empirical knowledge because of the sparsity of research on day care.

2. Despite this lack of evidence, or perhaps because of it, two types of rather polarized and influential ideologies are produced—one that emphasizes primarily the negative consequences of day care on the child and another that emphasizes the developmentally positive aspects of that care. This divergence can be traced to different theoretical systems, one that emphasizes the importance of keeping mothers and small children together and the other that emphasizes the value of allowing mothers to work outside the home and accepts as positive the external care of infants and young children.

But we must emphasize, with the "dual-socialization" orientation introduced early in this chapter in mind, that the evaluation of day care in isolation is in itself of limited value. What is crucial is not what is seen as a separate experience for the child in the day care center, but how this experience fits into the whole fabric of the child's experience. The larger question is how the experiences of the child in his or her several "dual-socialization" contexts are combined and integrated into a seamless whole.

NOTES

Jytte Juul Jensen, Danish expert in the European Community Network on Child Care, participated in the preparation of the section "Danish Day Care Policy." See also Jensen, 1991.

1. The usual translation of the Danish word *pædagogisk* as educational places inaccurate emphasis on the learning function; pedagogical is the more appropriate term in English, which refers to a primarily developmental perspective on the psychological and social development of children.

2. Only the most important programs have been mentioned in this section. For a more detailed presentation, see Langsted and Sommer (1988).

3. This case example from the Danish context is based on research material from the Nordic project "Childhood, Society and Development in the Nordic Countries," led by Lars Dencik. The authors are the Danish participants in this project.

REFERENCES

Andersen, B. H. (1991). *Børnefamiliernes dagligdag* (The everyday life of families with children). København: Socialforskningsinstituttet.

Anderson, B. R. (1984). *Kan vi bevare velfærdsstaten?* (Are we able to preserve the welfare state?). København: Amtskommunernes og Kommunernes Forsknings institut.

Andersen, D. (1988). *Kvinders samlede arbejdstid er lige så lang som mænds* (The total working hours of women are as long as men's). København: Socialforskningsinstituttet.

Andersen, D. (1990). *Hvad koster et barn—i tid?* (The temporal expenditure of having a child). København: Nordisk Ministerråd.

Bertelsen, O. (1991). *Offentlig børnepasning* (Public day care). København: Socialforskningsinstituttet.

Borchorst, A. (1988). "Kønsarbejdsdeling og børnepasningspolitik—En sammenligning af de skandinaviske lande" (The division of labor by sex and the policy of child care). *Tidsskrift for samfunnsforskning, 29*, 523–538.

Borchorst, A. and Siim, B. (1987). "Women and the advanced welfare state: A new kind of patriarchal power?" In Sassoon, A. S. (Ed.), *Women and the state: The shifting boundaries of public and private.* London: Hutchinson.

Bøgh, C. and Jørgensen, P. S. (Eds.) (1985). *Småbørn—familie—samfund. En antologi om småbørnsforskning* (Young children—family—society. An anthology about research on small children). København: Hans Reitzels Forlag.

Bøgh, C. and Parkvig, K. (Eds.) (1989). *Børne—og ungdomsforskning—Tendenser og perspektiver* (Research on children and youth—Tendencies and perspectives). København: SIKON.

Børnekommissionen. (1981). *Børnekommissionens betænkning* (The report of the Child Commission). Betænkning nr. 918. København.

Christofferson, M. N., Bertelsen, O. and Vestergaard, P. (1987). *Hvem passer vore børn?* (Who are taking care of our children?). København: Socialforskningsinstituttet.

Daginstitutionscirkulæret. (1976). "Socialministeriets cirkulære af 29.03.1976 om institutioner under kommunerne" (The circular of public day care from the Ministry of Social Affairs). København.

Dencik, L. (1989). "Growing up in the post-modern age." *Acta Sociologica, 32*, 155–180.

Dencik, L., Langsted, O. and Sommer, D. (1989). "Modern childhood in the Nordic Countries: Material, social and cultural aspects." In B. Elgaard, O. Langsted, and D. Sommer (Eds.), *Research on socialization of young children in the Nordic Countries—An annotated and selected bibliography.* Århus: Aarhus University Press.

Den sociale ressourceopgørelse. (1980 and 1991). (The social resource statistics). Statistiske Efterretninger. København: Danmarks Statistik.

Dunn, J. and Scarr, S. (1987). *Mother care/other care.* London: Basic Books.

Glavind, N. (1989a). *Hvor passes vore børn?* (Where are our children cared for?). København: BUPL.

Glavind, N. (1989b). *Småbørnsfamiliens hverdag* (The everyday life of families with small children). København: BUPL.

Gustaffson, L. (1988). "Barnets rettigheder i vort samfund" (The rights of children in our society). In U. Fasting, N. Michelsen, and D. Sommer (Eds.), *Man starter som lille*. København: Munksgaard.

Haavind, H. (1987). *Liten og stor* (Small and big). Oslo: Universitetsforlaget.

Kamerman, S. B. (1991). "Child care policies and programs: An international overview." *Journal of Social Issues, 47*, 179–196.

Jensen, J. J. (1991). "School-age child care in the Danish social context today." *Women's Studies International Forum*, (in press).

Jensen, J. J. and Langsted, O. (1988). "Age integration in an age segregated society: Mixed age groups in Danish day care centres." In K. Ekberg, and P. E. Mjaavatn (Eds.), *Growing up into a Modern World*. Trondheim: The Norwegian Centre for Child Research.

Langsted, O. and Sommer, D. (1988). *Småbørns livsvilkår i Danmark*, 2nd ed. (The living-conditions of small children in Denmark). København: Hans Reitzels Forlag.

Madsen, M., Lindahl, A., Osler, M., and Bjerregaard, P. (1991). *Børns sundhed ved skolestart* (The health status of the child entering school). København: Dansk Institut for Klinisk Epidemiologi.

Myndighedsloven (Act concerning minority and guardianship). København: Justitsministeriet/Schultz Grafisk.

Platz, M. (1988). *Familietid og arbejdstid—hvordan indretter vi os?* (Family-time and working-time—how do we arrange?). København: Socialforskningsinstituttet.

Sommer, D., and Dencik, L. (1988). "80'ernes småbörn i Danmark og Norden" (Young children of the eighties in Denmark and the Nordic countries). In Fasting, N. Michelsen, and D. Sommer (Eds.), *Man starter som lille*. København: Munksgaard.

Yearbook of Nordic Statistics. (1990). Stockholm and Copenhagen: Nordic Council of Ministries and Nordic Statistical Secretariat.

9

FINLAND

Eeva Huttunen and Merja-Maaria Turunen

Finland's 20th-century development into a modern industrialized country with the world's lowest perinatal mortality rate (6.2 per 1,000 births in 1987) has happened very rapidly. Earlier, when the Finnish economy was agriculture based, the living conditions of children were quite different. The number of children in families was large because the child mortality rate was high and the general life expectancy was shorter (79 years for women and 70 for men in 1988). In the agricultural setting women participated in the field work along with being responsible for household chores. Now that women in Finland have entered the work force outside the home as paid labor, especially in low-paying service and caretaking professions, caring has been professionalized. Despite improvements in their legal position, women have little power in the economic structure in Finland.

There exist conflicting interests in Finnish society—on the one hand the need to support and protect children and give them a good developmental start on life, and on the other the need to ensure economic growth and fulfill the demands of the labor market. This conflict can be seen in the urbanization of the country and in the demands placed on Finnish women.

THE URBAN POPULATION

Finland went through a rapid urbanization process. Sixty percent of those 15 to 19 year olds who lived in rural areas in 1960 had moved into cities by 1975. This resulted from a turbulent change in the structure of Finnish industries. Instead of jobs within agriculture and forestry, people now earn their livelihoods within the service, manufacturing, or construction industries.

This urbanization weakened the natural social support structure, as the working-age population moved into towns and the older people stayed in the rural areas. Care of children, disabled, sick, and elderly had to be arranged either by the family members of the small nuclear family or by other non-family networks, as extended family networks were no longer available. This urbanization process forced public services to provide care. In 1989 the social security expenditure (including pensions for the retired, disabled, and unemployed) was 25.7 percent of gross domestic product (GDP), an increase in constant prices of 96 percent over 1975.

WOMEN AND JOBS

Since the Second World War the majority of new students have been women. In 1990 51.0 percent of all students in universities were women. In 1989, 72 percent of all working-age and 90 percent of single-parent mothers were working outside the home. These percentages were 82 percent for mothers of children under four years old in 1990 and 80 percent for mothers of all children under school age.

Despite the official goal of promoting equality between the sexes (Act on Equality in 1987), far fewer women than men are found in top level jobs. Only 13 percent of upper-level management positions were filled by women in 1980. Routine office work and sales jobs are typical for women, as are all caregiving professions, both in nursing and day care. The occupations are also becoming more segregated by sex: a majority of men work in professions where other workers are men, and three out of four women work in professions occupied mostly by women. Though the economic inequality between the sexes is far less in Finland than in most other countries in the world, still women's salaries are on average only 72 percent (and within the public services, where most women work, only 64 percent) of men's salaries. Day care is still seen as women's work, needed because women are working, and as the child's educational right, with adequate resources adjusted to children's needs and wishes.

Finnish women are more likely to be employed full time than are women in other Scandinavian countries. Only 11 percent of women in paid work in Finland have part-time jobs, compared with the other Nordic countries, where approximately half of the women are employed part time. The unselfish, hard working woman is a Finnish tradition.

Women's full-time employment has led to a situation where in 1990 there were more part-time day care places offered than needed. One result is that Finnish children spend a very long day in day care. A 1984 study of children's development showed that 75 percent of children in day care in the second year of life and 85 percent in the third year of life stayed in day care for eight hours or more per workday.

Men rarely enter caring professions, and those who do leave soon or end up in administrative posts. For the development of both boys and girls it is very important to have men interested in working in day care, especially as the number of one-parent families grows (now 15 percent of families) and children often lack the opportunity for close contact and identification with men. There is concern about those adult role models that day care provides for both boys and girls.

Women in Finland are the majority of those in public employment, but still issues like part-time jobs, lower salaries, gender hierarchy within jobs, compromises between individual and career wishes, uneven distribution of household chores, and insufficient day care services are part of the web in which they are caught. In the 1991 parliamentary elections, 77 of 200 members elected were women. Future years will show whether this is a sign of a more equal sharing of power or of the weakening of the status of national parliaments as such bodies give way to male-dominated centralized decision making in the European Union.

Two very important factors will affect the development of Finnish day care and women's roles in near future.

1. A stagnation in economic growth reached Finland in 1990, forcing cutbacks in public expenditure. Social and health services will have less public funding available, and there is a trend toward seeking savings and instituting national economic corrective measures in these areas. This will lead to increased privatization of many services. There is concern about the dissolution of the welfare state and with it the diminishing solidarity of less powerful groups, like the poor, the disabled, the mentally ill, ethnic minorities, the elderly, women, and children.

2. The second factor is the increasing integration within Europe, and whether or not Finland will join the European Union. Statistics show that the status of women is lower in most European countries than in the Nordic countries, and public day care services lag far behind those in Finland. Progressive help to develop day care will be less likely when the comparison is made with other European countries, whose traditions are different and day care systems are less developed. The Finnish system is based on providing comprehensive services to all citizens, rather than only to problematic people or families at risk. A shift to systems supporting only especially needy groups of the population will enhance the inequality between different parts of population and may create circumstances on which there is a need to label people as problematic in order to legitimate the services given to them.

PRESENT CHILD-RELATED POLICIES IN FINLAND

About 5 million people live in Finland. Finland's annual population growth is 0.5 percent—one of the lowest in the world. There are 644,000 families with children, and 15 percent of these are single-parent families. The average family has only 1.7 children due to the fact that 47 percent of

Figure 9.1
The Division Among Different Family Supports

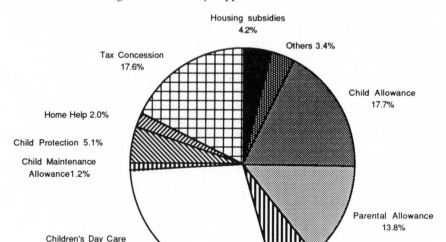

all Finnish families have only one child. Only 3 percent of families have more than four children. As the population growth has diminished there has been a growing emphasis placed on family policies and children's well-being.

The society's support to families for the costs of children is now estimated to be 20 to 25 percent, which is still far behind the agreed upon goal of 50 percent. The families with children are a central part of the active working population (56%). They also pay through taxes for those services they get from the society. Säntti (1989) points out that currently families with children pay more taxes than they receive in services. So the more these families work, the more money there is for all social services.

The distribution of expenditures to families with children is shown in Figure 9.1.

Housing subsidy. The resolutions of the 1987 family policy work group state that society should cover the extra increase in costs for housing of families with children. Although the housing subsidy helps, the housing situation is difficult for families with children, and they live in more crowded conditions than other families. Every third family with children had too little living space (more than one person per room) in 1981.

Parental allowance. The parental allowance consists of 275 days of employment leave. Of this total, paid maternity leave is 105 work days, of which 30 days are allotted before the due date of the baby's birth. The first three months are with full salary and after that are with 80 percent of the full income. After the maternity leave the paid parental leave begins, lasting for 170 work days, normally with 80 percent of full salary (depending on the employment contract). The minimum allowance per day for a person with no income is 60 Finnish Marks (FM), which totals to 1,495 FM per month (4 FM = 1 US dollar). The parents can divide the parental leave so that the father's share is up to, but no more than, 6.5 months. At this point about 35 percent of the fathers avail themselves of this opportunity, with most taking only 6 to 12 days off work after their baby's birth. Only 3.2 percent stay home for more than 12 days. In 1992 fathers were given an extra paid 6 to 12 days fatherhood leave. Adoptive parents are also allotted parental leave.

Child care leave. After the parental leave is complete, parents are entitled to child care leave until the child reaches the age of three. This allows the parent to be absent from her job, with the job protected, in order to stay at home with her child. No salary is paid for this time, but support is provided by the home care allowance. Only 0.6 percent of fathers used this option for extended care of their child. Forty-six percent of working mothers used this child care leave and 15 percent stayed home until their child reached three years of age. The minimum two months was used by 7 percent. The mean length of stay was 11.8 months. Parents are also entitled to partial child care leave; that is, to shorter work days until the child enters school or until the end of the year that the child is seven years old. They can reduce their work day by two hours, taken either from the beginning or from the end of the day. The loss of one's earnings due to shorter work days is compensated somewhat, with the partial child home care allowance. Parents can work shorter hours also during the child's first school year.

Home care allowance. The Child Home Care Allowance Law, passed in 1985, requires that parents be provided an economic alternative to taking jobs and having their children in day care. This allowance is paid monthly; 1,850 FM in 1991, with an increase of 370 FM for another child under seven years and extra support of 1,480 FM if the income of the parent is low. For parents working a shorter work day because of a child there is a partial home care allowance of 463 FM per month. From the home care allowance the parents have to pay their normal income tax, so that municipalities and the national government continue to get tax revenues.

In 1990 child home care allowance was chosen by 127,600 families, which was 83 percent of those eligible. Financially the home care allowance is much cheaper for the municipalities than is day care outside the home. The home care allowance has diminished the use of private family day care, but it has not had much effect on demand for municipal family day care. One way municipalities can influence the ratio between day care places and home care allowances is by adjusting the level of fees for day care. These fees have increased during the last few years, making the home care allowance a more tempting choice for some parents.

Maternity benefit. Since 1937 every mother has received a maternity benefit from the government, which can be taken as money (in 1991, 700 Finnish Marks) or in the form of a maternity package. The package contains basic clothing and bedding for the new baby as well as other baby equipment, the total worth of which is more than twice the cash sum. The maternity package with its informational booklet provides an excellent start for the first baby. Only 20 percent of mothers take this benefit as cash.

Child allowances. By 1948 Finland had initiated a child allowance system through which the State pays a subsidy to the parents that helps to compensate for the expenses incurred in child rearing. Parents are now paid this subsidy until the child turns age 17. The amount is calculated according to the number of children in the family, ranging from 4,392 FM a year for the first child to 10,104 FM for five children or more. An extra sum of 1,284 FM a year is paid to the parents of children under three years old.

Income tax deduction. A large part of the financial support for families with children comes through a special deduction in income tax. At the national level 13,200 FM is reduced from the parents' gross taxable incomes for the family with children between three and seven years of age. At the municipal level there is a deduction of 10,500 FM for each child under 17 years in the family. For the single-parent family with a child under 17 this deduction is 12,500 FM.

In 1988 there was an amendment to the Act on Contracts of Employment that allows parents of children under ten years four days to stay home to take care of a child with an acute illness. All employers do not pay salary for these days.

Child maintenance allowance. This allowance is paid to the lone parent, if the absent parent is not paying support for the child or if this support is less than the public child maintenance allowance. Currently this monthly payment is 549 FM for each child in the family (446 FM if the one parent is remarried or has a live-in partner).

Home help. This is assistance in which a municipal home help worker goes to the home and helps with household chores and child care when the family is in a crisis due to a parent's illness or social difficulties.

Child protection. This protection covers all the supportive measures given by the child protection agency, varying from summer programs for children to permanent foster arrangements in homes or institutions until the child is 18 or 21 years old.

THE FINNISH DAY CARE SYSTEM

The Children's Day Care Law of 1973 required that municipalities arrange or supervise day care to such an extent and in such forms as the need

Table 9.1
Number of Day Care Places in 1990

All day care places	222,600
Private places	8,600
Public places	214,000
Public day care centers	118,000
Public family day care	96,000

demands and to provide this care in the child's mother tongue (Finnish, Swedish, or Lapp). Because the law did not yet make day care a right, it did not force the municipalities to actualize the meaning of the law.

In 1985 the Child Home Care Allowance Law required that as of January 1990 municipalities had to provide a day care place after the parental leave was complete, if parents of children under three years did not choose the child home care allowance. In either case, the parent's job is now protected until the child is three years old.

On April 1, 1991 the law extended the day care right to the four-year-old child. Due to financial stagnation enforcement of this law was delayed until January 1993. From August 1995 the right of a day care place is to cover all children under school age (seven years). Table 9.1 shows the number of day care places available to Finnish families in 1990.

Finnish children start school during the year they turn seven. At this moment there are approximately 440,000 under seven years old. Of these, half are in day care and half at home. In 1988, 34 percent were in municipally provided day care; in 1990 this was 48 percent. The proportion of children in private day care centers and private family day care is not known exactly, but various sources indicate that it is less than 10 percent.

Although Finland currently has a very extensive day care center and family day care system, only children under three years of age are guaranteed a place in these settings. As long as the day care need is not met completely, the criteria for receiving places will be based on socio-economic and special educational needs. The children of parents who are employed full time because of economic need or are students, or the children of sick parents, are given highest priority. Special educational needs may be either a child's need for special education or early educational needs arising from deprived home circumstances.

The health care provided within the day care system is arranged according to public health laws. Services are provided by the local well-baby clinic nurses and local general practitioners or in larger municipalities by pediatricians. The day care system also gets services from the speech therapists and psychologists in the local health center, and children receive regular dental care within day care. All these health services are free of charge.

The Historical and Policy Basis of the Finnish Day Care System

Finnish day care has just celebrated its first centenary. The development of the system of day care and its content was most strongly influenced by the work of Froebel in the early 19th century. Froebel emphasized the meaning of education for small children and the guidance of mothers in the upbringing of their children. The roots of Finnish day care were founded also on the need to bring the children of poor families into guided education and away from the streets. The first Finnish kindergarten was founded in 1888, specifically for poor working-class children. Even then early education was seen in the context of social policy. Since then Finnish day care has been part of the social service offerings for families, and its administration has been embedded in the social welfare administration.

Although Finland was the first Scandinavian country to offer day care for children, the numeric increase in day care services was rather slow until the 1940s. An economic upturn in the 1960s and the willingness to give socio-political issues higher priority accelerated this development. The turning point in Finnish day care was the Children's Day Care Act of 1973, a law that stated that society was obliged to arrange day care for everybody who needed it.

The Children's Day Care Act (36/1973) specifies the day care system's main goal as supporting the home in its child-rearing role as well as working with the home to advance the childrens' balanced development. Historically the day care system has had two functions: (1) to fulfill socio-political needs, and (2) to fulfill educational needs.

According to the second article of the Children's Day Care Act, the socio-political duty of the municipal government is to guarantee "a proper day care arrangement suitable for a child's care and education, with continuous care at the time of day it is needed." In other words, day care makes it possible for parents to work, study, or be otherwise active outside the home.

Day care is directed at teaching the child. Day care gives the child long-standing, secure relationships, activities that will foster and support his stage of development, and a positive environment for growth. In addition, the child's individuality is emphasized. Children can come from very different backgrounds, which are to be taken into account. Preschool-aged children—specifically the six year olds—learn to work together in groups and acquire the skills necessary for primary school.

Although the goals of Finnish day care education are clearly formulated, the educational practices are not clearly founded on any special pedagogical or psychological theory. Day care is seen in its wider ecological context. The following are expectations for the setting and the caregivers:

- The child's care and educational environment must be safe, healthy, and home-like, and make possible close contact with nature.
- The child must have a permanent day care locale, which (together with the home) forms an organized and logical growth environment, where the care provided is suitable to the child's normal daily activities.
- In care and education the child must be shown morally appropriate models and must be protected from mental and physical violence and influences unsuitable for his age.
- The child must have permanent carepersons, who treat him lovingly, accept his individuality, and understand his developmental stages and needs.
- Education must offer the child the possibility for multi-faceted perceptions, activity totalities, and our cultural traditions. There must be a favorable opportunity to experience the changes in the seasons of the year, the commonplace, the festive, rest, and activity.
- The child must have suitable facilities and equipment for physical exercise and games, and experiences that enrich his development, in the form of activity periods and small tasks.

In a representative study of 315 children's development in day care, a research group analyzed the quality of material conditions experienced by these present. Of all day care places, 31 percent were estimated to be spacious, 52 percent adequate, and 17 percent crowded. In 97 percent of day care centers age-adequate play material was abundant, so the material tools for day care seemed satisfactory. Interestingly, the day care workers' satisfaction with their job did not correlate with the space available except in day care centers where the teachers expressed greater satisfaction when the localities were estimated spacious than in more crowded conditions. The municipal day caregivers working in their homes had more space available, but this did not seem to correlate with their satisfaction in the work.

Expectations and Demands of Parents

If the day care system is to realize its full potential in supporting the child's upbringing at home, parents must have the opportunity to clearly express their expectations regarding day care. To implement this the day care personal need to familiarize themselves with the background and needs of the children and their families. Parents are in the best position to know their own children and family situations, so their views must be taken into consideration in the planning and developing of day care activities.

Most of the parents whose children are in preschools think that the most important aim of preschool education is social education—teaching them how to interact with other children and adults. Those parents whose children are in family day care emphasize more emotional education, meaning that the child feels secure, learns to respect other people, and feels accepted as a person. In order for the education to be consistent, it is important that the day care staff and the parents be aware of each other's educational aims.

The emphasis on the emotional aspect in family day care reflects the general opinion that family day care is especially suitable for young children, whose need for secure attachment is essential.

Administration

Originally day care was guided and controlled by the National Board of Social Welfare, but in Finland a major decentralization process in administration is taking place within health and social service departments. In March 1991 the National Board of Social Welfare and the National Medical Board were combined into the Agency for Social Welfare and Health, which will focus its work on planning and development. The controlling and guiding activities will be transferred to local counties and municipalities. There will be a basic change in the control of funding for services. Municipalities will have more control over how to use government funds for all municipal services. There will be no other central control or guidance except those guidelines given in the laws themselves. Only those services that are guaranteed by law are assured of continuation; beyond those the municipalities themselves can decide how the funds will be spent. This is one reason why it is so important that the day care laws require the municipalities to provide day care services. Some municipalities may not place high enough value on the need to further develop day care, but instead put more resources into the financial support of the less expensive child home care allowance.

Family Day Care

The day care law (Law 36/1973) refers to family day care as care given in a family day care center, which can be a private home or home-like setting. Normally this is either the caregiver's home or the child's home. In "three family care" two to four families take turns providing their home as the care locale for a group of up to four children. Four is the maximum size of a family day care group, including the caregiver's own children.

In private day care the setting's physical properties have to be inspected and approved by municipal authorities before caring can begin. The family day care locale must provide at least seven square meters of play area for each child. Also there must be appropriate areas for hygienic care, eating, and undisturbed rest. The municipal day care supervisor controls, guides, and supports both the private and municipal day care givers. Private family day care is arranged by a contract between the family day caregiver and the parents, whereas the municipal family day caregiver is a public employee.

Practically all municipal family day caregivers have 250 hours of training. Besides this training their suitability for this kind of work is considered through interviews and home visits. There are regular meetings of the family day caregivers in a given area, and they also receive additional training through seminars.

Family day care's strong points are seen as its home-likeness and close contact with the other children in the group. There is also closer contact between parents and caregiver than in day care centers, where the highly qualified staff often remains distant from the parents. Parents feel that they can influence the content of family day care more than the content of the care in day care centers. Parents with irregular working hours enjoy the more flexible hours in family day care, which (on the other hand) may often tie the caregiver to the work for ten hours a day. Another positive factor is that the children learn to know the husband of the family day caregiver. Nowadays, when many children lack opportunities to identify with men, this can be very important. Children who have a tendency to experience recurrent infections benefit from the smaller group in family day care, as do children who are too restless in the larger day care center group. Younger children and some very shy children enjoy the closer physical contact with the caregiver.

THE DAY CARE CENTER

Finland has over 2,400 state subsidized public day care centers, serving 18 percent of all children under seven years old. There are also private day care centers, sometimes arranged by hospitals or factories for their own personnel, which are also subsidized by the state and function in ways similar to their municipal counterparts.

The following list illustrates the forms current in Finnish day care centers:

- Standard day care centers (part- and full-time care)
    groups for one to two year olds (maximum 12 children/group)
    groups for three to six year olds (maximum 20 children/group)
    preschool groups for six year olds (maximum 25 children/group)
    sibling groups for ages one to six (maximum 15 children/group)
- Day care centers for school-aged children (after school activities)
    first and second grade pupils (seven to eight years)
- Special day care centers
    for special groups of children in need of special care and education (special handicap or delays/disturbance in physical, cognitive, psychic, or social development)

- Open day care centers

  for children of different ages with their caretakers (mothers, childminders, grandparents, etc.), to support the upbringing of children and with guidance activities for the adults. Open day care centers operate in an open interactive process with the surrounding community, arranging and advertising activities for the whole child population of the area. The children must usually be accompanied by an adult. The maximum group size is 15 adults. This is a new and flexible way of providing educational guidance and is especially popular for parents choosing home care allowance instead of regular day care. About 1 percent of preschool children attend these services.

- Roving day care centers

  these are active in sparsely populated areas, providing mainly preschool activities for five to six year olds (maximum 25 children/group)

- Twenty-four hour day care centers and preschools

  open for extended hours for those children whose parents work on irregular schedules.

- Play clubs

  children attend these from once to five times a week for one to four hours. They can be arranged by the municipality, voluntary organizations, or the church. In 1985, 21 percent of preschool children attended private playclubs and 3 percent public ones. The maximum number of children in a play group is 15.

- Play equipment lending facilities

  these are often a part of open day care centers, but if 20 to 30 children in the area require this service, it will be provided separately. Family day care minders especially appreciate these services.

The size of Finnish day care centers varies from 5 to 100 children. While in exceptional cases there might be more than 100 children, the modern trend is to build small centers close to the child's home. Indoor space requirements for full-time day care range from six square meters per child for children over three years old to ten square meters for each child younger than age one. The equipped outdoor playground must provide at least 10 to 20 square meters for each day care place. Outdoor areas for children under three years and children over three years must be separated from each other.

Part-time care lasts four to five hours per day. In full-time day care children might spend as much as ten hours a day, depending on the working hours of parents. In bigger communities there are day care centers that provide night time and over night care for those children whose parents work in shifts. For rural areas the preschool is offered in moving day care centers, which children attend for a couple of hours on several days weekly.

In earlier years the daily schedules and programs were highly specific and rigid, but a strong developmental process within day care education now aims to loosen the tight programming and the rigid schedules. Meals and snack times are regularly scheduled, and smaller children have a chance for regular daily rest. Otherwise there is an emphasis on child-centered educational principles that support the child's own activity and self-regulation, which are supported, guided, and advised by the adult according to each child's needs.

Children with special developmental problems and/or with handicaps are integrated into regular settings. In practice integration takes place by reducing the number of children in the regular group so that one child with special problems uses two places. A special adult assistant may be included in the group, depending on the child's particular needs.

Day Care Center Staff

Each day care center must have at least one preschool teacher and two trained day care nurses or assistants. Each group also has support personnel. The Day Care Act prescribes the number of the staff members, and the child-staff ratios vary according to the age of children and the group type. The same norms apply to private day care centers as well.

- Preschool teachers receive three years of training at a teacher training college or institute, requiring a high school diploma.
- Social pedagogues have four years of vocational training.
- Child nurses have one year of training for high school graduates, or two and one-half years training for those who have finished the first nine years of comprehensive school. Training is approved by the Ministry of Social Affairs and Health.
- Municipal family day care minders have 250 hours of training arranged by the municipalities or other institutes.

Besides formal training, the personality and social background of the educator are important resources. The way a person is brought up is reflected naturally in choosing the job as an early childhood educator, as well as in the work itself. Finnish educational tradition has long been grounded in demands for obedience and respect for authority. With the changing of society, its ideas and norms about education are also changing. Today's educators are expected to bring up children in a very different way from the one in which they were brought up. The following personality features have been found to be common among day care personnel, especially preschool teachers: balance, interest in children and people in general, spontaneity, and creativity.

Teacher Training

Recent years have been demanding for those working in Finnish day care. The relatively low status given to jobs within day care, together with low salaries (given the level of training and demands of the job), have combined with the turbulent changes within the rapidly expanding day care sector to produce a drastic decrease in the number of applicants for day care teacher training programs during the last five years. In 1989, 50,000 people worked in the day care field, of whom 3,000 were not fully qualified. Sixteen hundred of the available posts (3.3%) were unfilled.

Despite this turbulence, personnel in the Finnish day care system are well qualified and highly educated in their field. Their actions as educators are based upon what they learn while in training: knowledge, skills, and attitudes. While in training the personnel learn both the theory of day care education and the latest research and its applications.

Teacher training has also played a role in the transfer of day care traditions. The day care pedagogy is born of and mediated through training. Up to now Froebel's theories of pedagogy have influenced both the contents and organization of the Finnish day care system, but one could ask if this indeed is sufficient to meet the situations of today's children and their families, or the demands of the future early childhood education.

The teachers of the day care personnel are themselves in a key position. It is very common in Finland that these teachers are also active in researching the day care system itself, which in turn helps to put the latest research and findings into practice. In addition to this, personnel working in the day care system are continuously receiving training and guidance from courses arranged both by the day care administration and by universities. The right to participate in in-service training is stipulated by law. In this way the staff is able to keep up with the latest developments and refresh their working knowledge.

ECOLOGICAL VIEWS IN DAY CARE EDUCATION

As mentioned earlier, one important goal of day care is to support parents in their child-rearing activities and to foster cooperation between parents and day care. One of the factors stimulating the emphasis has been the rise of ecological educational psychology as a new theoretical orientation. Urie Bronfenbrenner (1979) has played a key role in the development of this ecological framework. His orientation gives less emphasis to internal sources of psychological growth and more emphasis to education as a cooperative process among all the people who are involved in it.

The child develops while interacting in his environment and acts simultaneously in several reference groups. A day care situation should consider the quality of both the day care and the family settings, and relationships with friends, as children's growth environments. New and unique to the ecological education orientation is the stress on the importance of cooperation between those educating the child. Parents working and cooperating together create a kind of social network, where they both receive support and are able to better carry out their educational tasks, much in the same way as educators cooperate among themselves in day care centers. The support that parents receive from cooperation and interaction is conveyed on both formal and informal levels.

The aim of day care education is to support the educational task of the home. The only way this can be carried out is to first note the psycho-social background of the family and the needs and resources of the family. Parents must be accepted as the experts regarding their own child, and their voices must be heard. The parents are responsible for the education of their children. Because of this responsibility they have both the right and duty to influence day care education.

DOES DAY CARE MEET THE NEEDS OF CHILDREN AND FAMILIES?

Early education as part of social reality is in a state of change. The demands on early education continue to increase. These changes require an assessment of day care from non-traditional points of view.

Keskinen (1990) assessed the realities of day care from the staff's point of view in a questionnaire study focused on the working satisfaction, stress at work, and occupational identity of 610 day care educators, children's nurses, and day care students. Twenty-six percent of the day care workers were found to suffer from a number of psychosomatic symptoms, and 29 percent felt their work to be highly stressful. The most stressful factors were uncomfortable working postures, lack of time and noisiness at work, amount of responsibility, mental stress, and the low esteem with which others viewed their work. While most of the day care workers were satisfied with their work, 19 percent of both day care educators and children's nurses had frequently or continuously thought about changing their occupations.

In the day-to-day running of day care, many educators express contradictory feelings between how they would like to do things and how things are actually done in practice.

1. When the preschool group sizes are too large and are understaffed, the adults feel that they are mainly just watching and controlling the children. These adults feel that they have too little time or opportunity to give children individual attention. Under such pressures, situations can develop in which true child-oriented education remains only an ideal.

2. Another kind of conflict arises when the skills and practice received in training meet the everyday reality of day care and children's lives. Some of the staff have observed that many children are from homes that provide little support for emotional growth. The staff then has had to help children in the emotional sector, although staff training has emphasized intellectual development. The personnel feel that they are not well enough equipped to deal with the children who need this type of special care and protection.

From this viewpoint staff often feel that the present day care system was designed for balanced children who come from balanced homes.

3. Administrators and managers have their own expectations regarding the educators. Those advocating enlarging group sizes understand the staff's role as merely watching and controlling the children. In contrast to this view, caregivers see their role as being based on the children's needs, and they emphasize the importance of their roles as educators rather than shepherds or guards.

4. Pressures from parents can also be experienced as quite threatening. The problem comes from not knowing to what extent day care education should work independently in its own sphere and to what extent the views and desires of the parents should be heeded in the practical functioning of day care education. In principle, interested parents are considered a very positive factor. But if these parents are critical of standard operating procedures, friction and anxiety can result, even to the extent of undermining the whole foundation of day care.

THE STRENGTHS OF DAY CARE

From the points of view of both the parents and the children, the central strengths of the day care system are its educators, the relationships among the children, and their play activities. These are the cornerstones of pedagogy through which the educational aims of day care can be realized.

The Educators

Research has shown that if resources and structures are adequate, the success or failure of day care education is dependent on the educator's personality, as it affects relationships with the children and attitudes toward education. These factors are much more important than the contents of any educational program or plan. The educators must trust themselves, their skills and capabilities. Trust in other people, tolerance, and the ability to value differing points of view and opinions will also arise from this self-assurance. Herein also lies the basis for successful cooperation with the parents.

Children and Their Peers

The peer group itself is an agent of socialization. The average size of the Finnish family is shrinking, as are people's social networks. For children, day care offers "brothers and sisters" and the opportunity to learn to live together, to learn the social talents involved in developing their humanity. However, the views of those at the administrative level of day care regarding just how many "brothers and sisters" a child should have sometimes become extreme. There are no pedagogical grounds for having groups as large as those now found in Finnish preschools. In fact, trying to teach social behavior in large groups becomes self-defeating. Research has shown that children are overburdened by too many social relationships. At the same time, a peer group of appropriate size is very important for a toddler-preschooler in the development of his or her own identity. Not enough attention is being paid to the amount of effort involved in the development of these early friendships and their meaning to children. The turnover in many day care groups is high. Turunen et al. (1984) report that in only 4 percent of the day care groups studied had children experienced no changes in the group during the first three years.

Play

Day care's third resource is play. In day care the children learn about life and get acquainted with the world on a child's level through playing. In play children can find their own place in the community and can "test" their abilities in their relations with other children. Play is the basis of day care pedagogy, and the staff are well trained to help the children realize their potential in play.

THE FURTHER DEVELOPMENT OF DAY CARE

Both day care staff and parents feel that the nature of education is different in preschools and family day care. However, the main guarantee for quality day care in both forms of day care is the educator. The starting point for developing the content of day care further should be found in the underlying, distinctive characteristics that both types of day care—preschool and family day care—each have to offer, differences that are recognized by both parents and staff as being important. Family day care should not be molded in the same form as preschool day care.

Cooperation in Education

Early childhood education theory integrating the home and day care education emphasizes the cooperation of the two settings. How we perceive the child and childhood determines what we think the child needs and our understanding of the potential of education. We need to search more courageously than we have for a new social-pedagogical tradition, based on the realities of modern life in its varied forms and fitting the needs of today's children and families. The present challenge of day care is in the meeting of psycho-social problems, and the handling of them on an educational level. In the long run the quality of day care is not reflected in children's developmental levels or the high scores they may get in achievement tests.

According to research these differences even out in Finland during the first years of school. The quality of day care shows itself instead in the children's own opinion of themselves, the type of self-image and self-assurance day care develops in children.

Day care should not be regarded as merely a factor in labor market economics. But the idea that children do productive work during their long period of educational preparation, and that they have a right to demand stimulating working conditions, is still foreign to many adults. Adults require that childhood consist largely of schooling, from day care through secondary school; this is not a program constructed by the children themselves. Therefore, it is also the responsibility of the adults to honor the productive part played by children in our society and to see that the conditions they impose on children respect the special quality and social needs of childhood.

REFERENCES

Andersson, B. E. (1985). "Familjerna och barnomsorgen" (Families and Day Care). FAST-Project 36. Stockholm Institute of Teacher Education. *Faculty of Education.* Research Report 5.

Arajärvi, T., Malmivaara K., Martelin, L., Salenius-Laine, K., and Turunen, M. M. (1987). "Working mothers and day care in the development of 0–3 year old children." *Psychiatria Fennica,* 1987, pp. 19–31.

Bronfenbrenner, U. (1979). *The Ecology of Human Development.* Cambridge: Harvard University Press.

Bronfenbrenner, U. (1986). "Ecology of the Family as a Context for Human Development: Research Perspectives." *Developmental Psychology, 22*(6), 732–742.

Children in Finland (1/1988). *100 years of kindergartens in Finland.* The Central Union of Child Welfare and The Association of Kindergarten Teachers in Finland. Helsinki.

Cochran, M. (1982). "Profits and policy: Child care in America." In R. Rist (Ed.), *Policy Studies Annals,* Vol. 6, pp. 537–549.

Committee Report (1980). *Päivähoidon kasvatustavoitekomitean mietintö.* (Report of the Committee on the Educational Goals of Day Care), Vol. 31. Helsinki: State Publication Center.

Haataja, A. (1991). *Lone-parent families in Finland.* Ministry for Social Affairs and Health, Department for Research Planning. Helsinki: State Publication Center.

Huttunen, E. (1988). *Lapsen käyttäytyminen ja kasvuympäristö. Osa I: Perhe ja päivähoito kasvuympäristönä* (Child Behavior and Environment of Growth. Part I: Preschool and Family Day Care as Environments of Growth). University of Joensuu. Research Report of the Faculty of Education 20.

Huttunen, E., and Tamminen, M. (1989). *Day care as growth environment.* The National Board of Social Welfare in Finland. Government Printing Centre. Helsinki.

Huttunen, E. (1992). "Children's experiences in early childhood programs." *International Journal of Early Childhood*, Vol. 24, October (in press).

Keskinen, S. (1990). "Connections between internal models and working satisfaction, stress at work and occupational identity in day care personnel." Department of Psychology, Turku University, *Annales Universitatis Turkuensis* ser. C, tom 80, 225 pp., 52 A pp., Turku, ISBN 951–880–429-X.

Lahikainen, A. R., and Strandell, H. (1988). *Lapsen kasvuehdot Suomessa* (Conditions of Growth for Children in Finland). Helsinki: Gaudeaumus.

Lastentarha (2/1989). Vol. 52. (Kindergarten 2/1989). The Association of Kindergarten Teachers in Finland.

Law 24/1985. Laki lasten kotihoidon tuesta (Children's Home Care Support Act).

Law 36/1973, 304/1983. Laki lasten päivähoidosta (Children's Day Care Act).

Law (1991). Laki lasten päivähoidosta (Children's Day Care Act).

Niiranen, P. (1987). "Kikä on laatua lasten päivähoidostaf?" (What is quality in Child Day Care?). Publications of the National Board of Social Welfare 17. Helsinki: State Publication Center.

Ojala, M. (1983). "Lastentarhanopettajaksi kehittyminen I. Joensuu-tutkimuksen tausta" (The Professional Development of Kindergarten Teacher. Part I. The Background of Joensuu—Project). University of Joensuu. Bulletins of the Faculty of Education 37.

Rinne, R., and Jauhiainen, A. (1988). *Koulutus, professionaalistuminen ja valtio. Julkisen sektorin koulutettujen reproduktioammattien muotoutuminen Suomessa* (Schooling, Professionalization and the State: The Formation of the Educated Reproduction Professions in Finland). University of Turku. Research Report of the Faculty of Education A:128.

Säntti, R. (1990). *Hoitovapaan käyffö ja lasten hoitomuodon valinta* (The Use of Child Care Leave and Choice of Form of Child Care). Publications 1:1990, Ministry for Social Affairs and Health, Development Department. Helsinki: State Publication Center.

Säntti, R. (1989). Lapsiperheiden toimeentulo vuonna 1985 (The Livelihood of Families with Children, 1985). Publications 3:1989, Ministry for Social Affairs and Health, Planning Department. Helsinki: State Publication Center.

Sihvo, T. (1988). *Arki ja apu. Sosiaalihallituksen väestötiedustelun raportti I* (Everyday Life and Support. Population Inquiry Report). Publications of the National Board of Social Welfare 14. Helsinki: State Publication Center.

Sosiaalihallitus (1988). *Lasten päivähoidon vaihtoehdot* (The Alternatives in Child Day Care). The National Board of Social Welfare. Guide 1/1988. Helsinki: State Publication Center.

Turunen, et al. (1981). *Children's Development Study, Part I: The First Year of Life*. In National Board of Social Welfare, National Board of Health, University of Helsinki Child Psychiatric Clinic. Official Statistics of Finland, Social Special Research 32:72. Helsinki. State Publication Center.

Turunen, et al. (1982). *Children's Development Study, Part 2: The Second Year of Life*. In National Board of Social Welfare, National Board of Health, University of Helsinki Child Psychiatric Clinic. Official Statistics of Finland, Social Special Research 32:832. Helsinki. State Publication Center.

Turunen, et al. (1984). *Children's Development Study, Part 3: The Third Year of Life*. In National Board of Social Welfare, National Board of Health, University of Helsinki Child Psychiatric Clinic. Official Statistics of Finland, Social Special Research 32:102. Helsinki. State Publication Center.

Vuorela, U. *The Women's question and the modes of human reproduction. An Analysis of a Tanzanian Village.* Monographs of the Finnish Society for Development Studies No. 1, Transactions of the Finnish Anthropological Society No. 20.

10

FRANCE

Josette Combes

Imagine peeking into every French home on an ordinary morning and watching what happens to young children. Very quickly the observer would become aware of a variety of different rhythms of care and attention. Some children, just having awakened, will be taken by stroller, in the car, or on the subway to someone else's home. That person, who also has just begun her day, will give them a bottle, change them, and start a new day with them. Other children will spend the first hour of the day with their mothers, or both parents. The family will share the morning routines and then make its way to the day care center, where the child will join the other children with whom they usually spend their day. Still others, set down somewhere near their mother, will watch her attend to her household chores and will spend a few hours in a drop-in center while she goes shopping. Some of these children will spend between 10 and 12 hours outside their homes, while others will hardly go out at all.

A quick overview of such little moments in the lives of these children might leave this observer unclear about the causes of these differences in child-rearing patterns. Further analysis would reveal that the determining factor, beyond the uniqueness of each family, is the mother's involvement or lack of involvement in the labor market.

Our observer might try to draw conclusions regarding the harmful or beneficial effects that these various routines could have on the futures of these children. During the second half of this century, research in child psychiatry has been carried out in order to evaluate the conditions for harmonious development in children and the causes of its disruption. Findings oscillate between extreme positions: on the one hand, the continual presence of the mother is thought to be the critical factor in the child's development, and on the other, this continual presence is thought to prevent the child from developing autonomy at a sufficiently early age.

Child rearing and education are arenas that generate significant amounts of ideological confrontation, sometimes based upon scientific evidence but also built upon myths originating in the cultural, religious, philosophical, and political traditions of a given society. Before describing the French day care system, I will examine certain beliefs that provide the basis for French society, recognizing that the question of day care for the young child has only recently entered into the political sphere as an important social issue.

IDEOLOGICAL FOUNDATIONS

Social changes never occur suddenly and cannot be explained by a single cause. Each area of human knowledge—science, political context, philosophy, culture—provides input and receives feedback from the others. It is possible to create a multi-dimensional picture of the process by examining the intersection of the various developments of fields related to child care, beginning with the changing conception of childhood.

How the Child Becomes a Person

In French, the term "child" derives from the Latin "infant," which signifies "incapable." Until fairly recently this supposed "incapacity" gave a very particular status to the nursing baby and the young child. Its human quality was acknowledged only later, at what was considered a "sensible age," that is, around six to seven years old. Before this later stage the child was seen as living a precarious and vegetative life. Parental attachment was conditioned by the uncertainty of child survival and further complicated by the significant death rate of mothers linked to pregnancy and childbirth. The abandonment of children was a common occurrence, the illegitimate child was a social stigma, and the domestic economy was closely linked to laws governing the distribution of inheritance. The child was considered an economic resource, so infertility could mean social rejection for a woman. At the same time, too many children was a source of difficulty. The birthright, instituted to avoid the breakup of the inheritance, distributed resources according to the fraternal bloodline, leaving the youngest at a disadvantage. Daughters could provide the family with gratifying social alliances when they were lucky enough to have the necessary attributes, but they were also financial burdens, since they required a dowry for marriage. Mothers had no legal authority over their children and so could be deprived of their maternal function if the father so decided. At the same time, men were not bound to acknowledge their offspring and could abandon wife and child without suffering social consequences. These customs were found in all levels of society, although social position and wealth changed their impacts considerably.

Several changes took place in the 18th century that contributed to general shifts in understanding about children and parenthood. Scientific research was committed to finding ways to reduce the large number of deaths occurring in the first year of life. At the same time, the philosophy of enlightenment (Rousseau and others) heightened the general interest in education. One result was the production of a number of manuals on child rearing, which combined directives on hygiene with a moralizing discourse on how to be a good mother.

During this same period, the State sought to reduce the death rate among children in foster care by instituting the first measures for the registration of nurse caregivers. In order to be allowed to receive children, these nurses were required to provide a good letter of recommendation from the parish and to provide a minimum housing standard.

Starting in the 19th century, industrial development brought women into the workplace, away from the home and family. These factory workers, who could not afford to pay nurses, left their children at home or brought them along to their jobs, where the children would run small errands as soon as they were old enough to do so.

In 1841 a child labor law prohibited children from working, and the first "asylums" came into being. While the word "asylum" means shelter and refuge, in fact its use in the psychiatric context has given this term a pejorative character from which children's asylums have not escaped. Eventually these "asylums" were integrated into the educational system as nursery schools. Creches, which were established in the late 19th century with a charity function, became associated with welfare and attached to the welfare system.

After the First World War women were drawn into the labor market in large numbers. New creches were built, some by the industries themselves. A law requiring factories with more than 100 women older than age 15 to make special provision for breast-feeding, established in 1928, was never really enforced.

Financial allowances to protect mothers and children have a long history in France, having been instituted first in 1874. This original allowance was withdrawn in 1945, following liberation from German occupation, and replaced in 1946 with family allowance policies created for single mothers and homemakers. These policies favored the formation of large families, in an effort to repopulate France after World War II. They were accompanied by publicity glorifying the family and the mother's role in the home.

The 1950s brought contradiction. On the one hand, the dominant model was that of the mother in the home, with the social definition of a good father resting on his ability to support his wife and children. On the other hand, secondary and university education was more accessible to young women, opening more interesting career possibilities to them. This stimulated the re-entry of women into the labor force. France is now one of the European countries with the highest female employment rates (average of 50 percent, but 72 percent of women with a child under three years old).

Perspectives on the child have also changed radically during the past 100 years. Research in child psychiatry identified previously undetected competencies in infants and even in the fetus. Following the upheaval caused by Freudian theory, infancy emerged as a crucial period in the structuring of the individual. An understanding of the early origin of traumas created by difficulties in parent-child relationships underscored the importance of the first years of a human's life. Scientific investigation of biological phenomena has brought the close relationship between stimulation and development, and especially brain development, to light. While the mystery of the innate and acquired has not been fully unraveled, it has become possible to locate the defects caused by certain types of deficiencies, nutritional as well as those associated with the emotional environment of the child.

Finally, contraception has given children a different role and place in the family, by reducing the number of unwanted pregnancies and allowing for the planning of the number of children and their spacing in time. Children are no longer simply the embodiments of sexuality, but can represent plans, desires, and contracts of confidence—symbols of alliance linking the couple. Their number and sex no longer condition the economic and relational balance of the couple, but rather they may be chosen according to these circumstances.

Who Will Educate the Child?: Family and Collective Spheres

Women have traditionally been responsible for the care and education of the child, but until recently children have also been integrated into a large family network. Typically groups of brothers, sisters, and cousins were taken care of by mothers, aunts, grandmothers, and other older members of the family. The rhythms of these traditional arrangements included children involved in everyday chores, which they carried out by themselves as soon as their age allowed. Instruction only came at an older age and for a small minority. The majority received a religious education that prepared them to respect the moral values and social conventions of their time.

This dichotomy prevailed until the 20th century. With Jules Ferry came the "public school, secular and obligatory for all," as instruction was gradually replaced by education.[1] This phenomenon slowly took parents away from their instructional mission, especially as new generations gained knowledge that their parents did not have and prepared themselves for economic and social functions totally different from those of their ancestors.

The 18th-century church and charity-run nurseries (asylums) were created to take care of the children of the poorest families, with survival as the primary objective. They were established to counter the poor hygienic conditions prevailing at that time. The public day care centers and nursery schools that replaced these asylum nurseries inherited this prophylactic tradition. The State took on the preventive role in response to the poverty of families. About 40 years ago the interest of these centers shifted from the narrower concern with health and hygiene toward a more general interest in the child, evolving from the greater understanding of child potential discussed earlier. Since the 1960s this trend has accelerated, while at the same time the population of families served has changed. Day care centers that were previously viewed as for poor children were rapidly taken over by middle- and upper-class families, to the point where the proportion of poor families in public day care facilities is presently very small.

So the past half-century has brought an increasingly scientific and professional approach to child care at the same time that communal care has shifted from a narrow focus on poor families to a much broader involvement with the majority of French families. Professionalism was further advanced in 1973, with the establishment of a state Diploma of Early Childhood Education. These child care personnel have an essentially educational mission, complementing the health orientation of the pediatric nurses and pediatric nursing assistants who also work with preschool children. The significant point is that conceptions of the function and role of professionals with children are changing rapidly, both in terms of the needs and expectations of parents and the organization of society.

As their roles with respect to children have changed, professionals have had to find a new equilibrium in their relationships with parents. Parents in France have been allowed to enter the day care centers attended by their children only in the past 20 years. Previous to that time, the child was introduced into the day care center through a hatch in the door, his clothes were removed, and he was dressed in clothing provided by the day care center. In the evening, this procedure was repeated in the opposite direction. These methods of fighting epidemics and "bad" hygiene persisted, while the population of families using day care centers changed from "needy" to middle class. Slowly social pressure and the evolution of new concepts have made it possible for parents to enter their children's centers, first into rooms intended for this purpose and more recently into game rooms, bathrooms, and sleeping rooms. But the long tradition of exclusion has left repercussions. Despite all the directives and regulations set up to encourage the presence of parents within day care centers, this practice is still young, and relationships between parents and professionals remain relatively formal and very limited. Cooperative day care programs have been created in part as a reaction to the limitations in the parent-professional relationship.

From Centralism to Decentralism: The Transfer of Responsibility

The French attitude toward day care has had to evolve from compensatory and prophylactic, based on the deficits of families, to the notions of partnership and complementarity that recognize fundamental family strengths. Along with this transformation in social attitudes has come the need for changes in institutional framework.

France is one of the last countries in Europe to employ a very centralized system of service organization. As recently as the early 1980s family and educative policies for preschool children were still specified at the national level by the Department of Health, and care methodologies were determined by that departments's Management of Health and Social Action (DDASS). Regionalization was instituted in 1983, giving local councils the responsibility for methods of care and service provision. The result of this decentralization has been that the powers of planning and control have been shifted to the regions and localities, while the national department retains legislative control. National entities no longer have absolute authority, although they still define general areas of operation. One problem has been a lack of consistency in national regulations from one type of care arrangement to another. For example, the regulations applied to adult-child ratios vary significantly. In a day care center the ratio for two year olds ranges from five to eight children per adult, depending on the training received by the caregiver. But in a drop-in center this ratio is one adult for 20 children, and in the nursery school the teachers must manage with groups of 25 children with the help of a part-time aide.

Regionalization, while providing the potential for better meeting local needs, can also result in less systematic attention to those needs. Political traditions based on a notion of national homogeneity are not easily abandoned, and the political representatives with new responsibilities in this regional structure vary in their interest in the domains allocated to them. Thus great disparity exists both between regions and between municipalities within regions in the coverage of child care needs, depending on whether or not child care needs are considered of high priority.

The tradition of centralism is retained through caregiver and teacher training. Because schools of pediatric nursing and of teacher education remain under centralized supervision, national examinations are based on the assumption that programs are relatively similar, and they thus promote rather homogeneous educational ideas. This homogeneity is reinforced by the fact that young children pass from day care centers to nursery schools at a very early age (two years old in some cases), and the curriculum of the nursery school is still tightly controlled by the national Ministry of Education.

This shifting back and forth between centralism and local responsibility generates a number of difficulties, prominent among which is the lack of coordination between services dependent upon different sources of national supervision. This is most evident for relations between day care centers and nursery schools, where efforts to break down barriers remain weak and unsystematic.

Caring and Schooling

The preparation of children for nursery school is considered an essential objective in the mission of the day care center. At the same time, there is debate surrounding this issue, stimulated in part by statistics indicating that the earlier the child enters group care, the greater the chance of success at school. These kinds of data, which need further verification, are being used to justify access to preschools for two year olds.

In fact, the nearly universal schooling of children from four years onward is still very recent. Statistics now reflect the results of a system that has been changed both by the arrival of younger children and by an increasingly marked tendency to introduce types of learning until now reserved for children at primary school. There begin to be discussions of "academic failure at nursery school" and increases in the number of children considered not ready to go to primary school. At the same time, the presence of very young children at school has caused renewed thinking about the function of schooling, the types of teaching skills needed, and the day care alternatives available to families. This analysis has had some positive effects on pedagogy in nursery schools.

The entrance of two-year-old children into nursery schools has not met with universal approval either by early childhood specialists or by parents. But free entry to school does provide a viable solution for families that must have the child cared for outside of the home, and many families take advantage of it for this reason.

Public Education, Religion, and Culture

Religious education is totally independent of the educational system in France. Parochial systems can be subsidized by the state, but they belong to the so-called private sphere. The law requires that no form of religious education shall be delivered in public institutions, and no religious discrimination may be practiced.

Of course, France is traditionally Christian and practices certain Christian rituals, even when the religious dimension is toned down. Christmas and Easter are traditional holidays, the interpretations of which may vary according to the denomination of the staff. At the same time, the taboos of other religions may or may not be respected, for example, the forbidding of pork in food given to Muslim children.

Care of young children is at the center of discussion about respect for cultural differences and about adjustments necessary to encourage the transition between family culture and the larger culture. There tends to be a certain cultural standardization expected across day care programs. This is reinforced through the centralized training of personnel and through the integration of different approaches to the child and family. Certain precepts end up being adopted and applied across the board. These precepts may be very different from those that families accept for their own guidance; the differences between maternal and professional methods can be very significant. One of the most intense debates in recent years concerns the respect for individuality, the uniqueness of each child, as opposed to the application of a collective routine to which each child must be able to adapt. The presence of a significant contingent of children of different cultures exacerbates the debate. The stated purpose of nursery school is integration, but statements alone have proven incapable of fulfilling this objective. The need for earlier intervention, if this objective is to be reached in school, has become increasingly obvious.

Preschool group care facilities are little frequented by immigrant families. The reasons for this are not entirely clear, nor have methods to remedy the situation been found. There is evidence that the maternal role is experienced somewhat differently by western than by African and North African women. But cost and cultural distance are also determining factors. Thus immigrant families send their children to school at a very early age, in part because it is free. They wish to guarantee them every chance for academic success, but this relatively harsh insertion into the host culture can cause serious damage because neither the mother nor the child is generally prepared for or accustomed to separation.

It is appropriate to consider whether there might be methods that would better prepare these families for this separation. There is also a need to explore ways of familiarizing the children of immigrants with the cultural elements with which they will come into contact at school (language, books, games, etc.) at an earlier age. But this brings us to the ideological tension at the heart of this problem: the tension between assimilation (all children should be treated in identical fashion and abandon their family habits at school, especially language) and integration (children are products of different cultures, and it is a matter of encouraging the expression of the home culture and integrating it with the values of the receiving culture). Exclusion, the rejection of children because of their origins, is illegal. But rejection can be communicated in insidious ways, given ideological beliefs that are unsympathetic to the value of cultural diversity.

SERVICE COVERAGE

There were just over 5 million children under the age of six in France in 1990. Of these children, 2,372,100 were less than three years old. Twenty-nine percent of the newborn to three year olds and 98 percent of the children aged three to five were receiving some form of licensed or registered group care experience, and most of those were full-time arrangements. Table 10.1 shows the various types of care arrangements and the numbers and per-

Table 10.1
Children in Day Care and Preschool Programs

0-3 Year Olds*	Number of Children
Full-time Care	
Public day care centers	95,700 (4%)**
Family day care networks	53,200 (2%)
Registered family care providers	212,600 (9%)
Kindergartens	12,100 (1%)
Day care total	373 600 (16%)
Preschool centers (2 year olds)	260,000 (11%)
Part-time Care	
Drop-in centers	42,600 (2%)
Total 0-3 year olds	676,200 (29%)
3-5 Year Olds	
Public preschools	2,110,390 (86%)
Private preschools	294,084 (12%)
Total 3-5 year olds	2,404,474 (98%)

*   Sources: Service des statistiques des études et des systèmes d'information (1 Jan. 1989), and National Education Ministry (1990).

**   At least 3,500 of these children are in parental day nurseries. This figure is an underestimation because some parental day care centers are recorded in the statistics as day care centers (mini), having taken on this designation because it brings them a higher public subsidy and other benefits.

centages of children served by each type. The reader can see from Table 10.1 that less than 30 percent of French children under three years old are in care outside their own homes that is documented and monitored for service quality. Roughly the same number of newborn to three-year-old children are looked after by their mothers at their workplace (shopkeepers, etc.). The two-year-old children in preschool care make up a very significant proportion of those under age three in day care, and the use of this alternative continues to increase. This increase is generating controversy among both specialists and parents about the appropriateness of having such young children in a school setting that contains 25 children per classroom group. Many parents resort to this method in the absence of another better public alternative, primarily because it is offered at no charge to the parents.

PROGRAM DESCRIPTIONS

A variety of different program types operate within the French day care and early education system, especially for children under three years old. These include both center-based and family-based alternatives.

Public Day Care Centers

Designed to serve the children of working parents, these centers accommodate newborn to three-year-old children on a full-time basis. The centers are usually open from 7:00 A.M. to 7:00 P.M. during the five-day work week. Forty to 80 children are served at each locale. Sixty-five percent of these centers are sponsored by municipalities, 17 percent by regional governments, and the rest by associations and employers (particularly hospitals). These centers are directed by a pediatric nurse or by a nurse assisted by pediatric nursing aides, kindergarten teachers, and service staff. The programs may also include the services of a child counselor, a psychologist, or a doctor on a part-time or consulting basis. These programs are called mini-day care centers when they are accommodated in apartments and take care of smaller numbers of children. National requirements specify adult-child ratios of one to five for children not yet walking, and one to eight for those able to walk. These centers may take the form of parental day care centers, the operation of which is organized somewhat differently.

Family Day Care Networks

These networks bring together licensed family day care providers who take care of newborn to three-year-old children in their own homes. Each network typically involves about 30 providers, each of which may care for a maximum of three children in addition to her own. A network director is in charge of supervision, training, and coordination, and that person maintains contact with the families served primarily to collect parent fees. A provider and her children come together with others at a drop-in center or kindergarten on a regular basis, to encourage the socialization of the children in larger groups and provide opportunities to train family day care providers in child development techniques.

Independent Licensed Family Day Care Providers

These caregivers operate in their own homes but without being tied into a formal network. They are also allowed to care for no more than three children in addition to their own. A specially trained pediatric nurse visits each home at least four times a year, and sometimes more frequently.

Parental Day Care Centers

These centers are administered by a group of parents, who take turns as volunteers along side the professional staff, to further stimulate and provide additional assistance to each group of children. Parents also play an active role in center policy making. The parental centers are less expensive to establish and run than are regular public day care centers. They have developed quite well in rural areas, where the cost of public day care centers is too high for small villages and towns. Parental centers have recently been adapted to the needs of immigrant families.

Cooperative Day Care Networks

These operate in the same way as family day care networks, except that the parents administer the programs and act as employers. This is a very recent system, pilot tested mainly in the Rhône area, which is expected to increase in popularity.

Rotating Home Day Care Centers

These operate in rural areas. Families take turns hosting a group of newborn to three-year-old children (five to seven) one day a week, with the assistance of a day care provider paid by the families.

Drop-in Centers

These centers care for infants and toddlers on an irregular basis—by the hour or half-day. Some part-time working mothers use this system on a regular basis. Typical attendance is about 18 visits per year. Three quarters of these programs are integrated into another service organization (welfare community center, day care center, mother and infant welfare program, training center for women, preschool, etc.).

Preschools

These programs are primarily for four and five year olds, but increasingly serve two year olds as well (see Table 10.1). They are financially supported by the National Ministry of Education for the costs of teaching staff and educational materials and by municipalities for service staff and the maintenance of premises. The core program runs from 8:30 A.M. to 4:30 P.M., with three morning and three afternoon hours of activities. The emphasis is on language arts and developmentally appropriate exercises, games, dancing and singing, crafts, and play. A preschool teacher with advanced training is assisted by a part-time aide in working with 25 children. Lunch and naptime staff provide the teachers with two hours at mid-day for lunch and class preparation.

Activities Centers

These are "wrap-around" programs for children of preschool age, providing care before and after school, and during vacations and other free-time periods. They are designed to permit drop-off times as early as 7:30 A.M. and pick-up times as late as 6 P.M. These programs are run by youth counselors, some of whom have specialized training.[2]

Foster Homes

Twenty-four hour family-based care for children whose parents have been temporarily or permanently deprived of their parental rights or have a limited capacity to fulfill those responsibilities.

DAY CARE COSTS

Table 10.2 provides an overall picture of child care expenditures in France during 1987. Parents pay about 20 percent of child care costs from their own incomes. Approximately 39 percent of the cost is covered by national agencies, and another 5 percent comes from payroll taxes on employers. The remainder (about 36%) comes from local taxes. In general, parents pay on a sliding scale based on family income. Public preschools are free, but parents pay for before- and after-school programs.

A number of incentives are designed to encourage family day care providers to become licensed. Licensing provides the caregiver with social security insurance, unemployment insurance, and maternity leave. Costs associated with these benefits are paid by the parent, who is then reimbursed by the government. A minimum wage is guaranteed by law, with higher payment negotiated according to what the market will bear. Additional allowances for food and supplies are guaranteed. In addition, some parents who use licensed providers are paid something for doing so, as an incentive to discourage the use of unregistered caregivers. The optimistic estimate is that about half of the family day care providers in France have licenses.

The public day care centers and family day care networks are much more expensive to national and local governments than independent family day care because the governments contribute far more subsidy to these programs. From the parents' point of view, the result is that the public center and family day care system alternatives are less costly than private arrangements. For instance, a family with one child in full-time care and an income of $1,600 per month would pay about $180 a month in public center care, $152 monthly for a family day care mother tied into a formal network, and

Table 10.2
Child Care Expenditures in France, 1987 (Billions of U.S. Dollars)

PUBLIC AND PRIVATE SHARES (AND SOURCES OF REVENUE)

| | Total | Public | | | Private |
		National (mostly value-added tax)	National Family Allowance Fund (employer payroll)	Local (mostly land tax)	(Parents)
Preschool	5.0	2.8	0.0	1.7	0.5
Infant and Toddler Care	1.87	0.0	0.37	0.6	0.9
Group Care (primarily centers and family day care networks)	1.3	0.0	0.3	0.6	0.4
Licensed Family Day Care	0.57	0.0	0.07	0.0	0.5
Preventive Maternal and Child Health Care	0.25	0.0	0.0	0.22	0.03
Total	7.12	2.8	0.37	2.52	1.43

sources: Caisse Nationale des Allocations Familiales; Institut National de la Statistique et des Etudes Economiques (IN SEE); Protection Maternelle et infantile.

$460 per month for independent family day care (based on 5 Francs = 1 U.S. dollar).

The reader can see from data in Table 10.1 that the predominant form of care for children under three years old is family day care. While this is often interpreted as an expression of family choice, it also stems from the absence of other alternatives. The status of registered family day care providers is low, and theirs is the most costly day care option, due to the lack of public subsidy. Because the cost is so heavily born by parents, reducing the cost to the state, the Office of the Secretary of State for Families has recently decided to undertake the improvement of training and status of family day care providers.

CAREGIVER TRAINING

Pediatric nurses direct the public day care centers. Their training consists of the State Nursing diploma (two years beyond secondary school), plus one additional year of specialized training. Emphasis is on public health, child development, and administration. Much of the caregiving in these centers is done by pediatric assistants, who have a year of training beyond completion of at least the basic school examination (nine years of schooling). This additional training combines child care theory with practice in the field.

Family day care providers are not obliged to have any training. Licensing approval is based on a visit to the home by a doctor, who conducts an interview designed to assess the applicant's aptitude for looking after children. If they become part of a family day care network, these caregivers receive in-service training from the director of the network, who is likely to be a pediatric nurse.

Preschool teachers receive two years of training beyond the Baccalaureate (the final secondary school degree). This additional training is provided by teachers training colleges, which are governed by the national Department of Education. This course of study primarily focuses on pedagogy. These teachers receive the help of nursery school assistants, recruited by the local municipalities, who receive no training.

The training of people who look after young children, and especially of family day care providers, is presently at the center of national debate. The authorities are taking issues associated with early childhood more and more seriously, and at the same time, directors and caregivers are increasingly concerned about needing more relevant knowledge. As noted earlier, training programs tend to be very homogeneous and may adapt poorly to new forms of child care organization. Concerns are expressed about (1) the appropriateness of the training for those preschool teachers supervising two-year-old children, (2) the absence of attention in the pediatric nursing syllabus to the parent-professional relationship, (3) the relative balance between health and pedagogical education in that same curriculum, and (4) the separation between training institutions, which results in no common core syllabus for different categories of caregiver/teacher.

PEDAGOGY IN EARLY CHILDHOOD

As pointed out earlier, understanding of the young child's development has evolved considerably during the last two decades. New principles have followed from this knowledge, which increasingly provide the basis for organization and curriculum design in care centers. Several of the main themes currently guiding planning are outlined below.

The Importance of Adjustment to Mother-Child Separation

Day care centers and preschools provide periods of adaptation that allow the mother to remain near the child, time for him to get used to his new surroundings, and time to overcome the absence of his mother without too much trauma. This period must allow the child and mother to become acquainted with the world and people who will subsequently become part of their daily life. The length of this period varies from center to center. Some day care centers make it obligatory, while in others it is simply recommended. For nursery school adjustment time may include a period in June that precedes the start of the program in September and then a length of time that can vary from one to several days or even a month.

The Importance of Stimulation

Important progress has been made in providing living space and educational materials for the young child according to his developmental needs. Recognition of the importance of psychomotor needs has generated appreciation for the necessity of enough space for walking around and for climbing structures, and for the separation of play spaces from sleeping areas. There has been a growing tendency to permit free access to games, rather than trying to organize them for the child, and thus to rely more on the spontaneous activity of the child. Water games, the pool, and the bath have become part of activities commonly offered to children. Music and manipulation of musical instruments, books, language games, painting, modeling with clay, and the like make up the panoply of activities now organized for children.

However, professionals continue to oscillate between relatively opposed attitudes: whether to allow the child the power to choose a game or to suggest a structured activity to him. Caregivers wonder about the balance to be sought between asking the child to do something, making suggestions to groups of children, and the complete provision of freedom of choice to the child. Clearly this balance must vary to some extent according to the needs and capacities of each child. Meanwhile, the caregiving staff is not always sufficiently trained to develop a variety of activities, and so in most day care centers an early childhood specialist is responsible for leisure-time activities oriented primarily to developmental outcomes. Along the same lines, in family day care systems where family day care providers come together in groups, activities are organized with developmental aims in mind.

In 1989 an agreement was signed between the Ministry of Social Affairs and the Department of Culture in order to develop artistic development activities in care centers, especially to train parents and professionals in this approach.

Mixed Age Groups

Children may be grouped with children of the same age or placed in mixed age "sibling" groupings. Same age grouping has prevailed for many years and still remains widely used, especially for infants. The adoption of one or the other grouping method is not always motivated by pedagogical issues, but rather by staffing or facility constraints.

The Parent-Professional Relationship

After a long period of having been forbidden even to visit the center, parents can now be part of certain moments of day care center life. This also gives them an opportunity to communicate with professionals around and about their children. Once again the quantity and quality of this exchange varies from one locale to another. Often this relationship with the family is badly handled by professionals, who may adopt unenthusiastic or even hostile attitudes with respect to dialogue or feedback. Development in this area is still too recent for its future direction to be judged. Parental day care centers, which are based on parent-professional partnership, naturally encourage this exchange. Preschools are almost closed to parents, with the exception of formal matters such as parent boards that intervene to a limited extent.

EXPERIMENTING WITH NEW WAYS TO ORGANIZE CARE

Despite a very rapid growth curve for day care services in France, the types and quantity of care available are unable to meet the needs of the society. Supply is very uneven, characterized by a concentration in large cities. Forty percent of facilities are found around Paris, serving about 20 percent of the population. Rural areas are at a great disadvantage.

The Parental Day Care Center

Several new kinds of child care enterprises have come into being to compensate for the absence of satisfactory solutions. One of these innovations, the parental day care center, was referred to briefly earlier in the chapter. This approach has shown a very rapid development, not only as evidenced by the number of such centers created over the past decade, but also in terms of the uniqueness of their operation and underlying pedagogical ideas.

In the 1970s, during a time of experimental alternatives, parents decided to collectively take care of their children. From several isolated experiments the activity increased rapidly, thanks primarily to a media campaign. The result was that the authorities began to support such an innovation and to encourage the formation of an Association of Child-Parent Collectives (A.C.E.P.) as a federation for the provision of technical support, promotion, and effective negotiation.

In ten years the movement has developed to the point where more than 700 facilities were recorded in January 1990—day care centers, drop-in centers, and combined systems. Rather urban in origin, the activity rapidly expanded to rural areas and small towns, where the parental day care center has proved to be one of the only financially viable kinds of community care.

Beyond the need to resolve the problem of care for their child, the motivation of parents has been:

• To encourage a flexible transition between the family environment and the community, organizing small units of life where children and adults learn to know one another.

• To maintain responsibility for the education of their child, by actively participating in pedagogical orientation and in the daily organization of the care center.

• To promote a pedagogy of development that integrates less professionalist contributions, provided for through the creativity of groups of parents.

• To be initiated into parenting within a network of parents, by an informal means of exchange with professionals, through the sharing of different ideas and information, and by deepening their familiarity with early childhood.

• To rebalance parental roles within the family, encouraging the involvement of fathers in daily chores as well as in the care center.

The parent-professional partnership that forms the basis of parental day care centers naturally encourages the parent-caregiver exchange, since parents participate regularly in the leisure activities of the group of children, and decisions concerning program structure are generally made jointly by parents and professionals.

It is interesting to see how rapidly this type of care arrangement has been integrated into the national system. A set of 1981 regulations officially recognizes parental day care centers within a defined legal framework, specifying their obligation to pay skilled personnel, to comply with safety standards established by the municipality, and to serve a number of children determined by the capacity of the premises. Under these conditions, such care centers can be set up in apartments, public, or private facilities. The procedure for financing the programs is relatively well established, generally 40 percent from the National Family Allocations Fund and 60 percent from local communities. To cover operations, parental day care centers receive a service grant identical to that of family day care networks, and theoretically they receive a subsidy from the municipality and regional council. With respect to the latter, this system is far from being generally established, and for new parent groups this often presents obstacles. In general, these day care centers survive on tight and precarious budgets, despite low costs compared with other facilities.

Parental Day Care Centers and High Risk Families. Since 1986, the ACEP has led an experiment in the adaptation of the parental day care center system to areas that have a population showing significant risk indicators: very low income, heterogeneous ethnic origins, and so forth. The objective has been to provide care centers to young children adapted to their needs, so that mothers could engage in a process of professional and social integration. For most of these families, remaining above the poverty line depends upon the wife's salary, either in addition to or in place of the husband's income. The national percentage of families with a single parent in France—headed mainly by women—has been estimated at 10.2 percent, and this figure appears to be increasing steadily. Immigrant families represent 6.9 percent of the total French population, but they are highly concentrated in certain areas, especially in urban settings. Almost three quarters of the foreign population belongs to the working class, and 10.6 percent of the unemployed are foreigners.

In such a context, the principle of early prevention is naturally receiving more and more emphasis. The objective of parental care centers in this regard is to sensitize families very early to the importance of the mobilization of educative skills around children, in order to help them to develop and sustain their competence. The early introduction of books, music, and the importance of language are themes that can be taken up in an informal way with families, within the framework of their participation in the day nursery. This kind of sensitization is all the more beneficial if mothers have the means to develop at the same time, to reinvest themselves in a self-improvement or professionalization process.

For immigrant families, the question of "culture shock" also needs to be seriously considered. Educational approaches that encourage a familiarization with the receiving culture (French) while at the same time showing respect for the expression of the individual's cultural background are still far from being mastered. Studies of multi-culturalism are recent in France. These researchers study the phenomena that are at work in the communication between cultures, but in general, conflict situations are better defined than those of cooperation and mutual assistance.

It is probably at an early age that intercultural alchemy can be best observed and mastered. But the staff at the heart of this process is largely unequipped in terms of training and preparation for this role. This is likely to be one of the major issues addressed in the future.

Parent-Child Centers

A new approach to families has emerged through the work of Françoise Dolto, a French child psychiatrist who has been influential in expanding awareness of the significance of the first years of life. In 1979 Dolto created the "Green House" (Maison Verte), a meeting place for parents and children, open free to families. Early childhood professionals with primarily psychoanalytical training were available to welcome families and listen to them. Dolto has emphasized above all the significance of language and the benefits of putting situations into words when a relational difficulty arises. Thus the parent-child center is a setting for socialization and transition, where parents are not allowed to leave the child in favor of other activities. It is a place where the child begins to open up to the world—but within the security of the continued presence of his mother, father, or nurse. The adults present can exchange with professionals or with other parents and can learn ways of supporting the developing autonomy of the child. Because these centers do not charge a fee and have no public subsidy, they face many financial difficulties.

Grouping of Services Provided for Young Children

Responding to government initiatives, certain municipalities have taken the initiative to group several types of services in geographic proximity, in order to facilitate the breakdown of barriers between them, and to encourage a more integrative approach to the support of families. This takes the form of a Family and Child Services Center, which provides medical care for infants, a day care center, a drop-in center, a preschool, and sometimes a recreation center.

CURRENT PERSPECTIVES

France is certainly one of the Western countries with the foresight to give high priority to the developmental needs of its young children. But we are now at a point where there is a serious need to revise certain of our basic principles—especially involving the homogenization of educational practices—in order to allow innovation and partnership to further enhance the quality of resources made available to families. The authorities encourage innovation, that is, they invite civil society to show imagination in creating solutions for the needs it expresses. But after a period of relative autonomy, these innovative experiments are very quickly faced with a paradox. Either they fit into the existing public services framework and conform to pre-established regulations that suppress their innovative characteristics, or they maintain their innovate principles of operation and are cut off from public funds and either disappear or are forced to become elitist in their recruitment. Parental day care centers are at the present time in this phase. The National Family Allocations Fund (CNAF), imposing standards modeled on those of public day care centers, is forcing administering parents to adopt a logic of operation that contradicts the principles of self-management. In the same way, certain municipalities are requiring that parental centers obtain the status of mini-day care centers in order to be eligible for local financing. But this means that the early childhood professional technically in charge must then become a "director" and in turn is required to be a pediatric nurse. This contradicts the entire premise of the parental day care center, where the professional is not to direct, but rather to provide technical assistance and support to the governing parent group. Thus integration into the larger system may distort the very pedagogical and functional processes created precisely to introduce variety, flexibility, and partnership into a system that has tended to suppress such characteristics.

At the same time, the institutional environment is beginning to concern itself with finding alternative solutions to problems posed by academic failure in children, and new ways to encourage the integration of marginalized families. Working in the interests of young children and their families appears to be more and more acceptable as a pertinent angle of approach. Social workers are interested in this strategy and recognize their lack of skill in this area. There is recognition of the urgent and fundamental need to better understand how to bring together different cultural influences and modalities, to determine what systems might govern the mixing of cultural influences, and to discover the psychological enhancement and disturbances that will result from these complex social activities.

The opening of European economic frontiers in 1992 can offer an opportunity to change directions in relation to some of these challenges. At the same time, because France is considered one of the best equipped countries in the Common Market in terms of child care, there is fear that the uncertainty of this economic "leap forward" will reinforce in authorities a kind of wait-and-see attitude that will slow development, rather than stimulate it. One wishes that the innovative experiments that have borne positive results in France might inspire similar approaches in other countries. Recognition of common challenges across cultures would reduce the isolation and marginalization within official structures that so often accompanies such change efforts and could lead to greater coordination of such activities within as well as between the Common Market countries.

FUTURE CHALLENGES

Despite a range of incentives designed to stimulate expanded coverage, the parental demand for center-based day care has yet to be met. According to a recent survey, at least twice as much provision will be needed to meet the need.

Some parents seem to prefer the family day care alternative, but it is difficult to determine whether this is true preference or justification resulting from the lack of alternatives. The national and local governments are encouraging family day care because it costs those entities less than other options. From the family's point of view, however, cost is a disincentive to choose private family day care, especially considering the fact that unregistered care is unmonitored and may be of low quality. The State has launched a series of measures to attract unregistered caregivers, including improved fringe benefits, training, and professional status. The hope is to reduce the "black market" and encourage more women to provide child care in their homes.

Preschools meet virtually all the demand in the three- to six-year-old age range, and serve two year olds to some extent as well. But the general feeling is that these programs are not well equipped to serve the youngest of these children, and even when supplemented to serve children living in low resource areas, the teachers in these programs face very large classes (in some cases as many as 30 to 35 children, some very young).

Parental day care centers increasingly have become a preferred solution in small towns and villages, well received both by parents and by professionals eager to play an active part in creating their own job opportunities. The professionals in these programs find that their role is not confined only to child care; they are bringing new energy into local social support networks and contributing to the revival of sparsely populated areas by serving as an attraction to young families.

There is more general indication that parents are receiving more recognition as playing an important role in the educational process. Most recently the Deputy of Education circulated a letter to all schools, stressing the fundamental role of parents in education and reminding the schools of parents' right to be associated with the schools and to good relations with teachers. But teachers continue to be resistant and the schools have not publicized these opportunities.

The major change occurring over the past decade has been in the popularity of early childhood issues. Politicians now see value in mentioning these issues in their speeches.

There is general agreement that early childhood education is effective in combating the handicaps and failure associated with being reared in a high-risk environment. Unfortunately, the poorest families in France have little access to day care services, either because of their cost or because of the cultural gap between the center routines and family child-rearing patterns. Much remains to be done to provide these families with access to day care of higher quality, provided in a partnership of respect.

Finally, it is important to continue to support the initiatives of parents, not only because they make direct contributions to the services they help to develop, but also because their solidarity together strengthens that network of adults committed to collective responsibility for all the children, and further strengthens advocacy on behalf of education as a high priority for French society.

NOTES

1. Jules Ferry (1832–1893), a dedicated advocate of free secular education, became the French Minister of Education in 1879. His program of educational reform, carried out between 1879 and 1882, brought France a national public school system providing free, compulsory, and lay elementary education.

2. "Study time" is provided at the school for those primary school aged children needing supervision after school hours.

REFERENCES

Association des Collectifs Enfants Parents. (1988). *L'enfant, une responsabilité partagée* (Children, a responsibility to share). Actes du Colloque. Paris: A.C.E.P.

Associate des Collectifs Enfante Parents. (1990). *Les crèches parentales, services de proximité, pôles de solidarité* (Parental day care centers, neighborhood services, poles for solidarity networks). Actes du Colloque. Paris: A.C.E.P.

Battagliol, A. F., and Jaspard, M. (1987, Dec. 16, 17). Séquences de la vu familiale, évolution des rapports familiaux (Family life sequences, evolution of family relationships). Rapport communiqué au Colloque. *Temps et durée dans la vie professionelle et familiale* (Time and duration in professional and family life). I.D.E.F.

Bouyala, N., and Roussille, B. (1982). *L'enfant dans la vie: une politique pour la Petite Enfance* (Child in life: a policy for early childhood). Rapport du Secrétariat d'Etat à la Famille. Paris: La Documentation Française.

Colleret, Y., and Félix, M. (1988). *Les modes d'accueil des enfants en France* (Child care in France). Rapport aux Communautés Européennes. Paris: I.D.E.F.

Combes, J. (1987). *Création de structures d'accueil à participation parentale en milieu défavorisé pour enfants de O à 6 ans* (Parent's day care cooperatives for disadvantaged families). Compte rendu d'enquête préliminaire. Paris: A.C.E.P.

Combes, J. (1989). *Les structures d'accueil des jeunes enfants à participation parentale en milieu interculturel* (Parent day care cooperatives with migrant families). Rapport d'évaluation. Paris: A.C.E.P.

Gervet, J. F. (1983). *Les désir du père dans les crèches parentales*. Mémoire de psychologie clinique. (The father's desire in parental day care centers). Paris: Université René Descartes, Paris V.

Gervet, J. F., and Grillet, H. (1986). *Guide pratique des crèches parentales* (Practical guide for parental day care). Paris: A.C.E.P.

Hamel, D., Temple, P., Gerassy, J. M., and Priest, H. (1980). *Les modes de garde innovants de la Petite Enfance: les groupes Enfants-Parents* (The innovative day care resources for early childhood: Children and Parents groups). Paris: A.C.E.P.

Hatchuel, G. (1989). *L'impossible choix: les modes de garde des jeunes enfants* (The impossible choice: child care resources). Synthèse de l'enquête du CREDOC. Paris: C.N.A.F.

"Innovations dans le champ social." (1986). (Innovations in the social field.) *Informations Sociales* N 2. C.N.A.F.

Laroque, P. (1985). *La politique familiale en France depuis 1945* (Family policies in France since 1945). Ministère des Affaires Sociales et de la Solidarité. Paris: La Documentation Française.

Leprince, F. (1985). *L'accueil des jeunes enfants: les actions des Comités d'Entreprise et des Associations Parentales.* Thèse d'Economie Sociale. (Child care: The action of joint Production Committees and of Parent Cooperatives). Paris: Université Panthéon Sorbonne, Paris I.

Leprince, F., and Frenet, F. (1989). *Accueillir les jeunes enfants. Comité d'Entreprise des Crèches Parentales* (Welcoming young children. Joint Production Committees and Parent Cooperatives). Espace Famille N 3. C.N.A.F.

Malewska, H., and Gachon, C. (1988). *Le travail social et les enfants de migrants, Racisme et identité.* Recherche-Action CIEMI. (Social work and migrant children. Racism and identity). L'Harmattan.

Moss, P., and Philipps, A. (1989). *Qui prend soin des enfante de l'Europe? Compete-rendu du réseau des modes de garde d'enfants.* (Who is taking care of the European Children?). Commission des communautés européennes.

Passaris, S., and Schiray, M. (1983). *Le mouvement des crèches parentales et ses rapports avec les institutions* (The parental day care movement and its relation to institutions). Paris: C.I.R.E.D.

Passaris, S., and Schiray, M. (1984). *Eléments pour une politique de l'accueil collectif de la Petite Enfance favorisant la participation parentale* (Elements for child care policy encouraging parental involvement).

Richardson, G., and Marx, E. (1989). *A Welcome for Every Child: How France Achieves Quality in Child Care.* Report of the child care study panel of the French-American Foundation. New York: French-American Foundation.

11

GERMANY

Rudolf Pettinger

The topic of day care for children is assuming great importance in the present discussions concerning the reunification of Germany, in socio-political and especially in ideological debates. It is precisely within the arena involved with supplementing the family's contribution to child rearing that socio-political developments have followed different paths in the different parts of Germany.

In the German Democratic Republic (GDR) early collective education of children was developed from an ideological base, as a way to have early influence upon the development of the consciousness and behavior of the young and to free the mother to pursue her own career in the workplace on an equal footing with men. In the Federal Republic of Germany (FRG), on the other hand, priority has been given to raising children exclusively within the family, and supplementary child care in the first years of life is seen exclusively as a measure to relieve families in distressed circumstances. The secondary role given in the FRG to day care for children outside the family reflects the thinking that led to the emergence of the "Child Protection Policy" in Germany 150 years ago.

Because of the low level of development of day care facilities for children in the FRG, the level of employment of mothers is significantly lower than in other Western industrialized countries. However, because of the change in value placed on the gainful employment of women and their own desire to work outside the home, the debate about child care facilities has been opened up anew in the reunified Germany, and questions about the possibility of combining rearing a family with pursuing a career outside the home are being asked again, and more pressingly, in the debate on family and social policy.

The question of the rearing of young children has always been a subject for ideological discussion. The middle-class family model, where mothers gave up gainful employment outside the home to bring up their children competed with the picture of the mothers who were employed because of family circumstances (e.g., single parents) or for social reasons (hardship, need), or whose children were looked after in institutions or by childminders. Only the middle-class family model was seen as valid. Now, however, there is a trend toward identifying the different ways of rearing (within the family in the FRG and collectively in the GDR) with the two social systems, so it is easy to overlook the fact that the needs and circumstances of families, of mothers as well as children, have transcended political systems. On the one hand, one sees examples in Western and Northern European democracies of well-developed day care systems for very young children, which in the FRG have previously been considered typical only of the East European socialist countries. On the other hand, in some previously socialist countries, such as Poland, one sees a rather low level of development of day care for children, rather similar to that in the Federal Republic.

THE EMERGENCE OF DAY CARE AND PRESCHOOL EDUCATION IN GERMANY

The clearest causes of the emergence of facilities for very young children were the neglected children of the poor, working population. This issue had been articulated early in the 19th century:

We have never failed to appreciate that children in their tender years are best cared for within the family, provided that it, and in particular the mother, has sufficient time, the right sort of love and wisdom to bring to bear on the task. But there are in the urban areas and in the large towns, a large number of parents who, through earning their daily bread, with factory work and other occupations must spend a great part of their day away from the home, and there are homeworkers whose work is so arduous that they are unable to care for and supervise their children, so that the latter are left to themselves for most of the time. Some of these are locked up, where they vegetate passively in musty air, or often injure themselves by climbing on the furniture, by burning themselves in fires or cutting themselves with knives and such like, so that their bodies and souls, instead of being cared for and developed, wither and die at an early age. Yet others of these neglected children spend most of their time in the alleyways, where their ears, mouths and hearts are exposed to wickedness of every kind, that should forever remain foreign to them, and where the basis of brutality, promiscuity, laziness, impurity and immortality are laid, which poison all nobler seeds, often for the rest of their lives.

Finally there are everywhere not a few parents who, even if they had enough time to bring up their children, simply do not have the wisdom to do it properly. Rather, they raise them badly by either being too soft or too hard. For example, they take the normal childish urge for activity for destructiveness and try to suppress it through ill treatment because it requires a great deal of supervision. Instead of trying to guide their natural sense of joy and exuberance, they smother it because it is too noisy. They leave the great receptiveness of the childish mind to believe in and love the heavenly Father and the divine friend of all children undeveloped because they themselves are so far removed from it. (T. Fliedner, 1836 from Erning 1976, p. 54f.)

French and English institutions were taken as models for the institutions into which these children were placed. The large number of literature references—nine in 1848 alone with many more in succeeding years—demonstrates the different concerns and educational approaches followed. The basis of this variety lies also in the number of small states in the Germany of that time, as well as in the social activities of the church, and in the work of the independent societies and of the workers' movements.

The institutions were initiated predominantly by societies whose members belonged to the middle classes, the nobility, or the clergy. Through these institutions they pursued primarily humanitarian and charitable ideals, the moral, civilizing, and religious improvement of the poor, and the protection of children from negative influences and the drift into criminality. Later on the reasons for their foundation were socio-political and social—the indirect effect on the parents through the children, and the gain in State security through the improvement in the level of education of the poor and through their social integration.

Despite their common historical roots, care facilities for preschool children have developed differently. On the one hand, institutions and facilities for the care of newborn to three year olds have been unable to shake off their origins as provisions for families in distress. Their utilization remains very selective and takes a back seat to family-based care. Kindergartens for three to six year olds, on the other hand, were able to establish themselves as educational institutions alongside of the family, to set their own child-rearing goals, and to demonstrate their social worth. Their future existence is undisputed, and attendance in them, at least in the last preschool year, has become the norm.

THE LEGAL FRAMEWORK FOR PRESCHOOL PROGRAMS

Until very recently the definitive legal basis for preschool services has been the "Jugendwohlfahrtgesetz" (Youth Welfare Law). Starting in January 1991, however, the basic framework became the new "Kinder- und Jugendhilfegesetz" (Child and Youth Assistance Law), or KJHG. This law governs not only the furtherance of children's creches, day care centers, kindergartens, and after-school care facilities, but also child-minding (family day care) provision (Sections 22–25). In fact, in accordance with the KJHG, future child-minding arrangements will no longer require the approval of the Jugendamt Youth Department, although the situation with respect to institutional types of day care remains unchanged. This inconsistent treatment of the different kinds of day care provision could lead to a lessening of recognition for and promotion of child minding.

In contrast with the earlier Youth Welfare Law, the KJHG places more emphasis on educational provision in the facilities provided and allows for care based on parental initiatives alongside of the professional child care provision. In so doing the law codifies a reform movement that had established itself during the previous two decades—the foundation of self-help facilities, partly due to the inadequacy of those available and partly because the existing programs were rejected on grounds of value. The KJHG introduced the concept of "subsidiarity," the notion that the solution of the problem of caring for children lies at the organizational level immediately above that of the family. This incorporates the numerous reforms of parental initiatives and self-help measures into the public education and advisory services (Section 26 KJHG). It takes into account the requirements for ideological plurality in the services provided.

The KJHG itself governs only the legal framework, which should ensure a unified development of services within the federal structure of Germany. The power of the individual states to implement the law, concerning things like program implementation, mode of operation, and support, has not been abdicated. Thus the KJHG will not lead to further development or expansion of service provision. The responsibility for providing a range of facilities to meet day care demands is left to the states and communes, who bear the official responsibility for implementing the Youth Assistance Law.

Because of the costs involved, the establishment of these facilities must be considered in long-range terms. The KJHG will not change either the position and social prestige of day care on the one hand or the priority given to child rearing in the family on the other. What was written in the "Deutsche Bildungsrat" (1970) in its "Structural Plan for Child Rearing" remains unchanged: "It is the commonly held view that during its first three years of life, a child's development is best furthered if its family provides an understanding and stimulating environment. It is hard to see how children of this age can experience more stimulation outside such a family. For 3–4 year-olds, however, this conclusion is no longer valid" (p. 40).

In the majority of the federal states, kindergartens function as a part of the education system, under separate laws. The individual laws governing kindergartens regulate such things as premises, operation, educational standards, personnel, and official recognition. The introduction of the KJHG will not affect the level at which the states regulate their own kindergartens.

DAY CARE AND KINDERGARTEN PROGRAMS IN GERMANY

Both ideology and practice dictate that the care and education of German children younger than and older than age three be considered separately.

Those two sections of this chapter are followed by a brief discussion of after-school care for school-aged children.

Day Care for Children under Age Three

The specialist report for the eighth "Jugendbericht" (Youth Enquiry), 1990, points out that the provisions for children under three years are increasing perceptibly in educational and socio-political significance for children and families and are being encouraged as part of the regional social infrastructure. This change is primarily a product of the altered circumstances of families and children, but it also results from changed ideas and experiences regarding the developmental and learning potential in the first years of life.

At the same time, it is important to emphasize that up to now, in what has been West Germany (FRG), there has been no wish to change the practice of day care for very young children. Its back seat role to family-based care, and the use of strict criteria based on family circumstances to limit admissions to centers, will continue. Those admission criteria include the need to work due to poverty, the fact that both parents are studying, or of single-parent family status.

The situation in the former GDR is completely different. There child care in creches (centers) for children under three years old has been the norm. The provision of a wide net of facilities to care for preschool children and school-age children has been seen as a prerequisite for the assimilation of the mother into the work force. It can be inferred that in the future, however, because of increasing unemployment among mothers, the lack of funds on the part of local communities, the dismantling of social facilities in the workplace, and increasing charges to parents for day care, there will be a considerable reduction in the availability of these facilities. These changes deserve some elaboration before I discuss the facilities available for very young children and outline some policy alternatives to the use of those facilities.

Changes in Employment and Family Structure. More women, and particularly more mothers, are now employed than has been the case in the past. The increase in the proportion of working mothers is even greater than the general increase of women in the work force. There have been several opposing trends in the period under discussion.

- Women start work later, as a result of longer and better education.
- The proportion of women in gainful employment in middle age (35–55) has risen significantly, which suggests that this employment is increasingly planned and seen as a lifelong commitment, in contrast to earlier years when it was seen as a phase of strictly limited duration.
- The value of gainful employment to women has risen significantly. This is in part

a result of longer and better schooling, increasing professional qualifications, and more demanding employment activities. But it is also a result of greater family instability, that is, an effort to be more financially independent and less dependent on their partners. Other important motives for the employment of more mothers are participation in public life, the possibility for social contact that a job offers, social prestige, and accepting of responsibility, and personal satisfaction.

- The employment of mothers is significantly different, however, in the amount of part-time work they take up. About one mother in two with a child under three in the former Federal Republic works less than full time. Employment of mothers has not only increased the demand for day care facilities; it has also caused the admission criteria of the programs to be broadened, in part because the employment is stimulated by growing economic need.[1]

The number of children in families is falling. Two clear trends have been observed in the former FRG since 1970:

- The number of children living alone in their families has increased sharply, to 31.5 percent in 1989.
- The number of families with three, and especially of those with four or more children has decreased sharply during the same period.

These changes suggest that the experiences children have with siblings (i.e., contact with children their own age) has been greatly reduced. In their families children experience intense parental attention. They find themselves in a situation that tends to be excessively demanding, and they lack sisters and brothers who might provide support and relieve strain, or at best that support is provided by only one sibling. It therefore falls upon social organizations to provide facilities and opportunities for children to meet and interact with others their own age.

This trend to fewer children also interacts with career patterns, as any break in career to raise children is shortened. Thus the motivation to combine child rearing with work outside the home is increased.

Types of Programs and Amount of Coverage for Children under Three. The most common types of institution-based programs for children newborn to three years old are "Krippen" (creches), "Krabbelstuben" (toddler groups), and "Kindertagespflegestellen" (day care centers). Among the family-based approaches are "Familientagespflegestellen" (family day care centers), "Tagesmutter" and "Pflegenester" (childminders).

For children up to three years old there is a distinct shortfall in provision within the FRG. With 28,353 places in creches, care is provided for only about 3 percent of children up to age three. Figure 11.1 shows changes in provision since 1970. This provision has remained more or less constant over the last 20 years. This level of provision relegates the Federal Republic of Germany to the bottom of the list within the European Community. Beyond this official, or at least officially regulated, provision, there is a

Figure 11.1
Places in Creches and with Childminders in the Former FRG

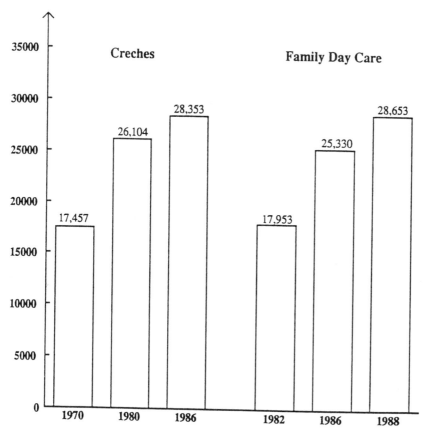

private day care sector, which is organized independently between individual families, without the knowledge, approval, or supervision of the responsible authorities. The size of this "market" is estimated to represent roughly an extra 25,000 places, but this is not a reliable figure as it includes older children. Thus there is provision for only 4 to 5 percent of all children under three when all the possibilities are taken into account. As a proportion of the children of working mothers, this represents about 14 to 16 percent.

As these figures imply, the simple employment of mothers is still not in itself a sufficient criterion for admission into a creche or day care center. Much more account is taken of the economic need related to a mother's involvement in the work force. The result is that the population served by creches is biased toward the economically weakest families, and above all single parents and immigrant families.

An assessment of the available creches shows a concentration in the larger cities. Two thirds of the places in creches are concentrated in Berlin, Hamburg, Munich, and Stuttgart, with the overwhelming majority of places available in Berlin. Berlin is also the only city that has engaged in the development of day care services with the aim of meeting the demand. Only one percent of the creches in the former FRG are located in smaller towns and in rural areas.

In the area of child minding, by way of comparison, there is a much wider distribution of facilities. Thirty-seven percent of registered child-minding places are in the rural districts. From this we can conclude that child minding, which normally only involves a few children, is also available in less populated areas. The structural advantages to this type of care lie in the close proximity to the families concerned, the low level of financial investment required (because it takes place in people's homes), and the possibilities of individual arrangements between childminders and parents.

If so few places for newborn to three-year-old children are available in the formal and informal day care sectors, where are the very young children of working mothers cared for? From a representative survey carried out 15 years ago, it is known that about half of these children are cared for by grandparents or older siblings, while about 18 percent can be looked after by the mother while she works. While these arrangements may sound rather ideal, it is important not to view them in an overly positive light. Parents hand their children over to the care of grandparents with a certain amount of ambivalence. For many the grandparents are not the first choice, and if there were other possibilities available, some of these parents would prefer to use them.

All in all, it is clear that the number of day care places provided by the public sector in the former FRG is insufficient, especially when one considers the changes in family structure and the changes in employment outside the home.

The value placed on day care facilities in the public sector is low. Day care continues to exhibit an emergency character and the strong social selection it acquired at the start of the 19th century.

In contrast, the former GDR government considered creches an essential prerequisite for mothers, so that they could take their places in the work force. In 1989 there were spaces available in creches for 80.2 percent of children up to age three in the GDR, and these were normally full-time places.

The Quality of Care Provided in Creches. Schneider (1989) concludes that in the Federal Republic of Germany "The quality of child care in present day institutions and by child-minders is very variable" (p. 117). Unfortunately the FRG lacks comprehensive research upon which to base a clear statement about the nature of that variability. Existing evaluations are based on regional analyses and, above all, on reports of personal experience and subjective judgments.

I stressed earlier that the care of very young children outside the home is characterized by its primitive state of development. For many years pedagogical efforts were oriented simply to meeting physical needs and ensuring safety. The priority given to parents in matters relating to upbringing led correspondingly to the avoidance of educational provision by day care programs.

More recently this picture has altered significantly, although there continue to be differences between individual facilities, and further improvements are still necessary. The following illustrations provide a sense of the changes and improvements that have taken place.

Individual municipalities (e.g., Berlin, Munich) have submitted and adopted development plans encompassing the requirements for and the further development of child care facilities for very young children. In addition, these plans take account of the equipment required for the facilities and of their modes of operation. These efforts at least indicate a recognition of official responsibility, and define the standard of care to be aimed for.

The expansion in public-sector provision for child care stands in contrast to the significant decrease in workplace provision and the stagnation of services provided by the societies (charities, etc.), especially church sponsors. It is reasonable to assume that expansion by these sponsors is seen by them to be inappropriate on ideological grounds.

Far-reaching changes in provision have come about through the establishment of self-help groups and parent initiatives. While these undertakings were partially a response to the insufficient care facilities available, they also addressed issues of program practice. In the 1960s and 1970s, as these initiatives were starting, they saw themselves principally as a form of protest against the modes of operation in the established institutions. Changes manifested themselves in the form and content of educational activities, better opportunities for parental involvement, and an open admissions policy (or at least in the use of political consensus to determine what limits to place on admission).

In these early stages the institutions and self-help provisions were often started and maintained by parents who could not meet the criteria for admittance to the official facilities. By contrast, present day initiatives and self-help groups see themselves primarily as a pragmatic remedy to the practical problem of insufficient provision.

The focus of present day reform efforts is on the improvement of professional training and qualifications of staff in creches and day care centers. Whereas previously, mostly personnel employed in creches were trained only to provide basic care, the number of workers with training in education is rising. However Schneider (1989, p. 117) complains that there continues to be a lack of appropriate preparation for the job of the group educational leader responsible for the smallest children. The improvement of the staffing situation is coupled with measures for in-service training of creche personnel, although this is not universally available. Training is dependent on funding agencies and is organized to take account of the trainee, of individual interests, and of the possibility for time off from employment through the use of substitute caregivers. The work methods in creches and day care centers have improved, through better age-grouping, a broader educational program, a need-oriented educational approach, and through improved accommodations within the institutions.

Schneider (1989, p. 118) expresses regret that there is still no consistent concept of creche education, resulting in an educational approach designed to serve kindergarten children. This approach is not appropriate for the more exploratory needs of younger children, which require greater emphasis on physical activity.

Any improvement in education levels in creches is naturally limited by the motivation of the staff, who are particularly badly paid, have a high rate of turnover, and again are overworked because of staff shortages.

Day Care Provision by Childminders (Family Day Care). There is a lack of comprehensive, scientifically based literature about the situation with regard to childminder care, but one can only agree with the following statement from the model project "Tagesmutter" (day mother or childminder) carried out from 1974 to 1979: "The care services are as different from one another as the life-style, qualifications, and living quarters of the child minders themselves" (Schneider, 1989, p. 118). With this in mind Germany intends to develop standards for child minding. Child minding, especially that which exists as a private arrangement between two families, should be more firmly established as an institution, and its educational framework should be improved in the following ways:

- Provision of preparatory and in-service training for the childminder.
- The establishment of local childminder support groups to exchange experiences, further training, and represent their interests to the "Jugendamt" (Department of Youth).
- Provision of educational care and advice from experts.
- Better pay and social security conditions for childminders.

The results of the model project referred to earlier indicate that children receiving a high level of substitute care with a childminder suffer no impairment of development when compared with children raised in their own families. But the work of Gudat (1982) also indicates that if children are introduced to care by strangers during the second year of life, there are often problems in settling down and some slight behavioral disturbance may appear.

The model project resulted in the adoption of certain structural measures for child minding: in-service training, the organization of child-minding support groups, and better payment for the childminders. But this has not led to a general improvement in child minding; the level of attention given to childminders from the local authorities continues to be very low.

When there is discussion of the relative advantages of center- versus family-based care, the primary advantage associated with institutional forms of care (creches, day-care centers) is the guarantee of service even if staff members are ill. Other positive features include the fact that care is provided in larger groups of children, that "surrogate mother" relationships (where the child can form stronger emotional bonds) do not develop, that there is a sliding scale of charges for parents, based on income, and that the creches receive state subsidies. In the case of child minding, by contrast, individualized care, the relationship of trust with the childminder, the individual agreements about the time of care, and the proximity of the minder to the child are emphasized. Because the childminder usually has children of her own, who are about the same age as the child she cares for, the child experiences a feeling of what it might be like to have siblings. Many of these children come from single-parent families, and it is in the childminder's family that they experience the adult male role. Because the child is cared for in the childminder's own home, the male partner is able to participate in some of the daily routines of the child-minding process.

But the model project also showed clearly that successful child minding is much more dependent on the quality of the relationship between mother and childminder, on their mutual acceptance of one another, and on their having similar ideas on the rearing of children, than is the case with professional creche personnel. This is not due necessarily to the closer relationship of mother and childminder and the increased competition for the child's affection, but also reflects the different decisions reached by the two women concerning the course their lives should take. The childminder has for the most part opted for the role of housewife and mother, while the mother has opted to remain in her career.

Changes in the amount of day care provision provided by childminders (family day care mothers) since 1982 in those German states formerly in the FRG were shown in Figure 11.1.

Alternative Family Policies. It is important also to recognize that the expansion of day care for very young children in Germany has slowed because alternative policies have been introduced and have been expanding in preference to day care. Parental leave and allowances are of particular importance in this regard.

All fathers and mothers can claim maternity/paternity pay for the first 24 months of a new child's life. For the first six months they receive 600 Deutsch Marks; after that the level depends on family income. In certain of the German states (e.g., Bavaria, Baden-Württemberg) there is also an allowance from the state payable after six months. For the first 36 months mothers or fathers who have given up work, or reduced their working hours (maximum 19 hours per week) in order to look after a child, are guaranteed their job back at the end of this time. Parental allowance/leave are claimed by 97 percent of parents entitled to them (although only one percent is claimed by fathers). Because of this, the demand for day care for children in the first year of life has fallen significantly.

Because more mothers with young children continue to enter the work force, and since leave payments have until recently stopped at one year (and in the future will stop at 24 months), it will be necessary in the future to expand day care services for children in their second and third years of life. The recognition of this need has led to demands that parental allowance/ pay be prolonged until the child enters kindergarten at the end of the third year.

As the time period for which one can claim these benefits is expanded, it must be assumed that some of the parents of two year olds, and even more of the parents of three year olds, will give up the benefits and return to work. A strictly one-sided policy, which further increases leave benefits without any expansion of day care facilities for very young children, again limits the range of options, which had been extended by the introduction of parental allowance/leave. The establishment of only a single role for mothers does not do justice to the wide variety of actual life-styles and family circumstances, for which a range of family- and socio-political policies and programs is required.

Another way of expanding the options open to German mothers has been through time-off provisions, which guarantee a return to work at the end of the statutory leave period. Under these agreements mothers (or fathers) can stay out of work longer to bring up their own children, without fear of losing their jobs. Time-off provisions range from one year to ten years. This option is offered particularly by major industrial companies, but it is also available in the public sector. These workplace initiatives especially encourage the long-term commitment of women to a particular employer, which is seen as important in light of the anticipated shortage of workers resulting from long-term demographic changes (work force depletion in the 1990s).

Empirical investigations have also uncovered the fact that families seek day care for children not only because of parental employment. Non-working mothers also express a desire to have their children occasionally cared for in day care centers or other group settings. They want occasional, flexible, time off for themselves and the opportunity for their children to play and learn in groups of children their own age. Parent/child centers, mother and toddler play groups, and mother and family centers, among other models, go some way toward meeting these needs. These alternatives have developed over the last ten years, sometimes without official backing. They should not be considered genuine child-minding facilities, but they do offer opportunities for regular attendance once or twice a week and serve particularly as preparation for kindergarten.

Kindergarten Education for Three to Six Year Olds

"Kindergartens are establishments in the area of pre-school education. They support the development and education of children from the end of the third year until school age" (Article 1, Bavarian Kindgergarten Law). As I indicated at the beginning of this chapter, these programs have their origins in the social upheavals of the 19th century. Kindergartens, more than any other preschool facilities, have freed themselves from their original aim of simply protecting children. They are now viewed as opportunities for learning and education that prepare children for school. The changes in the way kindergartens see themselves have, however, also resulted in their developing a certain institutional inertia, which has led them away from the child care needs of working parents. Kindergartens are primarily child-oriented in their organization and do not take account of family needs.

During the 1960s ideas of "compensatory development" for socially disadvantaged groups re-established a socio-political aim dating from the earliest days of institutional child care. However, disappointment with the results of compensatory development programs in the USA has also led to a reorientation of the aims of kindergartens in the Federal Republic of Germany. "Characteristic of this concept are the orientations toward the actual living conditions of children and families and toward the daily experiences of children, instead of artificially-organized learning, the fact that children live together in mixed age groups, the involvement of parents, and the firm grounding in the community (the situational approach)" (Achter Jugendbericht [Youth Report] 1990, p. 97).

In 1970, with the establishment by the Deutsche Bildungsrat (German Educational Council) of kindergartens as the first phase in the education system in the FRG, there came a sudden increase in the number of places available. This led to a significant increase in the level of attendance among three to under-six year olds, and among children over six not yet attending school. Overall in 1986, 78.9 percent of children benefitted from a kindergarten place, whereas in 1965 only 31.8 percent attended. However, the high rate of provision must be broken down further:

- Attendance increases with the age of the child. In 1988 attendance percentages ranged from 34 percent for three year olds to 83 percent for five year olds in the Federal Republic. This range is shown in Figure 11.2, which also includes an overall comparison with the German Democratic Republic.
- The level of provision varies considerably among individual states, from 54 to 100 percent. The major population centers are better served than are rural areas.
- The actual attendance rate of three to under-six year olds is lower than these figures suggest because there are also some children under three and some of school age, but not yet ready for school, attending kindergarten.

Figure 11.2
Kindergarten Attendance as a Percentage of Three Age Cohorts

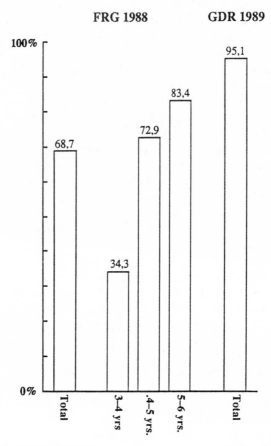

Criticism of the kindergartens on the part of parents has less to do with the work they do than with the number of places available, the attendance hours, and their social make-up. These concerns stem from the following facts. With the increasing birth rate of recent years, the waiting list for kindergartens has grown in many places. Because of the demographic evolution of residential areas (the tendency of the population of an area to age), there is an additional imbalance in the demand for kindergarten places. The institutions seem unable to adapt to the changing geographic pattern of demand, and the funding agencies have largely failed to convert the superfluous premises to other uses.

Most kindergartens offer only half-day places, or morning or afternoon places without lunch. Full-time places in 1984 were provided for only 12 percent (9 percent of three to six year olds have access to full-time kindergarten places) and they are almost all concentrated in cities. The kindergarten attendance hours are not geared to the needs of their working parents, so these parents must either make further arrangements for their children outside kindergarten hours, or they must take on limited part-time work. The majority of employed mothers make additional arrangements: grandmothers, neighbors, or relatives care for the children until the mother returns from work.

The social make-up of kindergartens has not changed, despite the sharp increase in numbers. Socially disadvantaged families, immigrant children, and the handicapped are still underrepresented.

The greatest cause of friction between parents and kindergartens at the present time derives from the institutional thinking behind the administration of kindergartens. Their rigid curriculum- or theme-based work practice and limited hours of operation, determined by statutory guidelines and the working hours of teaching staff, contrast sharply with the needs of families. The hours of kindergartens are geared to a "normal" family routine—a complete family with a non-working mother—which to a large extent no longer exists. Clearly the care of children and the relief of the parents from the burden of child rearing is no longer the raison d'être of kindergartens. Nowadays the emphasis is on their educational function. As Colberg-Schrader and Derschau note, "The service customarily provided presupposes the permanent availability of the parent" (p. 39).

Current discussions are aimed at increasing the flexibility of kindergarten provision, and especially the expansion of care to two and three year olds, and at providing longer attendance hours. Of course, this presupposes a willingness on the part of the staff of kindergartens to address themselves to the problems faced by families, and also a willingness on the part of the funding agencies to support the idea of working mothers and their demands. In the case of the churches, which run the majority of kindergartens in the FRG, this willingness cannot be assumed.[2]

Kindergarten costs paid by parents are on the increase. These charges depend on the amount of daily care provided and on attendance hours, but they depend also on the funding agencies and on state subsidies for staff and equipment. As a rule, parental contributions are low, but these costs may be one reason for the low attendance rate of children from poorer families and from families suffering the effects of unemployment.

Latchkey Centers

The roots of the latchkey center (after-school care) in Germany also reach back to the 19th century, when providing care for school children was seen as the answer to child poverty caused largely by the full-time employment of parents and sometimes of children themselves. In the FRG the latchkey center has been unable to free itself completely from these roots. It is still largely a provision for disadvantaged children, and the admission criteria are geared toward families with two fully employed parents, one-parent families, children with learning difficulties, and children with social problems. This negative image of the facility is tied to the low level of provision available, which makes selection according to social criteria necessary, and with the position of the facility in relation to the schools.

In 1987 there were only 102,000 places available in latchkey centers in the FRG, which means that a mere 4.4 percent of primary school children aged six to ten years had access to this service. Although there was a rapid increase in the number of places available in the 1970s, since then there has been real stagnation. The availability of these centers varies considerably between the different federal states and above all is concentrated in cities. Two thirds of all places are to be found in cities with a population of more than 500,000.

Only the State of Bremen has its own legislation governing latchkey centers. In the other federal states the facilities have up to now been provided in accordance with the Jugendwohlfahrtgesetz (Youth Welfare Law). Beginning in 1991 this regulation shifted to the KJHG (Child and Youth Aid Law), which leaves the further expansion of the facilities largely to the individual communities. At the planning level, a rapid expansion is seen as necessary because of the changing role of women in the workplace and the change in family structure (the increasing number of single-parent families and the increase of families with only one child). There is, however, no evidence that these plans are being made.

As Figure 11.3 indicates, the situation in the former German Democratic Republic is quite different. As with creches and kindergartens, there is almost full provision—in 1989, 81.2 percent of children in the first four years at school (to approximately age ten) were cared for in these centers. The latchkey center is seen in this part of Germany as a socio-educational facility, although it has not managed to develop an independent concept of its work in terms of leisure education for children and young people. The scholastic demands, especially involving homework, the necessity for individual help with learning, and the stimulation of the children dictate the everyday activities of the centers. Even the time spent at the centers is determined by school hours (children attend the centers before and after school). In addition, these latchkey centers are often unsuitable for use as leisure activity centers for children and young people because they are housed mostly on school premises outside of school hours or in the neighborhood of kindergartens. In spite of this close association with schools, there is often very little cooperation between the two, and initiative in this regard comes almost exclusively from the center staff.

From the staffing standpoint there has been an improvement in the existing programs. The number of employees possessing socio-educational training has increased, and groups are smaller, so that opportunities for individual help and attention have improved. This strengthening of the staff has also

Figure 11.3
Attendance at Latchkey Centers as a Percentage of Six to Ten Year Olds
(Primary School Classes 1 to 4)

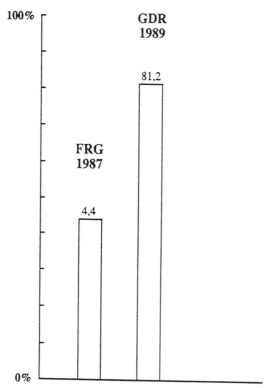

had costs, that is, shorter working hours in general and an increase in part-
time work for center staff.

THE OUTLOOK FOR DAY CARE IN GERMANY

In that part of Germany that was formerly the Federal Republic there is
a general lack of provision for all of the day care programs described in
this chapter. This must be considered a shortage even when one considers
the historical and ideological background as it developed in the 19th century.
The expansion of facilities has simply not kept pace with developments in
the employment of mothers. But today there is a further need for these
facilities brought about by the changes in family structures, including the
increase in single-parent families, the reduction in the possibility for care
provided within the extended family (grandparents), and the increase in the
number of families with only one child where these children need contact
with their peers. For most of the available facilities the admission criteria

for the few places available are extremely restrictive and serve to maintain the image of care facilities as being for socially disadvantaged families and children.

Only kindergartens have managed to free themselves from this image because their educational purpose as an extension of rearing within the family is widely accepted and because kindergartens have become an integral part of the education sector. The educational task of the kindergarten, its more positive social selection (attendance begins earlier and increases with the educational level of the parents), and the increasing professional qualifications of its staff have all helped to validate it as a "mainstream" institution.

The further expansion of care facilities is widely accepted as necessary, but a rapid change is not likely. At present the expansion already achieved is being jeopardized by the low level of attractiveness of work in day care, which is caused by poor pay and low social prestige in comparison with that of teachers. In the case of childminders there is a lack of opportunity for them to further develop their organizational structures, to ensure the quality of care, to improve their pay, and to safeguard their industrial rights. One can infer a decrease in official interest because in the future, under the new law, no official approval of child-minding arrangements is required.

The biggest changes in the near future are likely to take place in those federal states formerly in the GDR. Changes in the labor market there (increasing unemployment, part-time work) will lead to a reduction in the demand for care facilities, and the falling away of social supports in the workplace, including day care, will reduce the number of available day care places. To what degree these reductions will occur is not yet clear.

The demand for officially guaranteed child care facilities will, however, remain higher in the former German Democratic Republic because the possibility of leaving children in the care of relatives and neighbors is simply not there to the extent that it exists in the rest of Germany. Greater financial need in addition to the desire to retain their achieved career status will lead women and mothers in the former GDR to hold on to their places in the work force to a greater extent than in the former FRG.

NOTES

This chapter was written during the events leading up to German reunification. Because the envisaged separate chapter on the situation in the former German Democratic Republic was dropped, an attempt has been made to incorporate some of that information here. An evaluation of the quality of that information is not possible because I have no way of assessing the validity of the available literature.

I would like to thank Frau Lilli Haag for the preparation of this chapter and Mrs. Ruth Stewart for the English translation.

1. The employment of women in the former GDR has dropped from over 78

percent in 1989 (mostly full time) to a point where unemployment is rather high (especially among women).

2. About 70 percent of kindergartens in the former FRG are run by the welfare arms of churches and local parishes. In the former GDR they have been run by the National Ministry of Education and Science.

REFERENCES

Arbeitsgruppe Tagesmütter, D.J.I. (1980). *Das Modellprojekt "Tagesmütter"— Abschlußbericht der wissenschaftlichen Begleitung* (The model project "Day Care Mothers"—final report). Stuttgart: Kohlhammer (Bd. 85 der Schriftenreihe des Bundesministers für Jugend, Familie und Gesundheit).

Beller, E. K., and Stahnke, M. (1989). "Ein Modell der Kleinkind Pädagogik und seine empirische Evaluation" (A model of early childhood pedagogy and its empirical evaluation). In E. K. Beller (Ed.), *Forschung in den Erziehungswissenschaften*, pp. 231–237. Weinheim: Deutscher Studie Verlag.

Blüml, H., and Schneider, K. (1988). "Kleinkindererziehung—allein Sache der Familien?" (Early childhood education—concern of the family only?). In Deutsches Jugendinstitut (Ed.), *Wie geht's der Familie?* pp. 291–296. Müchen: Kösel.

Colberg-Schrader, H., and von Derschau, D. (1991). "Sozialisations feld Kindergarten." (Socialization in kindergarten). In K. Hurrelmann and D. Ulich (Eds.), *Handbuch der Sozialisationsforschung* (4th ed.). Weinheim: Beltz.

Dammann, E., and Prüser, H. (Eds.) (1981). *Quellen zur Kleinkinderziehung* (Historical documents of early childhood education). Müchen: Kösel.

Der Bundesminister für Jugend, Familie, Frauen und Gesundheit (Ed.) (1990). *Achter Jugendbericht* (The Eighth National Youth Report). Bonn: Bundestags-Drucksache 11/6576.

Deutscher, Bildungsrat. (1970). *Empfehlungen der Bildungskommission: Strukturplan für das Bildungswesen* (Recommendations of the Educational Commission: Structural plan of the German Educational System). Stuttgart: Klett.

Deutsches Jugendinstitut (Ed.). (1988). *Tageseinrichtungen für Kinder.* (Day care institutions for children). Müchen: DJI-Verlag.

Erler, G., Jaeckel, M., Pettinger, R., and Sass, Jr. (1988). *Kind? Beruf? Oder Beides?* (Child? Work? or Both?). Hamburg: Brigitte-Verlag.

Erning, G. (Ed.). (1976). *Quellen zur Geschichte der öffentlichen Kleinkinderzeihung* (Historical documents of public early childhood education). Kastellaun: Henn.

Grossman, W. (1987). *Aschenputtel im Schulalltag. Historische Entwicklungen und Perspektiven von Schulsozialarbeit* (Cinderella in the school routine. Historical development and perspectives of school's social work). Weinheim: Beltz.

Gudat, U. (1982). *Kinder bei der Tagesmutter: Frühkindliche Fremdbetreuung und sozial-emotionale Entwicklung* (Children in family day care: Early child care and the social-emotional development of children). München: DJI–Verlag.

Institut für Entwicklungsplanung und Strukturforschung (Ed.). (1989). *Beruflicher Wiedereinstieg und Weiterbildung für Frauen* (Women's vocational re-opening and further development). Hannover: IES.

Kinder- und Jugendhilfegesetz. (1990). (Child and Youth Assistance Law).

Martin, B., and Pettinger, R. (1984). "Frühkindliche institutionalisierte Sozialisation" (Early childhood socialization in institutions). In J. Zimmer (Ed.), *Erziehung in früher Kindheit*, pp. 235–251. Stuttgart: Klett (Bd. 6 der Enzyklopädie Erziehungswissenschaft).

Moss, P. (1988). *Childcare and equality of opportunity*. Consolidated Report to the European Commission (unpublished).

Reyer, J. (1983). *Wenn die Mütter arbeiten gingen* ... (When mothers were working ...). Köln: Pahl-Rugenstein.

Schneider, K. (1989). "Tagesangebote für Kinder unter 3 Jahren" (Day care offerings for children under 3 years). *Blätter der Wohlfahrtspflege*, 136 (May), pp. 115 ff.

Statistisches Bundesamt (Ed.). (1990). *Familien heute, Strukturen, Verläufe und Einstellungen* (Present structures, developments and attitudes of families). Stuttgart: Kohlhammer.

Verband für Evangelische Kindertagesstätten in Berlin. (1980). *Blick über'n Zaun* (A view over the fence). Berlin.

Winkler, G. (Ed.). (1990). *Frauenreport 90* (Womens' report '90). Berlin: Die Wirtschaft Berlin GmbH.

12

HUNGARY

Mária Neményi

Before treating the social welfare institutions that came into being with the development and dominance of capitalism at the beginning of the 20th century, it is important to point out that in the first half of the 19th century, on the eastern fringes of the Hapsburg Monarchy, Hungary offered a fine model of "social political" aspirations deriving from a sense of noblesse oblige and aristocratic commitments to charity. The first kindergarten in Hungary, founded by Theresa Brunszvick in 1828 and based on the example of infant schools in England, was an instance of charity nourished by an aristocratic ethos. This kindergarten opened the door to the development of a nursery school system that became internationally significant for the period.

The first kindergartens of the Hungarian capital city were sponsored by the Ladies' League, an informal organization founded by women of rank. Soon a training school for kindergarten teachers of Vienna, Graz, and Linz became organized under the influence of the Hungarian initiative. The first kindergarten law was framed at the end of the 19th century, aimed at encouraging the care of three- to six-year-old children in state, communal, denominational, and private kindergartens, with special attention to training for acceptable behavior, cleanliness, and spiritual and intellectual development. In fact, this law made kindergarten attendance compulsory, a requirement not yet realized to the present day.

Although a state network of kindergartens began to be built at the turn of the century, the few overcrowded nurseries were not much more than checking rooms for children. Development of a network of state nursery schools began at the turn of the century but was slowed by economic constraints. The kindergarten network remained limited and of low quality. While state, community, and church-related kindergartens were operating, life in those settings was determined by their overcrowded conditions. Average group size was 80 to 120 children, and equipment was of poor quality. Education and training of the children were impersonal and routinized.

The second kindergarten law was framed in 1936. It removed the kindergartens from the authority of the minister of religion and education and put them under the control of the ministry of the interior. Kindergartens were then regarded as institutions with which to carry out goals related to social welfare and hygiene. By 1938 there were 1,140 kindergartens and summer camps in Hungary, but they were able to take in only one quarter of the eligible age groups, and generally only for four to six hours a day. Only 7 percent of the kindergartens provided full-day care.

Apart from these institutions there were also private kindergartens for the children of urban intellectuals and the well-to-do middle class. Some of the private kindergartens were based on the Montessori system, while others introduced educational reform principles or the increasingly fashionable psychoanalytic approach to kindergarten.

Despite the fact that they were to be found only in a few kindergartens and children's homes, and referred to only in a small proportion of the specialized and popular literature on the subject, these approaches had a long-term effect on parental views about child training. Although the dominant ideology of post–1948 Hungary was to reject and ban such middle-class disciplines, in particular psychoanalysis, it is not difficult to detect their later influence, even in the work of specialists and kindergarten educationalists who disavowed their adherence to these tenets.

CHILD CARE POLICIES AND INSTITUTIONS SINCE 1948

Amidst the efforts to create a balance of power in Europe after World War II, Hungary was thrust upon an entirely new political, economic, and ideological platform. Election fraud in 1947 and 1948, challenges to the authority of Parliament, and politically rigged trials began to make clear what the decisions at Yalta would mean for life in Hungary.

No family would remain unaffected by the changes that occurred in Hungary following 1948, "the year of the change." The first steps taken by centralized authority—land reform, nationalization, and full employment—brought drastic alterations to Hungarian society. Extensive industrialization, imposed without consideration for Hungarian conditions, compelled large masses of the population to abandon their agricultural activities to move to newly created industrial centers. This industrialization and urbanization process began the dissolution of peasant family life, until then built on rural traditions, independent farming activities, and property ownership. At the same time the men forced into industry were unable to support their families on their wages. This unnatural economy demanded masses of untrained labor, thus stimulating the full-scale employment of women.

Employment was not only an economic but also a political necessity. The centrally controlled economy, operating with full employment, was expected to automatically end inequality and indigence. The overcentralized party state did not recognize the particular interests of different social groups and the operation of independent organizations. It used social welfare policy in an oppressive manner to deny the legitimacy of individual and local community autonomy.

The new state had reservations not only about pre-war family policy, but also about the institution of the family itself, in part because of its religious character. Moreover, according to the opinion of the ruling party, the family carried on the conservative structure of class society—male dominance, female vulnerability to that dominance, and the authoritarian education of children. Finally, the family was seen as keeping individuals from "high-rated" community activities.

Although these aggressively anti-family arguments characterized only the first years of communist takeover, the slogans glorifying the substitution of family functions with state services and advertising the replacement of family life with the community education of children survived for an extended period. Their effects can still be felt. During the past 40 years the value of communal training has become absolute and is generally accepted.

The first reaction of Hungarians to these coercive changes was to reduce the size of their families. Although the decrease in the number of children has continued for the past 100 years, a faster rate of decline is correlated with the radical post-war transformation of Hungarian society.

The Hungarian constitution of 1949 specified the equality of women and declared the equal rights of men and women in politics, employment, and schooling. Soon, however, family stability and its social value became recognized as a concern. This concern was in opposition to those anti-family interests identified earlier as contributing to the drop in the birth rate.

The state responded to this conflict in various ways. Legal provisions were made to support expectant mothers and the mothers of small children, including work reductions, extra leaves, and financial benefits. In 1953 a resolution of the Council of Ministers banned abortion and required that the courts treat this issue with the utmost severity. The result of these decrees was an increase in the birthrate. But they also produced undesirable results. In the short term there were medical, social welfare, and political tensions; the long-term effects have been cycles of sharp drops in the birth rate and baby booms that have caused continuing difficulties in social welfare and in kindergarten and school policy.

Child Care Assistance and the Child Care Allowance

The totalitarian dictatorship and arbitrary economic policy of the 1950s and the accompanying coercive demographic policy became untenable after 1956. Despite the failure of the revolution of that year, measures placing greater emphasis on individual interests became necessary. The raising of living standards become a central political aim. However, there was no reassessment of centralized planning and management from above in the field of social welfare policy (although in the economy, where the need for reform was recognized sooner, some advances were made in this respect).

After the easing of the strict abortion law of 1953, the number of births went down suddenly and then steadily. The increasing employment rate of women, the improvement in public health, more schooling for the general population, greater upward mobility, urbanization, and the emancipation of women were also instrumental in the reduction of the fertility rate. More recently the high divorce rate is also usually mentioned among the reasons for this decrease. The suddenness of this demographic shift led the government once again to institute comprehensive new policy measures. Maternity leave, with payment equal to the regular salary, was provided for working mothers and is now available for five months after delivery. In addition, working mothers receive a one-time cash grant for every child and are also entitled to a family allowance if they have at least two young children. Single mothers are entitled to a family allowance even for one child.

Until the mid-1960s the increase in the female employment rate exceeded the rate at which children's institutions were established. Then came the period when the post-war, post-abortion law baby boom generation reached the age of fertility and employment. This coincided with some years of economic stagnation, leading social and economic policy makers to decide that the country needed some reduction in female employment. This shift was also in tune with the opinions of physicians and psychologists both abroad and at home, who were emphasizing the importance of close mother-child contacts for development in early childhood. It was also clear that the development of additional creche capacity would be very expensive.[1] Thus social welfare measures were deemed necessary to diminish the threat of demoralization inherent in unemployment, which is "incompatible with socialist ideology," and to reduce the cost of institutional child care in money, buildings, and labor, while at the same time satisfying the health and psychological expectations of the time.

Child Care Assistance. The system of child care assistance introduced on January 1, 1967 was developed to serve this complex set of goals. At the time of its introduction, this benefit consisted of a stipend at about 40 percent of the average monthly earnings of women. Later the amount paid rose and increased for each additional child. But despite occasional supplementary increases to compensate for rising prices, it has equalled an ever lower percentage of the average wage.

According to preliminary calculations, if half or two thirds of the economically active women availed themselves of this opportunity after the end of their five-month maternity leave, the cost to the state of the assistance would be less than the combined cost of sickness benefits paid to employed mothers for the illnesses of their children, the time lost on the job for feeding their babies, the lower performance of mothers who return to their jobs after the maternity leave, and the added costs of maintaining and increasing creche capacity.

In the first year it was introduced 67 percent of the mothers entitled to child care assistance availed themselves of the benefit. During the first ten years the number of claimants increased, peaking in 1977. It then began to decline along with the decreasing number of births. Benefit users were relatively young and less educated, and more claimants stayed at home with the first child than with later children. There were fluctuations also in the duration of time various groups of women opted to stay at home on the assistance. Only about one quarter of white-collar and professional women chose to stay at home until the end of the entitlement period, whereas the majority of mothers doing physical work in several shifts availed themselves of the opportunity.

After the experiences of the first 15 years, the child care assistance benefit was extended to the members of agricultural and industrial cooperatives. In the case of chronically ill or defective children, the entitlement lasted until the child was six. Later the assistance was declared a parental right, thus officially recognizing the role of fathers in child rearing, and making them eligible to stay at home with their children.

The introduction of the child care assistance benefit clearly exerted a demographic influence. Many parents decided to delay having children until they became entitled to the benefit. In the case of parents who wanted to have two or more children, the period between the births was reduced. Consequently, 71 percent of all children were born to mothers between 20 and 29 years of age and the proportion of women giving birth over the age of 30 decreased. However, the effects of the child care assistance policy were not as expected. The timing of introduction proved to be wrong, as the delivery of babies from a populous age group was limited to a relatively short time period. This caused another population boom, which will lead to additional cycles in the birthrate.

Despite its undeniably positive aspects, and its uniqueness as a model in the European context, the child care assistance benefit became a cause for concern with some sociologists and psychologists. The reason for this concern involves the child care assistance policy as a factor in restoring the traditional role and subordination of women. By comparison with the economically active husband, the wife's role shifts from one of equality and financial independence to one of economic dependence, and she is expected to cope alone with the problems of the family and of housework. This situation is contrary to the life course expectations and self-improvement goals of some women and may cause dissatisfaction, loneliness, and frustration. It may consequently become a source even of neurosis, alcoholism, or severe depression, and thus it may determine the further course of a marriage. Today most women realize the importance of early mother and child relationship. However, the new generations of women, who were reared themselves as children of working mothers, are largely unprepared for raising their children and running their households at the same time, as they have not had the necessary parental models. Consequently, child rearing means for many women a series of unsolvable tasks, feelings of incompetence, feelings of inferiority, and worsening circumstances.

The Child Care Allowance. In the 1980s the continued low level of fertility and the social stratification of the recipients of child care assistance (little schooling, lack of skills, relative youth, etc.) gave rise to the creation of an altered form of help for mothers. The child care allowance was introduced in March 1985. Its value is equal to 75 percent of the mother's or father's average monthly pay, and it is received after the expiration of the five-month maternity leave. Although the lowest and highest monthly amount of the allocation that may be given is fixed (it cannot be less than the lowest old-age pension and cannot be more than its double), and although it does not increase with the number of children in the family, it is a higher benefit than is child care assistance. Initially the allowance was to be paid until the first birthday of the child; more recently it has been extended to the 18-month birthday.

One reason for establishing this earnings-linked allowance was the belief that it would motivate parents to have a second or third child. Another reason was to give recognition to the higher earnings resulting from additional years of employment or more schooling. An advantage to being tied to wages is that the allowance is less likely to lose its value over time. But the child care assistance benefit may be more advantageous for parents earning lower wages, or with larger numbers of children under three. Families can choose the form of support that they prefer. Once the child care allowance period has expired, mothers may opt to stay at home on child care assistance until its application period has expired.

In January 1985, the year that the allowance was introduced, 221,000 women were at home on the child care assistance program. By the end of 1985 that number had been reduced to 150,000, while concurrently the number of allowance recipients continued to increase steadily.

Creches and Kindergartens as Child Care Settings

In Hungary day care is provided to children under the age of three in creches, and the children from three years old to school age in kindergartens. Because they are quite different, each of these two children's institutions is addressed separately in the pages that follow. The numbers and percentages of children served in the two settings are provided in Table 12.1.

Creches. Working mothers in Hungary have access to creches as day care arrangements for children between five months and three years of age. The

Table 12.1
Preschool Children in Day Care (Number and Percentages)

		1970	1980	1988
Creche (6 mo.-3 yrs. old)	Number	41,771	69,768	44,362
	Percent	9.5	14.8	11.9
Kindergarten (3-6 yrs. old)	Number	227,279	478,100	393,735
	Percent	51.5	77.9	86.0

policy establishing creches and infant homes in 1948, and later the 1951 decree by the Council of Ministers increasing female employment in production, prescribed the expansion of the network of creches and called for the organization of creches at industrial plants and offices with over 250 women employees working a given shift. By the end of this period one fourth of all creches belonged to factories and companies and operated under the control of local councils, although following centrally established programs.

In 1945 only about 150 creches operated in Hungary, and they were capable of serving only 0.2 percent of children up to three years of age. By 1965 nearly 1,000 creches provided placement for 9.2 percent of the age group. However, as mentioned earlier, the increase in female employment rate exceeded the development rate of children's institutions. The consequence was overcrowding, frequent illnesses (which usually meant that the working mother had to stay at home), and selectivity in creche admissions.

The content of work at the creches was centrally regulated, as prescribed by the Ministry of Health. The main task was maintenance of the physical health of the children and the provision of home-like, permissive, and affectionate care for babies. The daily schedule was structured by periods of potty training, feeding, and sleep.

Creche placement must have been favorable for the physical development of children in families with low socio-economic status. Generally, however, the probability is that the emotional and social development of children institutionalized at an early age suffers from so much time spent away from their parents. At the time of expansion of the creche network, no comparative studies were made of children cared for in creches versus those reared exclusively at home, and nothing was heard from psychologists (psychology having been pushed underground as a "capitalist pseudo-science"). Thus support for these hypotheses is available only from data collected in the early 1970s. They show that at the time of kindergarten admission (three years old) children who attended a creche previously are less physically developed than those who were kept at home. Their ability to relate to adults is poorer, but their relationships with other children and their adapt-

Table 12.2
Percentage of Children from Birth to Three Years Attending the Creche

1960	7.4%
1970	9.5%
1980	15.7%

ability are better. The speech development of the two groups is similar, although more children in the creche group stammer or have other speech defects. At the same time, the creche group children are better in motor development, manual skills, learning ability, and creativity. However, the creche group shows a number of symptoms—such as eating and sleeping problems, bed wetting, nail biting, and speech defects—that may derive from their early separation from the parental home, from the less personalized relationship with the nurse, and from the overcrowded conditions of most creches.

Table 12.2 shows a decline between 1980 and 1988 in the percentage of newborn to three-year-old children enrolled in creches. The meaning of this trend can be understood in part in terms of the policy changes discussed earlier—financial child care assistance and allowance—that have encouraged mothers to look after their children at home. However, these changes have not reduced the demand for creche care significantly. Creche capacity continued to increase until 1985, while the number of children sent to creches decreased. But the number of children served by each creche has been reduced to improve the quality of care, which has actually kept the creches filled above 100 percent capacity. Creches in the large Hungarian cities are almost unbearably crowded, particularly in certain districts and new housing areas in Budapest.

Kindergartens. Children who have passed their third birthday and are physically and mentally fit may be admitted to kindergarten and attend kindergarten until the age of six. In 1945 the kindergartens were transferred to the then recently established Ministry of Public Welfare. In this period the most urgent task was to create normal conditions for child survival. War-damaged kindergartens were restored, and kindergartens with full day care were hastily organized. Soon there was a working schedule for kindergartens and day centers. Erzsebet Burchard published her *Practical Child Protection*, which provided the work schedule for the kindergartens and day centers of the period.

Two women had a special impact on the pedagogical philosophy of kindergarten care during this period. Erzsebet Burchard, who had founded the Montessori-type kindergartens in Hungary between the two world wars, participated with the commitment of a true progressive in working out the kindergarten program for the Ministry of Public Welfare and the new Kindergarten Bill. Alice Hermann (wife of Imre Hermann, a well-known psychoanalyst) disapproved of both the training drills in the "reactionary" kindergartens and the progressive but individualistic kindergartens of the time, preferring instead a "third type" kindergarten built on Makarenko's educational principles, which emphasize the educational force of living in a community.

The kindergartens were nationalized in 1948. This put them all under uniform leadership. The educational slogan of the period was: "In a community, through a community, and for the sake of the community."

In 1953 the Ministry of Education authorized the use of some formal education as a method of kindergarten training. The 1953 Kindergarten Law, the third in the series of such laws, instituted unified educational aims for all kindergartens. Thus the responsibility of the kindergartens is to educate and train young children according to the aims of socialist pedagogy, to care and provide for them, and to prepare them for primary school. According to the 1953 law, the kindergarten is primarily an educational institution providing training and instruction, and only secondarily does it fulfill social welfare functions. The education of children into "fit and healthy, cultured and patriotic adults who love their homeland and show courage and discipline" is to be realized in this setting.

Local councils, factories, offices and institutions, companies, cooperatives, state farms, and social organizations were permitted to set up kindergartens. The cost of kindergarten organization had to be provided from the central annual budgets and their operating expenses had to be provided from the budget of the sponsoring organization.

Professional writings on kindergartens and their history dated from the 1950s through the 1970s proudly stress that through the education of socialist kindergarten teachers and the retraining of older teachers it was possible to get rid of the negative aspects of the earlier regime. Alice Hermann points out that the religious and especially the authoritarian educational style of earlier times had been banished to a great extent, although bourgeois educational principles stressing the spontaneity of individual development were also out of favor. Nonetheless, looking back on that period it appears that the personalities and qualifications of the people who created the educational programs for the kindergartens had sufficient force to ensure the survival of the progressive trends that had developed in the field between the two world wars. Thus the kindergartens were child centered and offered the most desirable and attractive forms of individual and group activities for each age group. They were characterized by a cheerful and playful family atmosphere.

It is important to note the role of kindergartens in employment policy during this time. The primary role of kindergartens was to solve the day care needs of children with working mothers. Figures on the establishment and regional distribution of new kindergartens have always reflected regional trends in the demand for female labor. In the 1950s large-scale development took place first in Budapest and somewhat later in the provincial towns, whereas in the villages and rural settlements this growth in kindergarten services was delayed until the 1970s. Use of kindergartens as an employment policy consideration was in competition with its social welfare function, according to which the kindergarten is a centrally financed universal benefit to which anyone has access through payment of a nominal charge. In fact, kindergarten has become not a civic right but an employment-linked right, granted only to families where both parents work.

In the 1970s the position and role of kindergartens, and of the basic kindergarten program that had been compulsory in all "socialist kindergartens" since 1957, were re-examined. The new program was introduced in 1971, during a period when kindergartens were 150 to 200 percent oversubscribed and desperately short of qualified kindergarten teachers. The aims of the new kindergarten program included closer adjustment of the kindergartens to the real needs of children and closer adjustment to the family. Any preparation for school was to be based on the age and development of the child. As a continuation of family rearing and creche training, the kindergarten was to help children raise the level of their physical development, community feelings and discipline, and knowledge of the environment necessary for entering school.

Although the goals emphasize that children be mature enough for school attendance, rather than prepared for school, kindergartens have assumed a role in school preparation. Children are placed in three different groups in the kindergarten according to their age and development. In the "toddlers" group the little ones have no formal activities, but in the middle and preschool groups the children have to take part in certain school preparation activities. The societal pressure to maintain the instructional aspect of kindergartens comes, on the one hand, from overburdened primary schools, and on the other, from parents who also expect professional preparation for school attendance. However, as not all children go to kindergarten and kindergarten is not compulsory, the end result is that the children of disadvantaged families start school with accumulated and multiplied handicaps. The kindergarten has thus become the place of preselection for school. Children who cannot keep up with kindergarten requirements are placed in special kindergartens. If deemed simply not yet ready for school, they remain in the kindergarten and begin school a year later. This delay places their school careers in serious jeopardy.

The virtually full employment of women during the 1970s, when 78 percent of women between the ages of 15 and 54 were active outside of the home, necessitated the expansion of the kindergarten network. Table 12.3 shows the percentage of three- to six-year old children attending kindergarten between 1960 and 1988.

By 1988 total kindergarten capacity had nearly doubled. Today about 40,000 children, 86 percent of the age group, go to kindergarten. This general picture masks continuing inequalities in the admission and the qual-

Table 12.3
Percentage of Hungarian Children from Three to Six Years
Attending Kindergarten

1960	33.7%
1970	51.5%
1980	77.9%
1988	86.0%
1988	11.9%

ity of service, however (distance to the center, qualifications of staff, etc.). Mothers with several children find it more difficult to take on jobs, and consequently their children are often not entitled to day care in creches or kindergartens. Many hamlets and small villages are without kindergartens. The children of mothers staying at home on child care assistance are often still refused kindergarten placement because of lack of room. Despite the high proportion of children in kindergarten attendance, only about one third of the children of families in the lowest income bracket go to kindergarten.

These facts again call attention to the inability of the kindergarten to eliminate hidden selection mechanisms, which result in barring the children of the neediest social strata from the kindergartens. Thus the kindergarten does not fulfill its function of equalizing social opportunity through preparation for school. If the accent were on this social welfare function, the kindergarten could be a means of overcoming social handicaps and poverty-generated inequalities. In order to fulfill this function the kindergarten would need to give preference in admission to the children of the neediest families. As mentioned earlier, the reason this does not happen is due to the legal requirement that mothers be employed in order to entitle their children to kindergarten. Socioeconomically disadvantaged families often contain many children, and the women in these families are relatively less likely to take on employment. A second, partly related reason for the survival of inequalities lies in regional differences that are disadvantageous to small villages and hamlets. Two thirds of all Hungarian villages with a population of under 1,000 still do not have kindergartens. This discriminates against 17,000 to 18,000 children.

Gypsies, the largest and most disadvantaged ethnic minority group in Hungary, are the people whose children are least likely to go to kindergarten or will spend less time there than other children. The half million Gypsies in Hungary live in the most backward settlements of the country—often in slums—and work at unskilled jobs or occasional labor. They have had very little schooling, and some of them do not even speak Hungarian. In the case of their children the school obviously fails at its role of providing equal opportunities. The relative handicap born by Gypsy children who start school with such cultural and linguistic gaps has increased rather than decreased by the time they finish primary school. They are the least likely of any group in Hungry to reach secondary school and especially to attend a college or university.

Thus, the "socialist kindergarten" has not been able to provide equal chances for all Hungarian children. On the contrary, this child care system contains both overt and concealed selection mechanisms and has become in fact an institution for reproducing social advantages and handicaps.

PROBLEMS AND DYSFUNCTIONS

Hungarian state policies involving children and families, as they have evolved since the Second World War, have displayed complex and often conflicting interests and motivations. At the beginning of the socialist transformation it was a matter of political interest to favor collective over more individualized family training. The family was not seen as able to transmit the norms acceptable to the new society. This necessitated the creation of an alternative institutional framework. More recently social interests have made an emphasis on the advantages of family-based education and on women acting out their mothering role fashionable again. Thus during the initial period of intensive economic development, economic interests were satisfied by the increasing employment of women, and the emancipation of women was regarded as being in the interests of society. Then in the period of transition to an intensive economy, and again in the period of economic stagnation, the reduction in female employment again served economic interests. Thus the seemingly contradictory interests and arguments voiced in the "socialist" ideology of Hungarian society correspond largely to two distinct—and contrary—phases of economic and social development.

In the aggregate, the social and social welfare activities connected with children in Hungary offer a favorable picture. In the different areas of state concern there has been gradual numerical improvement over the past 40 years, and impressive amounts of both qualitative and quantitative growth can be seen. The introduction of the Child Care Assistance policy attracted worldwide recognition, and its supplementation with the Child Care Allowance is generous state support for working mothers, as is the extensive network of children's institutions. The family allowance for families based on number of children means an acceptable income, although it cannot keep abreast of the inflation rates of recent years.

At the same time, this favorable overall picture masks the significant differences that have developed in the living standards of families based on the number of the children they contain. In 1975, for instance, if the average income of childless families is defined as 100 percent, the families with one child that year reached only 79 percent, two-child families 67 percent, and three-child families 56 percent of that level. By the 1980s this discrepancy had increased further.

The assertion that less and less attention has been paid to the interests of children is also obvious in other kinds of data. In 1972 children constituted 33 percent of the poorest tenth of the country's population. In 1982 a full 41 percent of this stratum was made up of children. Although these poor families are actually entitled to assistance for raising their children, this support is received only occasionally. This type of relief assistance is made particularly difficult to obtain because the families themselves have to petition for help, and whether a grant is given or not depends on the attention and assessment of social workers, teachers, and council employees. Although in 1982, according to the provisions of the law, families containing at least 300,000 children should have received this additional support, less than 10 percent of those children benefited from such grants.

Institutions for children are another important form of social welfare benefits. I have discussed the fact that, since the introduction of the Child Care Assistance and Child Care Allowance, the demand for creche placement has slightly decreased, and the proportion of children taken to creches for day care remained almost on the same level over the past ten years—about 10 percent of the age group concerned. Although the kindergarten network is extensive, it is the children of large families, with mothers who for this reason are not employed and opt to stay at home on Child Care Assistance, who are denied access to this type of institution. Because this program not only provides day care, but also ensures the beginning of socialization and preparation for school, this means an irreparable handicap in the later school career of children who have not attended kindergarten. Village and hamlet children—and large Gypsy families wherever they live— are the hardest hit by these defects in service provision. All this reveals a value judgment that silently exists in the Hungarian society and public thinking today, according to which those families merit support whose children are likely to be well adjusted and in fact successful in society in the first place, who are likely to contribute to society. Those who are not expected to do so well according to prevalent social standards—Gypsies, deviants, and the extremely poor—should receive less social support, according to this viewpoint. Thus, instead of generating a kind of positive discrimination aimed at narrowing the social gap, the prospects are quite high that disadvantages will be conserved and even reproduced.

At the same time, we are now witnessing the collapse of an overcentralized, overbureaucratized, and overideologized party state. During the 1980s an increasing number of endeavors have been undertaken to correct the uniform operation of a social welfare policy that has proven unsatisfactory for those who diverge from the median—in either the positive or the negative direction. For instance, we know that cumulatively handicapped families with several children usually fall through the holes in the protective network of existing social policy. If these families are lucky enough to benefit from some form of social welfare, those benefits are scattered and oriented only to a single acute problem of a particular member of the family. Thus the problems of these families are divided among the various institutions—the health system, the judiciary, and other social authorities—and often the children become institutionalized.

It takes attention to each family as a whole to provide special and effective social support to disadvantaged families. This idea has given rise in Hungry to efforts to build a network of complex family care units, which have not existed until now. At the same time, the need was recognized for providing high-level integrated training for social workers. The few family care centers that were established in the 1980s have not been able, however, to help more than a very small proportion of those who need this new type of complex care.

The churches, which until now were largely barred from contributing to social care, are gaining an increasing role in providing help to those who are the most handicapped. Apart from their traditional activities, like running children's homes and caring for the aged, the churches are now active in caring for and rehabilitating young drug addicts.

Realizing the inadequacies of the state's treatment of the problems of Gypsies, Gypsy and non-Gypsy intellectuals have initiated the formation of an independent organization that, in addition to working out long-term social welfare objectives, is also creating special programs—summer camps, youth clubs, and kindergartens for Gypsies—that are already doing valuable work both in care and education.

The Foundation for the Support of the Needy (SZETA) operated for a long term as an opposition group, barred from publicity, although it was active in charity campaigns. In the past few years such charitable organizations have also worked out political and social welfare programs to ameliorate the position of the handicapped.

At the same time, new types of creches and kindergartens responsive to the free enterprise ideology and to the special attitudes toward child raising of certain parents are also being set up with increasing frequency. Well-to-do parents send their children to private kindergartens that sometimes even provide some foreign language instruction, usually only during the morning hours. There are private kindergartens based on teaching principles that have existed for a long time but have not been recognized in Hungary, like the Waldorf approach. We are also witnessing local initiatives and volunteer work by the parents of children in local kindergartens, in order to influence teaching methods and ideologies.

Now that the failure of socialism as a social system has been recognized, the entire system of policies and programs for children will certainly undergo fundamental changes that parallel changes at the political level. Some of the political parties now operating legally, or restructuring themselves on entirely new foundations, have their own social welfare programs. In the society of the future, which will probably be based on the operation of a market economy, we can expect the development of a new pattern of social insurance and new institutions of social security. It is to be hoped that in the Hungarian society of the future the right to existence and the rights to healthy conditions, social security, and human self-fulfillment will become universal.

NOTE

1. The term "creche" is equivalent to the term "day care center." See Chapter 1 for an overview of terminology.

REFERENCES

Bársony, Magda. (1976). Az óvodai nevelés kialakulása, hazai története és a fóbb óvodapedagógiai irányzatok, Budapest.

Burchard, Erzsebet. (1945). *Practical Child Protection: The Work Schedule for Kindergartens and After School Day Care Centers.* Budapest: Ministry of Social Welfare.

Ferge, Zsuzsa. (1987). Szpciálpolitika ma és holnap, Kossuth, Budapest (szerk: Ferge Zs., Varnai Gy.).

Ferge, Zsuzsa. (1982). Családpolitika, családgondozas (in: Oktatásrol és társadalompolitikáról, MTA Szociológiai Intézet kiadványa).

Hermann, Alice. (1965). Az óvoda es az óvónóképzes fejlödése a felszabadulás után (1945–60).

Hermann, Alice, and Komlósi, Sandor. (1972). Early Child Care in Hungary, Gordon and Breach, London–New York–Paris, International Monograph Series on Early Child Care.

Kulcsár, Kálmán. (1981). A népesedés befolyásolásának lehetöségei. In Népesedés és népesedéspolitika, Budapest, Statisztkai Kiadó vallalat.

Müvelödésügyi Miniszterium beszamolója a cigánység iskolázási adataival, 1985.

Neményi, Maria. (1989). A család szociális reprezentáiója, kutatási beszamoló, MTA Szociológiai Kutató Intézete, kezirat.

Sándorné, Dr., Horváth, Erika. (1986). A gyestöl a gyedig, MNOT és Kossuth, Budapest.

Szalai, Julia. (1982). Néhány adalék a gyermekvárással, szüléssel és a kisgyermekes családokkal kapcsolatos hazai szociálpolitika helyzetenek elemzéséhez. In Oktatásról és társadalompolitikáról, Budapest.

Szalai, Jùlia. (1985). Mire kell az óvoda és kinek? Nök és Férfiak, MNOT–Kossuth (szerk.: Koncz Katalin).

———— 13 ————

INDIA

Sukhdeep Gill

Traditionally caring for children in India has been a responsibility of the family. An organized national effort to provide child care services is of recent origin. Although women have been working in industry, plantations, mining, agriculture, and the unorganized sector for many years, support to them and their children through organized day care services has been neglected. There are multiple reasons for such neglect and apathy, which need to be understood in the context of historical and cultural realities, the caste system, child-rearing beliefs and practices, family traditions, female work participation, and the status of women within the family and society. The rapidity of changes in demography, migration, family size and composition, education, employment, and various other factors influencing the lives of women during the post-independence period, and the growing understanding of the links among all these factors, has underscored the importance of viewing programs for the development of women and children in the larger framework of social and economic change and development.

THE ADMINISTRATIVE STRUCTURE IN INDIA

India is a union of states consisting of 25 states and 7 union territories. The central government is run by a parliament, made up of a lower and an upper house (Lok Sabha and Rajya Sabha, respectively).

The states are governed by state legislatures based on the parliamentary form of central government. They are further divided into districts, managed by District Administration Committees for the various government departments. The union territories are entirely under the legislative and executive control of the central government, although headed by the president of India or an official (governor) appointed by him. At the grassroots level there are blocks comprising urban and rural areas. The management of urban areas is carried out by a municipal committee or municipal corporation depending on the size of the population. Village assemblies (*Panchayats*) act as governing bodies in the rural areas.

Although the Indian constitution is federal in form, it is unitary in spirit. The real power is vested in the central government. While governing bodies at the various levels (states, union territories, districts, and blocks) derive power from the Constitution, they act primarily as agents of the central government and are responsible to that government either directly or indirectly. The constitution provides the central government with the power to issue directives to the states, the implementation of which is at the discretion of the state governments.

IDEOLOGICAL FACTORS INFLUENCING CHILD CARE POLICIES AND PROGRAMS

Historically India has been hospitable to numerous groups of immigrants from different parts of Asia and Europe, who became an integral part of the Indian mosaic. The population of India is racially diverse, containing elements from six main racial types: the Hegrito, the Proto-Australoid, the Mongoloid, the Mediterranean, the Western Brachycephals, and the Nordic. Diversity is seen, therefore, in the patterns of rural as well as urban settlement, community life, and forms of agricultural operations. More than 22 languages are recognized. There are striking differences between groups in kinship, marriage rites and customs, inheritance, and the general mode of living.

Despite this multiplicity of subcultures, some values and traditions seem to have become stable over time and generalizable across regions. Caste, family, the status of women, and authority based on age hierarchy and gender are some of the most pertinent arenas in which a high degree of continuity is seen.

The Caste System

India is known to have over 3,000 castes and subcastes, intricately organized in a complex system of social stratification. In the traditional society, the caste system was based on an ascriptive principle of social stratification that determined an individual's occupation. The origin of the system is found in the laws of Manu (400–1100 B.C.), where four castes (*Varnas*), *Brahmin*, *Kashtriya*, *Vaishya*, and *Sudra*, were graded in hierarchical order. The *Brahmins* were the priests, the *Kshatriyas* the warriors, the *Vaishyas* the merchants, and the *Sudras* the menial "untouchables," lowest in the caste hierarchy. The functional interdependence of these groups has been pre-

Figure 13.1
Caste System in India as Adapted from Srivastava (1968)

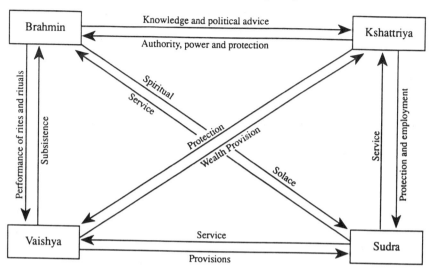

sented in Figure 13.1 In addition to determining occupation, each caste group maintained its distinctiveness by keeping to its own strictly defined limits and rules regarding marriage, social interaction, and behavior, motivated by the concepts of purity and pollution. Although the laws of Manu are considered to have placed equal importance on different occupations and the people belonging to each caste group, over time the untouchables became regarded as outcasts and were kept segregated from society.

In contemporary Indian society, although theoretically each caste seems to have a definite place in the social hierarchy, in reality the hierarchy has not remained static. Rules forbidding persons from higher castes to accept even food or drink from members belonging to castes lower than their own have weakened in the post-independence period, especially in the urban areas and in the younger generations. Changes have also come by virtue of the improved status of the middle and lower castes, due to geographic mobility, adoption of the ritualistic practices of higher castes, and improved education and economic conditions.

However, recent years have brought an increase in the political exploitation of the caste hierarchy to enlist political support. In order to protect their own economic and political interests, elite from the dominant sociopolitical strata are indirectly propagating caste solidarity and cohesion, which allows them to maintain their own status under the guise of social welfare. Therefore, while government efforts project a commitment to uplifting and mainstreaming people from lower castes, the caste hierarchy is being reinforced in the process.

At the societal level, the caste system remains a major factor influencing family cohesion. Even at the present time, the caste hierarchy has a considerable impact on the utilization of services provided for the welfare of children and families. For instance, families from higher castes prefer caregivers in day care to be from compatible castes. Caste boundaries are adhered to, especially in rural and less developed areas, in the utilization and even location of welfare services initiated by the government. Caste gradation has for a long time ensured that families from upper castes could obtain lower caste people as domestic servants, thereby solving any child care problems that might exist. The continuation of these practices in modern Indian society has been an important factor in stimulating government policies to provide day care for children from lower class families.

The Family

Diversity in the family ranges from the rich but declining tradition of the joint or extended family, where all vulnerable individuals (children, orphans, widows, elderly, etc.) are taken care of as a shared responsibility, to the urbanized self-sufficient nuclear family unit. Family form varies by cultural context, need, and family ties.

In the past, the roles of all the members of joint families were very well defined and segregated. The joint family system was based on authority and power vested in the eldest earning male member. The husband, who worked in collaboration with other adult male members, was viewed as the breadwinner of the family and expected to be educated and well informed. The wife was expected to manage the domestic routines under the guidance and authority of the eldest female member. Thus women's roles were subservient, except in the case of the eldest woman or the mother-in-law, who had limited powers in areas such as cooking for the family, household work allocation, and selection of a bride for her sons or grandsons. However, the final word remained with the eldest male member, the head of the family. By its very structure and functions, the joint family demanded unquestioned obedience to and identification with its system. The child, too, was expected to respect this code of conduct.

The young and inexperienced mother was guided in child care by the older, more experienced women. In the event of child illness the elders, especially the women, took over the responsibility of nursing the sick child. Family support was invariably available if the mother was unwell or had to go out of the village or town. Familial concern for the child's welfare, especially for boys, was founded in the expectation that the child would provide social security to the parents in due course and perpetuate the family name.

In addition to the fundamental responsibility vested in the family, society lent active advice and support in times of need. The priestly class designed practices and measures in the religious context, thereby ensuring compulsory obedience.

In the 20th century, under the influence of technological and social developments, the pattern of family living underwent drastic changes. Mechanization and modernization of industry nearly destroyed small-scale family handicrafts and cottage industries. The spread of education, the division of land holdings due to growing population pressures, the increasing cost of living, and the shift toward measuring one's status in terms of material goods induced large-scale migration from rural to urban areas in search of work. This migration tended to break up the joint families affected by it.

The proportion of nuclear households has been reported to vary from as low as 34 percent to as high as 78 percent in different regions of India. The range is similar in urban and agrarian settings, although extended households are more common in rural areas.

These changes in the family structure have resulted in several problems related to child care. On the one hand, there is the absence of familial support. On the other, where ties with the patrilineal kin are actively maintained, traditional authority remains unquestioned. The value of family unity and interdependence is upheld, which results in the maintenance of caste boundaries along with other traditional values.

In addition to the family structure, it is important to mention the traditional values placed on age and gender hierarchy within the family. The older the person, the higher has been his status and authority. Wisdom acquired through experience is held in high esteem. Deference for older people is the most consistent aspect of socialization. The supremacy of the male is another cultural reality whatever the ecology of the social group. Even in communities where the women may be the breadwinners, the male is considered superior.

Women and Work

For centuries women in India have played a multitude of roles in ensuring the proper functioning of the family. There have been no major changes over time in these roles or in the division of labor in the family. Housework has invariably been considered a "women's domain." A large majority of Indian women spend most of their time on household chores. Occupational status has always been severely constrained by home and family, such that despite having long working hours and being involved in a variety of jobs, women have remained inside the home. Long hours of daily work bring them no monetary return and do nothing to enhance their prestige in the family or society. Since the culture glorifies women's role as wife and mother, and considers their employment a failure by the family to provide for their needs, women withdraw from work outside the home as soon as the low-class family attains prosperity. For this reason child care has not been a

major concern for the upper caste/class families. Since socio-political development of governmental plans and policies has also rested with upper
caste members, male or female, there has been a lack of sensitivity to the
child care needs of a vast majority of low-resource families.

In addition to household chores and child care, about 54 percent of rural
and 26 percent of urban women, although classified as non-working, are
engaged in supporting the family economy through such activities as collecting fodder, firewood, and cow dung; caring for animals; maintaining a
kitchen garden; and tailoring and weaving.

In the past two decades, women have begun to account for a larger
proportion of the overall rural labor force. This increase is most marked in
agriculture, where the overall proportion of female to male cultivators has
gone up by one third from 1971 to 1981. In rural areas, as men are diver-
sifying out of agriculture into other areas, women are taking their place. In
addition to the pressure of poverty on rural households, the growing inten-
sity of agriculture, multiple cropping patterns, and increasing landlessness
have been viewed as some of the reasons for this shift to female work
participation in agriculture.

In 1983 the number of women workers nationwide was estimated to be
98.4 million. Eighty-nine percent of these women are engaged mainly as
laborers in agriculture. In urban areas, the household industries and other
service sectors account for the largest proportion of women workers. In all
90 percent or more of women workers are engaged in the unorganized
sector, mainly as self-employed wage earners. Work participation rates for
women have increased tremendously, with 24 percent being employed in
the rural areas and 11 percent in urban areas in 1981. An increase in wage
employment has been noted among all groups of women up to 59 years of
age. General female work participation is projected to increase from 67.4
million to 105.7 million by the year 2000.

Female work participation has left few non-working adults to care for
children, especially in low-income families. The burden of child care is
usually borne by older siblings, mostly girls, who are in turn deprived of
their own schooling. However, due to economic pressures even female child
labor has been on the increase in the recent past. In the period from 1971
to 1981, rural female child labor increased by 30 percent throughout the
country while during the same period male child labor dropped by 8 percent.
A large number of girls are put to work in the family fields while boys are
kept in school or trained in vocational skills. In urban areas, male child
workers have increased by 20 percent and females by 60 percent.

As a result of these changes, the availability of older siblings to care for
the younger children has also been affected adversely. In many cases, mothers have no option but to take children to work sites (construction or
agricultural fields) where older preschool children (three to five years old)
watch over the babies. Similarly, in the case of the middle-class working

women, the availability of relatives (grandmothers) for child care has diminished due to the increasing number of nuclear families. Only in the higher income groups, where a more leisurely life-style and joint family living are more prevalent, do young children still receive warmth and alternative care from several caregivers.

THE EMERGENCE OF CHILD CARE PROGRAMS IN INDEPENDENT INDIA

During the period since India's independence from the United Kingdom in 1947, both the government and the voluntary sectors have played a role in the development of child care programs.

Government Efforts

After India's independence in 1947, the government's concern for the child was first reflected in the Indian Constitution, which laid down in Articles 24, 39, and 45 that

No child below the age of fourteen years shall be employed to work in any factory or mine or engaged in any other hazardous employment. (Article 24)

The state shall in particular, direct its policy towards securing ... (c) that children of tender age are not abused and children are not forced by economic necessity to enter a vocation unsuited to their age or strength: (f) that children are given opportunities and facilities to develop in a healthy manner and in conditions of freedom and dignity and that childhood and youth are protected against moral and material abandonment. (Article 39)

Provision for free and compulsory education for children ... The State shall endeavor to provide within a period of ten years from the commencement of this constitution for free and compulsory education for all children until they complete the age of fourteen years. (Article 45)

Of the above, Article 39 (f) is the most significant on two accounts: child development is to be secured by creating the requisite facilities, and the child is to be protected from neglect.

Child care has also been provided for in the five-year plans formulated by the National Planning Commission, beginning in 1951. As early as the second five-year plan (1956–1961), the need to provide day care services for children of large numbers of women working outside the organized sector was recognized. The Central Social Welfare Board (CSWB), established in 1953 and entirely funded by the government, has been involved in promoting and expanding day care services in rural as well as urban areas, through its grant-in-aid program in general and welfare projects

(1967) in particular. State Social Welfare Advisory Boards came into being at state levels, which coordinated with the national CSWB on one hand and their respective state governments on the other. During the third plan (1961–1966) the CSWB started integrated preschool projects in urban areas, which also included day care creches for preschool children in urban slums.[1] A scheme called "Creches for the Children of Working and Ailing Mothers" was launched in the fifth plan (1974–1979) to encourage participation of voluntary organizations in the establishment of these services. The scheme provides day care services that include health care, supplementary nutrition, sleeping facilities, immunization, play, and entertainment for newborn to five-year-old children who are left uncared for when their mothers go to work. It provides assistance to voluntary organizations for running such creches, reimbursing 90 percent of the cost on approved items. The sixth plan (1980–1985) urged the establishment of creches in hostels for working women, state and central government offices, public sector undertakings, residential colonies, and at construction sites. Emphasis was also placed on the setting up of creches both for children of women in regular establishments and for agricultural and migrant labor families.

Even though these efforts came quite early in the post-independence period and were well conceived, a host of factors, such as the burgeoning rate of population growth, illiteracy, social underdevelopment, financial constraints, and inconsistency of emphasis on various aspects of the child welfare in five-year plans slowed the pace of achievement. An underlying cause of this situation was recognized as the absence of a national policy on children, as a result of which there was no clarity regarding the strategy for approaching and realizing the constitutional goals. Therefore, after several years of debate within and outside the government, a National Policy for Children was adopted in 1974. This policy emphasizes adequate services for the optimal physical, mental, and social development of children starting at conception, with special attention to comprehensive health and nutrition, free compulsory evaluation, physical education, games, and other recreational facilities. Announcement of this national policy gave impetus to programs in certain priority areas. The International Year of the Child in 1979 created further awareness and resulted in the establishment of a National Children's Fund in the central government and in the states.

Efforts by Voluntary Organizations

In the voluntary sector, the early recognition of the needs of working women from low-income families led to child care facilities in the form of rural preschools in 787 villages of Tamil Nadu State in 1962 (the number has now grown to include almost all of the 13,000 villages in the state). These "kappagams," or day care centers, were conceived as the most elementary and low-cost form of child care possible. Housed in thatched huts or sheds, staffed by local women with little or no education who were paid at a very modest rate, and equipped with the barest minimum of play materials, the centers were intended to care for children two and a half to five years old, for half a day or the whole day as the need required, while their mothers worked in the fields. With very limited resources and no training, the workers were mostly mere child minders. Some activities involving songs, stories, and games, with little attention to reading, writing, and arithmetic, were included for the older children. No concept of infant care existed. After 1971, the program was strengthened with the addition of supplementary feeding.

Two important developments in the later part of the 1960s and early 1970s played a crucial role in significantly changing the approach to the care of children. The first was the growing awareness among academicians and policy makers of the impact of poverty on the lives of children, along with a gradual understanding of the possibilities of countervailing intervention strategies. This led in 1975 to the launching of the first comprehensive program called Integrated Child Development Services (ICDS). The second was the individual initiative of one woman, Meera Mahadevan, who began to experiment with caring for the children of women laborers in construction and set in motion a chain of events that led to the government's scheme of Assistance to Creches for Working and Ailing Mothers.

Child Care Legislation

Following independence, child care found a place in the organized sector, in the form of day care services, when the Factories Act (1948), the Plantations Act (1951), and the Mines Act (1952) came into force. The Plantations Act laid down that a creche is to be provided by any plantation hiring a minimum of 50 female workers, and the revised Factories Act (amended in 1976) stipulates the same provision for 30 or more women workers. The Mines Act has specified that a creche be provided wherever women are employed, regardless of their number. Further highlighting the kind of environment in these creches, all these acts require that "in every factory where more than the stipulated number of women workers are ordinarily employed, there shall be provided and maintained a suitable room or rooms for the use of the children under age six of those women. Such rooms shall provide adequate accommodation, shall be adequately lighted and ventilated, shall be maintained in a clean and sanitary condition, and shall be under the charge of women trained in the care of children and infants." The act further specified that the state government concerned should make rules prescribing standards related to all of these conditions. The Factories Act went further in requiring the provision of free milk or refreshment or both for children, and it required employers to provide facilities for mothers to breast-feed children at necessary intervals.

The more recent Contract Labour Regulation and Abolition Act, passed in 1970, provides for creches to be located within 50 meters of every establishment where 20 or more women are ordinarily employed as contract labor. The guidelines for the physical characteristics of the facilities to be provided specify minimum standards for building, indoor and outdoor space, and other basic amenities along with qualifications of the staff. In addition, requirements for medical check-up and health records are laid down, as are the conditions of inspection. In 1980 the Interstate Migrant Workers Act was introduced to ensure the welfare of migrant workers.

However, there are a number of loopholes in these laws. Implementation has been left to individual employers in a capitalist framework, hence making it almost inevitable that the laws would be obeyed more in letter than in spirit and that mere "paper" compliance would result rather than a satisfactory welfare activity. The employers either avoid hiring women, or if employed keep them scattered, temporary, or casual, or employers show less than the requisite number of working women on the muster roll. There is no network of specialized supervision to ensure that the creche is functioning. A locked room with a few mats, charts, and boards does exist on some work sites, factories, and plantations. Satisfied that a creche facility exists, the visiting labor officer leaves the details to the employers. Assurance of quality day care for the children of the women working in the unorganized sector, not covered by a legislative provision, is a more distant dream.

EXISTING CHILD CARE STRATEGIES

Efforts to provide child care services are directly related to how the work status of women is defined. Because only 10 percent of all working women are in the organized sector, and because evasion of the law is frequent in those few work sectors where legislative action has been taken, the number of children of working women who have been reached through any form of formal child care arrangement is very small. An overview of the coverage provided by different types of day care and early childhood education provision is presented in Table 13.1.

In view of the increasing number of mothers in the work force, and the estimated 33 million children in need of day care, the facilities provided for child care are far from adequate. The different types of child care arrangements reported by lower-class women indicate that the mother is the major caregiver (67 percent rural, 57 percent urban) for both male and female children less than one year old. This percentage decreases to about 47 percent when children reach six years of age. Grandparents and other relatives emerge as the second largest category of caregivers (20 to 25 percent urban, 15 to 20 percent rural). In a few cases either unrelated persons or servants take care of children. In both urban and rural areas the range of children left unattended varies from 2 to 11 percent.

Table 13.1
Coverage of Day Care and Early Childhood Provision in India

	Number of Children
Needing alternative care	33 million
In alternative care	
Day Care Center	.2 million
Other early childhood programs	9.8 million
(I.C.O.S. and Balwadis)	
Family-based care	not documented

The above data clearly illustrate that while the work pressures of the mother have increased considerably, her caretaking role has not undergone a major change. Although other family members and unrelated adults account for a part of the child care options available to women, the extent to which they can extend such support is highly questionable in light of prevailing socio-economic pressures. Therefore, the traditional model of informal care within the extended family and community is being replaced by paid care in the formal settings.

The child care services available to children of working women in these formal settings fall into four categories: statutory sector, voluntary sector, private sector, and other child care support sector. As these sectors are regulated differently and operate with very different motivations, and other child support programs are quite different from creche facilities, each is treated separately below.

Day Care in the Statutory Sector

In keeping with the legislation described earlier, day care facilities are to be provided for the mothers working in mines, tea plantations, and factories. A number of investigators have conducted studies that have thrown light on the quality of these services. Because they respond somewhat differently to their statutory obligations, mining operations, plantations, and factories are distinguished in the presentation that follows.

Creches in Coal Mines. Women employed in coal mines constitute more than 50 percent of women in all mines. In 1984 there were 45,774 women in the coal industry, making Coal India Ltd. the largest single employer of women in India. However, the management in mines is almost wholly male dominated. Among officials and managers of the coal mines, welfare is seen only in terms of the infrastructure, which includes housing, hospitals, dispensaries and clinics, and bathing and washing places. Although separate figures are not available for creches, the records indicate that creches have a negligible status. For instance, at Bharat Coking Coal Ltd. there are only 64 creches serving 16,500 women workers, which highlights the very marginal nature of the creche operation. Among the mining officials, the use, non-use, or capability for use of the creches does not seem to cause any great concern. Empirical evidence has shown that these creches operate only for half a day, typically from 7:00 or 8:00 or even 9:00 A.M. until about noon, closing after the distribution of the midday meal. This part-day approach contradicts the very purpose of the service. Labour welfare department officers and inspectors concerned with implementing, supervising, monitoring, or evaluating welfare activities assign creches a very low priority.

Creches on Plantations. The plantations clustered in the hilly areas of the southern and eastern states of India are the second largest organized work sector in the country and have the highest proportion of women in their labor force (46 percent of the work force in tea, and 37 percent in rubber estates). Because they are far away from villages and other settlements, the usual practice has been to recruit whole families and settle them on the plantations, where men and women are paid equal wages. Along with housing, other benefits such as medical facilities, elementary schools, rations, and entertainment are provided by the employers. The extent to which these facilities are made available varies from estate to estate in different parts of the country.

The National Institute of Public Cooperation and Child Development (NIPCCD) estimated the presence of 500 to 1,000 children under six years of age on each of these estates. In almost all cases both husband and wife were working as laborers. During the peak season their older children were also employed as temporary hands, leaving young ones unattended.

One investigator reported existence of two kinds of creches in Assam, an eastern state: Central creches for children aged three and older with arrangements for kindergarten education, and satellite creches spread over the work areas for infants under three years of age, to enable the mothers to feed them during the work day. These arrangements were in line with the recommendations of a special committee set up in 1962. However, the investigator found no children in any of the facilities. The creche rooms were invariably found locked, and when opened were either empty or found to be used as storehouses for routine items. The satellite creches were just thatched roof areas with an abandoned look, which were sometimes used for storing the tea leaves plucked during the day. Creche attendants were either non-existent or consisted of one of the laboring women with no special training.

The management of these plantations mentioned parental apathy, illiteracy, lack of awareness of the importance of education, unwillingness to send children to the creche, and limited social education as reasons for the non-existence of the creches. However, the parents and labor leaders disagreed, mentioning the lack of equipment, facilities, untrained workers, unsuitable hours of operation, and disinterest of the management in running the creche.

The situation in the southern states, however, was reported to be quite different and far more encouraging. The NIPCCD study involved 15 large estates in three states and found creches functioning in all of them, in several cases with more than one creche per estate. Regrettably, it does not mention the figures relating to coverage, number, and the attendance of children in these creches. According to Labour Bureau figures, there were 144 creches in Karnataka, 400 in Kerala, and 154 in Tamil Nadu in 1980 and 1981.

Creches in factories. In the early days women working in factories brought their children along, which resulted in mothers' reduced concentration on the work at hand. Therefore, the management felt the need for starting creches away from the work site, to minimize mothers' distraction so that the quality of the product would improve. Another reason for starting creches related to mothers regularly giving opium to their infants, to make them sleep long hours without disturbance, thereby adversely influencing the development of children—"the future labor force."

The information on day care in the industrial sector is scanty, due on the one hand to the resistance of employers to provide data, and on the other to the lack of focus on child care dimensions in the studies that have been conducted. The presence of a room that fulfills the legal obligation to provide creche facilities, and an accompanying attitude of indifference toward child care, are seen among employers.

However, a study of the women in public sector industries in the period from 1968 to 1975, including textiles, electronics, pharmaceuticals, heavy electricals, and watches, reported that where creches existed they were often unsatisfactory. While in some cases (e.g., the cotton textile industry) provision was extensive, in other cases (e.g., municipal scavenging workers, building workers, port, dock, and cement workers) there was none. Lack of trained staff and poor conditions and equipment were reported in particular. Another study of the textile industry in Bombay in the early 1970s revealed that most of the factory creches maintained the minimum standards laid down by the Factories Act in relation to lighting, ventilation, space, equipment, salaries of workers, and presence of trained nurses. None, however, attempted to provide any form of preschool education or stimulating activity for children above the age of three. In all cases, the size of the creche was very small, the average attendance of children being only 11. Three fourths of the 16 units studied in detail had fewer than ten children, while three creches had only one child each. The study also brought out that for every 100 working women in the factories concerned, there were only 7.1 children in creches. In some cases, especially in the industrial units in Bombay, nurses or midwives are inappropriately employed in creches. At the same time, outstanding day care services have been provided by certain firms in the private sector, which have a long tradition of labor-related welfare service (e.g., Tata, Godrej, Glaxo, and the pharmaceutical industry in Bombay).

Day Care in the Voluntary Sector

In the 1950s, a majority of creches were run by four national voluntary agencies, the Indian Council of Child Welfare, the *Bhartiya Grameen Mahila Sangh*, the *Bhartiya Adimjati Seva Sangh*, and the *Harijan Sevak Sangh*. In addition, other agencies such as the Red Cross, religious trusts, and church-related organizations accounted for a sizable proportion of the creches. In response to the strong need for child care arrangements for the children of low-income working mothers unable to afford paid care, a scheme of creches/day care centers for the children of working and ailing mothers was launched by the national government in 1975. The scheme aims to provide for the basic needs of children, such as supplementary nutrition. There is a provision to release grants to various organizations through the Central Social Welfare Board to provide creches for the largest possible number of children. There were 1,411 such creches in 1981, of which nearly 65 percent were functioning in rural areas. Used mostly by employed women, these creches also serve the children of unemployed mothers.

Among the various voluntary organizations that are contributing significantly to the provision of day care for the children of working women in the unorganized sector, the effort referred to as "mobile creches" deserves special mention as an innovative, needs-based effort. Mobile creches were initiated in 1968 in response to the plight of children of migrant laborers involved in construction work in urban areas of New Delhi. Living conditions are deplorable in the labor camps where these children live. Small cramped huts leak with the slightest rain. Heaps of rubbish are seen all around the hutments. In addition to living in such a shabby environment, young children are not able to spend much time with their mothers, who are under constant economic pressure to earn, in addition to the usual household burdens they carry. Younger children are looked after by older siblings, who may be no more than five or six years old themselves. Common amenities available to the local population of the urban area (schools, hospitals, etc.) are not accessible to these families, due to their illiteracy, lack of confidence, and constant mobility. Despite the Contract Labour Act of 1970, the construction workers have not been able to ensure a minimum wage or any of the other facilities to which the act entitles them. It was in the context of such first-hand knowledge about the children of construction workers that the idea of mobile creches was born. Mobility was vital because the creche needed to be moved as the construction laborers moved to new sites. These creches function in sheds or uncompleted parts of buildings on a particular construction site for as long as the construction lasts. At any given time there are about 50 such creches in operation in New Delhi and Bombay, including two or three in Pune. A full-day program is run by a team of four to five workers for 50 to 150 children in the age group of newborn to 12 years, six days a week. An effort is made to provide age appropriate programming, along with serving the nutritional, health, and sanitary needs of these children.

Private Provision of Day Care

Day care services are required by all women, whether they are working in the organized or unorganized sector. The Committee on the Status of Women in India produced a report in 1974 stating that maternity and child care benefits are available to only half the women workers in the organized sector. The other women in the organized sector (mainly in services) do not get creche facilities because they are not covered by labor laws. For the 90 percent of all women who are in the unorganized sector, existing facilities are especially inadequate.

In the absence of a relative willing or able to provide child care, and given the cost and perceived unreliability of paid care at home by servants, day care in a family setting is fast becoming a popular child care arrangement, where housewives provide day care facilities for middle-class working mothers. The housewives are mostly middle-aged women, who after having fulfilled their own parenting responsibilities, feel that they are now equipped to provide day care. Requests from working mothers in the neighborhood, economic gains, meaningful utilization of time, and preventing loneliness are some of the reasons that these women begin to provide this service.

Although there is no documentation or directory of such arrangements, family day care is found in a number of the cities and towns where a majority of mothers work in office jobs. For example, a preliminary survey undertaken in Ludhiana city, a leading industrial town in India, revealed no provision of day care facilities in a single factory (out of 75 contacted), whereas more than 50 private family day care programs were identified.

There is no legislative system controlling the development or supervising the quality of family day care. Thus the type of care varies from one program to another. Other important considerations, in addition to the amount of space available for day care, are the number of children served, their ages, and the equipment available.

OTHER CHILD CARE SUPPORT PROGRAMS

Apart from the formally recognized day care facilities, there are other programs which, while not initiated with the care of children with working mothers as an objective, serve that purpose to some extent by relieving the mother of the child care role for at least a part of the day. A brief description of some of the major programs is included here.

Integrated Child Development Services

A growing awareness of the impact of poverty on the lives of children, along with an interest in their overall protection and development, culminated in 1975 in the innovative Integrated Child Development Services (ICDS) Program. Starting with 33 experimental projects spread throughout the country, ICDS now has more than 1,600 projects in operation. The program reaches out to young mothers and their children under six years of age to provide a package of preventive and development services through outlets called *anganwadis*. Although focused on the all-around development of the preschool child, ICDS is also the largest scheme providing part-time creche facilities to children in rural and tribal areas, and in slums. In some states, the *anganwadis* are reported to operate as full-day child care arrangements, in response to the needs of working women.

Balwadis

The *Balwadis* (Child Education Centers) program was intended to promote the education of three- to six-year-old children in rural areas. However, many of the centers are also urban or semi-urban in location. *Balwadis* are run or assisted by agencies such as the Central Social Welfare Board, the Indian Council of Child Welfare, state governments, and municipal authorities. Although no census or survey exists to provide data on the coverage provided by this program, it is estimated that 20,000 to 25,000 centers serving 600,000 to 700,000 children are in operation. The National Perspective Plan for Women, 1988–2000 provides a more conservative estimate of 5,045 *Balwadis* in all of India, serving about 230,000 children.

Nursery Schools and Kindergartens

Clustered mainly in urban areas and run privately, nursery schools and kindergartens focus on the education of children between two and a half and five years of age, relieving the mother of child care responsibilities for three to five hours daily. However, the utility of these programs is limited to the middle and upper classes only. Due either to poverty or to lack of awareness and the placing of low priority on education, the families from low income groups do not generally enroll their children in these programs.

A TYPICAL DAY CARE PROGRAM

A typical day care program established to serve women working in the mines has been described as follows by Mina Swaminathan in her book *Who Cares?: A Study of Child Care Facilities for Low Income Working Women in India* (1985). The creche was staffed by a woman in charge and a helper, plus a part-time cook, all paid at statutory wage rates. The creche was in a pleasant building consisting of two large rooms, a bathroom, toilet, kitchen, and storeroom, all fronting on a veranda, with a large open air courtyard which could have been used as a play space. The furnishings consisted of several cribs placed end to end in one of the rooms, with simple bedding, a first-aid kit, and a few charts on the walls. There was no sign of linen for changing, spare clothes for the children or any other equipment required for handling young babies, nor any toys or play equipment. In the kitchen there were a few utensils for cooking and for eating, but little evidence of their use. Most interestingly, there were only three children present, all 4 + years old, who did not seem to be regular attendees. These children were apparently going to spend the whole morning sitting quietly until food was served. There was also no evidence whatever of any regular contact with parents, for educational or any other purposes.

A Bengali speaking woman able to speak little Hindi had been in charge of the creche for nearly 30 years, and the *ayah* (helper) for a shorter time. The woman in charge claimed to have attended a short training course many years ago, but could not remember very much about the content. No refresher courses appear to have been given, nor was there any technical monitoring, supervision, or guidance by professionally qualified persons. The person in charge did not have a concept of what a program for young children should include, but conceived of her job as child minding. There was no evidence of any health program. Sick children were not brought to the creche and would not be kept there. If a child felt sick in the creche, it was taken to the nearest dispensary and the parents sent for. The Medical Office was supposed to inspect the creche regularly, but the extent to which this had actually happened was not clear.

Food seemed to be the only conceivable remaining activity in the creche, and possibly the only attraction for those children who might attend. It was very difficult to get any information about the amount and kind of food given to the children. There were no menu charts or records of amounts provided. Repeated enquiries failed to bring out the existence of any standards or limits either on a cost or calorie basis per child, or of guidelines laid down by health authorities. The staff mentioned that toffees and sweets had to be given to bring children to the creche and to keep them there. How often this was done and whether anything else was provided on the day the sweets were given was not clear. All workers and officials, however, maintained that money was not a constraint, that food and milk were served as and when needed at the discretion of the person in charge, who was free to make the menu, purchase foods and milk in the required quantities, and get bills reimbursed.

FUTURE PLANS AND PERSPECTIVES

"In the context of the need, the availability of day care in India today may be a tiny achievement. Yet it may be considered admirable precisely because it has taken place in the context of attitudes largely antithetical to it and represents a triumph of progressive forces in the ongoing conflict between modernizing and conservative forces" (Swaminathan, 1985, p. 131).

Concerted efforts are required to bring about much needed changes in the prevailing attitudes and myths regarding women's work pressures and the adequacy of informal supports for child care. A realistic appraisal and acceptance of the prevailing situation, coupled with the encouragement of innovative needs-based programs and increased funds, will be required if the situation for women and children in India is to improve.

Availability of Services

It is evident that child care facilities have not increased in proportion to increases in the number of working women in either the organized or the unorganized sector of the economy. This gap has long-term repercussions, not only for young children, but also for other family members. Education of older siblings, and especially females, has been sacrificed to the provision of child care.

Existing child care facilities lack flexibility in their design and operation. The rigidity of these programs makes adaptation based on local needs difficult, especially in the unorganized sector. In the statutory sector, loopholes in existing laws and the indifferent attitude of employers have had an adverse effect on the provision of child care. In order to eliminate the discrepancy in the provision of child care within the organized sector, provision of a creche wherever 30 persons (men and women) are employed should be made mandatory. Since the government employs a large number of women, child care facilities should be provided in and around such government offices.

To sum up, while the prime concern of the mothers is to ensure the safety of children in their absence, government has attained only partial success in providing day care through legislation and grants. The employers' concern is limited to safeguarding their statutory obligations, and in the unorganized sector, care is viewed more as a business rather than as a developmental program for young children.

Quality of Care

The care of young children involves much more than simply providing food and shelter. It is very important to ensure the quality of care wherever day care is provided. There is a strong need to cultivate positive attitudes in the various categories of creche workers and other employees, and to educate them regarding the needs of young children and the methods best suited to attend to these needs. Steps to ensure compliance with laws related to the quality of child care are urgently required. Strategies such as the licensing and training, supervision, and monitoring of family day care providers should also be considered seriously, as this kind of group care is growing rapidly, especially in urban areas. The fact that the National Perspective Plan of Women (1988) has for the first time emphasized the importance of flexible hours of program operation to suit the needs of working mothers, an integrated approach for overall development in child care, and the training of the workers involved in day care centers is a hopeful sign.

Service Integration

Educators and social welfare experts are of the view that resources from the various sectors should be pooled to provide centralized day care near railway stations, bus stops, and the like, where the service can be accessible to all mothers irrespective of their work situations. Keeping in mind the diversity of family and community life in India, there is a strong need to adopt a multi-model approach, so that the most suitable alternative can be implemented in a given situation. The possibility of providing day care near primary schools or residential areas has to be explored as well.

Child Care Administration and Program Delivery

Child care, by its very nature, is a small-scale and localized operation that has to respond to the needs of women, children, and school-aged girls. A three-tier structure is recommended as a way of balancing flexibility in program delivery with the economies of scale provided by larger institutional structures. The actual running of the day care service should be entrusted at the local level to organizations like *balwadis* and *anganwadis*, *mahila mandals*, *panchyats*, cooperatives, and unions. The supervision, funding, training, and monitoring should be entrusted to intermediate level organizations, like voluntary agencies, district authorities, municipal authorities, charitable trusts, and public-sector undertakings. At the apex level, there should be an umbrella organization functioning as an autonomous body, similar to the labor welfare boards under the joint auspices of the Ministries/ Departments of Women and Child Development, Education, and Labor.

Valid and Reliable Information about Need and Provision

There is an acute problem regarding the data base pertaining to the actual number of working women in India and the proportion of those women in the organized and unorganized sectors of the economy. It is widely accepted by now that the counting of females as workers in the census and in the National Sample Survey Organization suffers from serious enumerational and reporting drawbacks, but the lack of alternatives forces reliance upon these sources. In addition, there is a serious lack of demographic data on family composition, family income, and availability and utilization of services. Similarly, data regarding the number of children in need of alternative care, the requisite nature and duration of such care, and the extent of coverage of children in existing programs is not comprehensive. Besides quantitative data, there is very limited information regarding the functioning of existing services and the impact of these services on the development of growing children and families.

Existing child care facilities reach only a tiny fraction of those in India in need of such supports. There is a great deal yet to be accomplished. The existing policies and future plans of the government, a growing sensitivity on the part of professionals, and the increasing awareness among the working classes of their rights all represent positive trends. However, conscientious implementation of the recommendations being made at all levels will be required if significant changes in the well-being of children and families are to be achieved.

NOTES

The author wishes to acknowledge Dr. Baljit Kaur, reader, M.S., University of Baroda, India; Dr. R. Murlidharan, professor, National Council of Educational Research and Training, New Delhi, India; and Dr. Mina Swaminathan, India for their valuable suggestions in the preparation of this chapter.

1. In India creches are day care centers serving children from birth through age five. See Chapter 1 for a full overview of service types and definitions.

REFERENCES

Aliyer, S. A. (1990). "Agenda of Priorities for Women." *Indian Express.* January 7.

Anandalakshmy, S. (1980). "Day Care Centres." In *Profile of the Child in India: Policies and Programmes.* New Delhi: Ministry of Social Welfare, Govt. of India.

Anandalakshmy, S., Joshi, P., and Jain, D. (1989). *Creches in the Voluntary Sector in Delhi: A Report.* New Delhi: Ministry of Human Resource Development.

Centre for Social Studies (1985). *Caste, Caste Conflict and Reservation.* New Delhi. Ajanta Publications.

"Child in India." (1985). *A Statistical Profile.* New Delhi: Ministry of Welfare.

Datta, A. (1989). "Creches—Only Alternative." *The Tribune*, p. 3, October 15.

Datta, V. R. (1989). "Family day care: Answering the Needs of Working Mothers and Their Children." Paper presented in seminar by OMEP-India, Baroda.

Datta, V. R. (1989). "Quality Child Care." Paper presented in seminar by OMEP-India, Baroda.

deSouza, A. (1979). *Children in Creches: Day Care for the Urban Poor.* New Delhi: Intellectual Publishing House.

Gopal, A. K. (1983). *Creches on plantations.* New Delhi: National Institute of Public Cooperation and Child Development.

Iswaran, K. (1978). *A Populistic Community and Modernization in India.* Delhi: Vikas.

Khandekar, M. (1976). *The Disadvantaged Pre-Schoolers in Greater Bombay.* Bombay: Somaiya Publications.

Krishnan (1990). "Competence—The criterion." *The Tribune*, December 9, p. 8.

Kumar, R. (Ed.) (1988). *Child Development in India: Vol. 1. Health, welfare, and management.* New Delhi: Ashish Publishing House.

Luthra, P. N. (1979). "The Child in India: Policy Provisions and Practices." In S. D. Gokhale and N. K. Sohoni, (Eds.) *Child in India* (pp. 89–103). New Delhi: Somaiya Publications, Pvt. Ltd.

Mukherjee, R. (1977). *West Bengal family structure 1946–1966: An example of the Viability of a Joint Family.* New York: MacMillan.

Muzumdar, K. A. (1989). "Brief Historical Evaluation of Child Welfare in India." Paper presented in seminar by OMEP-India, Baroda.

Nakhate, V. S. (1987). *The Orientation Training Programme for Workers of Private Creches in Greater Bombay.* Bombay: Tata Institute of Social Sciences, Unit for Child and Youth Research.

Nakhate, V. S. (1987). *Family Day Care in Bombay.* Bombay: Tata Institute of Social Sciences, Unit for Child and Youth Research.

National Perspective Plan for Women, 1988–2000: A Perspective from the Women's Movement. (Report of debate, 1988, August.) New Delhi: Government of India.

Rani, T. (1992). *Status of day care services in Ludhiana City.* Unpublished Master's Thesis. Punjab Agricultural University, Ludhiana.

Shramshakti. (1988). *A Report of the National Commission on Self-employed Women and Women in Informal Sectors.* New Delhi: Ministry of Human Resource Development.

Singh, G., and Savara, M. (1980). *A Case Study on Child Care Facilities in Metropolitan Bombay.* Bangkok: Asian and Pacific Centre for Women and Development.

Srinivas, M. N. (1980). *India: Social structure.* Delhi: Hindustan Publishing Corporation.

Sriram, R. (1988, July). "A Teaching Module on Child Care Services as a Social Support for Women." Paper presented at the International Workshop on Women, Households and Development, Baroda.

Srivastava, H. C. (1968). *Studies in Indian sociology.* Vol. 1. Varanasi: Samajshastra Prakashan.

Swaminathan, M. (1985). *Who Cares? A Study of child care facilities for Low Income Working Women in India.* New Delhi: Indraprastha Press.

Swaminathan, M. (1987). "Day care: Problems and Strategies." *The Primary Teacher.* 12 (4), 16–21.

UNICEF (1988). *The State of the World's Children.* New York: Oxford University Press.

World Health Organization. (1983). *New Approaches to Health Education in Primary Health Care* Technical Report, No. 690. Geneva: Author.

14

ISRAEL

Abraham Sagi and Nina Koren-Karie

The number of working mothers in Israel has increased sharply in the last several years, a change that has led to increasing demands for child care services outside the home. This circumstance is characteristic of most developed countries. Because of it, considerable attention has been given in recent years to research in the area of infant day care and its implications for child development.

The major areas of research in this regard involve the effects of daily separation from the mother on the emotional and social development of the child, and the relation between the qualitative variables of the day care center (e.g., caregiver training, size of day care group, and physical, emotional, and cognitive environment) and such developmental measures as cognitive development and interaction of children with adults and peers. Some of these studies have investigated the combined effects of family environment with day care exposure on the development of children. Whereas researchers are in general agreement that exposure to day care has no negative effects on cognitive development, recently there has been an ongoing debate regarding the effects of day care on the socio-emotional development of infants. The traditional view, primarily inspired by psychoanalytic and ethological perspectives, is that non-maternal care in the first years is likely to result in negative effects. However, most studies during the 1960s and 1970s have not produced support for this contention. Thus during the last decade the dominant view has been that day care centers had no detrimental effects on infants.

Belsky (1988), who disseminated the notion of no-effect about a decade ago, has lately reassessed the evidence and concluded that the extended stay of children in day care centers, especially prior to the age of one year, may lead to a higher level of socio-emotional vulnerability in these groups of children. This reversed conclusion is based primarily on his critique of the research methodologies employed in earlier research. Consistent with attachment theory, the facts as reassessed by Belsky are claimed to be somewhat more problematic. His evaluation has been supplemented by recent studies that are more properly designed, suggesting that intensive non-maternal care is more likely to result in infant-mother avoidant attachment relationships and in higher levels of aggression and non-compliance. According to his view, attendance at a day care center for periods over 20 hours per week, especially in the first year or life, may incur a higher level of vulnerability in these infants, suggesting that they will experience more insecure attachment relationships. It should be noted in this regard that most infants and toddlers at day care centers in Israel remain there for weekly periods of about 35 hours or more, so that they automatically fall into the category of being at risk according to these findings.

Research regarding the direct impact of day care centers on child development is currently focused on specific characteristics, including the influence of the child's age when entering the day care center on the infant-mother attachment relationship, the effect of the child's gender (with main findings indicating that boys are more vulnerable to situations of stress), and whether there are short- versus long-term effects of day care center attendance. In any event, the main concern remains that extensive non-maternal care, particularly in the child's first year of life, increases the likelihood of developing avoidant infant-mother attachment.

As expected, the topic remains controversial. A number of recent publications have raised serious concerns about the validity of Belsky's conclusions. The major concerns include insufficient empirical evidence, inadequate consideration of the various complex ecologies pertinent to the issue, and the meaning of attachment research, carried out in the past 20 years, as pertaining to adaptation in general and to infant day care in particular. Therefore, as opposed to the contention stressing immediate negative effects of day care centers on children, a number of researchers have adopted the "early background" approach. According to this view, the negative consequences observed in day care children can be related to family, personal, and environmental variables that exert their influence on children prior to their being placed in the center. These factors may differ in the group of day care children, when compared with the same factors operating on children being kept at home. From the point of view of this approach, it is in fact the family-environmental ecology to which children were exposed prior to contact with the day care center, rather than experience at the day care center itself, that may be responsible for their greater vulnerability under conditions of group care.

Many questions remain unanswered, leaving both the notion of the "negative effects hypothesis" and the "no-effect hypothesis" equally plausible.

This controversy has certainly paved the way for potentially more sophisticated, ecologically based studies to be carried out in the future.

Most of the research addressing this controversy has been conducted in the United States. The discussion would be enriched by information generated in a country such as Israel, where the modal attachment insecure group is different from that observed in the United States of America (i.e., the ambivalent insecure versus the avoidant insecure). Fein and Fox (1988) have suggested that for methodological reasons it would be advantageous to carry out studies on early infant day care in nations where the day care system is more homogeneous, since the broad spectrum of day care styles characteristic of the United States may not yield strong effects for program quality. At one end of the spectrum, studies such as those conducted in Sweden may illuminate the issue from the point of view of a nation where the provision of quality infant care has been put forward as a clear-cut public policy. At the other end, it would be also informative to consider societies where, although infant care is provided as a basic service, there is inadequate concern with the emotional quality of such care. Israel serves as a case in point to illustrate this latter condition.

SOME DEMOGRAPHIC INFORMATION

The population of Israel has nearly doubled in the past 30 years, from about 1.9 million inhabitants in 1961 to about 3.7 million in 1989. About 90 percent of all Israelis live in urban settings, a percentage that has remained constant over time. Of the urban dwellers, somewhat more than half live in cities with more than 100,000 inhabitants. More than 80 percent of the families living in the rural areas occupy either cooperative settlements of individual farms (Moshavim) or collective settlements (Kibbutzim).

Israeli society, like that of other industrialized countries, is characterized by substantial growth in the percentage of working women and mothers. For example, in 1967, 1970, 1980, and 1989 the female population participating in the labor market consisted of approximately 25 percent, 27 percent, 39 percent, and 47 percent, respectively. Mothers with children under the age of one do not deviate from this trend. Here too there is an increase, from 21 percent in 1970 to 52 percent in 1989. Thus, being a mother of young children is gradually becoming less critical in the decision to assume a paid-work responsibility.

Whereas the demographic trends in Israel are consistent with those observed in other countries, Israeli society exhibits unique socio-cultural features to be considered when discussing child care issues. Israelis, for the most part, place heavy emphasis on the centrality of the family and the welfare of children. The Holocaust experience has caused many survivor parents to overprotect their offspring as a way of compensating for their own childhood deprivations and for ensuring the survival of their children.

This conviction, however, seems to be perceived rather than real in the present-day context.

In light of this, and given the nation's need to encourage more mothers of young children to participate in the labor market, one would expect that a more genuine interest would be shown by policy makers in the establishment of quality non-maternal care programs. Along the same lines, heightened parental involvement in the application of various early education programs, including day care centers, also would be expected. However, close study of the facts reveals a somewhat different picture of both public policy and parental involvement; that is, there seems to be a discrepancy between the perceived conviction and the actual performance and policy regarding the scope of services for families and children in Israel. This discrepancy can be understood, in part, in its historical context.

HISTORY OF DAY CARE IN ISRAEL

The early immigration to Israel was made up primarily of young people who left their countries of origin for the purpose of founding a new society. Although they wanted their children to be "non-Diaspora" new Israelis, the majority of these early settlers did not yet themselves speak Hebrew and were still influenced by attitudes formed in the Diaspora (pre-Israel communities outside Palestine), so they tended to regard the figure of the educator as representing a major sociological model for their children. Yet they did not really examine the exact nature of the educational curriculum that was provided to their children. Because of the many economic problems they faced, the principal concern at the time in establishing day care centers was to free mothers to work outside the home. Thus the day care centers that were established by women's voluntary groups during the early years of settlement in Israel developed as a branch of the welfare system of the country (together with services for orphaned children), as a measure for offering shelter to needy children or to children of working mothers. Day care centers in Israel developed without genuine reference to educational ideology. They developed as a response to the requirements of parents to be free to go to work, rather than answering to the needs of children.

During the 1950s, with the influx of immigrants, the function of day care expanded. More public attention was directed to the fact that in many communities of immigrants there was a growing number of children who did not receive sufficient parental care. The voluntary women's organizations, which still held exclusive responsibility for developing group care arrangements, responded by providing better nutritional and physical ecologies for the children. Another aim, albeit less emphasized at the time, was to help young children integrate into Israeli society. Prior to the establishment of the State of Israel (1948), education in the country was in the hands of the community. Following independence, education became a public matter under state management and legislation. The Compulsory Education Law (September 1949) applies to children of five years of age and over. Children were sent to school from the age of six. However, it was decided to implement the law in regard to children from the age of five, so that youngsters whose immigrant parents spoke no Hebrew and did not bring up their children according to modern educational values would be prepared to meet the requirements in the nation's schools. Even so, gaps between the various groups in the population still remained, and there was a growing awareness of the need for longer periods of preparation for immigrant children, so that they might be ready to take their place successfully in the educational system. This policy of integration, in conjunction with a growing consciousness of the importance that the early childhood years have for intellectual development, resulted in the extension of the country's preschool educational system to include children aged three to five years.

During the 1970s this latter trend received increased attention when the government became more involved in the establishment of day care centers. This change was the result of governmental concern about the deepening of social gaps and the intergenerational transmission of poverty. Thus, appropriate preventive measures were taken to compensate for developmental deprivations of children during their first years of life.

Policy makers believed that immigrants were unable to meet the basic social and cultural needs of the new society, and that it was therefore the role of public agencies to take an active part in the acculturation process. Consequently, more funds were allocated to establish day care centers. Also, in the 1970s a governmental interest in the reduction of social service consumption increased. It was believed that by enabling more women to become active members of the labor force, fewer families would be dependent on the welfare system. The establishment of more day care centers was seen as an indirect method to achieve this end.

It should be noted that an important impetus to this development was provided by the social events, taking place mainly in Jerusalem, known as the "Black Panthers" movement. These Black Panthers were Sephardic Jews, immigrants from Islamic countries, who felt that Israeli society had neglected their successful integration.

Among a number of social acts the government had taken at that time was the building of a large number of day care facilities throughout the country. To this end, the Ministry of Labor offered financial support and equipment to the women's organizations that were then still running such facilities. The ministry also offered to pay two thirds of the cost of maintaining the children that had been referred to day care centers by welfare agencies. The declared aim of the day care centers continued to be that of preparing problematic children and of giving assistance in cases of family deprivation, as part of the effort to close the social gaps. A survey undertaken in 1971 revealed that 73.3 percent of the caregivers and supervisors at day care centers in the country had no professional qualifications. These day care personnel were therefore hard put to implement the declared goals of these facilities. Despite the essentially educational idea underlying the policy of correcting and compensating for shortcomings in children's early years, in order to reduce to a minimum a child's inadequacies in dealing with the school system, it appears that no rigorous examination was made regarding the educational strategy by which these goals were to be achieved. Thus, in practical terms, the main goal of day care remained that of freeing mothers for work outside the home.

Nevertheless, because day care centers were perceived as being vital, considerable budgetary investment was applied toward their development. However, most of these resources were invested in building facilities rather than in the children themselves. The aim originally was for the Ministry of Education eventually to take over responsibility for the whole enterprise. But for political considerations, authority in the matter was distributed among three ministries: Education, Labor, and Welfare. The Education Ministry assumed responsibility for the day care of children older than three, and the Ministries of Labor and Welfare (which had at the time been joined under a single administration) took on the job of attending to the day care of children younger than three. This situation is still in force. Government policy remains to leave the organization, administration, and maintenance of day care centers in the hands of women's organizations and to encourage and extend financial support to them so that they can expand their activities.

The fact that most day care centers are being operated by women's organizations adds another function, though not necessarily a child-focused one. As already noted, it has been always stated that as many women as possible should be assisted in liberating themselves by means of entering the labor force, thereby strengthening their economic independence. It is not surprising, therefore, that the criteria for admission to day care centers are maternally oriented. Perhaps one of the best illustrations of this tendency is that centers adjacent to large factories and public institutions are made available mostly to children of female rather than male employees.

The increased availability and visibility of day care facilities and the government subsidy making day care settings a relatively inexpensive service, coupled with the normative social value placed in Israel on the promotion of early peer interaction, all caused as a by-product the popularization of infant day care among a growing number of middle-class families, who began to consider it a viable solution for their needs.

In sum, although day care centers in Israel were established with commendable aims in mind, they have not succeeded in achieving a sufficiently high qualitative level of service. The majority of personnel are still without professional education, although some supplementary training that might better qualify them for the job is currently being provided. A gap has developed between services offered by the Ministry of Education for the education of three to five year olds, and services supplied by the Ministry of Labor and Welfare for day care for children under the age of three. Rosenthal (1992) has proposed that this gap may have resulted as a consequence of the differing social aims of the systems. Kindergartens are conceived of as fulfilling a national purpose; namely, the closure of social and educational gaps between different social groups. These institutions have therefore received substantial budgets for their operation and a considerable allotment of resources. Day care centers, on the other hand, were perceived as furnishing a service to families in need and assisting working mothers, rather than being dedicated to a broad educational enterprise of national significance. For this reason, although some priority has been given to a number of day care centers in the country, neither their quality nor the needs of the children they service have received major attention. Many needy sectors in the country's population require budgetary consideration, and in the competition for resources, the needs of day care centers have not necessarily received very high preference in this regard.

DAY CARE CENTERS IN THE 1990s

There are about 1,000 day care centers in Israel today, most of them operated by women's organizations. The largest organization is NAAMAT (Voluntary Working Women), accounting for approximately 65 percent of the facilities. This is a section in the General Workers' Union, and it replaced the Union of Working Mothers that had founded the first day care centers. The second largest organization is WIZO (Women International Zionist Organization) accounting for approximately 30 percent of the centers. Last, EMUNA is a religious women's organization, responsible for the remaining 5 percent.[1] It should be noted that there are also private day care centers, as well as settings run by local authorities, although there are relatively few. About 970 day care centers were in operation in 1988 and served approximately 55,000 children, representing 19 percent of the total population of children in this age group. Of these, 41,000 were the children of working mothers, and 14,000 were from disadvantaged families and referred to day care by welfare services. We have no additional statistical data regarding the proportion of children at municipal and rural day care centers because the women's organizations do not publish their figures in monthly statistical reports.

Financing and Regulation

Since day care centers have become popular and in high demand, every center has to set aside 25 percent of its places for welfare families. The cost of operation is shared by the organization and the parents, 22 percent to 78 percent respectively. The portion paid by the parents is the actual full tuition fee, which is approximately $325 per month. Each year the Ministry of Labor and Welfare determines the level of subsidy provided to families defined as in economic need, based on the average income in the labor market. These families receive partial support according to income. It is interesting to note that not until recently was the woman's income taken into consideration, and it is only since the 1980s that the entire family's income has been considered. Also, the level of payment for day care is determined by type of neighborhood, family size, developmental problems of the child, mother's employment (with preferential treatment being given to mothers employed in industry), hours at the workplace, and years of residence in the country. So mothers who reside in a good neighborhood, receive a reasonable salary, whose children are in good health, and who neither work in industry nor are recent immigrants are expected to pay the full cost of day care.

At the present time, despite increased governmental involvement in day care financing, these programs have remained the traditional domain of women's organizations, and they are not based on any universal policy or social legislation. This is reflected in the fact that the only legislation pertaining to day care centers is concerned with ensuring their physical conditions, primarily prescribing the conditions for registration and licensing, without reference whatsoever to issues of caregiver training, supervision, and the like.

By law, moreover, the operation of a day care center is licensed by the Minister of Labor and Welfare. And since it is the case that until the 1988 school year the ministry had not made the operation of day care centers conditional on the receipt of a license, in effect all day care facilities in the country have been operating without licensing. Few inspections of day care centers are undertaken by the ministry, and when these are carried out they follow no consistent pre-established plan. Nor do local officials submit detailed reports to the ministry about the results of such inspections or recommend measures to correct irregularities, to the extent that such may have been observed. More rigorous inspection is indeed plainly called for, based on the serious irregularities uncovered in samples from a survey conducted by the Labor Ministry in 1987. For instance, on receipt of funds from the Labor Ministry's development budget, the women's organizations are under an obligation to apply the money toward the purchase of equipment and the maintenance and repair of day care facilities. However, the ministry makes no effort to verify that these funds have actually been used for the purposes for which they have been designated. The same absence of supervision is evident in that the women's organizations at times require money from parents in addition to a registration fee and monthly attendance fees. Such additional payments are justified to the parents on the grounds that they are needed to purchase equipment and maintain the facility, although these expenses are supposedly covered by the ordinary fees that have been collected. The Ministry of Labor has taken no steps under its own initiative to identify these day care centers, nor has it taken any measures against those centers that have been found to charge additional fees.

Societal Attitudes and Beliefs

Regarding the needs of the child beyond mere physical necessities, the stated goals as described by officials in these organizations (as well as by parents) are the facilitation of linguistic skills and a stable and well organized daily routine, including the acquisition of social manners and socially adjusted behaviors. It is strongly believed that infants can benefit from extended social interaction with their peers. Although compulsory education in Israel begins at age four, many children in the two- to four-year age range have been integrated into the educational system. Because Israelis favor introducing children into the school system at a very early age, the Ministry of Education has set aside increasing resources for infant education. As an example of the importance that Israeli parents assign to their children being in a group context even during their infant years, we cite the case of a group of parents wishing to enroll their children at a new private day care center and who applied to us for advice concerning the establishment of such a facility. In our conversation with the group, they explained that the particular facility they had in mind offered more flexible hours, laundry service, more meals, and a larger variety of modern games than other day care centers. For all these services, parents would pay a monthly fee equal to the amount that would otherwise be spent for a private caregiver at home. The parents maintained, however, that they were intent that their children (who were aged only 12 to 15 months) should be in a group setting in which they could play with children of their own age. This incident well illustrates social norms in Israel. These seem to be the central themes in guiding the actual performance in the center, although we do not have as yet systematic empirical data regarding this issue.

It appears, then, that day care centers, as a service for middle-class communities, perceive their role as strengthening the intellectual and interpersonal capacities and pay little attention to intimate emotional dimensions. As a result, notwithstanding the declared enrichment goals of day care centers, these institutions have no systematic educational programs. The preeminent concern remains the needs of parents rather than the needs of children. This is made particularly evident by the decision in 1980 to cut budgetary allotments to day care centers. The committee that took part in the decision, as well as the representatives of parents, preferred to see an increase in the number of children per group, so that attendance fees should remain unchanged. This decision accords with the general approach of opening additional day care centers (quantitative criterion) rather than improving already existing facilities (qualitative criterion).

Many of the supervisors at the middle- and high-management levels believe that day care centers are the optimal service available to children of working mothers. They hold that compared with home-based non-professional care on a one-to-one relationship basis, group care is monitored by extensive supervision and professional guidance. While this might partially be the case, it is not clear whether intimate emotional aspects of development receive adequate attention.

Quality of Care

Very few studies have been conducted in Israel on the quality of care at day care centers. Since the 1971 survey, the women's organizations have established a guidance plan. Although they make efforts to implement it regularly, in reality it is not being practiced very frequently. In any event, no systematic training program has as yet been developed in this regard, and available funds are invested in equipment rather than in the training of staff. We observed earlier that the Ministry of Education, which oversees the education of children over age three, ensures that kindergarten teachers are qualified for the job. This effectively means that infants are subject to the risk of poor quality care.

Caregiver Qualifications. Infant care providers, according to their "job descriptions," should be warm, sensitive, and loving persons. It is not evident what measures are indeed employed to ensure these standards. As a rule, all care providers are expected to be mothers themselves, with a minimum of ten years of formal education. They are irregularly exposed to in-service training and workshops, primarily focusing on various aspects of early education, religious holidays, first aid, nutrition, and personal hygiene. Although there is an early education component built into these activities, emotional development seems to be inadequately covered. To deal with the problem, teachers' colleges today have undertaken to qualify kindergarten teachers for dealing with the newborn to three-year-old group. However, graduates of teachers' colleges are generally not employed at day care centers because of the poor working conditions at these facilities. Thus low salaries, large groups of children, inadequate training, and unqualified personnel combine to negatively influence the quality of day care service, in particular that of infants.

Stability of Caregivers. Another important dimension of care is the stability of caregivers in their job. The wages of care providers are relatively low and caregiving is considered a low-prestige activity. Nevertheless, there is a relatively high stability of care providers. As of today, about 80 percent are in their present positions between eight and ten years. In the absence of systematic data, it would be premature to determine what might be the best correlates associated with this stability. The leaders of the organizations maintain that they have been able to recruit warm and loving individuals who, despite their low income and prestige, enjoy their work. Thus they attribute the stability to this satisfaction. An alternative explanation would be that this is a relatively weak, unskilled group of women who prefer to maintain their tenure, hence securing a stable income, albeit small, rather than seeking other jobs that might not necessarily result in a better income and social benefits.

Caregiver-Child Ratio. Although there are differences between the NAA-MAT and WIZO systems in the formula used to establish ratios of children per caregiver, the average ratio is eight to one. In practice, a group may consist of 16 to 25 infants, and thus most children are cared for by two to three caregivers during any given day. Although the socio-emotional implications of being cared for by two to three primary caregivers, in addition to the parents, need to receive further attention, it appears that the adult-infant ratios are less than optimal. Also, the formation of "classes" of infants causes in reality each of the caregivers to be responsible for more than eight infants. Therefore, one of the most noticeable results is a setting in which custodial care seems to dominate.

Research findings by Ricciuti (1977) indicate that for children under the age of two, the optimal ratio of caregiver to children is between one to three and one to five, and that for children three to five years old, the ratio should not exceed one to six. The evidence indicates that infant caregivers are more responsive when dealing with smaller groups of children. Ruopp and Travis (1982) found that when working with larger groups of children, caregivers are preoccupied with supervision. They also suggest that the more children a caregiver has in her charge, the greater the emotional distress experienced by the children. Size of setting has an impact as well. For example, it has been found that at day care centers serving more than 60 children, greater attention is given to overseeing behavior than to encouraging positive interpersonal relationships. When these aspects are considered in the Israeli context, we find that according to the standards set in 1984 by a committee made up of representatives of the Ministry of Labor and Welfare, the Finance Ministry, and the women's organizations, day care centers must meet the requirements of having four classes, a staff size of 11.75 staff positions, and a total of 99 children. Due to the size of such facilities and the large number of children cared for in them, Israeli day care centers are more likely to be concerned primarily with supervision.

As if this were not serious enough, a 1987 survey of 200 day care centers throughout the country revealed that in many of these facilities the staff was much smaller and the number of children in attendance was greater than is required by ministry standards. The level of care furnished by the staff failed to meet the requirements as well, since caregivers were unlicensed professionally, in violation of official standards. A number of examples will convey the extent of deviation from official criteria. For instance, in the case of the aged-two and under group, deviations from the standard ranged as high as 73 percent. Thus in classes for which the standard allows up to 22 children per class, as many as 38 children were found. For groups up to the age of three, the standard allows 27 children per group. However, many instances were found of groups consisting of 36 children. And where the standard permits only up to 15 infants, there were cases of 19 to 21 infants to a group. The Office of the Controller issued warnings to those programs. However, the controller's report furnishes no documentary evidence of any measures instituted by the Ministry of Labor to correct the violations found by the survey. Careful analysis reveals that the number of personnel employed fell below the requirements of the government standard, thus enabling the women's organizations to pay staff more than the standard wage. Although raising the pay of day care staff is certainly important, in this case it was done at the expense of the children and of the quality of care.

Group Size. Obviously custodial care is not only the result of undesirable infant-adult ratios. The size of the child group is a major variable in defining the quality of day care. Staff dealing with small groups can respond personally to each child, identify a child's individual needs and respond to a child's signals rapidly and efficiently. Travers and Ruopp (1978) suggest that for children under the age of eighteen months, the optimal group size should not exceed eight infants, and for children under the age of three years the number should not exceed 12 for one group. As already noted, the size of most groups in the Israeli day care system does exceed these numbers. In the case of these large groups, opportunities to devote optimal attention to each child are highly circumscribed. Quite apart from the fact that groups under day care are not at optimal size, a special problem is posed by the organization of work at day care facilities, the effect of which is to force children and staff to remain in such large groups throughout most of the day.

Caregiver Training and Supervision. Of major importance as well is the training of caregivers. There is general agreement that merely having a warm personality is insufficient to ensure the quality of care given to a child. The years of education accumulated by a caregiver are a major factor in determining the quality of care received by children over the age of three. As noted, it is indeed the case that only qualified personnel are given the responsibility for children in this age group. With respect to infants and toddlers, the factor that particularly affects the quality of care is staff training designed to meet the specific demands of the job, as well as supervision and guidance in the course of work. Rosenthal (1990) found that caregivers in Israeli family day care who received personal supervision once a week spent more time in developmental interaction with the children under their charge, were more successful in generating a feeling of security in the child, and were more amenable to providing an educational environment for the child.

A committee has been established, at the initiative of the Fund for Equal

Opportunities, whose purpose is to set standards for care. Difficulties have been put in the way of realizing this goal. The Ministry of Finance objects to the requirement for training of caretaking staff, on the grounds that raising professional levels may result in demands for higher pay. Moreover, with the Ministry of Education confining itself to the needs of children over three years of age, and qualified kindergarten teachers staying out of the day care system, the infant population at day care centers is at the greatest disadvantage among day care children in terms of receiving quality care.

In sum, various correlates—including the basic rationale for establishing infant day care programs, the stated goals, the background of the care providers, the attitudes of the organization as well as those of parents—all seem to affect the nature of care provided. The evidence (based on good anecdotal observations, albeit insufficiently researched) indicates that the daily routine is quite hectic, consisting primarily of custodial care, with minimal attention to the emotional needs of the children.

As stated earlier, parents do not emphasize the emotional component of child care and do not appear to be highly involved in other segments of the educational system either. Despite liberal legislation that allows Israeli parents to determine approximately 30 percent of the structure and content of the elementary and high school curriculum, parents do not seem to take advantage of this powerful mechanism to influence the educational welfare of their own children. Rather, they prefer to assume that all educational needs of their offspring are properly handled by the educational system. Clearly, this observation applies to school education and seems to reflect some parental indifference regarding the quality of care provided to their children. If this can be generalized to preschool education, which we believe is indeed the case, the implications for the welfare of very young children might even be of more concern because of the emotional component that is so emphasized in the child development literature. At a minimum, parents should determine whether custodial care is properly performed. Many parents enroll their infants in day care centers without even visiting these settings prior to enrollment. Based on caregivers' reports, mothers often inquire whether their infants have eaten or slept well, but very seldom do they ask questions about their infants' emotional adaptation and reaction to the center.

THE FORMAL EDUCATION SYSTEM

Thus far, we have focused primarily on children from birth to three years old. We have also specified the differences between the educational programs for infants and older children. It should be recalled that the day care system in Israel is not part of the formal public education program. However, some familiarity with public education in Israel can assist the reader in understanding the day care system itself.

Table 14.1 shows the numbers and percentages of Israeli children attending nurseries and kindergartens. About 75 percent of two year olds are using these facilities. This is a relatively high rate of attendance, but many of these facilities are private rather than public. A rather sharp increase is noticeable for children ages three and four. Almost this entire population is using public facilities.

The preschool public system (three to five years of age) is organized around a half-day schedule, with between 30 and 35 children to a nursery school class and sufficient space, games, and teaching aids. All nursery school teachers are licensed and have an unlicensed assistant at their side. The system is administered and supervised by the Ministry of Education, which is responsible for qualifying the personnel, setting the curriculum, directing the program, and paying the salaries of the staff. Programming is principally addressed to improving intellectual skills. Private nurseries operate in parallel with the public system. The teachers employed in them are qualified as well and work under the supervision and control of the Education Ministry. This is also the situation in nursery school classes at day care centers. The day care system for children over the age of three is thus well organized and follows a well-defined plan, although the emphasis continues to be on the cognitive aspects of development and the preparation of children for school, whereas the socio-emotional aspects are relatively neglected.

As regards the formal educational system for school-age children (over five years old), its curriculum is also based on a half-day schedule. Kindergarten and elementary school classes are active for an average of four and a half hours per day, with the number of hours increasing to six per day at the high-school level. This circumstance constrains mothers to work at part-time jobs or to look for alternative arrangements for the care of their children in the afternoon. The latter alternative is usually arranged by hiring private caregivers. In rural settlements, learning facilities exist for children during after-school hours, where for an additional fee paid to the local authority, children can prepare their school work under a teacher's supervision or take part in other extra-curricular activities. In other areas one-hour extra-curricula activity periods are provided by the local authority. Thus all children over the age of three enjoy the advantages of an organized educational framework.

It should be noted that 87 percent of children at day care centers are under three years of age and therefore do not enjoy the supervision and planning furnished by the Ministry of Education. Thus as already suggested, the infant population appears to be the most exposed to the risk of not receiving qualitative treatment. Today the Education Ministry contains a branch with jurisdiction over infant education that corresponds to the branch that oversees compulsory education. In recent Ministry of Education publications the years from birth to six years old are defined as preschool age. This would indicate a commitment on the part of the ministry to attend

Table 14.1
Children in Kindergartens,* by Children's Age and Origin (Absolute Numbers and Percent of Population)

	1976/77		1988/89**	
	Asia-Africa Origin	Total	Asia-Africa Origin	Total
AGE 2: Total	12,200 (39%)	34,400 (49%)	11,500 (67%)	56,300 (75%)
public kindergartens	5,300	6,900	8,700	33,300
private kindergartens	6,900	21,500	2,800	23,000
AGE 3: Total	24,700 (79%)	57,100 (86%)	16,600 (93%)	72,700 (96%)
public kindergartens	15,400	29,100	14,300	56,400
private kindergartens	9,300	28,000	2,100	16,300
AGE 4: Total	29,900 (95%)	62,400 (96%)	18,100 (97%)	73,300 (99%)
public kindergartens	27,100	54,300	18,100	70,700
private kindergartens	2,800	8,100		2,600
AGE: 5***	31,300	63,800	18,600	71,300

*   Incl. day nurseries

**   Among Non-Jewish population attended kindergarten in 1988-89: About 25% of age 3, about 53% of age 4, and about 85% (an estimate) of age 5 - altogether about 40,400 Children.

*** Most attended public municipal kindergartens.

to the needs of an age group that was earlier regarded as being outside the ministry's active scope. This is a positive development; however, this new policy is still not well organized and systematized. Attention and funding have yet to shift to meet the needs of day care children and staff.

DAY CARE IN THE KIBBUTZ SYSTEM

In contrast to the day care system in its current state, which may fail to meet basic standards of quality care, especially for infants, a day care system has evolved at kibbutzim that furnishes better care in terms of group size, adult-child ratio, staff qualifications, and suitability of equipment. The kibbutz is no longer a new phenomenon to sociological and psychological research. Its uses as a natural laboratory for research in these fields have been discussed by Beit-Hallahmi and Rabin (1977). Each kibbutz is a cooperative community with an average of about 100 families in residence. Kibbutz members, both men and women, work in agricultural and industrial enterprises belonging to the kibbutz. The profits belong to the kibbutz as a whole, and members are provided with living facilities, food, clothing, and other necessities and services on an equal basis.

In all kibbutzim, women return to work six weeks after the birth of a child and the newborn is placed in the kibbutz "Infant House." Note the difference in terminology. In towns children are put into day care centers, whereas at a kibbutz the corresponding institution is given a name that implies that it is an actual home for the child. Such is the kibbutz perspective, and such is the experience of kibbutz children as well. This is not a setting where children merely attend, but rather a home in which they live.

When the first kibbutzim were established, their founding members aspired to build a new society, different from that in the Diaspora where they had formerly lived. One of the features of change concerned sleeping arrangements. Along with the ideological transformation, changes of an ecological nature also developed that influenced attitudes toward sleeping arrangements for children. Because both the parents worked in places at a great distance from their living quarters, often rising very early to begin their labors, arrangements had to be made for the care of the children during the long hours that the parents were at work. In response to the collectivist ideology and the need for infants to be cared for in the absence of their parents, kibbutz babies were together with their parents only between the hours of 4:00 p.m. and 8:00 p.m. Education was an issue of major concern to the kibbutz movement, and kibbutzim devoted a great deal of thought and considerable resources to the creation of a physical and educational infrastructure of the very highest quality. So when we consider the institution of the kibbutz Infant House in its present form, we are in fact dealing with a setting that perhaps offers the best quality of care in the country and that meets the criteria for optimal infant care.

There have been recent changes in kibbutzim regarding the division of child-rearing labor between Infant House and family home. There are a few kibbutzim in the country at which children still sleep at Infant Houses, away from their parents. But there is a general tendency to return to the family model. While a consideration of all the aspects of the changeover from common sleeping arrangements to sleeping with parents would be beyond the scope of this chapter, it should be noted that where children sleep with their parents, their total time at the kibbutz facility is from 7:00 A.M. until 4:00 P.M. Following this, the children return to the family home. This current arrangement at kibbutzim therefore allows us to observe quality day care in a family setting. However, even this type of kibbutz day care services differs in a number of qualitative aspects from the sort found in towns.

The kibbutz "Infant House" physically consists of two bedrooms, each designed to hold three infants. Each child has its own bed and its own toys, together with a cupboard for personal effects. This arrangement gives each child sufficient private space and an area for making contact with peers. This differs from the arrangement of urban day care centers, where there is a large roomy hall with an eating area, a playing area, and a sleeping area with beds packed close to one another and no personal space for each individual child. Adjoining the bedrooms of the kibbutz facility there is a kitchen and dining room designed to receive all six children and their caregivers. In addition, there is also a playroom designed for games both in and out of doors, which is equipped with a large variety of playthings. The same equipment is found in ordinary day care centers but there is used by a far greater number of children.

During the day, children are cared for both physically and educationally by the child caregiver (Hebrew: s. "metapelet," pl. "metaplot") and the teachers of the kibbutz. Because the metaplot are also members of the kibbutz, they feel more committed to the children, and therefore try to express more warmth and more nurturing in their relations with them than do their urban counterparts, who work in exchange for a salary. Very possibly the difference has to do also with the fact that kibbutzim prefer metaplot to be mothers themselves. This is also the case in urban day care centers, but in the kibbutzim this is seen as motivating metaplot better, since their own children are being looked after by caregivers who are mothers as well. However, this idea is not always put into practice in kibbutzim, where the position is not regarded as carrying very much prestige, so that kibbutz women tend to shy away from doing such work. Increasingly, therefore, the job is being done by young women in the kibbutz who are as yet unmarried and without children, or by volunteer kibbutz guest workers from abroad. Although this situation does create some problems, the kibbutz staff of caregivers remains on the whole quite stable. We noted that staff turnover in urban day care centers, too, is minimal. But this similar circumstance results from different causes. In the case of kibbutzim, the economic reasons accounting for urban caregivers holding on to their jobs do not apply, and kibbutz metaplot have alternative options for work that their urban counterparts do not. There is reason to assume, therefore, that stability on the job in kibbutzim may derive from factors having to do with qualitative concerns and with job motivation.

The size of the group in kibbutzim is smaller than at urban day care facilities (1:3). Moreover the Infants' House is located inside the kibbutz, which makes the children's parents more accessible than in towns. The kibbutz arrangement for children therefore coincides with Etaugh's (1980) proposal that the family day care center represents a better solution to the problem of supplementary care. Indeed, the findings of recent research by the author and colleagues (1990) on the quality of child care arrangements at kibbutzim reveal their positive emotional and social effects on kibbutz children.

Reference was made earlier to Belsky's (1988, 1990) concern for the developmental risks to which children are exposed when remaining for long periods at a child care facility during the early years of their lives. Kibbutz infants would seem to fall into this category, since they are placed in child care facilities as early as their sixth week of life and remain there for about 50 hours per week. The quality of care was found to be the same both at kibbutzim where common sleeping arrangements are the norm and at kibbutzim where the child sleeps at home. However, our findings (1990) suggest that the incidence of infant-mother attachment insecurity is higher at those kibbutzim in which common sleeping arrangements are the rule (family sleeping arrangements: 20 percent insecure-attachment versus 80 percent secure; common sleeping arrangements; 48 percent insecure attachment versus 52 percent secure). In other words, greater vulnerability to infant-mother insecure attachment relationships in kibbutz children was not the result of their being kept at a day care facility, but depended on whether sleeping arrangements were at the "Infant House" or in the parents' home.

The conclusion that we reach in this connection relies on the early background hypothesis set out at the beginning of this chapter. In the case of infants younger than one year of age placed at a day care center offering good quality care, no negative effects in terms of attachment insecurity are found, even if the infant is left at the setting for long periods of the day. The data in this regard do not necessarily contradict the conclusions of Belsky, who was primarily concerned with non-optimal day care facilities. He maintains that for facilities offering lower quality care, the variable of child's age may be considered one determinant of the level of vulnerability to attachment insecurity effects (Belsky, personal communication). If the day care facility offers a low quality of care, it can trigger attachment insecurity in a child who comes from a vulnerable environment. Possibly such children are more sensitive to poor quality group care than are children whose relationship with their parents at home is receptive and warm. Indeed the recent data collection on day care facilities offering a high quality of care both in Sweden and in kibbutzim reveal no negative influences on the child.

It is worth noting that kibbutzim today have begun to make their day care facilities available to the residents of towns, and the response on the part of the public has been significant enough for the effects already to be felt in lower registration figures at urban day care centers. The competition may be positive. But the situation may also develop into one in which two levels of quality of day care will be offered: high level day care, available to those children whose parents can afford to pay the fees charged by kibbutzim; and low level care, for children from less advantaged families. In that way Israel may come to resemble those countries where there is no homogeneity in the quality of day care.

CONCLUSION

A widespread increase in the use of day care centers is currently under way in Israel. As more and more mothers are entering the work force, the need to place their young children in some kind of care arrangements has become an accepted and common phenomenon. Day care centers provide care for children for eight to nine hours each day and are only in part government supervised. Although in the past, day care was almost the exclusive realm of disadvantaged families, today it is also provided in large factories, hospitals, and universities. This allows mothers to work full time and feel at ease knowing that their children are being cared for in some kind of educational framework. Thus, day care centers provide an answer to the needs of mothers from all strata of Israeli society.

However, it is not clear to what extent the needs of the infants themselves are being sufficiently considered. In this respect there seems to be a discrepancy between stated concern and the actual performance regarding the centrality of the child among the various daily priorities of a turbulent society like Israel. Although most Israeli parents are certainly eager to provide the best for their children, the actual outcome may be somewhat different. Economic, social, and security constraints seem to play a dominant role, leaving insufficient time, energy, and motivation to more carefully check the quality of the service provided. Paradoxically, there seems to be a reduced emotional availability and accessibility in the face of real concern for precisely these social-emotional investments.

Consequently, the outcome may well be the transmission of ambivalent parental feelings. Inadequate attention to the emotional needs of children at the policy level, coupled with insufficient parental involvement in promoting the emotional quality of care, may contribute to what might be conceived of as an emotionally low-quality day care system for Israeli infants and toddlers.

Irrespective of this concern, day care is a service very much in demand, and it might well be assumed that this trend will continue in the future. The major question that presently needs to be addressed by decision makers at the policy and educational levels concerns the quality and standards of day care, and not whether it is good or bad for child development. Therefore, we must turn our efforts to improving day care at all levels of implementation. A general plan should be formulated for the proper training and supervision of caregivers, focusing on both cognitive and emotional aspects of the children under their care.

NOTE

1. There are some additional organizations operating infant day care programs, but their number is marginal.

REFERENCES

Ainsworth, M.D.S. (1985). "Patterns of infant-mother attachments: Antecedents and effects on development." *Bulletin of the New York Academy of Medicine, 61,* 771–791.

Ainsworth, M.D.S., Blehar, M. C., Waters, E., and Wall, S. (1978). *Patterns of attachment: A psychological study of the strange situation.* Hillsdale, N.J.: Erlbaum.

Anderson, B. E. (1992). "The effects of day care on cognitive and socio-emotional competence in 13-year-old Swedish children." *Child Development, 63,* 20–36.

Anderson, C. W., Nagle, R. J., Roberts,W. A., and Smith, J. W. (1981). "Attachment to substitute caregivers as a function of center quality and caregiver involvement." *Child Development, 52,* 53–61.

Barglow, P. (1985). "Other-than-mother, in-home care and the quality of the mother-child relationships." Paper presented at the biennial meeting of the Society for Research in Child Development, Toronto.

Barglow, P., Vaughn, B., and Molitor, N. (1987). "Effects of maternal absence due to employment on the quality of infant-mother attachment in a low-risk sample." *Child Development, 49,* 929–949.

Beit-Hallahmi, B., and Rabin, A. L. (1977). "The kibbutz as a social experiment and as a child-rearing laboratory." *American Psychologist, 32,* 532–541.

Belsky, J. (1988). "The effects of infant day-care reconsidered." *Early Childhood Research Quarterly, 3,* 235–272.

Belsky, J. (1990). "Parental and non-parental child care and children's socioemotional development: A decade in review." *Journal of Marriage and the Family, 51,* 885–903.

Belsky, J., and Rovine, M. (1988). "Non-maternal care in the first year of life and the security of infant-parent attachment." *Child Development, 59,* 157–167.

Belsky, J., and Steinberg, L. D. (1978). "The effects of day-care: A critical review." *Child Development, 49,* 929–949.

Blehar, M. C. (1974). "Anxious attachment and defensive reactions associated with daycare." *Child Development, 45,* 683–692.

Bowlby, J. (1982). *Attachment and loss: Vol. 1. Attachment* (2nd). New York: Basic Books.

Clarke-Stewart, K. A. (1983). "Interactions between mothers and their young children: Characteristics and consequences." *Monographs of the Society for Research in Child Development, 38* (607 Serial No. 153).

Cochran, M., and Robinson, J. (1983). "Daycare, family circumstances and sex differences in children." *Advances in Early Education and Day Care,* Vol. 3, pp. 47–67. JAI Press Inc.

Crouter, A. C., and Perry-Jankins, M. (1986). "Working it out: Effects of work on parents and children." In N. Yogman and T. B. Brazelton (Eds.), *In Support of Families.* Harvard University Press.

Etaugh, C. (1980). "Effects of nonmaterial care on children: Research evidence and popular views." *American Psychologist, 35,* 309–319.

Fein, G., and Fox, N. (1988). "Infant day-care: A societal issue." *Early Childhood Research Quarterly, 3,* 227–234.

Howes. C. (1983). "Caregivers' behaviors in center and family daycare." *Journal of Applied Psychology, 4,* 99–107.

Kontos, S. J. (in press). "Child care quality, family background, and children's development." *Child and Youth Care Quarterly.*

Kuggelmas, J., and Simoni, R. (May 1983). "A survey of the functioning and needs of Schwartz graduates working in group services for infants and toddlers." A report presented to the JDC-Israel, Jerusalem, The School of Social Work, Hebrew University.

Lamb, M. E., Hwang, C., Bookstein, F. L., Broberg, A., Hult, G., and Frodi, M. (1988). "Determinants of competence in Swedish preschoolers." *Developmental Psychology, 24,* 58–70.

Main, M. B., and Weston, D. R. (1981). "Security of attachment to mother and father: Related to conflict behavior and the readiness to establish new relationships." *Child Development, 52,* 932–940.

Prescott, E., Jones, E., and Kritchevsky, S. (1967). "Group daycare as a child rearing environment." *Final Report to Children's Bureau.* Pasadena, Calif., Pacific Oaks College.

Ricciuti, H. (1977). "Effects of infant daycare experience on behavior and development." *Policy Issues in Daycare.* U.S. Department of HEW.

Richters, J., and Zahn-Waxler, C. (1988). The infant day-care controversy in perspective: Current status and future directions." *Early Childhood Research Quarterly, 3,* 319–337.

Rosenthal, M. K. (1990). "Social policy and its effects on the daily experiences of infants and toddlers in family daycare in Israel." *Journal of Applied Developmental Psychology, 11,* 85–104.

Rosenthal, M. K. (1992). "The historical and cultural context for the development of daycare in Israel." In M. Lamb, K. Sternberg, C. P. Hwang, and A. Broberg (Eds.), *Daycare in context: Historical and cross-cultural perspectives.* Hillsdale, N.J.: Erlbaum.

Rosenthal, M. K., and Shimoni, R. (1985). "Criteria defining quality of care in daycare centers." *Society and Welfare, 6,* 147–160 (Hebrew).

Ruopp, R. R., and Travers, J. (1982). "Janus faces daycare: Perspectives on quality and cost." In E. F. Zigler and E. W. Gordon (Eds.), *Day care: Scientific and social policy issues*, pp. 72–101. Boston: Auburn House.

Rutter, M. (1981). "Social-emotional consequences of daycare for preschool children." *American Journal of Orthopsychiatry*, 51, 4–28.

Rutter, M. (1982). "Social-emotional consequences of daycare for preschool children." In E. F. Zigler and E. W. Gordon (Eds.), *Day care: Scientific and social policy issues*. Boston: Auburn House.

Sagi, A. (1990). "Attachment theory and research from a cross-cultural perspective." *Human Development*, 33, 10–22.

Sagi, A., Lamb, M. E., Lewkowicz, K. S., Shoham, R., Dvir, R., and Estes, D. (1985). "Security of infant-mother, -father, and -metapelet attachments among kibbutz-reared Israeli children." In I. Bretherton and E. Waters (Eds.), "Growing points in attachment theory and research." *Monographs of the Society for Research in Child Development*, 50, (1–2, Serial No. 209), 257–275.

Sagi, A., and Lewkowicz, K. S. (1987). "A cross-cultural evaluation of attachment research." In L.W. C. Tavecchio, and M. H. van Ijzendoorn (Eds.), *Attachment in Social Networks*, pp. 427–454. Amsterdam: Elsevier, North Holland.

─────── **15** ───────

ITALY

Rebecca S. New

Contemporary Italy distinguishes itself from other Western nations in a number of ways, not the least of which is a generally shared belief that the early education and care of young children is "a social responsibility, involving not only the parents, but the whole society," including both state and local governments (Moss, 1988). A nation once labeled as a "backward society," Italy now has pre-primary programs for all three- to five-year-old children in most communities.

With the goal of approaching an understanding of the socio-historical events, cultural values, and standards of child rearing that have contributed to the contemporary child care system in Italy, this chapter will draw upon several bodies of literature: anthropological studies of Italian families; historical treatments of family configurations, social relations, and patterns of child care; sociological studies of contemporary Italian households; and the burgeoning women's studies literature on the Italian feminist movement.

HISTORICAL AND CULTURAL FACTORS

While it is problematic at best to speak of Italy as having a singular cultural identity, given the historically strong emphasis on regional diversity, certain common denominators continue to surface in studies of contemporary Italian society that may be seen to play a role in the establishment, interpretation, and utilization of child care policies in Italy. Three key factors have been (1) the strength of kinship and family ties as a model for social relations, (2) the history of social policies and legislation aimed at defining women's rights and responsibilities, and (3) the (sometimes competing) roles of the state and the Roman Catholic Church in interpreting and providing for the period of early childhood. The continued presence of these features, in interaction with prevailing regional differences (in economics, family demographics, political and social attitudes), suggests that much of what is current in Italian child care reveals lessons and values drawn from its past.

While chroniclers typically refer to two major events as central to the evolution of Italy's child care system—the national unification that took place barely a century ago and the social upheaval that accompanied the contemporary Italian women's movement—the discussion will begin with a depiction of traditional Italian interpretations of the family, the roles of women, and the care of young children.

The Nature of the Family

While modern historians of the Italian family challenge much earlier work as uninformed and stereotypic, there is a general consensus that the concept of *patria potestas* (male head of household) describes the "fundamental institution underlying the structure of Roman society" (Lacey, 1986). The definition of *familia* included all of those dependent on the head of household, encompassing a range of quasi-familial relations. To some, the Roman state itself was a family. These features have continued to characterize the essence of Italian family life in subsequent centuries.

Throughout most of recorded Italian history, family journals, religious archives, notarial acts, and tax surveys combine to portray a society in which the strength of family ties has remained independent of family structure. Even though regional differences in economic development and family structure are well documented, and the gradual emergence of the nuclear family household in many parts of Italy has challenged the multi-family arrangement as the norm, the solidarity of the family "in its larger definition" (Klapisch-Zuber, 1985) has repeatedly been confirmed by economic and political historians. Concepts of *parenti, amici, vicini* (kinship, friendship, and neighborliness) have defined the parameters of social relations, referring to the many relatives and associates on whom an individual's well-being depended.

The Roles and Rights of Italian Women

The principle of *patria potestas* firmly established the state's limited view of women's lives, and Roman law emphasized that the primary purpose of marriage was to produce children. The Roman government offered a variety of incentives to encourage procreation, and Roman coinage promoted ideals of motherhood, one of which was the concept of *amor maternus* (motherly love). Yet there is evidence even in this early period of women's discontent over the narrowly conceived interpretations of their roles and legal rights; and the first recorded women's protest took place in 195 B.C.

Women's status has remained problematic throughout most of Italian history, in spite of growing acknowledgement of the importance of the maternal role fostered in the 13th-century Cult of Mary. Even as women were expected to devote themselves to child rearing, mothers' rights to their own children have often been limited. For example, a woman's in-laws were traditionally granted custody of children upon the death of her husband. The practice of wet-nursing, common throughout much of Italian history, was often orchestrated by men to allow for conjugal relations in a period in which it was believed that a new pregnancy would taint the mother's milk. Thus while a good mother was defined as one who would never abandon her children and would instead devote herself to their upbringing, the structures and strictures of the patrilineal society often compelled her to do otherwise.

Conceptions of Early Childhood

One measure of the value of children is the extent to which they are visible and differentiated in the remnants of any given society. Imagery of children is abundant in Italy, where ancient epitaphs and adoring *putti* adorn the façades of centuries-old architecture, and everywhere, it seems, examples of the Madonna and child compete with contemporary advertisements. Yet even as public records denote a modest investment on the part of the state in the procreation of children, there is also a marked ambivalence in state attitudes subsequent to birth. Infanticide and infant abandonment remained common throughout much of Italian history, often without legal sanctions.

The lack of attention to the plight of children is apparent in a variety of gruesome statistics associated with the Renaissance, even as experiences of childhood varied greatly according to sex and social rank. Amidst a high infant mortality rate, the practice of putting children out to nurse remained widespread. Children who survived the first years of life experienced a "brutal entry" into a society that exploited child labor.

Interest in the well-being of the very young infant, "so fragile that no one had dared consider him before" (Klapisch-Zuber, 1985, p. 113), was first sparked by the humanist movement. A new emphasis on the period of early childhood was reinforced by 14th- and 15th-century portrayals of the infant Jesus and the use of children in place of the traditional lame beggar in depictions of charity. Adults' more sympathetic view of childhood was apparent in the use of well-fed *putti* to adorn public buildings and the erection of the first official orphanages.

As social doctrines of primogeniture and *patria potestas* (which appeared in every statute prior to unification) continued to exclude women from familial succession and to drastically reduce their rights, church reforms at the Council of Trent had major consequences for the well-being of infants and young children. The sharpened distinction between wed and unwed mothers, seen as directly related to the transmission of property through male lineage, resulted in hidden pregnancies and the secret disposal of illegitimate children. Thus it is more painful than ironic that at the beginning of the 19th century infant abandonment was at its peak, with mortality rates so high that there was little difference between abandonment and infanticide. While the increase in abandonment was attributed to the rise in illegitimate births, poor mothers also placed children in orphanages, where they could receive care at the church's expense. Such practices, along with high overall infant mortality rates, attest to the difficulties of child-rearing in a society that included few means of actual support for mothers and children, especially those without the sanctity of marriage.

It was within this context that the first Italian attempt at early childhood education was launched. Motivated by the distressing circumstances of orphaned children, Ferrante Aporti opened his *askili carita* in 1831, since referred to by Pistillo (1989) as the "first modern Italian preschool." His methods made an impression on educators and garnered support for the concept of preprimary education. In the same period Giusepe Sacchi opened free facilities for children of working mothers, who were viewed as a more competitive labor force because they were paid less than men. As the proportion of women within the labor force increased, enlightened industrialists began to build child care facilities rather than submit to any regulation of female labor. In the meantime, however, public support for preschools declined.

From this abbreviated view of Italy's rich and tumultuous past, a picture emerges that reveals a continuity of Italian interpretations of the family and scant progress in elevating the status of women or improving the lot of young children.

Unification

Long after most countries in Western Europe had developed into coherent nation-states, Italy remained a "motley collection of kingdoms, principalities, duchies, city states, and dependencies" (Hellman, 1987, p. 9). By 1870 the unification process had joined groups of diverse social systems, cultures, and languages. Yet there was little comprehension among a majority of the people (74 percent of whom were illiterate) of being Italian at all.

An Italy united under Piedmontese rule was highly advantageous to the North, which quickly became an industrial power linked to the rest of Western Europe. In Central Italy, where the multiple-family household had reached its highest level, traditional forms of sharecropping were undermined by northern policies of fostering commercial agriculture, and class antagonism sharpened. These changes, enhanced by anti-clerical sentiments, enabled anarchism, socialism, and communism to set roots in Tuscany, Emilia, Romagnolo, and Umbria. In the feudal South, land-owning aristocracy joined forces with the industrialist North, leaving the most oppressive social and economic structures intact. Taxes and labor supported northern industrialization, and the South became even more peripheral to the national interest.

The reconciliation of different legal and cultural traditions in the various regions and the establishment of state power over the Church was daunting in a society undergoing such rapid socio-economic change. Much debate centered around family law; yet the status of women following unification was, in many respects, no better than before. The Pisanelli code, essentially the same as the Napoleonic code enacted earlier in the century (1804), limited *patria potestas* over adult offspring and offered equal entitlement of inheritance to sons and daughters. Yet the code actually increased the husband's control over economic and personal property and established the equivalence between familial and male honor and between male honor and the "moral" behavior of women. Thus while men in Italy were being transformed from subjects into citizens, the concept of "good wives and mothers" became the criteria for judging women of all classes.

By the close of the 19th century, Italy's high infant and child mortality was finally being defeated, although more slowly than in other countries in northern Europe. Fertility limitations were reducing the rates of abandoned infants. By this time Froebel had introduced his teaching methods, which quickly earned high acclaims. Yet preschool[1] education remained a low priority, and any further development of preschools was left up to private enterprise, with the Roman Catholic Church the most common provider. Rejecting Froebel's "protestant invention," the church emphasized the charitable aspect of its preschools. The state concurred, turning over the few preschools developed in the first half of the century to the Ministry of Interior. Preschool methods developed by the Agazzi sisters stressed the emotional relationship between the child and the teacher, while those developed by Maria Montessori in her *Casa dei bambini* in Rome stressed the importance of sensory motor development. By the end of the century, there was growing debate among advocates of these various approaches.

TWENTIETH-CENTURY ITALY

The beginning of the 20th century was characterized by extensive debate on women's status in the family and society, and profound political and social changes in the definition of rights and the individuals entitled to such rights. Regardless of family type, complex households remained more common in all social classes in Italy than elsewhere in Western Europe. From a legal point of view, laws on family relations remained essentially the same until the fascist regime, even as ethnographers began to note the strong domestic position held by women, especially in the South. Patterns of infant care were influenced by a new legal theory that children had rights of their own. While the wealthy continued to use wet nurses, public policies provided more benign treatment of unwed mothers by granting subsidies for the child.

The active recruitment of women into the labor force led to an examination of child care and working conditions for women. The protection laws of 1902 and 1907, which forbid night work and provided compulsory unpaid maternity leave for four weeks after delivery, ostensibly established women's right to work, earn equal pay, and be independent of their families. They were also interpreted as defending women from exploitation and enabling them to fulfill their duties as mothers and wives, and they were eventually used to justify the exclusion of women from employment. While the rules against female labor in factories were temporarily lifted during World War I, there remained a long list of occupations from which women were excluded by law. Reform legislation extending women's legal rights was cut short by the onset of fascism.

Fascist Interpretations of the Maternal Role

The fascist regime did not require much new legislation to send women back home; the subordination of women to their family responsibilities had already been well established. Inspired by the glory of the Roman Empire, Mussolini defined the family as a "social and political institution" with responsibilities directed toward state interests. Women's private lives came under increasing scrutiny amid concern over declining fertility rates; the issue was crudely addressed in Mussolini's "battle for births" (Craig, 1972). Unmarried mothers also received fertility awards, and the *Opera Nazionale per la protezione della Maternita e Infanzie* (ONMI) was created to lower the infant mortality rate (still double that of Germany, France, and Great Britain) and to encourage maternal behavior such as breast-feeding. The practice of nursing one's own child had finally become commonplace, and women who refused to comply with such norms were considered "bad mothers."

Fascist reform of public education resulted in the government endorsement of first the Montessori and then the Agazzi method (already well established in the Catholic Church) as "the method of the Italian preschool system" (Pistillo, 1989, p. 158). By 1933 most preschools were run by religious orders.

Child care policies that grew out of these circumstances during the first half of the century are itemized in Table 15.1. The serious methodological inquiry into various approaches to working with young children that initially characterizes this period is juxtaposed with the remarkable indifference of the national government to the number and conditions of preschools outside of the fascist period. Much of the progress that was made in the quality of preschool programs was under the auspices of the Roman Catholic Church,

Table 15.1
Child Care Policies in the First Half of 20th Century Italy[1]

1902	Minimum working age set at 12 years; women permitted to suspend work during pregnancy
1904	National Union of Educators for Infancy calls for transfer of preschools to Ministry of Education
1910	Ministry of Education denounces pitiful state of preschools as well as staff qualifications
1911	Italian Union for Public Education convenes to debate the merits of the Montessori and Agazzi methods
1913	Law passes instituting two-year technical secondary schools (scuole pratiche magistrali) for training of preschool staff
1914	Committee of experts reorganizes preschool provisions, gains approval of New Programs
1923	Gentile Reform Law passed under Fascist rule, renaming asili (charitable shelters) to scuole materne (maternal or preschools)
1925	Opera Nazionale Maternity e Infanzie (ONMI) established for needy mothers and children
1945	Government decrees Programs and Instructional Models to be Implemented in Elementary and Preschools
1947	National Committee for School Reform notes poor quality, custodial nature of preschool settings; urges improved teacher-training system
1948	Constitution established, guaranteeing religious instruction in Catholicism as integral to public education
1950	Agazzi method proclaimed "the method" for Italian preschools by Minister of Public Instruction; Law No. 860 passes; custodial services for children of working mother

[1]Sources include Corsaro & Emiliani (1992); Moss (1988); Pistillo (1989); Rankin (1985); and Saraceno (1984).

which emphasized a custodial function directly related to the importance of the maternal role.

CONTEMPORARY ITALY

At the conclusion of World War II, Italy was in a state of physical ruin as well as humiliation. The nation's subsequent transformation from "a relatively poor and predominantly agrarian country into one of the world's major industrial economies" was accompanied by dramatic changes in the Italian political scene that occurred "more rapidly and were more widespread in their effects than in any other Western European country" (Agnew,

1990, p. 772). These changes entailed complex ideological debates among at least three major political parties (the Italian Communist party, the Italian Socialist party, and the Christian Democratic party), the Roman Catholic Church, and the Italian women's movement, with differing interpretations of each at regional and national levels. The eventual outcomes of this culturally bound exchange were many, among them the current state of affairs with respect to child care policies in Italy. The issue of citizen's rights, including those of children, was a major focus of initial post-war political activity, as represented in the 1945 law granting women the right to vote and the 1948 law guaranteeing free and compulsory public education through grade five. During the ensuing "Italian Miracle" of the 1950s and 1960s there was an epidemic of public building, increased availability of public schooling, and a sharp rise in female labor force participation. At this time the term "three Italies" was coined to acknowledge the economic and ideological demarcations between the industrial Northwest, the radical Northeast-Center, and the impoverished and undeveloped South. Throughout Italy, the dramatic increase in nuclear family households coupled with a continued decline in births led to a growing concern about children's opportunities for socialization. The church and political forces had distinctively different opinions regarding these issues.

The shift in the Italian economy from an agricultural base to industrial production drew peasants off the land and women into the labor force at a time when women's roles were still being described as inseparable from family functions. But as improved transportation and communication broke down the isolation of rural communities, the authority of village priests and other conservative figures was undermined. It was within this setting that women experienced a new level of frustration as they faced the contradictions of sexism that characterize a more modern society. These circumstances, in combination with the steady trend away from the extended family, provided women with opportunities for expression previously unimagined. Thus Italian women were highly susceptible to the subsequent appeals of the women's movement.

Italian Feminism and the "Hot Autumn"

Appropriately enough, the first document of contemporary Italian feminism (December 1, 1966) was a manifesto for the "demystification of patriarchal authoritarianism," with a focus on what became known as "the woman question" (Milan Women's Bookstore Collective, 1990, p. 35). This feminist activity accompanied protests by the working class of the unequal outcomes and lack of social welfare expenditures associated with the Italian "miracle." By 1969 labor militancy had reached a post-war high, and the social and political unrest exploded in the form of right-wing violence, massive strikes, and demonstrations—a period thereafter referred to as the "hot autumn." It was within this context that contemporary Italian feminists as well as the current child care policies emerged.

While the bulk of activities associated with the "hot autumn" focused on working conditions and wages, labor demands also reflected a new focus on the world beyond the factory. Thus protest movements demonstrated for broad reforms in social services, including affordable housing, day care centers, and increased avenues for participation in local government by all citizens. These causes were successfully championed at the local levels by parties of the left, and by the mid-1970s dissatisfaction with the Christian Democratic rule was widespread. Thus the setting in which the Italian women's movement grew had the advantages of a strong leftist culture, as well as the problems associated with traditions of resistance and aims of socialism that had been defined in the masculine voice.

The Italian women's movement redefined "women's personal problems" as public issues, reinforcing the trends that began as part of the broad transformation of Italian society in the 1960s. Results of their efforts included a transformation in "attitudes, behaviors, culture values . . . and the collective unconscious" of Italian society (Hellman, 1987, p. 206). These changes in attitudes were reflected in a spate of new laws called the "most advanced of Europe" (Birnbaum, 1986, p. 206), which centered on issues of abortion and divorce, paternity leave, and family rights. The context within which laws for preschools (1968) and day care (1971) were established included the repeal of the punitive law against unfaithful wives (1968), the divorce law (1970), maternity and infant legislation (1975), the law clarifying equal family rights (1975) and equal pay and treatment of male and female workers (1977), and the law legalizing abortion (1978) among others. The growing solidarity of Italian women is most apparent in the defeat (1981) of the church-sponsored referendum to repeal the abortion law. The overwhelming victory was also a dramatic signal that Italy was no longer dominated by the values of the Roman Catholic Church, considered over the centuries to be the greatest unifying cultural force in Italy.

Thus the development of laws establishing preschools (see Table 15.2) was intertwined with demands for social reforms. Much of the resistance centered on the concerns, expressed by the church-backed Christian Democratic party, that state schools would detract from present private schools and further contribute to the decline of the family. Amid prolonged debate, the bill for state preschools was passed in 1968. A victory for the left, the bill nonetheless contained many compromises, including the provision of religious education (as outlined in the *Orientamente* published the following year) and an all-female staff, thereby retaining the custodial interpretation of preschool functions. While an underlying premise supporting the need for preschools was to compensate for shrinking opportunities for social relationships that had previously characterized Italian families, an accompanying ideology emphasized the importance of collaborating with—rather

Table 15.2
Child Care Policies in the Second Half of 20th Century Italy[1]

1960	Communist party proposes direct state involvement in preschool education
1962	Region of Emilia Romagna votes to construct first four of series of preschools through the region
1964	Minister of Public Instruction reports on disastrous state of teacher training in scuole magistrali
1968	Law No. 444 passes in Parliament, officially requiring female staff and establishing government's role in preprimary education
1969	Guidelines for Educational Activities in State Nursery Schools is approved
1971	Law 1204 passes, providing for job protection during pregnancy, 12 weeks leave at 70% earnings, additional 6 months leave at 30% earnings
	Law 1044 establishes doctrine of state-supported day care for children less than 3 years; regional governments responsible for specifying caregiver qualifications
1972	Law 1073 provides state funds for non-state preschools
1974	Decreti Delegati establishes institution of governing bodies, norms regarding qualifications of administrators, teachers, and other preschool personnel
1977	Law No. 616 transfers responsibility of preschool construction to regional government; staff payrolls, materials and equipment remain national responsibility
1978	Law No. 463 abolishes positions of co-teacher and assistants, specifies procedures for hiring
1991	Revised edition of 1991 Guidelines for Educational Activities in State Nursery Schools is published

---

[1]Sources include Corsaro & Emiliani (1992), Moss (1988), Pistillo (1989), Rankin (1985), and Saraceno (1984).

than substituting for—the family. To the consternation of educators, teacher training was not addressed.

Throughout the 1970s and 1980s, women continued to join the work force. The visibility of the women's movement brought about the acceptance of work for women, even those with children, as normal and legitimate. The approval of a compulsory *paid* maternity leave (Law 1204) in the same year that state-supported day care was established (1971) had a dramatic impact on women in the work force. These laws also combined to reveal state interpretations of the needs of infants and young children: before the age of nine months, children belong in the home under the mother's watchful eye; beyond that age, day care centers join preschools in achieving the aims of socialization previously fulfilled by the family.

Having described the socio-political setting of the transformation of child care policy in Italy, it is important to acknowledge the more immediate context of contemporary Italian families, where deeply rooted traditions have been passed down from generation to generation.

The Contemporary Italian Family

The cultural significance attached to Italy as a "country of families" (Sirey and Valerio, 1982, p. 179) is apparent in such simple facts as the extent to which family life determines the daily routine in small villages and urban centers throughout Italy. In spite of a rise in the number of women and children living in single-parent households, procreation remains a cultural priority in many parts of Italy where childless couples are referred to as *sposi* ("newly-weds") (New and Benigni, 1987).

While the extended family household no longer represents the typical domestic arrangement, the significance of the nuclear family unit as a basic social unit continues to be challenged. Amid studies emphasizing the continuing importance of the politics of kinship in the 20th century, the isolation of the nuclear family from the overall system of its relations is considered both distorting and misleading. *Parenti, amici, and vicini* remain a reality in the lives of Italian families, as friends, neighbors, and extended family members come and go freely from each other's homes.

The Modern Italian Mother

In spite of dramatic changes in Italian women's status, a continuity with traditional cultural values remains in evidence within women's political efforts as well as the home. The challenge of confronting the cultural expectation of female dedication to the benefit of others characterizes the feminist literature, even as feminists operate within a system of values that takes others into account. How else can we explain the hundreds of thousands of women from all political and economic spheres who joined together to defend the abortion law?

Ambivalence in the modern interpretation of women's roles is apparent in legal respects as well. While a 1977 law extended to working fathers the right to parental leave, a subsequent bill addressed to a "crisis in the family" praised women as the "first and unsubstitutable educator of the next generation" (Birnbaum, 1986, p. 138). These contradictions are apparent in studies across Italy that continue to show the mother as responsible for the organization of family life regardless of her salary or employment prestige. Although some have not acknowledged the discrepancy, studies also suggest that mothers' work within the home has actually increased as a result of the reduced availability of extended family members and the bureaucratic nature of contemporary domestic tasks. The label *doppia presenza* ("double presence") has been used to describe the two sets of responsibilities (home and employment) assigned to the modern Italian mother.

Perhaps the most critical determinant of the condition of women within Italy remains the unvarying and well-defined nature of child care. Even with all of Italy's advanced maternity leave legislation, the predominant cultural value—that it is better for the young child to have its mother at home—prevails in definitions of appropriate parenting. Thus Italian women continue to define a "good mother" as one who does not abandon her children.

Views of Children and Child Care

Concepts of infant vulnerability are based on historically high infant mortality rates (especially in comparison with other Western nations), which were still apparent as recently as the 1950s. Patterns of child care throughout the first years of life remain characterized by conspicuous attention to physical needs (including feeding, grooming, and protection from danger). In the ideal, such care takes place amidst a dense social setting that provides many and varied play partners in addition to nuclear family members. That such a setting is expected to occur naturally within the child care environment is reflected in the lack of a tradition of organized play groups.

There is a clear and articulated interest in children on the part of adults, with the rights of children to participate in the full spectrum of community living apparent in their presence at adult functions throughout the day. The broad interpretation of the Italian family is apparent in numerous studies where extended family members (grandmothers and aunts), friends, and neighbors provide assistance in infant and child care on a daily basis.

This constellation of cultural values, implied in definitions of family, interpretations of women's roles, and standards of adequate child care, is also visible in contemporary Italian child care policies.

CONTEMPORARY CHILD CARE IN ITALY

The current public child care system divides children into three age groups: zero to three, three to six, and six to ten years. In spite of national legislation for day care (for children from nine months to three years) and preschool (three to five year olds), different bureaucracies control services, and the availability varies across the state. In brief, the older the child, the more universal the services.

Day Care

The 1971 Law 1044 defines day care as a social right of all children and mothers, with priority given to children of working mothers.[2] Implementation throughout Italy remains uneven in part because of different aims embodied in the law, including those of assisting working mothers with the care of their children as well as offering all children an early education and group experience. Varying availability is also likely the result of the requirement that regional and local governments, in collaboration with parents, manage the services. With the vast majority (77 percent in 1983) of day care centers in the more densely populated north-central region, centers in the south remain under construction or reported as "not fully functioning" (Corsaro and Emiliani, 1992). Yet even in the wealthier northern regions day care is insufficient. Some of the gap is currently filled with private centers; industry supported facilities remain the most common in the north. In the south, most private programs are run by the Catholic Church. Many Italian families also continue to utilize extended family members. Thus, while the original aim of ultimately providing for 6 percent of children has not yet been reached nationally, current views are that such a figure grossly underestimates the need.

Until very recently, an assumption that young children need less specialized attention and professional handling has been prevalent in the organization and staffing of day care centers. Thus requirements have been for female caregivers, seen as vicarious mother figures, and their training has entailed what some (e.g., Saraceno, 1984a) have considered a vocational approach. While families that do not use day care facilities generally cite the traditional belief that mother is best, and emphasize the risk of early separation, more recent attitudes reflect the rationale for day care as an extension of opportunities for socialization.

A deficit view of the nuclear family ("characterized by exclusive and limited relationships . . . not sufficient to guarantee full development of the child") is reflected in the grave concern currently being expressed regarding the lack of a universal day care policy for children who are "socially isolated" with "no other children to play with and no adult other than the mother to relate to" (Saraceno, 1984b, p. 358). This cultural value attributed to children's socialization needs has also contributed to increased recognition of the educational significance of the day care center (Mantovani, 1982; Rankin, 1985), with concomitant implications for teacher qualifications.

Generally speaking, the younger the children, the lower the staff have been paid and the less specialized training they traditionally received. The new national contract, however, provides teachers in *asilo nido* with the same pay and conditions of teachers in *scuola materna*; furthermore, it gives caregivers the title of *educator* in acknowledgment of their educational role. Day care remains characterized by longer days for children than are typically experienced in preschool settings, a situation seen as increasingly less justified given the change in roles from custodial to educational.

Preschool

There is little ambivalence on the part of parents to send children to preschool. Seen as a right of citizenship for all children of three to five years, the state goes so far as to subsidize licensed private programs if public ones do not meet the demand for services. Although that policy remains controversial, especially since most private centers are church affiliated, the inexpensiveness and wide availability reflects the notion that all Italian children are expected to attend preschool as a normal part of growing up.

An important feature of current efforts to improve the quality and availability of preschool services is the distinction between state and non-state *scuole materne*. Non-state preschools, originally under the dominion of the Catholic Church and thus characterized by a custodial and religious mission, are now operated by a variety of religious, private, and local organizations, with no clear consensus on either their characteristics or their aims in spite of the supervision provided by the Ministry of Education. State-funded preschools, on the other hand, have been compelled until quite recently to comply with the 1969 guidelines, one of which is to prepare children for elementary school. Through this combination of services, from 80 to 90 percent of Italian children were attending some form of preschool by 1980. Today, a combination of state, municipal, and private centers serves close to 100 percent of preschool-aged children in most communities.

In spite of differences associated with the various governing and funding bodies of state versus non-state preschools, there are a number of features that characterize current preschool efforts in Italy. A basic belief in the importance of the preschool age period as a "never-to-be-had-again moment" has generated a national consensus regarding the importance of preschool attendance. Another major characteristic of Italian preschools, the importance attributed to cooperative decision making between homes and schools, is reflected in the ideal of the *gestione sociale*, a concept peculiar to Italy that refers to the way in which staff, community, and parents run the school.

Preschool teacher qualifications remain as specified in the 1969 guidelines, with numerous variations at the regional levels. While somewhat more stringent than requirements for day care teachers, teachers in non-state preschools (*scuola materna*) are required only to have a diploma from a secondary school. Elementary teachers may also teach in preschools if they pass an examination. Teachers in state preschools must also meet additional qualifications, as outlined in the 1968 Law 444, including one year's practice teaching and an oral and written competency test. Currently, in-service training for preschool teachers in Italy is dependent on the initiative undertaken by individual teachers, or programs designed by the preschool system within a particular provence.

The new 1991 *Orientamente per la Scuola Materna* (*Guidelines for the Preschool*) proclaims much of what has been advanced during the two decades following the establishment of preschools. Notably missing is any inclusion of religious education, while major additions focus on the increased understanding of the nature of the child. The theoretical premise of the guidelines outlines a conception of the child that is far removed from the earlier, more provincial point of view. The subject of the child's rights, the role of the school in protecting those rights, the changing nature of the Italian family, and the continuing importance of continuity—both within the school setting and between the home and the school—are discussed at length. Consistent with the Italian tradition of mainstreaming special needs children into regular classroom settings, issues of diversity and integration are expanded to include children of ethnic and linguistic minorities.

Conceptions of child development as described in the new guidelines reflect the expansive developments in the field, and academic domains such as reading and language arts are incorporated into broader discussions of communication and symbol systems. While advocates of the term *scuola d'infanzia* failed to win replacement of the more custodial label of *scuola materna* in either the title or the content of the new guidelines, it is clear from the theoretical description of the new Italian preschool that the aims are significantly expanded from the 1969 interpretation.

CONTEMPORARY ISSUES

Given the premises stated in the first portion of the new guidelines, the lack of attention to the means necessary to achieve the stated goals is disappointing to those who have worked to create exemplary preschool programs over the past three decades. There is no mention, for example, of the need for in-service teacher training, nor the importance of having adult collaborators (such as two teachers in each classroom) to enable teachers to work with children in the manner suggested by the theoretical orientation. While attempts are underway in the Italian legislature to establish new requirements for early childhood teachers, the debate also entails issues of regional versus national requirements, and the role of the university in teacher training.

The implementation of laws related to child care and early education have been inconsistent at best. Today there is considerable pressure to pass the responsibility for early childhood education, at the national level (in the form of day care and preschools), from the Ministry of Health to the National Education System as a means of addressing the problem of implementation.

Another interpretation of the inconsistent implementation is the extent of regional diversity, which raises additional concerns. In part because of the long and indigenous roots of many of these regional differences, and surely because the entire unification episode was more an extension of one region's dominance over the rest of the country than a bonding together of the nation, Italy has retained its history of geographical fragmentation. As such, the outmoded notion of *campanilismo*—a world view that does not extend beyond the bell tower (campanile) of the village church (Hellman, 1987, p. 10)—continues to reflect reality. Thus the impact of national laws on child care has varied according to region. In spite of tremendous gains at the national level, there is a wide regional variety in philosophy, funding sources, and administrative policies. Adequate day care remains a scarcity in the south, and this has been attributed to sub-cultural beliefs regarding the young child as well as economic consequences of the political decentralization law of 1975.

The final few pages of this chapter will be devoted to a description of an infant/toddler and preschool program that exemplifies the impact of regional characteristics on the conception and implementation of child care policies in Italy.

CASE STUDY: REGGIO EMILIA

The region of Emilia Romagna in northern Italy has the most highly developed and well-subsidized social services in Italy and is widely recognized for its innovative and high quality public child care programs. Located in the setting where first the Socialist, and later the Communist parties established their base of strength, Reggio Emilia has been described as "red as any city in Italy" (Hellman, 1987, p. 111). During World War II it was the center of the resistance movement, where men and women from every social class were drawn into the struggle to liberate northern Italy from fascism. The tradition of women cooperating together, a long-standing characteristic of Emilian and Romagnolo peasant life, easily transformed into post-war activities.

One such activity was the creation of the city's first cooperative preschool to meet the needs of working parents. In 1963, well in advance of the 1968 national law, Reggio Emilia took over the cooperative schools and opened its first municipally funded preschools. Today the city has 22 municipal preschools and 13 infant/toddler centers serving, respectively, 50 percent and 37 percent of the population. The inclusion of state and private facilities brings the proportion of children served to 100 percent and 40 percent respectively. While most communities provide similar availability of services to children in the preschool (three to five years) age group, the proportion of children under the age of three that attend infant/toddler centers is in dramatic contrast to the rest of the country.

Features of the Reggio Emilia early childhood program expand upon cultural values and traditions described previously, including the emphasis on cooperation between the home and the school, the rights of children and their families to high quality care, and children's need for social relations to replace those no longer available within the nuclear family.

Reggio Emilia's interpretation of high quality child care reflects a theoretical heritage reminiscent of other progressive educational programs, with theorists such as Kilpatrick, Dewey, Bronfenbrenner, Isaacs, Wallon, Frinet, Vygotsky, Bruner, Piaget, the post-Piagetians, Hawkins, Gardner, Maturana, and Varela identified as influential. Thus this community-based program includes an integrated curriculum that is characterized by long-term projects and an emphasis on children's many symbolic languages, features that have attracted world-wide attention (New, 1990; Kanrowitz and Wingert, 1991) and are described in greater detail in a forthcoming publication (Edwards, Gandini, and Forman, in press).

A major program goal is the facilitation of exchanges among and between *adults* as well as children; thus the physical and social structures of the schools are designed to promote social interactions. Concerns for the psychological significance of the physical environment are apparent in the attention given to the use of space in and out of the classrooms, which are arranged around an open central area considered similar in importance to the town *piazza*. These policy features make possible the quality of exchanges between children as well as the practice of keeping the same group of children together for a three-year period. While the latter practice is common throughout Italy, the former (two teachers working together) is less often found in preschool classrooms in other parts of Italy. This practice creates a community in which adults and children are a rich source of support, friendship, and information for one another.

A commonly shared belief is that *no one has a monopoly on what is best for children*.[3] There is a strong tradition of community support for young children and their families, which is apparent not only in the consistent and high level of funding provided for the program, but the degree of commitment to shared decision making by teachers and parents. In Reggio Emilia, the *gestione sociale* is not just an opportunity; it is a reality evidenced by parent and community involvement in the decision-making processes at the individual schools as well as those at the policy level. Reggio Emilia has also assumed a leadership role in the planning and implementation of teacher and staff development, and has emphasized the value of the school as a laboratory for teachers.

CONCLUSIONS

The above case study is far from typical in terms of Italian child care and early education. There is much to make Reggio Emilia distinct, not the least of which is a view of the child as capable of achieving heights unimagined by adults—a far cry from the more fatalistic view of children's development often expressed in Italy. Yet even Reggio Emilia's child care and early education program provides testimony to the influence of Italy's larger cultural heritage as outlined earlier: (1) the broad definition of and importance attributed to the family as a model for social relations, (2) the importance of women's roles as both subjects and instigators of social change, and (3) church and state contributions to the interpretation of children's needs. Indeed, the success of the Reggio Emilia early childhood program may be considered a result of the extent to which they have been able to capitalize on these indigenous features of the Italian culture.

The Italian feminist movement's collective voice regarding child care was loud and clear. Rejecting the notion of "socializing" all the functions of the family, Italian women demonstrated for working conditions and child care policies that would enable them to "eat with our own, and to have time to stay with children" (Birnbaum, 1986, p. 134). By insisting that they did not want "child care parking lots" (Dalla Costa, quoted in Birnbaum, 1986, p. 35), Italian women used their solidarity to push for more radical change in Italian society. This political strategy has been translated today into an emphasis, in national child care policies, on collaboration among adults. Parent-teacher relationships such as those found in Reggio Emilia also enlarge upon the model of extra-familial individuals historically incorporated into the Italian family. Finally, the rejection of the church emphasis on the child's custodial needs is apparent in the importance attributed by the state to the rights of the child, as a unique citizen, to a high quality educational experience. These values have culminated in the prevailing view that a child's social and intellectual development are dependent on a collective social process, a perspective that characterizes the aims and the means of contemporary Italian child care policy.

NOTES

1. In this chapter, the terms "preschool," "nursery school," and *scuola materna* all refer to Italian programs for four to five year olds. Because the last year of Italian preschool is the equivalent to kindergarten in the United States, some have suggested the term "pre-primary" as a more accurate descriptor. In most cases, I retained the use of the term "preschool" to be consistent with the vast majority of the references cited.

2. The terms "day care" and *asilo nido* will be used to refer to all-day programs designed for infants and toddlers under the age of three.

3. Sergio Spaggiari, personal communication, June 15, 1987.

REFERENCES

Acquaviva, S. S., and Santuccio, M. (1976). *Social structure in Italy: Crisis of a system.* Boulder, Colo.: Westview Press.

Agnew, J. A. (1990). "Political decentralization and urban policy in Italy: From "state-centered" to "state-society" explanation." *Policy Studies Journal, 18* (3), 768–784.

Avanzini, B., and Lanzetti, C. (Eds.) (1980). *Problemi e modelli di vita familiare— a study in the urban environment* (Problems and models of family life: A study in the urban environment). Milan: Vita e Pensiero.

Balbo, L. (1978). *La doppia presenza* (The double presence). *Inchiesta, 32,* 7–11.

Balbo, L., and May, M. P. (1976). "Women's condition: The case of postwar Italy." *International Journal of Sociology,* Vol. V (4), 79–102.

Barbagli, M., and Kertzer, D. (1990). "An introduction to the history of Italian family life." *Journal of Family History, 15* (4), 369–383.

Bassnett, S. (1986). *Feminist experiences: The women's movement in four cultures.* London: Allen and Unwin.

Berkowitz, S. G. (1984). "Familism, kinship and sex roles in Southern Italy: Contradictory ideals and real contradictions." *Anthropological Quarterly, 57* (2), 83–91.

Bettio, F. (1988). *The sexual division of labour: The Italian case.* Oxford: Clarendon Press.

Birnbaum, L. C. (1986). *Liberazione della donna: Feminism in Italy.* Middletown, Conn.: Wesleyan University Press.

Bradley, K. R. (1986). "Wet-nursing at Rome: A study in social relations." In B. Rawson (Ed.), *The family in ancient Rome.* Ithaca, N.Y.: Cornell University Press.

CENSIS. Ministry of the Interior (1984). *The condition of childhood between family and institutions.* Rome: Uffocio Studi Ministero dell/Interno.

Center for Educational Research (1989). *An historical outline, data and information.* Municipality of Reggio Emilia: Department of Education.

Cornelisen, A. (1976). *Women of the shadows.* Boston: Little, Brown, and Company.

Cornelisen, A. (1980). *Strangers and pilgrims: The last Italian migration.* New York: Holt, Rinehart and Winston.

Corsaro, W., and Emiliani, F. (1992). "Child care, early education, and children's peer culture in Italy." In M. Lamb and K. Sternberg (Eds.), *The cultural context of nonparental care arrangements.* Hillsdale, N.J.: Lawrence Erlbaum.

Craig, G. D. (1972). *Europe since 1914.* New York: Holt, Rinehart, and Winston.

Donati, P., and Cipolla, C. (1978). *La donna nella terza Italia.* (Women in the third Italy.) Rome: Editrice A.V.E.

Douglass, W. A. (1980). "The South Italian family: A critique." *Journal of Family History, 5* (4), Winter, 338–358.

Edwards, C. P., Gandini, L., and Forman, G. (Eds.). (in press). *The hundred languages of children: The education of all the children in Reggio Emilia, Italy.* Norwood, N.J.: Ablex.

Edwards, C. P., and Gandini, L. (1989). "Teachers' expectations about the timing of developmental skills: A cross-cultural study." *Young Children, 44* (4), 15–19.

Fraser, J. (1981). *Italy: Society in crisis: Society in transformation.* London: Routledge and Kegan Paul Ltd.

Gandini, L. (1991). "Not just anywhere: Making child care centers into "particular" places." *Beginnings: The Magazine for Teachers of Young Children, 1,* 17–20.

Giovannini, M. J. (1981). "Woman: A dominant symbol within the cultural system of a Sicilian town." *Man, 16,* 408–426.

Hellman, J. A. (1987). *Journeys among women: Feminism in five Italian cities.* New York: Oxford University Press.

Herlihy, D., and Klapisch-Zuber, C. (1978). *Tuscans and their families: A study of the Florentine catasto of 1427.* New Haven, Conn.: Yale University Press.

Kantrowitz, B., and Wingert, P. (1991). "The best schools in the world." *Newsweek,* December 2, 50–64.

Keefe, E. K. (1977). *Area handbook for Italy.* Washington, D.C.: American University Foreign Area Studies.

Kertzer, D. (1984). *Family life in central Italy, 1880–1910.* New Brunswick, N.J.: Rutgers University Press.

Kertzer, D. (1991). "Gender ideology and infant abandonment in nineteenth-century Italy." *Journal of Interdisciplinary History, 22* (1), 1–25.

Klapisch-Zuber, C. (1985). *Women, family, and ritual in Renaissance Italy.* Chicago: University of Chicago Press.

Lacey, W. K. (1986). "*Patria Potestas.*" In B. Rawson (Ed.), *The family in ancient Rome.* Ithaca, N.Y.: Cornell University Press.

Levi, G. (1990). "Family and kin—A few thoughts." *Journal of Family History, 15* (4), 567–578.

LeVine, R. A. (1974). "Parental goals: A cross-cultural view." *Teachers College Record, 76,* 226–239.

Livi Bacci, M., and Breschi, M. (1990). "Italian fertility: An historical account." *Journal of Family History, 15* (4), 385–408.

Mantovani, S. (1978). "Current trends in Italian preschool policy." *International Journal of Behavior and Development, 1* (2), 175–191.

Mantovani, S. (1982). *Asili-nido psicologia e pedagogia* (Infant-toddler centers: Psychology and education). Milan, Italy: Franco Angeli.

Maraspini, A. L. (1968). *The study of an Italian village.* Paris: Mouton and Company.

Merzario, R. (1990). "Land, kinship, and consanguineous marriage in Italy from the seventeenth to the nineteenth centuries." *Journal of Family History, 15* (4), 539–546.

Milan Women's Bookstore Collective (1990). *Sexual difference: A theory of social-symbolic practice.* Bloomington: Indiana University Press.

Miller, P. M., New, R. S., and Richman, A. (1982). "Social ecology of infant development in Italy and America." Paper presented at International Conference of Infant Studies, Austin, Texas.

Moss, L. W. (1981). "The South Italian family revisited." *Central Issues in Anthropology, 3* (1) 1–16.

Moss, L. W., and Cappannari, S. C. (1960). "Patterns of kinship, comparaggio, and community in a South Italian village." *Anthropological Quarterly, 33,* 24–32.

Moss, P. (1988). *Childcare and equality of opportunity: Consolidated report to the European commission.* London: London University.

Neri, S. (1991). "La continuita' educativa" (Educational continuity). In G. Rubagotti

(Ed.), *Gli orientamenti 1991 per la scuola materna* (1991 Guidelines for the nursery school). Milan, Italy: Fabbri Editori.

New, R. (1984). "Italian mothers and infants: Patterns of care and social development." Doctoral dissertation, Harvard University.

New, R. (1988). "Parental goals and Italian infant care." In R. A. LeVine, P. Miller, M. West (Eds.), *Parental Behavior in Diverse Societies*. New Directions for Child Development, no. 40. San Francisco: Jossey-Bass.

New, R. (1989). "The family context of Italian infant care." *Early Child Development and Care, 50*, 99–108.

New, R. (1990). "Excellent early education: A town in Italy has it!" *Young Children, 45*, No. 4. Washington, D.C.: NAEYC.

New, R. (in press). *Bello, buono, bravo: Italian early childhood*. New York: Guilford Press.

New, R., and Benigni, L. (1987). "Italian fathers and infants: Cultural constraints on paternal behavior." In M.E. Lamb (Ed.), *The father's role: Cross-cultural perspectives*. Hillsdale, N.J.: Erlbaum.

Oppo, A. (1990). " 'Where there's no women there's no home': Profile of the agropastoral family in nineteenth-century Sardinia." *Journal of Family History, 15* (4), 483–502.

Parente, M. (1991). "Societa' attuale e scuola materna" (Actual society and the nursery school). In G. Rubagotti (Ed.), *Gli orientamenti 1991 per la scuola materna* (1991 Guidelines for the nursery school). Milan, Italy: Fabbri Editori.

Pistillo, F. (1989). "Preprimary education and care in Italy." In P. Olmsted and D. Weikart (Eds.), *How nations serve young children*. Ypsilanti, Mich.: High/Scope Press.

Rankin, M. (1985). *An analysis of some aspects of schools and services for 0–6 year olds in Italy with particular attention to Lombardy and Emilia-Romagna*. Unpublished CAGS thesis, Wheelock College.

Saraceno, C. (1984a). "Shifts in public and private boundaries: Women as mothers and service workers in Italian daycare." *Feminist Studies, 10* (1), Spring, 7–29.

Saraceno, C. (1984b). "The social construction of childhood: Child care and education policies in Italy and the United States." *Social Problems, 31* (3), 351–363.

Sirey, A. R., and Valerio, A. M. (1982). "Italian-American women: Women in transition." *Ethnic Groups, 4*, 177–189.

Smith-Curtis, D. (1989). *Early childhood programs in Denmark, England, Spain, Italy, and Australia*. Unpublished master's thesis. California State University, Northridge.

United Nations, Statistics Office. (1957). *Demographic Yearbook*. New York: Department of Economics and Social Affairs.

Velarso, G. (1991). "La famiglia, la scuola, i diritti del bambino" (The family, the school, the rights of the child). In G. Rubagotti (Ed.), *Gli orientamenti 1991 per la scuola materna* (1991 Guidelines for the nursery school). Milan, Italy: Fabbri Editori.

Viazzo, P. O., and Albera, D. (1990). "The peasant family in northern Italy, 1750–1930: A reassessment." *Journal of Family History, 15* (4), 461–482.

—— 16 ——

JAPAN

Edith Lassegard

Day care and preschool programs are currently expanding more rapidly than any other level of education in Japan. These programs have nearly doubled in number each decade since 1960, and presently the highest level of expansion is for the care of infants and children up to three years of age.

Recent population trends and significant societal changes have contributed to the current demand for formal child care programs. Many of these changes have elicited the concern of educators, government officials, and economists as Japan attempts to cope with severe labor shortages, a steadily declining birthrate, and an increasingly aged population.

It appears that the direction of future change is largely dependent on the behavior of Japanese women. The government is both encouraging women to participate more fully in the work force, as well as calling for an increase in the birthrate. Although the majority of women continue to drop out of the labor force to take up family responsibilities, this trend has been changing considerably in the past few years, as more and more young women choose to pursue career opportunities.

Child care, therefore, has become a focus of national concern. Parents are presented with an increasing variety of program alternatives for children six years old and younger, although these programs may not necessarily meet family needs. Unlike the compulsory education system, which begins at the elementary school level and is built around a highly standardized curriculum and system of examinations, options at the preschool level can be characterized by a diversity in philosophy and methods. This may come as some surprise to those who are familiar with Japanese education, widely known for an emphasis on entrance examinations, rigidity in methods and curriculum, and a high level of academic achievement. Yet an analysis of preschool programs reveals a number of alternatives for children, despite uniform government licensing standards.

This complexity is due in large measure to the substantial proportion of private preschool programs, both licensed and unlicensed. It is also due to the often opposing theories regarding child development and childhood education that underlie program content. In addition, there are increasing differences between programs in terms of cost and criteria for admission. These differences have some educators apprehensive that the egalitarian principles of the Japanese school system are threatened.

RECENT POPULATION SHIFTS

For the past few decades, Japan has experienced a substantial increase in urban population. The migration peaked in the 1960s when millions of people moved into urban industrial areas. During the past 15 years, however, the difference between the movement into large city areas and out into more rural areas has declined considerably. Today, more than one fifth (20.5%) of Japan's population of roughly 122 million people lives in large cities of more than a million inhabitants.

Although in 1960 about half the population (51.6%) lived in cities with more than 50,000 people, by 1985 that figure was close to 70 percent. This is largely due to the urbanization of industry in Japan, which has produced extremely dense populations in the largest industrial cities (e.g., Tokyo, Yokohama, Osaka, and Nagoya).

According to Akio Tanosaki (1989) a major result of the overcrowding of large industrial cities has been the rapid development of neighboring cities surrounding the most densely populated industrial areas. Because of this expansion, many workers do not reside in the city where they work. In fact, by 1985 a considerable number of these suburbanized areas had expanded to have more than three times their estimated population in 1960. Examples of cities that have become, in effect, large suburbs for major industrial cities include Chiba (which grew from a population of 242,000 in 1960 to 789,000 in 1985), Funabashi (from 135,000 to 507,000), and Sagamihara (from 102,000 to 483,000).

During that same time period, the four most populated industrial cities (Tokyo, Yokohama, Osaka, and Nagoya) experienced proportionately less population growth: Tokyo only shows an increase of 44,000 people (from 8,310,000 to 8,354,000), Yokohama and Nagoya evidenced less than a 20 percent increase, and Osaka actually decreased in population during that 25-year span. These figures demonstrate the shift in recent years to areas surrounding these major cities as workers and their families move further from work to avoid the high cost of living and crowded conditions.

As a result of these population shifts, long distance travel to work is therefore becoming increasingly common. In large metropolitan areas such as Tokyo, it is not at all unusual for workers to commute more than two hours each way. Some workers commute for nearly four hours each morning and night. Commuting time has a great impact on child care arrangements and on the employment choices of women who plan to have children.

CHANGING FAMILY STRUCTURE

Due to the large numbers of young couples who have settled in or around large industrial cities like Tokyo, Yokohama, and Osaka, the proportion of extended family members living together or even nearby has declined considerably. A number of social concerns have resulted from this increase in the proportion of people in nuclear family units living away from other family and community members. Most of these concerns involve quality of life issues, especially for children and for the elderly.

Social Isolation. One social concern that has been noted recently by a number of educators is the increasing dependency of families on the education system not only for their children's upbringing and development, but also for the well-being of the mother. Due to the time demands of business on most fathers, combined with the decreasing involvement of extended family and community members with youth, the young non-working mother is often left alone to interact with her child. Because the strength of the bond between the Japanese mother and child has been remarked upon by researchers for quite some time, this involvement between mother and child cannot be seen as a strictly new phenomenon. However, lessened contact with other family and community members combined with the great decrease in number of children per family (as well as the relative ease in taking care of the modern household) has in many ways intensified this mother-child relationship in recent years. According to some researchers, because the Japanese mother is "judged socially on the success of her children" (Goodman, 1990), this intense involvement can result in the mother's competing with other mothers over the attractiveness of their children's lunches, or it can result in her becoming a "Kyoiku Mama," or "Education Mother" (a term used for mothers who strive to develop their children into academic successes).

Education mothers have been widely discussed in the media in Japan and also in Western research literature, usually shedding a negative light on mothers who are intensely involved in motivating their children to succeed in school. But at the same time, these Kyoiku Mamas are also given a great deal of the credit for the academic success of Japanese students. Most of this research focuses on the potential effects this mother type may have on the development of her children—whether or not the benefits of encouragement and motivation outweigh the negative results of overstudying on social skills and personality. Less attention has been given to the psychosocial aspects of the mother's situation.

Another possible result of the social isolation of young mothers is that they may look to the preschool for friendship and guidance, particularly in new urban communities. Parent Teacher Association groups consisting of mothers of preschool children tend to be service and socially oriented rather than administrative. Members typically gather to help organize events such as sports festivals and dramatic productions. Many preschools also offer other activities such as volleyball clubs to mothers. Some observers view this involvement as a sign of the isolation and uncertainty of young mothers and the need for a higher level of community support.

Rising Housing Costs. Not only do young couples typically live away from their parents and other family members, but also the housing situation in urban areas tends to be very crowded and expensive, making it difficult for young parents to accommodate a child of their own. Many couples cite lack of space as a major reason why they choose not to have another child.

Decrease in Birthrate. The birthrate in Japan has been steadily declining since the early 1970s when the so-called echo boom occurred as the World War II baby boomers began to have their own children. In 1990 the birthrate had dropped to 1.53, its lowest level in the post-war period. Even the third peak in births expected around the turn of the century is not likely to approach the 2.1 birthrate needed to maintain the current population.

According to a spring 1991 article in the journal *Japan Update,* some of the most commonly cited reasons for the low birthrate include:

1. The heavy economic burden of raising children.
2. The difficulty employed women experience in raising children.
3. The shortening of potential child-bearing years due to later marriages.
4. New lifestyles emphasizing the work and living patterns of the husband and wife.
5. Increasingly difficult housing problems due to rising land prices.

Recently the national government has reacted strongly to the continued reports of a declining birthrate. Prime Minister Kaifu Toshiki, in his March 2, 1990 address, called on Japanese citizens to have more children. Since then, the ruling Liberal-Democratic Party began proposing incentives to have larger families that included such things as a more comprehensive system of maternity leave, a tax deduction to double-income families with children, and funding for after-hours care in elementary schools ("Twilight Stay").

These incentives have not been completely well received by women in Japan, many of whom scoffed when the tax deduction (of about $30 per month) was announced. Quite a few Japanese women have expressed resentment toward these government policies to increase the birthrate. According to Asahi Shimbun writer Arioka (1991), this resentment stems in part from the government campaign during the war to "breed and multiply."

For these reasons, it appears doubtful that these measures by the government will have much success in terms of motivating young people to change their family plans.

Later Marriage. Besides housing costs, another factor that may have a negative effect on the birthrate is the trend of later marriage both for men and for women. In 1985 men, on average, began married life as they approached 30 years of age (29.5 years old), which is well over two years past the marriage age of men in the 1950s and 1960s. Women continue to average a few years younger than men when they marry, as evidenced by the estimated marriage age of about 26 for females in 1985. Furthermore, indications are that many young people are opting to remain single and that men are having an especially difficult time finding marriage partners.

Aging Society. One reason that the low birthrate has been a great source of concern for educators, business leaders, and policy makers has been the life expectancy rate in Japan, reported to be the highest in the world. By all estimates, Japan's future population is predicted to decline in number, with increasing proportions of elderly people.

For a number of years a tremendous amount of public dialogue and long-range planning efforts have been generated in preparation for Japan's increasingly aged population. The lack of living space in urban areas is expected to have a significant impact on the elderly, since married children who wish to invite their aging or ailing parents to live with them are often faced with the difficult situation of having very little room for their parents to stay. This also means that grandparents are seldom available to provide child care services, especially in urban areas.

Given that young couples in Japan frequently find themselves living in small, expensive apartment complexes isolated from family and community supports, it is not surprising that the decision to raise children must be considered carefully. The rapid changes in family patterns and community structure that have accompanied industrialization now have economic planners worried about having enough young workers to support the increasingly aged society in the years to come.

Demand for Labor. Companies in Japan have already demonstrated a demand for workers that is being unmet, causing some corporations to expand their operations to other countries, and others to shut down due to lack of labor. This labor shortage is also evidenced by the current low unemployment rate of about 2 percent and by the increasing efforts to recruit middle-aged women as temporary workers and female college graduates into non-traditional occupations.

It is evident that the declining birthrate paired with a greater life expectancy combine to make labor supply an increasingly important public issue in the years to come. However, the encouragement of young women to enter the labor market in order to help fill employment needs is seen by some as ultimately unwise because of the seemingly conflicting need for an increase in birthrate. This demand for women to be productive in the work force as well as reproductive for the benefit of the economy and society increases the complexity of the issues surrounding motherhood and employment.

Women in the Work Force. Female labor participation in Japan has risen steadily during the past few decades, as documented in the Rodohakusho publication put out annually by the Ministry of Labor (Rodosho). Women now make up over 35 percent of the total work force in Japan. However, because this figure includes part-time and temporary as well as full-time work, it may be misleading. In fact, although there seems to be close to the same proportion of males as females who are regular employees in the 15 to 24 age range, well over one third of the female workers between 25 and 54 years of age can be categorized as part time or temporary.

Traditional occupations for women have been in the service industry, in clerical work, and in textile and food manufacturing. Only recently have women taken administrative and other professional positions in Japan. Young working women are still stereotyped by some people as simply spending time working while waiting for a husband ("koshikake shigoto"). In 1986, the Teikoku Data Bank reported that in Japan less than 4 percent of the company presidents were female. This figure was seen as an optimistic sign for women, since the existence of more than 25,000 female company presidents in 1986 represented more than double the number found in 1981.

In observations of female labor force participation by age, a clear "M" shape appears. As is shown in Figure 16.1, there is a pronounced dip in the rate of female participation in the workplace during the prime childbearing years (between the ages of 25 and 35 years). This trend supplies consistent evidence of the high dropout rate of women once they marry and become mothers. The "M" shaped curve also gives evidence of the re-entry of many middle-aged women into the labor market, at least on a part-time basis.

Although other industrialized countries, such as the United Kingdom and the United States, have historically experienced female labor participation curves in similar "M" shapes, this pattern has been changing in these countries to resemble the curve found in Sweden, where there is no evidence of a drop in labor participation for child rearing. As can be noted in Figure 16.1, the rate of female workers in the labor force in Japan drops from a relatively high rate of participation (nearly 75 percent of all women in their early twenties) to approximately half of all women in their mid-thirties. Then a sizeable number of women in their late forties return to work, presumably once their children are old enough to take care of themselves.

In 1985 the Japanese government enacted the Equal Opportunity Act, which proclaims equal opportunity for men and women in employment, job assignments, and promotion practices. Although this Act has been criticized for a lack of enforcement measures for corporations that discriminate on the basis of gender, quite a few companies responded to the issue of

Figure 16.1
Female Labor Participation by Age in Six Countries

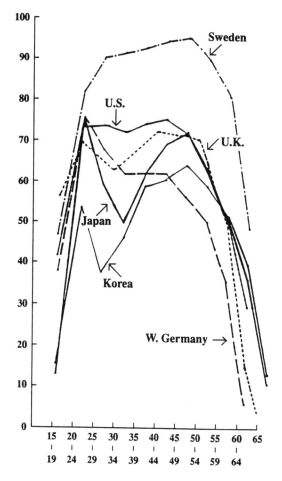

Japan (1989); Sweden, U.S., Korea (1987); W. Germany, U.K. (1986); Rodoryoku Chosanenpo, 1989; ILO, *Yeark Book of Labour Statistics* 1988.

equal employment soon after it was passed. In many companies, for instance, job categories and recruitment practices were broadened to include women.

In addition, a large number of companies began to use a path system, where new employees are given a choice of "tracks" they wish to pursue within the company. For example, the career path (or "sogo shoku") responsibilities might include plenty of overtime and the probability of job transfers to other cities. The traditional female office worker (or "OL":

Office Lady) position, by contrast, would most likely involve shorter hours, greater stability in terms of work location, and more flexibility for family concerns.

Of course, this path system could be seen as a way for companies to provide equal "opportunity" without actually modifying work conditions that prevent most women from pursuing careers, such as mandatory job transfers to other areas and inflexible hours. It is a fairly common corporate practice to ask upwardly mobile workers to take a new position that involves leaving behind family and moving to a new city ("tan-shin funin"). Not surprisingly, most women, even those who have university degrees, opt for traditional female office worker positions.

Yet stories of successful women who have chosen careers have been widely publicized, encouraging even more women to enter the career track. Companies are increasing efforts to recruit talented women for management-track positions because of very favorable accounts of exceptional female administrators, and also because of a recent shortage of college-educated young men.

Still, the decision to become a career woman in Japan is a tough one. It is thought by many that a woman who pursues a career is, by definition, giving up having a family. Accounts of ambitious Japanese women who have made it to high positions typically portray them as hardworking and single; if they are married, they are usually childless. Most men and women in Japan consider career demands and taking care of a family as incompatible roles for women to undertake. Recently the government called for an extension of the duration of maternity leaves, which is anticipated to have a significant impact in terms of making it possible for mothers to be able to maintain their position at work. However, the criticism has been made that in many cases maternity leaves are granted without salary.

Commuting time is another factor that greatly influences choice of work, especially for women who have, or plan to have, children. Arrangements with day care centers are especially difficult when both parents have to commute long distances. Only a few licensed facilities have evening hours.

There is some sign that the situation is improving for working mothers, as day care centers as well as elementary schools begin to provide programs that include lengthened hours to accommodate children with working parents. In addition, there are indications that younger business people, both men and women, are opting to leave work earlier than their fathers did. Trends in the attitudes of Japanese youth toward increasing interest in family time and personal fulfillment have been noted by some as a concern and by others as a favorable sign that fathers are getting to know their children better. Still, in the corporate culture the term "family man" (or "my-home shugi") is still a label applied to individuals who are thought of as less likely to be promoted because they are too involved with their families.

CHILDHOOD EDUCATION PHILOSOPHY AND METHODS

Despite similarities in licensing requirements for day care programs in Japan, a great diversity of methods can be found in various programs across the country. These methods are often based on philosophies reflecting the influence of Confucian, Buddhist, and Christian principles, as well as foreign theorists such as Froebel, Montessori, Rousseau, and Piaget.

Japan has had a long history of integrating developmental theories and educational practices from other countries into its own systems. For instance, developmental education ("hattatsushugi") is said to have been introduced into Japan over a hundred years ago during the Pestalozzian movement in the United States. This movement is reported to have introduced a child-centered approach and to have had a major influence over educational theory, teaching methods, and curricula.

A number of Japanese theorists in the field of child development have also been influential in the development of innovative programs for children. One example is Saito Kimiko, the founder of Sakura-Sakurambo Hoikuen, a well known day care program in the Saitama prefecture. Saito Kimiko reportedly developed this program after integrating her own research on Japanese culture with philosophies from other sources, such as the ideas of the Swedish feminist Ellen Key and the education reformer Nadezhda Konstantinova Krupskaya.

Following the Second World War, the education system was modified greatly, based on the American model. During the occupation of Japan, the new education structure included the establishment of a 6–3–3 ladder system (in place of the dual track system), universal co-education, and entirely new curricula and textbooks.

One value that characterized this time period is the idea of equal opportunity for education. The post-war baby boom resulted in very rapid increases in enrollment at the preschool and elementary school levels, and a great expansion in educational facilities. Since the end of World War II, the number of students attending school in Japan has increased so much that by 1980 virtually all children completed the nine years of compulsory education, with 92.4 percent going on to senior high school.

Today, the proportion of students that enroll in high school approaches 100 percent, and in 1989 the percentage of four and five year olds who participated in some sort of nursery school or kindergarten was reported at 94.4 percent. These figures for non-compulsory education attendance provide evidence of the widespread accessibility of education.

Although the egalitarian nature of education in Japan has been much praised, critics have pointed out the disparity between day care programs that serve mainly lower income children and the "enriched" (and very expensive) programs attended by children of wealthier families. "Tracking" *within* schools may be virtually non-existent, yet the schools themselves may form a hierarchy. This may be the case especially at the preschool and university levels, where the private sector plays a large role. The variety of day care or preschool programs available in Japan can be seen as a mixed blessing—providing more flexibility in the options available in terms of methods and theory but at the same time making it possible to have greater social class-related disparities between programs.

The Japanese government makes a substantial investment in education, amounting to 18.4 percent of the total government expenditure in 1985. As reported by Ichikawa (1991), comparative studies during the past decade have ranked the Japanese government as the second highest (following Australia) in terms of proportion of resources allocated to education and the highest (along with Belgium) in terms of total expenditures. However, these expenditures are allocated mainly to compulsory education, an approach that, according to Ichikawa, has "resulted in the financial sacrifice by both ends of Japan's educational spectrum—preprimary and higher education" (Ichikawa, p. 80). Because of this some researchers consider it necessary to make preschool compulsory in order to improve the system.

TYPES OF CHILD CARE PROGRAMS AVAILABLE

In the following analysis, an outline is given of the types of child care and preschool programs currently available in Japan. The first two types of programs described, Yochien and Hoikuen, are regulated by the government. The commercial programs outlined are unregulated.

Yochien

In the late 1800s schools for young children ("yochien") were developed for the purpose of giving youngsters the appropriate skills to assist their transition to primary school. The first yochien opened in 1876 and was reportedly headed by an instructor from Berlin who had been trained in Froebel's theories of kindergarten education. These initial yochien programs were geared mainly to children of upper-class families, since education before this time had been largely the privilege of the wealthy ruling class.

During the years following, the numbers of yochien continued to increase steadily, and accessibility grew for middle-class children as well. In 1947 the Diet passed legislation formalizing yochien as an educational institution and they were placed under the control of the Mombusho (Ministry of Education). According to Tobin, Wu, and Davidson of the East-West Center in Hawaii (1989), the number of yochien has continued to rise dramatically in post-war Japan, from roughly 6,000 programs in the 1940s to over 14,000 in the 1980s. Similarly, the percentage of children attending yochien had risen from 7 percent of three to six year olds in 1948 to 66 percent in 1977.

Lately there has been a slight decrease in the proportion of children enrolling in yochien due to the increased numbers of working mothers. Mothers with full-time jobs often experience difficulty if they wish their children to attend a yochien program. Until very recently most yochien only admitted children from three years of age to the age of six, creating the need to find alternative types of child care while the children are younger. Also, the hours of operation of most yochien are normally rather rigid, offering classes that typically finish by three o'clock during the week and at noon on Saturday.

Although some working parents transfer their children into yochien when they reach the age of three or four, there remains the general expectation that the mother (or, at least, another family member) of a child attending a yochien program will not only see her child off at the bus stop in the morning, but also will be there to greet him when he returns (more than 70 percent of children attending yochien travel to school by bus). Because of these factors, yochien programs largely serve children of middle-class families in which the mother is not employed outside the home.

The age range and the direction provided by the Ministry of Education prompts the comparison of yochien to the kindergarten system in the United States, although such comparisons are problematic due to curriculum differences and the large proportion of yochien programs that are private. According to Mombusho statistics, over three fourths of the children attending yochien are enrolled in private programs, which vary considerably in cost and method.

Even though the Ministry of Education (Mombusho) standards are uniform for all yochien, public and private programs are viewed very differently by parents, teachers, and researchers.

Expenses. Parents of children attending yochien are usually charged a flat rate for each year, regardless of income. Private yochien often are very expensive and elite, offering extras such as violin instruction, swimming lessons, an English teacher, or specialized learning programs. In fact, private yochien programs have been reported to charge fees that are, on the average, four times higher than any other type of preschool program.

When the Japanese government in 1972 initiated a ten-year campaign to promote education at the yochien level, 6,000 new yochien were built, and private yochien were encouraged to incorporate as educational foundations in order to be eligible for government funding. Most yochien, public or private, currently receive a yearly subsidy per student from Mombusho. Yet, enrollment has been decreasing during the past few years, due to the reduced birthrate as well as the competition from other programs better suited to the needs of working mothers.

Local governments, including the 47 prefectural and 3,440 municipal governments (listed in 1988) must undertake the responsibility for financing preschool programs, although they are heavily subsidized with national funding. These subsidies are adjusted according to each area's budget, making educational spending very similar between regions despite wide variations in economic development. In 1985 local governments received approximately one third (34.6 percent) of their funding for education from the central government, 20.7 percent of this from specific grants for education. Although private preschool programs are subsidized by the government as well, the percentage contribution toward the total operating costs made by the government to private programs has declined significantly in recent years.

Hoikuen

Whereas yochien programs are most often compared to kindergarten programs because of their structure and instructional content, hoikuen are most often referred to as equivalent to a nursery school in the United States. Hoikuen were first opened in 1890 to fill the needs of poor children with working mothers. These schools were often set up as assistance programs for the impoverished by American missionaries or local municipalities. Some industries found it profitable then, and still find it profitable now, to provide hoikuen programs as a company benefit to female workers. In this way, hoikuen have been responding to the needs of working mothers since the beginning of industrialization.

In 1947, the same year that yochien were formalized and placed under control of the Mombusho, a child welfare law was passed that defined hoikuen as welfare facilities. Hoikuen were placed under the regulation of the Koseisho (Ministry of Health and Welfare). At that time fewer than 2 percent of Japanese five year olds attended hoikuen. That proportion has since greatly risen to 25 percent in 1977 and to 30 percent in 1985. This, not surprisingly, reflects the increasing numbers of mothers in the labor force. The increase also reflects major changes in organization that have taken place recently in hoikuen programs.

Although the stigma of hoikuen as existing for lower-class children persists, two factors are currently offsetting this impression. First, hoikuen programs usually enroll infants and children up to six years of age, and there has become less distinction between the final years of hoikuen instruction and yochien instruction. The Koseisho (Ministry of Health and Welfare) has made great efforts to upgrade the hoikuen curriculum so that it is on par with yochien as far as preparation for primary school. Regulations for hoikuen programs parallel those set forth by the Mombusho in regard to curricula, health and safety, and equipment. Second, professional women are entering the work force in increasing numbers and placing their children in hoikuen. This further blurs the stigma of hoikuen as only providing for the children of poor families. Although some families choose to transfer their children to yochien after they reach three years of age, many now opt to let their children remain in the hoikuen rather than remove them.

Although more professional women are choosing to place their child in hoikuen, this does not erase the stereotype of hoikuen programs as serving children of poor families. In many cities, instead of integrating the children of working-class parents with children of professional parents, there has been the establishment of elite hoikuen with strict entrance requirements. Many private hoikuen programs have been developed to give children a head start for examinations. These programs have strict admittance requirements that might include special interviews and a mandatory IQ test for the mother.

Hoikuen are more heavily subsidized with government funding than yochien. The tuition that parents pay is typically based on a sliding scale according to taxable income, sometimes making hoikuen more expensive for wealthy families than yochien with fixed fees.

Teaching at Hoikuen and Yochien

Until recently, the training requirements given by Koseisho and Mombusho for hoikuen and yochien teachers were very different, making the possibility of Koseisho-certified teachers finding positions in yochien very low. Today, however, there exists more overlap in certification requirements for yochien and hoikuen teachers, so that the majority of instructors in hoikuen are now certified to teach in yochien as well. These requirements usually consist of two years of college education with coursework in such subjects as child development, health, and music. Preschool teaching is very demanding in terms of time and energy, due to the very long hours and the stamina needed to teach large classes of small children. Class sizes of 30 or more children are quite common in Japanese preschools.

Teachers of children in yochien and hoikuen are typically female and earn less than teachers at other levels of education, although they still earn more than they would in other traditional female occupations. Both the salaries and the working conditions in public schools tend to be better than in private yochien and hoikuen. Teachers working for private programs sometimes report additional parental pressure to provide elaborate displays of their children's activities and progress.

Careers in yochien or hoikuen teaching are normally only four to five years in duration, but this can vary depending on the type of program and its administration. Although approximately one fifth of the largely female teaching staff may stay on as administrators, most teaching staff do not rise to the position of director, which is commonly held by a man.

The Authorization Process. Anyone wishing to establish a hoikuen or yochien must seek authorization at the prefectural level (or the metropolitan level in Tokyo and Osaka). Hoikuen must additionally receive the approval of the mayor, who bases the decision on national standards and a judgment of area need. Yochien must be approved by the area's board of education through a similar process. A number of community programs remain entrenched in the somewhat difficult process of becoming licensed for quite some time.

Commercial Programs: "Baby Hotels"

One type of child care that has become available in some cities in Japan has recently received a great deal of attention in the media. These are "baby hotels" ("beibi hoteru"), which often charge by the hour and remain open 24 hours a day. Their existence demonstrates a need for child care outside the normal working day hours. These programs have been established mainly for children whose mothers work in service occupations such as sales, nursing, and the entertainment industry. Single mothers who work off hours in Japan often have a very difficult time finding care for their child or children, especially in urban areas where it is less likely that there are other family or community members available to give child care assistance.

Baby hotels are not normally regulated or licensed by an educational authority and workers do not necessarily receive any special training. This suggests that the level of care can vary considerably depending on the particular management or worker. Because these controversial commercial establishments are not licensed, it is difficult to document how widespread they are. One Koseisho survey in 1980 found 587 baby hotels caring for over 12,000 children; yet there were estimated to be as many as three times that number in operation.

In the early 1980s public attention was focused on certain incidents involving neglect and death of children left in baby hotels, generating great response in the media. Articles in newspapers and magazines described the custodial care given in certain baby hotels and the lack of training of the workers employed by baby hotel managers. Subsequent research revealed that 90 percent of the 130 deaths that occurred in child care establishments between 1968 and 1982 were in unlicensed programs.

STRENGTHS AND SHORTCOMINGS

One of the major strengths of childhood education in Japan has been its rapid popularization. As is shown in Table 16.1, in 1950 less than 10 percent of children four and five years old attended yochien, and hoikuen were attended by an even smaller number of infants and children. Since that time, however, the numbers of children in both yochien and hoikuen has steadily risen.

The percentages in Table 16.1 demonstrate the comprehensive use of

Table 16.1
Proportion of Four and Five Year Olds Attending Yochien and Hoikuen
Programs in Japan

Programs in Japan.

	1950	1975	1989
Yochien	8.9% (183,052)	63.5% (1,310,732)	64% (999,286)
Hoikuen	2%*	25%**	30.4%
Total %	10.9%	88.5%	94.4%

sources: from Annual Reports from the Ministry of Education (Mombusho) & from the Ministry of Health and Welfare (Koseisho)

*1947
**1977

early childhood education among four and five year olds, although this education is still voluntary and not without cost for parents. The reader can see that in 1989, a full 94.4 percent of all youth four and five years old attended some form of formal education program.

No longer are day care and preschool education programs either the privilege of children from wealthy families or assistance for very poor families. Opportunities to attend a variety of programs currently exist in most cities, and the high proportion of children who attend some sort of day care or preschool demonstrates the widespread availability of these programs.

This is not to say that early childhood education cannot be made more democratic or egalitarian. There is room for enrichment in the quality of programs for children, especially if government and local authorities recognize the experience and ideas of civilian educator groups and scholars. However, it is evident that great progress has been made during the past few decades toward the ideal of equal opportunity in education even at the preschool level. The next necessary step would be to make early childhood education compulsory.

Another strength of the day care and childhood education methods practiced in Japan has been the way in which children have been prepared to be productive citizens in industrial society. Children learn the value of group cooperation, of hard work, and perseverance. This preparedness has contributed to the economic success of current day Japan. At the same time, there is an emphasis on both the cognitive and emotional aspects of child development.

One problem with the types of programs available to children is the large difference in tuition between privately established schools and public ones. Although hoikuen fees are usually based on a sliding scale, private yochien programs charge a flat rate that is often extremely expensive. This undermines the quality of equal opportunity to education because many of these elite schools aim to give children a head start with enriched learning programs. This sort of disparity tends to weaken the principles of the public education system by stimulating early competition for educational achievement among children and parents.

Another problem pertains to the low salary preschool teaching staff receive. Although annual salaries of teachers and nurses in licensed day care and preschool facilities are considerably higher than wages found in many other female-dominated occupations, if salary were considered on an hourly basis, workers in child care (particularly in private preschool programs) earn much less than their counterparts in other service industries. Because of the lack of compensation for the long hours, quite a few experienced teachers quit. Therefore, it is becoming more and more difficult to retain knowledgeable teachers.

A complicating factor is the divergence of government policies between the Ministry of Education (Mombusho) that governs yochien and the Ministry of Health and Welfare (Koseisho) that governs hoikuen. There still remain many institutional differences between the policies set forth by these two branches of the government (e.g., school hours and curriculum) despite recent efforts to make them more similar. Recent movements to unify hoikuen and yochien programs into one ("Yo-Ho Ichigenka") have not yet been successful, although advocates now have some government backing. This unification proposal needs to become more of a public concern or it may not go beyond the slogan stage.

In addition, a polarization can be found in the curricula provided by private school systems. On the one hand, there exist preschool programs with extremely good equipment, aiming to educate small numbers of highly talented children. On the other hand, there are many schools that emphasize socialization with others and a free play educational style. This polarization of methods and materials reflects also the consciousness of parents, who may become confused as to the correct learning environment for their child. Since these two orientations co-exist in the parent's mind, it is very difficult for parents to find a compromise orientation toward child development and education. Although this type of confusion might provide the impetus to search for improvements in child care methods and innovative educational methods, prolonged confusion may not produce favorable results.

Finally, there is a lack of consensus regarding what child development goals are most desirable. Most teachers and parents do not hold a definite detailed image of desirable childhood education. This may be due to the lack of a definite consensus concerning the future of Japanese society. It also may be due in part to a lack of agreement, especially within public preschool systems, regarding how to implement guidelines set up by the national government. For instance, the revisions of the guidelines and course of study for yochien outlined by the Ad Hoc Council on Educational Reform created during the Nakasone administration were intended to "internationalize" methods and make childhood education curriculum more "information-oriented." However, the best implementation of these changes has not yet been agreed upon. Until these issues are resolved among school administrators, many parents must passively submit their children to the present educational system rather than working toward the improvement of day care and preschool programs.

The future of early childhood education may depend on the extent to which teachers and parents can make the systems more independent from political and industrial influence. Corporate interests have a great influence upon early education in Japan, and commercialism plays a significant part in terms of program choices at this level. Increased education and information for parents and teachers would prove beneficial for program planning and informed decision making.

Many people are actively involved in child care issues through organized participation in citizen and labor groups, parent and teacher associations, and women's organizations. A number of these groups were involved in fighting the budget cuts for child care initiated by the Nakasone government in 1985. Other groups have been attempting for quite some time to unify the yochien and hoikuen systems, with the slogan "Yo-Ho Ichigenka." Furthermore, for decades great debate has been waged over whether or not preschool education should be compulsory. In 1970, when the Central Council of Education proposed the idea of compulsory education at the preschool level, parts of the education establishment were in strong opposition, particularly private preschool administrators.

It is important to distinguish policies put forth by the government, actual practices in preschool education programs, and current issues in movements generated by teacher, parent, and other citizen groups. Clearly, child care remains an important and controversial public issue. Child care is also an issue of great importance for the decision makers in the government, particularly as the decreasing birthrate, the labor shortage, and the aging population continue to be national concerns.

NOTE

The discussion of strengths and shortcomings is based largely on the comments of Yamazaki Shoho, former professor of education at Shizuoka University, and Kaneda Toshiko, professor of childhood education at Shizuoka University. Also included is input from Sekiguchi Teiichi, visiting scholar in the Cornell University School of Industrial and Labor Relations, on leave from Chuo University, Tokyo.

REFERENCES

Arioka, J. (1991). "Fewer Babies: A Private Matter?" In *Japan Quarterly*, January-March, Vol. 38:1, pp. 50–56.

Ato, M. (1991). "The Decreasing Birth Rate: Background and Prospects." *Nihon Rodo Kenkyu Zasshi* (The Monthly Journal of The Japan Institute of Labor), August: 33: 8.

Beauchamp, E. R. (1991). "The Development of Japanese Educational Policy, 1945–1985." In E. R. Beauchamp (Ed.), *Windows on Japanese Education*. Westport, Conn.: Greenwood Press.

Boocock, S. S. (1991). "The Japanese Preschool System." In E. R. Beauchamp (Ed.), *Windows on Japanese Education*. Westport, Conn.: Greenwood Press.

Brause, S. (1990). "Love and Marriage." Reproduced from KG Monthly, November and December: p. 217. In *Japan Update*, Winter 1991.

Chung, B. (1988). "Labor Market Demand for Working Mothers and the Evolution of the Day Care System in Japan." *Sociology of the Family*, Autumn, Vol. 18: 2.

Cummings, W. (1980). *Education and Equality in Japan*. Princeton, N.J.: Princeton University Press.

Devos, G. and Wagatsuma, H. (1973). *Socialization for Achievement: Essays on the Cultural Psychology of the Japanese*. Berkeley: University of California Press.

Fujimura-Faneslaw, K. and Imura, A. E. (1991). "The Education of Women in Japan." In E. R. Beauchamp (Ed.), *Windows on Japanese Education*. Westport, Conn.: Greenwood Press.

Goodman, R. (1990). *Japan's "International Youth": The Emergence of a New Class of Schoolchildren*. Oxford: Clarendon Press.

Harada, Saburo. (1987). "The Character of Children and the Character of Schools." Reproduced in *Japan Update*, Summer, pp. 3–7.

Ichikawa, Shogo. (1989). "Japanese Education in American Eyes: A Response to William Cummings." *Comparative Education*, 25:3.

Imada, S. (1991). "Josei no Kyaria to Korekara no Hatarakikata." ("Careers for Women and the Future Way of Working Life"). In *Nihon Rodo Kenkyu Zasshi* {The monthly journal of The Japan Institute of Labor), August: 33, No. 8.

Imamura, A. E. (1987). *Urban Japanese Housewives: At Home and in the Community*. Hawaii: University of Hawaii Press.

Ishida, H. (1989). *Kigyo to Jinzai* (Companies and Human Resources). Tokyo: Hosodaigaku Kyoiku Shinkokai.

Japan Update. (1987). "The Age of Women." From the Nissan Parts Co., Summer, pp. 8–9.

Japan Update. (1991). "Japan Heads Toward Negative Population Growth." Spring, pp. 4–9.

Kawashima, S. (1984). *Yami ni Tadayou Kodomotachi* (Children Who Wander in the Darkness). Tokyo: Ayumi Shuppan.

Kotloff, L. J. (1988). "Dai-ichi Preschool: Fostering Individuality and Cooperative Group-Life in a Progressive Japanese Preschool." Ph.D. Dissertation, Cornell University.

Lebra, T. S. (1976). *Japanese Patterns of Behavior*. Honolulu: University of Hawaii Press.

Lebra, T. S. (1984). *Japanese Women: Constraint and Fulfillment*. Honolulu: University of Hawaii Press.

LeVine, R., and White, M. (1986). *Human Conditions: The Cultural Basis of Educational Development*. New York: Routledge and Kegan Paul.

Lynn, R. (1988). *Educational Achievement in Japan: Lessons for the West*. Armonk, N.Y.: M. E. Sharpe.

Mombusho [Japan Ministry of Education, Science and Culture]. (1985). *Monbu Tokei Yoran* (Handbook of Education Statistics). Tokyo: Mombusho.

Okuyama, A., Sodei, T., Fujii, R., and Nitta, M. (1991). "Child Care Leave and Related Issues." Panel discussion. *Nihon Rodo Kenkyu Zasshi* (The Monthly Journal of The Japan Institute of Labor), August: 33: 8.

Prime Minister's Office. (1983). "Present Status of Women and Policies: Third Report on the National Agenda Program." Tokyo: Foreign Press Center.

Rodosho [Ministry of Labor]. (1989). *Rodohakusho*. (Yearbook). Tokyo: Rodosho.

Schoppa, L. J. (1991). *Education Reform in Japan*. New York: Routledge.

Shoji, M. (1983). "Early Childhood Education in Japan." In G. Lall and M. Bernard (Eds.), *Comparative Early Childhood Education*. Chicago: Charles C. Thomas.

Simmons, Cyril. (1990). *Growing Up and Going to School in Japan: Tradition and Trends*. Philadelphia, Pa.: Open University Press.

Simons, Carol. (1987). "They Get By with a Lot of Help from Their Kyoiku Mamas." *Smithsonian*, 17: 44–52.

Tanosaki, Akio. (1989). "Contemporary Cities and Industrial Change." Translated by Mark A. Riddle. *Japanese Economic Studies*, Winter, 1990–91.

Tobin, J. J., Wu, D.Y.H., and Davidson, D. H. (1989). *Preschool in Three Cultures*. New Haven, Conn.: Yale University Press.

Tsuda, Masami. (1985). *Jinji Romu Kanri* (Personnel Management and Industrial Relations). Tokyo: Hosodaigaku Kyoiku Shinkokai.

Usui, N. (1990). "Between War Cry of Career and Whisper of Sweet Home." Reproduced in *Japan Update*, Winter 1991.

White, Merry. (1987). *The Japanese Education Challenge: A Commitment to Children*. New York: Free Press.

Yano, K. and Yano, I. (eds.). (1986). *Suuji de Miru: Nihon no Hyakunen*, 2nd ed. (From a Statistical View: One Hundred Years of Japan). Tokyo: Koseisha.

Yoshida, K. and Okubayashi, K. (Eds.). (1991). *Gendai no Romukanri*. (Contemporary Personnel Management and Industrial Relations). Kyoto: Minerva Shobo.

17

KENYA

Lea I. Kipkorir

THE PHYSICAL SETTING

Kenya covers 583,000 square kilometers of East Africa and borders the Indian Ocean for 400 kilometers. The country is almost bisected by the equator and has diverse physical features—savannah, tropical, equatorial, glacial, and volcanic landscapes. Rainfall is adequate only in small scattered areas of the country and water remains one of the main obstacles to agriculture and good health. Less than one third of the land is suitable for agriculture, which together with tourism forms the mainstay of the country's economy. The rest of Kenya is arid and semi-arid.

POLITICAL, DEMOGRAPHIC, AND ECONOMIC CHANGES

Kenya became part of the British East Africa Protectorate in 1895. While building the Kenya-Uganda railway between 1895 and 1902, the British found the country ideally suited for settlement by the white man and his family, and this settlement was encouraged. Kenya was seen as a British settlement similar to Australia, Canada, and New Zealand. Some Indians were brought in as laborers to build the railway, and others came as traders. Kenya became a British colony in 1920 and was ruled by the British until it achieved independence in 1963. The country thus became a nation with three racial groups: African, Asian, and Caucasian.

The country is politically and administratively divided into eight provinces. These are in turn divided into 41 districts with subsets of divisions and locations. The district unit is the focus of administration as it is the center of planning and implementation of government programs.

Kenya has one of the fastest growing populations in the world. A population that had been 5.2 million in 1948 became 10.9 million in 1969 and 16.1 million just ten years later. The 1990 estimate is 25 million people, with a growth rate of 3.8 percent. The rapid population growth is due to a combination of a decline in overall infant mortality, a general rise in the standard of living, improvement of maternal and child health, high fertility rate (7.7 in 1984), and increased life expectancy.

This high population growth has strained the resources of the country, particularly in the provision of services to meet such basic needs as health, education, and employment. This has been the case especially because of the fact that of the total population, 50 percent is under the age of 15 years. As early as 1967 population control measures such as family planning were introduced to curb the high growth rate.

The urban population has grown from 10.2 percent in 1970 to 16.7 percent in 1987, a much more rapid rate of expansion than that of the rural population. Migration from rural areas has been the main cause of this growth, creating severe shortfalls in the provision of such services as water, housing, health and school facilities and has contributed to the growth of urban slums.

About 80 percent of the Kenyan population lives in rural areas. The majority of these people are concentrated on that 20 percent of the lands with medium and high agricultural potential. Thus these areas have suffered from serious population pressures, and land has been fragmented to units so small as to be almost economically infeasible. Many people are engaged in subsistence agriculture. Those in the arid and semi-arid areas (80 percent of the land) practice pastoralism, whereas fishing constitutes the major activity of those around the lakes and coastal areas.

Agriculture is the most important sector in Kenya's economy, contributing about 35 percent of the gross national product and employing about 70 percent of the labor force. Productivity in agriculture has at times been severely affected by weather conditions, such as drought and floods, and by the fluctuating commodity prices for cash crops, such as tea and coffee.

To alleviate poverty and unemployment and curb rural-urban migration, the informal sector is being developed in small trading centers and promoted by the government and other development agencies. This sector consists of semi-organized and unregulated activities undertaken mostly by the self-employed, both men and women, who operate in open air markets, carrying out such activities as trading, tailoring, carpentry, weaving, blacksmithing, and general repair work. Efforts are being made to strengthen the financing and management of these activities. For the majority of Kenyans, non-farm job opportunities will be in this sector in the future. Another sector being promoted is that of cooperatives.

CHANGING SOCIALIZATION PATTERNS

There are more than 20 linguistic communities in Kenya. Although these communities have different customs, beliefs, and practices, in all of them the mother, as the first person in contact with the child, has played a significant role in establishing a warm interpersonal relationship. This relationship was then extended to the other members of the family, particularly to the older siblings, grandmothers, and other relatives. The child was brought up in a social environment that offered him love, care, and security. In this social arrangement the family catered to all the physical, social, emotional, and educational needs of the child.

The introduction of the cash economy and different settlement patterns have eroded this stable and secure environment. This process of disintegration of family units was quickened by the migration of men to urban and large-scale farming areas in search of paid employment, leaving women as the heads of their families as well as breadwinners and mothers.

Today the rural areas have experienced major changes in the organization of economic activities that affect child-rearing and socialization patterns. The changed settlement patterns have removed grandparents from the extended family environment, thereby removing support for the child. Today parents living in separate nuclear families have to rely on paid helpers.

The rapid expansion of educational opportunities, particularly at the primary school level, has resulted in the majority of children aged six and above attending primary school, thus removing another traditional source of child-rearing assistance.

Land shortage has also created a class of landless, rural dwellers who earn their living by working in the large tea, coffee, sugar, or sisal plantations, where they work from dawn to dusk. These parents cannot afford the services of childminders, so their older children go to school while the younger ones are left alone. These are the children who go without sufficient food and suffer from nutrition-related diseases.

Nuclear families in urban areas either employ a childminder or lock their children up at home. Even the childminders have often proved unsatisfactory, as some are young themselves and do not know or care about how to look after a baby. The single parent (a new phenomenon in Kenya) is emerging, and she too is in need of child care services. These indeed are parents and children in need of a setting that will provide good, affordable child care while the mothers are at work.

Employment of Women

Eighty-eight percent of Kenyan women reside in rural areas, and most of them are economically active. Traditionally women still contribute most of the labor required to cultivate food crops on family holdings and much of the labor in small and medium-sized holdings devoted to the production of cash crops. Even when women are not busy with economic activities, they are occupied with household duties, which also contribute to the living standards of the households. Thus it is not useful to maintain the distinction between economic and non-economic activities in this context, and usual estimates of female participation rate in the rural labor force are misleading in this regard.

In contrast to the situation in rural areas, women's representation in modern wage employment in urban areas has always been low. It is important to note that those women who are in formal employment receive only two months of maternity leave, which means that their need for assistance with child care resumes shortly after the birth of the child. In recognition of the contributions made by women, the Kenyan government has deliberately instituted policies and programs that try to place women at the center of development by allocating resources and supporting donor agencies and non-governmental organizations (NGOs) that participate in women's programs.

Maendeleo Ya Wanawake

The Maendeleo ya Wanawake (progress of women) Organization was formed in 1952 with the main objective of improving the economic, social, and political status of women in Kenya. The organization has encouraged its members, through group activities, to participate fully in development efforts and in uplifting the welfare of families, especially in rural areas. The groups promote a variety of voluntary services and self-help projects among women, including health and family planning programs, food production and processing, environment and energy conservation through improved cooking stoves and the planting of trees, leadership training programs, income generating programs, and improved housing for their families.

These groups have also initiated development projects such as group ownership of land, and the building of institutions such as preschools, orphanages, and small-scale industries. Still another objective of the organization has been to help the needy, the disabled, and disadvantaged women and children.

There are other women's organizations that work in urban areas, and others are affiliated with international groups. The total membership in all these groups is estimated at 1 million women.

FORMAL EDUCATION

Formal education was introduced to Kenya by European Christian missionaries toward the end of the 19th century. Initially the goal was to promote evangelism, but later education became an instrument for the development of skilled labor for European farms and clerical staff for the colonial administration. A racially divided approach to education was adopted, with Europeans as first priority, Asians second, and African students as last resort. The European educational system, which was based on British traditions and received more resources, had as its main objectives the preparation of youth from European families for leadership positions. The Asian and Arab systems were aimed at producing clerical staff for the colonial administration. The African system tended to develop as a hybrid of academic, technical, and vocational components designed to serve the various needs of the colonial power.

Missionaries built the schools, managed and supervised them, determined the curriculum and influenced the direction of education policy, with only a small grant subsidy from the Department of Education. Besides school education, the Government provided facilities for technical and higher education in the East African region through the establishment of Makerere College in 1922 and the Royal Technical College in Nairobi in 1956.

Racial segregation in education was abolished in 1960 as the country moved closer to independence. With the attainment of independence in December 1963, a Ministry of Education was created and the school system in Kenya was brought under a localized standard curriculum and public examinations.

AFTER INDEPENDENCE

The government acted swiftly to plan and relate education to national needs and aspirations. The national concern was the training of more human resources to enhance economic development, more equitable distribution of national income, closer integration to bring national unity, and the amelioration of national disparities.

The government's main objectives for education, both then and now, are to foster national unity, serve the needs of national development, develop and communicate the rich and varied cultures of Kenya, prepare and equip youth with the knowledge, skills, and expertise necessary to enable them to play an effective role in the life of the nation, and provide for the full development of individual talents and personality. Education must also promote social justice and morality, and it must foster positive attitudes and consciousness toward other nations.

In 1989, 30 percent of Kenyan children three to six years old (802,000 children) attended preschools. About 5 million children were in primary schools, 500,000 youths in secondary schools, and just over 30,000 students attending universities.

The Education of Women

The number of girls at all levels of education has been rising steadily over the years. In primary school the percentage of enrollees who were girls rose from 35 percent in 1964 to 50 percent in 1990. At the secondary level the rise has been from 30 percent in 1964 to nearly 50 percent in 1990 in some districts.

The proportions of girls enrolling in secondary education are low when compared to those enrolling for and completing primary school. The reasons for this trend are, first, that the average cost of educating a girl in Kenya is higher than that for educating a boy. Given the low average family incomes, many girls are unable to attend secondary schools due to parental financial constraints. A second reason arises from the relative shortage of secondary school facilities for girls as compared to boys. Third, a number of girls drop out of school due to pregnancy, and in some communities due to early marriages. In 1990, 30 percent of university students are women, a notable rise from the 15 percent recorded in 1973.

Since literacy is a basic necessity for personal development, it is important to raise the literacy rates of any given population as one of the efforts to facilitate development. The adult literacy programs in Kenya are intended to assist those who have not attained formal education to acquire the skills of reading and writing in at least one language.

In 1967 a selective literacy program was launched in Kenya, catering to only a few districts and a limited number of participants. A functional literacy program was introduced on a mass scale in 1978 when it was discovered that only 38 percent of women and 61 percent of men could read and write in at least one language.

HARAMBEE SPIRIT

There is much in our African heritage, especially concern and respect for others, the Harambee spirit, the dedication to integrity, and the respect for the family, which we must maintain. Indeed, we must strengthen these traditions because they, together with development, are the principal means by which we can enhance the moral and material well-being of our children. And it is through our children that we build the future of the nation.

—1963 speech by President Jomo Kenyatta

With political independence at hand in 1963 the people of Kenya adopted the motto "Harambee," the Swahili word meaning "let us pull together." This motto embodies the concept of mutual responsibility extended from the family to the community and to the whole nation. It is a phenomenon deeply rooted in African traditions.

In this way Kenyans were urged to pull together all resources available, both human and material, to build the nation. This early vision of the need for true partnership and cooperation between the government and its people, non-governmental agencies, and international organizations was based on the realization that the government could not achieve the targets of development alone. From then to the present, all national development plans have underlined this appeal, that the people reduce their expectation of what the government can do for them and instead become true partners in development, attempting to match or supplement government effort. Today Kenya stands proud of these early efforts by its people, symbolized in many Harambee preschools, primary and secondary schools, health centers, churches, water projects, cattle dips, and institutes of technology. In some areas of development, and particularly in early childhood education, the people's efforts have surpassed the government contribution.

EARLY CHILDHOOD EDUCATION AND CARE

In 1990 there were 15,469 preschools in Kenya, where 20,696 teachers worked with 802,000 children. Nearly all of these programs have been developed in the past 27 years, which represents a phenomenal rate of growth.

The first nursery school in Kenya was established in Nairobi for European children in 1942. A nursery school for African children was first built in 1948. Thus these facilities developed along the racial lines described earlier. By 1970, 16 day nurseries had been built in Nairobi, serving children two years of age and older. These nurseries were run by staff who had undergone a course of study in either child care or nursing. The nurseries operated year round on a 7 A.M. to 5 P.M. schedule, with meals provided, every day except Sunday. These nurseries were seen as a health service, where personal hygiene and good health habits were promoted. Doctors visited regularly, and there was heavy emphasis placed on protective foods and vitamins. Activities consisted of both indoor and outdoor play, for which there were plenty of materials, songs, stories, and hymns. Clearly this was a service available to a few well-to-do families, who valued it and could afford it.

Elsewhere in the rural areas, and especially after 1963, many were responding to the Harambee call by setting up preschools. The parents, and especially the mothers, organized themselves into groups to build and manage the centers. The centers were small, simple in structure, and catered to children from the village. One of the mothers was chosen as the "teacher," and the children were brought to the center while the other mothers went to work. As there was no provision for lunch, some children brought food while others went without it. The activities were mainly games, songs, and dances, and a few "ABC"-related activities. A small fee was charged, which went to the teacher as her salary, or the mothers would make payment through services like tilling the teacher's garden or selling her produce for her at the market.

In the late 1970s, with increased competition for entry into primary schools, parents began to put pressure on the teachers to "teach" the children. Formal teaching was introduced. Although there were an estimated 300,000 children attending preschools in 1970, there was as yet no viable training program for preschool teachers, no supervision, and no clearly established program of activities. In urban areas many of the preschools not run by churches or the local public authority were operated for profit.

Types of Program

Institutions caring for three- to six-year-old children in Kenya are referred to by various names.[1] Kindergartens are found mainly in urban areas. They are privately run and costly. Day nurseries and play groups are also to be found in the urban areas. The fee for these services is not as high as for the kindergartens.

Day care centers and nursery schools are found in rural areas. A majority of them are managed by parents' committees and some are assisted by local authorities.

Preschool units or reception classes are usually attached to and managed by primary schools. These only serve children aged five and older who are preparing to enroll in the first primary grade at the same school. A majority of these are found in urban areas.

Sponsors and Services

Currently the following sponsors and agencies offer preschool education services:

1. Parents/committees/local community. They are responsible for putting up buildings and furniture.
2. Church organizations. Nursery schools are built on church compounds or use church buildings as classrooms during the week. Some churches employ teachers and some assist with a feeding program.
3. Firms, estates, and corporations. Some have established preschools for their employee's children. They also employ the teachers and provide the equipment.
4. Voluntary organizations (Lions Club, Red Cross, Child Welfare Society). They have initiated the construction and running of preschools.
5. Women's organizations such as Kanu Maendeleo Ya Wanawake, YWCA, and Women's Guild, which run some institutions for young children.
6. Private communities/individuals. These are individuals and private organizations who organize and manage preschools mostly in urban areas. They are responsible

for the provision and maintenance of the physical facilities, furniture, teachers' salaries, school management, and teacher training sponsorship.

Why the Demand for Preschools?

Several studies and surveys have been carried out to determine the reasons for the rapid growth in preschools in Kenya. Three factors stand out clearly. The first is cognitive. Kenyan parents value education very highly and would like to see their children do well in formal schools. They see success in schooling as a channel of access to better occupations and higher life-styles. Most parents therefore assume that exposure to preschool experiences will substantially improve performance at the primary and subsequent levels of education. Such parents have explicit expectations of what should be taught at the preschool level. They want their children to have competence in languages (English and Kiswahili), basic number concepts, and literacy.

The second concern of parents is in the psychomotor area: parents are aware of the many health hazards that could affect the children's growth and development. They require that children not only be fed but also receive other health related services like inoculations. Safety of the child is also important to parents, and working mothers want the program to take responsibility for the custody of their children.

Social-emotional concerns are the third factor influencing parents. Education is a life-long process that begins at an early age with socialization into the values, norms, and attitudes of a society. In many communities, integrity, sociability, generosity, ethics, and concepts of honor are among the qualities constantly nurtured in children. Given the major changes in the organization of economic and social activities affecting Kenyan child-rearing patterns described earlier in this chapter, parents look to preschools for support. Preschools are the first institutions outside the home where children meet with non-family members. They do play an important role in reinforcing the socialization process already started at home.

Clearly preschool institutions play a very important role in Kenyan society. Upon realizing this, the government has continued to be involved and concerned with the development of preschool education, in order to ensure that quality services are provided to the children, the teachers, and the community.

GOVERNMENT INVOLVEMENT IN PRESCHOOL EDUCATION

The Kenyan child has a broad range of guaranteed rights and services. Over 60 government statutes determine the manner in which children are to be treated.

Government's concern for the development of preschool education began in the 1960s when the Ministries of Health and Home Affairs were charged with the responsibility for vaccination, treatment, and other preventive health measures, and for giving education in child care to mothers, teachers, and communities. The Ministry of Local Government, through the local authorities (county councils, municipalities, and town councils), established some preschool buildings, employed some teachers and supervisors, and in some cases provided equipment and learning materials. In some areas these local authorities provided health services and meals and organized in-service courses for their teachers.

In 1966 the Ministry of Culture and Social Services became responsible for the coordination, training, and supervision of preschool education. The ministry began to register and supervise virtually all private and self-help day care centers, and courses for training nursery school teachers were established in several parts of the country. There was, however, a lack of qualified trainers and supervisors.

Teachers and supervisors were trained in four national institutions beginning in 1968. However, the output of this effort was limited to 120 teachers per year. Many of these trained teachers preferred to work in urban areas where salaries were slightly higher. The rural programs, which had the most need, continued to function with untrained teachers. To help the teachers, a handbook on day care centers was published by this ministry in 1970.

The Preschool Education Project

Until this point in time the Ministry of Education had not been actively involved in preschool education. But in 1971 the ministry, together with the Bernard van Leer Foundation, launched the Preschool Education Project at the Kenya Institute of Education. The purposes of the project were threefold. The first goal was to prepare a cadre of officers, expert in modern preschool methods, who could assume the responsibility of promoting and supervising Kenyan nursery schools. The second objective was to document, through research, the educational and social gains of children exposed to such programs. A third purpose was to establish initially a small number of "demonstration" or model preschools in disadvantaged areas that embody the best features of modern preschool practice.

The objectives clearly borrowed heavily from the then current models based on the 1960s approaches to early childhood education. In order to operationalize them, the project set out to devise a teacher training program for upgrading early childhood education in Kenya, identify and train nursery school personnel for occupying supervisory roles, develop an experimental nursery school curriculum (matter, method, and instructional materials), and organize and conduct research activities in significant areas.

The project had three distinct phases. The first, conducted in Nairobi, sought to develop evaluation schemes. It was conducted at the Kenya Institute of Education, working with established nursery schools and day care centers within the city. The second phase sought to extrapolate the model and adapt it for application in more disadvantaged areas beyond Nairobi. The third phase involved wider dissemination of the program into three carefully selected rural areas. This phase was problematic in that the areas had diverse ethnic languages and a range of child development and child survival problems far beyond what had so far been encountered. The model had to be adapted to meet the different needs. At the end of the project ten years later the following had been achieved:

1. In-service training for some 200 teachers sponsored by local authorities in five districts.

2. Evolution of an on-the-job training model that upgraded the quality of the teachers without removing them from their working context. The training was planned and administered in their working environment. It was participatory in that trainees were encouraged to contribute to their own training. This approach required that the facilitators (trainers) be familiar with the environment in which training was taking place, so that the community could participate.

3. Improved ability by the teachers to cater to children's needs. They became more competent in planning and organizing activities and they changed their teaching styles from formal to more informal approaches. They also acquired decision-making skills and became more confident in choosing and directing their class activities.

The on-the-job model also facilitated commitment and participation of the parent teachers, trainers, and local leadership. This ensured self-generation and continuation of the program even at the end of the project's intensive participation. Using local initiatives and resources, the trained teachers were able to train many more teachers.

The teachers, trainers, and the community were all involved in curriculum development. This facilitated recognition and respect for the contributions of the parties involved, thus releasing a wealth of ideas and energies in a developmental process that was relevant and meaningful to all participants.

Another important feature of the project was the partnership and linkages among individual parents, local communities, local authorities, the government, and external agencies. All contributed to enriching the preschool project by providing resources, finances, and shared wisdom.

Of particular interest was the involvement of the community in the project. The project communicated a new interest in and commitment to early childhood education at the community level by enlisting the support of community organizations, local councils, women's groups, and voluntary bodies.

For teachers, the project developed a number of support materials, including a teacher's and trainer's guide, an in-service syllabus, and slides and tapes. A national guideline for early childhood education was developed for the institutions with the following objectives:

- To provide an informal education geared toward developing the child's mental capabilities and physical growth.
- To make it possible for the child to enjoy living and learning through play.
- To enable the child to build good habits for effective living as an individual and a member of a group.
- To enable the child to appreciate his cultural background and customs.
- To foster the spiritual and moral growth of the child.
- To develop the child's imagination, self-reliance, and reasoning skills.
- To enrich the child's experience so as to enable him to cope better with primary school life.

Implementation on a Broader Scale

Preschool education officially became a function of the Ministry of Education in 1980, and the ministry was charged with responsibility for the registration, supervision, and inspection of preschools; the training of teachers and supervisors; curriculum development; advisory services; and the formulation of policy guidelines.

The first national Preschool Education Seminar was organized in June 1982, at the end of the experimental phase of the Preschool Education Project. Participants in the seminar examined the trends in preschool education and discussed ways of mobilizing resources and coordinating the inputs of different sponsors and partners, in order to increase and improve the quality of services to the preschool child. Recommendations were made involving the formulation of policy guidelines, teacher training, curriculum development, research, and supervision. The seminar group also recommended that the emergent preschool education model be disseminated nationally.

To carry out these responsibilities the ministry established a national committee, the Early Childhood Implementation Committee, which advises the ministry on policy issues and the general development of the program. A Preschool Section was also set up in the ministry, with two units. The Headquarters Unit deals with all administrative matters regarding coordination of all partners, the registration of preschools, the management of government grants and funds from external donors, and the provision of early childhood personnel at all levels. The Inspectorate Unit is concerned with the maintenance of the program's professional standards. It coordinates the inspection and supervision of schools and training institutions, as well as the teachers undergoing training, and it administers teacher examinations.

THE NATIONAL CENTER FOR EARLY CHILDHOOD EDUCATION

Based on a 1982 National Seminar recommendation, the Ministry of Education decided to launch the National Center for Early Childhood Education (NACECE), to coordinate and continue the development of training programs, and to provide a national support system for early childhood education. With the support of the Bernard van Leer Foundation, NACECE was established in 1984 at the Kenya Institute of Education.

The Functions of NACECE

The National Center for Early Childhood Education is responsible for the development and dissemination of professional ideas, educational materials, and services for early childhood education and care. This involves the training of early childhood education personnel; curriculum development and dissemination; the identification, design, execution, and coordination of research into early childhood education and care settings; the provision of services to agencies involved in early childhood education; the coordination and liaison with external and internal partners; and the dissemination of information about the needs and development of the preschool education program.

District Centers for Early Childhood Education

The National Center for Early Childhood Education works in conjunction with District Centers for Early Childhood Education (DICECE). These district centers ensure that training and awareness programs are brought directly in contact with preschool children and their families. This is done through the training of teachers and other personnel at the district level and the development of relevant preschool curricula. The DICECE also supervise and inspect preschool programs in the district and involve the local community in those programs. These centers participate in evaluating local programs and carrying out basic research on the status of preschool children in and out of preschool settings.

Training

Years of experimentation and research during the Preschool Education Project revealed that training should not be limited to trainers and teachers. In order that personnel function effectively it was important that those in their working environments also be trained to give support and guidance. Therefore training was extended to parents, counselors, local leaders, local authorities, and local communities.

The Training of Trainers

The course of training for DICECE trainers consists of residential and field experience components spread over a period of nine months. The residential session consists of a total of 12 weeks divided into a number of sessions. The rest of the nine month period is spent in the field, either training teachers or monitoring their activities, which includes curriculum development workshops and seminars for field officers, parents, and teachers. Trainers also conduct action research in selected areas. The residential sessions are held in different parts of the country. This gives the trainers exposure to different cultures and environments.

The training of trainers also employs the participatory approach in which the trainers contribute to their own training. To achieve this, the course is mainly organized into seminars and workshops to facilitate full participation by all. The trainers are expected to initiate discussions, share experiences, and initiate group and individual projects.

Training through experience and practice is also used in order to make the trainers more sensitive to problems and issues in early childhood and also to give them skills in managing early childhood services and training teachers. They also carry out research on various aspects of early childhood education and care. Part of these investigations involves the collection of information and the formulation of recommendations and strategies for improving and developing early childhood programs. During training, emphasis is placed on practical aspects of the course. The trainers develop materials and demonstrate their use in preschools.

The work of the trainers is, however, closely related to the way their communities perceive them before, during, and after the induction. The respect and authority that the trainers have in their communities continues to be a propelling force in all of their activities. They are able to mobilize their communities to improve preschool facilities, pay teachers, start feeding programs, and improve the welfare of their children.

The training is done by the staff at NACECE, assisted by specialists who act as resource persons, particularly during the residential sessions. About 150 trainers have undergone the induction course.

The Two-Year Teacher In-Service Course

Training of teachers is a key function of NACECE and DICECE. The majority of the preschool teachers in Kenya have as yet received no training.

Teachers undergo a two-year in-service program. The course consists of six residential sessions of a total of 18 weeks. These sessions are held during the school holidays. Trainers give on-the-job assistance to the teachers during this time. The following areas are covered during the residential sessions:

A. Child development

B. Preschool curriculum

    1. Planning, organization and class management

    2. Arts and crafts

    3. Music and movement

    4. Physical and outdoor activities

    5. Language activities

    6. Environmental activities

    7. Health and nutrition

C. Community involvement and school administration

D. History, development, and status of preschool education in Kenya

E. General knowledge

F. Field experience

The trainers also monitor the provision of a rich learning environment, child stimulation, the fostering of overall growth and development, and the involvement of the community. In community involvement, teachers are expected to solicit and guide the community in providing suitable facilities and learning materials, in establishing feeding programs, in administering child immunizations, and in providing safe and adequate socialization.

The on-the-job aspects of the training are crucial to the success of the early childhood education program. In this way the decentralization of the early childhood education program is brought to the grassroots level. Children, teachers, parents, and community members contribute to the development, testing, and implementation of new ideas. Under these circumstances the teacher is expected to play a catalyst role. She is not just a "teacher" but also a researcher, curriculum developer, community worker, family support, and agent of change.

Other Training Programs

One center in Nairobi carries out Montessori training. Only a small number of teachers are trained, and they teach in those few schools using the Montessori method.

The Kindergarten Headmistress Association, an organization of privately owned kindergartens in Nairobi, conducts a training program for the teachers in those centers. The association also works to develop and maintain high standards in its kindergartens through the examination and certification of teachers.

EARLY CHILDHOOD EDUCATION CURRICULA

"It is...a common phenomenon to find preschool children in Kenya chanting nursery rhymes and poems like 'London Bridge is Falling Down,' 'The Little Snowman,' and 'Going to London to see the Queen,' " observed a commission on education in 1976 about the state of the early childhood education curriculum in Kenya. Not that these rhymes are no longer sung by some children, but now there are hundreds of others more meaningful, relevant, and understood by teachers, parents and children.

The debate on the relevance of the curriculum to the Kenyan culture has continued for many years. Kenya is made up of many ethnic groups and hence is a complex cultural setting. Different ethnic groups have different cultural traditions, social norms, values, and beliefs. However, there are many customs that cut across many ethnic groups. Curriculum development at this level has been designed both to reflect the norms and values of Kenya as a nation as well as to focus on the special needs of children from different cultural settings. One of the educational goals for education in Kenya emphasizes the need to respect, foster, and develop Kenya's rich and varied cultures.

The development and dissemination of curricula is an important component in the implementation of the NACECE/DICECE program. Although some centralized curriculum was developed under the Preschool Education Project (e.g., the "Guidelines for Preschool Education in Kenya, 1984"), there has been continued need for both centralized and decentralized curriculum development, which guarantees that the needs of trainers, teachers, and children of different cultures and environments are met while at the same time ensuring the maintenance of acceptable overall standards.

In developing the curriculum, the program has adopted the participatory model whereby trainers, parents, and local communities are involved. This approach liberates the trainer and the teachers from following the preschool curriculum rigidly, and it encourages them to improvise and to utilize the physical and human environment without restraint. In addition, the participatory approach develops confidence, a sense of achievement, and satisfaction in all those involved because they feel that they have contributed to the learning of their children.

Localized Curriculum

It is because of the cultural diversity described above that centralized curriculum development cannot adequately serve all the cultural patterns represented in Kenya. In view of this, NACECE recommended that preschool teachers, parents, and local communities be helped to establish a conceptual framework and develop skills that they can use to make decisions and identify curriculum materials relevant to the preschool children and their families within their local contexts.

Within DICECEs a curriculum development team is made up of DICECE staff, teachers, field officers, parents, and other members of the community. The team has to be familiar with the people's ways of life, including their culture, social values, social norms, and physical environment. Two types of localized curricular content have emerged:

Teacher/Parent made materials. The environments around both the home and the school provide a wide range of materials and objects with which children can work and play. Basic materials like water, sand, wood, and clay found in the nearby environment are useful in preschool learning and play activities. These materials also provoke the children to interact freely and unconsciously with other children and teachers, and therefore help their language development. Due to the importance of materials in preschool activities, the program has put a lot of emphasis during training on the collection and development of such materials. The trainers guide the teachers in how to develop such learning and play materials as toys, picture cards and books, number cards, letter cards, blocks, pegboards and weaving boards, balls, and ropes.

Folklore. The program has developed books of stories, poems, games, and riddles in various local languages. The process starts with the training of the DICECE trainers by NACECE staff. They are taught how to solicit support, how to select resource persons, and how to determine which are the best methods to use in order to collect needed information. By 1990, books of stories, poems, and riddles had been published in 21 mother tongues. The DICECE teams initiate the process of mobilizing parents, local leaders, teachers, and children to identify, collect, and collate materials related to their oral culture and traditions. The team identifies resource persons who form the district editorial team, which gets technical assistance from the experts at the Kenya Institute of Education. Through this process community-based stories, poems, rhymes, games, dances, and children's songs are identified and compiled. The final editing, graphics, and printing are coordinated and undertaken by NACECE in consultation with the relevant DICECE trainers.

Other materials that have been prepared and are in the process of being published include manuals in the following areas:

1. Management, organization of preschool centers, and language activities.
2. Creative activities, music, and movement.
3. Mathematics and environmental activities.
4. A health education manual focused on personal hygiene, child health, common childhood diseases, health records, child safety, and food production preservation, storage, and usage.
5. Child development.
6. Materials development.

A number of films and videos have been developed that are used during training and in creating awareness at all levels.

STRENGTHS, SHORTCOMINGS, AND CHALLENGES

Considering the relatively recent history of early childhood education and care in Kenya, much has been accomplished. This is true especially in relation to the development of viable training programs for the various categories of people involved with child care, the production of low cost and relevant preschool curriculum materials, the creation of awareness in parents and communities of the need for the full development of the child, the establishment of partnerships, and the commitment of the government to assist where possible in further strengthening early childhood programs.

These can be seen only as initial steps. There are still shortcomings, and some of these are substantial. Currently only 30 percent of children between the ages of three and six are attending preschool. Coverage needs to be extended to all children. Children under three who need this type of care are not included at all. Their mothers need this kind of assistance in order to be able to participate in other activities.

The quality of care and education in existing facilities needs to be greatly improved, in terms of physical facilities, the training of personnel, and the provision of play and learning materials. Some minimum standards have to be established and mechanisms for enforcing them set. Efforts must be made to extend center care to full-day coverage, with the provision of meals, especially where the distances between the center and the children's homes are great.

Salaries for teachers are another area of concern. Most of the teachers are employed by the parents, with low salaries and irregular payment. They get no additional benefits and so some are not highly motivated and often leave teaching when offered more permanent employment. Some centers are large, with over 60 children and only one teacher. Under such circumstances the teacher cannot provide quality care, and activities tend to be done in groups in a dull and repetitive way.

Of the over 20,000 teachers, only about 30 percent have had any form of training. Expansion of training capacity is needed. Trainers and other high-level personnel need additional training at the university level. Currently there are no university programs in early childhood education in Kenya, so most of the upper-level staff are trained outside the country. The need to train personnel for leadership in early childhood education has intensified.

Although initial steps in designing and developing relevant early childhood curricula have been taken, much more needs to be done, especially in the production of manipulative concrete play and learning materials. A distribution system must be identified, and mass production of these materials undertaken, so that affordable materials are available to children both within and outside the centers.

The training teams operate from temporary sites. If these teams are to have a lasting impact it is important that they have permanent sites, where they can design and develop models of various aspects of programs for local communities and demonstrate the production and use of acceptable materials, the preparation of healthy foods, and other such activities to parents and other community members.

Finally, research and documentation are still lacking. While much has been done, there is still little information about the impact of the early childhood programs on the development of the child, the value of different training models, alternative ways of providing education and care, program financing, and other possible inputs into the curriculum (including language differences in different communities). The overall program, as it has evolved thus far, needs to be carefully studied, evaluated, and documented.

NOTE

1. Most children under age three are cared for by a parent or by an "ayah" (hired maid).

REFERENCES

Bernard Van Leer Foundation. (1984–1985). *Alternatives in Early Childhood Education and Care.* Special Report: Kenya—Harambee and Early Childhood Education.

Economic Management for Renewed Growth. (1986). Government Printer, Nairobi.

Gakuru, O. N., Riak, P. F., Ogula, P. H. R. and Njenga, A. W. (1987). *Evaluation of the NACECE-DICECE Programme.*

Kabiru, M. (1989). *Early Childhood Education in Kenya—A Case Study for the Eastern and Southern Africa Regional Consultation on the World Conference on Education for All.*

Kenya Institute of Education. (1982). *Report on the National Seminar on Pre-school Education and Its Development in Kenya, Malindi, 13–19th June 1982,* October 1982.

Kenya Institute of Education. (1987). *Early Childhood Education in Kenya: Implications on Policy and Practice.* Jadini Seminar Report 31st August–4th September.

Kenya Literature Bureau. (1985). *Women of Kenya, Review and Evaluation of Progress.*

Kipkorir, L. I. and Mwaura, L.P.K. (1988). "Partnership in Development: Experiences in Early Childhood Education in Kenya." *Towards a Brighter Future,* p. 77. Bernard van Leer Foundation, The Hague.

Ministry of Education. (1984). *Guidelines for Pre-school Education in Kenya.* Jomo Kenyatta Foundation.

Ministry of Education. (1986). *The Status and Future of Pre-school Education in Kenya—A Policy Perspective.* Jomo Kenyatta Foundation.

Ministry of Education. (1987). *Education in Kenya.* Information Handbook. Jomo Kenyatta Foundation.

Republic of Kenya Sessional Paper No. 6 (1988). *Education and Manpower Training for the Next Decade and Beyond.* Jomo Kenyatta Foundation.

UNICEF. (1989). "Situation Analysis of Childhood and Women in Kenya."

United Nations Department of International Economic and Social Affairs. (1980). *Women.*

University of Nairobi. (1982). *The Impact of Development on Women in Kenya.*

———— **18** ————

MEXICO

Kathryn Tolbert, Elizabeth Shrader, Doroteo Mendoza, Guadalupe Chapela, Aurora Ràbago, and Robert Klein

Day care for children is an issue confronting every society, whether traditional and agricultural or modern and industrialized. Traditional societies usually organize such care within the prevailing kinship and residence system, allowing men and women of childbearing age to fulfill their work obligations. Modern societies tend to evolve mechanisms for the non-familial provision of child care that permit the incorporation of girls and women into the educational system and the formal and informal work force. Mexico is a society in cultural and demographic transition, increasingly more urban, industrialized, and segmented. Historic, social, and economic changes, including rural-to-urban and international migration, female labor force participation, female-headed households and the resultant feminization of poverty, and changing family structures have had a tremendous impact on the supply and demand of child day care services in Mexico.

HISTORY

Historically, the first known day care center in the country was founded in Mexico City in 1937 as part of the "Volador" market and served the child care needs of women vendors. The Austrian Empress Carlotta of Mexico founded in 1865 the "Casa de Asilo de la Infancia" to provide care for the children of her court attendants. In 1869, the Empress founded "El Asilo de San Carlos," a day care center offering food and supervision to the children of working women. Carmen Romero Ruio de Diaz, wife of the late 19th-century dictator Porfirio Diaz, founded "La Casa Amiga de la Obrera," a day care facility for working women that survived through the revolution of 1910 to 1920.

These efforts are within the Mexican tradition of political figures' wives lending official support to programs that benefit children. The wife of the Mexican president is the titular head of the national social welfare agency, DIF (Desarollo Integral de la Familia or Integral Family Development), and the governors' wives are the titular heads of the social welfare agency at the state level.

The official involvement of the Mexican government in child care began with the post-revolutionary constitution of Mexico, drafted in 1917. Article 123 of the Mexican Constitution specifically guarantees the right of working women to day care services for their children. The evolution of this right into service provision has been worked out through the various federal laws regulating labor and social security benefits. By the early 1970s, all female government workers and all female workers who were enrolled in the social security program had a right to day care services provided by the state. Additionally, salaried male workers with social security, minor children, and no female partner also were given the right to government-provided day care. Such services extend by law to private sector and parastate employees and must be provided by employers of more than 45 workers, usually through agreements with social security. However, the commitment of the state clearly is to provide day care for the children of female workers, not for all women, nor for all workers, nor for all children in need of day care services.

In the 1970s the regulation of norms, programs, space use and allocation, supervision, and control of all government day care facilities was placed under the direction of the Ministry of Public Education. The law emphasizes the concern that day care not be custodial, but rather be dedicated to the development of the child and that it include the following components: nutrition services; preventive and therapeutic medical, psychological, and social services; age-appropriate educational and play activities; and parental involvement.

DEMOGRAPHY

Despite official government support of day care for salaried workers, child care options are limited for poor Mexican women. Mexico is a country undergoing rapid urbanization, development, and modernization while simultaneously experiencing severe economic crisis. Interest in day care issues in Mexico has grown out of recent research on women, low income households, and urban services in the region, and the concern with the apparent accelerated entry into the work force at mid-decade of married women, due to the severe economic crisis of the 1980s in Mexico. Sociologists have documented the growing role of women in the formal and informal labor markets as well as an increase in female-headed households and poverty due to male unemployment and work-related emigration. These conditions imply a considerable increase in the need for daytime child care arrangements, a need to which neither the public, social, nor private sectors are prepared to respond.

The age structure of women employed in the work force in Mexico is such that the highest rates of female employment over the last 20 years are of women of reproductive age. Figures regarding women and work in Mexico in the 1980s indicate that approximately 30 percent of women over the age of twelve are employed, with a higher percentage of women employed in urban areas. For women of reproductive age, labor force participation averages 37.4 percent. The total female work force over age 12 was measured at 27.8 percent for the 1980 census.

Sex-specific employment figures are not disaggregated by the number or age of children that a working woman may have. However, the demographic data show that despite dramatic declines in the birthrate for women in all age groups over 20, the pyramidal age structure of Mexico's population is such that the absolute number of women of reproductive age has increased. Therefore, despite a decline in population growth rates, the absolute number of young children has also increased. About half the women working in Mexico are married, separated, divorced, or widowed, and many care for families with small children. With increasing numbers of women of reproductive age participating in the work force, it is clear that the number of children with mothers who work is also increasing and that they are presumably in need of some kind of non-maternal child care during some part of the day.

Many Mexican women work because they are poor and need the additional income. The current trend is toward increased participation rates by older women, married women with children, and women with less schooling. Poverty is often reinforced by the fact that Mexican women are concentrated in the lower paid jobs that fall outside the sectors that provide day care in Mexico. Women with primary education or less tend to be workers in factories, piece workers, street vendors, and domestic servants, all positions with little job security and that do not include the Mexican social security benefits of health services, pensions, and day care. Many Mexican women are limited to part-time employment, often not by their own choice.

Paradoxically, the poorest married women may be the least likely to seek remunerated employment. A study of wives of Mexican men with different incomes and occupations found that the lower the husband's income, the less likely was the wife's participation in waged labor. One explanation may be that for poor women with limited resources, skills, and education, labor force entry costs that include child care exceed their earning potential.

Other costs of labor force participation, such as time and transportation, tend to be greater for low income urban workers. Most poor workers live in peripheral slums that have sprung up around Mexico's cities and must travel to areas of greater employment opportunity in urban centers. The cost of daily movement to and from the home and the work site, even with heavily subsidized public transportation, may be as much as one fifth to one third of a minimum daily wage and may take between three to five hours a day in travel time on public transportation during rush hours. Work days that include commuting time may be as long as 12 or 14 hours.

CULTURE

Many poor women and families on the periphery of urban areas are relatively recent immigrants who may be cut off from the extended support networks that exist in their ancestral towns or villages. Urban Mexican families are moving away from the extended structure more prevalent in rural communities to the nuclear structure more prevalent in urbanizing areas. These changes affect the demand for day care insofar as the availability of free child care from family and household members is reduced.

Similarly affected by the decline in available free child care are those families now headed by single mothers. Single female-headed households include those families headed by women without male partners as well as those families where the sole wage earner is a woman, an increasingly common situation given the level of internal and international male migrant movement and of unemployment in Mexico. The incidence of female-headed households in Mexico has increased from a reported 12 percent of households in the 1970s to as high as 25 percent in the 1980s. Mexican women increasingly are entering the labor force as well as heading their own households. These phenomena may be related, as single female heads of household tend to participate proportionately more in the labor force than do mothers in union. As noted above, however, women tend to be employed in low paying jobs, and as sole wage earners they are more likely to be living with their children in poverty.

In response to the decline in available free child care from family and household members, female heads of households tend to initiate adaptive strategies to compensate for the loss of income and child care services provided in an extended family structure by creating alternative support networks of relatives and friends, especially relying on the woman's mother. However, these network relationships may be unreliable or disproportionately demanding of the woman's limited time and resources. The woman participating in this social network may, in return for child care, be required to give emotional and instrumental support to other members of the networks (e.g., doing favors or chores, lending money, mediating arguments, or handling family crises). This need for reciprocity often does not allow for a full-time or even regular work schedule and may result in frequent changes in child care arrangements and dysfunctionally stressful interactions.

The conflicting demands of women's domestic, maternal, conjugal, and occupational roles usually result in the "double day," where women work full time outside the home and are still primarily responsible for child care and housekeeping. The working woman contends not only with her husband's demands, but also with society's demands that she be responsible for domestic chores and child rearing. Time studies have show that for women participating in economic activity outside the home, the amount of domestic work, including child care, is not reduced.

There are many barriers to affordable day care for poor Mexican women. A lack of available day care facilities in marginal neighborhoods reinforces poor women's inability to obtain child care while they receive schooling or job training, seek employment, or are employed. Women bear the primary transportation costs of taking the child(ren) to and from the day care site. High operational expenses of facilities in Mexico increase the direct costs of, and thereby reduce access to, private day care. Government sponsored day care in Mexico is only open to female workers with social security benefits, thereby effectively excluding the urban poor and unemployed. However, not all barriers to quality child care services are externally imposed. To be wise consumers of child care, parents need to be informed of what is available, what is quality care, and what to demand. Many low income mothers do not have adequate knowledge or information regarding day care and the needs of their children, thus limiting their ability to make informed choices and appropriate child care arrangements.

There is a cultural perception in Mexico that a "good" mother does not leave her child in the care of strangers. Institutional day care in particular is perceived as harmful to the child, a place where the child will be ignored, unloved, neglected, or mistreated. Indeed, one of the most important characteristics that an institutional child care provider should have, according to potential users of the service, is that the caregiver be known to the parents.

The lack of accessible, affordable, quality child care often results in untenable situations for poor women and their children. Young children may be taken to the workplace, left in the care of other young children, or left alone. Such conditions may lead to increased developmental, health, and safety risks for children inadequately cared for, as well as to an increase in stress and a decrease in real economic advancement for poor women and their families. These situations for poor working mothers and their children are practically universal where the state does not or cannot provide comprehensive day care, as is the case in Mexico.

The sections of the chapter that follow present an overview of Mexican day care policies, regulations, and programs, with conclusions regarding improved day care access for low income and working mothers and their children. Where possible, we have made generalizations for the whole country. But for several reasons the focus of recent day care research has been in Mexico City, whose distinctive characteristics must be borne in mind when discussing Mexican day care issues. Mexico City is arguably the most populous city in the world, with a corresponding magnitude of urban problems. While other Mexican cities, particularly those along the northern border region, may have faster population growth and higher female labor force participation, Mexico City remains the principal locus for rural-urban migration, where women are consistently employed at higher levels than the national average. As Mexico's political and economic center, the capital consumes by far the greatest share of the nation's financial, natural, and human resources. Mexico's urban complexity is characteristic of urbanization throughout the developing world, with significant consequences regarding policy implementation and program design in all areas of social reform, including day care.

EXISTING POLICIES, FINANCING ARRANGEMENTS, AND REGULATIONS

In describing day care policies and programs in a country as large and complex as Mexico, it is useful to make distinctions between day care services offered by the public, social, and private sectors. While non-maternal child care strategies encompass a variety of options, including home day care, family day care, center-based day care, and after-school care, each provided by a variety of caregivers, the focus here is on day care provided outside the child's home by someone other than a relative.

Public Sector Day Care

Public sector day care may be defined as child care services provided by government or parastate institutions, which include the Mexican Social Security Institute (IMSS), the State Employees' Health and Social Security Institute (ISSSTE), the agency for the Integral Development of the Family (DIF), its counterpart in the Federal District (DDF), and various ministries and parastates such as the Ministry of Education (SEP) and Mexico's petroleum producer, Pemex. IMSS services are available to private sector workers while ISSSTE provides services to government employees. Both are financed through contributions from employers, employees, and the government. The DIF and DDF sponsor social welfare programs for the working poor, which are financed through federal tax revenues. SEP's and Pemex's services are available to those entities' employees and are employer-employee financed.

The public sector plays a vital but limited role in caring for the nation's children. A significant portion of the government's own personnel, as well as many privately employed female workers, depend on the service, but there is no economically feasible way to expand this costly model beyond its user-specific financial base.

The DIF and DDF are the designated providers for the children of the working poor, but despite figures on official demand for these services, it is clear that these children continue to be underserved throughout Mexico. The joint day care capacity in Mexico City of DIF and DDF is approximately 20,000 places for *all* children under five, compared to the estimated 500,000 children from birth to three years of age in the metropolitan area whose mothers work. In the border region, the waiting list for IMSS day care is so long that some facilities have ceased accepting names. Day care capacity is woefully inadequate, even when private day care centers and kindergartens are taken into account.

The critical policy concept in public sector day care in Mexico is the provision of services to *women who work* and their children. Day care is available to assure tranquility for the woman worker to increase her productivity, not to increase her training or employment opportunities to better compete in the marketplace. Interestingly, it is the service and not the policy that is child centered, with its focus on the cognitive and socio-emotional development of the child through integrated curricula guided by specialists.

The policy and the service work extremely well for insured women workers and their children, who are entitled to 90 days of paid maternity leave, then day care from the moment they return to work until their children enter first grade. Quality of day care is excellent and the Mexican government is a leader in services to women workers in the hemisphere. However, the service leaves out the vast majority of poor children, whose mothers are uninsured or employed in the informal sector. These mothers and children have little or no access to institutional child care, and frequently the results are inadequate and unsafe conditions. Policies aimed at *workers* and not at *children* are likely to be incomplete in terms of equal opportunity and social justice.

Social Sector Day Care

Social sector day care may be defined as child care services provided by individuals, agencies, and institutions that work for the public good, in a non-profit or trust relationship with their clients, constituents, members, or beneficiaries. Common examples would be religious organizations, charitable institutions, clubs that raise and distribute funds for social causes, private voluntary agencies, and philanthropic foundations.

An important distinction between the social and public sectors in policy and financing is that often in the social sector the benefit of day care to children who live in marginal areas is considered advantageous to low income mothers and children, with preference accorded to working mothers, those looking for work, or those whose children would benefit from the experience when the home environment is inadequate. This model is reflected in the public sector only in the DIF and some DDF centers, where day care services are attached to job training programs for mothers.

While the efforts within the social sector are noteworthy, often innovative, and always well meaning, they are extremely isolated and local, serving small communities or groups. No organizations exist to coordinate these efforts in policy making, public relations, or fund raising, or for sharing lessons learned in community involvement, training programs, financing strategies, child development, or pedagogical techniques.

Financing is the primary obstacle to successful social sector day care efforts for low income families. Those social sector day care projects that succeed invariably do so with initial and sometimes on-going funding from donor agencies. Due to the high costs of rent, maintenance, and salaries, social sector programs are not profitable. Costs may be reduced, however, through the use of donated space, community participation, training of "mother/educators" and program administrators by volunteer experts, and the availability of adequate start-up funds from donors.

Social sector day care is essentially unregulated, and data banks regarding these services do not exist. Day care centers in the social and private sectors may be registered with the Ministry of Public Education, but this is not mandatory. While the extent of its overall impact and importance cannot be accurately measured in terms of the number of users, it is clear that social sector day care represents an important part of total day care provision in Mexico. This sector may be the most effective potential provider for poor women and children in the near future, due to government foreign and domestic debt and the policies of privatization of the economy.

Private Sector Day Care

Private sector day care may be defined as child care services provided by individuals, groups, associations, and corporations as a profit-making business. In Mexico, this sector, like the social sector, is difficult to inventory because of the lack of coordinating agencies, public policies, and regulations.

Unregulated private sector day care results in large differences in facilities, quality, and price structure. As in the social sector, registration with the Ministry of Education is not mandatory for for-profit day care centers; therefore it is difficult to quantify private sector day care providers or users. The number of formal and informal "family day care" homes is even more elusive. In many areas, "Jardines de Niños" (kindergartens) are available, but they are also exempt from registration. They serve mostly the middle and upper classes, as their fees and hours make them inaccessible to low-income working mothers.

Private day care services offer a range of fees and physical settings, from expensive and luxurious to somewhat less expensive and acceptable. Price seems to have little to do with services but much to do with the area in which the center is operated. Private day care fees range from 40 percent to 200 percent of the minimum wage. It is clear from these figures that private day care is unobtainable for the working poor and is not a cost-effective alternative for government workers or private employees.

Essentially, private sector day care does not serve the poor, even in more marginal areas of the city. The fact that day care is unprofitable except under circumstances of home-ownership and home-based day care makes it unlikely that the private sector will be a large provider of day care in the future in Mexico, either to the working middle class or to the working poor.

PROGRAM DESCRIPTIONS

Day care programs vary widely throughout Mexico in terms of the quality of care, caregiver training, and additional services offered. Many day care facilities go beyond custodial care to include child-centered curricula designed to enhance the child's cognitive, psycho-social, and physical development.

Appropriate staff training and management skills are important elements of quality day care facilities, especially for community-based centers that benefit the poor. Caregiver training may be minimal, as in the case of family day care situations where a woman simply opens her home to a few additional children, or it may be quite extensive, as is the case for many publicly regulated or for-profit centers. However, whereas low income parents are often concerned with staff background and education, due to economic considerations these parents often must base their decision upon other selection criteria, such as affordability, proximity, or convenience. Even less of a concern is evaluation of day care staff and curricula using objective measures to standardize activities.

Mexican day care providers frequently offer additional services to reflect parental needs or desires. Wealthy consumers of private day care may seek classes for the gifted or foreign language instruction. Working-class and low-income parents may have access to job training, income generation projects, or adult education classes associated with their day care center. Parenting skills courses, psychological counselling, well-baby clinics with medical referral, and alternative care for sick, disabled, or school-age children may also be available, although no single day care center offers all of these associated services.

Below are more detailed descriptions of day care services provided by the public, social, and private sectors in Mexico. A brief overview of each sector's program characteristics is included as Tables 18.1, 18.2, and 18.3. While these descriptions are by no means exhaustive, particularly for social and private sector day care, they are generally representative of the types of day care programs available.

Public Sector Day Care

The government is the largest provider of day care in the country. The Department of the Federal District (DDF) and the Mexican Institute of Social Security (IMSS) are the largest providers in the capital, while IMSS is the largest provider at the national level. The quality of public sector day care services generally is high, based on staff professionalism, staff-to-child ratios, the adequacy of physical plants, level of cleanliness, and commitment to the children. The centers are recognized by workers at all levels as providing excellent care, and the demand for entry is often greater than the supply, especially at the toddler and preschool age levels. Waiting periods for admission can range from several months to a year.

Social Sector Day Care

Social sector day care in Mexico is notably omnipresent and invisible. It is omnipresent because it seems that almost every urban community has at least one project, put together with community, church, educational agency, foundation, or private donation assistance to help the mothers and children of the community. It is invisible because it is impossible to assess the role played by these centers in fulfilling day care needs in Mexico. Numerically, social sector day care serves a miniscule percentage of the population of children under six. In terms of social impact, however, these centers may represent the seeds of social change for women by dignifying their need or desire to work, legitimizing the community's concern for its children, and bringing together women with similar needs to form meaningful associations with women beyond their kinship group, often for the first time in their adult lives.

No large social sector agency offers day care to the Mexican public. Social sector participation is an unorganized, unregulated, unpredictable event, and its impact in terms of availability to mothers and children in need of day care cannot be determined. In lieu of national statistics, two case studies are presented as successful models, although it is important to note that failed social sector efforts are not available for analysis; probably many more fail than succeed.

Case Study I: Centro de Desarrollo Infantil Santiago Ahuizotla (CEDISA). This day care center, serving 60 children between the ages of two and six years, is located in the town of Santiago Ahuizotla in one of Mexico City's poorer areas. It is adjacent, however, to areas of greater wealth in the State of Mexico. This proximity has led to the social resource-sharing between neighboring communities that characterizes CEDISA.

The idea for the center grew out of the experience of women from the socio-economically advantaged areas giving classes in "Christian reflection" to a group of mothers and children in a neighboring but extremely poor

Table 18.1
Characteristics of Public Sector Day Care in Mexico

Service Provider	IMSS	SEP	ISSSTE	DIF	DDF
To Whom Service Provided	Children 45 days to 6 years of female private enterprise employees; or IMSS' female employees; or male employees with custody and no female partner	Children and female SEP employees (teachers and educational administrators)	Children of female government employees	Children of uninsured working poor; or low income parents attending job training workshops	Children of female DDF employees; of uninsured working women in Mexico City
Financing	Employer and employee contributions	No data	No data	No data	No data
Tuition Fees/Child/Mo. US$ Equiv.	No direct fee payments by parents	No direct fee payments by parents	No direct fee payments by parents	No data	No data
Total Number of Centers	256	36 (Mexico City only)	37 (Mexico City only)	44 (Mexico City only)	205 (Mexico City only)
Total Number of Children Enrolled	40,313	5,959	6,630	3,740	14,607
Average Number Children/Center	158	166	179	85	71
Waiting List as % Enrollment	116% (official); 300% (unofficial)	26%	51%	18%	4%

Table 18.1 (continued)

Service Provider	IMSS	SEP	ISSSTE	DIF	DFG
Staff Training	Trained dietician, preschool teachers, child care workers, auxiliary nurse, administrators, s, secretary, part-time psychologist and social worker	Trained dietician, preschool teachers, child care workers, auxiliary nurse, administrators, secretary	Trained dietician, preschool teachers, child care workers, auxiliary nurse, administrators, secretary, social worker	Fewer than 1 in 14 staff members has technical or professional child care training; high absenteeism; little more than custodial care	
Direct Staff-Child Ratio	1:5	1:8	1:8	1:10	1:20
Associated Services	Psychological and social work support as needed for individual children and families; full-time nurse on site	No data	No data	Baths, laundry, tortilla mill, government-subsidized food market, barbershop, job training	Most centers are located near markets where mothers work
Overall Quality	Excellent	Excellent	Excellent	Acceptable	Poor

Table 18.2
Characteristics of Social Sector Day Care in Mexico

Service Provider	Case Study 1: CEDISA	Case Study II: Nezahaualpilli Center
To Whom Service is Provided	Children ages 2 to 6 years of working women from community	Community Children
Financing	Tuition fees and private donations	Donations from foundations and individuals
Tuition/fees/child/month in US $	$14.40	No data
% Min Equiv. Wage	18%	No data
Operating Costs per month	$1,500 not including donated space and utilities	$3,600 not including donated building, rent and taxes
Staff Training	Mother/educators from community trained in Montessori techniques; advisory board of outside experts for administration, fund raising	Mother/educators from community trained in child development; expert consultants in education, management, financing; part-time accountant
Direct Staff-to-Child Ratio	1:15	1:15
Associated Services	Two meals, growth monitoring, medical referral, parenting skills courses, half scholarships & employment for mothers, and community organization	Pre-school day care, primary secondary, and adult education, street children outreach program
Overall Quality	Good	Good

parish. In exploring together the "needs of the community," the women from Santiago Ahuizotla identified child care as one of paramount importance and, not insignificantly, a culturally appropriate focus for their income generation and community development efforts.

The women decided to provide day care and preschool education in Santiago Ahuizotla to the children of mothers who worked or who had no appropriate options for child care. The women from the advantaged area would donate their time as members of the consulting committee, organizers, fundraisers, and links to the professional education community. The women of the town would contribute their time to be trained and to serve as remunerated mother/educators.

According to data collected by the project, the town of Santiago Ahuizotla has a population of approximately 105,000 inhabitants, principally manual laborers earning minimum wage and their dependents. Over 80 percent live in rented housing, largely rooms shared with other families. There are an estimated 19,000 children under age six, and the average family size includes six to seven children. There is a reported increase in female labor force participation since the economic "crisis" in Mexico, due to increased male unemployment, hyperinflation, and female headship of households. Prior to CEDISA's inauguration, child care options were limited to two kindergartens for children four to six years of age and one child care center for students enrolled in a local vocational school. Young children in the community are often left home alone, many reportedly tied to their beds to keep them "safe."

The project began in 1983 with the training of mother/educators in Montessori techniques. Initially, locating a suitable site and reconditioning it for child occupancy proved the biggest obstacle. A building was donated by the Santiago Ahuizotla parish after years of negotiations with the church hierarchy. Start-up funds were raised from the Dutch embassy, a Belgian foundation, and individual contributions.

During the first four years of operation, the center became well organized and essentially self-financing, with half of the budget from parent fees and half from individual donors. However, the center requires continuous fundraising efforts to meet its budget. Due to space and staff limitations, the addition of an infant nursery is the only major objective CEDISA has not met. Other difficulties include funding for the purchase or repair of materials, late fee payment by parents, and staff disagreements. The consultants have handled the latter with regular biweekly staff meetings and staff training on interpersonal dynamics and work relationships.

Evaluating staff quality is difficult in social sector day care projects such as CEDISA. While many staff members lack the formal education in child development and pedagogy required by public sector institutions, specialized training of mother/educators can compensate for this "educational deficit." Also, one may argue that mother/educators are more sensitive than teachers from outside the community to peer observation and parental participation and more receptive to supervision and in-service training.

CEDISA is an example of cooperation between volunteers and community leaders to serve the community. Project success is due in part to the volunteers' dedication and sensitivity to community needs, the community women's participation in the initial needs assessment, the incorporation of community members as staff personnel, the provision of professional consultant and administrative help, and the ability to enlist donor support at the institutional and individual level.

Case Study II: Nezahualpilli. The Nezahualpilli Center is part of an enormously ambitious community development project focused on child care and primary school education. The project is located in the City of Nezahualcòyotl, in the State of Mexico on the eastern border of the Federal District of Mexico City. Densely populated, more than 1.5 million people live in poverty conditions, most of whom are recent immigrants from other Mexican states. Children of working mothers often are left alone or in the care of older siblings, many of whom cannot attend schools due to overcrowding, academic underachievement, or unaffordable school costs. The streets are described as "full of children with nothing to do."

Nezahualpilli Center staff estimate that 30 percent of community residents are workers with fixed employment, while 60 percent are employed in the informal sector as street vendors, flame eaters, car washers, beggars, and prostitutes. Roughly 10 percent are estimated to be homeless families or abandoned women and young people. Community problems include severe unemployment, drug addiction, youth gangs, robbery, and rape. The women of the community described themselves as "doubly exploited and marginalized, by society and by their husbands," forced to work to feed their children by washing clothes or doing textile piece work.

The Nezahualpilli Center, established in 1982 with funding from the Centro de Estudios Educativos, the Ford Foundation, and individual donors, offers infant and toddler day care, alternative primary and secondary school, and an outreach program for street children. The center's model of community development relies on participatory and democratic administration by community members, with selective use of outside consultants for technical assistance in curriculum development, management skills, and mother/educator training.

The center has served over 1,000 children, enrolling 180 preschoolers per year, and employs 20 people, 19 of whom are mothers from the community. Consultants donate time to the center, and one accountant is hired part time by the center. Operating costs are approximately U.S. $20.00 per month per child. However, real costs would be higher, since building, rent, and taxes are absorbed by the Centro de Estudios Educativos. Financing for materials and salaries remains an issue.

Curriculum evaluation was based on standard measures of cognitive development. Based on this formal evaluation, the center's educational curriculum is effective. Materials and teaching are adapted to the community experience, and it is likely that the children involved suffer less "culture shock" between their Nezahualpilli experience and home than do other economically disadvantaged children who leave their community to attend less culturally sensitive day care.

The center is at an important point in its development, having survived a process of innovation, doubt, and resolution. Through the process, the center has decided to expand Nezahualpilli's program objectives, thereby creating a need for capital funds. Unfortunately, precious direct service time is spent in fund-raising activities. However, the women are sincerely committed to the center's continued success. Their vision of the community is an impressive combination of an acknowledgment of the enormous social and economic problems and a fierce pride about providing opportunities for women and children through community efforts. The impact on the community, while small in numbers, is large in terms of offering hope and pride to mothers and a chance for education to the children.

Lessons Learned. There are several factors common to successful community-based day care programs. They include problem identification and problem solving by low income women, community involvement in all stages of program implementation, collaboration with external volunteer consultants, and mother/educator training. Similarly, such programs face critical limitations, principal among them building costs, staff conflicts, and financing. These characteristics of success and these limiting factors are shared not only by the CEDISA and Nezahualpilli projects, but in case studies found throughout the literature.

Despite the obstacles, there are several important lessons to be learned regarding social sector day care for Mexico. The first is the need to tap into altruistic motivation through the use of volunteers, both community members and outside experts. A successful model project instills a sense of community pride, with repercussions far beyond the immediate goals of benefiting participating women and children. Community participation at all levels, including building construction by community volunteers and employing mother/educators, is key to community acceptance. The community then has a stake both in the success of the project and the overall control of educational and administrative quality.

However, the unique combination of people and circumstances that help form successful centers such as CEDISA contributes both to their appeal and unreplicability. To have a multiplying effect, associations of day care providers might be organized to develop mechanisms for reducing the cost of food and materials through cooperative arrangements. These associations could also provide a forum for the exchange of ideas and experiences among participating staff, administrators, consultants, and parents. The associations should not become a platform, however, for the selling of specific ideologies and techniques: community development projects often fail when implementation philosophies are imposed from without rather than expounded and tested from within.

To the extent that social sector day care is primarily run by women, employs women, and allows women time for schooling, income generation, and meaningful association with other working women, then community-based day care could be a powerful tool for development. The concept of "empowerment," which seems to be associated with the positive effects of female education on fertility control, child survival, and household decision making, may explain the similar benefits of community-based day care on women in the community, both for those mother/educators who provide and those mother/consumers who utilize its services. Unlike many "income generation" or "women in development" projects that may put women into competition with men for scarce jobs, or place women in conflict with cultural or family norms, child care projects tend to be compatible with women's roles and can be a more rapid, less divisive way to increase women's income, work experience, and status in the community, while providing role models and role changes that lead to the broader empowerment of women. However, one pitfall has been that child care as a profession is generally underappreciated and underpaid, and care should be taken that women who participate in day care as an income generation project are not further marginalized economically.

The quality of child care services must be defined in terms of the community's available alternatives, taking into account minimum standards and optimal care. The Nezahualpilli Center shows how dedicated community mothers, aided by educational consultants, can provide excellent preschool and primary education as measured by standardized tests. The value of the socialization experience and the positive attention received by the children versus being left alone or in the care of young siblings is indisputable. Parental involvement in their children's preschool education also has been shown to contribute to the parents' own personal development, to the children, and to the community. Social sector day care has an inherent advantage over private day care for the poor in that there is a built-in check-and-balance system for quality control between outside dedicated volunteer consultants and community-based staff, whose interests and responsibilities go beyond a simple employment arrangement.

The major concerns regarding these case studies are those of safety, accident prevention, and the ability to respond appropriately to a medical emergency. While such limitations exist throughout the community, those offering child care services must address health and safety issues through appropriate staffing and financing of the centers, particularly since Mexican day care is not regulated by any public health agency. While health and accident prevention services involve additional expense, they also offer opportunities for collaboration between government and community agencies.

One untapped resource could be the use of day care centers as internship sites for graduate students in medicine, nursing, psychology, and social work, who are required to perform one year of social service in their profession before receiving their degree.

The biggest stumbling blocks to social sector day care are housing costs and self-financing. The expenses of community-based social sector day care are generally less than those for public and private sector providers due to their location in less expensive areas and training of non-professional staff. It seems essential for social sector financing to have start-up and building costs, as well as any capital improvements or expansion costs, provided by an outside agency. Operating costs are generally covered by donations and tuition fees. Financing innovations, such as enlisting community construction skills for building centers and sharing community facilities already in existence, need to be developed.

In general, community-based day care implemented with external assistance for financial support and continued professional liaison seems the most promising model of satisfying future child care needs in Mexico. Philanthropic foundations and international agencies should concentrate on providing assistance to centers to organize provider associations and networks of consultants, which in turn could foster expansion of model programs. Additionally, development projects involving women sponsored by donor agencies should take day care into account, both as a service provided to working women and as a means of generating income.

Private Sector Day Care

Private day care fills a need for women who want child-free time and who have money to pay for child development services. Many private centers and family day care homes function as interim facilities for women trying to enroll their children into IMSS, ISSSTE, or other public centers to which they have a right, but for which the wait may be up to one year. Family day care is often advertised through word of mouth in the workplace, or through unofficial, informal referral by the public day care center staff itself.

As in the social sector, private sector day care is unregulated; therefore it is difficult to assess its pervasiveness or impact. For example, with a population of over 19 million people, Mexico City has only 30 private day care centers registered with the SEP and 37 advertised in the Mexico City telephone book. Other listings or information regarding day care, if these exist, are not widely available to the public.

Data from a non-exhaustive survey of 12 private day care centers in Mexico City indicate that program characteristics, including services offered, staff-to-child ratio, and staff qualifications are quite similar across sites. Only one center required the purchase of insurance by parents of children in its center, and that center also had available a pediatrician and

Table 18.3
Characteristics of Private Sector Day Care in Mexico

Service Provider (Social Class)	High middle*	Middle**	Low middle***
To Whom Service is Provided	Child 45 days (youngest) to 6 years (oldest)	Children 45 days (youngest) to 6 years (oldest)	Children 10 days (youngest) to 6 years (oldest)
Financing	Private tuition fees	Private tuition fees	Private tuition fees
Tuition fees/child/month in US $	$52.73 registration fee plus $80-182 per month	$30-77 registration fee plus $44.91 per month	$33.37 registration fee plus $40-58 per month
% min Wage	40% to 100%		
Staff training	Teachers; nurse-maids; administrators	Teachers; nurse-maids; administrators	No data
Direct staff-to-child ratio	2:7 to 1:15 depending on age and center	1:5 to 1:10 depending on age and center	1:15 to 1:10 depending on age and center
Associated Service	Two to three meals (all); on-site pediatrician (one case); after-school care to 8 p.m. (one case); Montessori method (one case; English (one case)	Two meals to three meals (all); transpiration (one case); Montessori (one case)	Two meals
Overall quality	Good to excellent	Good to excellent	Good

*represents summary data for 4 centers in Mexico City

**represents summary data for 6 centers in Mexico City

***represents summary data for 2 centers in Mexico City

nurses. In general, requirements for admission and sick-child policies are similar to public day care, and staff ratios are acceptable, being, on average, similar to public day care.

Private day care users had few complaints, though some suspected that the educational credentials of the staff were not as professional as claimed. There were no reports of child abuse or mistreatment. However, one of the frequently mentioned fears regarding private day care is mistreatment of children.

The fact that day care is unregulated in Mexico means that there may be great disparities in facilities and quality as well as price structure. However, child care as a career in Mexico implies one to four years of specialized post-secondary school education. Child caregivers in the private and public sectors must have these credentials and job placement is competitive. It appears that the quality of staff training as advertised at private centers, at least in Mexico City, is generally acceptable.

STRENGTHS, SHORTCOMINGS, AND CHALLENGES

The question of who is minding the children in Mexico is one that will become increasingly important in the 1990s as more married women enter the work force than ever before. Public sector day care systems are already overburdened, and the private sector is not sufficiently large to handle the excess demand. There is cause for greater concern for poor women and children, as neither sector has responsibility for them, and social sector efforts remain sporadic and unorganized. It is imperative that intersectorial cooperation be enlisted to confront this problem as it relates to other women's development and child welfare issues, such as female education, job training, and economic opportunity, and youth who find refuge in drugs and gangs.

It is unlikely that the government can meet the day care demand of its constituents, both insured and uninsured, due to the high costs of the service and the growing population of women workers in the lower income groups. Cooperation with the private and social sectors is desirable for increasing day care supply and improving the quality of services to non-insured users. The public sector's historical position as a provider of excellent day care and its ability to call together community leaders to address social problems make it an indispensable partner in achieving widespread community participation.

There are several ways to increase the availability of quality, inexpensive child care facilities. One measure would be to encourage the establishment of small-scale, licensed family day care homes through tax breaks and child-minder training. A second measure would be to help establish community-based centers by providing professional consultants in education and health to community groups willing to run centers. A third measure would be to coordinate especially marginalized groups of women workers, such as street vendors and domestic workers, to establish services appropriate to their needs in collaboration with social sector and community groups. A fourth measure would include community-based day care as part of women's income generation projects, both as an integral benefit for working women and as a means of generating employment.

Several policy recommendations are suggested by the results of the preceding overview of day care in Mexico. First, the issue of inadequate day care supply must be addressed by the public, social, and private sectors in a coordinated effort. Such an effort should involve government and non-governmental agencies with expertise in the area. It could take the form of conferences, discussions with concerned community groups and providers, and the formation of providers' associations. The goal would be to formulate policies that stimulate day care provision for children while strengthening the contribution of pertinent health and educational authorities.

Second, intersectoral cooperation must include the flexibility to design models of day care services and financing that are appropriate for the mothers and children served. Issues to be addressed include determining the best role of each sector in day care provision and financing; creating models for intersectoral cooperation; locating services according to community needs and characteristics; training and recruiting staff; providing ancillary services (medical, psychological, vocational); developing curricula; and finding means to finance day care, especially means outside the social security system.

Finally, the role of non-governmental agencies and foundations should include the support and organization of research, conferences, and service provision regarding day care and the assessment of the needs of economically disadvantaged working women and their children. Disseminating such work is critical to placing day care on Mexico's policy-making agenda.

REFERENCES

Acevedo, Maria Luisa, Jose Iñigo Aguilar, Luz Maria Brunt, and Maria Sara Molinari. (1984). *Estudio de las estrategias de cuidado infantil en el area metropolitana. Informe final.* Unpublished report, The Population Council, Regional Office for Latin America and the Caribbean, Mexico, D.F.

Atlas de la Ciudad de México. (1987). Mexico City: Departamento del Distrito Federal y El Colegio de México.

Barbieri, T. de. (1984). "Incorporaciòn de la mujer en la economia de América Latina." *Memorias del Congreso Latinoamericano de Poblaciòn y Dessarrollo,* Vol. 1. México, D.F.: PISPAL.

Bonilla de Ramos, Elssy. (1981). *La madre trabajadora.* Bogotà: Centro de Estudios Sobre Desarrollo Economic. September.

Campbell, Frances A., Breitmayer, Bonnie, and Ramey, Craig T. (1986). "Disadvantaged Single Teenage Mothers and Their Children: Consequences of Free Educational Day Care." *Family Relations* 35:63:68.

Chant, Sylvia. (1988). "Mitos y realidades de la formacion de las familias encabezadas por mujeres: el caso de Queretaro, Mexico." In Luisa Gabayet, et al. (Eds.), *Mujeres y Sociedad: Salario, hogar y accion social en el occidente de Mexico.* Guadalajara: El Colegio de Jalisco, CIESAS del Occidente.

Denmen, Catalina A., Professor and Research Director, Department of Health and Society, Colegio de Hermosillo, Sonora, Mexico. 11 November 1990. Personal Communication.

Diamond, Franna. (1982). *The Child Care Handbook: Needs, Programs and Possibilities.* Washington, D.C.: The Children's Defense Fund.

Direccion General de Estadistica. (1980). *Estadisticas sobre la mujer.* Mexico City: Secretaria de Programacion y Presupuesto.

Duley, Margot I. and Mary I. Edwards (Eds.). (1986). *The Cross Cultural Study of Women.* New York: The Feminist Press of The City University of New York.

Elu de Leñero, Maria del Carmen. (1988). *La salud de la mujer en Mexico Cifras comentadas.* Mexico City: Programa Nacional Mujer y Salud, Sector Salud.

End. (1982). *Encuesta Nacional Demográfica.* Mexico City: Consejo Nacional de Poblacion (CONAPO).

Enfes. (1989). *Encuestga Nacional sobre Fecundidad y Salud. 1987.* Mexico City: Dirección General de Planificación Familiar, Secretaria de Salud.

Engle, Patricia L. (January 1986). "The Intersecting Needs of Working Mothers and Their Young Children: 1980 to 1985." Unpublished paper, Department of Psychology and Human Development, California Polytechnic State University, San Luis Obispo, California.

Furqua, Robert W. and Dorothy Lebensohn. (April 1986). "Parents as Consumers of Child Care." *Family Relations* 35:295–303.

García, Brigida and Orlandina de Oliveira. (1990). "Cambios en la presencia femenina en el mercado de trabajo, 1976–1987." *IV Reunion Nacional de Investigacion Demografica en Mexico.*

Gonzalez de la Rocha, Mercedes. (1988). "De por qué las mujeres aguantan golpes y cuernos: un analisis de hogares sin varon en Guadalajara." In Luisa Gabayet, et al. (Eds.), *Mujeres y Sociedad: Salario, hogar y accion social en el occidente de Mexico.* Guadalajara: El Colegio de Jalisco: CIESAS del Occidente.

Gonzalez de la Rocha, Mercedes. (1986). *Los recursos de la pobreza. Familias de bajos ingresos de Guadalajara.* El Colegio de Jalisco: Guadalajara.

Gonzalez Salazar, Gloria. (1980). "Participation of Women in the Mexican Labor Force." In June Nash and Helen Icken Safa (Eds.), *Sex and Class in Latin America.* J. F. Bergin: Brooklyn.

Haskins, Ron and Johnathan Kotch. (June 1986). "Day Care and Illness: Evidence, Costs, and Public Policy." *Pediatrics* 77 (6 Part 2): 950–982.

Holman, Nicole and Margaret Arcus. (April 1987). "Helping Adolescent Mothers and Their Children: An Integrated Multi-Agency Approach." *Family Relations* 36: 119–123.

LACWC: Latin American and Caribbean Women's Collective. (1980). *Slave of Slaves: The Challenge of Latin American Women*: London: Zed Press.

Lindblad-Goldberg, Marion and Joyce Lynn Dukes. (January 1985). "Social Support in Black, Low-income, Single-Parent Families: Normative and Dysfunctional Patterns." *American Journal of Orthopsychiatry* 55(1): 42–57.

Martinez Manautou, Jorge (Ed.). (1987). *Analisis del Costo Beneficio del Programa de Planificación Familiar del Instituto Mexicano del Seguro Social*. Academia Mexicana de Investigación en Demografía Médica: Mexico City.

McMurray, Georgia L. and Dolores P. Kazanjian. (1982). *Day Care and the Working Poor: The Struggle for Self-Sufficiency*. New York: Community Service Society of New York.

Myers, R. and Indriso, C. (February 26–27, 1987). "Women's Work and Child Care." Paper prepared for the Rockefeller Foundation Workshop "Issues Related to Gender, Technology, and Development."

OEF. (1979). Overseas Education Fund of the League of Women Voters. "Child-Care Needs of Low Income Mothers." In *Final Report: A Synthesis of Recommendations from an International Conference, In-Country Workshops, and Research in Six Countries*. Washington, D.C.: OEF.

Pedrero, Mercedes and Teresa Rendón. (1982). "El trabajo de la mujer en México en los sesentas." In *Estudios sobre la mujer: El empleo de la mujer. Bases teoricas, metodologicas y evidencia empirica*. Secretaría de Programacion y Presupuesto: Mexico City.

Perez Alarcón, Jorge, Abiega, L., Zarco, M., and Daniel Schugurensky. (1986). *Nezahuapilli—Educación Preescolar Communitaria*. Centro de Estudios Educativos, A. C., México, D. F.

Rábago, A., Mendoza, D. and Shrader, E. (1989). *Encuesta sobre la disponibilidad y necesidades de cuidado infantil. Ciudad de Mexico. 1988*. Unpublished final report, The Population Council, Regional Office for Latin America and the Caribbean.

Robins, Philip K. (March 1988). "Child Care and Convenience: The Effects of Labor Market Entry Costs on Economic Self-Sufficiency Among Public Housing Residents." *Social Science Quarterly* 69:122–136.

Roldán, Martha. (1987). "Class, Gender, and Asymmetrical Exchanges Within Households." In L. Beltrán and M. Roldán (Eds.), *The Crossroads of Class and Gender: Industrial Homework, Subcontracting, and Household Dynamics in Mexico City*. Chicago: University of Chicago Press.

Schmink, M., Bruce, J., and Kohn, M. (Eds.). (1986). *Learning about Women and Urban Services in Latin America and the Caribbean*. A Report on the Women, Low-Income Households and Urban Services Project of the Population Council. New York: The Population Council.

SEP. (1982). "Secretaria de Educacion Publica. Que es un centro de desarrollo infantil?" Internal document, Secretaría de Educación Publica, Mexico City.

Shrader Cox, E. (1989). "Supply, Demand, and Models of Day Care Services: A Review of the Literature." Unpublished report, The Population Council, Regional Office for Latin America and the Caribbean.

Shrader Cox, E. and Mendoza Victorino, D. (1990). "La doble jornada: Percepciónes por parte de hombres y mujeres sobre el trabajo femenino." In *La Psicologia Social en Mexico: Vol. III*. Asociacion Mexicana de la Psicologia Social: Mexico City.

Tienda, Marta, and Jennifer Glass. (August 1985). "Household Structure and Labor

Force Participation of Black, Hispanic, and White Mothers." *Demography* 22(3):381–394.

Tolbert, Kathryn. (1990). "Availability and Need for Daycare Services in the City of Mexico." Unpublished report, The Ford Foundation, Regional Office for Mexico and Central America.

Turner, Pauline and Richard Smith. (April 1983). "Single Parents and Day Care." *Family Relations* 32:215–226.

NICARAGUA

Annabel Torres

Song of Hope

One day, the fields will stay
green and the earth black,
sweet and wet. Our children
will grow tall on that earth
and our children's children.

And they'll be as free as the
mountain trees and birds.

Now we plow dry fields, each
furrow wet with blood.

—Daisy Zamora,
Nicaraguan poet

Nicaragua is located in Central America, between the Pacific Ocean and
the Caribbean Sea. Neighboring countries are Costa Rica to the south and
Honduras to the north. Rich in natural resources, most of which are still
to be exploited, Nicaragua can easily support its population of approximately 3 million people on its 128,875 square kilometers of land area. Once
a colony of Spain, the Nicaraguan people are an Indian and Caucasian racial
mix that shares the Spanish language and the heritage of Christianity.

The model of imperialist domination upon Nicaragua since the beginning
of the 20th century has resulted in a long history of misery and led ultimately
to the populist revolution in 1979. This model was accompanied by a series
of dictatorial regimes, the cruelest of which was led by the Somoza family,

who used the riches of the country for their own gain, making no investment in the development and welfare of the Nicaraguan people.

In 1979 the Sandinistas ousted Anastasio Somosa Debayle Somoza and installed a new government, introducing land reforms and providing public services to the Nicaraguan people in the form of medical care and literacy programs. The Sandinista government introduced a mixed economy to the country and took a non-aligned stance in international politics.

In general, the Nicaraguan revolutionary process was based on maximum participation of individuals within group decision-making processes, with the goal of reaching communal solutions. Integral, community-based philosophy and treatment approaches also formed the foundation for Nicaraguan child care programs. This chapter provides an overview of the programs for children initiated and developed by this government during the past 11 years, with particular reference to underlying policies and to the characteristics of the programs evolving from those policies.

NATIONAL POLICY FOR THE CARE AND PROTECTION OF MINORS

During the 46-year rule of the Somoza family there were no government programs that actually provided services for children, although a Tutelary Law for Minors existed. In 1973 the Somoza government promulgated the Tutelar Law for Minors, establishing a Tutelary Court created exclusively to address the problem of antisocial minors. The personnel linked to this court took a psycho-social diagnostics approach and placed the youth in centers that had no legal authority, as they were under the direction of religious or private groups. Because attention was based on the technical aspects of the situation, the focus was on the legal rather than the social dimensions of the problem.

However, after the 1979 triumph of the Sandinista Popular Revolution the Nicaraguan government and people established the welfare of children as a fundamental policy priority and social concern. The Nicaraguan commitment to children was operationalized through both large-scale government child care programs and alternative projects by non-government organizations in support of the government's vision of child welfare. Popular revolutionary slogans such as "The Children: the Pampered of the Revolution" and "For Social Problems, Communal Solutions" also reflected the growing public and political awareness of the primacy of integrated social services, especially for children.

On August 8, 1979, less than three weeks after the end of the revolution, the National Government of Reconstruction established the Nicaraguan Ministry of Social Welfare (INSBBI). The government quickly reformed the existing Tutelary Law of Minors and specified the Social Welfare Ministry's responsibilities and jurisdiction regarding the care of children as the following:

1. Assessment of problems facing children and their families.
2. Development of preventive counseling and education for children.
3. Administration of child care centers (Tutelary Law, No. 39, Decree III, Article I. October 1979).

During the 11 years that followed the Ministry of Social Welfare functioned in two principal areas—welfare and social security. Evaluation of the ministry's effectiveness in responding to the needs of the community it is intended to serve was an important part of its growth process. As a result of this process, the ministry underwent a major restructuring in April 1989, to increase management efficiency and to guarantee the participation and systematic presence of the institution throughout the country. To insure community access to the services of the ministry, zonal teams were formed, each with the responsibility for several neighborhoods within the same area. This provides the greater amount of community involvement that is fundamental to legitimate social-political transformation and to addressing the root causes of social problems. These teams investigate and evaluate the social needs and problems of their respective zones and then plan, supervise, and evaluate projects designed to respond to local circumstances. They are also responsible for measuring the impact of preventive programs operating within their jurisdictions.

Child Care Approaches

The plan of social welfare with respect to minors and family utilizes three principal approaches: preventive education, protective care, and re-education. The preventive function involves supervising children in situations that put their capacity for physical and psychological development at risk. The protective function is carried out by providing a defense against any physical, psychological and/or sexual abuse, abandonment, or any other situation that puts the physical and/or moral well-being of the child at risk. The re-education process involves providing counseling, support, and education to children under 15 years of age who have violated the law.[1]

Underlying Beliefs about Children and Society

In Nicaragua the child is considered an active product of society. For this reason a child's needs must be considered within his or her historical and social context. Children's circumstances are shaped not by the children themselves but by the family and social context in which they develop.

Although it is the child who receives the greatest attention in many of the Nicaraguan child care programs, considerable emphasis is placed on assessing the child's environment as a whole. This holistic, psycho-social approach emphasizes a social and communal focus. Solutions to children's needs are sought through the involvement of the entire community and through consideration of the full range of social, economic, and cultural factors. This community involvement process implies the need:

- To be conscious that the problem of the young child is a social problem. For this reason it requires visits and meetings with those responsible for the local social welfare program, neighborhood leaders, natural leaders, and parents.
- To have self-diagnosis sessions with parents, leaders, and local promoters, based on participative research.
- To carry out educational activities with parents, promoters, and minors.
- To analyze the problem in collective form and define with whom and how to solve it. This process involves close relationships among state, local, and communal groups.

PREVENTIVE AND EDUCATIONAL CHILD CARE PROGRAMS

These programs fall into two major categories, those designed to promote basic child well being and those aimed specifically at high-risk children.

Child Care Programs for Newborn to Six Year Olds

A variety of rural and urban programs have been developed to monitor and promote children's early development. The responsibility for these programs has been assumed by the state, non-governmental centers, work centers, members of the community, and cooperative combinations of these forces. The Ministry of Social Welfare has trained the technical advisors and staff of these children's centers and programs. Other state ministries work directly with children's projects in their respective areas of expertise. For instance, the Ministry of Education developed the learning guides used for the educational development of three- to six-year-old children, and the Ministry of Health provides education and care regarding health and nutrition.

The main objectives of these programs are to offer educational, nutritional, and health care to children whose parents are engaged in the defense and economic activity of the country, and to work with the community to develop infant care practices that reduce the frequency of childhood disorders and problems. Thus they contribute to the consolidation of neighborhood organizations that promote popular participation in actions directed toward the elevation of the well-being of the child.

Six principal sets of activities are emphasized in all of the preschool programs. "Directed action" involves efforts directed toward the development of children's auditory, visual, observational, and creative skills. Teachers carry out these activities in groups or subgroups according to age. "Independent activities" consist of imitational games that make use of object, movement, and instructional materials to teach children to complete projects independently. "Daily routines" are the activities that insure basic care, such as feeding, clothes changing, washing, and health control. "Productive and work education activities" are directed toward three to six year olds and use the preschool work guide as a basis for instruction. "Nutritional support" provides the children with nutritionally balanced lunches and snacks. The community or the parents often help to provide the food for these meals. Finally, three principal approaches are utilized in what is called "family and community work": (1) formation of Parents' Committees that directly participate in the operation and coordination of the centers; (2) parental participation in the physical maintenance of the building, and repairs and construction of the furniture; and (3) education of parents as family and community leaders through talks, cultural activities, and workshops.

There are five child care programs in Nicaragua aimed at the basic well-being of preschool children. Each of these program types is described below. Special attention is given to the child development center because of the institutional support given to this approach and the more comprehensive services it provides.

The Child Development Center

Consciousness of the importance of the first six years of life has led in Nicaragua to the creation of child development centers. These centers assume the responsibility, together with the working father and mother, for guaranteeing the physical, psychic, and social stimulation that will assure the optimal development of young children. The number of Nicaraguan children enrolled in child development centers is shown in Table 19.1, presented by age and geographic location.

Child development centers provide care and instruction for children from birth to age six while their parents are at work. Two types of programs accommodate parental work schedules: those for the children of daytime workers, which operate between Monday through Saturday from 6 A.M. to 1 P.M., and those for the children of parents working at night or at jobs located far from the center, who arrive at the center at 6 P.M. and remain overnight.

Eligibility. Children of parents working in institutions and work centers within the center's district and those residing in the district whose parents

Table 19.1
Enrollment in Child Development Centers

Age	Location	
	Rural	Urban
Nursing (45 days to 16 mo.)	475	795
Toddler (17-36 mo.)	621	1,430
Preschool (3-6 yr.)	2,386	2,038
Total	3,482	4,263

work elsewhere are eligible. Priority is given to low-income families and those with no alternative child care arrangements.

Age groupings. Children are organized in classrooms and groups by age. In the first year of life nursing infants are divided into four groups: 45 days to 3 months; 3 to 6 months; 6 to 9 months; and 9 to 12 months. Children are kept under "first year" care until they can walk, drink, and eat without help. In the second year infants are divided into two sub-groups: 12 to 16 months and 16 to 24 months. Groupings in years 3 to 6 correspond with the age of the children.

Educational emphasis. These educational child care programs emphasize popular creativity and imagination, and they make a special effort to utilize culturally appropriate curriculum and educational tools.

Parent-center relationship. These centers do not intend to replace the care of parents through their services. The parents of the children in center programs maintain primary responsibility for care and must actively participate in center activities. Three principal approaches to involving parents were outlined earlier: Parents' Committees, parental participation in building and furniture maintenance, and parent leadership training and education. Parents are expected to participate in the administration of the center and in curriculum development. The parents must attend meetings and participate in courses organized by adult educators as well as center directors. Special efforts are made to maintain consistency between the norms and values of the center and the home environment.

It is also the responsibility of the parents to give financial support in accordance with their income and to support the maintenance and improvement of the center. For example, in one child care center there was a need for five tables and thirty chairs, but no funds with which to make the purchase. In a subsequent meeting with parents, two carpenters among the group offered to make the furniture while others found donors for the materials.

Relationship between the community and center. Given the extremely limited financial resources of the State, the survival of each child development center must be ensured through the contribution by the community of material and human resources. Realizing the necessity of child care services, community members voluntarily support the centers through activities such as sewing sheets and clothing, providing carpentry work, and completing reports and census forms.

Relationship between the center and the family. The parents pay a monthly fee according to their income and the general responsibilities they might have in relation to the program. Due to the limited resources of the center, the parents are permanently organized to carry out activities that contribute to its maintenance and infrastructure. They assist at the periodic conferences and workshops given by the directorate of the center, thus giving the parents themselves an opportunity to become true educators of their children.

Organizational structure supporting child development centers. The Ministry of Social Welfare's Department of Child and Family Management directs the child development center programs on the national level. A local Management Council works with a coordinator to make decisions regarding each individual center. This council consists of the coordinator, nurse aides, teachers, and representatives from the Parents' Committee.

Example: The Melania Morales Child Development Center

Located in the third district of Managua, the Melania Morales[2] center opened its doors in June 1988. The center serves 300 children between 45 days and 6 years old with a staff of 48 people, including the director, teachers, and administrative and service personnel.

The objectives of the center are (1) to facilitate the incorporation of women into the work force and the social undertakings of the country; (2) to contribute to the physical, psychological, social, and intellectual development of children; and (3) to improve the child-rearing capacities of parents. The center is administered by a group consisting of the director, the person responsible for each group of children, and representatives of the parents groups. Priority for admission is given to children whose mothers are working in production, education, health services, or military service.

The center is open from 6:00 A.M. to 6:00 P.M. Children are grouped in one year increments (45 days to 12 months old, one to two years, etc.). Each age group has a daily schedule involving different programs and activities. This schedule is explained to the parents, so that they can continue with the same program at home and on days when the children do not attend the center.

Content of the daily programs varies according to age group. During the first year of life the emphasis is on emotional contact, language stimulation, and movement activities. In the second and third years of life physical, moral, sensory, and aesthetic education are stressed. Once the children are preschoolers (4 to 6 years old), the focus shifts to organization and preparation for formal education. These older children concentrate on structured cognitive thought, acquisition and organization of language, and work programs in the socio-affective, psychomotor, and basic knowledge areas.

Parents pay monthly on a sliding scale based on family income. More well-off parents also come to know the problems of children with limited resources and how they can help these boys and girls. Some parents, for example, donate their own children's used clothing to those in need. There are also those who can donate food to share with malnourished families and provide food for these families when the center is not in session.

The Ministry of Social Welfare provides the center with food staples (rice, beans, milk, cooking oil) and provides salaries for the workers. Responsibility for program regulation, curriculum development, and staff training is shared by the Ministries of Social Welfare and Education.

Evaluation of the Melania Morales Child Development Center is very limited. Very basic indicators, like very low attrition and the fact that many malnourished children soon became healthy—attest to the effectiveness of the program. But it is evident that a more in-depth evaluation of the program is needed.

Other Preventive Child Care Approaches

Four other child care arrangements can be found in Nicaragua. In the first of these, called *work center child services*, working parents, employers, and the state cooperate in the development of child care services located at the workplace. The institution or employer assumes responsibility for center maintenance, furniture, and equipment. Parents provide clothes, nursing bottles, and toys. They also give voluntary economic support and contribute a day of unpaid work to the program. The state is responsible for training the center staff.

Communal child services are child care programs developed and run by the community itself, without direct government or workplace assistance. A grassroots organization of community residents provides salaries for center personnel and is responsible for the administration and general maintenance of the center. Parents who use the services make financial contributions and bring necessary materials, such as mattresses, hammocks, chairs, and cribs. Other members of the community provide technical support, such as carpentry. The community organization assumes the responsibility for the functioning and general maintenance of the center.

Child's family services are those in which one family assumes responsibility for several other children from the neighborhood. The participating children are usually from families without a caregiver during parents' working hours or without a healthy home environment (e.g., with alcoholic parents). Although the parents make an economic contribution to the caregiving family, this arrangement generally is largely based on the co-operation and solidarity of women and families within a particular community. The State offers training to these caretakers in the areas of nutrition, sensory stimulation, educational techniques, and recreational, cultural, and sport activities.

Preschool centers have been established to provide children between the ages of three to six with an environment that fosters social growth and contributes to their basic development. They are intended to identify children with possible learning disabilities and provide opportunities for corrective action. These centers are open for four hours each day. They are established in various locations, including annexes to local primary schools, community centers, private homes, and child development centers. The Ministry of Education is responsible for the curriculum and general operation. The State, the community, or parents assume the responsibility for the administration and finances, either individually or through a collective effort. In both urban and in rural areas welfare services are provided by the Ministry of Social Welfare, and health services by the Ministry of Health.

Child Care Programs for School-aged Children at Risk

The marginalized sectors of Nicaraguan society face economic problems that are manifested in social symptoms affecting family unity and the adequate development of family members. Typical behaviors in these family crises include the physical abuse of women and children, alcoholism, abandonment, and prostitution.

A child growing up in an environment of economic marginalization and family crisis is at great risk. It is quite possible that such antisocial behavior as theft may be seen as a viable way to contribute to family income for a child without economic resources or marketable technical skills. Since 1980, the revolutionary government has worked to develop preventive programs for children "at risk" between the ages of 7 and 15, and it has enlisted the active participation of community members living close to these centers of programs.

The fundamental objectives of these programs are to reduce the number of "street children" in Nicaragua and to develop the norms, values, and social habits in these children that will permit them to live productively within society. Mechanisms have been established for an integrative relationship between the community and the center. The community must understand the problem of these marginalized children and contribute to the development of a practical education program in vocational workshops and basic technical training.

Two major programs have been developed for children at risk—preventive centers and street educator programs.

Table 19.2
Enrollment in Preventive Centers

<u>Age</u>

6 to 9 Year Olds	1,280
10 to 13 Year Olds	1,305
Total	3,245

Preventive Centers

Preventive centers were created to address the problem of child laborers and street children. Established in areas with the greatest concentrations of these children, these centers maintain an open atmosphere in which children can participate according to their own needs and schedules. Table 19.2 shows the number of children served in 17 preventive centers, in two age categories.

Center activities. Both formal and "reinforcement" education is provided for children. Formal classes teach the same curriculum as in the regular primary school but are accelerated to compensate for the children's abbreviated school schedule. Other classes work to reinforce children's more formal education (if they are not participating in a regular school) by improving study habits and providing general guidance. Children aged 6 to 12 participate in pre-vocational workshops, while those aged 13 to 15 learn a trade in vocational settings. Children also participate in cultural and sports activities in an effort to help them achieve balanced personal development. Cultural classes offered include painting, drawing, and dancing.

Nutritional assistance is provided through the Ministry of Social Welfare. Often the parents help to provide the food and to maintain the center.

Center organization and functioning. In addition to child laborers and street children, juvenile delinquents, young drug addicts, and the children of alcoholics, prostitutes, and criminals are also eligible for center care. The child goes voluntarily to the center with the parents' consent after a social worker has studied the case and made such a recommendation. The community also participates in the decision and to the financing of the program.

The Child and Family Department of the Ministry of Social Welfare assumes responsibility for the centers. They are open daily from 8 A.M. to 5 P.M. The minimum staff consists of a director, workshop instructors, educational staff, and kitchen director. There is also a support team made up of representatives from each of the following groups: parents, workshop staff, teachers, youth, and community organizations.

Work with the family and community. A parents' assembly is organized to strengthen the links between parents and center, and to improve the relations between the child and his family. This assembly also stimulates in parents a sense of responsibility for their children.

Home visits are made when children show signs of mistreatment, are especially undisciplined, or are absent from the center for long periods of time.

The center's work with the community is performed through visits by local coordinators to learn how to help families with serious problems. Meetings are held to sensitize the community to the problems of youth and to identify solutions that involve community members as active participants.

The Street Educator Project

This program was instituted by the Ministry of Social Welfare in 1987. The principle objective of the program has been to give attention to working youth and to those children wandering about the markets of Managua, Nicaragua's capital city. The idea of the street educator is to undertake preventive and educative work in the same environment where the child works or participates in other survival activities.

Street educators adopt working hours that acknowledge the reality of the market areas. Their interest is in children or youths who are selling, begging, stealing, collecting food scraps, or just "hanging out." They are particularly concerned with adults who manipulate these children to beg or steal, who organize and direct criminal gangs of both sexes, and who morally or physically mistreat these children.

State and community responsibilities. The state assumes responsibility for defining the objectives of the educators and/or social workers, and the payment of their salaries. The state is also responsible for finding financing for the different projects, in support of program development.

The educators and/or social workers look for support from and the involvement of the sellers and other merchants in the market. For example, in the case of children who steal in order to eat, merchants are encouraged to offer some kind of work to the children, so that they can earn their nourishment with dignity. Women are found to serve as substitute mothers for children who have been abandoned by their parents and have adopted the marketplace as their home.

One of the main objectives of the project is to develop a new understanding among the merchants regarding their responsibility toward the social problems of children who have been deprived of the real joys of childhood and have never experienced the happiness of knowing a close family relationship. While much progress has been made with these endeavors, there is a long and winding road yet to travel.

SYNTHESIS AND EVALUATION

"Children, do you know what a gardener does with flowers? He takes care of each flower. He waters it every day and cuts away the roots that might destroy it. You children are for the Revolution as the flowers in the garden.

Do you know what every human being does with his eyes? He takes care of his eyes more than any other thing. He protects his eyes above all because it is sensible to do so. You, children, are the eyes we take care of with great affection, with much love, with great self-sacrifice.

Flowers, eyes, bright suns—you are all of this, you are the pampered, the loved ones."[3]

These words of Commander Thomas Borge capture the philosophy of the Nicaraguan Revolutionary government regarding the care and development of all the Nicaraguan children. During the ten years of the revolution, the government, non-governmental organizations (both national and international), and community organizations have developed a variety of programs to serve children and youth. Due to a lack of resources, adequate evaluation of the impact that these combined efforts have produced has not been carried out. There is also the need to study and debate the educational and work methodologies being used with children in these programs, to assure the opportunity for the full participation of the general population and thus guarantee the fullest possible development of those children who make up the majority of Nicaraguan youth.

Most of the child care projects in Nicaragua have the following characteristics in common:

a. Recognition of the economic, social, and cultural circumstances of the children they serve.

b. Development of pedagogical and educative processes that sharpen parents' awareness and understanding of the proper ways to care for children and youth.

c. Formation of groups of community educators at a local level who can give care to children who remain in their homes.

d. Development of participatory researchers among the residents of marginal communities trained to detect developmental problems in local youth.

e. Organized work by those promoting youth development in order to find solutions within the community for meeting the needs of children and youth.

f. A strong commitment to the participation of the parents in the care and maintenance of the centers serving children and youth.

g. An effort to develop feelings of understanding and concern for the education and development of children in the general population, so that parents and the community give positive support to the various child-related projects.

The experiences described here have been significant at a national level for the simple reason that revolutionary policy was designed to favor the development and welfare of all the people, the majority, rather than a privileged few. When the Sandinistas lost the national elections in February 1990, political power passed into the hands of representatives of a liberal bourgeois ideology. The challenge now is to maintain and deepen the achievements won in the revolution, in this case those achievements related to the full development of the whole child. This is the challenge for Nicaragua, and for all the "underdeveloped" countries—the arduous but worthy goal of maintaining policies that benefit all the people, so that "Our children will grow tall on that earth, and our children's children" (Daisy Zamora).

NOTES

1. At Ministry of Social Welfare's preventive centers throughout the country, these youths receive counseling and education regarding social and moral issues aimed at promoting integral and balanced personal development. The ministry coordinates this program with other state institutions and community organizations.

2. Melania Morales was a sociologist and social welfare worker killed by the Contras in 1988.

3. Intervention of Thomas Borge in the First Encounter of the Police and the Children, December 8, 1989.

REFERENCES

MED. (1981). Guia de aprendizaje para el nivel Pre-escolar. Ministerio de Educaciòn.

INSSBI. (1982). El papel del Educador. Diciembre.

INSSBI. (April, 1983). Línea de Trabajo con la Familia de los Menores en Situaciòn de Riesgo. Departamento de Programaciòn.

INSSBI. (Junio, 1983). Sistemas de Control de los Proyectos Preventivos. Departamento de Programaciòn.

INSSBI. Exposiciòn de la Ley Tutelar de Menores y el Centro Tutelar de Menores. Departamento de Programaciòn.

INSSBI. (Julio, 1983). Linea Reeducativa. Departamento de Programaciòn.

INSSBI. (Agosto, 1983). Manual de Funcionamiento para Proyectos para Menores en Situaciòn de Riesgo.

INSSBI. (1983). Documentos Normativas de los CDI.

INSSBI. (Noviembre, 1984). El Institucionalismo. Departamento de Programaciòn.

INSSBI. (1985). Guía de Estimulaciòn del Lenguaje. Departamento de Promociòn y Supervisiòn Tutelar de Menores.

INSSBI. (1987). Taller a Promotores Populares. Barrio Ariel Darce. Departamento de Evaluaciòn Psico-Social.

INSSBI. (1987). Proyecto Piloto de Capacitaciòn a Promotores Populares. Direcciòn Tutelar del Menor.

INSSBI. (1987). Proyecto: Estructura de Tutelares Zonales. Direcciòn Tutelar del Menor.

INSSBI. (1987). Proyecto: Formaciòn de Promotores Populares. Direcciòn Tutelar del Menor.

INSSBI. (1987). Acciones Sociales de lay Ley Tutelar del menor. Departamento de
    Evaluaciòn Psico-Social.
INSSBI. (1987). Nuevas Alternativas de Atención al menor. Direcciòn Tutelar del
    Menor.
INSSBI. (1989). Conceptos Sicos del Psico-Social. Direcciòn Tutelar del Menor.

20

NORWAY

Ingerid Bø

Far to the north in Europe, bordering the North Sea is the country of Norway. Looking down from an airplane one sometimes wonders how this can be a country for human habitation: treeless high mountain plains and crevices, snow-capped mountain tops, glaciers, thousands of lakes, rivers, long narrow fjords lined with steep mountains and tumbling waterfalls, rocky islands all along the coastline. But look carefully and you also see green valleys, deep woods, sandy beaches, and cultivated fields. Weather and light are as varied as the landscape, and farthest north include midnight sun in the summer and midday darkness in the winter. The 4.2 million people primarily live along the coast and waterways, with the majority settled in the southern half of the country where the capital, Oslo, and most of the other larger cities are found.

Traditionally a land of fishing, forestry, and farming, then industrialized with the help of a wealth of hydroelectric power, Norway today is characterized by the oil production in the North Sea and other activities associated with life in a western post-industrial society.

Constitutionally the country is a monarchy with a parliamentary government. As a Nordic welfare state it offers a rather wide selection of publicly funded social welfare programs. In keeping with strong egalitarian traditions, many of the welfare policies are universal in orientation—they are for everybody.[1] This service is maintained with a high level of direct taxation of the working population and of work organizations, a 20 percent sales tax added to the cost of goods and services, and a variety of special taxes.

Among the welfare policies adopted for the benefit of families with young children are parental leaves, child allowances, health care service, state guaranteed child alimonies for single parents, rent subsidies—and day care service. High quality day care, developed under public auspices and supported by public means, is regarded as something all children should be entitled to, regardless of who they are and where in the country they live. In practice we have not reached this goal. Demand still far exceeds supply, there are regional and social differences in access to day care, and there is a shortage of trained personnel.

FACTORS INFLUENCING RECENT GROWTH IN DAY CARE SERVICE

In Norway, as in most Western European countries, the recent decades have seen a significant increase in the demand for extra-familial child day care. This demand has been ascribed largely to various changes in family patterns. Particularly important has been the increase in dual-earner families, a pattern that emerged in Denmark and Sweden beginning in the 1950s, and in Norway somewhat more recently. The increase in single-parent families taking place during the same period also contributed to the growth in demand for day care services. Figure 20.1 shows the change in number of adults and number of employed in Norwegian families with preschool children from 1964 to 1990.

In a comparison of the Scandinavian countries, Leira points out that "A connection is generally assumed to exist between these two processes: the mass entry of mothers into the labor market, and the public intervention in day care provision" (1987, p. 9). However, the degree of synchronization between labor market policies and day care policies varies from country to country. Whereas in Denmark and Sweden the combining of motherhood and employment was facilitated by large-scale public investments in child care, in Norway the public provision of care came too late to be of special importance in furthering the employment of mothers.[2] On the contrary, the cause-effect relationship was reversed, with the increase in the proportion of wage-working mothers contributing to the increase in the demand for public day care services, and eventually to the involvement of the government in service provision.

This lag is illustrated by the fact that a little over 70 percent of mothers with children from newborn to age six are now employed, while only 34 percent of the children have access to group day care. About 38 percent of these mothers work full time. Looking at the youngest group (birth to two years) we find 68 percent of mothers employed, with about 43 percent of these in full-time jobs, and provision of day care places for only 13 percent of the children. Also the increasing number of women enrolling as students in higher education has had an impact on demand, both directly during the years of study, and indirectly through the fact that the proportion of work participation increases with increasing education.

In spite of this mass entry of mothers into the marketplace, either for jobs

Figure 20.1
The Number of Adults and the Number Currently Employed in Families with
Preschool Children

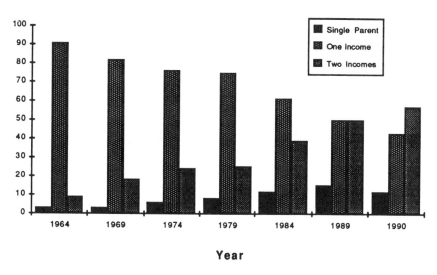

Year

Source: Gulbrandsen and Ulstrup Tønnessen, 1991

or for their education, fathers have generally neither increased their responsibility for domestic work and child care nor reduced their work time in the labor market. This situation has obviously meant strain on mothers and consequently on marriages and children. Access to good day care is a necessary but not sufficient condition to enable mothers to hold a job outside the home or to study on equal terms with men.

The increase in dual-earning, dual-studying, or work-and-study families is not the only development in Norwegian society that has increased the need for public day care over the last decades. An increase in motor vehicle traffic is making the outdoors an unsafe place for children's play in many places. Mechanization of farming is making even farms dangerous places to live. Many neighborhoods have little to offer children in the way of human contact and stimulating activities, located as they often are at some distance from the world of work. With a national average birth rate below two children per family, more families must look to other settings, such as day care centers, to find playmates for their children. The fact that more families now move away from their places of origin to new workplaces often brings strain and increased need for support. The option of grandparent care for children has largely vanished either because both grandparents already have jobs or because they live far away. Increases in difficulties with the marriage and with the family economy are other tendencies that have increased demand for day care and made the government aware of the necessity for involvement on behalf of children and their parents.

The demand for public day care provision also has grown out of national economic needs. Norwegian social budget policy was designed with the assumption that a certain proportion of the population be working for wages, including significant numbers of women in the work force. The labor market's own need for workers supported this policy.

Among the forces contributing to the public provision of day care has been the government's ideological stand on various socio-political issues. One such issue is support for the development of more egalitarian gender roles. Another involves a national commitment to ensure jobs that permit settlement in rural districts. It is widely accepted that this effort cannot succeed unless it includes the offer of public day care in those areas. Also the concern for equal rights to growth and development for children from various social, cultural, and geographic backgrounds and for children with handicaps requires government involvement in day care. Finally, there is the basic view that commitment to public day care will serve the interest of the welfare state as such.

In spite of all this, public child care in Norway has been slow in its development compared to the rest of Europe. Leira (1987) has explained this relative slowness by three factors. The first is relatively late industrialization and urbanization. Public day care followed these processes to a large degree—originating in cities and only gradually spreading to the rural districts. The second factor has been a slower increase in the labor market participation of mothers, and the third socio-cultural traditions that leave the responsibility for early socialization to the family. These three factors are obviously not independent of each other. For instance, it is likely that both the traditions mentioned and late industrialization are part of the reason for the slower increase in women's labor market participation.

These traditions are now in transition. Where day care used to be considered a solution to be used only when it was not possible to care for the child in the family, there is now wide acceptance of the view that high quality day care is an opportunity children need. When parents are asked what they need in order to manage both work and family well, a place in public day care has top priority. This does not mean that the value attached to family as early socializing agent is gone, but rather that public day care now is viewed much more as a help for rather than a competitor with the family.

THE PRIVATE/PUBLIC DISTINCTION

At the outset initiative for collective day care came from private organizations and individuals. The public sector did not really enter the arena until after World War II, more than a century after the opening of the first day care center.

Starting in 1947 the national government passed a series of measures that implied some supervision, guidance, regulation, and economic support for the day care field. In 1959 a national committee was established to investigate and discuss the need for day care institutions for children, and to propose a system of public grants. Following the committee proposal in 1961, a system of guaranteed grants came into effect to support the running of centers (1963) and the construction of buildings (1966), and to secure access to favorable loans in the Norwegian National Housing Bank (1969). These financial incentives acted as an impetus to growth.

A new government commission to evaluate the future development of day care for children started its work in 1969 and put forth a proposal for a Law Governing Pre-schools. When this law was passed in 1975 as the Law Governing Kindergartens it provided the basis for steady expansion of the public role in day care provision. Various other commissions have continued to look at the development of day care and of family policy as a whole (FAD 1973–1974, 1984–1985, 1987–1988, 1988).

Even after the government became heavily involved in the provision and management of day care centers and in the regulation of the day care field, private organizations have continued to play an active role. As recently as 1975 half of the day care centers in Norway were still private, and in 1989 this proportion was 40 percent. Through a system of rights and demands, not the least of which is economic support with public funds, Norway has welcomed the initiatives of voluntary organizations and other private bodies in day care provision. Provided that the facilities are approved by the public authorities, fulfilling certain requirements for number of children accommodated, hours per week per child, staffing, and criteria for admission, the center is entitled to a public-private mix in financing.

Day care centers owned by organizations but with financing from both the local municipality and the state presently make up the major part of private day care. Another type of private involvement is through what is called an "alternative basis of financing." This implies that employers who want to provide day care for their employees contribute that portion of the cost that is otherwise provided by the local municipality. These employers are then entitled to the same national support as other approved centers.

Alternative financing may be done in different ways:

1. Employer provides and manages a center.
2. Employer buys a number of places in an existing public or licensed center.
3. Employer buys and finances a number of places in the municipal day care system.

In the cases where an employer is providing a center, the community no longer controls the criteria for admission. In this case, parents connected to certain employers can get day care before other families with equally strong needs. Also, groups of parents and other private bodies have now established centers, with state support, that are without community control of admission. Recent surveys show that while center day care in Norway is used more by highly educated parents than by other groups, this is wholly explained by the distribution of places in these private centers. This equity problem must be weighed against the advantage of arriving at full coverage at a quicker pace through private supplement to the public provision. At present the national government believes that the pressing need for day care justifies the continuation of the alternative financing mechanism. The fact that public involvement in day care came relatively late and coincided with a new wave of privatization in society at large may in part account for this openness to private solutions in a country maintaining public responsibility to secure full coverage.

There is a small sector of publicly approved and subsidized family day care in Norway and a large sector of unregulated family day care. A short description of these services is provided later in the chapter.

LOCAL VERSUS CENTRALIZED PLANNING AND CONTROL

Administratively the country is divided into 20 counties and about 450 local municipalities. According to the 1975/83 legislation, the division of responsibility between these bodies and the central state is as follows: *Local* authorities at the municipal level are charged with the responsibility for planning, provision, distribution, and some aspects of the management of day care. *The county* approves the facilities and has a supervisory function on behalf of the national ministry. The county also provides guidance concerning construction, as well as the practical, economic, and educational aspects of the work carried out in centers. *The ministry* has the highest supervisory function. This involves the development of informational materials, the responsibility for research and development, and the distribution of the state support to those running the centers.

One requirement that has turned out to be of special significance is that each municipality provide an elected day care board or council. Where before parent groups and other organizations, together with teachers and health personnel, were the only consistent voices in support of the day care cause, now there was a public council with the right and duty to forward the interests of day care. The local leader of the organization for housewives, who had been timidly knocking at the door of the district administrator, found herself on a public board in a much more powerful position. One of the responsibilities for these boards was to develop comprehensive community plans for building day care centers. The planning has turned out to be a valuable method of attracting attention and generating discussion—valuable, but not yet strong enough to secure needed additional coverage.

Recently the national government introduced several new developments to increase the influence of local authorities. Starting in 1990 the authority to approve new centers was given to the municipality rather than to the county and state. Space requirements set by the state are now guiding norms, no longer mandatory, meaning that the municipality rather than the state decides how much room to provide for each child and controls standards for other aspects of the physical environment of the center. Furthermore the municipality, not the county, now provides exemptions from the requirement that the director of a center be a fully qualified teacher. The aim of these changes is to secure greater flexibility and local variety. The fear, particularly among preschool teachers, is that as the day care system moves toward full coverage, decisions about staffing and space will be driven more by economic considerations (keeping costs down) than by quality standards.

In apparent contradiction to this tendency toward decentralization, we observe a growing shift to stronger central control of program content. A national plan for work with six-year olds has been developed (FFD/UFD, 1990), and work is underway to create a national plan for content requirements in day care as a whole.

FORMS AND FIGURES

Main Program Types

Leira (1987) describes four main program forms that characterize day care in Norway.[3]

a. Public day care in center settings.
b. Public day care in private homes, called family day care.
c. Private day care controlled and approved by public authorities and supported economically by public means (usually in centers).
d. Private, unregulated day care (usually individual and in private homes).

In December 1989 close to 130,000 children newborn to seven years of age, 34 percent of all children in this age group, were enrolled in one of the forms of center care (A and C), about 65 percent of these in type A and 35 percent in type C. This includes special groups for six year olds. At the same point in time 2.4 percent of the age group were enrolled in public family day care (B). Data concerning private unregulated day care are less certain, but a recent survey estimated that 17 percent of children newborn to six years of age have this kind of care in a family setting, 4 percent are in "park care" (supervised outdoor care), and 4 percent in "other" kinds of non-parental care. This leaves 41 percent of the children in parental care.

The Organization and Staffing of Centers

Each day care center has a board, on which the owners, the parents, and the employees are represented. The center director has the right to meet with, address, and make proposals to this board but may not vote unless she is an elected representative. The authority of this board is limited to the internal structure and functioning of the center. Besides being represented on the board, the parents are formally related to the center through the parent's council, which is comprised of all parents whose children attend the center. The council is an advisory body that can discuss and give advice on all questions relevant to the children and the parents. Often it elects three to five representatives as a working group.

The day-to-day management, overall planning, and work organization are the responsibility of the director. This person, who is required to be a qualified preschool teacher or the equivalent, has the formal contact with other public services and with the parents, and she participates in the allocation of available places. In larger centers the program leaders (head teachers) are also required to have preschool teacher training. No formal training is required for other employees. In 1989, 25 percent of the total staff nationwide were trained preschool teachers, 48 percent were "assistants," and 20 percent were "other employed persons."

Grouping of children within the center has to a large extent been as follows: newborn to three year olds, three to five year olds, and five to seven year olds. In the last couple of decades professionals have argued that there are social and educational advantages to wider age groupings, and there has been some tendency to organize groups containing the total age-spectrum found at the center, with specific activities for narrower age ranges.

Norms for staffing in public and regulated private day care centers apply to the ratio of qualified staff to number of children. The recommendation is that there be no less than 2 adults per 14 to 18 children aged 3 to 6, and per 7 to 9 children under 3 years old. When attendance is for more than six hours per day, one of these adults is to be a preschool teacher. Where hours are shorter, a larger number of children per caregiving adult may be permitted. Nationally the average number of adults to children is one to four in public day care and one to six in regulated, private day care.

Care in Homes

Family care was brought into the public domain in the 1970s, in order to improve quality and to introduce rights and obligations for the benefit of both families and caregivers. Public family day care may be organized either in connection with an existing day care center or as a separate unit. Thirty children and their caregivers make up one unit, which is provided with its own director. Each family caregiver may care for up to five children of preschool age, including the caregiver's own children. The person employed as the caregiver, typically a woman, has terms of employment corresponding to those of assistants in public day care centers. The parents pay the same as for public group care and have the same rights.

No formal training is required for employment in public family day care, but some municipalities offer courses, and supervision is provided by the director, who is a qualified preschool teacher. Most of the supervision is given when the caregivers make weekly visits with their children to the center. During this visit the adults also may benefit from meeting each other, thus counteracting the feeling of social isolation that is often a problem for home-caregivers. At the same time the children get access to center equipment and to activities in a larger group.

Public family day care has clearly not developed to the point where it has replaced the informal unregulated arrangements. Unregulated family care continues to be the most commonly used form of day care, primarily because of the shortage of public facilities. Leira (1987) notes that both experts and parents are worried that the existence of a considerable "shadow market" in child care will reduce the efforts of central and local governments to provide public day care.

PROGRAM GOALS AND CONTENT

Law and Ideology

Since 1975 group day care has been regulated by special legislation. Lov om barnehager—literally the Act Governing Kindèrgartens ("children's gardens")—defines "barnehage" as a daytime activity based on educational principles for children of preschool age. According to official Norwegian terminology, all forms of public child day care and approved private day care are now termed "barnehager."

This choice of terms has ideological significance. The original proposal for the new law used the word "preschools," but the ensuing parliamentary debate and vote indicated that the majority did not want programs for young children to be called schools. The feeling was that a name has meaning that is likely to shape program content and that day care institutions for small children should not be like schools, but rather have an emphasis on free and creative play. This concern can be traced in part to the ideas of Friedrich Froebel and his "kindergarten." While the early "child asylums" in Norway (from 1837) emphasized the preparation of children for school and adult life, the Froebelian kindergarten, which came to Norway in the 1890s, was designed with the idea that childhood is important in itself and that day care institutions should help the abilities and aptitudes of each child unfold through play and creative activities.

As new day care centers were created, some were called "barnehage" in keeping with the Froebelian tradition, and others were called "daghjem" ("day-homes"), with more elements from the care traditions of the old asylums and creches. The post–World War II years saw a blend of the two pedagogical traditions. When the Norwegian parliament in 1975 chose "barnehage" as the official term to be used for all day care institutions, this can be said to be an official stance to protect this particular blend, which the majority felt would be endangered by the notion of school for young children.[4]

A basic assumption in today's welfare state ideology is that it is important to strive for human integration in our society. Integrating care and education in one institution serves the aim of creating social integration—an alternative to class-divided institutions. Social integration is brought out again when policy states that whenever it is thought to be for the best of the child and the family, the child with special needs (due to various physical, social, and psychological handicaps) is entitled to life in her own family and neighborhood, and a place in a regular day care center with enough extra help to develop her potential. A part of this integration ideology maintains that children who do not have special problems will benefit from life with those who do.

Integration in regular day care is also public policy for another special group—the children of new immigrants. During the last two decades, Norway has experienced immigration of a new kind and magnitude, with immigrants outnumbering emigrants and coming from countries outside Europe and North America. These children have priority access to day care. In order to meet the need also to develop their language and culture of origin, the national government has instituted a policy of economic support to provide native language teachers for immigrant children within the center. State support is given on the condition that the local community covers part of the cost.

Work for integration is closely tied to the goal of giving all children an offering of equal value. To get equal value more must be offered to some than to others. When the law requires priority of access and rights for special help to those with special needs, this is an expression of the concern for equity.[5]

Belief in the importance of the family as an early socializing agent is reflected in Norwegian legislation, which states that parents have the main responsibility for their children—the pedagogical mandate—and that day care is there to support parents. The Act of 1975 specifies the staff obligation for close cooperation with the children's home and gives goals and structures for parent involvement. Even so, the fact that a state policy for childhood exists and professional educators work with young children most of their waking hours challenges the parent mandate and is a break with the traditional division of labor between state and family. Leira (1990) talks of this as a quiet cultural revolution.

Starting in the late 1960s, there was a heated public debate in Norway about whether the opening paragraph of the national day care legislation should include a part on religion. Arguments in favor held that when the majority in the electorate supports the state church (Protestant Lutheran), it is appropriate that they should be guaranteed adherence to the same set of values in public day care as are provided in church and in the schools. The need for consistency between values in home and day care and for continuity between day care and school influences calls for the same adherence from the point of view of efficient learning as well as personal security.

The opponents argued that in a society that is no longer religiously homogeneous, a specific religious content would produce inconsistency and lack of continuity between home and public settings for a great many children, thus creating insecurity rather than security and confused rather than meaningful learning for the children. There was also the feeling that the very young age of the day care children required special restraint regarding inculcation of values outside the home.

The opponents won the first round in the debate, and the 1975 law said nothing about religion. But the debate continued, and in 1983 a clause was added stating a further aim: "Public day care shall help to give children an upbringing in accordance with basic Christian values." Instructions further specified that "day care shall build its activity on the fundamental ethical values anchored in Christianity. The ethical guidance given should consider the age, maturity, and home-milieu of the children. Day care shall mediate central Christian traditions as they are expressed in, for instance, the important Christian festivals" (FFD, 1990, my translation).

Although religion is not an issue that plays a major role in the daily life of most day care centers, it deserves mention because a formal tie to religion in day care is rather particular to Norway. In practice it comes across mostly through traditional content connected to Christmas and Easter. Instructions explicitly state that the clause on Christian values should not hinder private day care centers from deciding that they want no tie, a stronger tie, or a different tie to religion.[6]

Fields of Program Activity

In instructions accompanying the law, the goal of providing a good environment for children's activity and development is further specified to include individual and group care and support, self-expression, stimulation, learning, and ethical guidance. These concepts represent processes that are interconnected in various ways. The pedagogy of the day care center should build on a holistic concept of learning, where care, play, and learning in the more limited sense are integrated. Five fields of activity are delineated in a handbook provided by a governmental commission (FAD, 1982): care, play, experience of nature, creative activities, and work.

Care. Apart from the obvious need for care to satisfy fundamental physical needs, children need physical and psychological care and support from adults in order to develop basic feelings of security and self-worth and the confidence to venture into the world and learn about it. They also need to experience this care in order to learn to be caring themselves. Knowledge and experience in how to receive and give care are again prerequisites for the ability to express friendship and reconciliation and to solve conflicts in peaceful ways.

The Norwegian view is that day care institutions should focus clearly and strongly on caring for each individual child. They must consciously strive to help the children understand and accept their own and other peoples' feelings. Equally important goals are teaching the children to care for each other as well as for adults, and to use care situations as occasions for training in language and other skills.

Play. Play is seen as the most typical activity for children, of value in itself and essential for their development. Among the many conditions of importance for play in the day care center, the following are emphasized: the social relations in the group of children, the attitudes toward children's play among the adults, impressions and experiences in the lives of children, equipment and materials, time, and space.

The staff are responsible for consciously striving to develop the best possible conditions for play. Preschool teacher training involves in-depth study of these conditions and the methods of meeting them. To prepare themselves for work in this area, students must also learn about theories of play and about the importance of play as a way of being and a source of physical, emotional, social, and cognitive development in children.

Outdoor life and nature. Outdoor life is an important aspect of Norwegian culture in general, and it starts early. Based on a belief in the healthiness of fresh air, many parents take babies out to sleep part of the day even during the colder parts of the year (down to minus 10° C.), and certainly want them to play outside every day as they grow older. A day without some time outdoors is in some sense a lost day. Outdoor life is almost invariably related to nature. The role of outdoor life in Norwegian day care centers must be seen in the light of this general interest. Swedish researchers comment on the fact that emphasis on being outdoors and using the outdoors is seen more in Norway than in the other Nordic countries.

Preschool teachers are expected to have insight into the various functions outdoor activities may have for children's development. The national handbook on day care work points out that nature allows:

• Many-faceted training of the senses.
• Reality based formation of concepts—about animals, plants, natural processes, weight and quality of materials, etc.

- Room and materials for self-initiated research, creative expression, and play.
- Development of knowledge about and a relationship to the elements (water, earth, air, fire, sky and stars).
- Variety of experiences through seasonal changes.
- Activities aimed at awareness of the beauty found in nature and the forming of attitudes of responsibility for the environment.
- Physical expression to strengthen body and health at all times of the year.

To be able to promote these functions, the staff must have interest, experience, and knowledge about nature as well as about children and their way of thinking and learning. The pedagogy of the outdoors has a place in research as well as in the training of preschool teachers.

Creative activities. Three fields are delineated:

- Expression through picture, colors, form, and materials.
- Talking together, storytelling, and reading.
- Song and music, dance, drama, and movement.

In all these areas children need opportunities to express themselves in a variety of ways and to use their creative and communicative abilities. At the same time they need to receive and learn to appreciate other people's forms of expression—among their peers as well as in wider circles of time and place. The staff must arrange for and support such experiences and is urged to stimulate an experimenting attitude and to give boys and girls equal opportunities.

Work. The emphasis on play in our day care culture is significant both because of the value of play and as a timely reaction to the not so distant past, when many children were tied up in long, hard, work days that threatened their physical health and kept them not only from playing but also from going to school. But through our eagerness to protect children from too much work, and as the world of work has generally shifted away from the family, we have arrived in a situation where too many children have too limited contact with work, both as observers and in their own practice.

The developing day care institution mirrored the distance between children and work. Although a certain number of duties for the children was always involved, through the 1960s work for children was not a concept in much focus in the pedagogy of day care. In the seventies a counter-trend appeared. It was maintained that we underestimated children's ability to work and their joy from work, and that we underutilized the source of knowledge, skills, and self-confidence and of community with adults that can be found in wider access to adult work life and in doing useful tasks at home, in the day care center, the neighborhood, and greater society. Moreover, these work experiences give essential material for children's play.

Work, play, and learning are interrelated and should all be found in children's lives.

The five activity areas discussed above form the official specification of core content in Norwegian public day care, including what is recommended for publicly regulated day care in homes. I want to draw attention to two other themes—children's culture and local culture—both running through the other areas to some extent and both related to a development in society at large concerning the concept of culture. Through public debate and official documents, the emphasis was expanded from the notion that culture consists of the knowledge and expressions of the most talented representatives of various fields to a much broader concept. "The concept of culture broadly understood is about how people create, work, and express themselves as this is shown in things, social traditions, relationships with nature, and ways of living in general. Culture signifies human forms of expression and ways of living together and provides an important foundation for feelings of identity and belonging" (FAD, 1982, p. 68, my translation).

Children's culture. In Norway it is often emphasized that children have their own culture that is different from the adult culture. Several researchers have studied the content of children's culture in games, rhymes, riddles, songs, stories, and drawings. This culture is transmitted between the children; for instance, through play. Since play is an important element in public day care, it is obvious that these institutions perform an important role in promoting children's culture. At the same time, this culture is transmitted above all from older to younger children. To the extent that day care centers are age segregated, and only cover the first six years, they may also represent a threat to the maintenance and development of children's own culture. Alertness to this situation requires the use of wide age groups in activities within day care and for contact between day care and settings for older children, like schools.

Involvement with culture in day care is thus not only a question of letting the children get to know and share adult culture, but also a question of the children's own particular contribution to the lives of adults and to our culture in general. Gullestad (1990) calls attention to the importance of not assuming that children's culture is unitary. There are many cultures—a social and cultural variety—and as the value of children's cultural activities now has been carefully established, it is important to move on from the global concept of "children's own culture" to an analysis of that variety.

Local culture. In the early 1970s there was a growing awareness that day care centers seemed to be too homogeneous across the country. Toys, songs, stories, and activities were the same everywhere and were more tied to city-life, where public day care started, than to the small-town and rural areas where it gradually spread. Day care culture was to a great extent shaped by the training institutions for preschool teachers and their common emphasis on developmental psychology rather than on subject matter. Day care culture also tended to function in a rather isolated way—as an institution apart from the local community culture.

Awareness was followed by a growing interest in making day care centers an integrated part of the local culture. This meant placing more emphasis on children and staff going out into the local community as well as greater stress on bringing elements of this culture, and its people, into the daily life within the institution.

Working for local integration was also seen as important for the continuity between home and center life, a continuity that will influence the children's identity development and feelings of basic security. Emphasis on local culture is seen as being especially related to the goal of involving parents (Haug, 1982). Parents, more often than staff, come from the local area and have knowledge and skills representing its culture. They can be a resource to the center in bringing what they know—as well as interesting things they own—to the work with staff and children. Tapping this resource can also be a means of achieving a partnership, where each party has special strengths to bring to the relationship, thus increasing the chances that it will function well and last.

TRAINING

The training of preschool teachers is carried out at educational colleges. The entrance requirement is a high-school diploma. The course sequence presently requires three years and involves both supervised practical training in centers and theoretical studies. Throughout all three years pedagogy is a main subject—including early child development, history and theories of education, educational methods, and some themes from other areas such as sociology, social psychology, child psychiatry, and special education—all adding up to one and a quarter years of full-time study. Other subjects are music, arts and crafts, drama, natural sciences, religion/ethics, Norwegian literature and language, physical education, and social studies—also adding up to one and a quarter years. Students have a choice of content for the equivalent of one half year and thus get a chance to concentrate on an area of special interest. Various additional courses are offered for optional, continued training and specialization. A fourth mandatory year has been suggested, just a few years after the increase from two to three years took place.

Alternative roads to qualification as a preschool teacher are now being offered, to make formal training more accessible for untrained staff and others who need to work for income while they study. This is done by adding an extra year to the studies and placing much of the supervised practical training within the existing part-time job. In some instances this takes place in a decentralized manner, with a college responsible for offering courses to groups of students who live, work, and study in the districts at some distance from the school. Courses are then given by visiting teachers and—in some instances—partly through telecommunications and mail.

Day care "assistants," for whom no formal training presently is required, currently make up close to half of the staff in Norwegian day care centers. Some of these assistants may have some relevant training, for instance as "children's nurses," but most do not. In some communities assistants are now being offered courses designed to give them a basic foundation of formal knowledge for work in the field.

STRENGTHS AND SHORTCOMINGS

Public day care in Norway (including the publicly approved private care) is generally considered to be of high quality. But the scarcity of it is a major shortcoming, both for all those children seeking entry without success, and for the many employed parents who must find another alternative. But scarcity has negative consequences also for the people who are inside the system. Parents who know they have to apply each year worry about whether they will keep their place, and so they may feel hesitant about voicing criticism or getting involved with people and activities at the center. With a large turnover of children, personnel also may be more reluctant to involve themselves with the families. This way the scarcity of places becomes a threat to quality. To counteract some of these problems, some communities now admit children for two years at a time or even for the full period up to school age. The weakness to this approach is that it becomes still more difficult for other families to find a place.

The scarcity may also influence quality when following the criteria for admission results in groups that are heavily loaded with children needing special help or with family backgrounds containing specific strains. And certainly quality is affected when scarcity creates pressure to create more spaces at lower cost.

Local responsibility for provision of child day care—while in tune with a deep-seated Norwegian belief in the value of local autonomy and variety— is in some ways a threat to equity, as some municipalities are particularly low on economic means or have put low priority on public day care. Equity also is at stake when the cost of a place is so high that for some parents this is reason not to apply for or keep a place. (In general parents carry about 30 percent of the cost.)

If Norwegian day care as a sector has had limited resources, it is fair to say that resources at the center level are quite good, particularly when seen in an international perspective. Most centers have localities specifically designed and equipped for the purpose. They have a home-like appearance with several rooms and a child-oriented play area outside as part of the center.

The personnel situation causes problems. There has for years been a great unmet need for qualified preschool teachers, and there is a great turnover of personnel in the field. Vicious circles are established where deficits and instability make for more of the same, with negative consequences for all parties: staff, children, parents, and neighborhood. Another aspect of the situation is that preschool teachers as a group have a narrow range as regards their sex (almost all women), age (young), and work experience. This lack of variation may function as a weakness in adult work conditions as well as in the educational potential of the setting for children. Low pay, physical strain, and insufficient amount of in-service supervision and training may also count among the negative elements of the work situation for preschool teachers. Even though the last few years have seen some improvement in stability, preschool teachers still leave day care on a scale that should be a cause for concern.

In a recent analysis of Norwegian day care for four to seven year olds in international perspective, Kjørholt, Korsvold, and Telhaug (1990) point to the cautious use of authority and of demands for achievement in the Norwegian educational program—an unwillingness to use external pressure, for instance competition, which might motivate but could also stigmatize children. One question raised is whether we should re-evaluate our understanding of children's needs. Are children's lives in our part of the world today so marked by consumption, both materially and culturally, that they have a stronger need than before for more systematic and well-planned challenges? Is there a way to generate some constructive challenge while avoiding destructive pressure?

Internationally there is a tendency toward greater academic emphasis in educational programs for children below school age. This trend is also found in Norway, if in a moderate form. New interest in more systematic work with school-like or school-preparatory activities is paralleled by a tendency to move day care administration on a municipal level from the social to the school sector. The hope is that this development will make day care a better learning environment for children and help them to a better start in school, and that it will increase the prestige of the day care sector. But warnings are heard, saying that the day care sector's traditional independence from school is a strength. If we give it up, we will lose our special blend of caring and education. Day care must remain a place with much emphasis on children's play and creative self-management. Unwillingness to start structured concentration on cognitive tasks early does not have to mean a de-emphasis on education, but rather the promotion of the manifold development of the whole child—a broad concept of learning.[7]

Publicly specified main goals and fields of activity were described earlier. The fact that we have worked more consciously through the last decade on the formulation of goals and have an ongoing debate on what the content of day care should be is in itself a strength. Even if practice does not always measure up to the goals, what the goals are will make a difference over time. At the same time we need to be continually evaluating practices.

The goals for our day care specify both individual and social development, but in practice there has been much focus on the individual child. Lamer (1990) has expressed concern at a tendency to think that social development is taken care of just because many children are gathered in one place. There is a growing understanding of a need for more systematic work to promote pro-social skills and attitudes.

An area where realities often fall short of intentions concerns parent involvement. Examples can be found of centers that work well with parents, but by and large there is a rather superficial cooperation between staff and parents, and parents have not in practice been influential in Norwegian day care. Weaknesses can be found both in staff and parents' understanding of the whys, hows, and whats of this work—and consequently in ability to convey insight and interest. Adding to the difficulties is the fact that families with young children are often in short supply of both time and money.

As public day care moves toward full coverage and plans are launched for a full-day program for school-aged children (see note 3), questions are being asked about what the growing extent of institutionalization and organization of childhood will do to our children and families. Will children's capacity to create their own activities suffer when so much is organized and structured by adults? How will a lack of opportunity for self-management influence childhood and human development? Will increased institutionalization of children's lives weaken their ties to adult work life and their interaction with society at large? And will parents in full-time employment play enough part in the lives of their children?

How the day care institution and the schools are developed will make a difference in this situation, as well as how we develop other aspects of our society. Work-life reforms and support for the creation of ties between settings—including parents' active involvement with children and staff within day care and school—are some of the issues at stake.

PLANNING FOR THE FUTURE

The supply of day care—the challenge of the waiting lists—is currently a key issue in the field of support to families. It is a stated government goal to reach full coverage shortly after the turn of the century. The municipalities have been required to develop renewed plans specifying their building program for each year for the first four years and then for 1996, 2000 and 2004. Data from all the municipalities will form the basis of a national plan (FAD, 1989).

Economic support from the state will increase to nearly 40 percent of total operating costs. If this, along with information about the values of group day care, does not lead to sufficient growth in the number of places, the government will consider introducing legislation to make day care provision mandatory for the local authorities (FAD, 1987–88; FAD, 1989). A recent parliamentary debate showed strong opposition to such a step. At the same time, politicians are moving full coverage up on their list of priorities, stating that some quality may have to yield temporarily in order to finance the quantity. There is a considerable amount of tension between politicians and professional day care personnel. These professionals are also committed to full coverage but fight against a compromise of quality.

How much is "full coverage"? This depends on several conditions like birthrate (which has increased somewhat lately after a low period around 1980), length of paid leave at childbirth (which should increase from 6.5 months to 12 months within the period), age of school start (will it be lowered from seven to six?), and demand from parents (expected to be around 90 percent of all one to six year olds). Regularly revised and updated plans will be made to reflect changing conditions.

The ministry stresses the importance of personnel development for the further growth of group day care. Various ways of stimulating recruitment and stability in the profession are being tried out, such as increasing the capacity of the educational colleges, offering alternative roads to qualification, personal stipends, supplementary or refresher courses for teachers who have been out of the profession for some time, and improved supervision and support for local innovation. Concerning quality, it is argued that there is a need for further development of leadership in day care—in relation not only to children, but also to co-workers, parents, and surrounding institutions. In this connection the issue has been raised of changing the preschool teacher's role to one of more work with the various groups of adults—and less direct work with children. While being interested in training for leadership and supervision, the preschool teachers are opposed to the idea of less direct work with children and leaving that to staff with less training.

Educational planning is an issue of special importance for quality. Since 1983 it has been mandatory for each day care center to develop a plan for the year, and this has in some instances been followed by some more general planning at the municipal level. Parallel to this there has been a growing call for a national curriculum plan in day care, and the government has begun to develop such a plan.

During the last 15 years there has been a good amount of research and development done in the day care field, for instance, on programs for six-year olds; programs for immigrant children; planning; the relationship of day care to neighborhood; parental involvement, and issues of educational method (Hyrve, 1988). The government has underscored the necessity of increased support to research in the day care field and presently directs its resources into three main programs:

1. A five-year national program (1988–1992) managed by the Norwegian Council for Applied Social Research as part of a larger program "Children of the Welfare State." The research on day care is focused around three main themes: (a) day care as a societal institution, (b) provision, and (c) the inner life of day care centers.

2. County-level organization of innovation projects in day care and evaluation of these efforts.

3. Special projects initiated and/or financed by the ministry concerning administration and management in center day care, family day care, and economic issues on micro and macro level, particularly cost-benefit analyses.

In closing I would like to return to the question of values. In a discussion of common problems in the day care field in the Nordic countries, the conflict between day care for the sake of the children versus care for the sake of society or the world of work is brought out. The point is made by Vedeler (1975), Dencik, et al. (1988), and others that it is time for the labor market and society's family policy to adapt to the needs of children and their families to a greater extent than is the case today. Whether parents' demand for day care actually turns out to be 90 percent and whether the demand will be for full-day or for part-day openings, will depend on the development of policies and programs across this wider board.

A report by Hagen and Hippe (1989) on challenges to the welfare state concludes that the main challenge for society in the years to come is to free up more time for child care (Hagen and Hippe, 1989). Which solution will best serve both parents' and children's needs? Four different strategies are discussed:

1. The state can, through cash transfers, longer leaves of absence, six-hour workday, or by paying parents to stay at home, buy parents' freedom from the labor market so that they can themselves take a larger part of the child care.

2. The state can invest more in care-work as paid work in the public sector—meaning more day care openings and more public family day care.

3. The state can through direct pay or various sorts of tax deductions, subsidize families with children so that they may buy child care in the market.

4. The fourth model could be the East European one, where day care tied to the parents' workplace is part of the pay for work.

Another issue will be how these strategies interact with various other values and practices, not the least concerning gender roles. The first strategy, for more time for parents to care for their own children, will have a different meaning for children, families, and society at large if it involves fathers and mothers taking an equal share of this increased time for children compared to a traditional solution where mainly the mother would be responsible for this time. Fathers in Norway still have not shown that they are ready to take their share. Although the Norwegian welfare state supports the ideological aim of men and women sharing responsibility for care work, some of the system practices hinder change in that direction. One such practice is that of according more comprehensive and generous benefits to citizens who participate in wage work than to those who engage in vitally necessary but unpaid care. Leira (1989) points out that this creates a "dual concept" or "gendering of citizenship," which gives preference to men's instead of women's activity patterns. A discussion is taking place about the need to change this social structure.

What direction will our thinking and feeling take concerning the best way to care for our children, and what priority will be put on these issues when it comes to action—on the part of the government, on the part of various societal institutions and on the part of parents in various cultural and political niches? The strategy—or combination of strategies—chosen will decide the future development of public day care.

NOTES

1. The universal orientation makes Norway an *institutional* welfare state as distinguished from welfare states classified as *residual* or *marginal*, which offer a limited set of policies for a limited part of the population (Leira, 1990).

2. Leira (1989) made an in-depth study of this process.

3. Not included here is the "leisure-time center," where seven to nine year olds (who now have short school days) spend the hours before and after school while their parents work or study. With room for less than 6 percent of the age group in these institutions, there is a great shortage of places. A new full-day service at school is planned to solve this problem, and various models are being discussed.

4. The professional title "preschool teacher" was established before the law came and has remained.

5. It is also clear that integration is not always the best response to special needs. Special institutions are needed for some children.

6. Historically the tie to religion has been much stronger in our schools. Whereas school at the outset had a clear religious motivation, day care has been guided not by religion but by the behavioral sciences.

7. The ambivalence between ties to school versus independence is shown in the fact that central administration is carried out by the ministry responsible for family affairs, not the one for education.

REFERENCES

Balke, E., Berg. B. and Fagerli, O. (1979). *Barnehage—heim—lokalsamfunn.* (Day-care—Home—Local Community). Nærmiljø Barnehage Prosjektet. Rapport nr. 10. Oslo: Forbruker-og administrasjonsdepartementet.

Bogen, H. (1987). *Barnepass—drøm og virkelighet* (Child Care—Dream and Reality). Fafo rapport R4:87, Oslo.

Dencik, L., Bäckström, C. and Larsson, E. (1988). *Barnens två världar. (Children's Two Worlds)*. Esselte Studium AB, Falköping.

Evenshaug, O., Hagesæther, G. and Hallen, D. (1975). *Føskolen i fokus. En artikkelsamling* (Preschool in Focus: A Book of Readings). Luther forlag: Oslo.

F.A.D. [Forbruker-og administrasjonsdepartementet]:

(1973–74). *Barnefamiliens levekår* (Living Conditions of Families with Children). Stortingsmelding nr. 51, 1973–74.

(1982). *Målrettet arbeid i barnehagen. En håndbok* (Goal-Oriented Work in Day Care: A Handbook). Oslo: Universitetsforlaget.

(1984–85). *Om familiepolitikken* (On Family Policy. Stortingsmelding nr. 50.

(1987–88). *Barnehager mot år 2000* (Day Care Towards Year 2000). Stortingsmelding nr. 8.

(1989). *Barnehageplanlegging mot full behovsdekning. Utvikling av nasjonalt utbyggingsprogram* (Day Care Planning Towards Full Coverage: Development of a National Program of Construction). P–0792.

F.F.D. [Familie og forbruker departementet]. (January 1990). *Lov om barnehager med forskrifter* (Law on Day Care with Regulations). Q–0511 TRE.

Flising, B. and Johansson, I. (1984). *Förskola i Norden. Slutrapport, Diskussion om och exempel på pedagogisk verksamhet* (Preschool in the Nordic Countries, Final Report, Discussion of and Examples of Educational Programs). Stockholm: NORD.

F.A.D./U.F.D. [Forbruker-og administrasjonsdepartementet/utdannings-og forskningsdepartementet]. (1990). *Pedagogiske tilbud til 6–åringer Veiledende Rammeplan* (Organizational programs for 6 year olds. Supervisory Work Plan). Oslo: Universitetsforlaget.

Grude, T. (1987). "Det begynte med barneasylene" (It Started with the Child Asylums). In E. R. Tømmerbakke and P. Miljeteig-Olssen (Eds.), *Fra asyl til barnehage. Barnehager i Norge i 150 år* (From Asylum to Day Care, Day Care in Norway for 150 years). Oslo: Universitetsforlaget, pp. 23–63.

Gulbrandsen, L. and Ulstrup Tønnessen, C. (1990). *Småbarnsfamilier ved inngangen til 1990-årene: Yrkesaktivitet, barnetilsyn og familieøkonomi* (Families with Small Children at the Beginning of the 1990s: Work, Child Care, and Family Economy). Notat 1990:4. Oslo: Institutt for sosialforskning.

Gulbrandsen, L. and Ulstrup Tønnessen, C. (1991). *Småbarnsfamilier i dagens Norge* (Families with Small Children in Today's Norway). Notat 1991:3 Oslo: Institutt for sosialforskning.

Gullestad, M. (1990). 'Barnas egen kultur'—finnes den? (Children's own culture—does it exist?) *Barn*, 4, pp. 7–27.

Hagen, K. and Hippe, J. M. (Eds.) (1989). *Svar skyldig? Velferdsstatens utfordringer—partienes svar* (Answer required? Challenges for the welfare state—Answers from the political parties). FAFO-rapport nr. 092.

Haug, P. *Foreldre, barn og barnehage—samarbeid om oppseding* (Parents, Children and Day Care—Co-operation on Child Rearing). Oslo: Det Norske Samlaget.

Hoel, M. and Torgersen, U. (1991). *Yrkesløp og organisasjonsaktivitet blant lærere og førskolelærere* (Careers and Organizational Activity among Teachers and Preschool Teachers). Rapport 1991:4. Oslo: Institutt for samfunnsforskning.

Hyrve, G. (1988). *Barnehageforskning i Norge 1975–1987* (Day Care Research in

Norway, 1975–1987). Mimeograph, Dronning Mauds Minne, Høgskolen, Trondheim.

Joner, T. B. (1979). *Barnehagene—de nye misjonsmarker?* (Day Care Centers—The New Frontiers for Missionaries?). Oslo: Aschehoug.

Kjørholt, A. T., Korsvold, T. and Telhaug, A. O. (1990). *Pedagogisk tilbud til 4–7-åringer i internasjonalt perspektiv. En studie av England, Frankrike, Japan og USA* (Educational Opportunities for 4–7 Year Olds in International Perspective: A Study of England, France, Japan, and the USA). Norsk senter for barneforskning, Rapport nr. 18, Trondheim.

Lamer, K. (1990). *En, to, tre—ingen flere med* (One, two, three—No One Else. On the Mediation of Values in Child Rearing). Oslo: Universitetsforlaget.

Leira, A. (1987). *Day Care for Children in Denmark, Norway and Sweden.* Institute for Social Research, Report nr. 5, Oslo.

Leira, A. (1989). *Models of Motherhood, Welfare State Policies and Everyday Practices: The Scandinavian Experience.* Oslo: Institute for Social Research.

Leira, A. (1990). Visjonen om barndommen: Den nordiske velferdsstatsmodellen (The vision of childhood: the Nordic Welfare State model). *Norsk Pedagogisk Tidsskrift*, 6, pp. 290–99.

Linge, P. and Wille, H. P. (1980). *Barn i arbeid, lek og læring* (Children at Work, Play, and Learning). Oslo: Aschehoug.

N.O.S. [*Norges offisielle statistikk*]. *Official Statistics from the Central Bureau of Statistics of Norway*:

1990a: *Kindergartens (Day Care Centres) and Leisure Time Centres 1989.* Oslo/Kongsvinger 1990.

1990b: *Labour Market Statistics 1989.* Oslo/Kongsvinger 1990.

Pedersen, P. and Pettersen, J. (1983). *Fungerer våre barnehager?* (Do Our Day Care Centers Work?). Tromsø, Oslo, Bergen, Stavanger: Universitetsforlaget.

Rødseth, T. (1987). "Velstand og tidsnytting" (Affluence and Use of Time). *Norges offentlige utredninger 1987:9B. Vedlegg til arbeidstidsutvalgets utredning.* Oslo.

Vedeler, L. (1975). *Førskole og skole i samvirke. Rapport om førskolevirksomheten i de nordiske land. Overgang og samvirke førskole/skole.* (Preschool and School Working Together. Report on Preschool Programs in the Nordic Countries: Transition and Cooperation in Preschool/School). Nordiske utredninger nr. 15.

—— 21 ——

PERU

Jeanine Anderson

Day care is a relatively small service sector in Peru. But the provision of these services becomes highly complex when understood in the context of contemporary Peruvian society.

THE CONTEXT OF CHILD REARING IN PERU

Peru offers a great diversity of experiences to its young children. To begin with, the country's three markedly different geographical regions—Pacific coast, Andean highlands, and forested Amazon basin—make very different "homes" for the children born in them. The coast-born child will probably live in a town or city, go to school, watch television, play soccer or volleyball (according to sex), and acquire a relatively cosmopolitan outlook. The child born in the Andes may live in a provincial capital or regional center of agriculture and trade, but his or her family's access to services, communications, consumer goods, and the income with which to buy them will be far less than the coast child's. The Andean child may form part of a peasant village, speak Quechua or Aymara, and devote most of his or her time to helping on the family's small farm, perhaps sacrificing a primary education to those tasks. In the Amazon basin, the possibilities are even more extreme. Some children live in river towns—local administrative and commercial centers corrupted by the international narcotics trade before they could be properly integrated into national life—while others belong to tribal groups that actively reject that integration.

Much could be said about the socialization and welfare of Peruvian children in this wide range of contexts. Nonetheless, the subject of this book—day care—counsels a selective approach. In wealthier countries, day care is pertinent to school-aged as well as those under age six, to mothers pursuing an education or voluntary community activities as well as those working out of need, and is necessary in both urban and rural areas. This is not the case in Peru—not as yet. Day care is an urban service for the preschool-aged children of working mothers.

The discussion of any aspect of contemporary Peru, however, is framed by the prolonged economic crisis affecting this nation. Thirty years ago Peru was one of a group of middle-level developing countries in Latin America; today it is among the poorest. The immense foreign debt, stagnation of agriculture, mass unemployment, raging inflation, widening of the inequalities of wealth, and elusiveness of a political solution have brought in their train a decade of violence. Bodies in the plaza, illegal detentions, and revolutionary harangues in schools are realities too many Peruvian children have come to know. Meanwhile, as the country applied a structural adjustment program in August 1990, half of its 22 million inhabitants were estimated to be in need of emergency food assistance.

The backwardness of Peru's economy, with its heavy reliance on exporting primary products, is belied by a high level of urbanization. Almost 70 percent of Peruvians live in urban localities, a third of them in the capital city of Lima. Industry, health and educational services, and most government investment are concentrated in Lima and a handful of regional urban centers. Because of these imbalances, migration out of the countryside has been intense since the 1940s. Twenty years ago, only one in ten Lima-born children had both parents born in the city as well. Migrants must adapt to discrepancies between their value systems, those of the "old" settled, street-wise urban poor, and those of the dominant social groups.

Changing patterns of women's employment in the cities open another window on children's care and socialization. Overall, female participation in the labor force is 47.8 percent in Lima. Women begin to work early: their participation in the 15 to 19 year cohort is higher than that of men. While many withdraw temporarily during the childbearing years, the economic crisis has gone far to reverse that trend, such that the age distribution of economically active women is becoming increasingly like that of men. Women workers, however, obtain far lower incomes than men: on average, they earned 44 percent of men's wages in 1987. Nearly half of working women in Lima are in the urban informal sector. Of those in formal employment, 16 percent work in industry and 35 percent are white collar employees.

Above and beyond paid employment, poor women in Peru are increasingly called upon to dedicate time and energy to "community management" work. Each new formation of an urban shantytown demands the participation of the entire adult population in the tasks of laying out streets and housing lots, negotiating with municipal authorities, and even battling with police sent to evict them. The follow-up work of consolidating the settlement and equipping it with minimal urban amenities falls largely on women, who more frequently than men work at home or close to the settlement. They write petitions, organize marches, raise funds, mobilize community support, supervise building construction, and keep accounts of monies collected and spent. Such leadership roles have enormous potential value as a vehicle for the education and integration of women. There is reason to believe, however, that the time demands of community development, added to the high investment of energy in housework without basic services, create special risks for the young children of the most active women.

A final factor that must be singled out for its important bearing on child rearing and child care is kinship and family composition. In urban and rural Peru, nuclear family households are the norm. Nonetheless, Peruvians of all social classes seek to locate close to relatives, particularly siblings. Encouraging strong friendships among cousins and sharing the burden of child care are explicit considerations in this pattern. Adult brothers are a source of social support and financial aid for their sisters, especially should they be living alone due to widowhood, separation, or abandonment by their spouses. Among the urban poor, women head between 20 and 25 percent of households.

SOCIALIZATION PATTERNS

Just as the contexts of child rearing are greatly varied in Peru, so are patterns of socialization, but because town or village life in the rural Andes forms the cultural background of most of the urban poor, Andean child rearing is particularly relevant to the present discussion.

Andean babies enjoy close physical contact with their mothers. They are carried tightly wrapped in a cloth on their mothers' backs almost continuously through the first year of life, frequently through the second, and sporadically even longer. With hands and arms free, they pull on their mothers' braids, munch on a cracker, or wave a toy. As in other cultures that practice close physical contact between mother and the young child, their communication tends to depend heavily on non-verbal strategies.

In general, Andean children are socialized to assume high levels of responsibility at an early age. They work both as childminders and as their parents' assistants in the herding of sheep and alpacas, cultivation, marketing, and household tasks. Given the family's combination of multiple income-generating strategies, children learn the skills of planning, ordering priorities, and synchronizing their activities with those of others. Clear sex differences exist in the assignment of tasks to young children. A study using spot observation of five to seven year olds found girls engaged in chores in 46 percent of the observations and boys in 30 percent. In 10 percent of observations, girls were engaged in child care, while boys never assumed this responsibility. Nonetheless, caring for young siblings is an experience many adult Peruvian men recall with a certain satisfaction, and an unmarried uncle is an important figure in the emotional growth of children of both sexes.

Migrants to the city must adapt their child-rearing strategies to risks and opportunities they may not fully understand. A comparison of children of inner-city "old poverty" with children of the new shantytowns found, for example, a greater tendency of the "experienced" urban parents to restrict their children's movements, limiting them to the house or a tiny attached patio. Migrant parents, in contrast, often underestimate the social and physical dangers of giving their offspring the same freedom they had in the countryside. Children of three or four are sent on errands with little appreciation of the difficulties of orientation in a sea of identical straw shanties. Frequently, young children are left to their own devices for constructing meaning out of a wide variety of stimuli, many of them extremely violent; criminals who use the shantytown as a hideout, alcoholism, abuses by police and officials, inappropriate television programs, and wheeled water cisterns (trucks) that deliver a vital provision but often occasion fatal accidents as they careen through the settlement in pursuit of clients.

Though parents and older siblings are their primary socializers, most Peruvian children have a quasi-filial relationship with one or more sets of godparents. Some of these relationships may involve no more than a formal visit at Christmas and birthdays, but most are binding in highly significant ways. The institution of godparenting gives almost all children the possibility of a counterbalance to their parents' authority and the assurance of a temporary refuge in case things go badly at home. In addition, the practice of fostering is quite widespread in Peru. An oldest child may be "given" to the grandparents for raising, or an "extra" daughter may be entrusted to a family in the kin network that is in need of another hand for domestic tasks. More urban families may turn children over to public or church-supported foster homes. Such institutions, though intended for orphans, admit a large number of children with intact families whose root problem is economic need.

These patterns suggest that a global relinquishing of rights over a child is a practice more enshrined in Peruvian culture than the partial and temporary transfer of rights that day care implies. Something of the confusion about the rights and obligations of day care users and providers seems to have been caught in a 1981 study by this author of informal exchange of child care services in Lima shanty communities. Overall, 7.6 percent of the nearly 700 women interviewed said that they left their children with a neighbor when they needed to go out. In contrast, 26.3 percent left them with older siblings,[1] although these older siblings were often still children themselves and would have to turn to neighbors for help in any emergency. Half of the respondents felt that their neighbors did not intervene in any way when their children were at the neighbors' house, whether to offer a cracker, organize a play group, or protect them from blows and falls. The migrant mothers tended to send their children to neighbors' houses more frequently than they returned the favor—apparently a strategy for forcing the city-born to define the rules of the exchange.

Meanwhile, on the formal level of agencies and programs, a consensus with respect to the objectives and organization of day care services has proven just as elusive, as shall be seen in the discussion of day care policy.

SOCIAL POLICY MAKING IN PERU

Making social policy for a heterogeneous, culturally diverse population in a chronically poor country is a complicated enterprise. Peru's social policy has largely grown by accretion, often under the influence of external pressures, especially the recommendations of United Nations organs or industrial country models. The result is a motley collection of norms and institutions with poor mechanisms of coordination, monitoring, and evaluation. Sorely lacking is a public debate on the role of social policy in national development, in the protection of ethnic- and cultural-minority rights, or as a mechanism for combatting massive poverty.

Social policy is formulated in the Ministries of Health, Labor, Education, and Justice, and in specialized agencies such as the National Institute of Family Welfare (Instituto Nacional de Bienestar Familiar—INABIF). Both municipal governments and the recently created regional governments have a broad mandate for establishing and supporting social services within their jurisdictions. Frequently at odds with permanent policy-making bodies is the enshrined custom that licenses the wife of each newly elected president and mayor to organize her own special programs, often directed to children. Finally, a large number of private agencies also act with great autonomy in the social field, often (in recent years) with funding from international agencies. Again, no effective mechanisms exist to ensure that the programs and services they organize are consistent with national social policy goals, or that, as relatively well-financed pilot experiences, they generate critical data for informing future social policy making.

Such a context is hardly propitious for developing a progressive, coherent, publicly supported day care policy. Indeed, Peru has no such policy to date. Instead, it has patches of day care legislation slipped into various parts of the government machinery. The first of these is the Labor Law of 1918, created in response to International Labor Organization (ILO) recommendations of the period. This law, designed to protect breast-feeding, obligates employers to provide facilities for care at the workplace of children up to one year of age, wherever the scale of the industry guarantees a minimum number of beneficiaries (25 women employees of reproductive age, irrespective of their marital status). According to a stipulation probably never enforced, smaller enterprises and employers of pieceworkers are obliged to subsidize infant care in a place mutually agreeable to workers and management.

This law, tying day care to women's industrial employment, brought into being a stock of day care services estimated in the early 1970s to cover approximately 1 percent of the potential demand in Lima. Outside the capital city there was little or nothing. Alarmed at the growing number of children in self-care, the Ministry of Health created a working group to inventory facilities in Lima and design a new policy that would respond to the needs of poor families. Its work was cut short when the center of gravity in programs for young children shifted to the education sector. The current involvement of the Health Ministry in the day care field is limited to providing services for its employees in some of the largest hospitals, and, on request, sending health-post staff to examine the children in day care programs.

The Ministry of Education, then, became a third source of legal norms concerned with day care. Following a profound sectorial reform in 1972, early childhood education moved to top priority. The principal thrust, however, was promoting school readiness among older preschool children. A major program of non-formal preschool education was created, with important external funding and technical assistance. This program, which rests on community participation in donating or constructing a center and in selecting a local *animador/a* (teacher/caregiver), is known as PRONEI (Programa no-escolarizado de educaciòn inicial). At present some 315,000 four and five year olds are enrolled in PRONEI centers, and approximately 13,000 community men and women, in the rural Andes and Amazonia as well as urban shantytowns, work as animadores.

Overwhelmed by the demands of rapid growth in primary, secondary, and tertiary education, the Ministry of Education has never acted as a promoter of day care services. Instead, it has taken over the administration of a few centers created by community initiative, and, in 1985, of a large network of combined preschool and day care services established through a special program of the outgoing president's wife.

Despite its limited enthusiasm for day care, the Ministry of Education has a high profile in the field. Its philosophy of day care dominates the thinking of two key sectors: politicians and community leaders. According to this philosophy, preschool services are an "extension down" of the elementary school system, and day care is an "extension down" to one, two, and three year olds of the preschool. The child's day should be filled with activities mandated by the basic curriculum for early childhood education. This vision of day care as a first step in the child's educational career—almost ethereally disassociated from the family's need for substitute child care and the domestic routine of the real-life day care program—finds a happy niche in the thinking of many political leaders, from the national to the community level, whose limited understanding of child caretaking makes them seek connections to legitimated programs such as universal basic education.

If the making of laws for day care in the education sector is dominated by the teaching profession and its goals, day care norms in a fourth sector, the Ministry of Justice, tend to respond to the professional concerns of social workers. There, INABIF is charged with formulating a comprehensive family policy and administering a set of services and programs that translates that policy into action. INABIF recognizes two conditions that together justify the provision of day care: poverty and mothers' employment. When demand is especially great, some INABIF centers add a third filter and admit only the children of single mothers. Most of INABIF's day care facilities function as one of multiple family services housed in large complexes that draw clients from the surrounding district.

Municipal governments are a fifth source of norms and precedents in the day care field. They are called upon to "promote, establish, and support" day care centers, as one in a long list of social services that may command their attention. Unfortunately, their mandate far outstrips their current resources or any they are likely to deploy in the near future. Only a small minority of Peru's more than 1,000 municipal governments have gone into the day care business. Of metropolitan Lima's 42 district sub-divisions, six support and administer municipal day care centers.

All these patches of laws impinging on day care do not add up to a day care policy. No single unifying vision of the raison d'être of day care lies behind them, nor do they project any social consensus concerning its importance and role. The existing norms are supervisory, even censorious, rather than promotional. Nowhere do they assign a clear responsibility for ensuring that day care services actually meet the potential demand, or even for monitoring the relation between supply and demand. In the confusion and frequent defensiveness about prerogatives and jurisdictions, there is little room for cumulative learning or objective evaluations of on-going programs. Despite a history reaching back several decades, day care does not project a coherent image to the public.

Nor is day care legislation placed in the context of a set of legal norms designed to protect the working mother or promote gender equity in the labor force. Peru has very little work-family legislation overall. Women in formal employment have rights to a total of 90 days of paid maternity leave (45 before and 45 after childbirth) and to one hour daily for breast-feeding, assuming that their infants are being cared for close enough to make visits feasible. These rights are effectively exercised, however, only by a minority of economically active women. For self-employed and informal workers, there is no protection. Peru has no policy of child allowances, no paternity leave, and no parental leave to cover a child's sickness, except that understanding employers may wink at absences they know spring from that cause. In a country so poorly provided with basic utilities and so poorly served by health and educational facilities, having small children under one's charge is a severe disadvantage when competing for jobs.

With fleeting exceptions, Peru's existing day care legislation does not address the fundamental problem of financing day care services. The sectorial norms and the Law of Municipalities assume by implication that both investment in new programs and the operating costs of existing services should be financed from general budget appropriations. Day care, then, must compete for funds with a plethora of alternative programs, many with strong outside lobbies and well-installed internal administrative units interested in their survival. Employer-provided day care for infants is the only category of services whose funding is explicitly provided for by law, with the full costs assigned to the employer.

FINANCING DAY CARE SERVICES

Parents pay a very small proportion of the costs of day care in all except private, for-profit services. Ministry of Education, municipal, and INABIF centers charge daily fees equivalent to less than bus fare and use that source to cover less than 4 percent of the centers' operating budget. Other day care providers tend to follow their lead regarding user obligations. The occasional private philanthropy struggles valiantly to attract paying working-class families, achieve a mixed population of clients, and develop sliding fees. Meanwhile, middle-class, private day care users pay fees ranging from US $50 to $80 a month—nearly equivalent to a secretary's wage, and a third to a quarter of the earnings of many women professionals.

Day care provided by the public sector in Peru costs between US $100 and US $500 per child per year in basic operating expenses. The lower amount represents public expenditure in the Ministry of Education centers, where parents pay part of the cost of food, provide teaching materials, and donate labor for repairs, and where many replacement costs are simply not being met. The higher figure reflects the much higher investment in, and higher quality of, the services for government and para-statal employees, although the two publicly accessible day care centers of the Lima city government and some of the best furnished INABIF centers nearly match their outlay per child.

Altogether, the Peruvian government invested around US $2.2 million on day care services (both publicly accessible and for its employees) in Lima in 1989. The calculation can be made only for the capital city; nonetheless, publicly supported day care in any other part of the country is so limited that it would not add much to the total. Public spending on day care is a negligible part of the Peruvian national budget. Yet for a poor country that must use its resources well, it is inexcusable that spending takes place with so little coordination among agencies, so little public supervision or understanding of the benefits that derive from it, and so little relation to planned and conscious social policy.

DAY CARE PROGRAMS

Information on day care programs in Peru must be put together piecemeal, for there is no central register of centers or sponsors. Day care directors open registration each year without a backup list of nearby programs for referrals. The need to compile an inventory of day care services in the city of Lima was so evident that this became one of the first activities of the Acciòn Pro Cunas project, under the author's direction, in 1988.

Based on partial results of the inventory, this city of 7 million inhabitants has approximately 250 day care centers. These are listed in Table 21.1, classified by types of promoters or sponsors. Figures on Peru's second largest city, Arequipa, are included for comparison. There, a total of 19 day care facilities exist for a population of 635,000. Acciòn Pro Cunas estimates that Lima's present stock of day care centers provides care for some 10,000 children, about 3 percent of the city's potential demand.

About one third of Lima's day care sector is private, even "informal" in the sense that it is subject to almost no regulation by the agencies discussed earlier as responsible for day care policy. The fastest growing element of the private sector are the "for-profit" centers, which account for some 17 percent of the existing stock. "For-profit" should be construed in modest dimensions, since most such centers barely cover the costs of one or two teacher's salaries, a contingent of auxiliaries paid at domestics' wages, meals, and rent. Catering to middle- and upper-income groups, these centers tend to be established as private ventures by early education teachers. Frequently the center occupies part of the sponsor's house. They may enter into contract arrangements with private companies that, rather than create services, prefer to subsidize the care of their employees' children in out-of-house centers. Some have contracts with Lima's large hotels to provide drop-in care or baby-sitting services to tourists and travelers.

Employer-provided day care constitutes about a quarter of that currently available in the city. It is concentrated in two categories: private firms, accounting for approximately 5 percent of current supply, and public ministries, hospitals, universities, state and para-statal firms, jointly accounting for almost 20 percent. In its role of employer, the Peruvian government is currently the second point of most vigorous growth in day care provision in Lima. It is, of course, not irrelevant that the public sector employs a high proportion of women and is strongly unionized. As the price of private domestic service has risen beyond middle-class possibilities, white-collar working women have turned to day care. Their capacity to bring pressure to bear on employers is evident as well in the private banking sector.

Churches, regional and municipal governments, philanthropic societies,

Table 21.1

Day Care Services in the Cities of Lima and Arequipa (by Type of Sponsor)

Sponsor/administrative agency	Lima N	%	Arequipa N	%
Public sector				
Ministry of Education	87	35%		
INABIF (Ministry of Justice)	26	11%		
Public ministries (for employees)	15	6%		
Public and para-statal firms (for employees)	11	5%		
Hospitals (for employees)	10	4%	2	10%
Municipal governments	8	3%	3	16%
Public universities	3	1%		
Regional government			1	5%
Para-statal beneficence society			1	5%
Sub-Total	164	66%	7	37%
Private sector				
Private for-profit	43	17%	2	10%
Community-run, self-help	15	6%	1	5%
Private firms (for employees)	11	5%	1	5%
Churches	10	4%	2	10%
Philanthropic societies	6	2%	6	32%
Universities	1	-		
Sub-Total	83	34%	12	63%
Grand Total	250	100%	19	100%

*Some figures subject to confirmation.

and local communities occupy the lower rungs of day care providers. Not
only are their numbers small, but (except for some municipal day care) their
programs tend to be small as well. Each of these sponsors struggles alone
with the problems of developing a philosophy for the service, managing
relations with parents, recruiting personnel, and ensuring that there will be
food on the table from day to day. Only very recently have municipal day
care providers begun meeting together. Links do not exist even among the
few Catholic church organizations and religious orders active in this field.
It is worth noting that Protestant churches, in this overwhelmingly Catholic
country, are proportionately more involved in day care than Catholic parishes or orders.

Day care was not on the agenda of local community organizations in
1981. Today, with strong pressure on the entire family to go to work, the
priority attached to it might be different. The technical problems of ad-

ministering a day care program probably still outstrip the capacity of unaided community groups of the poor, however. Moreover, achieving acceptable quality requires subsidies. The women community leaders who initiate programs find that they have mounted a treadwheel of "tocando puertas" (knocking on doors): their time, rather than devoted to consolidating the program internally, is spent in going from foreign embassies to local philanthropic associations to government agencies, seeking small donations to keep the center afloat.

What is the supply of day care outside the capital city of Lima? Extremely little is known. INABIF has 26 centers in Lima and eight in all of the rest of the country. Rural day care is not a priority or even a topic of discussion in any agency involved in the field, public or private. In apparent contradiction, the network of village-level non-formal preschool centers is steadily expanding, some say under demand from rural women who use the two or three hours of sessions to cover a child care need. In the large cities of the Andes, mothers hold to the traditional ways, carrying babies on their back and leaving young children with other family members. Cuzco, for example, with a population of 275,000, has only three day care centers: a municipal center for workers in the principal market, and two INABIF facilities. Arequipa, straddling the coast and the Andes, with a mixed population of migrants, industrial, and white-collar workers, represents an intermediate situation (see Table 21.1). Distributed according to the type of sponsor, the city shows, in comparison to Lima, a higher profile for the municipal government, private philanthropic societies, and the Catholic church. The complete absence of the Ministry of Education as a day care provider is noteworthy, as is the very sparse presence of employer-financed programs.

MODELS OF DAY CARE SERVICES

Center-based day care in the only model of child care services officially sanctioned in Peru. At a level of popular attitudes, day care (*cuna*) calls up visions of rather splendid, specially constructed complexes of sleeping rooms and playrooms, full of large cribs and miniature tables and chairs, with "classrooms" for carefully stratified age groups. Why this should be so is difficult to explain, since for a shanty dweller or even a middle-class parent the likelihood of having been inside a day care center is remote. In any case, the only centers that might match that vision are a few of the largest INABIF facilities, a handful of foreign-funded projects, and the white-collar services of certain government ministries. The mass media, especially television, both from the industrial North and from more prosperous Latin American countries, would seem to be playing an important role in shaping day care expectations as in consumer tastes.

Nonetheless, family day care, in its various forms, is an important alternative model, both present and potential. Some of the private for-profit day care programs function as the center of a wheel of satellite family day care homes. This seems to come about when the center has more requests for placement than it can handle or has to turn away children with special needs. The center attracts the attention of women in the neighborhood who are interested in working as childminders in their homes. Centers and home-based caretakers that establish these arrangements do it with a sense of precariousness. No official agency is at present in a position to enter into relation with these family day care homes, whether for purposes of super-vision, licensing, training, or channeling any other kind of assistance. Of-ficially the service does not exist.

In poor neighborhoods, informal day care has demonstrated important qualities of flexibility and adaptability to the needs of the population. Family day care—essentially neighbor care plus a few experimental programs being implemented by INABIF private development organizations—is the only child care system at present that covers the real working day of the poor, which often begins before dawn and, after a grueling trip home on a crowded bus, ends with collecting the children, having a hurried meal, and falling into bed. Moreover, for those sensitive to the significance of "ecological" frames in child development, home settings, even in very poor shanty dwell-ings, have clear advantages over the typical public day care center. In these homes, tables and beds, floors, and walls are covered with the gear of the domestic and work lives of several family members of different ages. The house is permeable to the rhythms of the neighborhood; older children come and go, and a corral with chickens, ducks, and a pup or two is likely to be present in the next lot if not the caretaker's own interior patio. The center, in stark contrast, will probably consist of a large, high-roofed room with a few cribs and mats along the walls and a table or two in the middle. The efforts of teachers and aides to make the space interesting by hanging col-orful mobiles are largely in vain.

The experience of family day care throws into relief the shortcomings of center-based care in Peru at present: the rigidity of days and hours of care, the poverty of the centers as a physical locus for stimulating activities, the sense of obligation created in the user family, the oppressiveness of formal requisites and admission procedures, the exclusion of men (when many day care children are fatherless), the restricted vision centered on the single child under care, and the vast cultural distance between users and providers. Family day care systems show the direction that all day care should take. At the same time, family day care has problems of its own that must be resolved before it can be seen as an alternative for increasing the overall supply of day care in Peru. The exploitation and burn-out of the caretakers is one; another is the lack of legal recognition that prevents family day care programs from getting access to donated food and other occasional subsi-dies. Above all, much more must be learned about the compensatory education young children growing up in poverty in Peru need and the capacity of family day care to provide it to them.

DAY CARE PERSONNEL

A large, very heterogenous category of para-professionals forms the backbone of Peruvian day care staffs. Only about one third of existing day care services function with licensed preschool teachers, and another, occasionally overlapping, third has social workers present or associated with them. Extremely few programs have professional child care workers (*puericultoras*) attached, since that specialty was eliminated from university curricula in the early 1970s. No program is administered by a professional day care administrator: that training is simply not available in the country. The overall panorama is one of fuzzy lines of authority, uncertainty over the responsibilities different categories of staff should assume, low pay for day care workers, an almost total absence of opportunities for in-service training, and short or non-existent career ladders.

The appropriateness to day care of the training either teachers or para-professionals receive is highly questionable. In day-to-day behaviors and decisions, it is likely that both rely primarily on the natural socialization practices alluded to at the outset of this discussion. This has several implications. In suggests very effective skills for entering into close affective relations with individual children, maintaining a sensitive tuning to their emotional states, and circumventing conflicts in small groups. However, when the children are too many, the space too small, and tensions too great, caretakers may have insufficient resources for controlling the situation. The caretaking style may be overly silent, deficient in language stimulation (particularly in the case of Andean-born women with a cultural bias away from verbal communication with small children), compounded by a low level of competence in Spanish. But most dangerous of all would seem to be the conflict between the work ethic of the Andes and the seemingly purposeless activity of the children's center. Under the strain of this contradiction, many caretakers react with apathy and disorientation. They cannot structure activities for the children, nor do they construe their own role as "work," with all that implies in terms of organization and intentionality. In such cases, training is needed to help the women see the "work" in children's play and the seriousness and constructiveness of their own part in it.

FINAL COMMENTS: THE FUTURE OF DAY CARE IN PERU

As these pages have shown, even a small sector of service provision becomes enormously complex when set in the context of contemporary Peru.

In its search for a set of workable institutions that would support national development and overcome the periodic deadlocks of intense social conflict, Peru offers constant surprises. Awareness is increasing of the country's inescapable problem of child welfare, and the invisibility of day care as a topic of public debate could change dramatically. Out of the current mix of poverty with aspirations to membership in the group of Western democracies with responsible social policies, new openings on the problem of child care may emerge with unexpected rapidity.

Some of the features of Peru's existing day care system give a basis for optimism. One is its capacity to respond quickly to new needs through what is known locally as "informality," that is, mechanisms not sanctioned by law but rooted in traditional patterns of social exchange and social control. Informality provides the elasticity whereby preschool programs can give a de facto drop-in day care service to the young siblings of the four- and five-year-old enrollees. It permits the same programs to extend their hours beyond a half-day, add a lunch, and convert to a de facto day care program. The family home "satellites" that absorb the overflow of formal day care centers are another example of informality, as is neighbor care in its various forms.

A second, related reason for optimism is the continuing force of consensual norms based on "confianza" (trust) backed by social rather than legal sanctions. This substrate of consensual norms makes possible the expansion of day care programs in relative safety despite the impossibility of providing them with the support services they would be required to have in richer countries. Day care programs in poor neighborhoods of Peru operate entirely bereft of a second line of defense formed by the local fire department, telephone hot line, police, clinic, and insurance companies. Instead there is the child's local social network, and the willingness of (almost) all concerned to accept on good faith (most of the time) that the other parties to a child care arrangement are doing what is expected.

A final reason for optimism is the broad range of institutions committed to day care. Most are involved in a small and tentative way, but they display a spirit of experimentation and an important potential for growth in the future. This great variety of actors gives the field a disorderly appearance at present. Yet their diversity opens the possibility of eventually building a child care system with many different programs, differently organized, with different philosophies, and attuned to the diverse needs of a heterogenous population.

For this dream of a large and richly diverse child care system to be realized, two essential problems must be resolved, beyond those already raised in this review. One concerns parent and community involvement in day care. Both, at present, tend to be low and problematic. Day care in Peru has not galvanized a poor people's movement or mobilized feminists. In a country that desperately needs to close the gulf between social classes, day care services are almost perfectly class segregated. Gender differences and the fact that community leadership is almost exclusively male give too facile an account of why day care services have difficulty achieving a firm integration in local neighborhoods. These problems deserve study.

The second issue demanding attention before day care can meet its potential in Peru concerns its nexus to poverty alleviation and economic development. Day care has many possible uses as an instrument for addressing poverty: as a support service in employment programs; as a source of new jobs; as a mechanism for grouping children at risk; as a channel for early childhood education fine-tuned to the needs of poor children. Day care can be a potent vehicle for enrichment, understood not in a spirit of making the poor child an alienated copy of the privileged child of the suburbs, but as a means of spreading some of the advantages of the latter while reaffirming the poor child's cultural heritage and membership in a particular social group. As more non-poor families come to rely on it, day care might even be a means of promoting the social integration Peru's development also requires, and of transmitting to privileged children some of the advantages of the education and socialization patterns of the poor. Day care, here as at other points, offers promising new approaches to some of the more recalcitrant problems of contemporary Peru.

NOTE

1. As many as 33.5 percent left them with other family members (aunts, uncles, and grandparents), 13.7 percent left them alone in self-care, 0.3 percent left them in a day care center, and 18.4 percent reported that they always took their children with them when they went out.

REFERENCES

Anderson, Jeanine. (1982). Servicios espontàeos e informales de cuidado infantil en los barrios populares de Lima. Lima: SUMBI (Servcios Urbanos y Mujeres de Bajos Ingresos), Documento de Trabajo.

Anderson, Jeanine. (1986). 'Y ahora ¿Quién cuida a los niños? El cuidado diurno en Lima, 1981–1986. Lima: SUMBI, Documento de Trabajo.

Anderson, Jeanine. (1989). "Women's Community Service and Child Welfare in Urban Peru." In Leslie, Joanne and Michael Paolisso (Eds.), *Women, Work, and Child Welfare in the Third World.* Westview Press, pp. 237–253.

Anderson, Jeanine et al. (1982). *El desarrollo del Niño en contextos de transición cultural: Un estudio de cuatro zonas en el Perù.* Lima: Instituto Nacional de Investigaciòn y Desarrollo de la Educaciòn (INIDE), Peruvian Ministry of Education.

Anderson, Jeanine and Nelson Panizo. (1984). Limitaciones para el uso de los servicios urbanos por mujeres de bajos ingresos: transporte y seguridad. Lima: SUMBI, Documento de Trabajo.

Anderson, Jeanine, Blanca Figueroa, and Ana Mariñez. (1979). *Child Care in Urban and Rural Peru*. Report to the Overseas Education Fund, Washington, D.C.

Appenzeller, Christine. (1990). Personal communication.

Barrig, Maruja. (1989). *Mujer y empleo en Lima Metropolitana, 1979–1987*. Lima: Asociaciòn Laboral para el Desarrollo.

Bolton, Charlene et al. (1976). "Pastoralism and Personality: An Andean Replication." *Ethos* 4:463–481.

Bolton, Charlene and Ralph Bolton. (1972). "Techniques of Socialization Among the Qolla." Paper presented to the 49th Meeting of the International Congress of Americanists, Rome, Italy.

Bronfenbrenner, Urie. (1979). *The Ecology of Human Development*. Harvard University Press.

Delpino, Nena. (1990). *Saliendo a flote: la jefa de familia popular*. Lima: TACIF/Friedrich Naumann Foundation.

Gonzàlez, Verònica. (1989). El financiamiento pùblico del cuidado diurno en Lima Metropolitana. Lima: SUMBI (Proyecto Acciòn Pro Cunas).

Herencia Hinojosa, Cristina. (1987). "Identidad social en la dominaciòn cultural y de clase en el Perù: consecuencias para la identidad nacional." Manuscript.

Herencia Hinojosa, Cristina. (1990). Personal communication.

Lambert, Bernd. (1977). "Bilaterality in the Andes." In Bolton, Ralph and Enrique Mayer (Eds.), *Andean Kinship and Marriage*. Washington, D.C.: American Anthropological Association, pp. 1–27.

Lobo, Susan. (1982). *A House of My Own: Social Organization in the Squatter Settlements of Lima, Peru*. University of Arizona Press.

Lowder, Stella. (1973). "Aspects of Internal Migration in Peru." Doctoral dissertation, University of Liverpool. Cited in Roberts, Bryan. *Cities of Peasants*. Sage, 1978.

Moser, Caroline. (1983). "Evaluating Community Participation in Urban Development Projects." London: Development Planning Unit, Working Paper No. 14.

Myers, Robert and Cynthia Indiriso. (1987). "Supporting the Integration of Women's Productive and Reproductive Roles in Resource-Poor Households in Developing Countries." Paper presented to the Rockefeller Foundation Workshop on Issues Related to Gender, Technology, and Development.

Stahr, Margarita. (1987). Una experiencia psicoanalitica con niños en un contexto urbano-marginal: Lima. In *Los Niños de la querra*. Lima: IER José Maria Arguedas/National University San Cristòbal de Huamanga, pp. 137–155.

Vàsquez de Velasco, Carmen and Jeanine Anderson. (1989). Los para-profesionales en los servicios de cuidado diurno. In *Aportes para una política de cuidado diurno en el Perù*. Lima: SUMBI (Proyecto Acciòn Pro Cunas).

Zappert, Laraine Testa. (1976). *Socialization, Social Class and Economic Development: The Case of Peru*. Doctoral dissertation, Cornell University.

—— **22** ——

THE PHILIPPINES

Luz G. Palattao-Corpus

The goals and emphasis of child care programs in the Philippines are quite different from those of policies and programs in many Western countries.

BACKGROUND FOR PRESENT POLICY AND PROGRAMS

Several cultural and historical characteristics provide an important backdrop for present child care policies and programs in the Philippines. These include family values and patterns, population shifts, the current economic crisis, changing female labor force participation, and some history of the early childhood programs that preceded those currently in existence.

Family Values and Patterns

Historically, Filipino society has been family oriented. Early in the recorded history of the country families banded together for mutual protection and support to form a "barangay," or small village. The barangay was governed by a village council composed of male heads of families, usually led by the most senior or strongest family head, considered the barangay chieftain. Families were closely knit, with a patriarchal type of leadership. Women were considered important members of the household but were generally treated as second-class citizens. Their primary role consisted of keeping the home and was devoid of significant participation in decision making, even within the house. For this reason a wife is called "maybahay," meaning owner of the house, to indicate that she belonged to the house. In the barangay, activities like building houses and boats, planting and harvesting crops, and gathering fish caught in the fishing nets or fish corrals were done collectively, principally by the men, in what was termed the "bayanihan spirit." Similarly, child care during infancy was essentially the mother's responsibility, but as soon as the infant became a toddler this care became a family responsibility. Each family member, although primarily the females, took over whenever the mother was not available.

Three hundred years of colonization by the Spaniards did not make much difference in these child care practices, but it did introduce new concerns related to rearing children. The Spaniards introduced their language and their religion, and in the process they organized classes for teaching Christian doctrine to adults and children. The family became increasingly exposed to broader social influences, especially of the church, thus widening the horizons of women and children. Moreover, the effect of Western influence became evident in child-rearing practices as superstitions about the influences of evil spirits were gradually dispelled.

The American colonization at the turn of the century (1896–1946) brought more Western influence to what is now known as early childhood care. This influence was primarily in the areas of health, nutrition, sanitation, and education. Female participation in social activities was encouraged. Formal education was opened to men and women alike. Women began to leave the confines of their homes for school, church, and subsequently for community activities. With this new awakening, women began to recognize their role in society, got involved in economic activities, and pursued careers as men had been doing. Filipino women won the right to vote in 1935. At the same time, in spite of the increasing involvement of women in activities outside the home, child care remained a family affair because of the continued involvement of the extended family.

The family remains as the basic unit of present-day Filipino society. Concern for the family is enshrined in the Constitution of the Philippines, which states:

The State recognizes the sanctity of family life and shall protect and strengthen the family as a basic autonomous social institution. It shall equally protect the life of the mother and the life of the unborn from conception. The natural and primary right and duty of parents in the rearing of the youth for civic efficiency and the development of moral character shall receive the full support of the government. (Article II, Sec. 12)

Strong family ties and a strong sense of responsibility for the general welfare of family members continue to characterize present-day Filipino society. Family solidarity is a value that is most prized by Filipinos, and family interests are given first priority. This enables poor families to cope. Poverty is more bearable because of the sharing system, in which the food, no matter how meager, is apportioned among the members, with priority given to the children. Indeed, the family acts as a welfare agency. The very young, the very old, the jobless, and the infirm are figuratively "carried on the shoulders" of those who are able-bodied and productive. The family is also the custodian of the family honor and prestige, and as such exercises discipline over extended family members. This creates less criminality, less delinquency, more solidarity, and more goodwill. If an individual acquires wealth, honor or prestige, the rest of the family shines in reflected glory. At the same time, many of the ills noted in contemporary society have been attributed to this value of family solidarity. Nepotism in government is rampant despite stringent civil service laws and rules prohibiting the employment of relatives by the appointing official. In the private sector, the most qualified applicant for a position may be bypassed in favor of a less competent and less qualified relative. These practices, anchored as they are in "family solidarity," do not contribute to effectiveness or efficiency.

At the center of each family is the child. Children are highly valued and it is generally accepted that one important reason for getting married is to have children. Children are considered assets of their parents, who will ensure that the parents will be cared for when they can no longer care for themselves. This belief is perhaps the reason why the Filipino value of family solidarity ranks first and economic security last in studies on the value systems of Filipinos. Children are also inputs to the family's productive capacity—more hands to till the soil, to cast and pull the nets for fishing, to weave baskets and mats, and many other like activities. With the high premium placed on children, they are considered "gifts from God."

Because of the high value placed on children, early marriages are encouraged or even arranged by parents, especially in rural areas. Parents want to make sure that they will have many grandchildren to brighten their old age and perpetuate their family. This is one reason why the Philippine Population Program has not made much headway in population control.

Another major factor affecting population control is the influence of the Roman Catholic Church's stand on the use of artificial birth control methods. About 85 percent of the Philippine population is Roman Catholic. The Church allows only the use of natural means (the rhythm method) for spacing pregnancies. This method is well known for its ineffectiveness, especially in a culture where the male is not directly involved in family planning and fathering many children is evidence of machismo. Policy makers, program planners, and those implementing population control programs are limited by these moral constraints. The result has been the half-hearted implementation of government family planning efforts. In some cases family planning practices and educational messages have been neutralized or even reversed by a pastoral letter of the Catholic Bishop's Conference read from the pulpit during church services.

The population growth rate of 2.6 percent annually from 1980 to 1985 is one of the highest population growth rates in Asia and the rest of the developing world. Based on the 1990 national census, the Philippine population was 60.5 million. This means that there are about 7 million Filipino children between the ages of three and six years. About three fifths of these children live in rural areas.

The family is the first socializing agent, receiving the newly born baby and playing a vital role in developing his character and personality. While child care is the primary responsibility of the mother, in many instances that responsibility may be shared with or even taken over by a doting grandmother. Extended families still abound in the rural areas, and even in urban communities there continues to be a tendency for parents to persuade their newly married children to live with them. Many compromise by building homes within a compound, so that each nuclear family has an independent domicile but advantage can still be taken of the services of extended family members. In the rural areas, it is not unusual to find families ranging from great grandparents to great grandchildren living under one roof. In this context, child care becomes not only a nuclear family affair but an extended family system that permits young children to be carried around by older members of the family—sisters, aunts, nieces, cousins, and grandparents. There would seem to be no real need for extra-familial structures or arrangements for early childhood care in these situations, since these interactions between children and family members, while unstructured and unprogrammed, include physical caring and emotional and intellectual stimulation.

Population Shifts

As modernization diffused to the countryside, with improved mass communication and transportation, young men and women in these areas became aware of another kind of life in the urban centers, and young people left the farms to seek jobs in the cities. After some time these young people would return to their rural homes with success stories, both real and imagined. Ultimately, they would convince their immediate family to move with them. Increasingly, nuclear families moved to urban areas, beginning the breakdown of the extended family, with its child care support. Urban migration has been progressively increasing throughout the years. An annual rate of increase in urbanization of 3.8 percent from 1970 to 1975 became 5.0 percent between 1975 and 1980, and the level of urbanization of 37.3 percent in 1980 had increased to 41.0 percent by 1985.

The rural migrants to urban centers are usually poorly educated and lacking in skills for employment in well paying jobs. As a consequence, they would settle on any available land, whether in the public domain or privately owned. With no provisions for sanitary water, waste disposal, and electricity, these living conditions are deplorable. This "squatter colony" phenomenon appeared in Manila in the 1950s. The squatters became a significant social problem in the 1970s when squatter colonies mushroomed in the urban centers, as a result of the deterioration of the country's economy, giving rise to widespread poverty.

The Economic Crisis

The 1987 report, *The Situation of Children and Women in the Philippines*, describes this crisis and its impacts as follows:

The early years of the 1970s and the 1980s were hard times for the Philippines and the world economy. The oil price shock during the period caused severe recession, and this coupled with longstanding fundamental economic problems of the country worsened the already strained economic status of the country. The added burden of a large external debt increased the situation of poverty of the great majority of the population. The proportion of Filipino families living in poverty grew by 10 percentage points, from 49.3 percent in 1971 to 59.3 percent in 1985. In terms of magnitude, about 5.7 million families did not have basic necessities of life in 1985, valued at an average of P2,382 a month for a family of six.

Women, and particularly those in the childbearing age group, are hardest hit when there is widespread poverty. Not only are they expected to bear and care for their children, but they are also burdened with how to meet day-to-day family needs. Poverty has impelled the Filipino woman to add to her familial responsibilities a significant role as economic supporter of the family—sometimes as primary breadwinner, often as co-worker in meeting the family's economic needs. She usually has a major income-generating activity and then stretches herself further with supplementary tasks to further increase her income. These supplementary income-augmenting activities are necessary because her primary work is often seasonal, with fluctuating income. In a study conducted by PILIPINA, a non-profit civic organization of women, the women participants described the daily routine as beginning at 4:00 A.M., when a rural woman wakes up to tend to her animals and clean the yard. She prepares breakfast, and shortly after 7:00 o'clock she hikes off to work in the fields or to the streets to vend. After lunch she may attend to her laundry, but the rest of the afternoon is once more devoted to her income-producing work. In the evening, after cooking dinner, eating, and washing the dishes, she may still find time to engage in her supplementary income-generating task if she is not busy with the children. If she has children of breast-feeding or carrying age, the demands on her are even more strenuous.

Even when the woman is engaged in income-generating tasks she is not exempted from home management and child care. Most women in the PILIPINA study agree that their roles as wives and mothers are "normal and come with marriage." Some even suffer pangs of guilt and patiently bear additional tasks when production work infringes on their domestic obligations. In their own words: "It is difficult but it is needed." A number

Table 22.1
Female Participation in the Work Force

	Labor Force (in M)	Employment (in M)
Total	21.8	19.0
Women	7.8 (35.8%)	6.8 (35.8%)

Source: National Census and Statistics Office, 1986.

of women have even reached a point where they seem to be convinced that "playing a martyr's role gives fulfillment." Many, however, still look at their lives with mixed feelings of resentment, resignation, and a desire to change the normal order of things.

Women in the Labor Force

Empirical data gathered in recent years documenting the type and extent of economic activities performed by poor women, and their contribution to family income, have helped dispel the myth that women are full-time housewives. General trends since 1957 point to the increasingly substantial participation of Filipino women in the labor force. There are 34 million Filipinos 15 years of age and older, and 17 million of these are women. Table 22.1 shows that more than one third of the labor force is composed of women. The labor force includes those women without employment who are looking for jobs. Four million of the employed women are located in rural areas, with the remaining 2.8 million in the urban centers.

It is important to emphasize that the figures in Table 22.1 do not give a complete picture of working women in the Philippines, since most of them are considered homemakers and so are automatically excluded from national statistics on the economically active population. Furthermore, their contributions to the economy through household work are assigned no monetary value and therefore go unrecorded and unrecognized.

Nearly half (48%) of working women are married. The average age of women at the time of marriage is 22 years. The majority of women in the labor force have children.

Rural women comprise two thirds of the female populace. The majority of them work as seasonal farm workers and/or unpaid family workers. In the urban areas, women work in factories and services, often assuming the lowest skilled and lowest paid jobs. A sizeable majority of urban women belong to the non-formal sector. The work situation of these women has been described as having the following characteristics: "non-permanent and casual activities, lack of company and/or government regulations, small scale and less capitalized and self-employment" (National Commission on the Role of Women, 1985).

Many women in the non-formal sector enter into subsistence production that requires skills closely related to domestic duties or that allows the combination of work and child care. These jobs are income-augmenting work like laundry washing and household service for richer families in the neighborhood. This is done on a part-time or daily compensation basis. The working middle-class or even low-resource families living in urban areas must resort to hiring help for laundry and child care activities during office hours because they are separated from their extended families as part of the changing socialization patterns referred to earlier.

Employment overseas. As the economy of the country has further deteriorated during the past few years, triggered by the huge payments on external debts incurred by the previous administration and the instability of the new democracy, unemployment has worsened. The unemployment rate of 7.1 percent in 1985 had worsened to 9.2 percent in 1989. Underemployment was 31.2 percent in 1989, with underemployment in the rural areas twice that of the urban areas. With the lack of employment opportunities at home and the lure of high salaries offered by overseas employers, there is an exodus of Filipino men and women as contract workers abroad. The increased inflation has also caused a marked devaluation of the Philippine peso. Consequently, the salaries of the contract workers abroad become very high when converted to their equivalent in local currency. Thus, even professional women like teachers, midwives, and commerce graduates leave their low-paying jobs to become domestic helpers, baby-sitters, garment workers, clerks, and hotel workers overseas, for which there is high demand. Under these circumstances, more and more children are left to the care of one or the other parent, or in some cases with the grandparents, aunts, and cousins when both parents go abroad. In cases where there are no extended family members to care for the children, maids or "yayas" (child care givers) are hired as mother surrogates for working mothers. This alternative child care arrangement, which is the most common among the middle class, is made possible due to the improvement in the financial status of overseas contract workers. While there may be economic advantages to the children of overseas workers in terms of better nutrition, better educational opportunities, and professional health care, the maternal and/or paternal deprivation of such children may have untold negative consequences. If the present trend of emigration for employment continues or accelerates, there will be increasing demands for extra-familial or institutional types of early childhood care.

Precursors of Present Early Childhood Programs

Formal early childhood development programming in the Philippines began in 1924 at the Harris Memorial School, Manila, under the direction of an American missionary. Subsequently, other religious groups (primarily Roman Catholic and Protestant) established kindergarten classes in their sectarian schools. Civic organizations such as the National Federation of Women's Clubs set up playrooms in maternal and child health centers, where preschool-aged children could play while their mothers received prenatal or postpartum checkups. These playrooms were actually child-minding facilities designed to keep children occupied and in a safe place while their mothers were busy with health and nutrition concerns.

The Day Care Service, now a program of the Department of Social Welfare and Development under the Philippines' Urban Community Welfare Program, was established in 1964 as part of the UNICEF–Assisted Social Services Project. The first day care centers were organized in locations with an established community welfare program. At that time, the day care service focused on the social development of preschool children, rather than on the care of children while their parents worked.

In the 1970s supplemental feeding was included in the day care service due to the increasing incidence of malnutrition among preschoolers. There were 671 day care centers in 1972. Interest in the day care service as a strategy to combat malnutrition generated much needed funds, with the result that by 1974 the country had 2,658 day care centers. Support from voluntary organizations and parent groups increased.

By 1975 the local governments had funded 2,106 day care centers in implementing the Child and Youth Welfare Code, which resulted in a total of 3,390 day care centers under the Day Care Service program.

The Barangay Day Care Law (P.D. 1567) was passed in 1978, providing for the creation of a day care center in every barangay. This law also assigned the community the responsibility for setting up day care centers to serve its neglected preschool-age children.

The earlier focus on social development of preschool children in the day care service in the 1960s was expanded to include developmental stimulation of children in all areas of development (physical, intellectual, emotional, psycho-social, and moral-spiritual). The UNICEF-assisted undertaking called Early Childhood Enrichment Program (ECEP) was pilot tested in 1982 in three geographical regions of the country.

ECEP was expanded under the Second Country Program for Children, beginning in 1983. The expansion included the training of day care workers, home management technicians, and parent trainers. The third Country Program for Children (CPC III), started in 1988, sought the institutionalization of ECEP by the implementing agencies.

UNDERLYING CHILD AND FAMILY POLICIES

The most comprehensive law addressing early childhood care in the Philippines is Presidential Decree 603 (P.D. 603), promulgated in 1975 (otherwise known as the Child and Youth Welfare Code), which includes the following articles:

Article 1. Declaration of Policy. The child is one of the most important assets of the nation. Every effort should be exerted to promote his welfare and enhance his opportunities for a useful and happy life. The molding of the character of the child starts at home. Consequently, every member of the family should strive to make the home a wholesome and harmonious place, as its atmosphere and conditions will greatly influence the child's development. Attachment to the home and strong family ties should be encouraged, but not to the extent of making the home isolated and exclusive and unconcerned with the interests of the community and the country. The natural right and duty of parents in the rearing of the child for civic efficiency should receive the aid and support of the government. Other institutions, like the school, the church, the guild, and the community in general, should assist the home and the state in the endeavor to prepare the child for the responsibilities of adulthood.

Article 3 of the Code provides for the basic rights of the child:

a. To be born well.
b. To a balanced diet, adequate clothing and sufficient shelter, proper medical attention, and all the basic physical requirements of a healthy and vigorous life.
c. To a well rounded development of his or her personality.
d. To protection against conditions or circumstances that are prejudicial to his or her physical, mental, emotional, social, and moral development.

Article 9. Levels of Growth. The child shall be given adequate care, assistance and guidance through its various levels of growth, from infancy to early and late childhood, to puberty and adolescence, and when necessary even after he or she shall have attained age 21.

Article 10. Phases of Development. The child shall enjoy special protection and shall be given opportunities and facilities, by law and by other means, to ensure and enable the fullest development physically, mentally, emotionally, morally, spiritually, and socially in a healthy and normal manner and in conditions of freedom and dignity appropriate to the corresponding developmental stage.

Article 12. Education. The schools and other entities engaged in nonformal education shall assist the parents in providing the best education for the child.

Article 13. Social and Emotional Growth. Steps shall be taken to insure the child's healthy social and emotional growth. These shall be undertaken by the home in collaboration with the schools and other agencies engaged in the promotion of child welfare.

The foregoing provisions of law would seem to integrate child care policies with family policies. Initially day care services were child focused. While family participation is integral to any program for child welfare, before 1970 the day care service was defined as an independent program. The economic crisis of the 1970s, bringing with it the increased incidence of malnutrition, led to a broadened definition of the day care service as a part of the total care of children, including nutrition and health. Nutrition programs for families included projects/programs for income generation. With P.D. 603 in 1975 mandating a total integrated approach to child care, many agencies of government such as the Department of Local Government became actively involved in the establishment of day care centers. Hand in hand with the increase in early child care facilities, parent involvement became a need as well as a strategy to improve child care services. The inclusion of ECEP in the First Country Program for children, with funding assistance from the UNICEF, saw the expansion of day care services not only in terms of areas of concern (i.e., inclusion of early childhood stimulation in the physical, emotional, intellectual and psycho-social areas of development), but also in terms of the involvement of parents. Parents became involved not only in the provision of financial assistance to the day care centers and/or participation in the day-to-day operation of the center, but more importantly in parent education sessions for more effective parenting. The expansion of ECEP and its eventual institutionalization by the implementing agencies enhanced the integration of child care services with family directed programs: parent education, income generating projects, family planning, and health and nutrition programs.

In addition to the country program for children, there are many other government and non-government agencies implementing early child care programs. It has not been an easy task to integrate these child care services. The Council for the Welfare of Children was created by P.D. 603 to coordinate the implementation and enforcement of all laws relative to the promotion of child and youth welfare. It is also assigned the responsibility of formulating policies and devising, introducing, developing, and evaluating programs and services for the welfare of children. The mandate is there and the agency to carry it out exists, but the coordination and integration of programs and services for children still remain elusive.

DESCRIPTION OF PROGRAMS

Early childhood care services and programs in the Philippines may be categorized into two groups: informal, home-based programs and formal, center-based programs.

Informal, Home-Based Programs

The majority of young Filipinos are reached in the informal, home-based setting. This reflects the strong belief in the Philippines that child care is the responsibility of the family. The community at large is not expected to take on a portion of the burden of caring for very young children, especially if they are not yet of school age.

It has been estimated that about 79 percent of the children of preschool age are not reached by a formal type of early childhood care program. To remedy this situation, government agencies such as the Department of Education Culture and Sports (DECS), the Department of Social Welfare and Development (DSWD), and the Department of Agriculture and Food (DAF) (through the Bureau of Agriculture Extension [BAEx]) have launched programs designed to empower parents for effective parenting. The DSWD conducts a program called "Neighborhood Parent Effectiveness Assembly" (NPEA) for parents with newborns to 6-year-old children who are not enrolled in day care centers. Another group, composed of parents of children in the day care centers, is called "Day Care Service-Parents Group" (DCS-PG). Although the programs for both groups are essentially the same, the two groups are taught separately, and the emphasis in certain lessons differs to some degree in the two groups. Furthermore, when day care center parents meet, discussions about matters relating to the administration, funding, and other issues of the day care center will be discussed in the DCS-PG but not in the NPEA groups.

In the parent education program lessons on child care, health, nutrition, and the "whys" and "hows" of early childhood stimulation, songs, and nursery rhymes are shared among the parents. Through group discussions, parents (primarily mothers) are exposed to proper child-caring techniques and rearing practices. In addition, the social workers who generally serve as organizers and facilitators of these parent groups conduct home visits to see how mothers translate the knowledge and skills gained in the parent education sessions into effective child care. This home-based program reached a total of 490,670 parents between 1988 and 1989, indirectly benefitting approximately 981,340 children.

The DAF-BAEx home-based program reaches very young children in a similar way through parent education. While the BAEx program is focused primarily on malnutrition prevention and on effective home management (including income-generating activities for mothers at home), early childhood care and effective parenting was formally incorporated into the BAEx program in 1983, with funding assistance from UNICEF as part of the Early Childhood Enrichment Program (ECEP). The ECEP program sought to strengthen the delivery of early childhood enrichment services through the training of those delivering the services—day care workers in the case of the

DSWD and Home Management Technicians in the BAEx program. No data on the extent of the DAF-BAEx home-based programs is available.

Some informal arrangements involving efforts to enrich the ability of the caregiver to delivery early childhood stimulation were found to exist as alternative child care settings, as documented in research done by the Child and Youth Research Center in 1987. One of these arrangements consists of child-to-child care, wherein older children of school age teach groups of preschoolers on the backyard playgrounds or at home as part of their play activities. Another mode is for an itinerant community worker to circulate through the community, concentrating her efforts where groups of children from the same neighborhood are playing. She provides some learning experiences as part of the children's play, in addition to her regular health and nutrition services. The setting for these activities may be a backyard, a playground, or a home large enough to accommodate a group of children. A third approach is through the delivery of early childhood enrichment services using the mother-surrogate, who may be a member of an extended family or a neighbor. This is done by incorporating early childhood enrichment messages and techniques into the services extended by community development, health, and nutrition workers who do home visitation. The mother-surrogate ordinarily oversees the children's activities principally to insure safety (against accidents, fire, poison, etc.), while attending to the physical needs of the children. With some training in early childhood enrichment, the otherwise passive mother-surrogate becomes an active child caregiver. These informal settings need further development if they are to become effective, including the more formal education and training of the caregivers involved.

Formal, Center-Based Programs

The two primary center-based approaches in the Philippines are the Day Care Services and the Preschool Education Program (PEP).

Day Care Services. The Philippine Day Care Services is a total departure from the traditional Western concept of day care service, which provides child care to children for a whole day while their mothers are at work. The day care services provided by the DSWD for children two to six years old are described as providing supplemental child care, feeding, and early childhood stimulation to children whose mothers are not able to provide proper child care for reasons of employment, physical incapacitation, and/or intellectual or psychological inadequacies. The children are cared for by day care workers, with mother volunteers as assistants. The children stay in the center for two to three hours, five days a week, following the regular school calendar (June through March). Activities consist of supplemental feeding, daily living skills, socialization skills, and learning experiences in the fields of art, dance, music, and play. Pre-academic skills are taught in about 45 percent of the centers.

The physical facilities of about 40 percent of the centers include classrooms, outdoor play areas, and equipment for three- to six-year-old children. The day care program relies heavily on the direct service provided by one salaried adult child care worker per class. Eighty-two percent of these workers have no formal education training. Parent-volunteers provide additional services from time to time by preparing snacks and/or serving these to the children.

Funds for operating the day care centers are generated mainly from local governments (for 65 percent of the centers). Forty-eight percent of the centers obtain individual or institutional donations. Parents also contribute something for maintaining the centers.

Available data indicate that only one third of the barangays have such day care centers. In 1989, 11,555 centers were found operating, serving a total of 561,081 preschool-age children. With about 2.8 million preschool-age children potentially in need of this service, this represents only about 20 percent coverage.

Thus it has become apparent to day care advocates that the Barangay Day Care Law referred to earlier was not sufficient to mobilize local governments to open a center in each barangay. Because of this, concerned groups of professionals, parents, and educators sought the passage in 1990 of a new law, Republic Act 6972, establishing a day care center in every barangay for the total development and protection of children, including not just day care services but also services for street children, victims of abuse and exploitation, drug users, the disabled, and the like. The major factor making this law more powerful than its predecessor is a section mandating the appropriation of national treasury funds for day care worker salaries. Because the major cause of center closure has been lack of funds for day care workers, this new program should help sustain existing centers and stimulate the opening of new ones. Based on this law the Department of Social Welfare and Development set as a target the establishment of a total of 16,666 day care centers by 1991.

Another center-based day care service is provided by the Rural Improvement Club Children's Centers, spearheaded by BAEx and participated in by rural mothers trained by BAEx Home Management Technicians (HMT) in home making and child-caring skills. While the Rural Improvement Club runs these child care centers, the technicians train the mother/leaders to enrich their knowledge of child growth and development, and in the use of stimulating activities and materials to help children develop intellectually, socially, and physically. These centers accept three- to six-year-old children for one and a half to two hours a day for supplemental feeding and developmental activities. The program aims to help improve the children's health, nutrition, and psycho-social competence.

Day care service in factories and places of employment is still in the pilot stage. A few government agencies and private plants, encouraged by the Bureau of Women and Young Workers, set up on-site nurseries/child care centers. Some of the centers were eventually closed because of non-patronage. The working mothers found it very inconvenient to bring their babies along while struggling to get a seat in the crowded public transport system of the metropolis. They found it unhealthy for the baby to be exposed to dust and other environmental pollutants. It is believed that the setting up of plant-based child care centers is a practice culled from Western models. The community-based child care center would be more in keeping with the culture of the Philippines. While the Labor Code and the Child Youth Welfare Code provide for the establishment of child care centers to ensure the proper care of children of working mothers, there are no laws compelling employers to establish such programs. Child care facilities in places of work must still be the subject of collective bargaining agreements or other arrangements between employees and employers.

The Preschool Education Program. This program is the normal form of preschool education for children aged two and a half to six and is sponsored either by the public or the private sector. Public sector programs consist of preschool classes attached to the regular public schools that are normally held on the public school grounds and campuses. Programs in the private sector include preschools run by private individuals, institutions, church organizations, and corporations, which are registered with the Department of Education, Culture, and Sports.

The school-based programs for early childhood development are anchored in the philosophy that every child is a valuable commodity and therefore must be given opportunities to develop competencies and potentials early in life. The goal of these programs is to prepare the child for school. This goal is addressed through the teaching of pre-academic skills and arts, dance, and music, and through the provision of experiences designed to develop the child's skills in the various areas of growth (i.e., motoric, cognitive, personal-social, language, and value orientation). Where schools adopt specific teaching methods, like those of Montessori or Piaget, extensive sensory and motor experiences are provided to the children, in order to facilitate working alone and the development of independence. In a few private settings, medical services add another level of sophistication to the whole program.

Classes in preschools are held for two to three hours per session, five days a week, allowing for Christmas and summer breaks. Child performance is monitored individually. Results are reflected on report cards, which provide a common reference point for the school and the parents regarding the child. Beyond the financial obligations parents have in maintaining their children in the preschools, about 65 percent provide practical assistance to the school, sometimes as one-day volunteers.

The coverage of the formal preschool education program, as reported by the DECS in its latest statistical report (1989), is as follows:

Enrollment in Public Preschools   136, 843

Enrollment in Private Preschools   137, 263

These figures may not show the full coverage of the preschool education program since many private preschools are not registered with the DECS. But it has been estimated that only about 20 percent of three to six year olds receive some form of structured early childhood education.

REGULATORY MECHANISMS

The day care centers operated by the Department of Social Welfare and Development (DSWD) are under the direction and supervision of the social workers at the Bureau of Child and Youth Welfare. Those run by the Rural Improvement Clubs are under the supervision of the Bureau of Agricultural Extension in the Department of Agriculture and Food (DAP-BAEx). Privately run child care centers, including those sponsored by Rural Improvement Clubs (RICC), are not supervised by the DSWD. However, they may voluntarily seek DSWD accreditation.

The Department of Social Welfare and Development has set criteria for accreditation that classify day care centers on a scale of one to five stars, rated on the following six areas of assessment: stability of support, physical facilities, quality of day care workers, program activities/content of sessions, availability of program materials, and availability and utilization of records. After a center is accredited, periodic assessment is made by an audit team to ensure the continued quality of the program.

Preschool education is not a part of the formal educational system in the Philippines. However, in 1986, in an attempt to regulate preschool programs, the Department of Education, Culture, and Sports issued DECS Order No. 8, setting standards for the organization and operation of kindergarten schools. The standards set the age requirement for admission, class size, teacher qualifications, curriculum, and class hours, with a suggested program of activities. It also gave the specifications for the structure of the physical environment. The administration and supervision of pre-elementary education in the public schools is vested in the elementary school principals or school heads.

The private pre-elementary schools may seek a permit to operate if the school meets the minimum standards specified in DECS Order No. 8 s. 1986. If the school continues to operate according to standards for at least three years, it is granted a Certification of Recognition. This certificate may be withdrawn if in the course of time a school becomes substandard or violates reasonable rules and regulations.

PHILOSOPHIES AND METHODS ADDRESSING PROGRAM QUALITY

The formal preschool education program is not a part of the regular educational ladder. The Department of Education, Culture, and Sports (DECS), concerned at the problem of drop outs in Grade 1, would like to see preschool education for Filipino children aim at preparing them for formal schooling. The goal would be to narrow adjustment and learning gaps, thereby minimizing drop outs and eventually improving the achievement of elementary school pupils. Because the preschool program is not completely under DECS control, a coordinating council for early childhood education in the Philippines (CONCEP) has been organized to act as a coordinating body and an advisory arm of the DECS on matters related to preschool education. CONCEP is presently establishing criteria for accreditation of Philippine preschools. Meanwhile, the DECS, along with concerned parents, educators, and other groups, is advocating the inclusion of preschool education as part of the educational ladder. Legislation that would accomplish this goal is currently under consideration in the Philippine Senate. The hope is that higher quality in preschool education can be achieved if the program becomes an integral part of the educational system.

The Relationship Between the DSWD and the DECS

The children served by day care centers and nurseries are usually two and a half to four years old, but some are as old as five or six years of age. Children in formal preschools are usually five or six years old, but a few preschools also operate nurseries and playhouses or learning centers for two and a half to four year olds. Clearly there is overlap in the ages served by these two separate systems.

Prior to 1985, there was hardly any coordination between the two government agencies concerned with preschool children. Some DECS educators observed that day care centers were actually teaching children of preschool age to read and write, just as is done in Grade 1. A well-known exponent of quality preschool education observed that some preschool "enterprises" (schools run for profit) arrange their classrooms with children sitting in rows, with very little space for movement. Thirty to 60 are placed in a small classroom, with one teacher whose educational background is unsuited to working with young children and/or education. Workbooks and notebooks are used throughout the day, and the instruction consists almost entirely of lecturing and teacher-dominated recitation. Other educators have commented that the preschools were doing more harm than good because the Grade 1 teacher has to spend the first few months making the child "unlearn" the skills taught in the day care centers and nurseries.

In 1985, the Interagency Committee of the Early Childhood Enrichment

Program (ECEP), a project established as part of the Second Country Program for children, felt a need to establish linkages between the day care centers and the elementary schools, so that the knowledge, skills, and attitudes acquired by the children in the centers could match the expectations and requirements of the elementary educators. Accordingly, arrangements were made to involve the Undersecretary of DECS, the Director of the Bureau of Elementary Education, and the Director of Non-Formal Education in the deliberations regarding ECEP and other matters related to the total Day Care Program. Representatives of the DECS were also invited to join in monitoring field visits, to acquaint them with the different activities in the day care centers as well as to solicit recommendations from them regarding how learning activities in the centers could dovetail with the kindergarten curriculum of the Elementary Learning Continuum (ELC) of the Bureau of Elementary Education.

With the institutionalization of ECEP, the interagency committee membership expanded to include all agencies with early childhood care/education programs. Thus coordination between DSWD and DECS has flourished. The DECS now realizes that the Day Care Program is not just supplementary feeding of the poorest of the poor to "stave off hunger."

Although a certain level of cooperation has now been achieved by the two government agencies involved in early childhood care, there is still an unresolved issue of who should be responsible for licensing, accrediting, and supervising the day care centers. It is the thinking at the DECS that all kinds of programs/services with an education component such as ECEP must be supervised by DECS.

TEACHER TRAINING

Teacher education specifically for preschool teachers has not been established yet in the Philippines. Teachers working in the formal preschools usually hold a college degree in education, science, the arts, home economics, or family life and child development. This is particularly the case in those preschools belonging to the exclusive religious sectarian institutions and those that are privately owned and operated.

At the second National Conference on Preschool Education, held in 1988, the Coordinating Council for Early Childhood Education of the Philippines (CONCEP) presented the Standard for Preschool, which prescribes the following educational qualifications for teachers working with preschool children:

- a Bachelor of Science (B.S.) with specialization in family life and child development, or early childhood education, or kindergarten, or
- a B.S. degree in elementary education with 18 units of preschool education and 54 hours of practicum in preschool classes, or

- a B.S. or B.A. degree with disciplines allied to education or with 18 units of preschool education, or
- a Certificate in Preschool Education, achieved through a two-year preschool education study course.

CONCEP also specified the subjects comprising the 18 units in preschool education as follows:

Child study/growth and development	3 units
Philosophy, principles, techniques	3 units
Preschool program/curriculum development	3 units
Art in the preschool	3 units
Materials and equipment/physical set-up	3 units
Preschool administration and supervision	3 units

While the foregoing are the desired standards, proponents lament the scarcity of educational institutions offering preschool education courses. In metropolitan Manila, where the bulk of the teacher training institutions are located, only four colleges and one university offer such courses. Some state colleges and universities may include early childhood education as adjunct to their B.S. programs in education or psychology.

THE TRAINING OF DAY CARE WORKERS AND PARENTS

The day care centers under the Department of Social Welfare and Development are staffed by caregivers who rarely have more than a high school education. Many are parent volunteers who also have very little educational participation. To upgrade the knowledge, attitudes, and skills of day care workers and parents, the Early Childhood Enrichment Program (ECEP) instituted a continuing training program for day care workers, which consists of one-month live-in workshops for regional child development specialists (CDS). These specialists in turn train supervising social welfare supervisors. The supervising social welfare officers train day care workers (DCW) for one and a half months through on-the-job training (OJT). During this training day care workers with exceptional ability are identified. These are given additional training as day care worker trainers. These trainers in turn train other day care workers. The day care worker who successfully completes a one and a half month OJT is considered an accredited day care worker. An accredited DCW in an accredited day care center qualifies for the government subsidy of P500.00 per month.

According to the training manual, the training of DCWs includes the mission of day care centers; characteristics of children in day care centers at different age levels; their needs and how to meet those needs, planning activities for children; and developing indigenous playthings, storytelling, play, etc. Management of DCCs is also discussed. Since the start of ECEP I in 1983, it is estimated that almost half of the DCWs have had some training.

Parent Education and Training

One of the components of the ECEP is parent education. This is important because about four out of five preschool-aged children in the Philippines are at home. The Department of Social Welfare and Development, through the Bureau of Family Welfare, is at the forefront of this service. Called Parent Effectiveness Service (PES), this program serves parents of children in day care centers as well as those who are not in day care. Parents are given intensive training in early childhood development. The manual of the training program consists of three modules:

1. Early childhood development, which describes children from 0–11 months, 1–3 years, and 4–6 years. The characteristics of children at these different age groups are discussed, and their needs in all phases of development and how to meet these needs are taken up. Accordingly parents are taught how to make toys from scraps or from indigenous materials; they learn songs, poems, stories, and games that they can teach their own children. Early childhood stimulation is emphasized.
2. Parenting as a right and a duty. Here parents are informed about Philippine laws regarding families, parents, and children. Behavioral management of children (i.e., how to discipline, inculcate values, etc.) is taken up. Improvement of the husband-wife relationship is also covered.
3. Health care. This includes topics like growth monitoring, breast-feeding, oral rehydration, and immunization.

The manual also covers such topics as early detection of disabilities, herbal medicine, and accident prevention. About a million parents have been trained by the project since its start as ECEP I in 1983.

PERCEIVED STRENGTHS AND SHORTCOMINGS OF THE CHILD CARE SYSTEM

The Philippine early childhood development program has a number of strengths. First, the Day Care Program is a multi-agency concern. This commitment stems from the fact that there are sufficient laws and issuances to give the different agencies legal bases for their programs.

Second, there is a great deal of interest and concern that preschool-age children have access to day care services, which have now ceased to be thought of as just a "feeding program to stave off hunger" and are becoming appreciated as a well-rounded program aimed at total development of the young. Parents, community leaders, and professional groups are all supportive of early childhood development programs.

Concern for the quality of day care services has been evidenced by the combined efforts of DECS and DSWD to enrich the curriculum of centers, so that it dovetails with the expectations of the Bureau of Elementary Education, and especially with the kindergarten curriculum of the Elementary Learning continuum.

Finally, a mechanism for the integration of day care center and preschool programs has been set in motion. In the long term this should lead to a well-balanced, comprehensive system of early childhood development programs that prepares children well for elementary school and improves performance in later schooling.

There are also a number of shortcomings in the Philippine child care system as it currently exists that deserve immediate and long-range attention. One of the key issues raised in the PILIPINA study of the Day Care Service was the inadequacy of reach and quality of formally instituted day care programs. The quality of day care services is hampered by inadequacy in funding, in the poor qualifications of day care workers, and in provisions for program maintenance.

Another issue related to existing day care programs is their failure to address the needs of women as well as children, and especially women living in low-income families. Integration of women's needs will require greater flexibility than exists in current programs.

The lack of assurance that existing day care programs will be sustained in the long term is another shortcoming of the system. In general, day care remains an adjunct service, with its existence highly dependent on the availability of support from local government and other participation groups and organizations.

The accreditation question deserves further consideration. In the opinion of this author the Department of Social Welfare and Development should be empowered to compel all day care centers to be accredited.

Finally, there is the question of where child care programs fit within the priorities of Philippine political parties and leadership. While there are sufficient legal bases for these programs, there seems to be a lack of the political will needed to give substance to the laws.

REFERENCES

Bureau of Family and Child Welfare. (1985). *Self-Instructional Handbook for Day Care Workers*, Ministry of Social Welfare and Development, Manila, Philippines.

Bureau of Family Welfare. *Handbook for Parent Effectiveness Services*, Department of Social Welfare and Development, Quezon City, Philippines (available in mimeograph form, scheduled for printing).

Bureau of Women and Young Workers, Department of Labor and Employment. (1989). *Study on Maternity/Paternity Leave Benefits*.

Child and Youth Research Center. (1980). *The Values of Adolescent Filipine Students*. Department of Education, Culture, and Sports, Manila, Philippines.

Child and Youth Research Center. (1984). *The Present Economic Crisis and Its Impact on Parents and Their Children 0 to 6 Years*. Department of Education, Culture, and Sports, Manila, Philippines.

Department of Education, Culture, and Sports, Order No. 8. (1986). *Standards for the Organization and Operation of Kindergarten Schools*, Manila, Philippines.

Estelas, J. V., and Nunez, D. B. (1974). *Preschool Education in the Philippines*. Manila: National Bookstore and Publishers.

Lim-Yusen, C. (November 1987). *The Day Care Centers of the Department of Social Services and Development*, CONCEP Gazette, pp. 15–16.

Lim-Yusen, C. (1989). "The Effective Preschool Teacher." Paper read at the Fifth Asian Workshop on Child and Adolescent Development, Asian Institute of Tourism, February 11, 1989, Quezon City.

National Statistics Office. (1989). *Philippine Yearbook 1989*. National Economic Development Authority, Manila, Philippines.

Palattao-Corpus, L. (1987). *A Review of the State-of-the-Art of Educational Research the Philippine Experience Area 7, the Filipine Child*. PRODED Ministry of Education Culture and Sports, Republic of the Philippines, Manila.

Palattao-Corpus, L. G., (1989). "Philippine Care and Education for Children Aged 3 to 6." In P. O. Olmsted and D. P. Weikart (Eds.), *New Nations Serve Young Children: Profiles of Child Care and Education in 14 Countries*, pp. 255–271. Ypsilanti, Mich.: The High Scope Press.

Palattao-Corpus, L. G., Nuñez, D. B. (1986). *Situation Analysis of Early Childhood Education*. Department of Education Culture and Sports Child and Youth Research Center.

Pelicarpie-Mendez, P. (1987). *A Review of the State-of-the-Art of Educational Anthropology*. PRODED, Ministry of Education Culture and Sports, Republic of the Philippines, Manila.

Pierce, J. S., Celina, J., and Pierce, G. S. (1980). "The Major Ecological Factors Affecting the Slum Dwellers in Alaska, Ermita, and Sawang, Calere, Cebu City: Implications to Barangay Development." Unpublished masters thesis. Cebu State Colleges of Sciences and Technology, Cebu City, Philippines.

PILIPINA. (1989). *Why Day Care: Building Support for Woman's Work and Child Care*. Quezon City, Philippines.

Republic of the Philippines. (1975). *Presidential Decree 603 (Child and Youth Welfare Code*.

Republic of the Philippines and United Nations Children's Fund. (1987). *Situation of Children and Women in the Philippines*.

Republic of the Philippines and United Nations Children's Fund. (1990). *Situation of Children and Women in the Philippines*.

Sevilla, J. C. (1982). *Research on the Filipine Family: Review and Prospects*. Development Academy of the Philippines, Pasig, Metro Manila.

23

POLAND

Ewa Korczak

This chapter is written at a time when Poland is experiencing dramatic political and social changes that have significance for the capacity of Polish society to care for and educate its young children in the ways we would most prefer.

THE BACKGROUND FOR PRESENT POLICY AND PROGRAMS

The welfare of the child is at the heart of Polish guardianship law and is fully reflected in all its provisions. These protections are considered so important, not only from the parents' point of view but also from the standpoint of the state and society, that they are addressed specifically by the Polish Constitution.[1] From these constitutional rights flow the ideological assumptions of family law related to the protection and strengthening of the family, with particular reference to the welfare of the child.

The basic rules on which family and guardianship law are based in Poland are as follows:

1. Protection of the welfare and stability of the family as a highest priority for society.

2. Treatment of the welfare of the child as the basic determining criterion for settling conflicts within the family.

3. Protection of the right of each child to be brought up in a family.

4. Equal treatment of all children, regardless of the circumstances and conditions of their birth and origin.

5. Recognition of the fundamentally social character of child care.

6. Recognition of personal emotional ties as the basis of family relationships.

7. Separation of family relationships from the dominating role of property issues.

8. Recognition of the secular nature of all the institutions of family law.

It is important to note that this treatment of family and child rights is quite different from the views taken up until 50 years ago (prior to World War II), when family assistance and protection was seen only in terms of the help given to the family and child by public care or charitable institutions. The shift reflected in the Constitution of the Polish People's Republic is to give clear recognition of the family as the basic social unit, which fulfills very important socio-educational functions. It is for this reason that the Constitution guarantees the family legal protection and provides the child with specific subjective rights.

In 1976 amendments to Article 79 of the Constitution considerably widened the meanings of marriage, motherhood, and family protection. The rights of children born in and out of wedlock have been made equal, and the rights and duties related to alimony have been spelled out, giving all children legal access to the financial support necessary to provide the material conditions needed for basic living. Recently a State Alimony Fund has been established in Poland, through which a mother or other authorized person may obtain part of the adjudicated alimonies that have proven difficult to collect directly from the child's father.

The Rights of Women

The Constitution also addresses the need to provide women, especially mothers, with the conditions needed to enable them to reconcile professional with family responsibilities. Women's rights are most strongly emphasized in Article 78 of the 1976 formulation, which guarantees the right to work and salary equal with men, based on the idea of equal pay for equal work, the right to vacation, the right to respect and awards for outstanding achievements, and the right to fill public posts. On the "family" side of the work-family equation, Article 78 provides for the care of mother and child, the protection of pregnant women, paid leave before and after childbirth, the development of a network of maternity clinics, infant nurseries and kindergartens, and the development of a network of service institutions (canteens, laundries, etc.).

Considerable importance is placed on close contact between mother and child immediately after the child's birth. This need is addressed through leave periods for working women. In Poland mothers are granted leave for 16 weeks in the case of the first child and 18 weeks for the second and subsequent children.

Educational leaves are also available to parents, for a period of three years. These leaves allow the parent to take responsibility for the child's development and education until it reaches kindergarten age, that is, during the years when the family environment plays the most important role in the child's development. Financial benefits may be granted for two of the years, depending on the amount of per capita income in the family, up to 25 percent of the average income in the state sector. Single parents may receive such a benefit for the full three-year period, at an amount 60 percent higher than that of the married parent.[2]

When the process of caring for and educating the child works correctly, the state seeks to avoid any interference with it. The family is considered the most important social group in that regard, and keeping and educating children belong to its basic duties. These tasks must meet both the collective needs of the whole family and the individual needs of family members.

The Polish Family

In contemporary Polish society the most common family type consists of a man and a woman united by marriage and their minor children. The dominance of this nuclear family form is the consequence of socio-economic changes occurring in industrialized society. Changes in the Polish family structure over the past 50 years include decreases in the number of children, domination of the two-generation family form, and increases in the number of parental separations and incidences of single parenthood.

According to recent statistical data,[3] in 1984 there were 10,175,000 families in Poland, including 6,354,000 families with children. Of these families, 1,242,000 (19.5%) had a single woman as head of household, and 153,000 (2.4%) had fathers bringing up children alone. Of the 17,830,000 people in the Polish work force in 1988, 8,001,909 (45%) were women.

Linking Day Care and Family Policies

One of the basic assurances of a child's rights is the family and guardianship law outlined earlier, which results from fundamental constitutional guarantees. One assumption of this law is that social policies toward families will operate both in the interest of the family and the child. This means that particular mechanisms and activities must mutually benefit both the strengthening and happiness of the family and the broader needs of society. It is assumed in turn that successful family functioning guarantees success in the development and education of the child.

Thus, the state care policy is designed to help the family and in this way to help the child indirectly. Only in the case of children without a family does the state take over the caring, educational, and socio-legal functions of child rearing.

Particular priorities of Polish national family policy are the following:

a. Protection of the basic needs of families.
b. Equalization of the life chances of children from different environments.
c. Adjustment of both family and social mechanisms to facilitate women's professional work.
d. Provision for old age.
e. Dissemination of pension schemes.

From the child's standpoint, the policy aim of the State is to create the most favorable conditions for development, education, and preparation to participate in society. The basic strategies for accomplishing this are through developmentally focused prevention, protection against threats to development, compensation for the effects of handicap or disability and loss of family, and resocialization to correct for developmental or social abnormalities. The programs designed to carry out these strategies heavily emphasize the importance of activities that prevent developmental and educational threats to children. At the same time, a more and more common theme in care activities involves the fuller realization of children's rights. The concern is for reaching all children as fully as possible by increasing the breadth and range of activities supporting families.

The following rules of action guide the "tutorial-educational system" focused primarily on the needs of the child:

a. First priority for care provided to children should be given to the environment closest to their regular upbringing. This means the kindergarten, the school, within the family, or in the nearest surroundings, in order to provide children with the possibility of growing in natural family, cultural, and social conditions.
b. Care should be provided early in development and should be of a prophylactic character, to prevent the formation of abnormalities harmful for the child's health and education.
c. Placement of a child in a care, educational, or reform institution should take place only after exhausting all the other possibilities for help and care aimed at keeping a child in a family because the family is the most appropriate environment for assuring the correct development of a child.

For many years small children have been brought up exclusively in families. Only in the last century have major changes occurred in this respect, due primarily to the entry of mothers into the professional work force and the resulting need to leave children in the guardianship of educational institutions, nurseries, and kindergartens during working hours. The main contribution of kindergarten to family policy is in helping these parents by

Table 23.1
Nurseries and Kindergartens in Poland

Program	Age Served	Number of Programs	Number of Children	Percent of Children in Age Group
Nurseries	0-3 year olds	1,553	150,631	8.7
Kindergartens	3-6 year olds	26,358	1,322,400	49.5

providing for children in a well-functioning institution, awakening the educational interests of those children and complementing the educational culture parents are able to offer them.[4]

NURSERIES AND KINDERGARTENS IN POLAND

Working women and single parents are the first priority for the state in its efforts to establish and maintain nurseries and kindergartens. Table 23.1 shows the number of nurseries and kindergartens in Poland in 1989, and the numbers of children served by those programs.[5]

THE NURSERY PROGRAM

A nursery is a protective-educational institution providing help to working parents or others in the care of healthy children six weeks to three years old. The basic duties of a nursery involve assuring the child life conditions as close as possible to those of the child's home during the child's stay in the care setting. In particular, these duties include the following:

a. Educational, nursing, and medical care, with special emphasis on prevention.
b. Board, underclothing, and clothing.
c. Preventive medicines and first aid provision.

Organizational Structure

Nurseries in Poland come under the purview of the Ministry of Health and Social Care. They are divided into two types: those organized and run by district health departments and those attached to factories under health department supervision. Health department run nurseries serve the children living in a specified catchment area, and those linked to factories serve the children of employees (plus others if space allows).

Nurseries are established by constructing new buildings or by adapting existing structures. The area around each building is to include a large green area. In equipping the nurseries the general rules relate to comfort, functionality, cleanliness, and order. Appropriate colors are used to create an atmosphere and conditions similar to home settings, with monotonous white excluded.

Nursery attendance is organized in three different ways:

1. all day, for 10, 12, or 14 hours as the need requires;
2. shift times at those factories employing women in shifts;
3. 24 hours per day during the work week, with home stays on weekends and holidays. These work-week nurseries are intermediate between a nursery and a home for small children. The need for them comes from that percentage of mothers or single fathers who cannot provide a child with regular night-time care during the work week.

Nursery organization is based on the division of children into groups, as determined by educational and epidemiological needs. The number of groups depends on the number of children in the center, the number of rooms available, and on the planning of functional activities. The general rule is to organize groups of 12 to 20 children. Typically the division consists of

a. a group of babies (6 weeks to 11 months);
b. a group of toddlers (12 to 23 months); and
c. a group of older children (24 to 36 months).

When kindergartens are overcrowded, permission is given to include pre-school groups in the nurseries. These are groups of children three to four years old.

Properly organized nurseries include a full set of rooms for each age group. These consist of an anteroom into which the child is received and examined for illness (only healthy children are admitted); a changing room; a bathroom adapted to the child's age; a bedroom with permanent beds (or deck chairs, for two to three year olds); a playroom; and an isolation room, for children who fall ill during the day. A doctor is called in such cases, and the parent is contacted to fetch the child.

Each age group is assigned a nurse, a caregiver, and a helping attendant. These personnel are required to work 40 hours per week. The amount of staff in a given nursery depends on the number of children's groups. For instance, a nursery with up to 35 places (two groups), open for 10 hours each day, would employ three nurses and caregivers and two attendants. A nursery serving 56 to 80 children during the same 10-hour day would be staffed by seven nurses and caregivers and six attendants. A center of that same size running 14 hours per day would have 18 such personnel, half of them nurses and caregivers. The cost of care is divided between the parents and the state.

The Care and Educational Activities of Nurseries

Each group of children has a daily timetable. It is designed to provide life routines that take into account age and developmental level, appropriate amounts of sleep, number and nutritional value of meals, and the time needed for nursing activities and games. Protection against infectious diseases is very important, including regular health examinations and protective vaccinations. A doctor works in the nursery two to three hours every day. A psychologist may also be available two or three times a week to advise staff on the care of children in the different age groups and to carry out psychological examinations.

There is a general belief that, while education outside the family is provided by kindergarten, school, and out-of-school institutions, the nursery is simply a place to deposit very young children during the day. This belief stems from the fact that few people treat the nursery as a care-educational setting, very little research is conducted in such settings, and there is a lack of literature discussing the needs and problems of such institutions. Another contributing factor is the location of nurseries and kindergartens in two separate ministries—nurseries in Health and Social Care and kindergartens in National Education.

No fully defined concept of care-education exists to guide nursery activities. As a result, the quality of care depends on the inventiveness, competence, and willingness of the individual caregiver and her cooperation with the doctor and the psychologist. One result is a lack of continuity between the child's activities in the nursery and those experienced later in the kindergarten setting.

Preparation of Nursery Staff

Medical secondary schools carry out the preparation in care-educational work for nursery staff in Poland. This general and professional training provides a good basis for professional work with the small child and for further specialized training.

The general education takes place within the framework of the following subjects: children's anatomy and physiology; hygiene and work safety; basic psychology, pedagogy, and sociology; biology, with microbiology; and early childhood illnesses. More specialized training includes such subjects as caregiver methodology, practice in those methods, practice in technical-aesthetic education, and other practical classes. A total of 26 subjects are studied during the four-year course of learning, followed by examinations in both theory and practice for the diploma.

Changes in the program for preparing nursery caregivers are in the planning stage. Two versions of the revised program are currently under consideration, one that would retain the medical secondary school but reduce the number of subjects to 12, and the other that would create a medical unit designed to train nursery caregivers in two years.

THE KINDERGARTEN PROGRAM

Kindergarten programs in Poland provide care for children and assist parents who are working outside the home. Above all, however, these programs address important educational goals and are the first stage in the social system of education. About 60 percent of the kindergartens are in the country, with the remainder in cities and towns.

Starting in the latter part of the 1970s, several different forms of kindergarten organization were developed within the Polish system, in an effort to reach all six-year-old children.[6] At the present time the following forms of preschool education are operating:

- Kindergartens as free-standing educational institutions for children between the ages of three and seven. These programs are open year round, for nine hours a day. They are organized into three or four levels by age.
- Introductory classes, attached to primary schools. Known also as preschools, these serve only six-year-old children, and operate with a five-hour workday during the school year.

In the free-standing kindergartens children are grouped by age. Groups in urban kindergartens each contain about 25 children. Rural kindergartens tend to have smaller groups, with each containing 15 to 25 children.

The size of the kindergarten staff is determined by the state office of preschool supervision. Typically a given group has contact with two interchanging teachers because teachers working with three to five year olds have a 25-hour work week, and those with six year olds a work week of 22 hours. An additional helper is added to the group if it contains at least 15 three or three and four year olds. Administrative staff are hired in addition to those working directly with the children.

Parents cover the cost of meals at the kindergarten; the remaining costs are covered by the state.

The Training of Kindergarten Teachers

Until recently there have been four training sequences for kindergarten teachers:

1. A six-year program following primary school.
2. A two-year program following secondary school.
3. A five-year Masters Degree program at universities and teacher training colleges.

4. The "2nd degree" at the Masters level, consisting of three years of part-time studies at the university or teacher training college.

Recently, because of a drop in the number of children attending kindergartens caused by unemployment and the resulting fall in family incomes, many nurseries and kindergartens are being closed in Poland. This has led to an oversupply of kindergarten teachers, the closing of teacher training colleges, and limited admission to Masters-level programs.

Curricular Goals

These preschool programs are organized in accordance with a syllabus created by the Ministry of Education and the Institute of School Syllabi in 1981.[7] This educational program is directed at the child's education and comprehensive development, on the one hand, and at the general needs of economic life and the family situation on the other. These twofold purposes are linked by the simultaneous need to provide equal life opportunities to children from different socio-economic and cultural environments, and to eradicate the early social- and health-related causes of school failures. Kindergarten creates the possibility for daily contact, interaction, and cooperation with equals. This interaction is an important factor in both intellectual and socio-moral development. The contemporary family rarely creates the possibility for permanent contacts with other children, due to the lack of a sibling or to a large gap in age between children for the child, and to the disappearance of neighborhood ties (especially in urban areas).

The tasks of the kindergarten are to

- Ensure proper child development. This means that in the educational activities one should take into account mutual dependencies between the biological and mental development of the child, and between health, socio-moral, intellectual, and aesthetics education.

- Educate comprehensively and prepare for school. Preparation for school involves the achievement by the child of intellectual, physical, emotional, and social maturity. It is also necessary to develop a satisfactory amount of physical strength and a certain degree of psychological endurance in the child, to acquaint him with the norms of social behavior, and to develop the independence necessary to take up school duties.

- Help the family in bringing up and caring for the child. This means cooperating with the child's parents, in order to obtain, if necessary, some influence over the conditions and educational atmosphere at home, and communicating with the family regarding joint educational activities. Care activities lead also to the early discovery in children of deviations from general norms, which usually enables effective remedial measures to be applied in time to prevent serious long-term consequences.[8]

Methods and Content

The basic assumption of the kindergarten program is that the child's personality should be shaped in the course of his own activity, as manifested in contacts with the surrounding world.[9] This requires the conscious, purposeful, and planned directing of children's activities. The child is not only the object in this pedagogical system, but also the subject of education as broadly defined, that is, also containing the elements of training.

The educational program is aimed at the comprehensive development of an individual within a group, by shaping the attitudes, beliefs, interests, developing abilities and skills of the child, as well as gradually widening the child's knowledge base. Kindergarten shapes a child's personality by educating him within the nearest environmental circle—in the family and kindergarten group—and in gradually widening contacts with the surroundings.

Five major fields of educational interest make up the content of the program: health, moral-social development, intellectual development, technical skills, and aesthetic education. The content in each of these fields is integrally connected with the others, however, creating the possibility of simultaneous realization of the various contents.

Included in the field of health education are both the development of attitudes toward the health and safety of oneself and others, and the development of general motor abilities. Thus activities range from teaching and reinforcing the rules of safety to shaping the right posture and developing physical vigor. Moral-social education involves the development of characteristics like friendliness, honesty, and sense of duty, the strengthening of emotional ties with the family, and the training for both independence and the ability to cooperate and act for the benefit of others. Intellectual education includes developing the motivation for learning, providing language enrichment, teaching simple mental operations, developing the basic ability to read and readiness to write, shaping simple mathematical ideas, and training in the abilities connected with understanding the natural environment.

Technical education involves developing research and promoting interests and abilities, training for work and respecting the products of work, and becoming familiar with different ways of applying technology as subordinated to the needs of man. Aesthetic education includes enriching the experience and imagination, training sensitivity toward aesthetic values in nature, technology, and the arts, and shaping the ability to notice and compare visual, sound, tactile, and other phenomena.

Syllabus contents are provided separately for each preschool age group. Material for the three-, four-, and five-year-old children is worked out within the same structure, but with increasing levels of difficultly. However, the scope of content designed for the six-year-old children is formulated in the language of results related to the behaviors, efficiency, and information needed by a child entering primary school, while at the same time synthesizing all of the previous four years of experience in the kindergarten. Priority is given to socio-moral behavior and to separate treatment of tasks concerning initial reading ability, preparation for learning to write, and technical education.

Kindergarten also undertakes re-education activities with children whose early development has been uneven. The aim is to level existing environmental or developmental differences, correcting faults and abnormalities that occurred in the earlier development of the child and reducing differences in children's readiness for the start of formal schooling. In this way the program of education in kindergarten can be understood as a way of democratizing the educational system.

Recent Curriculum Reform

A new program of education in kindergarten has been recently worked out as a result of research carried out in Poland between 1987 and 1989. This program was introduced experimentally in the 1989–1990 school year and made a standard part of some kindergartens in 1992.

This modified program contains some new psycho-pedagogical assumptions about work with children of preschool age and changes in the content of education and learning. The key assumptions involve looking differently at the developing child in the educational process. The preschool period is viewed as one of the stages of the entire life course. All of these stages undergo development, and each should be the subject of educational stimulation. Like later stages, development in the preschool period is individual in nature, and so it is characterized in each case by different rhythms and rates. Learning takes the form of both spontaneous searching and work directed by the teacher. One essential element in the process of learning involves adults as the source of information about the culture. Based on these assumptions, the authors of the revised program propose that "the role of the educator consists, on the one hand, of mediating the transmission of cultural output, and, on the other hand, of enabling the child to preserve its own personal identity" (Kielar and Karwowska-Struczyk, 1989). Thus children are not to be only the receivers of the outside world; they must participate in creating knowledge and think out for themselves "methods" of gaining and constructing it.

The process of education is treated in the program as introducing the child to the nation's culture, helping the child into that culture, and facilitating the child's development. Education does not consist of speeding up development, but in enriching it and providing it with an experiential base. The child himself organizes the surrounding environs for his own activity and may be the initiator of various tasks and problem situations. He suggests the ways of realizing and solving them, setting the goal that he wishes to attain. In bi-subjective, coordinate integration with the teacher he sometimes occupies the central position, and sometimes he is subordinated. Always, however, the teacher and the child modify, harmonize, and coordinate their own activities to reach a common interpretation of reality and construct a common world.

The child is treated as a co-participant in educational situations. The child "may, in every situation, not only listen to and follow orders but also suggest and look for, may pose the problems, ask and not only answer" (Kieler and Karwowska-Struczyk, 1989). The teacher should release, modify, and develop particular mental activities of the pupil. The teacher's pedagogical work would consist in helping the child to create "his own world." The aim of the educational activity is supporting, enriching, co-creating the inner conditions of the child's self-development, considering its individual, genetic, and cultural determinants. Thus teacher-child interaction should take different forms. The following are suggested:

- The child presents the problem and includes the teacher and his peers in solving it.
- The teacher organizes the problem situation and waits until it is noticed and taken up by the child.
- The teacher puts the problem before the child, inviting him to act.

The problems offered by the teacher may be of a closed character, offering fixed knowledge about the world and the child's abilities, or they may appear in open form, stimulating the child's imagination and developing his cognitive independence and creative thinking.

STRENGTHS AND SHORTCOMINGS OF THE POLISH DAY CARE SYSTEM

Preschool education is an important link in the system of education in Poland, mediating between family and formal schooling. As the first stage in this social system, it is designed specifically to influence children relatively early in their development. This purpose is manifested in the specific organizational forms and methods of work found in Polish nurseries and kindergartens.

Particular forms of preschool education in Poland fulfill their tasks with an unequal degree of effectiveness. The highest level of educational effectiveness, both generally and more specifically in terms of preparing children for school learning, is reached by the independent kindergartens. The other, more abbreviated and simplified organizational forms of kindergarten are relatively less effective.

Access to the independent kindergartens is limited and unable to meet social needs. This was especially true during the 1980s for children in the three- to five-year-old age range and those living in rural areas. There is now justifiable anxiety that this situation will worsen, due to changes in the rules of payment for kindergartens. Because of the rapid upsurge in food prices in August 1989, the government decided that further financing of food expenses in kindergarten from the state budget was impossible. This meant an increase in fees to parents, which has produced severe hardship for large families, those with low family incomes, and single mothers. Many of the children from these families have stopped attending kindergarten as a result. In some provinces kindergartens have even been closed down. For example, six kindergartens were closed in the rural part of Radom province, and four of 100 kindergartens in Zamosc province are expected to close, depriving about 450 children of service. Katowice province will be hit especially hard because it contains an exceptionally large number of single mothers.

Reform of the Polish educational system will result in providing all six-year-old children with obligatory schooling. As a result, kindergartens will cover only three- to six-year-old children, increasing the chance of providing access to those younger children.

The effectiveness of our institutions of preschool education is also influenced by the excessive number of children cared for by each teacher and the shortage of qualified pedagogical staff. The first graduates of our university and pedagogical colleges received degrees as recently as 1981. These programs of study are not in high demand, in part because the preschool teacher's profession is not very popular or prestigious. This situation is improving now that two-year colleges of preschool education have been founded, training graduates, the majority of whom will take up jobs in the institutions of preschool training. The organizational and program changes in higher education affecting the training of kindergarten teachers do much to improve the staff situation in kindergartens.

Research has shown us that introducing the elements of systematic teaching into kindergarten led to excessive "didactization," which in turn had a negative influence on children, restraining the proper course of stimulation and masking shortcomings in their development. These findings were taken into account in developing the revised educational approach discussed earlier in this chapter.

Taking into account demographic forecasts anticipating a fall in birthrate, and thus decreasing numbers of children aged three to six, there are plans to gradually reorganize the system between 1990 and 1995 and to carry out intensive improvement efforts for programs and methods of education in kindergarten settings.

NOTES

1. The Constitution of the Polish People's Republic of July 22, 1952, addresses the protection of the child's rights and its welfare in Chapter VIII, and the basic

rights and duties of the citizens in Articles 79 and 80. Further changes were introduced in the Parliamentary Act of February 10, 1976.

2. For single mothers in difficult life circumstances, institutions are organized so that the mother can give birth to a baby and raise it until the family can become independent, usually with the help of this organization. Efforts are also made to find a substitute family for orphaned children and for the children of parents whose child custody rights have been taken away by the courts. In 1989, 161 mothers and their children were living in such homes.

3. All the data come from the *1989 Statistical Yearbook*.

4. Health services also play an important role in child care in contemporary Polish society. Modern medical and health care policy is concerned not only with saving children's lives, but also with optimum physical and mental development. Of primary importance is preventive treatment and early rehabilitation aimed at making it possible for handicapped children to live in normal environments. In Poland a health book received by parents shortly after the child's birth is designed to ensure continuity of health care. Data entered into it by health personnel provide information for the pediatricians taking care of a child at later life stages.

5. In addition to nurseries and kindergartens, three other main categories of guardianship institutions exist in Poland. Educational and curative care institutions for children with developmental handicaps include special schools, institutions for retarded children, and special institutions for deaf or blind children, or with other physical handicaps. Special educational institutions for children and youth include both home and school settings, some with boarding arrangements and some based in the community. Child and youth development settings include clubs and reading rooms, play areas, creative work centers, summer camps, and information bureaus.

6. *Raport o Stanie Oświaty w PRL* (Report on the state of education in the Polish People's Republic), Warsaw, 1973, pp. 194–195.

7. This educational program united two earlier program documents; the "Syllabus of education in kindergarten" developed in 1973, and an addition to this syllabus, published in 1977, called "The scope of contents of training and education for 6-year-old children."

8. M. Kwiatkowska and T. Topinska (Eds.), *Metodyka wychowania predszkolnego.* (Methodology of preschool education), Warsaw, 1972, pp. 24–25.

9. Education syllabus in kindergarten, Warsaw, 1981, pp. 5–10.

REFERENCES

Balcerek, M. (1981). *Instytucje opieki nad dziećmi i mlodzie* (Institutions of care for children and youth). Warsaw: Ministry of Education Publishing House.

Brzezińska, A. (1987). *Gotowość dzieci w wieku przedszkolnym do czytania i pisania* (Readiness of children at the preschool age to read and write). Poznań.

Cackowska, M. (1984). *Nauka czytania i pisania w klasach przedszkolnych* (Learning to read and write in the preschool classes). Warsaw.

Kakol, M. (1988). "Z badán nad warunkami adaptacji dzieci trzyletnich do przedszkola." *Wychowanie w przedszkolu.* 2 (From the research on the conditions of adaptation of three-year-old children for kindergartens. *Education in kindergarten.* 2).

Kielar, M. and Karwowska-Struczyk, M. (1989). "Informacja o projekcie nowego programu wychowania w przedszkolu. Poszukiwania nowej koncepcji wychowania." *Wychowanie w przedszkolu.* 7 (Information on the project of the new program of education in the kindergarten. Searching for the new concept of education. *Education in kindergarten.* 7).

Korczak, J. (1957). *Prawo dziecka do szacunku* (The selection of pedagogical works). Warsaw.

Kwiatkowska, M., Topińska, Z. (Eds.). (1972). *Metodyka wychowania przedszkolnego* (Methodology of preschool education). Warsaw.

Lobodzińska, B. (1974). *Rodzina w Polsce* (Family in Poland). Warsaw.

Miller, R. "Dostep do óswiaty i wyrównywanie startu szkolnego. Problem wezloey." 11.4, maszynopis (Access to education and leveling the school start. 11.4. Typescript).

Misiorna, A. (1987). "Spostrzeganie potrzeb drugiego czlowiek przez dzieci." *Wychowanie w przedskolu.* 10 (Noticing the needs of other men by children. *Education in kindergarten.* 10).

(1981). *Program wychowania w przedskolu* (Program of education in kindergarten). Warsaw.

(1980). *Program nauczania Liceum Medycznego. Zawód: Opiekunka dziecieca* (Program of teaching of Secondary Medical School. Profession: children's carekeeper). Warsaw.

(1979). *Raport o funkcjonowaniu instytucji prawnych w zakresie ochrony rodziny* (Report on the functioning of legal institutions in the field of family protection contained in the family and guardianship code). Warsaw: Ministry of Justice, typescript.

(1973). *Raport o stanie óswiaty w PRL* (Report on the state of education in the Polish People's Republic). Warsaw.

(1990). *Rocznik statystyczny* (1990 Statistical Yearbook). Warsaw.

Ratyńska, H. (1989). "Rekrutacja 89—zagrozenia i szanse." *Wychowanie w przedszkolu.* 10 (Recruitment 89–threat and chances. *Education in kindergarten.* 10).

Tyszkowa, M. (1989). "Wychowanie przedszkolne. Stan i kierunki przebudowy." *Problem wezlowy, seria nr. 13* (Preschool education, State and directions of remodeling. *Thematic reports series no. 13*). Warsaw-Cracow.

Wilgocka-Okoń B. (1985). "Glówne kierunki badań w pedagogice przedszkolnej." W. Okoń (Ed.), *Monografie pedagogiczne XLIX* (Main directions of research in preschool education. Okoń, W. [Ed.] *Pedagogical Monographs*, XLIX). Warsaw.

Wilgocka-Okoń, B. (1989). "Stan wychowania przedszkolnego w Polsce. "*Problem wezlowy, seria nr. 16* (The state of preschool education in Poland. *Thematic reports series no. 16*). Warsaw-Cracow.

Wolczyk, J. (1973). *Edukacja dla rozwoju. Niektóre problemy polityki óswiatowej* (Education for development. Some problems of educational policy). Warsaw.

Woznicka, Z. (1977). *Wychowanie przedszkolne w Polsce Ludowej* (Preschool education in Polish People's Republic). Warsaw.

Wroczyński, W. (1979). *Pedagogika spoleczna* (Social Pedagogy). Warsaw.

———— 24 ————

SOUTH AFRICA

Mildred Mkhulisi and Moncrieff Cochran

> There is a gulf that separates
> children from children
> those who eat well
> and those who are malnourished
> those who are healthy
> and those without health care
> those who are stimulated
> and those who live in apathy
> those who are happy
> and those who are despondent
> those who are curious, excited and eager to learn
> and those who enter formal school
> already at risk for failure.
> —Kaye Ter-Morshuizen
> Natal Training College, Pietermaritzburg

South Africa, because of her "apartheid" policy, is currently going through a transformation process. She is experiencing the "winds of change." This transitional stage is especially deeply felt in black education because it is just there that most injustices are experienced. The national government policy of "own affairs" institutionalizes inequality, creates confusion, and is a wasteful dissipation of human energy and material resources. The resulting educational system, compartmentalized by race and ethnicity, has deprived 86 percent of South African children—those classified as "non-white"—of the best quality and standard of education that every child deserves and ought to receive.

This chapter is written at a time of political transition in South Africa.

For that reason it is future oriented, designed to provide a basic reference in anticipation of a post-apartheid political system. But an understanding of future possibilities must be informed by history and build on present realities.

HISTORICAL BACKGROUND FOR PRESENT POLICY AND PROGRAMS

The Union of South Africa came about in 1910 with the uniting of four previously self-governing colonies of the United Kingdom, now the Cape, Natal, Orange Free State, and Transvaal Provinces. In 1961 the union became a republic.

The indigenous African population in South Africa includes eight distinct tribes,[1] speaking five different languages. Black Africans currently make up about 75 percent of the South African population. Political domination of this majority by a white minority began in the Cape Colony, which was founded in 1652 by the Dutch and taken over by Britain in 1806. The other three white-controlled colonies were established by the Dutch and the British during the 1840s and 1850s.

Two other racial and ethnic groups have significance in South African society. Those of mixed African and white ancestry are descended from white settlers and Africans who joined together during the 17th century. These people are referred to as "coloured" in current terminology.[2] The other group, now called "Asians," had its origins in India and (to a lesser extent) China. These people first came to southern Africa as indentured laborers brought to Natal during the 1860s to work on sugar plantations, and somewhat later as merchants.

Since the middle of the 17th century the European settlers and their descendants have steadily expanded their political and economic power through increasing segregation of those not defined as "white." These policies and practices, which were well established by the middle of the 19th century, received a further boost when the discovery of diamonds and gold led to the transformation of the South African economy.

Apartheid became official policy in 1948 with the ascendence of the National Party, in coalition with the Afrikaner Party (primarily descendants of Dutch settlers). While much of apartheid was little more than formalization of the policies of previous governments, the Nationalists hardened the racial lines that formed the basis of the policy and gave it a stronger ethnic focus. Adam and Giliomee (1979) state that "Afrikaners are taught that their ability to realize themselves depends on group membership and that the survival of the group depends on its acquisition and maintenance of control" (p. 79, as quoted in van den Berg and Vergnani, 1986). Van den Berg and Vergnani (1986) describe five consequences of apartheid policy for South African society:

1. The structuring of the political system operates to entrench the identity and interest of those defined as "white."
2. Access to economic benefits and to social services is extremely unequal, as an instrument of deliberate state policy.
3. The rule of law has been systematically eroded by the need for autocratic rule with the use of repressive security forces, as a reaction to resistance to apartheid policies.
4. The legitimacy crisis caused by policies contradicting religious values, common law traditions, and democratic principles has led to a chronic state of violent conflict, creating polarization both within and among the politically designated groups.
5. Most recently, social dislocation and confusion have resulted from the attempt by the state to broaden its base of support by incorporating the "coloured" and "Asian" sectors into the political mainstream without endangering the ultimate power of the Afrikaner establishment.

In 1983 the effort to broaden support for apartheid policies took the form of constitutional reform, which for the first time brought a racialist classification into that document through a system of "general" and "own" affairs. Van den Berg and Vergnani (1986) describe this system as follows:

> "General affairs" were those matters to be decided by all but which in effect left "white" decision-making power untouched. "Own affairs" were presented as matters to be decided by each group for itself, but which had to operate within the framework of parameters laid down under "general affairs," that is, as laid down by the ruling "white" elite, which also alone had decided on the allocation of "general" and "own" affairs in the first place. (p. 39)

"Blacks," who made up 73 percent of the population, were not even given that pretense of power provided by the "own affairs" permitted the "coloureds" and "Asians." All policies affecting their welfare continued to be under the central control of "general affairs." The administration of services to "blacks" is further complicated by the distinction between "national" and "independent" states, depending on the administrative status of those areas designated by the state as "homelands" for "blacks."

The "homelands" concept, which had first been initiated as policy early in this century, was refined and carried forward in the 1960s. The idea was to move all black Africans into geographic areas arbitrarily defined as "homelands," give these areas nominal "independence," and define their inhabitants as foreigners, requiring a passport in order to enter "South Africa." Implementation of this policy led to the treatment of black African men as migrant laborers, forced to live in male hostels in townships around the major cities and able to return to their "homeland"-based families only once a year. Ten such "homelands" currently exist.[3] Four have "independent" status, while the others are now "self-governing," thus leading to the distinction between "independent" and "national" referred to above. All are under the ultimate control of the central state.

Significant elements of all four statutory population groups rejected the new "power sharing" arrangement created by constitutional reform, leading to considerable violent resistance and social dislocation. Not surprisingly, the elaborate bureaucratic structures and regulations created to implement the new system in a way that assured continuation of complete "white" control have brought further confusion to already cumbersome administrative machinery.

For preschool children this policy context results in a stark set of real consequences. All South African children live in an artificial world, compartmentalized in ways that prevent normal interaction with the rich cultural diversity that the society has to offer its citizens. If they are not classified "white," then these children grow up under authoritarian threat, in environments that have become increasingly violent and even life-threatening. Resources are distributed so that black African children, who make up 85 percent of all South African children, receive the least, while their "white" counterparts (6%) receive the most. Thus preschool provision in South Africa can only be understood in the context of the ideology underlying apartheid policy. Cock et al. (1984) summarize this embeddedness nicely:

The neglect of child care in South Africa must be located in terms of the state's lack of concern with the conditions under which African labour power is reproduced generally. The neglect of state expenditure on child care is thus linked to a whole series of state policies such as the neglect of housing, education, health, pensions and welfare services generally for the working class. (p. 36, as quoted in van den Berg and Vergnani, 1986)

Changes in the Family and Women's Roles

Within the black African majority, cultural ideologies have given women a subordinate position, treating them along with children as minors. At the same time, women have always been held in high esteem in their identities as females and as mothers. Although traditional cultures grouped women with children when referring to them, this meant that they were to be given the best care, love, attention, and support. The ways that these societies have honored the birth of each child by nurturing the mother and the baby have underlined the traditional significance and importance of women.

The arrival of Christian missionaries in South Africa brought changes in African family and community structures and relationships. When children were baptized they acquired a new name, foreign to the family because it was unrelated to the specific incidents in family history that formed the basis for the family name. This reduced value given to family origins was further eroded as loyalty shifted to the "missionary fathers," and this in turn affected child-caring procedures. Behavior patterns became dependent on the missionary perception of how life should be organized and lived, leading to a shift away from one of the most treasured concepts in southern African cultures, the concept of child rearing as an experience actively shared by parents with the other adults and older children in the village throughout the stages of the child's development. (See also Chapter 30 on child care in Zimbabwe.)

Another powerful force in undermining traditional family structure has been the introduction of migratory labor. Instead of homes being erected next to the workplace, black African fathers wishing employment in South African industry must leave the homelands to which they have been assigned and live in single sex hostels or labor compounds. Ramphele (1989) describes these hostels as "beds" actually occupied by an average of 2.4 people, only one third of which are bedholders—the men officially renting the space. She describes each of the sections of these barracks as containing

six bedrooms averaging 4m times 3m, leading off a central narrow passageway, four of which contain three beds and two of which have two beds each. Thus for every 16 beds there is one toilet, three cold water taps, and two electric wall sockets. Given the average bed occupancy of 2.4, approximately 38 people share these facilities. (p. 21)

Ramphele documents the fact that some of these "beds" house whole families, the members of which have developed extraordinary creativity in surviving unimaginable space constraints. However, many men live in such conditions without their families, which they have left behind in the "homeland." While the full effect of such conditions on feelings of human dignity and self-image may be difficult to document, the impacts can only be very powerful and must have undermined the capacity of these men to provide material and emotional support for their families.

Under these conditions child caring became exclusively the women's role, and the fathers became "kind" strangers. In some instances the father was eventually alienated from the family, permanently lost to the "bright lights" of the urban modern environment. The woman became the sole provider, protector, and policy maker for the family. With fathers absent from the home for weeks or even months at a time, mothers were burdened with the dual mother/father roles of parenthood.

More recently the increasing severity of economic deprivation among "non-whites" has forced growing numbers of women into the labor market, where available jobs involve long hours at low wages. With industrialization and urbanization this has forced those families not forcibly removed to "homelands" to settle in the sprawling "black" and "coloured" townships that surround the major South African cities, where Black and mixed race

Africans are forced to live by the Group Areas Act of 1950 (which racialized residential areas by statutory group). Apartments and cottages are very small, allowing no room for those extended family members (grandparents, aunts, uncles) who traditionally played such an important child-rearing role in the family. This has forced employed mothers to leave even infants with strange childminders, people without any links to the norms and cultural traditions of the family. Typically the services of these childminders are exchanged for shelter, food, and the minimal wage needed to maintain their own destitute families. In this fashion children have become a secondary commodity, cared for largely by others or left to fend for themselves. Completely lost are the hospitality, respect, love, and loyalty that characterized traditional black African societies. Equally important has been the loss of a means by which to pass our cultural heritage from one generation to the next through traditional legends, folktales, or interesting informative rhymes. The warm fireplace, with all its educational values, has disappeared. The developing child can no longer share the wisdom and the skills of the elders.

These changes in family structure and functioning and the triple burden born by increasing numbers of women, brought about by economic and political forces beyond the control of the vast majority of South Africans, have resulted in a very high need for preschool programs. Such programs must be able to serve two extremely important purposes: the care of very young children in safe, stimulating environments while their parents are at work, and the exposure of older preschoolers to cognitively, linguistically, and socially stimulating environments that will prepare them for primary school.

A DEMOGRAPHIC PROFILE OF THE PRESCHOOL POPULATION

The current population of about 36 million South Africans is expected to increase to about 59 million over the next 25 years. Although the population growth rate is falling for all four statutory groups, the current rate for "blacks" (2.6%) is higher than that for "whites" (.9%), and the projected rate of decline is greater for "whites" than for "blacks." The result of the differences in these growth rates will be that the percentage of the population now designated "white" will decline from 14 to 10 percent over the next quarter century, while the percentage now designated "black" will increase from 75 to 81 percent. In fact, Grobbelaar (1987) projects that by the year 2015 a full 89 percent of all births will be to parents now designated "black," and even the births to those now designated "coloured" and "Asian" will outnumber those to parents currently designated "white."

There were about 6.4 million children age six and younger in South Africa in 1985. By 1995 that number will have increased to 7.5 million. Table

Table 24.1
Distribution of Newborn to Six-Year-Old Children, by Statutory Designation
(1985)

Designation	Number
"White"	538,000
"Coloured"	477,500
"Asian"	143,000
"Black"	25,248,000

[reported by van den Berg and Vergnani (1986) as derived from

Grobbelaar (1983)]

24.1 shows the distribution of those children by statutory designation in
1985.

Van den Berg and Vergnani (1986) point out that, based on existing
estimates of population growth, 17 of every 20 South African children will
be "black" in 1995 (assuming that such designations are still in force at
that time) and thus living in circumstances of political exclusion, social
disadvantage, and economic exploitation. At least half of these children are
living in families with incomes below the poverty line. Van den Berg and
Vergnani cite several South African studies documenting high rates of malnutrition and growth retardation among these children. They are unlikely
to receive proper medical care, often live in inadequate housing, and once
of school age will attend schools staffed by overworked teachers with little
formal teacher training.

CURRENT PROVISION OF PRESCHOOL SERVICES

State provision of preschool services takes place through the complex
administrative structure defined by apartheid policy as described earlier.
Alongside this state "system" is a diverse and increasingly large set of non-
state early childhood initiatives, which attempts to provide services to that
extremely poor and rapidly growing population that is put at great disadvantage by the way that state provision is organized. As will be seen below,
the term "non-state" is used as a heading under which to describe these
services because their diversity and variety prevents the formulation of a
more specific descriptive typology. Before distinguishing the services pro-

vided by these two sectors, we provide an overall picture of provision as a whole.

Table 24.2 presents an overview of the various preschool arrangements serving the 160,000 children officially recorded as enrolled in such programs in 1985. The data indicate official documentation of only about 160,000 preschool children in any sort of preschool provision, which amounts to only 2.5 percent of South African children age six and younger. Moreover, 61 percent (108,600 places) of this service is to "white" children, in a country where the preschool population is 92 percent "non-white." A full 20 percent of the "white" preschool cohort, but only .8 percent of the "non-white" cohort, received the provision reported by these government figures. Thus official provision is inversely proportional to need.

Types of Provision

Four types of child care programs are referred to in Table 24.2. The first of these, shown as "preprimary schools" in the table, are what Short refers to as nursery schools. The first nursery schools were started in the 1930s. Short reports that by 1939 there were 14 nursery schools in South Africa, including one for "black" children, and that by 1955 that number had increased to 150 subsidized schools. Nursery schools are primarily half-day programs seen as educational institutions aimed primarily at middle-class families. They fall under the jurisdiction of the Education Department at the national level. Short (1985) describes them as emphasizing free play and free expression, prevention of maladjustment, and socialization. The reader can see in Table 24.2 that all but 80 of the children served by state/provincial preprimary schools (nursery schools) were "white." The 80 "coloured" children attended the Athlone Nursery School, which receives more attention below under non-state provision.

"Creches" are day care centers, typically in operation for 8 to 11 hours a day. Seventeen centers operated in 1939, and 133 were reported in 1955, 85 of them for "coloured" and "black" children. The number of centers has increased steadily since that time. Short (1985) quotes Webber (1978) as distinguishing day care centers (creches) from nursery schools in the following way: "Unlike the creche, the nursery school supplements the home and is not a substitute for the home. Where the role of the creche is custodial, that of the nursery school is primarily educational" (p. 149). Short goes on to say that

because nursery schools were seen as educational institutions that had to be staffed by qualified teachers, they tended to become privileged middle-class institutions. Day care centers tended to become working-class institutions where the need for day care was greatest, but because parents could not afford the fees necessary to pay qualified teachers, the centers were forced to provide custodial care only. (1985, p. 47)

Table 24.2
Number of South African Children in Preschool Programs, by Statutory Group and Type of Program (1985)

Type of Preschool Program	"White"	"Coloured"	"Asian"	"Black"
Preprimary Schools	74,452	9,959	2,233	11,218
Provincial/State	11,149	80	-	-
Private	63,303	9,879	2,233	11,218
Provincially aided	36,044	8,187	960	9,988
Other private	27,259	1,692	1,273	1,230
Creches	20,001	4,838	185	16,864
After-school Centers	8,403	4	-	-
Preprimary classes at				
Ordinary schools	4,701	685	-	2,400
Special schools	1,043	359	-	170
Total	108,600	15,845	2,418	30,763

Note: "Black" figures exclude national and independent states. Only registered preschool institutions are included.

Source: Central Statistical Services, 4 June 1985: Educational Statistics 1984 and 1985. Summary Statistical News Release P23, Pretoria. Adapted for this chapter from the table on p. 55 of van den Berg and Vergnani, 1986.

Given these distinctions it is not surprising to find that day care centers in most of South Africa fall under the jurisdiction of the Welfare Department, rather than the Education Department.

Pre-primary classes are educational experiences provided primarily for five year olds in classrooms attached to primary schools. Their purpose is defined as school readiness preparation. The provision of this type of program for "non-white" children has increased significantly in the past five years as a result of a commitment by the various education departments (general affairs, "own affairs") to provide a "bridging" year for all five year olds under their jurisdictions.

Much of the actual provision of child care and preschool services in South Africa is not reflected in Table 24.2. The State Statistical Services have not included support provided to either the "national" or the "independent" states, where many black South Africans live. (In the latter case such assistance is considered "foreign" aid.) Van den Berg and Vergnani note that at least three of the "independent states" have begun to increase provision of preschool services in recent years. In Bophuthatswana the traditional split in jurisdiction between the Education Department and the Welfare Department has been done away with, and all preschool services fall under the Department of Education. There are currently at least 400 preschools in Bophuthatswana, with 85 percent of day care centers registered with the Educational Department.

There is also no reference to childminders, who provide the majority of the non-parental care received by South African children. Childminders care for up to six children in their own homes (or in some cases provide care in the child's home). This type of care will be discussed further below, under non-state provision.

State Provision

Very little state, or public, support of preschools comes in the form of direct, public provision of the service itself. In Table 24.2 only the provincial/state preprimary schools (nursery schools) fall into this category of service, and they serve only a relatively small number of children, almost all of them "white."

Most state support comes in the form of aid or subsidy, either education subsidies to the pre-primary programs serving older children, or welfare subsidies for children up to age three. Education aid and subsidies can come in two forms, either as salaries for teachers with approved qualifications or as a per capita subsidy, paid quarterly and covering roughly 20 percent of total costs. Welfare subsidies are paid for younger children, who must therefore be in full-time day care centers (creches). Here again discrimination by racial designation is very much in evidence, with qualifying "white" children receiving 1 South African rand per day, "coloured" and "Asian" children

.8 rand per day, and "black" children nothing, unless the local administrative board sees fit. In addition, in order to qualify for the subsidy, family income must fall below certain limits. But the limits are higher for "white" incomes than for those of "coloured" and "Asian" families, allowing a higher proportion of "white" families to qualify, even though need is greater among "non-white" families. Atmore (1986), in a study of 224 "black" families in the Cape Town area, found that 99.5 percent would qualify for subsidy using the "white" income limits, when in fact the Western Cape Administrative Board pays no subsidies at all to "black" families.

Non-State Provision

Given the inadequate and grossly inequitable provision of preschool services by the national and provincial governments, the voids to be filled by the non-state sector are indeed dauntingly large, especially in a country where the largest and neediest segments of the population are very poor. Understood in the context of an extremely repressive government regime, which can easily perceive community organization on behalf of children and families as a political threat, the program developments described below constitute one of the most extraordinary feats of social organization ever accomplished.

It is impossible to describe adequately the diversity and variety of the non-state organizations invented to address the child care needs of the South African majority. Therefore, we can only provide an overview of some major dimensions of service, in an attempt to help the reader understand alternative sources of funds, innovative approaches to care and support, program resource and coordination activities, and comprehensive community development undertakings. Efforts related to teacher training and to program regulation are described separately, in sections that compare non-state with state provision. The specific program examples given are illustrative; we are not attempting to be comprehensive.

Alternative Funding Sources

One might expect fees paid by parents to be the first recourse in response to inadequate support by the state. Indeed such payment, or in-kind contributions in lieu of payment, is an important source of income for most non-state programs. But these programs are serving the poorest of South Africa's families, and these families make up the vast majority of the total population, so there are severe limits to the revenues able to be generated through parent fees.

A number of foundations and international funding organizations have made very significant contributions to the financing of the innovations described below. One of the earliest to become involved was the Bernard van

Leer Foundation, based at The Hague in Holland and committed to supporting innovative projects designed to improve the opportunities of those children from birth to age eight least able to benefit from "mainstream" educational and development opportunities. The foundation is the principal beneficiary shareholder of the van Leer Companies, which produce packaging materials and products in 30 countries. This foundation has provided financial and technical assistance support to many of the most influential projects working with South African preschool provision, beginning in 1972 with the Athlone Early Learning Center (ELC) and including the Early Learning Resource Unit (based at the Athlone Center), the Border, Chatsworth, and Entrokozweni ELCs, and the rural, farm-based Ntataise project.

The Urban Foundation, set up following the 1976 Soweto uprising, promotes peaceful structural change in an urban context, related to community needs like housing, employment, and education. The foundation has become increasingly involved with preschool provision, in projects ranging from facility construction to caregiver training and child minding. All funds are donated by the private sector, permitting the perception by some of an attempt by Big Business to ensure the perpetuation of the capitalist system in South Africa.

The Rural Foundation for Community Development, established in 1983, aims at a broad range of community development efforts for farm workers. Funds come from the Department of National Health and Population Development, the private sector, and farmers. The foundation supports community "developers," who work with 4 to 40 farms in the development of day care centers (creches) or play groups.

World Vision is an international organization funded via individual sponsorship of children, donations from large companies, and fund-raising campaigns. In 1986 the South African branch was involved in 180 projects, with 70 percent of its funds devoted to preschool provision. Projects must be community based and usually involve churches, missions, or other organizations as co-sponsors. In addition to reaching children and families directly through child sponsorship, funds may be paid to a preschool as salaries or to feed the children.

About 30 percent of the budget of Grassroots, perhaps the most dynamic and fastest growing preschool organization in the Western Cape, is provided by Trade Unions.

ALTERNATIVE APPROACHES TO CARE AND SUPPORT

These innovative approaches extend full-time day care centers beyond custodial care, upgrade the services provided by childminders, and bring information and other supports to parents and children within the family setting.

The educare concept. Educare programs bridge the gap found in the state system between custodial day care and educational nursery schools by integrating full-day care with a high quality education program provided from 7 A.M. to 6 P.M. One of the largest organizations involved with preschool children in South Africa—Grassroots Educare Trust—provides direct professional and financial support to more than 60 educare centers, and, since 1986, to associated home-based educare-using childminders in homes located near the centers. Rooted in the U.S. Headstart program, Grassroots makes use of existing community resources and emphasizes strategies that keep preschool education in the hands of parents. Most programs serve the "coloured" and "black" communities. Considerable attention is given to training paraprofessional teaching staff, using ELRU in-service training materials.

The African Self-Help Association (ASH) provides over half the full-day center care in Soweto, involving at least 36 centers and over 4,000 children. The centers are guided by the Children's Institution Services of the Johannesburg City Health Department. Staff training is provided in various ways, including workshops, courses, and in-service training. Voluntary assistance is provided from the "white" community. Each center has a service committee elected from parents or interested community members, which assists the supervisor, helps with maintenance and fund raising, and has some say in the hiring of staff.

Child-Minding Services

Given the enormous shortfall in center-based preschool places described earlier, many township women offer to mind the children of working parents for a fee. These minders have functioned autonomously, with no coordination, training, supervision, or support. A number of projects have gotten under way over the past 15 years to provide an infrastructure for childminders that addresses these difficulties. Examples include:

Kleinvlei Childminding Project. Started in 1978 in a "coloured" area, these childminders each provide full-day care for a maximum of six children (the legal limit). Some specialize in infants, while others serve older children. Those with older children take them to the Kleinvlei nursery school for part of the day, where the childminders assist in the caregiving and teaching. A supervisor provides in-service training, and a number of the childminders have completed the ELRU TAP course.

Alexandra Childminding Project. Begun in 1981, the project's main activities involve educating childminders, visiting them to give supervision and support, health screening of minders and children, bulk buying, a toy library, monthly childminder meetings, and quarterly parent meetings. A project coordinator synchronizes the work of the minders, staff, and parents, and links them to training programs and workshops. Four part-time supervisors recruit new minders, make home visits, and encourage minders to attend training sessions. More than 50 minders are involved in the network.

The Childminder's Association. This association was formed in Soweto in 1981 to coordinate all child-minding services in and around Johannesburg. It is a voluntary organization that aims to upgrade and standardize services. A staff person is employed to coordinate the services and assist in recruiting new childminders. The association offers ongoing seminars to over 100 members.

Home Educare. Launched in 1986, trained Home Educare Visitors appointed by Educare Centers recruit Home Educare Workers (childminders), who join the staff of the centers as salaried employees. The visitor supports them with advice and training, equipment and food supplies, access to education, health, and welfare resources, admissions and fee management, and relief help.

Home- and Community-Based Education

Biersteker (1987) describes these programs as aimed directly at involving and supporting parents and communities in their roles as primary educators and caregivers of their own children. They include community play groups, parent education groups, and educational home visiting programs for parents and grandparents, in addition to educationally enriched child minding. The approach is seen as a cost-effective way of bringing preschool education to significant numbers of children in oppressed communities.

The most well-known prototype of this approach has been developed by the Early Learning Resource Unit (ELRU). It consists of parent awareness programs (12 brief talks and demonstrations), parent education programs (an in-depth series of workshops), home early learning programs (weekly home visits by a trained home visitor over one to two years), and mother-child group programs (weekly, two-hour, mother-run playgroups, short discussion sessions, and a toy/book lending library).

Preschool Resource Centers

These centers focus on coordination, training, and resource provision. Each center combines goals and activities in a somewhat different way. For instance, the Chatsworth Early Learning Center, serving low-income families in Durban, focuses on home- and community-based playgroups, and helps with center-based facilities. Preschools are viewed as a vehicle for community development, rather than ends in themselves. Their main activities include a mobile playbus program, a teacher and toy library, home-based playgroups, parent workshops and training, a health program, and management committee training. Increasingly, training has become the main focus of the center.

The Border Early Learning Center, located in East London, was established to provide coordination, training and resources for all preschool efforts in the Border area. This ELC also sees training as the most important element of its work. The Teacher Aide Program (TAP) involves weekly two-hour sessions for 11 months plus monthly workshops on Saturdays. Other BELC activities include a demonstration preschool, a yearly playfair, a preschool shop, and a theme box library. A day care advisory service has been established to help match children with caregivers, and counsel and train new day care mothers.

The Entokozweni ELC has branches in Moletsane, Soweto and in Alexandra. This ELC concentrates more on direct service, but provides the teacher training needed by the staff of those programs. Services include a baby program, nursery schools, a school readiness program, a large childminding project, home visitors, bulk buying and toy lending, and TAP training.

Coordination

A number of organizations have been created to facilitate cooperation among preschool-related projects and coordination of those efforts. For instance, the Association for Preschool Education, Care and Training (ASPECT) links various organizations and individuals in the Western Cape interested in the preschool field. ASPECT runs several large workshops each year, produces an annual newsletter, and provides an information and consultation service.

The Preschool Regional Liaison Committee (RLC), a voluntary association based in Port Elizabeth, attempts to coordinate and assist all the child care and preschool organizations in that area. Meeting twice a year, RLC members share ideas and resources and get to know each other. Similar committees have been established in Bloemfontein and Greater Durban.

The Southern African Association for Early Childhood Education (SAAECE) is probably the most widely representative organization in the preschool arena in South Africa. Founded in 1939 to buttress the nursery school movement, it now has broadened its mandate and has national headquarters in Pretoria. The SAAECE Council includes representatives of various societies for early childhood education, local authorities, state departments, and other national organizations. SAAECE has ten local societies for early childhood education (ECEs) that function quite separately, carrying out a variety of activities, from lecture series and courses to certification of centers maintaining approved standards, magazine publishing, and the running of toy libraries.

Consulting Support Organizations

These types of organizations support community-initiated projects in a variety of ways. For instance, the Western Cape Foundation for Community Work supports day care projects both administratively and educationally, including auditing services, administrative training for local committees, and educare training for workers. The foundation also runs two home-based projects and does more general promotion for the communities in which it is involved.

The Centre for Social Development (CSD), Rhodes University, provides assistance in establishing community-based facilities, offers in-service training, provides home-care facilities for deprived children, trains local leaders in management and fund raising, helps communities with job creation, and encourages students to become involved in local communities.

Community Development Organizations

These programs, operating in rural areas, use preschools as one means of enhancing the lives of rural women and the villages in which they live. The Zenzele Women's Association draws its membership from Zulu-speaking communities in Natal/Kwazulu. Zenzele (meaning "help yourself") clubs have established a substantial number of preschools, each serving about 35 children, in centers provided by the rural communities. Field workers chosen by the community are trained in a wide range of subjects (gardening, toy making, basic health, child care, etc.) and travel from club to club to give basic training and motivate members.

The Phambile Mawethu Community Development Program is a comprehensive community development project located in the Ciskei, one of the "independent states." Starting in 1984 people in various villages were consulted about the possible establishment of various community projects. One result was the opening of 40 preschools, in rural—often virtually inaccessible—villages. People nominated by the villagers were selected to undergo a TAP training program with the help of the Border ELC. The Ciskei Department of Education has paid the salaries of these teachers, and huts provided by the communities provide the premises. Malnutrition led in 1985 to a feeding scheme at the preschools and local primary schools, and the introduction of school and community vegetable gardens has been supported by local agricultural extension officers. Health training has been another important emphasis. The long-term goal of the project is to establish in 140 villages a preschool center, a health center, home industry/small business, a primary school, a community garden, and a community-run shop.

THE EDUCATION AND TRAINING OF CAREGIVERS AND TEACHERS

Short (1985) describes three training courses established for "white" nursery school teachers at training colleges in Johannesburg (1938), Cape Town (1939), and the University of Pretoria (1940). These programs ran either for three years after ten years of basic schooling, or they were a one-year post-graduate course. Short reports that, while remaining small, these training colleges were powerful in the nursery school movement and that until 1969 the University of Pretoria was the only South African university involved in preschool education.

The Anglican Mission established a training course for black African teachers at a nursery school in Johannesburg that was recognized by the Transvaal Native Education Department in 1938. This was a three-year course following the first eight years of schooling. Progress was made in the 20 years between 1938 and 1958, through the Transvaal Native Education Department, the Bantu Education Department, and the Natal Native Education Department. But in 1958 the mission schools that served as bases for these training programs were phased out by the government, leading to a decade-long lapse in training opportunities of any kind. The government started a one-year course for preschool assistants in Soweto in 1969, and similar courses—requiring eight years of schooling or a certificate in home management—have since been established in Rustenburg (Transvaal) and Umlazi (Durban).

"Coloured" nursery assistants were trained at the Athlone Nursery School in Cape Town as early as 1952. This training, which lasted 18 months and required eight years of basic education, continued—with a five-year break between 1957 and 1962—until 1972, when it became a two-year program leading to a nursery school teacher's certificate. The center has accepted 15 to 20 students a year.

Short reports that the training of "Asian" nursery assistants has developed very slowly, largely because the need has been small. She mentions a course for nursery assistants now being run at the M. L. Sultan Technical College in Durban.

Short characterizes the situation in the mid–1960s as one involving "a shortage of trained preschool workers of all kinds and at all levels, and inadequate training for African and Coloured staff" (1985, p. 50). In 1969 the Athlone Early Learning Center was established, and this was followed in 1978 by the creation of the Early Learning Resource Unit (ELRU).

It is important to recognize that the ELRU approach, which involves the design and implementation of innovative non-formal training programs, came about as a direct result of the lack of commitment and demonstrated inadequacies of state provision in the area of teacher education and caregiver training. ELRU programs include:

• The Teacher Aide Program (TAP), referred to earlier, which upgrades teacher aides already in the field using a set of four "Learning through Play" handbooks and workbooks. Training approaches include (1) a weekly part-time course at Athlone ELC, (2) gatherings of people from various centers for group sessions, practical work, and evaluation done in their own centers, and (3) staff training by center supervisors with ELRU materials and under ELRU supervision.

- The Preschool Training Program (PTP), which is a training program for center supervisors taken part time for a year.
- The Baby Care Program (BCP), for those caring for children under age two.
- The Home-Based Educational Development Program, a one year, part-time program for people, like home visitors, health workers, and community workers, who are interested in improving care and education in the home.

STANDARDS AND REGULATIONS

There is not enough space in a brief overview of this sort to devote much to discussion of this subject in the South African context. However, it is important to recognize that this is another arena in which innovations in the non-state sector have been required to compensate for barriers created by state government. Van den Berg and Vergnani (1986) state that "state preschool provision is characterized by insistence on *standards* that *are inflexible and totally unrealistic* for the great majority of those who wish to provide preschool services for their children, thus further consolidating inequality and deprivation" (p. 60).

The Children's Act of 1960 requires that any place of care serving more than six children is to register with the relevant welfare authority. This requires a health certificate, which in turn requires conformity with a great array of space, equipment, and staffing requirements, most of which are completely beyond the reach of many community-based programs. Thus non-state initiatives designed to provide the services the state is unwilling to provide are hamstrung by red tape and stringent standardization and regulation. Van den Berg and Vergnani point out that "stringent norms and convoluted procedures eliminate those who do not enjoy the knowledge about how to proceed from any chance of assistance from the state" (1986, p. 64).

Projects and organizations not financially dependent on the state have developed much more reasonable standards and design technical assistance to assist programs in attaining those standards. This is particularly evident in some of the "independent" states, which have some control over the requirements of the Departments of Education and Welfare. May (1987) reports that in Bophuthatswana until 1985 criteria for registration of creches (day care centers) were simply:

- good drinking water on site
- adequate and hygienic toilets
- shelter that was safe and not overcrowded
- adequate food
- minimum of one staff member with five-phase ECE in-service training
- a vegetable garden

Stricter requirements were introduced in 1986, but these still are tied to what is feasible within the resources of the local communities.

STRENGTHS AND SHORTCOMINGS

Understood in the context of an extraordinarily repressive government regime, the non-state provision of preschool services in South Africa represents one of the truly extraordinary feats of social organization accomplished in the modern era. This remarkably creative, large-scale response on behalf of the majority of South Africans provides a solid framework and a number of models for preschool projects in a non-racial, democratic society, and in fact for any social programs developed in post-apartheid South Africa. Most importantly, it demonstrates the clear understanding by the South African majority that preschool children and their families deserve, and society requires, community support for children in a variety of forms (centers, home-based services, etc.). The educare concept, the resource center approach, non-formal training programs, and a broader community development orientation will all be vital to the further development of this community mobilization and support.

But for all its strengths, there are many shortcomings to be found in the South African provision of preschool services, most of them legacies of apartheid. Even assuming that the racialist, "own affairs" approach to state service development and delivery is dismantled with apartheid, much needs to be done to improve the existing system. Van der Berg and Vergnani (1987) identify a number of general characteristics of the current service organization and delivery that must be addressed in future efforts, including:

1. The diverse array of government departments and bodies involved.
2. The insistence on standards that are inflexible and totally unrealistic, and the inhibiting bureaucratic requirements. The need is for program standards that protect the health and safety of children while leaving programs room to develop creative ways to maximize the use of available resources.
3. The lack of coordination and cooperation, not only between what are now state and non-state providers, but also among the various participants in the non-state sector.
4. Variation in the quality of non-state provision. Some programs are outstanding, while others offer little more than dedication and commitment. The overcrowding, low salaries, and lack of access to training that are legacies of a segregated system can be addressed quite quickly with the judicious application of more resources.
5. The necessity of a comprehensive, integrated approach to the needs of children whose housing, health, and nutritional needs are as great as their need for constructive social experiences and stimulating cognitive activity. Models for such an approach can already be found in the non-state sector.

6. The sheer shortage of provision. The question becomes how to provide services of reasonable quality to as many children as possible in as short a time span as possible.

7. The need for adequate funding mechanisms and a sharply increased flow of funds to programs using approaches with a record of success.

8. The importance of recognizing the value of "support systems" (home based and parent focused) as well as "delivery systems" (centers and childminders).

9. The desperate shortage of trained staff.

The winds of change are indeed blowing through South Africa. Most people hope that those winds will bring with them the emergence of a non-racial, democratic society. The social and political convulsions and deeply rooted divisions of the present suggest that such an outcome is by no means certain. What is clear, however, is that the roots of such a social order can be found in what is currently referred to as the "non-state" sector of the South African preschool "system." It would be fitting that organizations and approaches like Grassroots, Educare, ELRU, the South African Association for Early Childhood Education, Zenzele, and Phambile Mawethu should lead the way to a new South Africa, for that would be in the tradition of at least one great prophet, who predicted that "a little child shall lead them."

NOTES

The authors are especially indebted to Owen van den Berg and Tania Vergnani, from whose 1986 report and 1987 edited book of readings much of the material for this chapter was abstracted.

1. The Zulu, Xhosa, Sotho, Tswana, Shangaan, Swazi, Venda, and Ndebele tribes. Of these, the first four range in membership from 2 to 5.5 million people, with the other four containing between .5 and .9 million members.

2. In order to solidify economic and political control through racial separation, the white minority government has assigned every South African to one of four categories: "white," "coloured," "Asian," and "black." In this chapter these terms will be used in quotation marks to indicate that they refer to political rather than cultural designations.

3. Transkei, Bophuthatswana, Ciskei, Venda, Lebowa, KwaNdebele, Qwaqwa, Gazankulu, KwaZulu, and KaNgwane. The first four of these had been formally granted "independence" between 1976 and 1981. By 1986 the other six had been defined as "self-governing."

REFERENCES

Adam, H. and Giliomee, H. (1979). *The Rise and Crisis of Afrikaner Power*. Cape Town: David Philip.

Atmore, E. (1986). "Investigation into welfare subsidies payable to "white," "coloured," and "black" children." Preliminary unpublished report for the AS-PECT executive, Cape Town.

Atmore, E. (1987). "The myth of separate but equal provision of pre-school educare and care." Unpublished symposium paper. Pp. 174–178.

Bailey, M. "The development of a preschool child educare support structure in Natal/Kwazulu." In Owen van den Berg and Tania Vergnani (Eds.), *Door to the Future: The Preschool Child in South Africa.* Bellville, S. A.: The University of the Western Cape.

Biersteker, L. (1987). "Home-based alternatives in early childhood education." In Owen van den Berg and Tania Vergnani (Eds.), *Door to the Future: The Preschool Child in South Africa.* Bellville, S.A.: The University of the Western Cape.

Cock, J., Emdon, E. and Klugman, B. (1984). "Child care and the working mother: A sociological investigation of a sample of urban African women." Carnegie Conference Paper No. 115.

Grobbelaar, J. (1983). *Projections and Analysis of the South African Population for the Period 1980–2015.* Stellenbosch: Stellenbosch University Institute for Futures Research.

Grobbelaar, J. (1987). "The potential pre-primary school population of South Africa for the period 1980–2015." In Owen van den Berg and Tania Vergnani (Eds.), *Door to the Future: The Preschool Child in South Africa.* Bellville, S.A.: The University of the Western Cape.

Hulley, J. (1987). "Talent sharing: The story of "Zenzele" in Natal." In Owen van den Berg and Tania Vergnani (Eds.), *Door to the Future: The Preschool Child in South Africa.* Bellville, S.A.: The University of the Western Cape.

Lapping, B. (1989). *Apartheid: A History.* New York: George Brazillier.

Malepa, M. (1987). "Entokozweni Early Learning and Community Services Centre: Progress Report." In Owen van den Berg and Tania Vergnani (Eds.), *Door to the Future: The Preschool Child in South Africa.* Bellville, S.A.: The University of the Western Cape.

Masango, L. (1987). "The Alexandria childminding project: Parent involvement." In Owen van den Berg and Tania Vergnani (Eds.), *Door to the Future: The Preschool Child in South Africa.* Bellville, S.A.: The University of the Western Cape.

May, H. (1987). "Early childhood education in the Republic of Bophuthatswana." In Owen van den Berg and Tania Vergnani (Eds.), *Door to the Future: The Preschool Child in South Africa.* Bellville, S.A.: The University of the Western Cape.

Mermelstein, D. (Ed.). (1987). *The Anti-Apartheid Reader.* New York: Grove Press.

Ramphele, M. (1989). "Empowerment and the politics of space: The hostel dwellers of South Africa." *Radcliffe Quarterly,* June, pp. 20–24.

Rickards, J. (1987). "Grassroots." In Owen van den Berg and Tania Vergnani (Eds.), *Door to the Future: The Preschool Child in South Africa.* Bellville, S.A.: The University of the Western Cape.

Short, A. (1985). *Seeking Change: Early Childhood Education for the Disadvantaged in South Africa.* Ypsilanti, Mich.: The High/Scope Press.

van den Berg, O. and Vergnani, T. (1986). *Providing Services for Preschool Children in South Africa.* Bellville, S.A.: The University of the Western Cape.

van den Berg, O. and Vergnani, T. (1987). "Preschool provision in South Africa: An introduction." In Owen van den Berg and Tania Vergnani (Eds.), *Door to the Future: The Preschool Child in South Africa*. Bellville, S.A.: The University of the Western Cape.

van den Berg, O. and Vergnani, T. (Eds.). (1987). *Door to the Future: The Preschool Child in South Africa*. Bellville, S.A.: The University of the Western Cape.

Webber, V. (1978). *An Outline of the Development of Preschool Education in South Africa, 1930–1977*. Pretoria: South African Association for Early Childhood Education.

25

SWEDEN

Lars Gunnarsson

In 1985 the Swedish Parliament (Riksdagen) voted in support of a proposal by the Social Democratic Government that by 1991 all children between one and a half to six years old have the right to a place in public child care, as long as their parents worked or studied. If this goal is reached, and time has yet to tell, it represents the completion of a National Child Care Program that began at an organized level back in the early 1960s, when women were encouraged to enter the labor market in larger and larger numbers, creating a need for child care outside of the home.

The shape, content, and financing of this comprehensive child care program have been widely discussed by politicians, administrators, and parents for 30 years, and this discussion continues. But two stabilizing factors have been particularly important to the development of the program. First, child care policies have been closely linked to other family support policies, such as financial support to families with young children (child allowances, rent subsidies, parental leave programs, and public health care). Second, the Social Democratic Party has formed the government during all but six of these 30 years (the exception being the period between 1976 and 1982), allowing this party to put its ideas into action in ways that would not have been possible had the political situation been more unstable.

Following a long-lasting Swedish tradition, the government has launched several national commissions over the years that have been instructed to work out the foundations for political decisions aimed at creating an integrated family support system. Official reports from the National Commission on Children's Living Conditions and the National Commission of Family Support have all contributed substantially to political and public discussions in the area and affected the present status of family and child care policies in Sweden.

THE DIFFERENT FORMS OF PUBLIC CHILD CARE

Full-time care for preschool-age children is provided in the *day care center* for children whose parents work or study, or for children judged to be in "need for special support." Day care centers are usually open weekdays from 7 A.M. until 7 P.M. with some local variations. Most children spend seven to ten hours per day in the center. The *parent cooperative center* is a recent variation of this full-time, state-subsidized care center in Sweden. Parental involvement and participation are the cornerstones of this type of child care.

Full-time care is also provided in public *family day care homes,* where the family day care mother takes care of children from birth to age 12 in her own home, while their parents are working or studying. The children spend varying parts of the day in the family day care home, sometimes including evenings or weekends if parent work schedules include "odd hours." Another fairly recently developed alternative is the *"three-family system,"* which is formally classified as a family day care home. In this alternative, a children's nurse is hired to take care of three or four children in the home of one of the three participating families.

Part-time preschools (kindergartens) are intended for children in the four- to six-year-old age span. All Swedish municipalities are required to provide this type of part-time experience for their six year olds, and four and five year olds are accepted into the programs when places are available. The children usually spend three hours per day, five days a week in these pre- schools.

After-School Homes ("Fritidshem") are open to children 7 to 12 years of age whose parents are working or studying outside the home. Children enrolled in this program spend those parts of the day when they are not in school in the after-school home, and they also attend during school holidays. Due to shortages of places in many municipalities, only 7 to 9 year olds are eligible for this type of care in those locales.

"Open Preschools" are available to those preschool-aged children who are not enrolled in other forms of public child care. The municipality pro- vides space, equipment, and a preschool teacher, who assists parents who are staying home with their children to meet other parents in the same situation, while their children have the opportunity to interact with play- mates. These settings also provide opportunities for private or public family day care mothers to get together and share their experiences, or to ask the preschool teacher for advice. Parents or family day care mothers do not have to sign up to participate in the open preschool. They can drop in with

Table 25.1
Participation by Type of Care

Type of care	No. of children	Percent of children
Public child care	350,000	47%
Day care center	248,000	34%
Family day care	102,000	13%
Private child care	380,800	53%
Own home	330,400	45%
Out-of home care	50,400	7%

Source: Official Statistics of Sweden (1991)

their children at their own convenience, but they are not allowed to leave the children. They must stay and participate.

SWEDISH CHILD CARE COVERAGE

Table 25.1 shows the number and percentages of children from birth to age six in various forms of Swedish child care. As indicated in Table 25.1, 47 percent of all children under the age of seven are in full-time public child care, two thirds of them in a public day care center. Of the remaining 53 percent, most are taken care of at home by one of the parents (usually the mother). Seven percent of Swedish preschool children are taken care of in some private out-of-home arrangement (private family day care, relatives). The table does not provide any information about the use of "open pre-schools," of which there are over 1,600 in Sweden. A recent survey shows that 201,000 children and their caregivers visited an open preschool one or more times in January 1991.

Table 25.1 shows the distribution across different types of child care arrangements for *all* children under the age of seven. But the goal of the government is to provide public child care to those children "whose parents work or study." When we examine the statistics only for those children whose parents work or study, we find that 57 percent are in public child care, 11 percent are in care outside of the home but not in public care, and 36 percent are cared for in their homes by their parents. This last group also includes those six year olds who do not have a place in full-time child care but who participate in part-time preschool (kindergarten) three hours per day, five days per week. It also includes those infants taken care of in the home by their parents during the period of paid parental leave.

It is also worth pointing out that the older the child gets the higher the probability that he or she will be in a day care center, as compared to a family day care home, and large urban areas have considerably more places available in public day care centers than in public family day care homes, whereas the reverse tends to be true in rural, sparsely populated areas.

PERSONNEL AND EDUCATION

Four different types of personnel work in the Swedish public child care settings. Preschool teachers, children's nurses, and family day care mothers are hired by the local authorities to take care of children in day care centers, part-time preschools, open preschools, and family day care homes. "Leisure-time teachers" work with the 7 to 12 year olds in after school centers. The educational background and training of these four groups of staff members vary, as do the settings they work in and their professional responsibilities.

The *preschool teacher* completes a two and a half year college-level educational program, which combines practical fieldwork in centers and part-time preschools with theoretical courses focusing mainly on early child development, family sociology, teaching methods, arts, and crafts. After graduation, the preschool teachers are hired to work in day care centers, parent cooperative centers, part-time preschools, or open preschools. They are more likely to work with the three- to six-year-old children than with the newborn to three year olds, and they often find themselves working in teams with children's nurses, the other major staff category in these settings.

Children's nurses get their education in the Swedish secondary school, which has a nursing program as one of its two-year tracks. In addition to offering compulsory courses in mathematics, language, and social sciences, this program combines theory and practice to provide the students with the basic skills in child nursing and developmental psychology. After graduation these staff work in the day care centers, usually with the younger children. On the average, the salary of a children's nurse is about 90 percent of that of a preschool teacher.

Some children's nurses might also work in the homes of parents with young children, as part of the recently developed "three-family system." However, most of the public child care in home settings "away from home" is provided by *municipal family day care mothers*, of which there were approximately 34,000 in 1985. There is no centrally developed educational training program for family day care mothers, although according to the recommendations of the National Board of Health and Welfare, family day care mothers "should all, in the long run, have training equivalent to that of a children's nurse" (Broberg, 1989). Many municipalities offer 50 to 100 hours of mandatory course work as an introduction to the family day care occupations and provide guidance and support through specifically hired supervisors. The family day care home is always inspected and approved by the local authority prior to the hiring of the family day care mother.

Swedish children start school at the age of seven. During their elementary school years, they usually have classes from 8 A.M. to 1:30 P.M. every weekday. If their parents are working, they might be offered a place in an after-school center, where they will spend the afternoon with a group of 15 to 18 other school-aged children and two *leisure-time teachers* (Fritidspedagoger). The education and training of these child care workers is very similar to that of the preschool teachers—often the two groups of students take courses together.

Each day care center has a *director*, who is formally responsible for the activities in the center. This person is usually an experienced preschool teacher who has had some additional administrative in-service training. Center directors in a given area normally meet on a regular basis to share experiences, compare budgets and planned activities, and discuss problems of common interest. One such topic of discussion might be the difficulty in attracting men to work in the child care sector. In 1984, only 6 percent of the staff members in Swedish day care centers were men, not including a small number of young men who, as conscientious objectors, were doing compulsory public service in centers as an alternative to military training. It is a widely held belief among administrators and child care workers that more men in child care would not only diminish shortages in personnel supply, but also contribute both to making the day care centers a better work environment for adults, and most importantly, give the children a much needed opportunity to spend time in daily activities with adults of both sexes. Especially for preschool-age boys, the lack of same-sex adult role models working with children is seen as an obstructing factor in the effort to change traditional sex-role attitudes.

THE SWEDISH FRAMEWORK

From an Agrarian to a Post-Industrial Society

Although ranked fourth in Europe in geographical area, following Russia, France, and Spain, Sweden has a rather small population. Most of the 8.5 million Swedes live in the southern half of the country, especially in and around the three large metropolitan areas of Stockholm, Göteborg, and Malmö. The northern half of the country is sparsely populated, but the mining, lumbering, and water power available in this area of mountains, forests, and rivers have long represented one of the cornerstones of the Swedish economy, producing much of the raw materials and energy for the processing industries further south. Agriculture is concentrated in the southernmost parts of Sweden, where large, high-technology farms produce grain

Table 25.2

Distribution of Swedish Labor Force by Sector (1890, 1950, and 1980)

	1890	1950	1980
Agriculture and forestry	63%	20%	6%
Industry and construction	22%	42%	34%
Services, retail trade, transport, and communications	14%	38%	60%

(Source: Adapted from Moen, 1989, p. 23)

and meat in amounts well exceeding the needs of the population. In fact, advanced technology and these large cost-effective, production units of the Swedish agricultural industry have largely eliminated the small, family-based farms, which for hundreds of years were at the core of Swedish society.

Over the past 100 years the children of Swedish farmers, fishermen, and lumberjacks and their families have moved in large numbers to urban, newly industrialized areas, growing up to work in the factories and, later, in the expanding service sector. During this same period, Sweden has gone from being a country of emigrants (several hundred thousand Swedes, who could no longer make a living as farmers, left for the United States before the turn of the century), to becoming a country of immigrants. An estimated 10 percent of the population in the Sweden of today is first- or second-generation immigrants, mostly from southern Europe or Finland, who left their countries to find factory jobs in Swedish industry.

This transition from an agricultural to an industrial society, and from an industrial to a "post-industrial" society with a large service sector, is clearly illustrated in Table 25.2. While in 1890 more than 60 percent of the labor force was found in agriculture and forestry, that percentage had dropped to a mere 6 percent in 1980. In the service sector, the pattern is the reverse: today more than 60 percent of the labor force is employed in the areas of service, retail trade, transport, and communication.

If a "post-industrial society" is a society "marked by the ascendancy of the service sector, with attendant economic, technological, and social changes that transform the character of contemporary life" (Moen, 1989, p. 17), then Sweden clearly is an example of such a society. Moreover, the expansion of the service sector is largely a function of the increased number of people employed in the *public* service sector as administrators, teachers, nurses, child care workers, and the like. The public provision of child care and care for the elderly, of health care and of free education is part of the comprehensive Swedish social welfare system. The work carried out within these public domains is to a large extent performed by women.

The Changing Roles of Women

Over the past 25 years Swedish women have left the "homemaker" role and entered the labor market in full strength. In some cases they have done so out of a need to contribute in a situation of strained family economy and in other cases out of a desire to change the traditional male-female role division and work toward the development of more egalitarian gender roles. Several factors have influenced this change: (a) there has been a shortage of labor, and so it has been relatively easy to find a job; (b) costs of living have increased, making it difficult for a family to live on only one salary; (c) separate income tax assessment for husbands and wives (as of 1971) that has made it more profitable economically for women to work outside the home; (d) changing gender role ideologies in society at large, instigated to a large extent by strong women's organizations; and (e) the efforts of society to create a comprehensive support system for families with young children, a system designed to enable mothers and fathers to work outside of the home while at the same time feeling reassured that they could fulfill their roles as parents in a way that would give their children a good start in life.

Table 25.3 shows the change in labor force participation between 1970 and 1985 for men and women in the 20 to 64 age range. In 1985, 78 percent of Swedish women were in the labor force. The percentage for women with preschool-aged children is even larger (86%). But, as shown in Table 25.3, 43 percent of women are working part time, compared to only 6 percent of men. The ideological shift toward more equal gender roles, involving equal rights and responsibilities for both men and women to work outside of the home and to take care of children and domestic work, clearly has not affected the behavior of fathers as much as that of mothers. One out of three fathers does make use of the paid parental leave system during their child's first year, staying home to take care of the child for a month or two, and mothers and fathers are sharing about equally the right and responsibility to stay home and take care of a sick child (with 90 percent of salary losses covered by parental leave insurance). Moreover, recent research shows that fathers are increasing their share of domestic work when it comes to child care and cooking. Nevertheless, the step from theory to practice seems to be a long one for most Swedish men, and women are still doing most of the housework in addition to working outside of the home. Given this situation, a part-time job might be more attractive for women than working 40 hours per week and then using up their remaining energy on shopping, cooking, and cleaning. We might have to wait until the next generation before "equal rights and responsibilities" are lived up to in practice, but

Table 25.3
Male and Female Work Force Participation (Ages 20–64)

		1970	1985
Men:	Total percentage in labor force	85%	84%
	Full-time	79%	78%
	Part-time	6%	6%
Women:	Total percentage in labor force	50%	78%
	Full-time	38%	35%
	Part-time	12%	43%

(Source: Adapted from Ericsson, 1988, p. 125.)

the changes that have taken place in the lives of Swedish families during the past generation are already quite substantial. The "traditional Western family," with mothers as homemakers and fathers as breadwinners, is all but gone in Sweden. It has been replaced not by one "post-industrial family," but by several forms of families, each with special strengths and weaknesses.

The 20th-century transformation of the economic structure in Swedish society has been coupled with a lowered fertility rate, a decrease in family size, and the development of several different forms of families. Although the Swedish population has doubled over the past 100 years, from 4.3 to 8.5 million people, only the fact that immigration has been substantial has kept the population from decreasing during certain periods in the second half of the century. After several decades of declining fertility rates, reaching a low point in 1983 with 1.6 children for each women in her childbearing years, that trend now seems to be broken, and in 1988 the number of children born was the highest in 15 years. According to recent population estimates, this new trend is likely to continue, and a present rate of 2.1 places the Swedish birthrate close to the top among countries in Europe.

The Swedish Social Support System

To many people in other parts of the world, Sweden is probably thought of as a small "socialist" welfare state way up north, with high taxes, the

Nobel Prize, the midnight sun, and good athletes. The economic system in
Sweden is, however, clearly "capitalistic," based on principles of the market
economy, and about 90 percent of all companies are privately owned. Although a monarchy, with a king and a court, the form of government is
parliamentary, with elections to the Swedish Riksdag taking place every
third year. The "socialist" label often attached to Sweden is probably based
more on the fact that Sweden over the years has developed publicly funded
social welfare policies, which provide individuals and families with support
in a variety of ways. Public social insurances and health care, free education,
and a comprehensive system of supports to families with young children
are parts of these social welfare policies, financed by direct and indirect
taxes. Companies pay "employer taxes," sometimes earmarked for certain
social services, and a Swede working full time pays an average of 30 to 40
percent of his income in direct taxes. In addition, Sweden has a indirect,
23 percent state sales tax placed on goods and services.

There seems to be a general consensus among Swedes, and among most
of the political parties in Sweden, that while expensive, this comprehensive,
social welfare system is a necessary prerequisite for the establishment of a
society based on equality and a fair distribution of resources. The expanding
public child care program is part of that system, as are the paid parental
leave program, child allowances, state guaranteed child alimonies to single
parents, rent subsidies, and other state supports directed specifically toward
families with children. Some of these supports, like monthly child allowances, prenatal care, or free meals in the schools, are granted to all families
with children. Others, like income-related housing benefits or priority rights
to places in public child care for handicapped children are based on the
specific needs of individual families or groups of families.

The *paid parental leave program* is a "parental insurance" that entitles
parents (mothers or fathers) to stay home from work and take care of their
infants during a specified time period. The program includes several different
components. Established in 1974 as a modification of the maternity leave
program of 1937, it has been extended step-wise since then. When fully
implemented the program will give parents the right to stay home caring
for their child during 18 months following the birth of the child. (In 1991,
the insurance covered 12 months.) Parents themselves choose whether the
mother or the father is to become the caretaker; they both have the right
to take on the task. The parent who stays home to take care of the child is
economically compensated by the state with 90 percent of his or her salary.
To qualify for this compensation the parent has to have been employed for
at least nine months prior to the birth of the child. Other benefits from the
parental insurance include the right for fathers to ten days paid leave when
a new child is born, to take care of other children in the family, and to be
available as support to the mother. It also gives parents the right to take

up to 60 days off from work, with 90 percent pay, to care for a sick child at home and the right to spend two days per year with pay, in child care settings or schools to help the child better adjust to these settings.

All in all, the extended paid parental leave program is likely to make family requests for infant care outside of the home quite limited in the future. Most parents will make use of their right to stay home and take care of their babies from birth to 18 months, hereby removing the pressure on society to provide public child care outside of the home for these children. Recent statistics indicate that this is already happening to a large extent.

HISTORICAL ROOTS AND IDEOLOGIES

In a historical perspective, public child care is a fairly recent phenomenon in Sweden. The first infant creche was opened in 1854, but for more than a century the number of available places in centers was very limited. In 1935 about 4,000 children had a place in a creche. The major purpose of these early programs was to give inexpensive care to poor children whose mothers worked outside the home. These creches were usually organized and run by foundations or private organizations and were based on charity. In 1944, when limited public support was introduced, the name was changed from creche to day care center, and the National Board of Health and Welfare became the new supervising authority.

Before 1962, the major objective of day care centers was to care for the children of single mothers, as an alternative to placement in foster homes. Care in foster homes, where children were removed from their mothers and placed to live with a new family, was gradually replaced by care in foster day care homes, or family day care homes, where the children spent week-days in the home of a family day care mother but continued to live with their biological parents.

Foster homes, day care centers, and family day care homes were linked by a common objective. They were to care for children of single parents, and their presence was also based on socio-political considerations. Alleviating poverty was the primary political goal during the first six decades of the century, and in this respect the development of a public child care program was only a small piece of a much larger puzzle. Direct financial support to all families with children, paid in the form of child allowances, is an example of a reform that was more in line with the political aspirations of that period.

The link to social policy was made quite clear when the National Child Care Commission presented the results of its efforts in 1949. The attitudes toward public child care were hesitant, and only social reasons, such as support for single mothers, were accepted as justification for expansion of the system.

Only after 1962 did a systematic effort to build new day care centers begin. In 1965 about 15,000 preschool-aged children had a place in a public day care center or family day care home. In 1991 this number had reached 350,000, or 47 percent of the newborn to six year age group.

A different type of full-day institution was developed alongside creches, albeit on a small scale. The first infant schools started in 1836 had specific pedagogical goals in addition to social motives. These infant schools were few in number and were transformed eventually into creches. Their educational program was similar to those developed somewhat later in another parallel form of "child care," the kindergarten.

The first kindergartens in Sweden were started in 1890, with an educational program based on the ideas about children's development and learning of the German pedagogue Friedrich Froebel. Central to the Froebel pedagogical system for working with small children was the emphasis on children's play. Play provided children with opportunities to experience and construct their outer and inner worlds, and playing was seen as the child's tool to true development.

But Froebel also stressed that kindergartens were only to be seen as complements to the home and the family, and children were only supposed to spend parts of their days in these pedagogical settings. Part-time kindergartens represented a stimulating addition to home care, rather than alternatives emanating from social policy considerations. They were used mainly by families with financial resources above average, where mothers were not working outside of the home. It is worth pointing out, however, that the kindergarten movement was not only to be seen as a service to children from the upper and middle classes. In the period from 1904 to 1930, People's Kindergartens recruited children from socially disadvantaged families, in an attempt to "teach the children of the poor the importance of saving, contentedness, and good taste" (Johansson, 1983, author's translation). This form of social work grew out of a wish to dampen the growing class conflicts following the rapid process of industrialization and urbanization. In the words of the chairperson of the Swedish Froebel Association: "In these times, when hatred and envy between classes are boiling, there is so much the true kindergarten conductor can do, in her little circle, to quiet the hatred by showing that there is understanding, and that there is a willingness to help and to ease the burdens of the poor" (cf. Johansson, 1983, author's translation).

To some extent, the pedagogical system designed by Froebel has had to compete with the more structured, goal-oriented and work-based ideas introduced at the turn of the century by Maria Montessori. Montessori-based programs continue to operate in Sweden, but on a small scale. It is probably the adaptation to modern theories of child development, represented chiefly by Gesell, Erikson, and Piaget, that has helped Froebel-inspired methods of organizing daily activities in child care settings to survive and to continue to influence today's programs in early childhood care and education.

Yesterday's creches, foster homes, day care centers, kindergartens, and play schools had different roots and purposes. Today the situation is different. Following the report of the 1968 National Commission on Child Care and the 1975 National Preschool Act, the label "preschool" is now attached both to full-time and part-time child care in day care centers and to part-time preschools. The unified focus on care, socialization, and education implicit in this change of label was made explicit in 1987 by the National Board of Health and Welfare with the presentation of the Educational Program for Preschools.

The Shift Toward More Local Control

The "Educational Program for Preschools" formulates the goals of Swedish public child care and presents guidelines and recommendations to the local municipalities, which are responsible for implementing these goals. The program is aimed specifically at the activities in public child care centers (also referred to as "full-time preschools") and in part-time preschools. Additional guidelines have been developed for educational activities in public family day care homes and in the "after-school homes" for 7 to 12 year olds.

During the late 1960s and the 1970s, when the Swedish child care system was planned and launched on a large scale, detailed state rules and regulations governed the planning and organizing of the child care settings. In order to obtain government subsidies, the local authorities had to follow these rules and regulations closely, which included issues like the physical design of buildings, outdoor and indoor space requirements per child, group sizes, staff-child ratios, and personnel training. The strict enforcement of criteria for quality laid down by the 1968 National Commission on Child Care has resulted in public child care settings of uniformly high quality in Sweden. At the same time, local authorities, child care personnel, and parents often have found the system to be too rigid and unresponsive to the needs of individual municipalities, preschools, and families. During the 1980s there has been a gradual shift in responsibility for public child care from the national to the local levels. The guidelines and programs referred to above all reflect this shift. Even though national authorities like the National Board of Health and Welfare will continue to have a supervisory responsibility for public child care, manifested for example through the development of the educational programs and guidelines, more and more of the responsibilities for child care organization and activities have been placed at the local level. While the overarching ideology specified by the Social Services Act will continue to shape activities in child care settings, politicians and administrators at local levels and personnel and parents in individual child care settings now have considerably more freedom than previously to organize and develop programs of activities tailor made to suit the needs of the children in the particular settings.

PROGRAM GOALS AND CONTENT

The "prototypic" Swedish public child care setting is the day care center. One such center is described below.

The Swedish Day Care Center

The center we are using as an example serves families who live in apartment buildings in the surrounding neighborhood and is one of several in the area. The center was built in 1972. It is a one-story "standardized" wooden building and has 56 places available for children in four age groups: toddlers (10), 3 to 5 year olds (15), 5 to 7 year olds (16), and 7 to 12 year olds (15) children in the after-school program. In Sweden, some centers still group children by age in this manner. Most, however, are practicing a somewhat different "sibling-group" system, following the recommendations of the National Child Care Commission for non-age-segregated groupings. Basically the sibling group consists of 3 to 7 year olds or even two year olds, and each center might have two such groups. In many centers there is also an infant toddler group, although the need for child care outside of the home for infants is gradually decreasing, following the expansion of the Swedish Paid Parental Leave System.

Let us take a look inside the area for the five to seven year olds: two full-time preschool teachers and one half-time assistant take care of the children in this group. In this case there are 16 children in the group, nine boys and seven girls, and six of the children have only one parent at home. The parents all work full time. Most children arrive in the center at about 7 o'clock in the morning and are picked up by 4:30 P.M.

The indoor area is made up of five rooms. There is a large playroom, which is used most of the time for running, climbing, or structured group activities, but where some of the children take a short nap on floor-mattresses around noon. Another room with tables and chairs, an electric stove, and a sink is where the children do puzzles, bake cookies, and have their meals. The other three spaces are a small "doll-room," a "cozy-room" with pillows, books, and an aquarium, and a carpentry room.

The physical design of the areas for the young or older age groups in the center is fairly similar to the one described here, with age-related modifications. There is also a main kitchen in the center, where food for all the children is prepared, a staff lounge, and an office for the director.

Outside the children have opportunities to play "across the age groups." Play equipment consists of swings, sandboxes, jungle gyms, slides, tricycles, wheelbarrows, and the like. The ground is covered with grass, bushes, and sand. The whole area is fenced in, to prevent the children from escaping into "the world outside" with its streetcar tracks and heavy car traffic.

All in all, the physical and social design of this day care center is very representative of Swedish centers, the vast majority of which are created by the municipalities to meet the standardized requirements of the central government. Meeting these requirements, which regulate staff training, indoor and outdoor space per child, group sizes, adult-child ratios, and so on, is a prerequisite for obtaining state subsidies. The running costs for Swedish center care are divided among the state, the municipality, and the parents in such a way that the state and the municipality each cover about 45 percent of the costs, and the parents the remaining 10 percent.

Parent Cooperative Day Care Centers

A fairly recent addition to the Swedish child care system is day care centers started by parent cooperatives. As of spring 1989 there were about 500 such centers registered, serving a total of 7,000 children. Most of these parent cooperatives are found in Stockholm, Göteborg and Malmö, but more than 100 municipalities all over the country report the presence of one or more such center.

Parental involvement and participation are the cornerstones in this type of child care. Like the traditional centers, parent cooperatives are financed by money from the state, the local municipality, and the parents themselves. But since the parents are carrying out a substantial portion of the work in the centers, thereby reducing the number of trained staff members required, running costs per place are considerably lower, especially for the municipalities.

There is usually more variation in the daily routines and scheduled activities among parent cooperative centers, than among traditional day care centers. Parents and staff members plan the schedule together, and the mere fact that parents take turns working in the center results in greater variation. Parental participation in the day-to-day work in the center varies considerably. Usually each family sets aside two weeks per year for center work, and fathers are encouraged to do their share. Although many parent cooperatives were started as a response to lack of places in traditional centers, some are formed with specific educational goals in mind. Shared religious beliefs or an interest in special musical education are reasons why parents might gather and start a cooperative center. Thus far, an overwhelming majority of families making use of parent cooperative centers are two-parent families, with parents who are relatively well-educated, white-collar workers or professionals. The flexible working schedule that often goes along with these positions in the labor market makes possible the increased parental involvement required if parental cooperative day care centers are to function according to established goals.

National Guidelines and Recommendations

Reference was made earlier to the guidelines and recommendations presented in 1987 by the National Board of Health and Welfare as the "Educational Program for Preschools." The guiding principles brought forward in this program are based on a theoretical perspective in which the interactions between the child and the environment are seen as the driving forces of development. At the municipal level these principles are to be translated into local guidelines by politicians and administrators and, in a third step, into daily activities in the child care settings by the preschool teachers and children's nurses, ideally in cooperation with the parents.

Children are not passive recipients of influences from the environment. Through their acts and activities they test and develop their skills, knowledge, and understanding in relation to the environment. The child's own initiatives, curiosity, and desire to explore and test limitations make him or her an active participant in interactions with the environment. These interactions are constantly occurring and represent the central driving forces of development. (National Board of Health and Welfare, 1987, p. 21, author's translation)

This perspective on child development, which is based on historical traditions and experiences in the preschools, as well as research and theories, leads to the formulation of several general principles for the activities in the child care settings: (1) It is important that the activities be linked to the children's own experiences and developmental stage; (2) learning and development is occurring all the time, not only during structured learning situations; (3) situations involving basic care (feeding, diaper changing, carrying, hugging) are particularly important when it comes to fulfilling fundamental physical, social, and emotional needs, they represent the most intimate relationships between the child and the caregiver and are hence of great significance to the development of the child's perception of self in relation to others and ways of looking at relationships among people; (4) playing is the child's own concrete way of acting out and reflecting upon experiences and impressions from the environment, and it is very important to give children vast opportunities to play in the child care setting; and (5) when organizing activities it is important to take advantage of the fact that children in preschools (be they day care centers or part-time preschools) form stable groups, which meet every day for several hours. The group is the basis for daily activities and gives each child an opportunity to develop social skills and competencies through daily interactions with other children. In the Educational Program for Preschools, the importance of the group is also related to changes in society:

The group in the preschool, which today is largely replacing the groups of children who earlier played together in the village or in backyards, gives the children the opportunity to participate in a larger community than the family can provide. In being members of a preschool group, and having the opportunity to grow up and develop together with a group of peers, children in the preschool might be socialized into feelings of responsibility and solidarity, and develop friendships and lasting relationships. (1987, p. 49, author's translation)

Nature, Culture, and Society

The Educational Program for Preschools also specifies content areas of particular importance for the planning of activities. The areas specified are nature, culture, and society, and the contents of the daily activities in these areas are to be chosen in ways that correspond to the developmental stages of the children and the thoughts and interests expressed by them. Under the heading of "nature" the program stresses the importance of creating in all children a feeling of responsibility toward nature and a basic knowledge about human beings in an ecological perspective. Environmental protection is a central issue, and it is important that the children are given many opportunities to experience nature through field trips and walks in the woods. Knowledge about the ancient "Allemansrätt" (Right of Public Access) that gives Swedes the right to move around freely everywhere in nature, needs to be combined with internalized feelings of responsibility for the natural environment, starting in the preschool years.

Culture is an important part of identity formation, and the Educational Program states that the preschools shall contribute to helping children understand their own social and cultural milieu and that of others, and keeping alive the cultural heritage. Since language and other forms of communication are central to understanding and mediating culture, the development of language and speech, arts and crafts, music, singing, puppet theater, and dramatic acting are central parts of the daily activities in the child care settings.

It is important for the growing child to develop an understanding of the surrounding society of which she is part. This process can be facilitated if children in preschools are given opportunities to observe and participate in activities in the local neighborhood—at different workplaces, for example. Concrete experiences in the factory, post office, or bakery might make it easier to understand and internalize the basic values and norms of society. The fostering of democracy, equality, solidarity, and responsibility is an overarching goal in Swedish day care centers and part-time preschools.

PLAY AND WORK AS THE BASIS FOR LEARNING

We noted earlier that what characterizes program ideologies in Swedish child care is the dual focus on care and education. Both of these components are considered equally important and are integrated in the Educational

Program for Preschools. This becomes quite clear in the section of this program where methods for learning and socialization are addressed.

The activities in the preschools are to be seen from a broad pedagogical perspective where both daily care, play, work, and other activities are of importance for the development of the children.... Children do not only learn when adults have the intention to "teach." Since learning during the preschool years also takes place through imitation and identification, the behaviors, values, and attitudes of the personnel are crucial.... Learning in preschools should primarily be encouraged through play and work in natural circumstances. (1987, pp. 41–43, author's translation)

The importance of play for learning and development is stressed throughout the Educational Program. Experimenting and exploratory play is considered important, and especially stressed is role playing, where the children try out different types of adult roles. But in order for play to develop into something stimulating and creative, there need to be some sources of inspiration from which to gather play materials. Work is one such source. Concrete experiences from the adult world of work might be gathered through visits to parents' workplaces. There are also a number of work-related tasks that need to be carried out in child care settings. Watering plants, repairing broken toys, cooking, cleaning, and doing errands are all examples of daily activities in which children themselves might participate and learn new skills and responsibilities.

Parental Involvement

The Educational Program states quite clearly that the preschool is a complement to the home and that the family and the preschool are serving different functions for the children. Since the activities in child care settings are to take the living conditions of the children outside the preschools into consideration, it is important that the planning of these activities take place with cooperation between personnel and parents. Different forms of parent-staff interaction exist. When a child starts in a day care center, a week-long adjustment period is scheduled. During this period staff members might visit the child's home and the parents are spending time with their child in the center. This adjustment period sets the stage for future cooperation, and it is considered very important. When parents leave or pick up their children in the day care center, there should be an opportunity for small talk around the daily activities in the setting. Individual conferences are scheduled on a regular basis. During these meetings, usually 15 minutes long, parents and staff members have a chance to talk in more detail about matters affecting the child inside or outside the day care center. The paid parental leave program gives the parents the right to spend two days per year in the day care center and participate in the daily activities. Group meetings with parents and staff members are also scheduled a couple of times a year to provide opportunities for information sharing and discussion. Some parents attend these meetings with enthusiasm and engage in vivid discussions, while other parents feel left out and shy and find it difficult to participate. Picnics, field trips or "workdays," where parents and children together paint a room or replant the garden, might be more appreciated by some parents as ways of getting together.

Parental involvement is easier said than done. Clearly expressed as a goal in the Educational Program for Preschools, it works well in some day care centers. In parent cooperative centers it is even a prerequisite. But parental involvement is also related to the resource levels of the parents. Long hours at work and the additional responsibility for the home and the family may be more than enough physical or psychological burden for a day, leaving little energy to invest in discussions at the day care center, especially if the parent is confident that the staff in the center is doing a good job of caring for and educating her child.

ACCOMPLISHMENTS AND CHALLENGES

The Swedish National Child Care Program, which began on a small scale some 30 years ago, has today reached a point where "full coverage," defined as the goal that "all children between one and a half and six years of age have the right to a place in public child care if their parents are working or studying," seems likely to be fulfilled within a few years. It seems fair to state that specified state rules and regulations, college-level educational requirements for personnel working in day care centers, and a comprehensive national family support program are all factors that have contributed to a child care system with high standards. Longitudinal studies, carried out in Sweden in the 1970s and 1980s, show that children in full-time public day care centers, when compared to children raised at home, develop just as normally as, or sometimes even developmentally surpass, their home-reared counterparts.

The general consensus at the time of this writing is that public day care centers represent an important and much needed complement to home care, when parents are working or studying. Family day care homes will also continue to be available for families who, for one reason or another, choose this kind of arrangement. But surveys carried out among parents of preschoolers show that the day care center is the child care alternative preferred by most parents. The quality of the care and education provided in day care centers can be improved, however: rather than supporting additional research aimed at comparing effects on child development of child care inside or outside of the home, more money is now being spent on developing and evaluating the programs in operation within public child care settings. Municipalities can apply for state money to try out in individual centers new parent-staff communication programs, educational programs, organization development programs, and the like, and to evaluate such programs. This type of local program development and evaluation is aimed at improving the quality of public child care and at the same time is an attempt to decentralize what has long been considered by many to be a much too state-regulated area of public service.

However, three major challenges will have to be addressed and solved within the next few years if the goal of providing child care outside of the home for all families in which parents are working or studying is to be achieved. First, whereas some municipalities already are getting fairly close to meeting the need for places in child care settings, several are lagging far behind in their planning and realization of this goal. Second, the number of trained personnel to work in the expanding public child care sector is far from sufficient to meet anticipated needs. Third, large groups of families, where parents are working odd hours, evenings, or weekends, are presently almost excluded from access to public child care.

Lack of Places in Public Child Care

Certainly the 1985 Parliament decision to extend the public child care system to "full coverage" by 1991 has led those 284 municipalities that are responsible for the carrying out of this decision to intensify their efforts to create more places in public child care. This process has been slower in some municipalities than in others, depending on such factors as previous commitment to child care, population size and density, number of women in the labor force, number of parents working odd hours, willingness to increase local income taxes, and political majority in the municipal councils.

To provide politicians and administrators with information about the progress in the child care sector, the 1981 Social Services Act called upon all municipalities to develop regular plans to assess local needs for child care and outline strategies to meet those needs. Moreover, beginning in 1986, the National Bureau of Statistics has carried out annual national surveys of child care supply and demand. These plans and surveys reveal large differences in the amount and type of public child care available in urban versus rural regions, in areas with a high versus low percentage of blue-collar workers, and in municipalities with a high versus low work force participation by women. In the larger cities, where the percentage of women working outside the home is approaching that of men, and where large numbers of women are working in white-collar or service jobs (often in the public sector), the availability of public child care is high, and the children usually have a place in a public day care center. In rural, sparsely populated areas, where families live further apart, where the labor market structure often is quite different from that of the urban areas, and where child care traditions and attitudes toward public child care also tend to be different, the number of places in family day care homes outweighs the number in day care centers, and the percentage of children in public child care is lower than the national average.

Shortage of Personnel

The second issue causing major concern among politicians and planners is the shortage of trained personnel, which is becoming more and more acute as the child care program expands. In 1988 the estimate was that in order to meet the needs of "full coverage" child care, more than 30,000 new preschool teachers, children's nurses, and family day care mothers would be required.

The government is painfully aware of the seriousness of the personnel situation and is taking a number of steps in an attempt to alleviate the pressure. First, the number of students accepted into the college programs for preschool teachers is being increased. Whereas colleges in some regions find it difficult to fill the classes already in existence, programs in other parts of the country have two to four applicants per available educational slot, providing the demand for some expansion. The second effort is to encourage, through "reactivation courses," the return of personnel who have left the child care arena for other jobs, or to stay home and take care of their own children. It is estimated that 10,000 former child care workers are presently doing things other than working in jobs for which they were originally trained. A third approach involves making more money available for local municipalities to spend on in-service training and continuing education, in an attempt to increase interest and motivation among staff members in day care centers and prevent "escapes" into other job sectors. Finally, there is support for the development of specific "pedagogical programs" for centers, part-time preschools, and after-school centers, with a double goal: (1) to increase the quality of the programs, and (2) to upgrade the status of child care workers. The idea behind this second goal is that, with this new "curriculum" available, it will be easier for child care workers to describe and identify with their work, somewhat along the same lines as teachers in public schools are able to do.

The major reason for difficulties in recruiting personnel may well be the relatively low salaries they earn. The government has been reluctant to intervene in annual wage negotiations, knowing full well that substantial salary increases will limit the financial capacity of municipalities to expand their child care programs.

Unequal Access to Places

Access to and use of public child care are unequally distributed across different types of families with young children in Sweden. At present, working-class children and children in immigrant families are clearly underrepresented (about 10 percent of the Swedish population consists of immigrants), whereas children from white-collar families, families where the parents have an academic education, and children in one-parent households are overrepresented. In 1987, at the request of the government, the National Board of Health and Welfare conducted several studies to illuminate the reasons for this skewed recruitment to public child care. The results of these studies, published in 1989, point at several, often interacting, factors that explain this skewedness. Chief among those factors are tradition, motivation, and organization.

Tradition. Parents in working-class families and those in immigrant families (who often also have blue-collar jobs) tend to have more traditional and conservative attitudes and values in areas related to child care, housework, and work outside of the home. This traditional role division, with mothers as caregivers and household workers and fathers as breadwinners, is reinforced through close relationships with relatives from an older generation and through the exchange of services and information within a social network that tends to be more dense and homogeneous with respect to attitudes and values than are the networks of parents in middle-class families. With immigrant families, cultural and religious beliefs might also operate as forces conserving traditional sex role attitudes and making parents less likely to see public child care outside of the home as an attractive alternative. If mothers are working outside of the home, child care is often solved through various forms of informal arrangements, such as relatives or private family day care mothers, or by the parents themselves, who might try to schedule their working hours in non-overlapping shifts, so that one parent is always available for the children in the home. These families do not show up in the column of "unmet needs" in child care statistics, since they do not apply for places in public child care. However, as their children grow older, and "education" and "group-training" becomes more of an issue than "basic care," these families might reconsider their child care needs and try to enter their children into public day care centers, only to find that the available places have already been taken by middle-class families who were out early.

Motivation. About 10 percent of Swedish preschool-age children live in one-parent households, usually with their mother. Most single mothers are working outside the home, and they work full-time much more often than mothers in two-parent families. This is because they need to support themselves and their family financially. With no partner available to contribute to the family economy, the alternative to working for pay is to stay home and live on social welfare, an alternative not very attractive to most single mothers. Many municipalities give priority to single parents who need public child care, also contributing to the overrepresentation of this group.

Financial reasons are also important to mothers in two-parent, middle-class families who work outside the home. Additional motivation to join the labor market stems from the fact that the jobs available to these women, who usually have a college-level education, are likely to be more stimulating, better paid, more flexible with regard to working hours, and scheduled in ways more compatible to the operating hours of the public day care centers (7 A.M. to 7 P.M., weekdays), than are the jobs available to working-class women. Fathers and mothers in two-parent, middle-class families are also more likely than parents in working-class families to share attitudes and values linked to changing sex-role patterns, and the rights and responsibilities for both men and women to work outside of the home and to divide the household tasks among them (although not equally).

Parental fees for public child care might also affect the motivation for families to use day care centers or family day care homes. Local authorities decide on the principle for imposing child care fees, and several different systems are presently in operation, resulting in a large range in fees between the "cheapest" and the "most expensive" municipalities. Some municipalities charge on the basis of family income, where high-income families pay more than low-income families (who sometimes pay no fees at all). Other municipalities have a "standard fee," which is the same for all families. The effect of this variation in financing principles is that in some municipalities low-income families might find that public child care fees are too hard on the family economy, motivating them to try to find other, less expensive child care arrangements.

Organization. Even though differences in attitudes and values, motivation to work, or relative child care costs all are factors likely to contribute to the present unequal representation of children from different types of families, the single most important factor responsible for the unequal distribution is probably found in the actual organization of public child care. More than 80 percent of mothers with children under the age of seven work more than 20 hours per week. They often work odd hours (i.e., evenings, nights, weekends, or irregular shifts) as shop employees, nurse assistants, cleaning ladies, or bus drivers. Public child care, however, has hitherto for the most part been available only for families where parents work "regular office-hours," that is, weekdays 8 A.M. to 5 P.M. Statistics from 1986 indicate that 45,000 children under the age of seven (12.5%) have parents who work odd hours and would prefer public child care during evenings, nights, and/ or weekends. Most of these parents are "pink-collar" workers in the public or private service sector. Most municipalities are beginning to offer some public child care during odd hours, usually in family day care homes. Centers open at night are also beginning to appear in several locales. Children in these centers whose parents are working nights sleep in the center some nights per week and are also part of the day-time group during certain days. Although centers open at night were available in 50 municipalities in 1990, many critics feel that the labor market should be forced to adjust much more to the needs of parents with young children and schedule working hours that will not force these parents to work nighttime hours.

Until recently, the shortage of places in public child care has made it possible for the municipalities to put a lot of demands on families applying for such child care. To obtain an eagerly awaited place, parents usually have had to work full-time during weekdays. They have been expected to accept ideologies and activities in the child care settings without too many objections, being told that they belong to the "lucky few." With the expansion of public child care, and the demands placed on local authorities to meet the needs of all families, this situation might change. New alternatives to centrally regulated child care settings are beginning to develop, alternatives in which decentralized decision making, opening hours, parental fees and involvement, ideologies, and planned activities might be more geared toward the needs of individual families. Private, non-profit organizations, entitled to public support and offering cultural, educational, or religious alternatives to public child care, are likely to become more common. But in sheer numbers, these alternatives will probably continue to make up only a small percentage of Swedish child care, which will continue to be based on public day care centers and family day care homes.

POSTSCRIPT

Since this chapter was first written the "baby boom" has continued in Sweden. The addition of 25,000 new places in public day care centers during 1990 did not help much when birthrates reached new highs. Moreover, the government decided for economic reasons to postpone the last step in the expansion of parental leave insurance, resulting in about 25,000 more one year olds on center waiting lists who would otherwise have been at home with one of the parents for another six months. The goal of reaching "full coverage" has been postponed until 1993, and the government's "Action Group on Child Care" has suggested that the 1985 Parliament recommendation be changed into a binding obligation, in order to put more pressure on local politicians.

(August, 1991.)

REFERENCES

Andersson, B. E. (1989). "Effects of Public Day-Care: A Longitudinal Study." *Child Development, 60*, 857–866.

Andersson, B.E. (1992). "Effects of Day Care on Cognitive and Socio-Emotional Competence in Thirteen-Year-Old Swedish School Children." *Child Development, 63*, 20–36.

Broberg, A. (1989). "The Swedish Child Care System." In A. Broberg, *Child Care and Early Development.* Department of Psychology, University of Göteborg, Sweden.

Broberg, A., Hwang, C. P., Lamb, M., and Ketterlinus, R. (1990). "Child Care Effects on Socioemotional and Intellectual Competence in Swedish Pre-schoolers." In J. S. Lande, S. Scarr and N. Gunzenhauser (Eds.), *Caring for Children: Challenge to America*. Hillsdale, N.J.: Erlbaum.

Cochran, M. (1977). "A Comparison of Group Day Care and Family Childbearing Patterns in Sweden." *Child Development, 48,* 702–707.

Cochran, M. and Gunnarsson, L. (1985). "A Follow-up Study of Group Day Care and Family-based Childrearing Patterns." *Journal of Marriage and the Family,* May, 297–309.

Ericsson, Y. (1988). *Att vilja men inte kunna—Om deltidsarbete i Sverige* (Willing but unable—about part-time work in Sweden). Brevskolan.

Johansson, J. E. (1983). Svensk förskola—en tillbakablick (Swedish pre-school in a historical perspective). Liber, Stockholm.

Lamb, M., Hwang, C-P., Bookstein, F., Broberg, A., Hult, G., and Frodi, M. (1988). "Determinants of Social Competence in Swedish Preschoolers." *Developmental Psychology*, Vol. 24, No. 1, 58–70.

Leira, A. (1987). *Day Care for Children in Denmark, Norway, and Sweden*. Report 87:5. Oslo, Norway: Institute for Social Research.

Moen, P. (1989). *Working Parents: Transformation in Gender Roles and Public Policies in Sweden*. Madison: The University of Wisconsin Press.

National Board of Health and Welfare. (1987). *Pedagogiskt program för förskolan* (Educational program for pre-schools). Allmänna råd från Socialstyrelsen 1987:3, Stockholm: Allmänna Förlaget.

National Board of Health and Welfare. (1988a). *Kommunala familjedaghem* (Public family day care homes). Allmänna råd från Socialstyrelsen 1988:4, Stockholm: Allmänna Förlaget.

National Board of Health and Welfare. (1988b). *Pedagogiskt program för fritidshem* (Educational program for after-school homes). Allmänna råd från Social-styrelsen, 1988:7, Stockholm: Almänna Förlaget.

National Board of Health and Welfare. (1989). *Den sociala snedfördelningen inom barnomsorgen* (Social skewedness in public child care). SoS-rapport 1989:20. Stockholm: Allmänna Förlaget.

Official Statistics of Sweden (1991). *Barnomsorgsundersökningen 1991: Förskole-barn (0–6 år)* (The 1991 national public child care survey). Stockholm: National Central Bureau of Statistics.

Sandqvist, K. (1990). "Fäder och mödrar" (Fathers and mothers). In B. E. Andersson and L. Gunnarsson (Eds.), *Svenska Småbarnsfamiljer* (Swedish families with young children). Studentlitteratur, Lund.

26

THE UNITED KINGDOM

Bronwen Cohen

The United Kingdom had a population in 1988 of 57.1 million, which is expected to reach 60 million by the year 2011. It comprises four countries— England, Wales, Scotland, and Northern Ireland—historically united (with a unitary political system) since the 18th century but retaining (to varying degrees) separate cultural identities, minority linguistic and religious traditions, and, in Scotland and Northern Ireland, separate educational and legal systems. This diversity has been further enhanced by international migration trends; 4.5 percent of the population is now from other minority ethnic groups, predominantly West Indian/Guyanese Indian and Pakistani.

In 1973 the United Kingdom joined the European Community (EC), within which all citizens are free to live and work in any EC country on equal terms with nationals with no loss of social security rights. The closer integration of the European Community, resulting from the intended creation of a single market in 1992, and the adoption of the Single European Act have significant implications for future developments within the United Kingdom's educational and welfare systems. In particular, unfavorable comparisons in respect to day care provisions with many other member states within the European Community, and the European Commission's own program to improve provision in all member states, are beginning to influence policy developments in this area within the United Kingdom.

HISTORICAL BACKGROUND

The first day nurseries in the United Kingdom developed in the 19th century arising from concern over "day nursing" (child-minding) arrangements being made by women having to make formal provision for the care of their children as the industrial revolution drew them from agriculture, small workshops, and the home into more concentrated work in factories. A philanthropic factory owner, Robert Owen (founder of the cooperative movement in the United Kingdom) opened a nursery in 1816 in the mill town of New Lanark, and in 1850 the first of a number of nurseries run by charitable organizations was opened.

The First World War brought the first public involvement in the provision of day nurseries with the setting up of 108 day nurseries across England and Wales. At the end of the war, in 1918, Local Health Authorities were empowered by law to provide day nurseries or assist voluntary nurseries, and the 1918 Education Act also allowed local authorities to establish nursery schools.

The 1870 Education Act had previously required the provision of elementary schools in all areas. Neither act led to extensive provision. By 1938 there were only 4,000 places in public nurseries and just over 9,500 in nursery schools. The Second World War again prompted the development of social and fiscal policies to encourage women's employment. The Ministry of Labor proposed a range of provision, including shopping leave, factory canteens, an expanded school meals service, part-time work, and an increase in the provision of child care. By the end of the war there were 1,300 day nurseries in England and Wales providing places for 62,000 children, well over twice the number of places now available in local authority (public) nurseries. There were similar nursery programs in Scotland and Northern Ireland.

Even before the end of the war the nurseries began to be closed and within 20 years they had been reduced in number to only a third of those in existence in 1945. The nursery closures were based on the expectation that women would—and should—withdraw from the work force when the country's wartime and post-war economic problems diminished. This expectation was reflected in the system of social security developed in the early post-war period, in which women were provided for largely as dependents of men. Radical reforms recognized the cost of children, establishing a universal tax-financed family allowance system for all families with two or more children. This allowance, together with child tax allowances, was the principal basis of financial support for families until their replacement in 1975 by Child Benefit—a tax-free flat rate benefit paid to mothers in respect to every dependent child up to 16 or 19 if in full-time education. The reforms recognized the direct costs of children but did not address the wider requirements of families in bringing up children, such as child care services, because of prevailing perceptions of family roles. William Beveridge, who chaired the enquiry that established the principles on which the social security system was developed after the war noted: "The great majority of women must be regarded as occupied on work which is vital though unpaid, without which their husbands could not do their paid work and without which the nation could not continue" (Beveridge Report, 1942, p. 49). This "vital work" involved "ensuring the adequate continuance of the British Race" (Beveridge Report, 1942, quoted by M. Henwood and M. Wicks, 1986) and taking care of their husbands.

The closure of the nurseries was also influenced by post-war psychoanalytic theories that emphasized the dangers of separation of mother and child and favored, where care was necessary, individual rather than group care.[1] A Ministry of Health circular published in 1945 noted that "The right policy to pursue would be positively to discourage mothers of children under two from going out to work; to make provision for children between two and five by way of Nursery Schools and Nursery Classes" (Mayall and Petrie, 1983, p. 16).

A government report on nursery education in 1967 recommended that nursery education should be part time "because young children should not be separated from their mothers" and the limited provision of places in public nurseries was increasingly restricted to parents with only one child "where there was no option but to go out to work" or to those with broader health and welfare requirements (Cohen, 1990). This policy was continued by the Department of Health and Social Security, which took over responsibility for the nurseries for the Ministry of Health in 1970. As a result, local authority nurseries have only played a very limited role in meeting parental requirements for day care.

CHILDREN AND FAMILIES

In 1988 there were 10.7 million children under age 15 in the United Kingdom. This included 3.7 million children aged 0 to 4, 3.6 million children aged 5 to 9 and 3.4 million children aged 10 to 14. The under-fives population is projected to increase to 3.9 million by 1995 when the number of 15 to 19 year olds will have dropped by over 1 million from 1985, reducing the number of young people entering the labor market and increasing the demand for women's labor. Following a decline in the 1970s, the birthrate has increased from 11.7 (total births per 1,000 population of all ages) in 1977 to 13.8 in 1988 and is projected to fall again in the 1990s. Fertility rates dropped between 1971 and 1981 and have since remained generally stable, but below the replacement level. The total fertility rate in 1988 was 1.84.

Lone parent families have increased in comparison to all families with dependent children from 8 percent in 1971 to 14 percent in 1987, reflecting both a rising divorce rate and an increasing incidence of births outside of marriage. The proportion of families headed by a lone father has remained virtually unchanged.

PARENTAL EMPLOYMENT

Changing social attitudes combined with labor market demand have led to a considerable increase in women's employment. Marriage no longer ends paid employment for most women in the United Kingdom, and over 50 percent of all married women are now economically active compared with only 20 percent in 1951 and 10 percent in 1921. Childbearing itself involves shorter breaks, and a package of employment provisions introduced in 1975 included protection of pregnant women from dismissal and the right to be absent from work for a total of 40 weeks before and after the birth of a child—both provisions subject to restrictive qualifying conditions (legislative provision was also made the same year covering sex discrimination). An increasing proportion of women return to work between the births of their children and return to work sooner after their first birth than was the case 20 years ago. The most highly qualified women return to work sooner after their first birth, whereas clerical and sales workers are least likely to return to work within six months of the birth of their first child. For mothers of children over five, the time spent by children at school has facilitated a relatively high level of employment. In 1985, 29 percent of mothers with a youngest child aged birth to four years old were in paid employment. This rose in 1988 to 37 percent. For mothers of preschool children, difficulties in finding suitable, affordable provision have contributed to a very low rate of labor force participation but this is now rising.[2] About two thirds of mothers with children aged five to nine work fewer than 30 hours a week.

Lone mothers are less likely than married women to be in paid employment. The most recent statistics show that only 18 percent of lone mothers with a child aged newborn to four years were in paid employment in 1988. This is accounted for by the poverty trap created by the system of income support within the U.K. Social Security System, which does not take child care costs into account in any significant way, and by the greater difficulties lone mothers experience in making child care arrangements.

Men's employment participation remains largely unaffected by fatherhood. In 1988, 87 percent of fathers of children aged newborn to four years and children aged five to nine years were in paid employment. Only 2 percent of fathers of under-fives in paid employment were working part time. The working hours of fathers are increasing. In 1988, 80 percent of fathers of children four years old and under worked 40 hours a week or more and 35 percent worked 50 hours a week or more.

DEMAND FOR DAY CARE

Rising employment participation rates among women with children have contributed to the increasing demand for day care. That demand has been met to a very limited extent by the development of voluntary and private nurseries, and to a somewhat greater extent by childminders (who provide care in the minder's own home), but the majority of child care arrangements made by working women still involve the use of their husband or partner or other relatives. The relatives used to provide child care include fathers, grandmothers, aunts, uncles, and older siblings. Maternal grandmothers are the most common care arrangement used by women working full time, while for women working part time husbands/partners are the most common source of care. Over two thirds of all child care arrangements used by working women for their preschool children involve care by a spouse or other relative.

Although the use of relatives in some cases represents a positive parental choice, it more commonly reflects the absence of affordable alternatives. The gap between demand and supply of day care provision is documented in U.K. survey evidence at both local and national levels. A major survey carried out in 1974 by the then Department of Health and Social Security (and not yet repeated) found that some form of day care provision (defined as day nurseries, playgroups, childminders, creches, and nursery education) was wanted by mothers for twice as many children as were then receiving it. The survey found that 26 percent of children in the survey had working mothers, but a further 22 percent had mothers who said that they would have liked to work had they been able to find satisfactory child care arrangements. Later studies carried out by the Pre-School Playgroup Association in 1983 and 1985 found that the demand for provision has substantially increased in particular for educational provision and center day care (see Table 26.1). A recent survey of 1,000 families in the Strathclyde Region of Scotland found that of those mothers not working (72%) just under a quarter (24%) would choose to be at home if suitable affordable child care were available. Of the rest, 47 percent would have liked to work part time, 16 percent full time, and 13 percent would have chosen to undertake further education. The demand for provision was slightly higher among rural than urban families, reflecting a significant change in economic activity rates within U.K. rural areas.

The information provided by these surveys on parental preferences between different forms of provision is somewhat imprecise, reflecting confusion over terminology and the difficulties inherent in establishing preferences in the absence of clear models for provision. In general, they show that parents of older preschool children favor educational provision, although a major longitudinal study on child health and education that followed the progress of 15,000 children concluded that the benefits of preschool experience are not limited to formal educational services but include day care and playgroup experience. Surveys also show that many parents using childminders would prefer to use other forms of provision.

Table 26.1
Parent's Preferred Type of Provision (1974, 1983, and 1985)

	1974 (n=2501) %	1984 (n=367) %	1985 (n=400) %
Public nursery school/class	20	42	42
Public day nursery	7	10	11
Private nursery	NA	6	10
Playgroup	25	39	38
Creche	1	2	3
Mother-and-toddler group	NA	12	14
Childminder	3	4	3
None	37	10	10

Source: Cohen (1988)

However, one study that presented a more positive view of child minding also found that some parents may prefer it for children under age two.

DAY CARE POLICIES

With the exception of short-lived government day care programs developed to meet specific wartime requirements, government policies have in general envisaged only a restricted role for the provision of public day care. As public (local authority) nurseries closed down in the 1940s and 1950s, places in the nurseries became restricted to children with particular health or social requirements to the extent that even one-parent families frequently no longer have access to this form of provision. Current government policy emphasizes that day care for working parents is a matter for parents themselves to provide. "Our view is that it is for parents who go out to work to decide how best to care for their children. If they want or need help in this task they should make the appropriate arrangements and meet the costs" (Hansard Col 150, 12/7/88).

Current government policy also appears to support the view that day care for younger children should be family rather than center based. Draft guidelines circulated for (limited) consultation in 1985 recommended that

Children under the age of two years are not placed in large institutional nurseries offering group based care since their ability to cope with a number of different contacts with staff and other children, inevitable in such nurseries, will be limited.

Nurseries should only very exceptionally accept babies under the age of 11 weeks; it is strongly recommended that such young children be catered for in the family day care setting such as with a childminder. (DHSS draft guidance on day care provision for the under-fives, 1985. See Cohen, 1988)

The same draft guidance drew attention to the advantages for authorities of using forms of provision with "low unit costs," such as childminding which, "where properly supported, can provide an excellent level of care and which can be readily tailored to suit needs of individual families" (DHSS cited in Cohen, 1988).

The view expressed in the draft guidelines was strongly criticized at the time and the guidelines have not been published, but it reflects a not insubstantial body of opinion hostile to the use of day nurseries for young children and a declining, but nevertheless still significant, view among the wider population that children should be cared for by their mothers at home.

Labor market requirements are now leading the government to emphasize employer responsibilities in this area, but they have not yet caused any substantial government policy changes, although there is increasing pressure on and from within the party of government—the Conservative Party—to provide more assistance through tax and voucher systems. Within the principal opposition party, the Labour Party, a major review of child care policies has been taking place, and Labour Party policies now include local authorities' being obliged to provide comprehensive child care services for under-fives and out-of-school care for older children through partnerships between local councils, employers, and community groups "to make this cost effective with funding from central government to help finance new initiatives" (Labour Party, 1989). The Labour Party also proposes to establish the Department of Education and Science as the "lead" department for under-five education and care and to require each local authority to draw up a development plan in consultation with other providers and with parents, showing how they will achieve an integrated approach for under-fives services and a timetable for implementation (Labour Party, 1990).

While local authorities have increasingly withdrawn—with some exceptions—from the public provision of day care, except for children in special need, the legislative framework for public regulation of private and voluntary provision has been extended, although the resources made available have never been sufficient to fully implement legislative requirements in relation to regulation and monitoring. The changes that have been made have been reactive rather than proactive—a response to concern over standards of care or supervision—and as such have been symptomatic of the lack of an integrative and coordinated approach to child care provision or family policy. Within the area of services the relationship of nursery education to parental day care requirements remains largely unaddressed at a

Government level, although there have been some individual initiatives by some local education authorities in providing extended hours to meet parental care requirements. Similarly there has been no attempt to develop a coordinated work and family policy.

European Community Program

While policy development within the United Kingdom has been limited, the European Community Program in this area is of increasing significance. The European Commission has become involved with the issue of child care services through its program on equal opportunities. Under its first program on equal opportunities, the commission proposed that member states should be required to provide parental and family leave. These proposals have not yet been adopted. Under its Second Equal Opportunities Action Program, which ran from 1986 to 1990, the commission established a child care network that was asked to report on provision and policies, to make recommendations for improvement, and to initiate a program of positive action projects. The network recommendations to the European Commission included a legislative requirement on member states to develop publicly funded child care services for children at least up to the age of ten "with an ultimate objective of ensuring the availability of publicly funded services for all parents who are employed or training, either free at the time of use or at a price that all parents can afford, taking into account their income and other needs" (Women of Europe, 1990). The commission is currently preparing a recommendation for member states, to include guidance on day care policies and provision.

While the U.K. government continues to oppose a number of important initiatives by the commission in this area—most notably the European Commission proposals for parental and family leave—the European Commission program has had a considerable impact on the policies of the opposition parties.

DAY CARE PROGRAMS

Day care programs comprise local authority day nurseries, employer, community, and private day nurseries, child minding (family day care) provided by care workers in their own home, and care provided in the parents' own home by care workers known as "nannies." Some child minding is sponsored by the local authorities—in general the children or families involved have health or social requirements of day care provision. In addition to these day care arrangements, there are other services for preschool children, the most prominent being nursery schools and classes for three and four year olds. The scope of provision in these various categories is shown in Table 26.2.[3]

Public Day Nurseries

These provide full- or part-time care for children who are considered to be in need of extra help because of some developmental delay or because of the social or economic circumstances of their parents. They are run by local authority social service departments and (with the exception of a small number of jointly funded children's centers and a few authorities that are integrating services for under-fives) are quite separate from education departments. A growing number of local authority nurseries now offer no day care facility but provide a center that can be attended by children together with their parents (usually mothers), which offers activities for the adults and children. However, some local authorities are now seeking to open access to their nurseries to meet the needs of all parents. The Manchester City Council, for example, plans to develop 12 centers around the city to provide free full-time, part-time, and sessional care from age six months to 12 years. The city's financial difficulties have temporarily reduced the number of such centers, but the policy remains in place. Similar policies are operating or being considered by a small number of other authorities.

There are places in local authority nurseries for just under 1 percent of under-fives, and the number of places as a proportion of under-fives did not rise at all from 1985 to 1988—the most recent year for which complete statistics are obtainable.

Private and Voluntary Nurseries

These comprise a wide range of provision managed by many different organizations—community and voluntary groups, employers, private individuals, and (a recent development) commercial companies. All day nurseries have to be registered with the Local Authority Social Services Department, except those run by statutory bodies, such as the armed forces or hospitals. The majority of the nurseries provide full-time care for the children of parents in paid employment, training, or education. Community nurseries began to appear in the 1970s, often set up by frustrated parents unable to obtain day care and including in some cases black parents wishing to meet the particular needs of their children.

Table 26.2 indicates a significant increase (47%) in the number of places in these nurseries between 1985 and 1988. Although the statistics do not provide details of particular categories of nurseries, the most significant increase appears to be private and commercial provision. Over the earlier ten-year period (1975 to 1985) the number of places fell. This was accompanied by a fall in the number of children under age five, and as a consequence there was a small rise in the number of places as a proportion of under-fives.

Table 26.2
Childcare Provision in the United Kingdom (1975, 1985, 1988)

	1975		1985		1988	
	No. of places	No. per 1,000	No. of places	No. per 1,000	No. of places	No. per 1,000
Public Day Nurseries (pop. aged 0-4)	29,554	7.5	32,964	9.1	34,225	9.1
Private/Voluntary Day Nurseries (pop. aged 0-4)	27,600	7.0	27,533	7.6	40,378	10.8
Childminding (pop. aged 0-4)	88,766	22.5	144,908	40.1	189,054	50.4
Nursery schools/classes (pop. aged 3 & 4)			338,541 (17% full time)	230.0	359,310 (16% full time)	250.0
Primary schools (pop. aged 3 & 4)			295,202 (94% full time)	203.0	297,082 (93% full time)	203.0

Employer Run and Assisted Nurseries

Day nurseries run directly by employers were traditionally associated with manufacturing and textile industries. Current and anticipated labor supply problems, in particular relating to skill shortages, have brought renewed interest from employers. But it remains to be seen as to whether this will result in a significant increase in provision or whether such nurseries will outlast labor market shortages. One recent survey found that 3 percent of employers intended to introduce child care schemes, and a further survey carried out by the organization Working for Child Care found that an increasing number of employers operated or intended to operate a "hands off" approach with the facility run by a company on their behalf.

A further development in this area has been local authority interest in developing nurseries in partnership with employers and education and training establishments—avoiding the necessity for employers to seek assistance from commercial providers and enabling local authorities to meet some of their own priority needs within a more integrated and less stigmatized form of provision. Some of these developments are being assisted in the more economically disadvantaged areas by limited financial assistance available from the European Community's Structural Funds. It is, however, too soon to assess the significance of these developments.

Childminders

Childminders provide day care within their own homes and are required by law to be registered with the Social Services Department of their local authority. They are registered to care for no more than three children under age five (including their own children). The great majority of children are with childminders because their parents are at work or undertaking educational training, but a growing number of local authorities now sponsor the placement of "priority" children with childminders, sometimes as an alternative to day nurseries. In 1984, 2 percent of places for childminders were such sponsored children. It is estimated that approximately 20 percent of U.K. childminders are unregistered—in Northern Ireland the proportion is probably much higher.

Table 26.2 shows the substantial increase in the number of children cared for by such caregivers between 1975 and 1988. These children now constitute 5 percent of all children under five years old. Childminders are also used to provide care for school-aged children, before and after school and during the school holidays. The new Children Act provides that childminders providing care for children up to age eight will now have to register, encompassing some but not all of these arrangements. The increase in the number of childminders has placed a considerable strain on local authorities seeking to provide training and support. A number of surveys carried out in the 1960s and 1970s found the level of care to be very low. Partly as a result of this, local authorities began to provide preregistration training programs. There has been considerable work in this area, assisted by the establishment of a voluntary organization working on behalf of child minding, the National Childminding Association (NCMA). But the level of training and support does not now appear to be keeping pace with the increase in provision.

One factor contributing to this increase has been the development of schemes aiming to persuade employers to subsidize the use of childminders by their employees. One such scheme, operated by the National Child-minding Association in association with a commercial company, involves an employer purchasing child care checks to be used by employees with recommended childminders.

Nannies, Mothers Helps, and Au Pairs

These provide care in the parents' own home but are excluded from regulation and control (with the exception of nannies shared by more than two sets of parents). Therefore only limited information is available about them.

A 1980 survey found that 4 percent of all working women and 6 percent of women employed full time used this form of care. This suggests that there are at least 30,900 nannies in the United Kingdom and that they are a more significant area of provision than local authority nurseries. Almost all are female and many are very young. Mothers helps are usually expected to do some housework as well as child care, are less often in sole charge of children, and do not normally have any professional qualifications. Au pairs are generally not of U.K. nationality and usually work for short periods, six months to a year, to support themselves while learning English. Home Office regulations state that they should not work more than five hours per day as a general rule. They all live with the family. There is currently some interest in examining ways of providing more support for nannies. One European Community Child Care Action Project, based at Wandsworth Parents Information Center, will be seeking to provide guidance to parents and support for both baby-sitters and nannies.

Other Services for Preschool Children

Publicly funded educational provision for preschool children. Publicly funded educational services comprise nursery schools and classes and the infant classes of primary schools. Nursery schools and classes provide education for children below school age and are run by Local Education Authorities (LEAs). Nursery classes are attached to infant or primary schools.

The majority of places are for three and four year olds with a few places for two and five year olds. Most children (84%) attend part time. Sessions are usually from 9:00 to 11:30 A.M. and 1:30 to 3:30 P.M. for 40 weeks of the year. Only a very limited number of classes and schools have provision for extended hours to meet the needs of working parents.

Table 26.2 shows the number of children attending nursery schools and classes in the United Kingdom during 1985 and 1988. A quarter of three and four year olds now attend local education authority nursery schools—2 percent more than in 1985—but the proportion of children attending part time continues to increase. A further 20 percent of three and four year olds are in the reception classes of primary schools, predominantly fulltime. Fulltime school is usually from 9:00 A.M. to 3:30 P.M. for 40 weeks of the year. Very few local education authorities have adjusted their staffing ratios to take account of the growing number of children under five within reception classes, and a 1986 report found that no extra provision was being made in almost a half of all LEAs admitting four year olds at the beginning of the year they are four. There is considerable controversy attached to the policy of admitting these children early into schools. In Northern Ireland nearly a third of three and four year olds are admitted early into schools.

In addition to Local Education Authority provision, an increasing number of under-fives attend private schools. In 1988, 40,000 children under five attended "non-maintained" schools—5,000 more than in 1986.

Preschool Playgroups. Playgroups developed in the 1960s largely as a response by women themselves to both their own needs as mothers and the social requirement of their children. They provide sessional care for three and four year olds and in general rely on considerable help from parents in staffing the sessions. All groups have to be registered by local social service departments, and recommended staff-child ratios are one to six, including parents. The majority of playgroups are non-profit community or church groups run by committees of parents. A 1985 survey found that 29 percent were run on a commercial basis and 3 percent by social service departments. Playgroups have developed into a substantial area of provision. They provide places for around a third of three and four year olds and are probably used by more. A small number have extended hours—1 percent of groups in 1985. The Playgroup Association is now reviewing the role of playgroups in relation to the needs of parents in paid employment.

School-Age Day Care Services

Full-time nursery and primary school hours are generally from 9:00 A.M. to 3:30 P.M. for 40 weeks of the year. These hours of opening mean that parents have to make care arrangements for their children after school, during the school holidays, and sometimes before school, or substantially reduce their hours of work. A very small number of schools offer "extended

Table 26.3

Arrangements for the Care of School-Age Children (in Percents)

Type of Work Arrangement	Full-Time	Part-Time	All Employed Women
Husband	44	63	59
Grandmother	28	24	25
Other relative (a)	25	18	20
Childminder or friend	17	12	15
Nanny (b)	4	2	3
Other	4	3	3

(a) Includes older siblings.
(b) Defined as person employed in child's own home.

Source: J. Martin and C. Roberts, 1984

hours" schemes. In general the care function provided by schools is unacknowledged and often specifically rejected. As a result, most parents have to make use of informal arrangements, and this includes many mothers having to work part time. Seventy-one percent of mothers with children aged five to nine work fewer than 30 hours a week.

Table 26.3 shows the arrangements made by working women for the care of their school-age children during the school term, distinguished by full- and part-time work status.

In the last 15 years a small amount of provision has been developed to provide care for children out of school and during the holidays. A voluntary organization, the Kid's Clubs Network, has been established to promote this form of provision. However, a survey carried out by this organization in 1989 found that there were only 300 out-of-school clubs in the United Kingdom and that only 8,500 children during term time and just over 10,000 during the school holidays have a place in a club. More than a third of these clubs were in Greater London, and there is only one club in the whole of Wales.

In addition to these clubs, there is a growing number of projects developed for such purposes as providing opportunities for play and to keep children out of crime. These may be used by parents to provide care in the absence of other provision but are not care schemes and do not take responsibility for children. Following the Children Act 1989, local authorities have the duty to register and monitor standards of these services when provided for children up to the age of eight. Child care organizations lobbied strongly over this, arguing that day care settings required as great a level of care as residential settings, which are subject to regulation, and pressed for a Statutory Code of Practice to safeguard standards and safety. However, their proposed amendments on the bill failed.

Information Services

The complexity of parental child care arrangements, reflecting the low level of formal services and their fragmented structure, has contributed to the development of a small number of local information services aiming to help parents find their way around local services and facilitating a more informed choice (to the extent that this is available) between different forms of provision. There are probably less than 30 such schemes in the United Kingdom. Some of them have been set up in local authorities, in some cases by voluntary organizations, and a number of such schemes have been funded by the Department of Health as pilot projects—influenced by U.S. information and referral centers. One national voluntary organization, the Day Care Trust, is currently planning to develop local centers across the country—called Child Care Links—to both provide information and advice to parents and stimulate the development of more provision through working with local authorities and local child care groups.

REGULATION AND QUALITY CONTROL

Regulation now covers day nurseries, child minding, and a very limited proportion of nanny arrangements (those involving a nanny shared by more than two sets of parents). Regulatory legislation enacted in 1948 in England and Wales (the Nurseries and Childminding Act 1948; similar legislation exists in Scotland and Northern Ireland) was amended in 1968 to strengthen control over childminders and allow local authorities to provide them with support. Most recently, the Children Act 1989 again strengthens local authority powers in a number of areas, extending registration to nannies shared by more than two families—an increasing development in some parts of the country—and assuring effective regulation of day care providers for children up to the age of eight.

Day nursery regulation and standards cover accommodation, staff-child ratios, health, feeding, general care and staff training, and suggestions about play material and toys. The required minimum staff-child ratio overall for children under age five is one to five, and this ratio is reduced substantially where there are children under age two. The 1985 draft guidelines recommend a one-to-two ratio for children under age two, a one-to-four ratio for two to five year olds, and in practice local authority requirements vary considerably. The 1985 draft guidance also covers admission policies, optimum size, staff and staff training regime, curriculum, parental involvement, safety record keeping, and links with other services. A number of local authorities are themselves addressing this issue. In Scotland, Strathclyde Regional Council is funding evaluation research to broaden and extend criteria for assessment of day care programs.

Legislation provides an extensive framework for registration and monitoring and empowers local authorities in the provision of support, but resources available for these improvements are extremely limited. The expansion, in particular, of private day care has significant implications for regulatory and monitoring mechanisms. There is lack of clarity concerning the scope of local authority powers of enforcement (it remains to be seen whether the new Children Act will improve this), and growing recognition and concern that local authorities may not have sufficient powers of resources to effectively ensure high quality care. Government funding has supported the establishment of an organization of private and voluntary providers, a project that involves the examination of a voluntary accreditation scheme based on U.S. models. The relationship of such a scheme to statutory regulation and monitoring procedures is not yet clear.

CHILD CARE WORKERS

Local authority nurseries in general employ trained staff and make use of a small number of untrained students and other staff. Most of the staff in these nurseries have a nursery nurse qualification—a two-year course with a strong vocational content. There is little information on private and voluntary nurseries. Some local authorities require that a half or two thirds of staff should be qualified; some make no stipulation. Survey evidence suggests that most private and voluntary nurseries employ a reasonable proportion of trained staff, but a recent development has been the use of youth trainees—unemployed people on assisted government training programs.

No qualifications are required for registration as a childminder, although a number of authorities use their own courses and a course is now available through the Open University. Although courses are becoming more common, the National Childminding Association (NCMA) in 1986 found that only 22 percent of its members who responded to the survey had attended a course. The proportion of nannies who are qualified, in general as nursery nurses, is not known. All of these workers receive less than the average nonmanual female wage. In general local authority nursery workers and local authority sponsored childminders receive higher pay and better conditions of employment than child care workers in the private sector.

All local authority nursery workers receive paid holidays (about four weeks), belong to a pension scheme, and have access to state social security benefits. They work rarely more than 39 hours per week and sometimes less. Survey evidence suggests that private and voluntary nursery staff are less likely to belong to a pension scheme. In some cases their hours of work, when below the threshold of qualification, exclude them from many basic social security benefits. No information is available on staff turnover rates, but one report estimated that turnover, absenteeism, and sickness were high in local authority nurseries, possibly reflecting stress relating to the high proportion of high priority children within these nurseries. There is no information on turnover in private and voluntary nurseries.

Childminders in general work long hours; an NCMA survey found that over half were working 40 hours per week or more. Child-minding rates vary considerably, but the estimated pay is less than a half of the average female non-manual worker. Only childminders earning over the national insurance threshold and paying contributions have access to state maternity, employment, and sickness benefits and the basic state pension scheme. In general, minders receive no pay during their holidays. Turnover among childminders is thought to be high. In 1986 a survey of minders belonging to the NCMA, and therefore likely to be more committed than any others, found that only 27 percent had been minding for five or more years and nearly half had been on the job for less than two years.

A national research and development project was established in 1989 to prepare recommendations for new forms of vocational qualifications in child care based on employment led standards. The project, which is part of a broader "care sector consortium" set up by the training agency, is examining the range of occupations (including voluntary occupations) of those working with children under age seven and their families, the functions carried out, and the skills required, in order to prepare standards of competence. Although the project offers a solution to current confusion in the area, and (it is suggested) will improve access to the profession and facilitate transferability between areas of work, there is some concern that the exercise is being carried out in too much haste and that too few resources will be available for implementation.

STRENGTHS AND WEAKNESSES OF U.K. DAY CARE PROVISION

The early development of provision in the United Kingdom has undoubtedly brought some advantages in allowing the development of regulatory standards of care. The United Kingdom does have minimum registration requirements for both day nurseries and childminders, effectively preventing some of the worst child-minding conditions that promoted the first charitable nurseries. But more than 170 years after the opening of Robert Owen's nursery in New Lanark, day care provision has not achieved the acceptance and recognition required if it is to be properly supported, researched, and appropriately developed. A major element in this has been the lack of acceptance of mothers leaving their children in the care of others. Social prejudices against maternal employment have inhibited debate over day care policy. As a result, while education and health services have developed and been maintained as areas of public provision universally available, day care has never developed into an equivalent service but has increasingly been

restricted to disadvantaged groups, creating what is widely seen as a stigmatized form of care.

Mounting demand for day care over the last decade has not led to any
significant increase in real terms in public expenditure. Public expenditure
on local authority day nurseries, grants to the voluntary sector, and local
authority playgroups was in 1987 and 1988 only 0.027 percent of the gross
domestic product—slightly lower than the previous year and only slightly
higher than ten years earlier (0.024%). The proportion of children aged
five in local authority day nursery provision is now falling in England. Private
day care provision has been expanding, with the number of places in private
day nurseries now greater than local authority nurseries. But the increase
has been sporadic, and most significant in the more economically advantaged
areas. All this still means that there are nursery places in public, voluntary,
and private day nurseries for less than 2 percent of preschool children. The
increase in child minding has been significant, but the sharp increase in the
number of childminders is now severely testing the support and regulatory
mechanisms provided by local authorities in this area of care.

The political failure to address the issue of day care has resulted in an
expanding gap between demand and supply on formal services. The dearth
of affordable formal day care services has led to a heavy use of informal
arrangements and determines the hours and nature of employment undertaken by many women with small children. In these circumstances benefits
of regulation are necessarily limited as formal regulated services form only
a tiny island in a sea of informal care.

Ambivalence toward maternal employment has also undoubtedly contributed to the failure of educational services to come to terms with parental
requirements of care, although a further element in the separation of these
functions can be attributed to the separate administrative responsibilities in
government and local authority departments. The lack of policy coordination evidenced by the fragmented nature of services encompasses other
relevant areas of provision. There is no coordinated program or policy at
the government level in relation to services, working hours, and employment
provisions. The United Kingdom has no work and family program or coherent policies relating to these areas. However, as noted earlier, such a
program is beginning to be developed in the European Community. Integrative developments within the European Community, with the creation
of a single market by 1992, have focused attention on the need for improved
harmonization of working conditions within the community and are likely
to lend support to the development of the European Work and Family
Program. In the long term these European peace time initiatives are likely
to have a greater impact within the United Kingdom than the child care
programs associated with mobilization during the First and Second World
Wars.

NOTES

1. See, for example, J. Bowlby, *Can I Have My Baby?* National Association for Mental Health, Haden, 1958.

2. Compulsory school begins at age five in the United Kingdom.

3. Statistical information on day care programs is far from adequate, reflecting the lack of priority that it has been accorded. Within the returns of local authorities on their own public provision, no distinction is made between local authority nurseries that provide day care and local authority nurseries (often called family centers) that increasingly address what are seen as the broader needs of socially disadvantaged families and offer in some cases no day care at all. Similarly, there are no centrally available statistics that record the number of employer nurseries or community nurseries. Private and voluntary nurseries are recorded as one category. In addition, there is some variation in the recording of statistics between different parts of the United Kingdom.

REFERENCES

Bone, M. (1977). *Pre-school children and the need for day care.* London: HMSO.

Braybon, G., and Summerfield, P. (1987). *Women's experiences in two world wars.* London: Pandora.

Central Statistical Office. (1990). *Social Trends, 20,* London: HMSO.

Cohen, B. (1988). *Caring for children: Services and policies for child care and equal opportunities in the United Kingdom.* Report for the European Commission Child Care Network. London: Family Policy Studies Center.

Cohen, B. (1990). *Caring for children: The 1990 report.* London: Family Policy Studies Center, London.

Davie, C. (1986). *An investigation into childminding practice in North Staffordshire.* Report to Department of Health and Social Security.

Hansard Parliamentary Proceedings. London: HMSO. Column 150, July 12, 1988.

Henwood, M., and Wicks, M. (1986). *"Benefit or burden?"* In *Objectives and Impact of Child Support.* Family Policy Studies Center, London.

Kid's Clubs Network. (1990). *A patchwork of Provisions: Kid's clubs today.* London: Kid's Clubs Network.

Labour Party. (1989). *Meeting the challenge, make the change. A New Agenda for Britain.*

Labour Party. (1989). *A new future for women.*

Labour Party. (1990). *The best start. Labor's Policy in Education and Care for Young Children.*

Mayall, B., and Petrie, P. (1983). *Childminding and day nurseries: What kind of care?* London: Heinemann Educational.

Moss, P. (1988). *Child care and equality of opportunity.* London: Commission of the European Community.

Osborne, A., and Milbank, J. (1987). *The effects of early education.* A report for the Child Health and Education Study. Oxford: Oxford University Press.

Scott, G. (1989). *Families and under-fives in Strathclyde.* Glasgow: Strathclyde Regional Council.

Shields, J. (1986). "Age of Entry—Inequality of Education." In *Parents and Schools,* Vol. 47, Autumn.

Summerfield, P. (1984). *Women working in the Second World War.* London: Croome Helm.

Van der Eyken, W. (1984). *Day nurseries in action.* A report from the Child Health Research Unit. Bristol: University of Bristol.

Women of Europe. (1990). *Child care in Europe 1988–90.* Brussels: Commission of the European Community.

Working for Childcare. (1990). *Meeting the childcare challenge: Can the market provide?* London: Working for Childcare.

—— 27 ——

UNITED STATES OF AMERICA

Polly Spedding

"The relation of day care to family life is sometimes not understood by the general public."

—Urie Bronfenbrenner,
Cornell University, July 23, 1986

"Day care is not just for children, it's for working mothers. It's for fathers, so their wives can help support the family. It's for families, so their children can grow up in a healthy environment. And it's for people who don't have children, so the economy can run smoothly."

—Edward F. Zigler and Jody Goodman,
Yale University, 1982

"American parents recognize and accept the fact that they have primary responsibility for raising their children. They will, therefore, make every effort to retain that responsibility as they select caregivers to assist them with child care while they work."

—Moncrieff Cochran,
Cornell University, 1978

Child day care in the United States of America is closely related to the world of work, providing an essential support system to American families and to the American economy. In contrast to many other industrialized countries, however, the United States has no national day care "system" or single, clearly articulated federal policy concerning child care. The reasons for this lie at least in part in deeply rooted belief systems dating from the nation's early beginnings.

IDEOLOGICAL AND DEMOGRAPHIC PERSPECTIVES

Citizens of the United States often characterize themselves as a nation of "rugged individualists." Ideals of individual freedom, personal and family privacy, self-sufficiency (the "work ethic"), the separation of church and state, and the responsibility of the more fortunate to help the less fortunate—although not always realized in fact—are basic to the American culture. This ideological framework has its roots in the not-so-distant past (19th and early 20th centuries), when the nation was settled by immigrants who left their European homelands for the "New World" in search of freedom from religious persecution and oppression. Successive waves of immigrants came to the "land of opportunity" to carve out new lives, hoping to make their fortunes. Self-reliance was, and is, highly valued. The rights of citizens to freedom of worship, speech, and security in their persons, papers, and households are guaranteed by the U.S. Constitution, which also reserves to the states any rights not specifically delegated to the federal government. As we shall see in this chapter, these traditions and constitutional guarantees are strongly reflected in child care programs and policies as they exist in the United States today.

Interwoven with these ideals are a number of social, economic, and political concepts and concerns that are also part and parcel of the U.S. heritage. Traditional as well as constitutional divisions between the role of the federal government and the rights of the states give considerable autonomy to the states in the development and delivery of social programs. There is also a long-standing division between the roles of the "public" and "private" sectors. In addition, there is widespread ambivalence about women's roles and concern about the long-term effects of day care on very young children.

The United States of America is a vast nation, enclosing over 3.5 million square miles and containing almost 250 million people. The sheer size of the country is sometimes difficult to grasp, even for those who live and work within its borders. The land mass of the United States, for example, is only slightly smaller than either China or Canada. Populous states in the United States often contain more people than individual European countries; the population of New York State, for example, is approximately equal to the population of Denmark, Norway, and Sweden combined. The 50 states—each with its own governor, legislature, and judicial system—reflect variations in culture and traditions that are specific to their own geography and history. While the complexion of the nation's citizens is predominantly (84%) white, the "American melting pot" is growing more and more culturally diverse, due to increasing Black, Hispanic, and Asian populations.

The nation's economy is also diverse and is based on a long-standing tradition of free enterprise; that is, the freedom of private business to organize and operate for profit in a competitive system without government interference except, perhaps, for regulations that protect the common good.

Small businesses—employing fewer than 100 workers—make up almost 98 percent of the approximately 6 million U.S. employers. And although the United States is a heavily industrialized nation dotted with large population centers, much of the land is rural. Agriculture and businesses related to agriculture continue to be important components of the nation's economy. The ethnic diversity of the nation's cities is often in sharp contrast to the white homogeneity of many of America's rural and suburban areas. Traditionally, the nation's rural residents have held more conservative views than their metropolitan peers.

Family Patterns

A major influence on day care in the United States today has been the much documented change in the family itself. The family has been and continues to be the basic unit of American society, but the term "family" in contemporary America is often used to include a variety of traditional and less traditional life-styles, including households headed by married couples, unmarried couples, single parents, and same sex couples. Regardless of the family structure, however, the raising of children is clearly understood to be the responsibility of parents of other adult family members who serve in the parenting role.

The most dramatic change in the U.S. family has been the shift from the stereotypical family with wage-earner husband and stay-at-home wife (fewer than 20 percent of all U.S. families with children in 1989) to a majority of families (52 percent in 1989) in which both adult partners are employed outside the home. In addition, a growing number of families (17 percent in 1989) are headed by employed single parents, usually women. The economic status of many of these families, particularly those headed by women, is precarious; typically, women workers in the United States earn 20 to 30 percent less than their male counterparts. The effect on children is shocking: currently, 20 percent of the nation's children live in poverty; among children younger than age three, the percentage is even higher (23.3%). Day care is increasingly seen as an essential component in any effort to address the economic and social needs of families in the United States today.

Women in the Work Force

In the last 30 years, unprecedented numbers of American women have entered the work force: almost 60 percent of all the nation's women were in the labor force in 1988, accounting for almost half (46%) of the total. Over half of the mothers of infants are employed. By 1995, it is expected that two thirds of the mothers of preschoolers and three fourths of the mothers of school-age children will be in the labor force. The vast majority (74%) of employed women work full time. Despite the influx of women into the work force, the pool of potential workers is shrinking, a trend that is largely due to lower birthrates. Neither the proportion of women in the work force nor the lower birthrate are expected to change in the foreseeable future. As a result, U.S. employers are becoming more and more aware that family-oriented policies such as support for child day care can be in their own interest.

Changing Perceptions

Historically, women in the United States have always worked, both inside and outside of the home. But teaching, nursing, participation in the family farm or business, and volunteer work in the community have traditionally been viewed in a different light than other types of employment. A combination of forces—economic pressures on families, the feminist movement, and a shrinking labor supply—are gradually making profound changes in traditional points of view. Clearly, perceptions about the role of day care in relation to the family and the U.S. economy have changed. A major change in perception involves the understanding of what out-of-home child care is and for whom it is intended.

HISTORICAL PERSPECTIVES: DAY CARE AND EARLY EDUCATION

Historically, the out-of-home care and education of young children in the United States took two separate paths,[1] both of which evolved during the 19th and early 20th centuries. Both borrowed from the "infant school" and "kindergarten" movements in Europe, but one path led toward a negative identification with poverty and social welfare, while the other led toward a positive identification with affluence and education.

Day Care

The first path, day care, provided custodial full-day care for the children of underprivileged families, headed for the most part by widows and immigrants engaged in low-paying jobs due to economic necessity. In keeping with the traditional U.S. sense of responsibility for the less fortunate, coupled with the less altruistic motivation of reducing public assistance payments, day care (originally called "day nurseries") became part of the public welfare system. Regardless of economic and philosophical changes over time, it remains there today. Early day nurseries often had a strong moral tone and were frequently organized by church women. Thus, many day nurseries were located in facilities operated by religious institutions. Although the moral tone has diminished over time, religious institutions still provide sites for thousands of day care centers in the United States.[2]

In contemporary America, a number of changes have taken place: now the vast majority of families pay for all or most of their day care costs; day care centers located in churches and synagogues pay their way; and "developmental" day care has replaced "custodial" day care in theory if not always in reality. Nevertheless, services that carry the "day care" label are administered and regulated by all but one of the states through their designated "social welfare" departments. The exception is the State of California, which placed its day care and early childhood programs in the state's Department of Education and has only recently placed several new initiatives under the auspices of social services departments. Thus, because of differences in philosophies, funding, and tradition, and in the absence of clear-cut national policy, there is wide variation in both administration and regulation among the various states. Regardless of these state-to-state differences, the traditional view of day care has been that it belonged in the social welfare arena. As such, it was strongly related to the need for parental (usually maternal) employment and has long carried the stigma of poverty.

Early Childhood Education

The second path has been that of part-day "educational" programs for young children, which provided enrichment and socialization for the children of middle and upper-middle income families. This path is rooted in the nursery school movement and, historically, has had little or no relationship to parental employment. Where "custodial" day nurseries focused primarily on providing a safe environment and paid scant attention to children's developmental needs, nursery schools focused on enhancing the social, emotional, and cognitive needs of children. Thus, nursery schools were seen as belonging in the educational arena. In contrast to day care, however, nursery schools are rarely subject to governmental regulation. Most are privately operated and their use is seen as entirely a matter of parental choice.

Merging Pathways

By the mid–1900s, the "day care" and "early childhood education" pathways had begun slowly to intertwine. Research on the importance of the child's early years filtered into day care settings. Child psychology and, eventually, early childhood education became respectable courses of study; professionals trained in these disciplines entered the "day nurseries" as well as the "nursery schools." World War II found thousands of middle income mothers working outside their homes as part of the war effort; federally funded child care centers were organized as part of that effort. Although the majority of women returned to their homes after the war and federal funding for day care ended, many other women stayed in the work force.

The need for day care continued. These more affluent, sophisticated parents expected more than routine, "custodial" care for their children.

Programs for children from less advantaged families changed too. In the 1960s, the establishment of the national Head Start program for disadvantaged children became a centerpiece of President Lyndon Johnson's "War on Poverty." Head Start centers incorporated an educational philosophy into their comprehensive services for economically disadvantaged children and their families. The vast majority of Head Start centers, although licensed as day care centers, operated on part-day schedules similar to the nursery schools attended by children from more affluent families. In addition, Head Start was not tied to parental employment. The lines between "day care" and "early childhood education" were blurring.

Although philosophical differences may have diminished somewhat and day care has become more widely accepted as a support system for working parents at all income levels, the separation between day care and early childhood education has not completely disappeared in the United States. Much of the remaining separation has to do with ways in which child care programs are defined and delivered, which in turn reflect distinctions between "private" and "public" funding and delivery mechanisms.

CHILD CARE OPTIONS IN THE UNITED STATES

The following descriptions are intended to provide brief overviews of child care options in the United States. As such, they are necessarily general in nature.

Day Care Center. Provides group care for children in a non-residential setting for all or part of a day. Most centers enroll three to five year olds; a growing number also offer care for infants, toddlers, and school-age children. Some also offer kindergarten programs for five year olds. Most day care centers in the United States of America operate year round, five days per week, from early morning to early evening, with some local variations. Very few of these day care centers are in facilities built specifically for day care purposes: the majority are located in buildings owned by churches and other organizations; a few are at work sites; a few are in public schools. Day care centers in the United States are primarily private businesses and can be either "for-profit" or "not-for-profit" centers. In either case, they are usually subject to the regulatory system of their particular state.

Employer-supported or Employer-sponsored Child Care. Day care provided by or subsidized by an employer. Direct services may be provided by an employer in a day care center at or near the work site or purchased by the employer in one or more family day care homes. Indirect employer support may take the form of donations to child care programs, support for resource and referral services, and family-oriented personnel policies.

Currently, fewer than 1 percent of the nation's 6 million employers provide direct support for child care.

Family Day Care. Provided in a caregiver's home for all or part of a day. Care is usually year round, five days per week, early morning to early evening, with somewhat more flexible hours than day care centers. Most family day care providers accept children from infancy through school age; some limit enrollment to specific age groups. Most family day care providers are private entrepreneurs working under private arrangements made with parents; these providers often are outside any governmental regulatory system. Other family day care providers accept only publicly subsidized children.[3] Still others accept children from both fee-paying and publicly subsidized families. Providers who accept publicly subsidized children are more apt to operate within the regulatory system of their particular state, which usually limits the number of children in care. In some areas of the United States, family day care providers operate as part of Family Day Care Systems: networks of providers that are sponsored by a child-related administrative agency.

Group Family Day Care. Provided in a caregiver's home for all or part of the day by at least two adults and for larger groups of children than regular family day care. Care is usually year round, five days per week, early morning to early evening, with local variations. Most group family day care homes accept children from infancy through school age; some limit enrollment to specific age groups. Group family day care providers are usually private entrepreneurs. Some accept only children from fee-paying families; some accept only public subsidized children; others accept both. It is not currently known how many group family day care homes operate inside or outside of the regulatory system of their particular state.

Head Start. Federally funded, compensatory program for disadvantaged three to five year olds. This comprehensive program includes health, nutrition, education, social services, and parent involvement. Head Start can be part-day or full-day programs and often follow a school-year schedule. Most programs are center based (including public schools); some are home based. There is no fee to the parents. Children from families whose incomes are at or below the poverty level are eligible for Head Start services; some exceptions can be made for children with special needs. Currently, Head Start serves fewer than 20 percent of the eligible children in the United States.

In-Home Care. Full- or part-day care provided by an adult in the child's own home. If the care is on a regular, paid basis, the caregiver is considered a household employee. Most in-home caregivers perform light housekeeping tasks in addition to caring for children in the home. In-home caregivers are sometimes referred to as "nannies" or "baby-sitters." Very little is known about in-home care in the United States; it is rarely discussed in terms of child day care and is not subject to day care regulation in any state.[4]

Kindergarten. Virtually all states offer kindergarten programs for five year olds, usually through the public schools. (The compulsory enrollment age for public school in most of the United States is age six.) Some kindergartens are half-day programs, others full school-day programs. There are also some privately operated kindergartens and some kindergartens offered by day care centers. Regardless of the sponsorship, most kindergartens must meet guidelines established by the education department of their particular state.

Nursery School. Privately operated preschool that provides social and educational programming for three to five year olds. Nursery schools usually operate for three hours or less per session, two to five times per week, and often follow a school-year schedule. Most privately owned nursery schools are supported through parent fees. Some nursery schools are "parent co-operatives," requiring parent participation to administer the school and assist professional teachers in the classrooms. Nursery schools are rarely subject to day care regulations.

Public School Preschool. Over half the states currently offer some public school educational programs for disadvantaged four year olds and more are in the planning stage.[5] These are usually part-day programs, operate on a school-year schedule, and charge no fee to parents. Programs are often similar in nature and goals to Head State, but they are financed through state and local education funding rather than federal funds. The choice of whether to offer the program is left up to individual school districts. Some public schools in the United States also act as sponsors for federally funded Head Start programs.

School-Age Child Care. Planned activities and supervision for school age children (kindergarten to early adolescence) in the hours before and after school and at times when school is not in session. School-age child care may be provided by day care centers, family day care and group family day care homes, public schools, youth recreation groups, religious organizations, and other community groups. There is usually a parent fee.

In addition to the variety of child care options, a substantial number of American families provide their own child care—juggling jobs so that one adult is home with the children while another adult is at work, delegating child care responsibility to older siblings or relatives, caring for children at the workplace, or leaving children to care for themselves.

DATA ON CHILDREN IN VARIOUS TYPES OF CARE

Data on the actual numbers of children in the various forms of care are extremely difficult to obtain and, until fairly recently, have not been kept in any systematic manner. As a result, what data are available are subject to considerable interpretation. A 1987 survey by the U.S. Bureau of the Census is generally regarded as one of the more reliable to date.[6] A summary

Figure 27.1
Primary Child Care Arrangements of Preschool Children (8 million children)

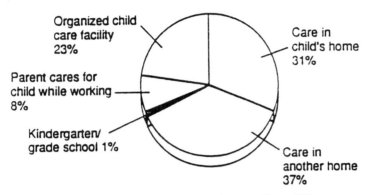

Organized child
care facility
23%

Care in
child's home
31%

Parent cares for
child while working
8%

Kindergarten/
grade school 1%

Care in
another home
37%

Source: Statistical Brief, U.S. Bureau of the Census, May, 1987

of the data from that survey is provided in Figure 27.1. According to the Census Bureau, more than a third of the nation's preschoolers (birth to age five) whose mothers were employed outside the home was cared for in family day care homes, including the homes of both relatives and non-relatives. Almost another third received care in their own homes, including care by relatives, in-home caregivers, or friends. About one quarter of these children was enrolled in group care settings, including both day care centers and nursery schools. The remainder were cared for by parents themselves, either at home or at the parents' work sites.

For school-age youngsters, the vast majority of children ages five and over are in public school for the major portion of the day. The arrangements made for those children when not in school are shown in Figure 27.2. The reader can see from the figure that secondary arrangements for the times when children were not in school included care in their own home, care in another home, organized group settings, and care by a parent at the work-place. The remaining children (an estimated 6 to 7 million preschool and school-age youngsters) are assumed to be in "self-care," taking care of themselves and sometimes their siblings while their parents are at work.

Whatever else one might make of the data, it seems clear that the majority of employed parents in the United States use home-based day care for their children. Whether this is by choice or whether it is dictated by the types of care that are readily available and/or affordable is a question that has yet to be satisfactorily answered.

PUBLIC-PRIVATE DISTINCTIONS

Child care in the United States has been described as a "mixed economy" in which privately funded and operated programs co-exist with totally public

Figure 27.2
Child Care Arrangements of School-Age Children

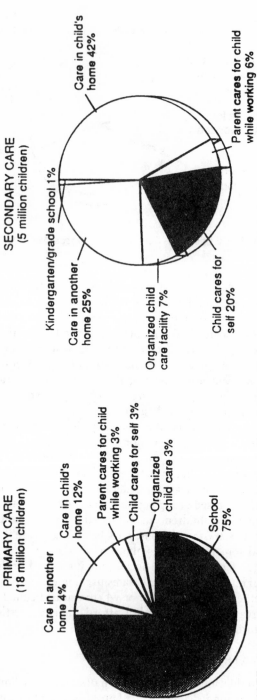

PRIMARY CARE
(18 million children)

Care in another
home 4%

Care in child's
home 12%

Parent cares for child
while working 3%

Child cares for self 3%

Organized
child care 3%

School
75%

SECONDARY CARE
(5 million children)

Care in child's
home 42%

Parent cares for child
while working 6%

Kindergarten/grade school 1%

Care in another
home 25%

Organized child
care facility 7%

Child cares for
self 20%

NOTE: Primary is the arrangement used most of the hours the mother is working; secondary is the arrangement used when
additional care is necessary during the mother's working hours.

Source: Statistical Brief, U.S. Bureau of the Census, May, 1987

programs. It has also been suggested that programs can be located on a continuum from the completely private to the completely public, with most somewhere in the middle.[7] As the descriptions of child care options suggest, several of the program types might be found at more than one point along the continuum, depending on how the programs are funded and administered, whether enrollment is open to all children or limited to children of specific groups, and even on various definitions of the terms "private" and "public."

For example, a school-age child care program operating independently and enrolling only children from fee-paying families would be placed at the "completely private" end of the "private-public" continuum. A similar program operated by a public school, with open enrollment and no parent fee, would be placed at the "completely public" end of the continuum. At points between the two would lie countless variations with mixed funding (parent fees, public subsidies, foundation grants, employer contributions), different types of sponsorship, and various enrollment policies.

American traditions of free enterprise and parental choice are clearly evident in the development, delivery, and administration of child care services across the nation. In the absence of any consistent national policy, a proliferation of public and private funding and delivery mechanisms have been, and continue to be, the norm. As we shall see, the regulation of child care provides another demonstration that variety is the "norm" that characterizes child day care in the United States.

THE REGULATION OF CHILD CARE

It has long been understood in the United States that it is the responsibility of government—at all levels—to protect its citizens and to regulate the free enterprise system when necessary to ensure the public interest. Attempts to establish federal guidelines for child day care have not met with success; instead, this regulatory responsibility has been left to individual states. The states have varied widely in their responses.[8]

In general, both family day care and day care centers are subject to state licensing regulations, but there is considerable variation in regulations from state to state, and the regulation of family day care is far less rigorous than that of day care centers.

Over half the states regulate group family day care. It is important to note that although either form of family day care is generally subject to state regulation, estimates are that 60 to 90 percent of family day care, nationwide, occurs in informal arrangements that are outside the formal regulatory system.[9]

State regulations for day care centers often do not apply to church-run programs, programs sponsored by public schools, recreational programs, nursery schools, and—in some cases—school-age child care programs.

In general, state day care licensing regulations set minimum standards for space, staff-to-child ratios, group sizes, health, safety, and staff qualifications. But licensing regulations do not guarantee quality. In the absence of federal standards, individual states have developed a wide range of "acceptable" minimum standards. For example, day care center regulations concerning the ratio of staff to children range from one adult to three infants in the most restrictive states to one adult to eight infants in the least restrictive, with the majority of states requiring one adult to four infants and one state having no requirement at all. Group size, considered by many early childhood specialists to be a critical determinant of quality care, is not specified in over half the states, is specified only for infants in several others, and varies widely in the remainder. One commonality in day care center regulations among the states is the required inspection of the facility before the license is issued, with periodic inspections thereafter. However, the regularity of post-licensing inspections varies.

Variations in family day care regulations are even more dramatic. A handful of states either do not regulate family day care at all or regulate only those that provide care for children from publicly subsidized families. In the states that do regulate family day care, some "license" homes, others "register" them, and still others use a combination of both licensing and registration. While both systems mandate minimum requirements, "licensing" usually includes an inspection of the home before the license is issued and periodic inspection thereafter. "Registration" requires the care provider to certify that the home meets the state's minimum standards, usually does not require an inspection before the home enrolls children, and may or may not require inspections thereafter. Because the safety of children is the underlying reason for day care regulation and the number (both minimum and maximum) of children allowed in family day care homes varies so widely among the states, the question of mandatory inspections is often hotly debated by early childhood specialists, policy makers, and practitioners. Beneath the rhetoric of the debates lies an ideological dilemma involving issues of the provider's right to conduct business, the privacy of the care provider's home, the well-being of children, and the responsibilities of parents and of government.

Another widely debated regulatory issue in both center-based and family day care is the question of how specific regulations should be about the daily program for children. Here again, there is wide variation. The majority of states require that day care centers provide "developmental" programs, but they are not always specific about what such a program should include. Regulations for family day care are, for the most part, even less specific.

As previously noted, part-day nursery schools are usually not subject to licensing regulations, although some states offer a voluntary registration system for nursery schools, and a few states have attempted to ensure that guidelines for part-day programs located in public schools meet or exceed day care licensing regulations.

In-home care providers are simply not mentioned in day care regulations. They are legally viewed as household employees since they are screened and selected by the head or heads of the households in which they work. It is generally assumed that employing an in-home caregiver is a luxury reserved for wealthier families.

In addition to state day care regulations—or, sometimes, in their absence—local governments in various parts of the nation also claim some regulatory jurisdiction over child day care services. These regulations usually have to do with health and safety, and they take the form of inspections for safe drinking water, sanitary kitchens, and adherence to local fire and building codes. In the case of family day care, local zoning regulations that prohibit the operation of businesses in residential neighborhoods have sometimes prevented would-be providers from opening their homes for the care of children.

CHILD CARE RESOURCE AND REFERRAL

In addition to—or perhaps because of—the variety of direct child care services in the United States, a growing number of community-based child care resource and referral (CCR&R) agencies have sprung up across the nation—some in systematic "networks," others operating independently. These CCR&R agencies help parents locate child care, recruit and train new providers, gather data about child care needs and services, offer technical assistance to employers, policy makers and others, and often take the lead in advocacy efforts for children, parents, and providers.

The expansion of child care resource and referral agencies has not been consistent from state to state; fewer than half the states have statewide networks of CCR&R agencies.[10] Although several states have begun to provide funding mechanisms for statewide networks of resource and referral services, most agencies that offer the services are dependent on their own fund-raising efforts for their continued existence.

In some areas of the United States, child care resource and referral is proving to be a popular option for employers who are interested in providing some form of child care assistance to their employees. Some employers contract for the service through community-based CCR&R agencies, while others provide the service through their own personnel offices.

ISSUES OF QUALITY

Concerns about issues of quality are certainly not unique to the United States. What may be unique is the variety and complexity of quality issues, given the number of part-day/full-day, in-home/out-of-home, costly/less costly, regulated/non-regulated child care options that exist across the nation.

Many of the issues have already been highlighted in previous sections of this chapter. By way of summary, I will restate two major concerns about quality of care and look at some attempts to address these issues.

First, there is no consistent, nationally regulated definition of high quality child care. Research efforts in the United States have consistently shown that well-trained child care workers, developmentally appropriate activities and routines, high ratios of adults to children, and small group sizes are critical to quality care.[11] As illustrated in our earlier discussion of child care regulations, these components of quality care are often missing.

In the absence of a comprehensive national policy and consistent regulatory standards among the states, three national early childhood accreditation/credential systems have been developed to address the quality of out-of-home care for America's children. All three were designed to promote program quality and worker competence beyond minimum standards.

One, a national voluntary accreditation system for early childhood centers and schools developed and sponsored by the National Association for the Education of Young Children (NAEYC), sets standards based on developmentally appropriate practices also developed by NAEYC and recognizes those programs that meet the standards. The standards include interactions among staff and children, curriculum, staff-parent interaction, staff qualifications and development, administration, staffing, physical environment, health and safety, nutrition and food service, and evaluation.

The self-study NAEYC accreditation system is open to center-based programs that serve ten or more children, have been in operation at least one year, and comply with their own state's licensing requirements. Eligible programs include day care centers, Head Start centers, nursery schools, and school-age child care programs. Since its inception in 1985, the NAEYC accreditation system has gained considerable strength. As of August 1991, almost 1,800 centers had been accredited. Over 100 centers begin the accreditation process every month. Currently, family day care homes are not eligible to participate.[12]

A second accreditation system designed specifically for family day care was developed and field tested in 1988 by the National Association for Family Day Care (NAFDC) and became operational in 1989. Designed to professionalize the field of family day care, the self-study system uses an "Assessment Profile for Family Day Care" which measures performance in seven categories: interaction, safety, health, nutrition, indoor play environment, outdoor play environment, and professional responsibility. Slightly less than 300 family day care providers across the nation are currently accredited, but many more are in the process. Accreditation is awarded by NAFDC following a process that includes self assessment by the candidates and both observations and evaluation by parents and NAFDC-trained "validators," who may be early childhood specialists or experienced family day care providers. Providers who participate must also meet whatever regulatory standards exist in their own states.[13]

A third system, administered by the Council for Early Childhood Professional Recognition, grants Child Development Associate (CDA) credentials to early childhood workers in a variety of settings, including both family day care and center-based programs. The CDA credential was developed in the early 1970s to meet the staffing needs of Head Start centers, but it has since been opened to workers in other child care/early childhood programs. It, too, is a self-study process that measures competencies in a number of functional areas, and it can be tailored to meet the individual needs and experience of participants. Each candidate for the CDA credential is evaluated by a team of early childhood specialists and parents. The team makes the recommendation that the credential be awarded. Nationwide, more than 30,000 people have been awarded CDA credentials.[14]

Despite increasing interest in these voluntary credentials and accreditation systems, a recently completed national study rates the overall quality of day care in the U.S. as abysmally low.[15] As previously noted, attempts to establish federally mandated standards have consistently failed, and the regulatory standards established by individual states vary widely.

Second, the quality of child care in the United States is seriously threatened by a shortage of qualified workers. Until very recently, discussions of the quality of child care workers in the United States have been based primarily on national research conducted over a decade ago and on a few recent, smaller-scale surveys from various sources in individual states.[16] The research has consistently underscored the importance of well-trained child care workers to quality care for children. In addition, the more recent surveys have increasingly shown concern over high turnover rates, low status, and low wages in various child care settings.

In 1989, the results of a carefully conducted National Child Staffing Study, based on extensive research in 227 diverse child care centers in five U.S. cities, were released to the public.[17] The study's findings not only confirmed earlier research on the critical relationship between well-trained staff and quality care, but added compelling evidence that the work environment for child care staff has deteriorated at an alarming rate.

According to the staffing study's report, child care teaching staff in U.S. day care centers have completed more years of formal education than the average U.S. worker, but earn poverty-level wages and receive only minimal benefits. Primarily because of low wages, staff turnover almost tripled in the last decade, reaching an annual turnover rate of 41 percent in 1988.

The study rated the quality of services provided by the majority of child care centers to be "barely adequate." Findings showed that children attending lower quality centers—particularly those with higher staff turnover—were less competent in language and social development than children in better quality centers. As the staffing study report makes clear, "In child care, children's experience is directly linked to the well-being of their care-givers. Good quality care requires an environment that values adults as well as children."[18]

The study concludes with five major recommendations designed to improve the quality of care for children and the work environment for child care staff:

- Increase child care teacher salaries.
- Promote formal education and training opportunities for child care workers.
- Adopt state and federal standards for adult-to-child ratios, staff training, education, and compensation.
- Develop standards within the various child care settings that would minimize disparities between different types of programs.
- Promote public education about the importance of well-trained, adequately paid child care staff.

It is important to note that the National Child Care Staffing Study investigation included only center-based child care programs and did not include family day care or group family day care homes. There is, however, little reason to believe that conditions in either form of family day care are any better than those found in center-based care, and a number of reasons to believe that conditions may well be worse. Surveys and reports on child care in the United States have consistently stated that family day care providers are more apt to have less training, earn less, and leave the child care field at even higher rates than workers in center-based child care programs. Therefore, there appears to be no reason to believe that the recommendations contained in the national staffing study report would not be equally effective in improving the quality of family day care across the nation.

At this writing, it is not yet possible to tell what effect the National Child Care Staffing Study may have on child care policies at either the state or federal levels. Prior to the issuance of the study's findings, a handful of states had established funding mechanisms designed to raise child care workers' salaries and thus enhance recruitment and retention. A few states had also made funds available for training child care workers. Both public and private sources of funding for resource and referral agencies have usually included the requirement that the agencies provide training for workers in a variety of child care settings. Some employers and benevolent foundations have also made funds available for recruitment and training efforts. Child care organizations and individual child care advocates have made concerted efforts to encourage parents to become more vocal about their child care needs and concerns.

What remains to be seen is whether the nation as a whole is convinced that non-parental child care is ideologically acceptable and that the issues surrounding child care affect children, their families, and the economy. If so, perhaps the nation will prove ready to commit itself to providing the resources necessary to improve the quality of child care services to its youngest citizens.

STRENGTHS, SHORTCOMINGS, AND CHALLENGES

Seen in the most positive light, the numerous child care options available to families in the United States today would appear to provide many choices and are in keeping with deep-seated traditions of individual freedom and family privacy. However, despite the variety of options and the helpful presence of resource and referral agencies in some states, it would be far from correct to conclude that all is well with child day care in the United States of America. Over the past several years, numerous task forces, commissions, committees, and researchers in various locations across the nation have drawn a dismal picture.[19] Their findings echo several common themes:

- Not all of the options for child care are available in all communities. In particular, day care services for infants, toddlers, and school-age youngsters fall far short of the demand.

- Not all families have access to all the types of care even when they are available. Narrow eligibility criteria and funding, transportation difficulties, and uneven distribution of CCR&R agencies all contribute to problems with accessibility to services.

- The cost of child care is higher than many families can afford to pay. Government subsidies have decreased dramatically in the last decade, and employer assistance, though increasing, is extremely limited.

- The cost of quality child care is higher than many programs can afford to provide. Child care workers are woefully undervalued and underpaid. In addition, other program costs have escalated in recent years.

- The qualifications of child care workers differ dramatically from state to state, ranging from no prior training or experience to four-year college degrees and/or extensive experience.

- The quality of care in all types of child care programming is highly questionable. In the case of family day care, the quality of the informal, unregulated care that currently provides the bulk of child care services across the nation is virtually impossible to assess. Center-based programs report high caregiver turnover rates, with severe difficulties in recruiting and retaining child care staff. In family day care, the situation is reported to be even worse.

- Day care policies are fragmented and sometimes contradictory. There is little or no coordination between programs and administering agencies at local, state, and federal levels. A specific concern is the need for full-day care for disadvantaged children currently enrolled in part-day "compensatory" programs (i.e., Head Start and similar state-sponsored early childhood programs) whose parents are employed in full-time jobs.

- The absence of a national policy on parental leave and the growing representation in the work force of parents with infants have created a twofold demand: one for more day care places for infants and toddlers, the other for serious consideration of parental leave policies in both the public and private sectors. Neither demand is currently being met.

CONCLUSION

The bewildering array of program options in the United States—operating primarily in a free enterprise system with an emphasis on parental choice and minimal governmental interference—clearly demonstrates the high value the nation places on self-reliance, freedom of choice, and personal and family privacy. But these concepts, held so dear, can also create a variety of problems for children and their families. Underlying many of the problems is an ideological dilemma that pits self-sufficiency and the work ethic against the traditional role of parents as primary caregivers for their children.

Contemporary observers of the scene—this writer included—have used the word "crisis" to describe the child care situation in the United States today. Clearly, the situation is critical. Questions of availability, accessibility, affordability, and quality cannot be ignored, for the well-being of children and their families is at stake.

Surely, in a nation known for its energy, empathy, and creativity, the problems that revolve around child care can be resolved. To do so will take concerted effort and, undoubtedly, a large monetary investment.

There are hopeful signs that the nation is beginning to respond. In 1990, after vigorous efforts by child care advocates, federal legislation was passed by both houses of Congress that will infuse over $1 billion into various child care services. The measure falls far short of what advocates believe is needed and does not require uniform federal standards for child care programs. It does, however, signify a willingness at the federal level to regard child care as a critical national issue and may lay the groundwork for more comprehensive measures in future years.

Also in 1990, federal legislation was passed that would have established a minimal parental leave policy. The legislation was promptly vetoed by President George Bush on the grounds that government should not interfere with private enterprise. It is widely believed, however, that the move for a national policy requiring some form of parental leave will be successful within the decade.

For the sake of children and families, the efforts and investments necessary to solve the dilemma of child care in the United States cannot be made too soon.

1. Observers have not always agreed about how clearly delineated the separate "paths" of child care and early childhood education have been, but numerous writers have attested to their reality. For a recent, detailed discussion, see Emily D. Cahan, *Past Caring: A History of U.S. Preschool Care and Education for the Poor, 1820–1965* (New York: National Center for Children in Poverty, 1989).

2. For a comprehensive discussion of the relationship between churches and child care, see Eileen W. Lindner, Mary C. Mattis, and June R. Rogers, *When Churches Mind the Children: A Study of Day Care in Local Parishes* (Ypsilanti, Mich.: High/Scope Press, 1983).

3. A variety of publicly administered funding streams at both state and federal levels are used to subsidize some or all of the cost of child care services for children from low income families. Eligibility criteria guidelines vary widely.

4. Lin Yeiser discusses in-home caregivers in *Nannies, Au Pairs, Mothers' Helpers-Caregivers* (New York: Vintage Books, 1987); other references are rare.

5. "Preschool" is a generic term in the United States commonly used to refer to any out-of-home educational programs for children younger than five years of age.

6. U.S. Bureau of the Census, "Who's Minding the Kids?" Statistical Brief SB–2–87 (Washington, D.C.: author, May 1987).

7. References to child care as a "mixed economy" and the "private-public continuum" are both from Alfred J. Kahn and Sheila B. Kamerman, *Child Care: Facing the Hard Choices* (Dover, Mass.: Auburn House, 1987) pp. 94, 112.

8. M. Therese Gnezda and Shelley L. Smith, *Child Care and Early Childhood Education Policy: A Legislator's Guide* (Washington, D.C.: National Conference of State Legislatures, 1989); Gwen Morgan, *The National State of Child Care Regulation 1986* (Washington, D.C.: National Association for the Education of Young Children, 1987); Deborah Phillips, Jeff Lande, and Marc Goldberg, "The State of Child Care Regulation: A Comparative Analysis" in *Early Childhood Research Quarterly* Volume 4, Number 2, pp. 151–179. (Norwood, N.J.: Ablex Publishing Corporation, June 1990).

9. The estimate that 60 to 90 percent of family day care homes are not regulated appears in numerous reports. For example, see Kahn and Kamerman, 1987, p. 205, and Children's Foundation, 1988, cited in Gnezda and Smith, 1989, p. 7.

10. Data on child care resource and referral services nationwide, by Cornell University graduate student Emilie Kudela, shows statewide networks in 19 states (personal conversation, January 1990).

11. Among the various research studies that have reported these findings, see especially Richard Ruopp, Jeffrey Travers, et al., *Children at the Center: Final Report of the National Day Care Study* (Cambridge, Mass.: Abt Associates, 1979).

12. National Academy of Early Childhood Programs, *Accreditation Criteria and Procedures* (Washington, D.C.: National Association for the Education of Young Children, 1984); also, Sue Bredekamp (Ed.), *Developmentally Appropriate Practice in Early Childhood Programs Serving Children from Birth Through Age 8*, expanded edition. (Washington, D.C.: National Association for the Education of Young Children, 1987).

13. Current information about the NAFDC Accreditation Program is included regularly in *Family Day Care Bulletin*, published by the Children's Foundation, 725 Fifteenth Street NW, Washington, DC 20005.

14. For a recent update on the CDA program, see Carol Brunson Phillips, "The CDA Program: Entering a New Era," *Young Children*, Vol. 45, No. 3. (March, 1990), 24–27.

15. Marcy Whitebook, Carollee Howes, and Deborah Phillips (principal investigators), *Who Cares? Child Care Teachers and the Quality of Care in America* (Oakland, Calif.: Child Care Employee Project, 1989).

16. The National Day Care Study (Ruopp et al., *Children at the Center*), published in 1979, has provided the benchmark study for quality in center-based child care programs. For examples of more recent studies and reports, see Dave Riley and Kathleen Rogers, *Pay, Benefits and Job Satisfaction of Wisconsin Child Care Providers and Early Childhood Teachers 1988* (Madison: University of Wisconsin, April 1989); Barbara Willer, *The Growing Crisis in Child Care: Quality, Compensation, and Affordability in Early Childhood Programs* (Washington, D.C.: National Association for the Education of Young Children, 1987); and Caroline Zinsser, *Day Care's Unfair Burden* (1986). For a review of pertinent research, see also Deborah Phillips (Ed.), *Quality in Child Care: What Does the Research Tell Us?* (Washington, D.C.: National Association for the Education of Young Children, 1987).

17. Whitebook, et al., *Who Cares?*

18. Ibid., p. 2.

19. For representative examples, see *A Report to the Governor of California* (California Child Care Task Force, 1985); *America's Child Care Needs* (Washington, D.C.: American Federation of State, County and Municipal Employees, 1987); *Child Care in Maine: An Emerging Crisis* (Augusta, Maine: Maine Department of Educational and Cultural Services, 1984); *Day Care: Investing in Ohio's Children* (Columbus: Ohio Children's Defense Fund, 1985); *Final Report of the Governor's Partnership for Day Care Initiative* (Boston: Governor's Office of Human Resources, Commonwealth of Massachusetts, June 1987); *Hard Questions/Straight Answers: Child Care Policy for New York State* (Albany: Governor's Commission on Child Care, October 1986); Karen Norlander, *Casting a Blind Eye: Regulation of Family Day Care in New York State* (New York: Child Care, Inc., 1986); Marcy Whitebook, Carollee Howes, and Deborah Phillips, *Who Cares? Child Care Teachers and the Quality of Care in America* (Oakland, Calif.: Child Care Employee Project, 1990); Barbara Willer, *The Growing Crisis in Child Care: Quality, Compensation, and Affordability in Early Childhood Programs* (Washington, D.C.: National Association for the Education of Young Children, 1987); and Caroline Zinsser, *Day Care's Unfair Burden: How Low Wages Subsidize a Public Service* (New York: The Center for Public Advocacy Research, September 1986).

REFERENCES

American Federation of State, County and Municipal Employees. (1987). *America's Child Care Needs*. Washington, D.C.

Bredekamp, S. (Ed.) (1987). *Developmentally Appropriate Practice in Early Childhood Programs Serving Children from Birth through Age 8*, expanded edition. Washington, DC: National Association for the Education of Young Children.

Bronfenbrenner, U. (1979). *The Ecology of Human Development: Experiments by Nature and Design.* Cambridge, Mass.: Harvard University Press.
Bronfenbrenner, U. (July 23, 1986). "A Generation in Jeopardy: America's Hidden Family Policy," testimony presented at a hearing of the Senate Committee on Rules and Administration.
Cahan, Emily E. D. (1989). *Past Caring: A History of U.S. Preschool Care and Education for the Poor, 1820–1965.* New York: National Center for Children in Poverty.
California Child Care Task Force. (1985). *A Report to the Governor of California.* Sacramento.
The Children's Foundation. *Family Day Care Bulletin.* Washington, D.C.
Cochran, M. (1978). "Parents, Work, and Social Policy." Unpublished manuscript.
Cochran, M. and Bronfenbrenner, U. (1979). "Childrearing, Parenthood and the World of Work." In C. Kerr and J. Rosow (Eds.), *Work in America: The Decade Ahead.* New York: Van Nostrand Reinhold.
Euben, D. and Reisman, B. (1990). *Making the Connections: Public-Private Partnerships in Child Care.* New York: Child Care Action Campaign.
Fein, G. G. and Clarke-Stewart, A. (1973). *Day Care in Context.* New York: John Wiley and Sons.
Gnezda, M. T., and Smith, S. L. (1989). *Child Care and Early Childhood Education Policy: A Legislator's Guide.* Washington, D.C.: National Conference of State Legislatures.
Governor's Commission on Child Care. (October 1986). *Hard Questions/Straight Answers: Child Care Policy for New York State.* Albany.
Governor's Office of Human Resources, Commonwealth of Massachusetts. (1987). *Final Report of the Governor's Partnership for Day Care Initiative.* Boston.
Hayes, C. (Ed.). (1982). *Making Policies for Children: A Study of the Federal Process.* Washington, D.C.: National Academy Press.
Hochschild, A. (1989). *The Second Shift: Working Parents and the Revolution at Home.* New York: Viking Press.
Kahn, A. J. and Kamerman, S. B. (1987). *Child Care: Facing the Hard Choices.* Dover, Mass.: Auburn House.
Kamerman, S. B. and Kahn, A. J. (1981). *Child Care, Family Benefits, and Working Parents: A Study in Comparative Policy.* New York: Columbia University Press.
Kamerman, S. B. and Kahn, A. J. (1987). *The Responsive Workplace: Employers and a Changing Labor Force.* New York: Columbia University Press.
Keniston, K. and The Carnegie Council on Children. (1977). *All Our Children: The American Family under Pressure.* New York: Harcourt Brace Jovanovich.
Keyserling, M. K. (1972). *Windows on Day Care.* New York: National Council of Jewish Women.
Lazar, I. and Darlington, R. (1982). "Lasting Effects of Early Education: A Report from the Consortium for Longitudinal Studies," *Monographs of the Society for Research in Child Development.* Chicago: University of Chicago Press.
Lindner, E. W., Mattis, M. C. and Rogers, J. R. (1983). *When Churches Mind the Children: A Study of Day Care in Local Parishes.* Ypsilanti, Mich.: High/Scope Press.

Macchiarola, F. J. and Gartner, F. (Eds.). (1989). *Caring for America's Children.* New York: The Academy of Political Science.

Maine Department of Educational and Cultural Services. (1984). *Child Care in Maine: An Emerging Crisis.* Augusta.

Marx, F. and Seligson, M. (1988). *The Public School Early Childhood Education Study.* New York: Bank Street College of Education.

Mitchell, A., Seligson, M. and Marx, F. (1989). *Early Childhood Programs: Between Promise and Practice.* Dover, Mass.: Auburn House.

Morgan, G. (1987). *The National State of Child Care Regulation 1986.* Washington, D.C.: National Association for the Education of Young Children.

National Academy of Early Childhood Programs. (1984). *Accreditation Criteria and Procedures.* Washington, D.C.: National Association for the Education of Young Children.

Norlander, K. (1986). *Casting a Blind Eye: Regulation of Family Day Care in New York State.* New York: Child Care, Inc.

Ohio Children's Defense Fund. (1985). *Day Care: Investing in Ohio's Children.* Columbus.

Okin, S. M. (1989). *Justice, Gender, and the Family.* New York: Basic Books.

Olmsted, P. and Weikart, D. P. (1989). *How Nations Serve Young Children: Profiles of Child Care and Education in Fourteen Countries.* Ypsilanti, Mich.: High/Scope Press.

Phillips, C. B. (March 1990). "The CDA Program: Entering a New Era." *Young Children,* Vol. 45, No. 3, pp. 24–27.

Phillips, D., Lande, J. and Goldberg, M. (June 1990). "The State of Child Care Regulation: A Comparative Analysis." *Early Childhood Research Quarterly,* Vol. 5, No. 2, 151–179. Norwood, N.J.: Ablex Publishing Corporation.

Phillips, D. (Ed.). (1987). *Quality in Child Care: What Does the Research Tell Us?* Washington, D.C.: National Association for the Education of Young Children.

Powell, D. (1989). *Families and Early Childhood Programs.* Washington, D.C.: National Association for the Education of Young Children.

Riley, D. and Rogers, K. (April 1989). *Pay, Benefits and Job Satisfaction of Wisconsin Child Care Providers and Early Childhood Teachers 1988.* University of Wisconsin.

Robinson, H., Robinson, N., Wolins, M., Bronfenbrenner, U. and Richmond, J. (1973). "Early Child Care in the United States of America." *Early Child Development and Care,* Vol. 2, No. 4, 359–582.

Ruopp, R., Travers, J., et al. (1979). *Children at the Center: Final Report of the National Day Care Study.* Cambridge, M.A.: Abt Associates.

Schweinhart, L. (1985). *Early Childhood Development Programs in the Eighties: The National Picture.* Ypsilanti, Mich.: High/Scope Research Foundation.

U.S. Bureau of the Census. (May 1987). "Who's Minding the Kids?" Statistical Brief SB–2–87. Washington, D.C.

Whitebook, M., Howes, C. and Phillips, D. (principal investigators). (1989). *Who Cares? Child Care Teachers and the Quality of Care in America.* Oakland, Calif.: Child Care Employee Project.

Willer, B. (1987). *The Growing Crisis in Child Care: Quality, Compensation, and*

Affordability in Early Childhood Programs. Washington, D.C.: National Association for the Education of Young Children.

Yeiser, L. (1987). *Nannies, Au Pairs, Mothers' Helpers-Caregivers.* New York: Vintage Books.

Zigler, E. F. and Goodman, J. (1982). "The Battle for Day Care in America: A View from the Trenches." *Day Care: Scientific and Social Policy Issues,* E. F. Zigler and E. W. Gordon (Eds.), Boston: Auburn House.

Zinsser, C. (September 1986). *Day Care's Unfair Burden: How Low Wages Subsidize a Public Service.* New York: The Center for Public Advocacy Research.

Zinsser, C. (1990). *Born and Raised in East Urban.* New York: Center for Public Advocacy Research.

28

VENEZUELA

Josefina Fierro de Ascanio, María Rosa Frias
de Orantes, and Ileana Recagno-Puente
Translation by Robin Urquhart

To understand preschool care policies and facilities in Venezuela it is necessary to understand how different sectors of the population have developed
different ways of life, which vary in terms of the opportunities they offer
for personal growth. These ways of life have their roots in Venezuela's
socio-economic, educational, and demographic histories. Both the conditions of family life and the public and private alternatives available for the
care and education of children have been affected by these factors.

HISTORICAL AND SOCIAL ANTECEDENTS

Venezuela is a country of contrasts. It has many natural resources, but
at the present time it is suffering an economic recession caused by the change
from a high rate of economic growth based on petroleum to a situation of
relative stagnation, with growing inflation and crippling foreign debt. This
is a country trying to build a democratic society in spite of extreme social
inequalities. With its institutions in crisis, Venezuela finds itself forced to
define the structural and functional changes that will both provide economic
independence and promote the well-being of its increasingly impoverished
population.

Looking back over the last 50 years, it is evident that Venezuela's rapid
transformations have not marched hand in hand, nor have they affected all
sectors of the population in the same way. This has led to inequalities and
imbalances, some of which have been overcome while others have worsened
with time.

Before the 1920s, Venezuela's economy was agrarian. The production
units were "haciendas"—large, privately owned farms whose products were
destined for both foreign and home markets. Alongside these was a system

of "conucos," small areas farmed by "campesinos," whose products were for family and local consumption. Ninety-six percent of the population still lived in their birthplaces.

During the Great Depression and in the 1930s, there was reduction in agriculture for export, and farm workers were forced to look for work in other areas. The discovery and exploitation of petroleum fields produced great changes, and Venezuela became dependent on that production. By the end of the 1920s petroleum had replaced coffee as the main export and source of revenue.

The economic structure of Venezuela changed again in the early 1960s. At that time the government established two main goals: (a) to stimulate and modernize agriculture and (b) to implement policies of import substitution and industrial diversification based on an expanding home market and state protection. At the same time there was migration to the cities, which offered new work opportunities. Cities grew rapidly, the majority of the population became urban, and marginal urban communities sprang up.

By the early 1970s Venezuela was considered to have achieved important political, economic and social development, and significant advances in health and social security, education, and projects for resolving its housing deficit. In the mid–1970s a new development plan emerged, given impetus by an emergent bourgeois class and supported by a rise in petroleum prices. This plan included: (a) a policy of industrial diversification for the development of a group of basic industries (iron, aluminum, petrochemicals, hydroelectricity); (b) increasing state intervention in the production of goods and services; and (c) a pricing policy as a means of controlling inflation. The state diversified its functions and created a system of official institutions organized on the basis of criteria derived from private enterprise.

Seen as a whole, the decade of the 1970s was a positive period for Venezuela. The petroleum industry was nationalized and its emphasis on export was reduced, in accordance with a policy of conservation of non-renewable natural resources. There were favorable increases in economic indexes. However, there was a reduction in social spending, in spite of the expansion of public spending. The growth of the economy in this process of dependent capitalism brought few improvements to the lives of most Venezuelans. Agricultural credits were awarded to big landowners and very few "campesinos" received economic help. A similar pattern occurred with industrial credits. Twenty percent of the population received 50 percent of national income, and 50 percent of the population—the poorest groups—received 14 percent. Simultaneous with the economic boom came the growth of the marginal "barrios."[1]

During the 1980s the policies of successive governments failed to control recession and inflation, which were accompanied by changes in world petroleum prices. The policies applied so far have not reduced the size of the population living in conditions of poverty. In 1989, there were 3,769 "barrios," an increase of 105 percent over 1978. So 61 percent of the urban population, 8,331,482 people, now live in these residential areas. The so-called adjustment of 1989, a series of measures for balancing the economy, fortifying exports, and reducing the pressure of foreign debt, was accompanied by a lack of decisiveness about how to face this accelerating impoverishment of the population. Official statistics showed unemployment levels of 7.3 percent in 1988 and 9.2 percent in 1989, and a 34 percent drop in income levels during the same period. In 1989, purchasing power dropped more than it had in the previous four years. A nominal salary increase that year was more than offset by inflation. The poorest sectors of the population have been hardest hit by inflation. The percentage of families living in conditions of extreme poverty rose from 55 percent in 1988 to 65 percent in 1989.

Although the government has introduced a series of measures to protect the neediest sectors of the population, these have been insufficient. Their coverage has been limited and they have emphasized compensatory stopgap measures not based on an analysis of the structural and functional origins of the problem.

DEMOGRAPHIC CHANGES

Venezuela is an underdeveloped capitalist country. This means that, along with other limitations, there is limited information available for research. Bolivar (1984) points out that these limitations are "due not only to the fidelity and the obvious commonplace errors of demographic data for underdeveloped countries, but also to the types of information available, since official bodies frequently don't undertake certain types of research for political, financial or supposedly methodological reasons" (p. 245).

In the last 40 years, there have been violent changes in Venezuela's population. Until 1941 population increase had been moderate, but in the 20 years following the Second World War its population doubled and then nearly doubled again in the next twenty years. Key factors affecting these changes have been changes in the birth and death rates.

Birthrate

The data in Table 28.1 indicate a steady growth in fertility up to 1961. This alone could explain the doubling of the general population in the 1941–1961 period. From that point a steady decline in the birthrate began, and it is expected to continue in the 1990s. Thus the doubling of the population between 1961 and 1981 can be explained by other factors.

The high birthrate prior to the 1960s is thought to be due to the prevailing conceptualization of the role of the woman as mother and homemaker. The socialization process reinforced this model, and the improved socio-eco-

Table 28.1
Birthrate in Venezuela (Live Births per 1,000)

1936	40,2
1941	41,2
1946	42,6
1951	43,5
1956	45,7
1961	46,3
1966	42,3
1971	38,3
1976	36,6
1981	35,0
1986	28,3

Source: Bolivar, M., 1989.

nomic conditions of a growing percentage of the population allowed women to stay at home. However, from the present time on it can be supposed that "the influence of sociocultural and psychological reduction factors will be greatly increased because of the restrictive socioeconomic circumstances brought about by the economic recession and the impoverishment of large sectors of our population" (Bolivar, 1989, p. 15).

One of the characteristics of this decline in fertility in Venezuela is that it is younger women between 20 and 30 who are having fewer children. This group participates heavily in the job market; perhaps having one or two children and having to go out to work has made this group realize how difficult it is to support a large family.

Another interesting characteristic of Venezuela's demographic behavior involves fertility among adolescents. Eighteen to 20 percent of the birthrate is caused by adolescent pregnancy. This rate is on the increase; it has risen from 13 percent in 1951 to 19 percent in 1987. The situation is worsened by the socio-economic characteristics of these adolescent mothers, the majority of whom come from the lowest strata of society.

In general, family size has been on the decrease, from 6.4 children in 1965 to 3.4 in 1985. Two thirds of this reduction are to be found in the more educated cohort of the 20- to 35-year-old age group.

It is important to note that these variations in the reproductive behavior of Venezuela's population are due more to economic, educational, psycho-social, and cultural factors than to any actions by the national government or private family planning programs.

Death Rate

The rapid population increase after the 1940s is a reflection not only of the increase in the birthrate discussed earlier but also of a reduction in the death rate, due to the eradication of endemic diseases. Prior to the 1940s the most frequent causes of death in the adult population were malaria, tuberculosis, and cardiopathies caused by the Chagas beetle. Gastroenteritis and diarrhea-related illnesses were the main causes of death in children. The creation of the Ministry of Health and Social Assistance in 1935 led to government medical and sanitary programs, which in conjunction with the economic boom brought about by petroleum improved health conditions in Venezuela. Life expectancy at birth has increased dramatically in the past 45 years, from 42 years in 1941 to 70 years in 1986. During that same time period the infant mortality rate has dropped from 122 to 27 per 1,000 live births.

These statistics are not homogeneous throughout the population. In the lowest strata, children are still dying from diarrheas or diarrhea-related illnesses that could be prevented by government action, and in the highest strata there has been an increase in deaths from cardiovascular diseases associated with the consumer habits of affluence.

Extreme Poverty

At the present time, the situation in Venezuela is deteriorating as regards the number of families living in conditions of extreme poverty. Official figures show that just in the first three months of 1989 this number jumped from 493,000 to 1,005,000 homes.

Current Population Statistics

The most recent population statistics (1988) gave Venezuela a total population of 18,272,157. Approximately 18 percent of this population was under six years of age, making pre-school children almost a fifth of Venezuela's population. Of these, more than half (about 1,800,000 children) live in urban barrios. With two thirds of the population under 29 years of age, Venezuela is a country of young people.

From a socio-economic standpoint, 80 percent of Venezuelan families live in the two lowest social strata, below the poverty line. Thus Venezuela is a country with a young, largely poor population, concentrated in a few cities, and particularly in Caracas.

LIFE-STYLES AND FAMILY STRUCTURE

From a historical standpoint, present Venezuelan family patterns are modified forms of those that developed during the colonial period. Socio-economic conditions under the Spanish colonial system did not permit the development of families on the European model. The general population did not marry. Some economically favored groups established two families: a legal one with a Spanish or a favorite Amerindian woman, and an illegitimate one with another Amerindian woman (or several in succession). This double standard contributed to a weakening of men's paternal and conjugal responsibility.

At the beginning of the 19th Century, less than 27 percent of the population had been married by the church. For the rest of the people the unions were as temporary or fairly stable concubines. These latter arrangements led to incomplete families, centered on a mother and her children (sometimes joined by other relations) and a sporadically present, temporary, or absent father.

In the 20th century the crisis in the rural economy, industrial production, and growth of the home market led large numbers of people to migrate to urban areas. These processes affected the life-styles of migrating families. After 1936 there was increasing acceptance of marriage, which was awarded protection by the Venezuelan Constitution in 1961. The present systems of labor organization and social security favor the establishment of stable unions as a basic nucleus for raising children. Thus many families in Venezuela are based on legally married couples. However, there continues to be a large group of families based on consensual relationships and another large group made up of couples with children from former unions. There are also many single-parent families, usually headed by the mother. The extended family is still more prevalent than the nuclear family, particularly in rural and marginal areas, and nuclear families tend to retain their ties to a wider family network.

An analysis of family groups during the last 20 years shows that there are now twice as many legal as de facto relationships. In 1988, of 3,605,229 families, 46 percent consisted of married couples, 23 percent of de facto couples; 21 percent were headed by a single woman, and 9 percent by a single man.

The Role of Women

Certain advanced groups of women have fought for the recognition of the fundamental role played by women over the centuries in the family and society, and for the enforcement of women's rights. However, the present situation of women in Venezuela reflects the country's contradictions. Relations between the sexes are characterized by domination-submission, the idea of women as sexual objects, and a lack of paternal responsibility. Prevailing socialization patterns, women's relatively low educational levels, and the lack of social support for their participation in the labor force have favored the development of these kinds of relations. Although conditions have changed as women have become more aware of their importance to the family and to their country, "machismo" is still prevalent at all levels, and especially at the lowest levels of Venezuelan society.

At the same time, considerable progress has been made in the status of women over the past 40 years. Total female illiteracy dropped from 55 percent in 1950 to 14 percent in 1981 and 12 percent in 1988.[2] During the 1950s less than 1 percent of university students were women. In 1985 this figure stood at 53 percent, and for many professions the majority of students are women.

Fifty years ago, very few women participated in the job market. Children were educated at home until they were seven. This situation has changed considerably. Women's overall participation in the work force was 30 percent in 1982 and 32 percent in 1988, showing considerable stability over the decade of the 1980s. Younger women are employed at a higher rate— 64 percent of the 15 to 24 age group are in the labor force. Women continue to have little access to high management posts.

The increasing incorporation of women into the work force has made child care institutions increasingly necessary. These facilities are important not only for mothers, but also because of the developmental and cognitive benefits that they confer on the child.

Policies Related to Women, Children, and Families

Venezuela's constitution (1961) makes the protection of the family a right of all citizens and a duty of the State. More recently (1986) the importance assigned to the family by many social programs has led to the creation of the Ministry for the Family. Its main purpose is to plan and execute policies to protect families and integrate them into the country's development processes.

Illegitimate children have long been objects of discrimination in Venezuela. In 1982, after 40 years of effort by women, changes were made in the Civil Code that gave the same rights to illegitimate as to legitimate children (surname, education, maintenance, and inheritance). The laws also protect adopted children and adoptive families. Adopted children have the same rights as other children. It is important to extend and promote adoption in Venezuela because of the growing number of abandoned children, mostly in the newborn to age 6 group. In 1987 there were only 2,256 adoptions and 1.6 million abandoned children under age 18.

In 1975 the First National Congress of Women recommended that society recognize how the conditions of work imposed on women provide little opportunity for their personal development, and obstruct their maternal functions. The following year a Feminine Advisory Committee to the Presidency was set up to evaluate the legal, social, and economic conditions of women in Venezuela and to prepare projects for achieving women's greater participation in Venezuelan society. The importance of this was emphasized in 1979 when the committee was replaced by the Ministry for the Promotion of Women.

Venezuela's laws give protection to mothers regardless of their civil status. This protection includes full salary for six weeks before and 12 weeks after the birth of a child, plus the right to return to their jobs for up to one year, two half-hour periods off work to breast-feed their babies in special rooms that must be provided by all businesses with more than 30 female workers, and the right to receive the same salary as other workers who are not breast-feeding. However, these laws are frequently ignored. Many groups are now working to have them enforced and extended to all working women.

Divorce is legal in Venezuela. The mother has automatic custody of children under seven years old. Divorce is on the increase: in 1981, 6 percent of couples got divorced and by 1987 this figure had risen to 22 percent.

SOCIALIZATION PATTERNS

Socialization patterns are enmeshed in the historical and local context and are affected by the socio-economic, demographic, political, and cultural factors currently operating in Venezuela. Certain of these factors appear to have had particular significance for the different socialization patterns seen in Venezuelan families.

Social Class

Differences in income and schooling seem to have the greatest influence on life-styles and patterns of upbringing. They affect the standard of living, nutrition, hygiene, life expectancy, education, employment, and habitat in complex interactive ways.

In Venezuela we can identify two main patterns of upbringing, one pertaining to the high and middle classes and the other to the lower and marginal classes, with some intermediate patterns. In high and middle-class families (20 percent of the total), children live in planned dwellings with adequate water and sewage systems. Their diet is good and their physical and intellectual development is similar to that of middle- and high-class children in the industrial nations. They have predictable sleeping, feeding, and bathing routines. Daily life revolves around school, which imparts ways of playing, language use, and free time activities that are appropriate to the parents' cultural norms.

In marginal families, dwellings are precarious, crowded, and suffer from acute lack of space. Incomes usually depend on unstable jobs, and weeks or months can often pass with no regular income for the family. There is no social security system to carry these families through these periods.

There is general acceptance of the precariousness of existence. The rainy season often produces landslides that flatten dwellings in the barrios, forcing people to leave suddenly for other areas. The dry season may mean several months without running water. Life for marginal children is chancy and unpredictable. In times of crisis like the present, both children and adults eat only twice a day, and then very poorly.

The Change from Rural to Urban Living

This change is a frequent one in Venezuela and has important effects on socialization patterns. Rural families transfer their poverty from the countryside to a marginal barrio lacking the services needed even for a minimally human standard of living. To reach such a standard usually means long years of struggle and the sacrifice of the children's educational opportunities. Conditions of dietary restriction and bad sanitation affect children's physical well-being as well as their future prospects.

Lacking so many things, both adults and children give priority to activities that satisfy the need for basic survival. There is little time for play. Feeding, bathing, and sleeping times are irregular. Most of the activities initiated by adults and children are in order to meet immediate goals.

In spite of these conditions, these marginal children may have access to better schools than those in rural areas, and to the variety of attractions and new experiences offered by the city. It is possible that their cognitive development will be stimulated, thus opening up new alternatives and goals for them (Recagno and Orantes, 1981).

Family Size

As in other countries, the less educated the parents, the larger the family. Thus, poor Venezuelans aggravate their difficulties. However, when mothers giving birth in state hospitals ask to be sterilized, this request is usually refused—even for women with five children—unless the mother is seriously ill.

In large families there are few adults and many children, and children usually have no adult supervision in the afternoons. Recent studies describe certain marginal barrios in Caracas composed mainly of nuclear families with many children from different fathers and a high turnover of father figures. Very few of these "fathers" and even fewer mothers in these barrios have stable jobs.

When there are many children in a family, the older sons often take care of the younger ones, to the detriment of their own education. In families of this type, the period of protection given to children is very short; as soon as they are able, they must help meet the family's subsistence needs.

Early School Drop-out

Families with good incomes send their children to good schools at the age of three or before, thus setting them off on the "cycle of excellence." However, preschool education is unavailable for the majority of the population, or offered in poorly run schools only after the child is over age five. Thus, most of the day for children living above the subsistence level is divided between school and watching television. Poor children, who have not yet entered school or enter at a later age (eight or more), share the vicissitudes of their parents' daily lives. They usually drop out of school early, thus losing any opportunities for achieving a better standard of living.

FAMILY ORGANIZATION AND LIFE-STYLE

Different life-styles can be found in social strata of Venezuelan society, defined by the socialization factors described above. In what might be called the structured life-style families have enough resources to provide hygienic and orderly habitats for their children, with those services necessary for stable domestic organization. Frequently the father is a professional and his income is more than enough to cover vital necessities, deal with emergencies, and make provisions for the future.

Most homes with a reasonable level of comfort include two parents, and often the mothers also have a profession. When the mother stays at home or has a stable arrangement with a day care center, grandmother, or other caregiver, this ensures that the children's daily routines are predictable, support the development of both children and parents, and facilitate later schooling.

Families living in the semi-structured life-style have fewer resources. Although their adult members may have some professional training, their jobs are less stable. They often live in cheap apartments or houses with few comforts, usually in consolidated barrios. The basic needs of the children are met, but schooling is very often irregular. Sometimes these families are forced to deal with emergencies, which they address with a variety of strategies. They move to less organized barrios or, in the case of single mothers, to their own mothers' homes. Many do not look for work when the father leaves them because they have to take care of their young children.

Families that do not possess enough resources to guarantee a minimum standard of development and nutrition for their children live what might be called an anarchic or chaotic life style. They usually live in "barrios" or makeshift housing, with many people crowded into very little space and almost completely lacking in domestic equipment. It is very difficult to predict the daily activities of the children in these families. The homes they live in are notorious in their communities because of their constant state of crisis. The families only manage to survive through the occasional help of neighbors, relations, or friends, or by re-forming into new couples. Most of these families are made up of a single woman and her children. Usually these women do not have a stable partner, regular work, or sufficient income to guarantee their children enough to eat.

In these homes it is difficult to plan meal hours and everyday tasks. They are in a constant state of emergency so that activities such as keeping oneself clean, housework, washing the clothes, or keeping bed time hours are rarely maintained.

Even though the children from these homes receive verbal messages that could promote better personal or social development, they have few opportunities for putting them into practice. Usually their schooling is limited and they have a high drop-out rate from primary school. When they grow up these children make up the bulk of the unskilled labor force. They have great difficulty in facing up to the challenge of attending to their own children and many of them reproduce the patterns of marginal upbringing they experienced when they come to form their own families.

MARIANA AND JUAN CARLOS

The daily routines of Mariana and Juan Carlos illustrate the differences between families with structured and semi-structured life-styles.

Mariana

Mariana will be four in September. Her parents are professionals, with the father working full time and the mother half time.

Mariana gets up at 7:30 A.M. Her mother is already dressed and has prepared breakfast and the bottle for Mariana's baby sister, who gets up at 6:15. The father gets up at 6:00, has a shower and a cup of coffee and leaves the house at 6:30 for Caracas.

Her mother starts work at 9:30. Before leaving for work, she must dress the baby, provide her with a bottle and vitamins, prepare the girls' lunch boxes, help Mariana get dressed and combed, and then take both children to the nearby day care center. This center is totally private. It serves 20 children between three months and five years of age. The center does not follow the official school curriculum, nor is it officially supervised. Nevertheless, the children are well supervised. Mariana has breakfast there and then takes part in activities such as painting, gymnastics, and clay modeling. She has lunch at twelve and then naps until her mother picks her up at 2:30 P.M.

At home, Mariana plays with her books or watches television while her mother prepares her own and her husband's lunch, eats, removes the baby's dirty clothes from the lunch box, tidies up the house, and gives the girls an afternoon snack.

The father returns between five and seven and eats when he arrives. At seven Mariana has a bath while her mother bathes the baby and the father (sometimes) does the dishes. At 7:30 the girls eat dinner, with the father feeding the baby. The baby goes to sleep between 8:00 and 8:30. Mariana stays awake playing with a jigsaw puzzle or drawing as the parents watch the news on television.

Mariana gets ready for bed between 9:00 and 9:30. After cleaning her teeth, she sometimes asks one of her parents to tell her a story or read to her in bed.

Even though her part-time job means in effect that this mother has two jobs, the work contributes to the economic and personal development of all members of the family. Little by little, the father has become more involved in looking after the girls and has learned to enjoy being a father and to think of his wife's needs. In this way, Mariana, her sister, mother, and father have contributed to one another's development, although the mother carries the heaviest load. For this family, the day care center is an important source of support for the parents' professional development and crucial for their capacity to manage within the economic crisis Venezuela is facing. A satisfactory standard of living would be impossible on only one salary.

Juan Carlos

Juan Carlos is five years old and lives in a barrio. He has four brothers with whom he shares two beds. The parents' and children's beds are separated only by a curtain. The mother wakes the children up just before dawn because they have to be at school by 7:00 A.M. Breakfast consists of a piece of corn bread and sometimes a piece of cheese, which she makes sure they take to school. If the water has arrived during the night or if it has rained, the children can wash their faces and drink some watery coffee before leaving. Milk has been difficult to get for some time and the mother only manages to buy it occasionally. The father, who begins his work as a cable hanger at 7:30 A.M., leaves the house before the children. He will be away all day because his work is far away and transportation is expensive. All the same, he does not complain because many people do not have work.

The house is a shack with three brick walls and one of corrugated iron.

A portrait of the saintly Jose Gregorio Hernandez hangs on one wall. The floor is grey cement. A little red sofa and three plastic basket-weave chairs are in the sitting room. On one wall there is a blackboard where the mother helps the older children repeat their lessons. Juan Carlos has to walk six blocks to school. He sets off with his older brothers. The four year old is still too young to go to school and stays at home. He is joined by a seven-year-old neighbor who was not given a place in school because he has only been living in the district for six months.

The school to which this preschool belongs is typical of conventional barrios public schools. The classroom has 30 chairs arranged around four rectangular tables, and a small piece of furniture with pigeon holes for each child and spaces for piles of notebooks and pencils. There are no toys, and the walls are painted uniformly in white and blue. When the teacher comes to school, and the normal program is followed, the morning begins with singing. The children clap their hands in time while they sing a folk song. After that there is a recess for breakfast. The children line up to receive a glass of milk, as established by a government program. At 10:30 A.M. they go back to the classroom, where the teacher hands each one a photocopied line drawing of three geometric figures for their notebooks.

After a while, most of the children are out of their seats and all are shouting from one end of the room to the other. To make herself heard the teacher has to shout at them to make them take their seats, do some arm exercises, and put their heads on the tables for a few minutes. This brings them to 12:30, when they pick up the classroom in preparation for the following day.

Every other day the teacher is late beginning the class. On these days the first activity is listening to a story, talking about it, and then making a drawing (for those children who have brought their drawing books). There is a fight over a pencil, and its owner punches someone. The teacher pays no attention because this type of aggression is frequent. After the nine o'clock recess, the teacher asks the children to pick up their things and go home, as she has to leave. This happens two or three times a week. The parents complain, but they are afraid to insist for fear that the teachers will take it out on the children.

Juan Carlos goes home alone through streets lined with little brick houses or corrugated iron huts. His mother makes no comment when he arrives and sends him out to buy vegetables in a nearby shop so she can make soup for lunch. Ingredients will be vegetables and pasta because the money will not stretch to buy meat.

Juan Carlos plays on the stairs in front of the house with other children from the neighborhood. When his brothers come home they eat lunch one by one, sitting at a wooden table in the kitchen. In the afternoon, the children continue to play on the stairs and take turns watching the small black-and-white TV tuned in to soap operas and Japanese robot cartoons. They often go down the street or visit their cousins who live nearby. If they find a ball to play with, it usually gets lost down the hill.

When she has a little free time from washing, ironing, and cooking for seven people, the mother tries to help nine-year-old Alicia, who has difficulty reading and is repeating second grade. Juan Carlos and the smallest children go to bed late, after watching soap operas and waiting for their father to return home around 9:00. After working eight to ten hours, he often has had to wait more than an hour for a jeep to take him to the barrio.

PRESCHOOL POLICIES AND PROGRAMS

In 1990 there were 3,684,516 children in Venezuela age six and under. Of these more than half lived in the barrios. Venezuela's Constitution and other laws establish that all children, without discrimination, should receive protection from conception to adulthood. Present-day circumstances, however, show an increasing lack of attention to children, not only in education but also in permanent social services, nutrition support efforts, and family support networks, which are almost nonexistent.

The first institution to establish policies on early childhood, the Venezuelan Children's Council (CVN), was created in 1936. The first preschool classes were set up in 1937 as annexes to two experimental schools. These schools established a training center for preschool teachers, and the following year the CVN set up its first preschool. From then until 1969 most preschool education was privately run in homes or small locales by untrained people or teachers. It was not until 1969 that the first official preschool program was published. Starting at that time, more preschools were established, but only 2.7 percent of the preschool population received services. During the 1970s the Preschool Department of the Ministry of Education set up 500 preschool classes. In 1974 the World Preschool Congress, held in Caracas, stimulated the extension of the preschool period down to infants and emphasized the need for comprehensive attention, including nutrition and health.

During the 1970s, as the preschool population reached 1,500,000, the Ministry of Education and some private institutions organized experimental care that tried to bring low-cost preschool services to a larger number of children. Those institutions were nonconventional and used voluntary workers supervised by graduated teachers. Examples of such institutions are the Meval kindergartens and the Book Bank Program (see Table 28.3 below).

In 1979 the interest in preschool education that had developed in the 1970s was reflected in a change within the Ministry of Education, from a Department to a Division of Preschool Education. In 1980 a decree was passed, making preschool education obligatory, but in 1986 the regulations related to this law reduced the obligatory requirement to five year olds.

Table 28.2
Preschool Care in Venezuela (1990)

Type of Care	Number of 0-6 year olds
Conventional*	956,537
Public	859,221
Private	97,316
Non-conventional	320,326
No Pre-school Program	2,407,653
Totals.....................	3,684,516

*The conventional system does not cover ages 0-2.

That same year the Ministry of Education's Advisory Committee for the development of plans and programs for preschool children made the following recommendations:

a. Attention to preschoolers should be comprehensive rather than simply educational.
b. With the appropriate training, the family and the community should be able to provide satisfactory preschool care and education.
c. Large school buildings are not necessary, especially when they are located far from where the children live.

The committee also established objectives for preschool education that would make preschool institutions instruments for promoting more general improvements in the quality of life in local communities. Like many such projects, this one still has yet to be put into practice.

The goal of serving 500,000 children proposed in 1975 was finally met in 1989, when the preschool population had already increased sevenfold. In spite of the interest and the efforts made to extend preschool education, at present conventional preschool education only reaches about 26 percent of the target population (see Table 28.2).

PRESCHOOL PROGRAMS

Table 28.2 provides general information about the preschool experiences of the more than 3.6 million Venezuelan children less than six years old. Very few day care services are available for children under two years old. Those that do exist are organized by institutions like public ministries, local governments, and the Children's Foundation. No more than 1,500 children from low-income families are served by those programs. These figures do not include children cared for in the Day Care Homes and the multi-homes programs, which are at present being expanded. The statistics available for those programs do not differentiate newborn to two year olds from other children under age six. Some semi-private infant care services with higher fees are offered by a variety of other institutions. There are also private services, such as that described earlier for Mariana, whose prices make them accessible only to people from higher income groups. Coverage includes nearly 50 percent of the three-to-six-year-old age group, but this includes a far higher percentage of children age five and six than age three and four. Thus the majority of the unserved children are in the newborn to two age range.

Three quarters of the children receiving services are enrolled in "conventional" programs: regular preschool centers run under public or private auspices. The remaining 320,326 children are in "nonconventional" programs: services provided in barrios by the Children's Foundation, the Ministry of Education, the Ministry of the Family, and several other organizations. The range and coverage of these programs is summarized in Table 28.3.

A Typical Conventional Preschool Program

The Educational Ministry's official preschool curriculum follows modern preschool guidelines. Its programs usually have adequate material resources and good teachers. Many of these preschool classrooms are in public or private schools. However, they are few in number and serve only a small sector of the population (see Table 28.2).

THE ROLE OF THE FIRST LADY

By tradition, the wives of Venezuela's presidents devote themselves to improving the lot of poor children. Initially this was done through social services run by the presidency and by the Bolivarian Foundation.[3]

In 1964, the First Lady established a Children's Festival and created a foundation with this name, which functioned along with the former Bolivarian Foundation. Throughout the five years of the 1964–1969 government, the Children's Festival Foundation's policies were to give indirect help to poor Venezuelan children and to support charitable institutions that gave direct attention or protection to children.

During the next government (1969–1974), the Children's Festival Foundation established as its main objectives the giving of attention, protection, and recreation to children, especially at Christmas time. Between 1970 and 1971, new elements were introduced in the foundation's activities, including

Table 28.3
Non-Conventional Care Programs for Marginal and Rural Preschoolers

Program	Coordinating Institution	Public	Private	Location	Number children served
Day Care Homes 1974	Children's Foundation,	X	X	Family homes in Barrios	101,986
	Ministry for the Family	X			
Meval "Maternal Gardens" 1974	Ministry of Education	X		Ad-Hoc buildings	1,608
The Family in Pre-School Education 1976	Book Bank	X		Adapted houses in Barrios	20
Child and Family Centers 1985	Ministry of Education	X		Locales in marginal Barrios	8,318
Pilot Attention Program for Preschoolers	Foundation for Trujillo		X	Houses, Parks, etc.	4,937
Community Learning Centers (CECODAP) 1986	CECODAP		X	Ad-hoc buildings	180
Global Attention for rural Pre-schoolers 1988	Ministry of Family	X		Houses in rural areas	830
The Family* Program	Ministry of Education	X		Locales Centers and other centers	201,976
Preschoolers'* Attention Network	Min. of Education & Min. of Family	X		Locales in Marginal areas	471
				TOTAL	320,326

*All programs provide daily care/education except those shown with an asterisk.

direct service programs such as holiday camps and indirect support via television series, publications, recreation programs, and museum visits.

In 1975, the Board of Directors defined new policies for the foundation and changed its name to the Children's Foundation. These new policies gave priority to permanent attention to children from marginal communities, and priority to a policy of preschool provision emphasizing day care homes, a policy that has continued to the present day. According to documents in the foundation, the Day Care Homes Program came into being because of the convergence of three factors:

a. Research results that demonstrated the importance of giving attention to pre-schoolers, and the lack of such attention in Venezuela.

b. Venezuela's affluence during that period, due to large increases in income from petroleum.

c. The government policy of full employment, which offered mothers the opportunity to go to work.

Because the Day Care Homes Program is one of the largest in Venezuela serving barrio children and families, and because it is popular with the present government, it is described in greater detail below.

The Day Care Homes

The Day Care Homes Program has suffered from a malady common to most family support initiatives in Venezuela. Continuity is unusual for such programs because projects "belong to the former government," and each new government wants to make its mark in history for its own projects. Because of this, many people in Venezuela feel that everything is temporary. Many institutions and projects have evolved according to the changes introduced every five years by a new government. The Family Day Care Homes Program was introduced in 1974. Over the next four years the program grew rapidly, until 3,000 such homes had been established. With the change in government, the new First Lady was more interested in other things and the program declined. This decline continued throughout the following government's term, until only 1,000 homes remained.

In 1989, the program was re-established. The present government has decided to provide the program with much greater support, in part through the Ministry for the Family (soon to be the Ministry for Social Development). This ministry will coordinate the program, which will be supervised by various Venezuelan institutions (universities, communities, etc.).

In 1987, socio-economic studies isolated several factors pointing to a critical and worsening situation in the nation. These factors included the deterioration in the quality of food consumed, drops in health conditions and educational indices, and an increase in the size of the population living under marginal conditions. In 1989 the government created a Committee for Fighting Poverty to design strategies for attacking these problems. The first phase of this committee's plan was to "give compensations to the large proportion of Venezuelans living in conditions of extreme poverty." This included health, nutrition, educational, recreational, and psychological attention for pregnant women and children under age six.

However, a new model has been adopted for the program, with the idea of expanding it en masse during the present government's five-year term. This new model is based on the following principles:

- The program should adapt the informal, naturally existing forms of child care already present within the community and as far as possible incorporate existing services. Emphasis should be placed on improving the positive aspects of these existing informal day care homes.
- The state should not give communities or families what they can find for themselves. Families and communities should only be provided with what they need. This is one of the most important principles of social development.
- Coverage should be rapid and massive.
- There should be maximum community participation. The program should belong to the family day care mothers and the communities rather than to an organizing institution.

This new model requires the cooperation of various individuals, organizations, and institutions. There are the day care homes themselves, which will operate in houses already located in the community. There are also multi-homes, which link several day care homes in a local community (one adult per ten children). This multi-home approach expands coverage more rapidly.

The family day care mothers will be specially selected and trained. Each one will take care of six to eight children under the age of six, from 6 A.M. to 6 P.M., Monday through Friday. If these homes lack the basic necessities for living, the program will be responsible for making necessary repairs. In addition, the day care mothers will be given the basic equipment needed for day care provision.

Family day care mothers will be chosen jointly by the state and by the mothers seeking care. The state will contribute those funds that cannot be supplied by the consumers of the day care service. The state contribution will include a special nutritional supplement.

The program will be coordinated at the national level by the Ministry for the Family. A National Advisory Committee will be presided over by the First Lady and include representatives from the Committee for Fighting Poverty, economic and religious institutions, the neighborhood, the community, and private child care and protection organizations.

This policy, aimed at massive expansion of the Day Care Homes Program, has as its goal the provision of care and education to 500,000 children living in extreme poverty by the end of this government's five-year term. Expansion has been taking place between 1990 and 1992 and will be consolidated from 1993 onward, until 42,000 day care homes are established.

Strengths and shortcomings of day care homes. Given this major commitment to family day care homes as a "nonconventional" strategy for bringing care and protection to poor children, it is important to be realistic about the strengths and shortcomings of such an approach, in order that the advantages be maximized and the disadvantages be reduced to a minimum. The positive aspects of this strategy, as stated by its proponents, are as follows:

1. The children will be taken care of by an adult receiving a certain amount of supervision and support from a technical team.
2. The children will receive a well-balanced diet, medical attention, and supervision.
3. The children will acquire social skills.
4. Nonworking mothers will be able to look for work.
5. Working mothers can be sure their children will receive adequate care and nutrition.
6. Working mothers will contribute to the expenses of their own children attending the day care homes.
7. Caretaker mothers will be able to include their own children in the program and receive an income. The program creates jobs.
8. The houses used as day care homes will receive improvements and repairs.
9. Isolated communities will benefit from the program.
10. The program will provide opportunities for parents and the community to participate in activities for the improvement of their children's development.

While this is an impressive list of possible accomplishments to be associated with the day care homes strategy, there are also reasons to be realistic about the approach. Evidence to date indicates, first, that the space available in these homes is very limited and restricts the natural activity of children in this age group. Second, the homes provide few materials and experiences that will stimulate much cognitive development, and with six to eight children to care for, do not have enough time to attend to each child's psychosocial and emotional development. Because she is also expected to buy, prepare, and serve the food, keep the children clean, and do the housework, it is impossible for the mother also to give attention simultaneously to so many children. The day care mother's interaction with the children is frequently restrictive and very seldom oriented to individual development. Third, because of constant price hikes, the amount of money available for buying the food necessary for a balanced diet will always be insufficient.

Finally, the technical supervision, support, and money for the caregiving mothers are not adequate to permit them to carry out what is a very complex role. There is very little contact between caregiver, the mothers of the children cared for, and the technical support team.

CONCLUSIONS

Slightly more than a decade ago, Venezuela was given the opportunity to accelerate positive social changes and give better attention to its child population. But this opportunity proved to be no more than a mirage. The country's economic dependence, and the fact that most of its social policies were designed to resolve problems caused by politicians' economic decisions, made it impossible to make better use of the enormous amount of money that was generated by petroleum exports.

Unfortunately, those affected most negatively have been the poor, who make up the vast majority of Venezuelans. As stated in a report presented to the government in 1986, "Venezuela has failed to achieve the social development to be expected from its vast material and human resources and democratic ideals" (Uslar Pietri, 1986).

Venezuela needs to take a lesson from history. The present economic crisis, its family life-styles, the increasing impoverishment of its population, and unequal opportunities offered to its children make it urgent to set up a social support network that will give all children real equal rights and opportunities for development. The educational system needs to be redesigned so that poor children have access to excellent quality preschool education and do not drop out. The rates at which Venezuelan children repeat grades and drop out of school are increasing alarmingly. They contribute to the growing number of functional illiterates, diminish people's access to work in an even more technological society, and create paralyzing individual frustrations.

The professionalization of women, their unquestionable and necessary contribution to production, their personal development, and their right to receive the education needed to fulfill their responsibilities at work and in the family make it imperative to introduce family support programs that will give them real and sufficient help. We have given special attention in this chapter to the Day Care Homes Program because of the importance assigned to it in the present government's plan for fighting poverty. However, we consider it only a transitional solution for the problems of attending to children in marginal areas. In time day care homes should be replaced by centers able to provide comprehensive care. Such centers could combine the positive aspects of both the conventional and nonconventional programs described here. The negative aspects of the day care homes would seem to make it difficult for the program to achieve the ambitious goals expected of it. We hope it will have some effect on nutrition and health, and stop the deterioration of those families and children who live in extreme poverty. Nevertheless, better attention to these two areas is no guarantee of stimulating children's overall development. Because the day care homes are immersed in the marginal way of life, they must to some extent reflect and propagate that way of life. Children need access to more ample care systems, those that provide comprehensive care and adequate teaching facilities. One of the recommendations in the chapter on teaching published in the report of the Third Symposium on the Study of Preschoolers in Venezuela (1986) was that "Formal and non-formal educational programs designed for children living in extreme poverty should have excellent teaching, at least as good as that available for more favored children. Such programs should give parallel medical, nutritional, sanitary and environmental care" (Fundación E. Mendosa, 1988, p. 520). Such systems should stimulate critical reflection in families and communities and the active search for solutions to problems, thus promoting self-development.

NOTES

1. In Venezuela "barrio" means unplanned family settlement, usually located on land poorly suited for habitation. Barrios usually do not provide essential services (water, sewage, electricity, transport), although these can develop as a barrio is consolidated into the central city. Barrios contain large numbers of marginalized families.

2. Single women who head families have an illiteracy rate that is three times the national average. Forty-eight percent of these women are employed. The rest consider themselves "housewives." These circumstances explain why families headed by single women are so often living in extreme poverty.

3. Created in 1936.

REFERENCES

Benaim Pinto, G. (1985). Informe. Proposición para establecer el Prap 4–5. (Proposal for the creation of PRAP 4–5). Reporte de la Comisión asesora del Ministro de Educación para el desarrollo de planes y programas dirigidos al Preescolar. Caracas, Venezuela: Ministerio de Educación.

Bolivar, M. (1984). Capitalismo y población. Estudio sobre el comportamiento demográfico en el Capitalismo desde la Revolucion Industrial. (Capitalism and Population. Study of Demographic Behavior in Capitalism from the Industrial Revolution). Caracas: Universidad Central de Venezuela.

Bolivar, M. (November 1989). Una contribución sociodemográfica para la superación de la crisis. Documento central. (A socio-demographic contribution to overcome crisis. Main document). Seminario Nacional Población y Desarrollo Social. Caracas.

Cartaya, V. and Garcia, M. (1988). Infancia y Pobreza. Los efectos de la recesión en Venezuela. (Infancy and poverty. The effects of recession in Venezuela). Caracas: Nueva Sociedad.

Castellanos, M. (June 7, 1990). Mas del 80% de los venezolanos vive en condiciones de pobreza. (More than 80 percent of Venezuelans live in poverty). El Nacional, pp. C–7.

Colmenares, H. (November 1, 1989). Crece la marginalidad. (Marginality increases). El Nacional, pp. C–1.

Diaz, J. R. (March 14, 1991). Solo 1,476,233 niños de 3 a. 6 años son atendidos como pre-escolares. (Only 1,467,233 three- to six-year-old children are attended as preschoolers). El Nacional, pp. C–4.

España, L. P. & Gonzalez, M. J. (1990). Empobrecimiento y Politica Social. (Empoverishment and social policy). S.I.C., 522, March, 62–64. Caracas.

Fierro, H. (1985). La Protección Legal de la Familia. (Family Legal Protection). In AVEPANE (Eds.), Retardo Mental. (Mental Retardation). Caracas: Universidad Central de Venezuela.

Fierro, J. and Vegas, L. E. (1985). La Acción Preventiva de la Educación Prescolar. (Preventive action of Preschool education). In AVEPANE (Eds.), Retardo Mental. (Mental Retardation). Caracas: Universidad Central de Venezuela.

Fundación Eugenio Mendoza (1988). El Pre-Escolar en Venezuela. III Jornadas. (The preschooler in Venezuela. Third Seminar). Caracas: Cromotip.

González de Lepage, M. (1988). Inventario de Programas No-Convencionales de attención al niño Pre-Escolar. (Unconventional Programs of Preschool. Attention: An Inventory). Caracas: Ministerio de la Familia.

Marcano, B. (October 1990). La Educación Pre-Escolar en Venezuela. (Preschool education in Venezuela). Trabajo presentado en las I Jornadas Audiovisuales Nacionales y Latioamericanas. AVEPANE. Caracas.

Mendez Castellano, M. C. (1991). La Familia en Venezuela. (Family in Venezuela). Invited Address. Graduate Program in Human Development. Central University of Venezuela. Caracas.

OCEI (1988). Anuario Estadístico de Venezuela 1987. (Venezuela's Statistic Yearbook 1987). Caracas: Presidencia de la Repùblica.

Pereira, I. and Escala, Z. (1989). La Mujer en Venezuela. (Women in Venezuela). Caracas: COPRE.

Recagno-Puente, I., and Orantes, M. R. (1981). Estimulación Audiovisual, Juegos Dirigidos y Desarrollo Mental. (Audiovisual Stimulation, supervised games, and mental development). Acta Científica Venezolana, 32, 437–447.

Recagno-Puente, I. (April 1988) La Organización Doméstica y el Rol de la Mujer. (Organization of home routines in women's role). Paper presented at the International Seminar Crisis y Sobrevivencia en Sectores Populares Urbanos de América Latina. Caracas.

Relemberg, N. S., Karmen, H. and Koheler, V. (1979). Los Pobres de Venezuela. (The Poor in Venezuela). Buenos Aires, Argentina: El cid.

Ruesta, M. C. & Barrios de Vidal, A. (1978). Evaluación Programas de Cuidado Diario. (Evaluation of the Day Care Homes Program). Caracas: Fundación del Niño-UNICEF.

Uslar Pietri, A. (Ed.). (1986). Reporte de la Comisión Presidencial del Proyecto Educativo Nacional. (Report of the Presidential Commission for the National Educational Project). Caracas: COPRE.

Vethencourt, J. L. (1974). La estructura familiar atípica y el proceso histórico cultural en Venezuela. (The atypical family structure and historic-cultural process in Venezuela). SIC, 37, pp. 67–69.

——— 29 ———

VIETNAM

Tran Thi Trong, Pham Mai Chi, and Dao Van Phu

Prior to 1945 the traditional Vietnamese family comprised many generations. Patriarchal in its structure, and based on an Asian feudal ideology,
the family was consciously supported and protected by all its members. This
membership lived in a closed group marked by a strong sense of mutual
assistance and a powerful attachment to the family's place of origin.

Within this framework, women played an important role in family and
social development. In the countryside, where more than 95 percent of the
population was concentrated, women made up an important labor force
because their aptitude for rice planting was much needed by the small-scale
agricultural economy. Women also played the main role in support and
self-sufficiency of their families through the practice of kitchen gardening,
animal husbandry, weaving, and other family-based trades. Despite these
key contributions, the social status of women was not recognized either in
law or through public opinion. Nearly 98 percent of the women were illiterate. Polygamy was legal, and free marriage was not tolerated. The *tam
tong* or "three obediences" rule required that unmarried women had to
obey their fathers, wives their husbands, and widows their sons. As the
peasantry was impoverished by exorbitant taxes and high rents and interests,[1] this made women practically the sole providers of their families, a
burden imposed on top of full responsibility for their children. Public opinion was tolerant of lazy, debauched husbands, but censorious of incompetent
women.

In the cities and towns, where workers, artisans, traders, and low-ranking
functionaries made up the larger part of the urban population, life was no
less difficult, but family ties were somewhat more relaxed. Nevertheless,

women fared little better. They worked hard and bore the brunt of household chores.

Happiness in the traditional family was measured by the number of children. Sons were favored, whereas daughter-in-laws were regarded merely as additional labor and vessels with which to bring forth progeny. Parents did not care for their daughters very much because they would one day be attached to other families. Similarly, a childless wife or.a mother without sons would be regarded as useless and might even be replaced by a concubine.

As large families were favored, it was customary for a woman to bear at least five and as many as eight children. Moreover, because of poverty, ignorance, and superstition, women were subjected to a rigorous dietary regime during their pregnancies, which did great harm to their health and to that of the foetuses.[2]

Children were the object of love in the close-knit family, following the old saying "Fatherless, you can always rely on your uncles—Motherless, you can turn to your aunts." Yet, because their parents were occupied with the many problems of daily life, children were often left to themselves without proper guidance. There was real difficulty in providing for a large family, leading to the general belief that as God had created the "elephants" he would give them "grass" to eat. The consequence was a very high infant mortality rate, especially in the countryside. Most children in rural areas suffered from malnutrition and had to begin work at the age of five or six.

CHANGES IN THE FAMILY AND STATUS AND ROLES OF WOMEN SINCE 1945

The August Revolution in 1945 put an end to the French colonial regime. The birth of the Democratic Republic of Vietnam, now the Socialist Republic of Vietnam, ushered in a new era, bringing with it far-reaching changes in family life, in the status of women, in child care, and in the education of children.

Article 9 of the first Constitution (1946) provided that "all power in Vietnam belongs to the people regardless of origin, sex, class or religion" and that "women are equal to men in all respects." The present Constitution, promulgated in 1988, declares that "women and men have the same rights in political, economic, cultural and social matters and in family life." It goes on to state:

The State and Society are responsible for the political, economic, cultural, educational, and professional upgrading of women. The aim is to give women a bigger and bigger role in society.

All citizens, regardless of nationality and sex, can vote from the age of eighteen and can run for the National Assembly or local People's Councils from the age of twenty-one. (Article 57)

The State will adopt labor policies suitable to women's conditions. Women doing the same jobs as men will receive the same pay. (Article 63)

The new Constitution also declares that "family is the cell of society," that "the State protects marriage and family," and that "marriage is based on the principles of voluntariness, progress, monogamy and equality between husband and wife." Also in this regard, Article 64 points out that "Parents are responsible for bringing up their children to become useful citizens. Children must respect their parents and must care for them. The State does not tolerate discrimination against children by parents." The 1980 Constitution (Article 47) also stipulated that "the State and society protect mothers and their children and encourage family planning."

These constitutional provisions have been followed by many decrees and legislative acts, most notably the Law of Marriage and Family[3] and the National Assembly Standing Committee's 1979 Ordinance on the Care and Education of Children.

The "New Life" that was developed during the 30 years of armed struggle to defend national independence and unity did much to radically change the character of the Vietnamese family. Members of the People's Army, most of them newly literate peasants, were largely responsible for the spread of these "New Life" notions throughout the country. Social barriers between the upper classes—functionaries and intellectuals—and the laboring people were removed. A whole new generation of professionals—political, military, scientific, and artistic—was established along with the establishment of agricultural cooperatives and State farms and the emergence of industrial centers and new settlements. The breakdown of the old social structure was completed by the displacement of many families during the war and the emigration of many others after the reunification in 1975.

Liberated women are now present in every sphere of social life. During the war they fought as hard as men did and constituted an important part of frontline labor. Moreover, women in production had to do both their own work and what was left behind by men taken into military service, along with taking charge of their children, their parents, and their parents-in-law.[4] With equal opportunity for education, women have been able to demonstrate their importance to society.[5] They now make up 48 percent of the work force in the public sector and from 70 to 80 percent of the labor directly engaged in agriculture, in the production of consumer goods, in handicrafts, and in the areas of trade, health, and education. Since its founding in 1946, the Vietnam Women's Union has done a great deal to enhance the political and social status of women, by helping them fight for equality and in making their role felt more strongly in family and social life.

All these changes have combined to give the typical family a completely new profile. Socialization is taking place very rapidly, especially in cities and other densely populated areas. Homes are no longer closed sanctuaries, but instead are open to information from the mass media, from the different professions, and from different parts of the country and the world. As a result, new elements are being introduced and backward practices replaced. The "nuclear" family is on the rise, a form in which women with higher political status and better education enjoy some degree of equality and have an important say in all matters.

These changes have brought much improvement in the care and education of preschool children. In general, parents now realize their responsibilities and cooperate well in performing their roles. As a rule, mothers have a greater role to play in the first years. The responsibility is gradually taken over by fathers as the children grow up. Nevertheless, it has become more and more difficult for parents to fully supervise their children. Some of the reasons for this are the following:

- The growing number of working mothers and of nuclear families, and the rapid spread of primary education. This has compounded the problem of day care.
- Threat of disease and accidents, due to the lack of development and unsanitary conditions in rural areas, the rapid population growth rate, and crowded conditions in the cities.
- In many low-income homes adults must be occupied primarily with making a living. As their knowledge of child care and education consists mostly of outdated experience and superstition, it often does more harm than good. In the mountains and other underdeveloped areas, harmful practices are still quite common.

Consequently, many children suffer from calory-protein deficiency, vitamin A deficiency, anemia, infections often resulting in chronic problems, physical deformation, and a high infant mortality rate.[6]

POLICIES RELATED TO THE CARE AND EDUCATION OF CHILDREN

There are three key principles that serve as the basis for all policies and measures regarding the care and education of children.

The Rights of Children

Beginning at birth, children are entitled to proper care and education. This principle stems from socialist humanism and from the view held by the State that man is the greatest asset in the construction of a socialist society. This principle is spelled out in policy as follows:

Children are a source of family happiness, the future of the country, the maintainers of the cause defended by preceding generations, the executors of all the tasks in the construction and defense of the socialist fatherland. (Ordinance of the Standing Committee of the National Assembly on the protection, care and education of children)

The protection, care and education of children is part and parcel of the responsibility towards the nation. It is based on adults' love for children and on justice. (Article 2, ordinance cited above)

All children are provided with protection, care and education, regardless of sex, nationality, religion, class and the social status of their parents or their guardians. (Article 3, cited above)

Children are entitled to good care and education. (Article 5, above)

They are entitled to health care and free medical treatment. (Article 8, above)

President Ho Chi Minh has pointed out that "trees are planted in the interest of the next decade; people are cultivated in the interest of the next century." This belief provides the rationale for the Vietnamese commitment to child care policies and programs.

A Policy of Joint Responsibility: Family, State, and Society

Following from this commitment to the rights of children is the second principle—that the family, the State, and society are all duty-bound to provide children with protection, care, and education. Two articles in the ordinance cited earlier make this explicit:

The family, the State, and society are all duty-bound to provide protection, care and education to children in accordance with their respective functions. (Article 4)

Joint efforts must be made by the family, the State, and society to create every condition for the constant improvement of education for children. (Article 5)

All of this is aimed at institutionalizing the principle that the entire people must join in child care and education. This joint effort consists of four basic elements:

1. Parents must fully discharge their obligations. This involves setting good examples for their children in every respect, providing them with good care, bringing them up properly, and giving them every chance to develop into useful citizens. The State and society will take appropriate measures to assist parents in carrying out these functions.
2. The Fatherland Front and member organizations should play an active part in motivating factories, trade unions, cooperatives, and businesses to contribute as

much as possible to this cause, and should make practical recommendations on how best to educate children morally and physically. The Ho Chi Minh Communist Youth Union, the Women's Union, the General Confederation of Labor and the Peasants Association should cooperate with one another to best carry out the roles prescribed for them in their own regulations.

3. The State Council has to plan this work on a national scale and take effective measures to ensure success. The ministries of education, public health, culture, and information are responsible for assisting the State Council in this task. These ministries should also join the Youth Union and the Central Committee for Child Protection and Care in making plans and recommendations for approval by the State Council. Local governments are responsible for carrying out tasks in their respective territories. Their responsibilities, to be carried out with the cooperation of mass organizations, include planning, supervision, and control.

4. Factories, cooperatives, and businesses are called upon to make contributions in money and means to the construction, maintenance, and upgrading of day care centers and nursery schools, and to other activities for the benefit of children of their employees.

The Protection of Mothers, Newborn Babies, and Infants

The third principle involves population education and family planning. The high population growth rate in Vietnam in the past few decades has combined with a low rate of economic development to exert great pressure on various aspects of social and economic life.[7] This pressure has been felt most strongly regarding the quality of family life, child care, and education. The promotion of family planning began in 1963 with a committee headed by Premier Pham Van Dong. In 1980 family planning was included in the Vietnamese Constitution. Then in 1981 the Council of Ministers stated the following objectives for population and family planning (Circular 29/HDBT):

• Two children at most for each family. One-child families are encouraged.
• Spacing: the second child should come five years or more after the first.
• Women should not become mothers before the age of 22.

In 1984 the Chairman of the Council of Ministers, empowered by the President of the State Council, decreed the establishment of the National Committee for Population and Family Planning under the charge of a Vice Chairman of the Council of Ministers. Each province, city, and special zone was provided with a population and family planning committee of its own, and family planning thus became a national policy. That policy is implemented in the following ways:

• To encourage family planning the State provides free advice and contraceptives, and has made abortion legal.

- Pregnant women are given free health checks regularly. They are also given advice on food and hygiene, and are exempt from heavy work and night shifts from the seventh month of pregnancy and for the first 12 post-natal months.
- During the 180 days that they are on childbirth leave, women receive full pay. Allowances are also paid for the first and second child, and in case of milk deficiency or miscarriage. No allowance is paid for the third child. During the first year of the child's life, the mother may have time off twice a day (30 minutes each time) for breast-feeding.
- Infants are to be given regular checks on growth rate, vaccinated against dangerous diseases, and protected from malnutrition.

A National Policy for the Development of Creches and Nursery Schools

These three principles, on the rights of children, joint responsibility, and the protection of mothers and infants, provide the philosophical framework for the national policy supporting the development of creches and nursery schools. A government circular issued in 1970 stated that "to develop creches and nursery schools is a big policy of the Government regarding women and children and is an important part of the collective welfare policy under socialism.... From 1971 it must be included in annual State plans, and quotas must be assigned to each locality and unit."[8]

Preschool education is also to be thought of as part of the national education system as pointed out by the National Constitution. "Education is placed under the management of the State which must see to a balanced development of the whole system including pre-school education, general education, vocational training and higher education" (Article 41).

Creches and nursery schools have the following responsibilities:

- To prepare children for general education. For the success of this, quality must be ensured and prescribed methods must be strictly observed.
- To cooperate with parents for higher effectiveness.
- To advise parents on how best to bring up their children.

The policy for the development of creches and nursery schools is based on six general guiding principles. The first, already referred to, is that development will involve joint efforts by the State and the general population. A second guideline stresses the importance of applying different program forms to suit local conditions. Third, program priority is to be given to children of working parents. Fourth, parents who can afford to keep their children at home are encouraged to do so for the moment. Special attention is attached to five year olds, in order to prepare them well for primary education.

A fifth guideline emphasizes the importance of greater efforts to provide health care on a more regular basis and implement effective measures to fight malnutrition. The sixth principle is that nurses are the organizers and guides of all activities of their charges, and that these children will attain self-development through their own activities. This goal is spelled out more fully later in the chapter.

The Ministry of Education is accountable to the Council of Ministers for the supervision of the whole child care development program, the compilation and publication of curricula and related materials, the training of teachers and the management of staff, the execution of plans, and the rewarding of meritorious people and units.

Care for All Children

Along with formal preschool education, another major concern of the State and society is education at home, as expressed through the activities of the Youth Union and the Women's Union. A number of movements have been launched with child-rearing education as a central role, including the "Five-Good" and "Three-Responsibility" titles during the 1960s and 1970s, the "New Culture Family" movement, the "Children of Good Health and Good Behavior" movement, many baby contests, the "Fund for Children," and the movement for "Mutual Assistance in Household Economy Against Malnutrition and Illiteracy."

PROGRAM MODELS SERVING PRESCHOOL CHILDREN

The program models attended by Vietnamese children under the age of six fall into five categories. Public creches provide full-time center care for children three months to three years old. Public nursery schools extend this care to three to five year olds. Private mini-creches, or family day care providers, provide home-based day care in family settings on a full-time basis. Part-time nursery school ("short courses") is available to five year olds unable to attend the regular preschool program. Finally, there are guided recreation groups for three- to five-year-old children unable to attend any other form of preschool program.

Public Creches and Nursery Schools

Creches and nursery schools are organized to ensure the overall mental, physical, psychological, and social development of children, help form their personalities as new participants in socialist Vietnam, and prepare them for school.

Creches. The children in public creches are divided into four age groups: 3 to 12 month olds, 13 to 18 month olds, 19 to 24 month olds, and 25 to 36 month olds. Milk, especially mother's milk, is stressed for the first two age groups. Mixed-age groupings may be found in places where there is little demand for day care (government offices, remote areas, etc.).

Thirty children is the maximum size for a group, with one attendant responsible for every six children. Normally, creches take in new children and adjust existing groups once every three months.

Creches operate six days a week. The hours of operation vary, with some centers operating ten hours a day, others for eight hours, and still others open to accommodate factory work shifts. Food is provided at the ten-hour programs, but parents who can afford to feed their children themselves are encouraged to do so. There are also seasonal creches operating during peak periods in agricultural production.

Nursery schools. Children in these programs are divided into groups of three year olds (25 children each), four year olds (30 children each), and five year olds (35 children each). Where grading by age is impractical, mixed groups are organized. Each group is placed in the charge of two teachers. Like creches, nursery schools operate six days a week.

There are also schools that combine the functions of a creche and a nursery school, and thus offer a better chance for the different age groups to mix for improved emotional development.

Children are admitted to the nursery school program at the beginning of every school year, which begins on September 5 and ends on June 2. Three year olds have the option of registering either in early September or in early February of the following year. Parents who wish to send their children to nursery school during summer vacation pay extra fees, at rates established locally.

Some places are provided with exclusive schools for five year olds who have no previous preschool experience. This program, to last for at least 26 weeks, is provided by the Ministry of Education.

Program Content

The development of a child is a complex, dynamic process involving the interplay of physiological, psychological, and social factors. Therefore, care and education should be combined judiciously, and methods should be devised to provide a broad education that will exert its full impact on the whole personality of a child. The primary way of doing this is through the organization of the children's activities. In this sense, creche attendants and nurses are the organizers and guides, and children are the initiators of their own activities.

It is important that the education of young children be a function shared by the formal preschool and the family. Therefore, in addition to working directly with children, the responsibility of creches and nursery schools is to provide parents with scientific notions of child care and education without interfering with family practices and customs worth preserving.

Creche and nursery programs must be designed in ways that will ensure the physical development of the children, as well as the formation and development of both psychological functions and general capabilities. Special attention should be attached to the safety and health of the environment, and to the creation of an emotional, moral, and aesthetic climate for the natural, healthy development of children. In the integration of children into community and national life, respect and encouragement should be given to their individual interests. The optional guidelines for creches and nursery schools provided by the Ministry of Education stress the following routines and activities:

- Personal and environmental hygiene: periodic health checks (every six months). Regular vaccinations. Differing dietary regimes for different age groups, with full utilization of local food sources to ensure maximum nutritional quality.
- Physical education: morning exercises, relaxation exercises, games.
- Fine motor activity: manipulation of objects and creation of forms with building blocks and by drawing, modeling, cutting, and other exercises.
- Language development: introduction to children's books and speech development through conversation, story-telling, singing, recitation of folk poetry, play acting, and other forms.
- Introductory mathematical concepts: the idea of sets, one to one correspondence, counting, recognition of geometric forms and of directions.

Other emphases include observation of nature and society, music education through rhythmic movements, listening to music, singing and dancing, and moral education. Instruction is given in groups (3 to 6 months, 6 to 12 months, 12 to 18 months, 18 to 24 months, 24 to 36 months, etc.) with due consideration to local climate and customs. Free play is stressed, using toys and games for creche-age children, and role playing and games for nursery-school children. During outdoor time children are left to play as they wish.

Only at nursery schools are classes held, and this only so that children get used to teacher guidance. Field trips and tours are other ways to provide educational experiences for the children, and festivities also provide important opportunities for learning and growth.

Caregiver Training

Preschool teachers play a central role in the development program of the day care system. These teachers are to receive basic formal training. Each province or city has two such training institutions, one for creche attendants, and the other for nursery school teachers. Training is also provided at Hanoi Teachers College and at two central schools for nursery school teachers.

The training of the attendants and nurses is covered by municipal or provincial funds.

Creche attendants and nursery school teachers working at government offices, factories, construction sites, and in urban areas are to be paid as government employees. In the countryside, they will be paid as agricultural workers. Creche and kindergarten payrolls and equipment are to be covered by both government funds (including proceeds from lotteries) and local resources, including parents' contributions.

Organization

As provided by the Council of Ministers, creches and nursery schools are designed to serve villages, city wards, public offices, and factories and other workplaces. They are set up on local request and with the permission of local authorities, and are placed under the supervision of local education departments.

Establishments that have made the request are responsible for the construction of school buildings, the maintenance of facilities, the conduct of plans for preschool education, the financing of all operations, and the welfare of the staff.

Health care for children is the responsibility of local medical stations. Municipal or provincial authorities may decide where and when doctors or medical assistants are needed.

Each creche or nursery school is to be assisted by a committee made up of the director of the school and representatives of the sponsoring unit, the local administration, trade unions, the Youth Union, the Women's Union, and parents. This committee is to help promote appropriate methods of child care and education, and mobilize financial contributions for the upkeep of the school. Another function of the committee is to strengthen parent-teacher relations and help improve the welfare of the day care staff. The committee is to meet every six months, with special meetings called by the chairman if needed.

Financing

Creches and nursery schools are funded according to the principle of "joint efforts by the State and the population." A number of schools are also given assistance in kitchen gardening or fish farming to help improve the children's fare.

Financial assistance has also been provided by international and national organizations and by overseas Vietnamese. From 1987 to 1989, the Department for Protection and Education of Children, in the Ministry of Education, received donations from seven international and national organizations. The biggest contribution, 93 percent of the total, came from

UNICEF. Of that amount, 17 percent went into training and research, and the rest into equipment and the improvement of the feeding program.

Quantity and Quality

In 1989 there were 28,122 creches in Vietnam, with an enrollment of 783,954 children. This included 15.3 percent of the newborn to three years age group. Nursery schools numbered 6,711, containing 63,027 classes serving 1,821,188 children. These schools reached 37.5 percent of the three to five year olds. These accomplishments demonstrate the great efforts put forth by the State and society. Nevertheless, because of economic constraints, investment is limited. Moreover, most models are too expensive for the State to afford. As a result, enrollment in creches and nursery schools has never exceeded 30 percent of the total newborn to five years age group.

Most of the nursery schools are located in city wards. They are usually overcrowded, sometimes exceeding the recommended numbers by as much as 150 percent. Most factories have their own nursery schools, which operate during the daytime only. Despite this inconvenience, these schools are much favored by parents because of their flexible timetables and more reasonable fees.

Most creches and nursery schools in the countryside operate during mornings and mid-day only. In regions with difficult climatic conditions (cold weather in the mountains and flooding in low-lying regions) schools operate seasonally. Quality may suffer as a result, but at least parents are freed to concentrate on their jobs.

The few half-day schools are found only in the southern part of the country. Programs covering the full newborn to six years age range are even rarer because they require more space than ordinary ones.

On the whole, preschool education is much more developed in towns, where large numbers of government employees, workers, and artisans live. In the countryside, development is uneven due to unstable incomes and limited resources. Least advantaged are the mountain regions and other places where economic production is mainly at the level of self-sufficiency.

Program quality is generally poor. In some instances it has decreased to an alarming degree in recent years. Good programs make up some 15 percent of the total and are located mostly in urban areas or in big enterprises. The rest of the centers are insufficiently equipped. In 1988 and 1989 food was provided at 61 percent of creches and 11 percent of nursery schools. But, on the whole, meals were inadequate in terms of animal protein, iron, and vitamin content. Other problems are the lack of room in urban preschools for children to play and the short supply of clean water for the rural programs.

Most alarming is the level of malnutrition. During surveys conducted between 1981 and 1988, both in the north and in the south, 44 to 48 percent of the children involved were actually affected by or were threatened by malnutrition. The situation was worst among children 13 to 18 months old. At schools providing only one meal a day the rate was 61 percent, versus 42 percent at schools providing two meals, and 35 percent at schools where three meals were served.

Only half of the creches offered an educational program. The rest simply provided baby-sitting services. In nursery schools, modelling with clay and drawing were usually absent for lack of materials or of competence on the part of teachers. Games were uninteresting, and speech development was neglected because of lack of appropriate methods. Instruction tended to be didactic rather than being suggestive as it should have been.

In the countryside, allocations from agricultural cooperatives have shown a decrease because of lack of funds. Moreover, now that farmers can plan their own work many have stopped sending their children to creches or nursery schools.[9]

The economic situation in Vietnam has been very difficult during the recent past. To cope with these changing economic circumstances, the Council of Ministers has called for new forms of preschool education to suit local economic conditions. The Ministry of Education also set the following goals for the 1989–1990 and 1900–1991 periods to ensure continuation and stabilization of preschool education in ways suitable to changing socio-economic conditions:

- Existing facilities must be consolidated. Targets should be adjusted to suit conditions in each region, with special attention to key areas where the need is real and where necessary conditions are available.
- Efforts should be made to motivate most of the five year olds to go to school to prepare themselves for primary education. Most of these children will follow the current program for nursery schools or the 26-week program for five year olds. The rest will follow a shortened program, for 36 periods only.

Private Family-Based Care

These programs are found in the cities and cater to children under five years old who cannot get access to care and education in the public system. The first of these private programs appeared in the mid–1980s. Recent surveys made in 80 wards in Hanoi, Haiphong, Hue, and Ho Chi Minh City revealed that some 57 percent were served by such programs. Day care homes containing two to three children were most numerous (44 percent). Next came the one child and four or five child groupings (each at 20%). The homes that catered to five children or more were less common. In half of the homes the children ranged in age from newborn to five years. Of the remainder, 39 percent catered solely to three year olds, and 11 percent to children from ages three to five.

Most of the family caregivers were advanced in age (84 percent over 50) and had little formal education (70 percent with primary education only). They all had good incomes, but most (82 percent) had received no formal training. Two thirds of the women wanted to continue to provide day care, but most (84 percent) did not want to attend child care related courses. The knowledge base was largely practical and included a number of incorrect beliefs and practices. Very little was known about the sciences of early childhood education or nutrition.

Because the parents using these private arrangements can afford to pay more, they expect better conditions for their children, in terms of space, hygiene, safety, care practices, and other matters, including more hours of care per day. However, many (40 percent) prefer to bring the food themselves rather than let the day care provider prepare it.

Generally speaking, children in private family arrangements show better physical development than those in public centers. Psychologically and socially, however, they are less developed, probably because of little contact with the outside world.

In 1987 the Ministry of Education moved to regularize private child care. The aim was to improve its quality and better meet demand in densely populated areas. Regulations were established regarding program objectives, forms of organization, modes of operation, rights of caregivers, the obligations of parents, and so on. These regulations include the following:

- Each private program is allowed no more than ten children, and no more than three of those children may be under 18 months of age.
- Caregivers must be recommended by local chapters of the Women's Union.
- Programs must meet minimum standards. In an effort to meet these standards they may request the cooperation of local authorities.
- Caregivers are to take advantage of professional guidance by local education and medical departments, and will be supplied with the necessary manuals.

Arrangements have been made at local education departments to provide professional guidance to private family caregivers, and appropriate manuals have been compiled by the Ministry of Education. By 1989 these requirements had been extended to 21 of the 40 Vietnamese provinces, affecting 1,157 family-based programs involving 5,331 children.

Guided-Recreation Groups

These programs are designed for children who cannot attend nursery schools. The aim is to stimulate the mental and physical development needed as preparation for primary school. According to regulations by the Ministry of Education:

- These groups will cater to children from three to five years of age living in the same neighborhood. Each group should consist of no fewer than six and no more than 15 children.
- Various options are allowed for locating the programs, provided that they are convenient to all the children wishing to participate.
- Toys can be borrowed from nursery schools or made with the assistance of primary school students.
- Group leaders are to be primary school students and other volunteers with formal preschool education in their backgrounds.
- Depending on local conditions, the children can meet twice a week year round, or during the summer months on a more frequent schedule.
- Each meeting should last no more than two hours, during which the children will learn singing, dancing, and drawing. They will also listen to stories, play games, and go on outings.

Guided-recreation groups are organized by local education departments. They are assisted by local nursery and primary schools. Thus far this program model is still in its early stages. Since 1989, 38 such groups have been set up for a total of 260 children.

Shortened Courses for Five Year Olds

Shortened courses are organized to benefit five year olds who cannot attend regular preschool courses. Each course is to be attended by no fewer than five and no more than 30 children. Lessons can be given in private homes, in school buildings, at club houses, in village communal houses, and in any other convenient location. In half-day schools, one teacher is responsible for each group. These caregivers may be formally trained, or teachers and students from secondary schools, or pensioners qualified in early childhood education.

Fees are to be agreed upon by parents and teachers, and financial assistance can be expected from public offices, factories, and other workplaces in the neighborhood.

The children meet two or three times a week, with each session no more than 150 minutes long. The group should meet at least 36 times during the year. Since 1989, 1,008 such courses have been organized in ten provinces for 20,909 children.

Other Related Projects

The rate of population growth in Vietnam has been high, putting a strain on the economic capacity of the country to improve the welfare of families with young children. Population control and family planning projects, and associated parent education, have been strategies aimed in part at reducing population growth. A primary health care strategy has also given priority to women and children, who make up three fourths of the population.

Population and family planning. This effort, directed by the Prime Minister, was started in North Vietnam in 1963 and later became nationwide. In 1975 the U.N. Fund for Population Activities (UNFPA) began cooperating with Vietnam. Since that time UNFPA assistance has been focused on:

- Combining protection of mother and child with family planning.
- Providing information on population and family planning.
- Collecting data on population.
- Population planning.
- Promoting women's activity in population and family planning and increasing their income.

The project has succeeded in helping bring down the natural population growth rate, improved the health of women and children in eight key provinces, and reduced the gross birthrate on a national scale. The mortality rate has also dropped.

Decision 162 of the Council of Ministers defines the functions of the National Committee for Population and Family Planning and provides for the organization of a national network of 300 technical centers in service of population and family planning, with an investment totaling 6.3 million dong (4,000 Vietnamese dong = 1 U.S. dollar).

Parent education. In 1986 and 1987, a parent education project was conducted on an experimental basis in one urban district in Hanoi and one rural district in Ha Nam Ninh province, with the assistance of UNICEF and UNFPA and financial aid from the Australian Government. This effort became a national project in 1988, with financial aid from UNFPA and UNICEF and technical assistance from UNESCO. It is now included in population activity programs undertaken by the National Committee for Population and Family Planning. The Institute of Early Childhood Studies and the Department for Protection and Education of Children are directly responsible for its implementation. The long-term objective of the program is to provide parents with accurate information about child care and education practices. Project goals are to:

- Improve the quality of life for children, especially children under six years old.
- Reduce the incidence of disease and the mortality rate among children.
- Lower the birthrate in the interest of long-term State population policy.

In 1988 to 1991, the effort has been to complete training for 18,000 creche attendants and nurses in 13 key provinces. These people in turn will help train at least 360,000 parents. Current activities of the project include conducting basic surveys in pilot provinces regarding daily customs and habits during pregnancy, in childbirth, in child rearing, and in running family affairs. Manuals are being compiled, and professionals trained. The training of parents continues, through four-month courses involving two one-hour lessons each month. An evaluation of the project was undertaken in 1991.

The primary health care strategy. The Alma Ata Declaration of September 12, 1978, which was an international commitment to a global health strategy (health for all by the year 2000) has received an enthusiastic response in Vietnam, where its contents are integrated into plans for the medical department at every level, backed by State plans. Many projects have been deployed on a national scale with international financial assistance. These include the Integrated Environmental Sanitation Program and projects for intestinal parasite control, for the prevention of viral diseases, for the prevention of malaria, and protection against venereal disease. Encouraging successes include a decrease in the incidence of viral diseases, a lower population growth rate nationwide (at 2.13 percent for the 1989 census, and at 1.7 percent in certain areas), and a lower mortality rate among children under one year of age and in the one to four age group).

Especially important features of this primary health care undertaking for women and children are the strategy for reducing malnutrition due to ca-lorie-protein deficiency, the supplementary food program, the expanded vaccination program, the diarrheal diseases control program, and the effort to provide a clean water supply and standardized latrines and bathrooms for families and child care programs in the rural villages.

STRENGTHS AND WEAKNESSES

Child care and preschool education have been made part of a human strategy in Vietnam and play a crucial role in the overall strategy for socio-economic development in the country. As such, these programs are provided within a policy framework that continues to be articulated and consolidated. This basis in policy ensures constant public awareness of the importance of these efforts and the political will to carry the necessary tasks to a successful conclusion.

Greater impact has been achieved by integrating preschool education into the national education system, through the mobilization of all governmental and popular efforts and by the diversification of child care models. Family-based and center-based forms have been developed, and a number of national projects have been initiated in earnest. As a result, more and more children have benefitted from a scientific approach to child care.

Child care and preschool education have also become more scientific and more relevant due to the application of achievements made in other socialist countries and by international agencies (WHO, UNICEF, and UNESCO) to results obtained by the Institute of Early Childhood Studies and to information obtained in recent basic surveys. In this same vein, pilot projects are under way in preparation for the reforms to be effected in the 1991–1995 period. Financial and technical assistance by international organizations has also been very important and has led to the initiation of many important projects.

At the same time, economic problems have often diverted official attention from child care and education. This is combined with the fact that for many years too much emphasis was put on the construction of very large facilities. The intention was to move very quickly in the areas of child care and education. However, this impractical approach led to sloppy development, inadequate infrastructure, and haphazard training.[10]

Another shortcoming has involved the slow rate of progress made in the care of children other than those currently receiving formal preschool education. Most projects of this sort are just getting under way. No successful models have yet been found for assisting underdeveloped regions of the country, where children are at greater risks. Attention to the handicapped child is also inadequate.

A better job can be done of utilizing all available resources. More contributions need to be solicited from private groups and volunteers, and much more can still be expected from parents. Research is not up to the mark, and investment in this field is limited. As a consequence, many problems remain unresolved.

Prospects for the Future

Success in the renovation of State and economic management in the past few years has provided a basis for further development of child care and education in the years to come. The demand for education is expected to rise as a consequence of the formation of a multi-sector economy, which is generating more and more jobs, and of the faster deployment of national programs of population and family planning. This will further stimulate child care services. Recent policies for the socio-economic development of mountain regions are expected to give a big boost to child care and education in those areas. Better approaches, improved implementation of projects with more effective international assistance, and greater contributions from the voluntary sector will help step up research, enhance parents' awareness, and extend services to all target groups.

NOTES

1. Most of the peasants were landless and thus had to rent land at rates that ranged from 40 percent to 80 percent of the value of the crop (higher in the south

than the north). In addition, personal taxes took three fourths of what could be gained from the fields.

2. Ninety-five percent of the population was illiterate. The number of primary school pupils account for 0.4 percent of the population and that of secondary school pupils, for only 0.0019 percent. Preschool education was nonexistent.

3. There are two such laws. The first was promulgated in 1959, the second, in 1987.

4. The wartime title of "Three-Responsibility Woman" was awarded to those who were simultaneously successful in production, household affairs, and fighting.

5. By 1947, 70 percent of Vietnamese women had become literate. At present, women account for 52 percent of the enrollment in primary and secondary schools, and 38 percent of university enrollment. They also make up 26.6 percent of the teaching staff at colleges and universities and 10.6 percent of the recipients of doctorate and masters of science degrees.

6. In 1988 the infant mortality rate (IMR) was 43 (per 1,000 live births) in the six northern provinces and 45 in the seven southern provinces (Department of Statistics).

7. Between October 1, 1979, and April 1, 1989, Vietnam's population increased by 11,700,000, for an annual rate of 2.13 percent. This growth should have been accompanied by an increase of 6.4 percent—8.5 percent in national income. The actual average annual income increase since 1980 has been only 5.4 percent.

8. Government Circular 170-Ttg, Sept. 22, 1970, on the necessity of stepping up preschool education (legal documents on preschool education, 1985, pp. 14–17).

9. According to the Department of Protection and Education of Children, the Ministry of Education, creche enrollment in 1988 and 1989 decreased by 239,738 places as compared with the previous year. There was also a decrease in nursery enrollment. At the same time, classes for five year olds showed a sharp increase. During the same period, 3,470 creche attendants and 2,089 nurses resigned to find better paying jobs.

10. A survey made of 13,912 nurses and 9,628 attendants showed that only 8.4 percent of the latter had received secondary-level training, mostly through courses from three to six months long. Of the nurses, only 23 percent had received secondary-level training. (Nguyên thi Dung, 1989)

REFERENCES

Ban nghiên cúu cái cách giáo duc mâũ giáo. (Ed.). (1985). *Môt sô văn bán pháp ui vê ngành giáo duc mâu giáo 8.1966–1.1984* (The legal documents on pre-school education, August 1966 to January 1984).

Bô giáo duc. (1987). *Chúóng triñh phát triên nhóm tré gia diñh 1988–1991* (Project for development of family day care centers, 1988–1991). Roneo. MOE archives.

Bô giáo duc. (1989). *Húông dân nhiêm vu năm hoc 1989–1990 Ngành bào vê–giáo duc tré em* (Guidelines for child protection and education in the 1989–1990 school year). Roneo. MOE archives.

Bô giáo duc. (Ed.). (1978). *Chúóng triñh mâū giáo cái tiên* (The improved curriculum for Nursery Schools).

Bô giáo duc. (Ed.). (1990). *Chúóng triñh chiñh ly chăm sóc và giáo duc tré tú 3–*

36 tháng ó nhà tré (The revised cirriculum for care and education of infants from 3 to 36 months of age in creches).

Bô giáo duc. (Ed.). (1990). *Qui định vê muc tiêu, kê hoach chăm sóc, giáo duc cúa nhà trè và trúóng mâũ giáo* (The Regulations of care and education objectives and programs in creches and kindergartens).

Bô giáo duc, Bô y tê, Tông công đòan Viêt nam, Hôi Liên hiêp phu nũ Viêt nam, Trung úóng đòan thanh niên công sán Hô Chí Minh, Hôi nông dân VN, and Hôi chū thâp đó VN. (1988). *Thông tú chung vê viêc chăm sóc nuôi dúòng vã giáo duc tré em tú 0 – 6 túôi* (Joint decision of the ministries on the care and education of children from birth to six years old). Roneo. MOE archives.

Bôytê—HSO (1988). *Hôi tháo chăm sóc súc khóe ban đâu phía Nam* (Regional seminar on the implementation of PHC concept, Ho Chi Minh City, November 22 to 25, 1988). Roneo. MOE archives.

Cuc báo vê—giáo duc tré em. (1987). *Húóng dân tô chúc lóp mâu giáo 5 tuôi ngăn han* (Guidelines for organization for short-term courses for five-year-old children). Roneo. MOE archives.

Cuc báo vê—giáo duc tré em. (1988). *Kêt quá điêu tra nhóm tré gia đính ó các tinh điêm* (Survey results of family day care centers in key provinces). Roneo. MOE archives.

Cuc báo vê—giáo duc tré em. (1987). *Tap hop tré vui choi co huong dan* (Guideline for the guided-recreation groups). Roneo. MOE Archives.

Cuc báo vê—giáo duc tré em. (1988). *Húóng dân tô chúc nhom tré gia đính* (Guideline for Organization of Family day care centres). Roneo. MOE archives.

Cuc báo vê—giáo duc tré em. (1989). *Báo cáo tông kêt chúóng trính giáo duc các bâc cha me* (Review of the Parent Education Program). Roneo. MOE Archives.

Cuc báo vê—giáo duc tré em. (1989). *Báo cáo tông kêt năm hoc 1989–1989 ngành báo vê - giáo duc tré em* (Review of school year 1988–1989). Roneo. MOE archives.

Cuc báo vê—giáo duc tré em. (1989). *Húóng dân thúc hiên chuyên đê chông suy dinh dúóng ó nhà tré, trúóng mâu giáo nhũng năm 1989–1991* (Guidelines for reduction of malnutrition in creches and kindergartens in the years 1989–1991). Roneo. MOE archives.

Đào văn Phu. (1989). "Giáo duc trúóc tuôi hoc phô thông" (Preschool education). *Nghiên cúu giáo duc,* 8.

Hiên pháp núóc Viêt nam dân chú công hòa. (1946). (Constitution of Democratic Republic of Vietnam.) Hà nôi.

Hiên pháp núóc Công hòa Xã hôi chú nghiã Viêt nam. (1980). (The Constitution of the Socialist Republic of Vietnam.) Hà nôi: NXB Pháp li.

Hôi đông Bô trúóng. (Quyêt định 23/HDBT, March 9, 1989). *Quyêt định vê môt sô vân đê câp bách trong công tác giáo duc và đào tao* (The Decision of the Council of Ministers on pressing problems in education and training). Roneo. MOE archives.

Lê thi Nhâm Tuyêt. (1975). *Phu nũ Viêt nam qua các thói đai,* 2nd ed. (Vietnamese women in successive eras). Hà nôi: NXB Khoa hoc xã hôi.

Luât hôn nhân và gia đính. (1987). (The Marriage and Family Law). Hà nôi.

Mai Kim Châu. (1986). "Ngúòi phu nũ trong gia đình nông thôn hiên nay" (Women in the rural families nowadays). In Trung tâm nghiên cúu khoa hoc vê phu nũ (Ed.), *Mây vân đê vê phân bô, sú dung đào tao và điêu kiên lao đông phu nũ*, pp. 160–164. (Issues on distribution, employment, training and working conditions of female labor). Conference Proceedings.

"Nghi quyêt cúa Bô chinh tri (Dang công san Viêt nam) vê môt sô chú trúóng chính sách lón phát triên kinh tê xã hôi miên nui" (The resolution of the CPV Political Bureau on some main policies of socio-economic development of mountain regions).

Nguyên thi Dung, Lúóng thi Binh, and Dô xuân Hoa. (1989). "Tinh hinh đôi ngũ giáo viên vá nhu câu gúi con ó các nhà tré, trúóng mâu giáo" (Teacher situation and parent needs to send their children to creches or kindergartens). *Nghiên cúu giáo duc*, 8.

Pham Mai Chi. (1989). "Vân đê báo vê súc khóe va giáo duc mâm non." (On child health care and preschool education.) Nghiên cúu GD, 8.

Pham Song. (September 5, 1989). Trích bài nôi truyên nhân ky niêm 20 năm UNFPA và 11 năm hóp tác UNFPA—Viet nam 16/8/1989" (The 20th anniversary of UNFPA and Eleven Years of UNFPA—Vietnam Cooperation, Press Conference, August 16, 1989). *Suc khoe*, 17/498.

Trân thi Trong. (1988). "Vê Giáo duc mâm non" (On early childhood education). *Nghiên cúu giáo duc*, 12.

Truong xuan Truong. (1986). "Vai trò ngúói bô trong môt só chúc năng chinh cúa gia đinh nông thôn hiên" (Paternal role in some main functions in rural families nowadays). In Trung tâm nghiên cúu khoa hoc vê phu nũ (Ed.), *Mây vân đê vê phân bô, sú dung, đào tao và điêu kiên lao đông phu nũ*, pp. 168–172. (Issues on distribution, employment, training, and working condtiions of female labor). Conference proceedings.

Uy ban bao vê bà me và tre em trung úóng (Ed.) (1977). *Điêu lê tam thòi vê tô chúc nhà tre* (Regulations for creche operation). Roneo. Archives of the Institute of Early Childhood Studies.

Uy ban bao vê bà me và tre em trung úóng (Ed.) (1984). *Chúóng trinh nuôi day tre tú 3–36 tháng ó nhà tre* (The program for rearing infants from 3 to 36 months of age in creches). Roneo: Archives of the Institute of Early Childhood Studies.

Văn kiên cúa Đang và Nhà núóc vê giáo duc tú 1975–1984 (1984). (Documents of Viet Nam Communist Party and government on education, 1975–1984.) Hà nôi: NXB Giào duc.

Viên nghiên cúu tre em trúôi túói hoc (Ed.) (1989). *Dú thao chúóng trinh cai cách giáo duc mâu giáo* (The tentative reform curriculum for nursery schools). Vol. 1, 2, 3. Roneo. Archives of the Institute of Early Childhood Studies (IECS).

Viên nghiên cúu tre em trúóc hoc. (Vol. 1, 1976; Vol. 2, 1981; Vol. 3, 1986; vol. 4, 1989). *Tuyên tâp các công trinh nghiên cúu khoa hoc* (The selected research works on child care and education). Roneo. Archives of IECS.

——— 30 ———

ZIMBABWE

Rosely N. E. Chada

> There were no professional schools or teachers in the traditional villages,
> nor any formal teaching except perhaps in morality. The child learned
> from various members of the family as he grew, mostly without realizing
> that he was being taught. Most often he learned from his grandparents,
> his mother and father, frequently sitting next to his grandfather or father
> in the evening at the fireplace or in the open fields, at the cattle pen or
> wherever a male activity was being pursued.
>
> (Gelfand, 1979, p. 219)

Extraordinary changes have taken place in Zimbabwean society since independence from Britain was achieved in 1980. These changes are bringing
early childhood education and care to the children of Zimbabwe in a much
more comprehensive and equitable way than had been the case during the
colonial period. At the same time, traditional patterns of socialization, as
described in the opening quote, are giving way to new structures and processes that must build upon, rather than replace, the underlying values and
roles providing historical roots for Zimbabwean culture.

CHANGES IN THE FAMILY AND SOCIETY

The traditional family structure was composed of the father as the head
of the family, the mother as the nurturer, the grandparents as sources of
wisdom and knowledge, the uncles and aunts as referees in family squabbles,
and brothers and sisters. Although the father appeared to have greater
decision-making power, the mother had great "behind the scenes" influence
on all major decisions. Most family matters required discussion and ap-

proval of both parents before action could be taken. The extended family lived in very close proximity to one another, permitting a degree of influence on and control of family members. Discipline was exercised on every member of the family, but cultural and economic inhibitions on women fostered female dependency on their menfolk. The later introduction of Christianity and colonial rule did not change the subordinate status of women because both the British culture and the basic teachings of Christianity incorporate patrilineal role relations.

Growing Up in Shona Society

Parents were expected to nurture the child as a matter of duty. Ultimately children were the responsibility of the family unit, the kinship group, and the community in general, and this included instilling discipline and good behavior in the child. However, any misdeed by the child was seen as a reflection of the moral standards of the parents, the closest people to the child. An individual's conduct toward the community was and still is an important aspect of Shona education. Gelfand (1979) points out that

Great emphasis was placed on teaching every child to show respect to others. This instruction started from his earliest years, so that by the time he was ten or twelve years old most children were thoroughly familiar with all the details of correct social behavior and proper attitudes towards people. Manners were and are still taught in elaborate detail. Bad behavior towards other people, family members or strangers was and still is promptly punishable mostly by rebuke. The various family members were intimately concerned with the inculcation of good manners. Those mostly responsible were the mother, father, grandmother, grandfather, the paternal aunt as well as the brothers and sisters of the child. (p. 220)

The Status of Women

The patrilineal nature of Zimbabwean society traditionally left very little room for female participation in socio-political activities outside the home, save in the economic sphere. Women participated in the economic activities side-by-side with their menfolk. At the same time, women were highly respected, particularly because of their childbearing role and the nurturing functions that they performed in the family. The mother was the embodiment of culture during the crucial early years of the child's development. She was and still is the first language teacher for the child and the giver of social values, until the child is ready to mix with others in the larger community.

The Status of Children

The coming of a newborn child has always been the happiest event in the family. Great interest in the newborn is shown by all family members, and soon the child learns the importance of the extended family. Particular importance was also attached to the way the child was brought up. While the more general responsibility for the upbringing of the child revolved around the grandparents, the paternal aunts, the brothers and sisters, and the father, the mother played the predominant role. From the first few weeks of life until weaning, the infant enjoys a very close relationship with its mother—closer than is normally seen in Western society. The mother keeps constant watch over the child's whereabouts, sleeps between the child and her husband, and carries the baby on her back. This physical proximity develops in the child a very strong sense of security, comfort, and confidence in the mother's tender care.

Another important and striking feature of the child's development takes place during the toddler stage after weaning, when the child leaves the world of the mother and is transferred to the care of the grandparents. The boy becomes the responsibility of the grandfather, and the girl of the grandmother. There they are taught the correct use of the language, social etiquette, manners, and behavior. At this stage they listen to the many tales told by their grandmothers, grandfathers, and parents. They begin to hear many proverbs, puzzles, taboos, and songs. They learn to play games for the development of mental, physical, and social skills. Stories were told that related to the child's environment, such as hunting for food, the wind, the rain, and relationships in the extended families. The grandparents were involved in passing on the family history, which is told in the evenings around the family fire.

The teaching of life skills was carried out separately based on the gender of the child. The boys were taught the ways of good fatherhood, the girls those of good motherhood.

The principle of teaching children that which they are capable of understanding at their level was very much in practice in the Zimbabwean traditional educational system. The impatience of the adults for children to be grown-ups was not tolerated. There was recognition of the child as a growing organism, following a timetable that could not be rushed. As Jean Piaget observed, "Nature would have children be children before they are men. If we invert this order, we shall produce a forced fruit, immature and flavorless, fruit that rots before it can ripen. Childhood has its own ways of thinking, seeing and feeling" (as quoted in Elkind, 1976, p. 41).

The British Colonial Period

The coming of British colonial rule resulted in a number of significant changes. First, there was a deliberate attempt to destroy or weaken the social fabric of Shona society, to create an environment for effective rule and to destroy the tradition of resistance that Zimbabweans had exhibited at the end of the last century. Second, an organized educational system was introduced through Christian missionaries. In this way the mission establishments became the centers of modernization and cultural destabilization. The Christian religion came into direct conflict with the traditional religion, which provided the basis of early childhood education. Children were removed from the traditional setting to a new world of the mission station. In some cases the moral behavior taught in Zimbabwean society, such as avoiding adultery and promoting the sanctity of marriage, were parallel with Christian teachings. However, in general the mission stations were committed to destroying the religious basis of our traditional early childhood practices. In many instances children found the missionary teachings at great variance with the traditional teachings, and so children found it very difficult to develop a unitary perspective of society.

The colonial education system was a major factor limiting African economic and political advancement. The colonial governments created an educational system that not only was segregated and inferior to that provided for European children, but it also was calculated to further the political ends of keeping the majority African population permanently under the domination of the minority European population. In a letter to *The Rhodesia Herald* written in 1912, the authors stated "that we should educate the native in any way that will unfit him for service. He is and always should be a hewer of wood and drawer of water for his master." Attitudes had changed very little more than a half century later, when in 1965 a writer to the same newspaper argued that, "by educating our African population we are committing political suicide, and sooner or later an African Government must come into being unless we do something about it" (quoted by Theodore Bull, *Rhodesian Perspective*, pp. 69–70). Thus the educational policy was geared to the economic, social, and political policies aimed at maintaining the ascendancy of the white minority. The educational system was carefully designed to educate Africans only to the level where they would be able to serve the labor needs of the white minority without threatening the political privileges of the white working class and the white leadership.

Another factor that disrupted the traditional mode of early childhood education was the creation of an abundant and cheap migrant labor pool through the expropriation of African land, which served to compel African males into white controlled cash sections of the economy in order to earn a living. The result was a deterioration of traditional family life, and thus of traditional early childhood education. The effects of this migrant system are still being felt in apartheid South Africa, following the creation of a migrant labor system from the Bantustans (see Chapter 24).

Modern Family Structure in Zimbabwe

There are two family structural arrangements now found in modern Zimbabwean society. One is the result of the migratory labor system mentioned earlier, in which the menfolk were drawn to the urban centers for employment, leaving all the traditional responsibilities of caring for the home in the hands of their women and children. This pattern has several serious difficulties associated with it. Women are unable to make binding decisions on major family issues until their husbands return on visits from the city. There has also been a fracturing of the strong extended family in this process. Traditionally, the father was the disciplinarian of the family. When he left for the urban centers, the responsibility for disciplining the children fell on the mother. The women have gradually adjusted to these new expectations. More recently, with the improvement of public transportation, the rural family has been reinforced, although not completely restored, as men are able to pay more frequent visits to their homes.

The other modern family form is urban based, emerging as a result of the more permanent settlement of blue- and white-collar African workers in and around the cities. These modern urban families are basically nuclear in structure, composed of the father, mother, and children. Extended family membership and obligations have declined in these families because the grandparents, aunts, and uncles no longer live within the immediate environs of the child, coming to the urban homes only as visitors. The loss of this extended family involvement has led to a decline in the stability of society, in the absence of any other way to provide a smooth cultural transmission of values and customs from the grandparents to their grandchildren.

With parents still adjusting to the new socializing roles now required of them, they have tended to leave the whole area of children's education to formal education institutions made up of people themselves unready for these new roles. The victims of this new vacuum in the education of the child are the children themselves, the results of which are evident in the deviant behavior they now more frequently manifest.

Women and Work in New Zimbabwe

These modern urban family structures and practices have encouraged many women to join the labor market. This means that they too can no longer be expected to play the traditional family role on a full-time basis. The need to find institutions to look after children while their mothers are at work has necessitated the expansion of early childhood education and care centers, especially since 1980.

The growing number of women entering the labor market on a full-time basis has been facilitated by several legislative provisions. The passage of minimum wage legislation has benefitted the majority of women, who generally occupied the unskilled category of the labor market. The Labor Relations Act of 1985, which prohibits discrimination on the basis of sex, creed, and for other reasons has enabled women to earn equal pay for equal work. The same law has provided mothers with maternity leave for a maximum of 90 days without the loss of job, while receiving 75 percent of their salary.

In the rural areas women are also now encouraged to participate in income-generating projects such as cooperatives, cash crop farming, and other personal income-generating activities. Thus the entry of an increasing number of women into the labor market both in the urban and rural areas has resulted in a great demand for early childhood care centers throughout the country.

THE ECONOMIC POLICY FRAMEWORK IN ZIMBABWE

Upon independence, the government of Zimbabwe inherited a socially, politically, economically, and technologically dualistic socio-economic system. On the one hand, it was composed of white-dominated, relatively capital-intensive, modern economic sectors including commercial farming, mining, modern manufacturing, and services. On the other hand, there existed a largely neglected peasant sector characterized by low per capita incomes, widespread poverty and disease, and an underdeveloped infrastructure.

The two sectors were not working independently of each other. The peasant sector served as a reservoir of cheap labor for the modern sector and at the same time provided a home and a living for children, women, the aged, and the disabled. As noted earlier, because they and their families could not subsist on the overcrowded and poor land that was allocated to them, able-bodied men had to migrate to commercial farms and to cities to seek wage employment. Since their families could not join them, more and more communal area households became de facto headed by women, with the husbands returning to visit them from time to time. This had a negative and, in many respects, traumatic impact on rural African families. Thus, the economic dualism that characterized the colonial period was evident in the inequitable pattern of income and wealth distribution between racial groups and between urban and rural inhabitants.

Government Economic Policy Response

In 1981 the government of Zimbabwe published an economic policy statement entitled "Growth with Equity," which was directed toward the attainment of a socialist and egalitarian society. This statement provides a framework for overall sectorial policies. It summarizes clearly the situation found at independence and the challenges that had to be faced:

> Government is determined to forge ahead with the task of building a progressive, non-racial and egalitarian society which draws on the energies and abilities of all its peoples, without regard for their race, color or creed. However, the restructuring of the economic and social framework of our society is an absolutely essential and imperative economic ingredient of the policy of reconciliation if that policy is to result in genuine and durable peace in our country and is to be conducive to economic development and prosperity for all our people.
>
> Above all, recognizing the confidence of all Zimbabweans in the future of their country and their desire to forget the past and build together a new nation, recognizing also the significant achievements already made in this regard, Government is determined to embark on policies and programs designed to involve fully in the development process the entire people, who are the beginning and the end of society, the very asset of the country and the raison d'être of Government. (Government of Zimbabwe, 1981, pp. 1–2)

The primary national objectives of the government, which form the framework within which all programs are to be implemented, include the following:

1. Achieve a sustained high rate of economic growth and speedy development in order to raise incomes and standards of living of all people and expand productive employment of rural peasants and urban workers, especially the former.

2. Create and maintain high levels of employment for Zimbabweans in all sectors and at all levels of skill and responsibility, and redress the historical racial imbalances in skilled employment.

3. Train, mobilize and utilize fully the country's human resources, which are its creative and greatest asset.

4. Democratize the workplace in all sectors of the economy by encouraging worker participation in decision making at the office and shop floor levels.

5. Provide, improve, and extend the rural economic infrastructure, with particular emphasis on the extension of marketing services, credit and agricultural factor input, and facilities.

6. Provide, improve, and extend social services (including housing, health and education) to lower income groups in the urban and rural areas; and consider possible schemes for social security services where they do not exist, bearing in mind the overall responsibility of the State for the welfare and well-being of its citizens.

Government Policies for Children and Women

Any analysis and examination of how best to meet the needs of children cannot be done in isolation from the roles and situation of women. The government's efforts to improve the situation of children and women have to be viewed in turn within the framework of national objectives and policy. There is clearly a linkage between poverty, malnutrition, disease and the demands placed on mothers by their onerous family and economic roles. If mothers are to adequately feed, care for, and raise their children in conditions of good health, they must have the materials, knowledge, time and energy to do so. Most mothers in Zimbabwe do not have these resources in sufficient amounts.

One of the immediately effective strategies that the government has adopted to improve the ability of women to care for the children in their households has been to reduce the burdens caused by inefficient technologies or poor access to such essential services as water supply, cheap and accessible energy, and sanitation, thus giving them more time to improve their knowledge and skills and to better care for their children. Community-based child care centers of various types, including the preschool institutions we shall be examining in more detail later, are one of the mechanisms for achieving this objective. They are of particular importance to urban women who lack the child care supports of extended family and communal structures that are more common in rural areas. However, their value in the rural areas has increased considerably as well.

The Enhancement of Women's Legal Situation. Zimbabwe's legal system is governed by two bodies of law: the indigenous customary law of the Africans and statutory law with Western origins. Customary law, which is unwritten, is subject to different interpretations and manipulation by different ethnic groups in the country, and even by those well versed in the law. The vast majority of women in the rural areas are governed by this law.

The question of women's role and status in our new society, as it relates to their place in national economic development, is at the crossroad. Steps are being taken to ensure that there is recognition that integration of women must not only be reflected in national macroeconomic policies but also be realized through the implementation of concrete projects. There is need for the development and presentation of macroeconomic policies with no gender overtones and biases against women, whose work has been recognized to be central to the success of those policies.

Yet the shapers of macroeconomic policies continue to underrate the economic contributions of women. One of the recurrent problems is the development of specific recommendations for educating policy makers to acknowledge and reflect the role of women in development, and provide means through which that crucial role can be enhanced within the overall development spectrum.

While the situation in Zimbabwe with regard to the effective integration of women in development has improved considerably since independence, a great deal of public education needs to be carried out before women can enjoy equal treatment and have equal access to opportunities in all areas of Zimbabwean life. One of the major achievements made in the government's effort to integrate women's issues into the overall development process was the creation of the Ministry of Community Development and Women's Affairs. That ministry, in conjunction with other government departments and non-governmental organizations, has done a great deal to promote the status of women by raising the consciousness in both men and women of the need to integrate women into development, and by carrying out various development programs involving women. In 1987 then Prime Minister (now President) R. G. Mugabe outlined the following legal measures undertaken by the Zimbabwean government to enhance the status of women in our society:

1. The Legal Age of Majority Act (1982), which gives both women and men full contractual capacity on attaining the age of 18, has since been raised to age 21. This act also makes provision for unmarried mothers to claim maintenance from the fathers of their children (as does the Customary Law and Primary Courts Act).

2. The Labor Relations Act (1985), which makes it an offence for an employer to discriminate against any employee or prospective employee on grounds of race, tribe, place of origin, political opinion, color, creed, or sex in relation to job advertisements, recruitment, creation or abolition of jobs, determination of wages and benefits, choice of persons for jobs, training, advancement, transfer, promotion, or retrenchment. Now women and men get equal pay for equal work. Prior to independence men and women doing the same kind of work, with the same qualifications, were remunerated on different scales.

3. The Labor Relations Act also enabled women to take 90 days maternity leave with up to 75 percent of their pay during the period.

4. The Matrimonial Causes Act (1985), which recognizes the direct and indirect contribution of women to family wealth, gives women a right to a share of that property upon divorce.

The new role and status of women has necessitated the adoption of community-level strategies to address one of their major traditional responsibilities, the care of children. The recognition of this need led to the creation of the national Early Childhood Education and Care Program (ECEC).

EARLY CHILDHOOD EDUCATION AND CARE: POLICIES AND PRACTICES

The education and care of the young child emerged soon after independence as an area of national concern in Zimbabwe, after many decades of laissez-faire philosophies and approaches during the colonial period. Perceptions of early childhood education and care as a downward extension of primary education and as a child-minding system outside the framework of human resources development strategies were quite common among the parents and even the early childhood educators prior to independence, and these conceptions still linger in the minds of many people in the field. One major task has been to broaden this view of the field.

The government policy on early childhood education and care is based on the premise that early childhood from birth to six years is the period in which human growth is most rapid and the child is most vulnerable and sensitive to environmental influences. This policy is also grounded in the belief that the needs of the young child are interdependent; therefore, any measures for his/her advancement must be based on a holistic approach to child development and must be implemented within the framework of an integrative structure. There is an increasing awareness now of the interdependence of all aspects of child development.

Government policy is based as well on the assumption that strategies adopted for early childhood education and care should take into account the situation of the family as a whole—the child's immediate environment. The policy recognizes that the physical, psychological, and educational aspects of young children cannot and should not be isolated from the general situation of the family, either for the purpose of seeking a clearer understanding or for the formulation of remedial measures. The policy and practice of early childhood education should not be seen as a substitute for the home. It is rather a complementary strategy to meet the needs that the family is unable to fulfill and to foster child-rearing practices that are conducive to balanced development. Thus the early childhood education and care system is perceived as a community enterprise, with parental participation in the familiar environment of the child's neighborhood.

The government's decision and desire to develop its own strategies for early childhood education and care derives from its historical experiences with its attempts to adapt the primary and secondary systems to the realities of post-independence Zimbabwe. In 1989, the Minister of Primary and Secondary Education, Hon. Fay Chung, made the following statement about the activities and plans of her ministry on preschool education.

We have 1.8 million pre-school children who are presently not well catered for and it is a virgin area where we do not have to pick up systems that were developed previously. So we can actually say we can move on to a completely new field and plan solutions which are not as constraining as our present primary and secondary system. The school system is very constraining because we can not move away very far from the models we inherited... in pre-school we are in virgin territory... and I think this gives us possibilities for very innovative approaches at the same time ensuring we have the highest quality. ("The World Bank Report: Education in Sub-Sahara Africa," 1989, pp. 41–42)

The government's policy on early childhood is aimed at meeting both child survival and development needs. The policy emphasizes the holistic and developmental approach to early childhood education and care through the satisfaction of the basic psycho-social needs of children—love, acceptance, belonging and security, achievement, self-reliance, recognition, self-esteem and independence, and finally self-realization and actualization to develop satisfactory interpersonal relationships and social interaction and in order to avoid behavioral disorders and social maladjustments.

Early Childhood Education and Care Program

The Early Childhood Education and Care Program (ECEC) is one of the major strategies the government adopted in order to achieve effective integration of women in development. Before 1980 early childhood education for black children in Zimbabwe was available only on a very limited basis. In 1982, the Ministry of Community Development and Women's Affairs was given the responsibility for coordinating a new early childhood education and care effort, building on the initiatives of local communities.

The plan was to establish children's centers in both rural and urban locations, incorporating the existing infrastructure where possible and building new facilities where they did not exist. These centers could be developed at health centers, community centers, the sites of non-governmental organizations, churches, and club centers. The expectation was that they would be staffed by volunteers from the local community.

The major tasks assumed by the Ministry of Community Development and Women's Affairs involved the development of relevant curriculum, the provision of training, improvement of the existing physical facilities, and the setting up of guidelines for standards control and supervision.

Before independence in 1980 there was no single agency charged with the development of policy for the provision of education and care services for the young children of all races in Zimbabwe. The result was that the programs on early childhood education and care throughout the country were conducted in an uncoordinated manner, with minimum government direction and intervention. Although the need for coordinating health and nutrition services through such structures as nurseries and creches was there, few steps were taken in this direction. The early childhood education and care approaches were imported from the industrialized nations, while suited to those conditions, were not appropriate for the cultural and economic environment in Zimbabwe.

The colonial governments were never particularly enthusiastic about becoming involved in the welfare of the young child. Most of the interventions prior to 1980 were simply framed in legislative enactments, with little effort to see that the laws passed were followed. For instance, the Smith regime passed The Children's Protection and Adoption Act in 1972 and the Nursery

Schools Education Regulations in 1973, but little effort was made to see that most of the children benefitted. While the above-mentioned act and regulations still provide the general policy framework within which early childhood education and care services are developed, the protection given under the law now covers children of all races, rather than simply those of the white minority.

On coming to power, the government of President (then Prime Minister) Mugabe introduced a comprehensive national program of early childhood education and care. A Commission of Inquiry into Preschool Activities in Zimbabwe Report of 1981 recommended that

since the community play-center is envisaged as the service center for the majority of preschool children, especially in rural areas, it would be appropriate for the Ministry of Community Development and Women's Affairs to be responsible for the overall coordination of the preschool activities. The Ministry could play a major role through their community development workers. The latter as innovators and advisers could provide the link between the play centers, the community and the home. (Government "Inquiry into Preschool," 1981, pp. 49–50)

Thus in 1982 the Ministry of Community Development and Women's Affairs was charged with the responsibility of running the program. This was the first step taken by Zimbabwe to develop its own strategies for early childhood education and care, with the clear recognition that the satisfaction of needs of children at every phase of life was closely related to the well-being of women.

The new National Early Childhood Education and Care (ECEC) program was based on a project agreement signed between the government and UNICEF in 1982, with UNICEF originally planning to support the program in a phasing-out process over a period of three years. This plan was later reviewed and extended to the end of 1989.

Objectives of the National Program. The general objectives of the post-independence national early childhood education and care program are as follows:

1. To provide all children, regardless of socio-economic background, with early childhood education and care, particularly in recognition of the fact that the first five years of life are crucial to one's future development, and that early childhood education prepares children to develop basic life skills essential for adulthood.

2. To adequately invest in national manpower development programs at the earliest possible stage since research has shown that children who have attended early childhood centers perform better in the formal educational system; to provide a safe place for creative play while parents, particularly the mothers, actively participate in other important national tasks.

3. To standardize the ECEC activities throughout the country.

The Legislative Framework. Early childhood activities continue to be regulated by the Ministry of Labor, Manpower Planning and Social Welfare and the Ministry of Education. The Ministry of Labor is responsible for the registration of all early childhood centers, and it is also charged with the responsibility for the welfare of children through the Children's Protection and Adoption Act of 1972. That act provides for:

a. the protection, welfare, and supervision of children;
b. the establishment, recognition, and registration of certain institutions and institutes for the reception and custody of children and families; and
c. the treatment of children after their enrollment in such institutions and institutes.

The Ministry of Education, through the Education (Nursery Schools) Regulations of 1973, was made responsible for the registration of all nursery schools. The provisions of these regulations state that no person or institution shall establish a nursery school unless he/it has informed the government of the proposed name and address of the preschool, the geographic area served, the number and age of the children to be enrolled in the school, the names, qualifications, and experience of the staff, and the planned curriculum and other activities. Thus, a nursery school will only be registered if the government is satisfied that

a. the nursery school premises, including any building in connection with the instruction or accommodation of the pupils attending, are suitable and adequate for the purpose, and conform to the standards defined above;
b. efficient and suitable instruction, including social training, is being provided at the nursery school, with particular reference to the number, ages, and sex of the pupils attending the school;
c. the principal or a senior member of staff is properly trained with recognized nursery school teaching qualifications or a minimum of five years teaching experience in a nursery school.

The minimum standards that have to be complied with for legal operation of early childhood centers are laid down in these two regulations. These minimum standards have been broadened to take into account the different circumstances prevailing in the urban and rural early childhood centers.

The Community-based Approach. A community-based approach is the basis for the establishment and operation of the early childhood centers throughout Zimbabwe. Besides ensuring the effective mobilization of local materials and human resources for development purposes, this approach is intended to strengthen the communities' planning and management skills. This is in conformity with the government policy of self-reliance and decentralized planning.

Table 30.1
Early Childhood Centers in Zimbabwe

Year	Rural Centers	Urban Centers	Total
1981	582	418	1,000
1985	4,000	500	4,500

Source: The Zimbabwe Report on the United Nations Decade for Women 1985.

Current Provision by the National ECEC Program

Table 30.1 shows the estimated number of rural and urban early childhood centers in 1981, and again in 1985. In 1981 only 80,000 children were benefitting from these programs. By 1985 this number had increased to about 200,000 children. This large increase in demand was a reflection of the great desire by women to participate in national economic and development activities, as well as an indication of their appreciation of the benefits of these early childhood education and care services.

The current provision of ECEC facilities and personnel only serves a small percentage of the newborn to age six group. This is due mainly to limitations in the financial, material, and human resources needed to launch a program of this nature. The goal of the Zimbabwe government is to have 50 percent of the country supplied with ECEC centers and trained personnel by the year 2000.

The Structure of the ECEC Program

The promotion of the micro-level planning and district and national level coordination and supervision has necessitated the creation of a five level management structure within the Ministry of Primary, Secondary Education and Culture. Emphasis in creating this structure has been on using existing administration and implementation structures and personnel as much as possible. Each children's center is managed by a preschool supervisor who operates in close liaison with the chair of the Parent-Teacher Association. This supervisor works under the general direction of the headmaster of the local primary school. The headmaster reports to the District Education Officer. That person is responsible to the Education Officer, ECE, who in turn works under the Deputy Regional Director of Primary Education. Regional Education staff members work directly with the Head Office of the Ministry of Primary and Secondary Education and Culture in Harare, the capital city.

The roles of the local Parent-Teacher Association are extensive and crucial to the development and maintenance of the local program. The association is selected by the community from local government officials, representatives of non-governmental organizations, parents, and the preschool teachers and workers. Responsibilities of the association include

a. mobilization of local resources, and maintenance of the center;

b. motivating parents to send their children to the center, and to be involved in center operations;

c. provision, management, and maintenance of buildings and equipment;

d. the management of financial grants from the government;

e. coordinating the provision of labor for building construction, in the form of moulding bricks and finding the builders;

f. ensuring that the premises are clean; and

g. paying the teachers' wages.

The degree of parent commitment, particularly in rural areas, is dependent on their perception of the role of early childhood education. At the time of independence the government declared that while primary education would be free and universal, early childhood education and care would continue to be a fee-paying service (although in the hands of the community or non-governmental organizations), with payment of teachers' salaries a community responsibility. This has created some problems with the parents, thus adversely affecting the operation of these programs. However, the fact that early childhood education is not free and universal at this stage of our development does not mean that the government places little importance on the program. The major constraint is financial. From a fiscal standpoint it is simply impossible to provide both programs on a free and universal basis at this stage of development.

Methods of Standardizing and Expanding Early Childhood Programs

It is important to restate that at independence there were no policy guidelines regarding this field of education, as early childhood education had been of little concern to the previous governments. Before 1980 community-based organizations, international non-governmental organizations (NGOs), and a few individuals were the prime movers of early childhood education in Zimbabwe. The absence of policy guidelines led to a lack of standardization of any aspect of early childhood education.

At independence, the following types of early childhood education centers predominated:

a. preschools, which were mainly rural child care centers offering a regular organized environment specifically oriented to the development needs of three to five year olds;

b. creches, which were day centers that provided a safe environment for newborn to three-year-old children and constituted a custodial service rather than a child development oriented experience;

c. nursery schools, which were largely urban educational institutions providing for the developmental needs of three- to five-year-old children under the skilled guidance of qualified teachers;

d. play groups, which were units of not more than 15 children with a mother supervising play activities; and

e. play centers, which were hybrids combining nursery schools and play groups. These centers were mainly community based with heavy community participation.

The new government needed to find ways of standardizing the activities of this great variety of early childhood program types, which included wide differences in physical facilities, a broad range of enrollments and teacher-child ratios, and sharp differences in staffing policies (ranging from the full-time volunteer paid no pay to the part-time volunteer with as little pay as $3.00 per month and the full-time teacher earning $300.00 per month). This situation required a rigorous, well-conceived process of establishing regulations, developing curricula, standardizing training, integrating staff policies, and building facilities.

Program Regulations

Regulations are a traditional means of ensuring minimum program standards. Perhaps the most comprehensive and detailed guidelines for ECEC programs in Zimbabwe are those that govern the operation of creches. These regulations require that within the building there be a playroom that provides three square meters of floor space per child. The resting spaces must include eight and a half cubic meters of space per child in an inside room and seven cubic meters of space on adequately ventilated verandas. The children's beds should be one meter apart. This standard does not apply to infants twelve months of age and under.

The regulations stipulate that the window should be at least 10 percent of the floor area in every room, that at least half of each window should be made to open, and that there be adequate crossventilation. There should be a stretcher or bed for each child. Each child should have a small chair and suitably low tables, and there should be adequate storage space for children's clothing. Separate sleeping accommodations are required for infants with 17 cubic meters of space per infant child.

Since the first problem of children is survival, the regulations are even more stringent on health standard requirements in the creches. The creche administrators/owners are required to provide an isolation room or sickroom for any children who fall sick. The regulations require that all sanitation facilities on the licensed premises be waterborne, including one water closet for every 15 children, small wash basins not more than half a meter above floor level supplied with hot and cold water, a bath with hot and cold water, and suitable facilities for cooking, storage and refrigeration, and serving of food. There should be an adequate and pure water supply on the premises. It is a requirement that the center have sufficient food of an approved standard of purity and wholesomeness and that detailed menus be made available for inspection.

Where a staff member or child falls ill due to any infectious disease he/she shall not be admitted into the creche until certified free from infection by a qualified medical practitioner.

There is to be an outdoor play area containing six square meters of space per child. These grounds are to be free of obstructions or other hazards likely to cause accidents, and made such that they facilitate easy supervision. The premises must be adequately and effectively enclosed, and provided with security. Measures must be taken to minimize glare and dust outdoors. Adequate and safe play equipment is also to be available.

It is obvious that these regulations were originally established for creches in urban areas. It would be impossible to meet some of the requirements in the rural parts of Zimbabwe, and so they have been adjusted to suit the special circumstances of those areas.

Curriculum

In 1986 the Government produced a *Curriculum Handbook for the National Early Childhood Education and Care Program.* The purpose of the handbook, as stated in its introduction, is

to provide guidelines about what should be taught to children in Zimbabwe from the ages 0–6 years. [The handbook] provides a useful introduction to ways of providing stimulating environments for children at this early stage of their lives. It is the Ministry's first attempt to provide and expand the standardized early childhood education and care program nationally. Its third objective is to inform parents, communities and the public of ways and importance of exposing children to early stimulating learning experiences. (p. 1)

The handbook promotes a holistic approach to early childhood education and care programs, encompassing health and physical development, intellectual growth, and social relations. This approach was captured in the preface to the handbook, written by the Minister of Community Development and Women's Affairs:

Children should be involved and participate in activities that stimulate all forms of development. It is hoped, therefore, that this handbook will encourage the creation of an early childhood education and care environment which promotes maximum development in all the six core curricular areas, i.e., physical, cognitive/intellectual, creative, social, and moral, emotional development and good health. (p. iii)

All of the early childhood centers are expected to use the material in the handbook for organizing their daily preschool curriculum activities. In this way the curriculum handbook has functioned as a valuable instrument for the provision of program quality.

The Training of Trainers

The second strategy the government adopted for standardizing early childhood education and care programs was to institute a "Training of Trainers of Preschool Teachers" program. This program was developed by the Ministry of Primary, Secondary Education and Culture to address the serious national shortage of trained teachers. The program had four objectives, all focused on better equipping the trainers of early childhood development teachers, supervisors, parents and communities with appropriate skills and knowledge. The first objective was to train teacher-trainers in the development, use, and implementation of the national curriculum for the child. A second goal was to train trainers to be more conscious of children and their special needs, through observation, recording, evaluation, and interpretation of behavior. Third, the program set out to train trainers to be conscious of and understand community needs. Finally, there was emphasis on equipping trainers with basic teaching and evaluation methods.

The trainers who go through this one-year intensive training program are in turn deployed to the various provinces to train the 18,000 child development teachers, supervisors, parents, and community members. This training is essential if we are to increase integration of the roles of the home, the ECEC center, and the community in order for the child to achieve maximum benefit. The trainers are provided with a training guide that should be used in conjunction with the *Curriculum for the Child Handbook*. The aim of the guide is to provide assistance to trainers in conducting workshops for early childhood education teachers and supervisors.

Those trained as teacher trainers are themselves qualified nursery school teachers. Two groups have so far gone through the program and been deployed in the provinces.

The Standard Early Childhood Center Facility

The third strategy for standardizing the delivery of ECEC programs was to provide grants-in-aid to motivate communities to build standard preschool centers. A standard preschool construction design was produced by a government architect to be used by all those who intend to build new early childhood centers. The grant-in-aid is for purchasing all building materials except bricks, which should be moulded by the communities. Such government assistance has achieved wonders in expanding early childhood education activities in rural areas. The grants-in-aid were meant to be a way of meeting the communities halfway in their self-reliance efforts, as well as fostering the spirit of initiative among communities.

One important reason for having a well-built early childhood center is that the facility becomes a multi-purpose community center. The early childhood education and care program has relationships with other social service systems. For instance, the Ministry of Health, through the village health worker and community related government department officials, often uses the childhood centers for such public activities as immunization, feeding schemes in times of drought, and inspection of water and sanitary conditions. In 1984, the Ministry of Health issued a sectional review and policy statement deploring imbalances in the delivery and utilization of health services in Zimbabwe. The statement enunciated a new policy aimed at equitable distribution of health care, with emphasis on community participation, decentralization of management, and the integration of curative and preventive services. The expansion of early childhood education became one of the strategies for spreading health care services to children in rural areas in particular. As a result, health services to children have increased considerably since independence.

The early childhood center has also been used to attack the problem of poverty and inequalities. Some of the existing centers, started as feeding points during the early years of independence, have continued to be used as feeding centers.

STRENGTHS, SHORTCOMINGS, AND CHALLENGES

Zimbabwe may be defined as a multi-racial and multi-cultural society. The social and cultural composition of our country has to a large extent influenced our approach to early childhood education and care. The integrated approach we have adopted in Zimbabwe is intended to ensure that these programs contribute to the mutual enhancement and maintenance of the multi-cultural values of our society. The ideal is to carry forward both the traditional and the modern cultural values of our society within programs focused on the child and the family. The family and community oriented approach that characterizes the policies and the program is an attempt to link our cultural values and beliefs with the policies and the early childhood education and care program in Zimbabwe.

Strategies for delivering the program to low-income families serve a primary objective, which is to provide all children, regardless of socio-economic background, with early childhood education and care services. Particular recognition is given in this regard to the fact that the first five years of life are crucial to one's future development and that early childhood education prepares children to develop basic skills essential for adulthood.

A real strength of this approach has been its emphasis on building government-community partnerships through the use of government grants-in-aid. Part of the success in establishing 4,000 ECEC centers in rural areas has stemmed from the responsibility assumed by local communities and individuals, who take ownership of each program. The government role, beyond the matching grant-in-aid, is coordination and regulation. All of these rural centers are still being run by parents' committees, with responsibility for the building, toilets, and safe water supply. For seven years after independence early childhood personnel provided their services as volunteers. Since January 1988 the government has allocated some incentive funds for supervisors and teachers working in rural areas.

The ECEC approach has also been well received in cities and towns, where the 2,000 existing centers cannot meet the demand for services. Some city councils (e.g., in Harare) are matching funds raised by urban districts to establish new centers, encouraging the same community development approach carried out in rural areas. Thus the greatest strength of the Zimbabwean ECEC strategy has been in demonstrating that when communities really value the contributions made by the preschool project, the policy of self-reliance is easily understood and practiced.

Shortcomings

The growth in demand for centers, and the mushrooming establishment of them, has had to be managed despite the severe economic impacts of the world recession, external debt crisis, destabilization activities by South Africa, and difficulties associated with recurrent droughts in Zimbabwe. The future of this national development effort will continue to be constrained by such factors.

Rapid expansion of the national program over a relatively short time period (12 years) has resulted in a shortage of early childhood professionals to teach in the 6,000 centers and to administer the overall effort.

Communities and individuals have often rushed to establish programs without a clear understanding of the professional needs and requirements of such child care efforts. The majority of rural ECEC centers operate without being formally registered and certified.

Future Challenges

The major challenge for the Zimbabwean government is to develop a viable, good quality ECEC system based on clear policy about what professional development is needed to ensure benefits for the children served. Specifically, this means attention must be given to the 18,000 untrained

ECEC personnel currently teaching young children. Thus the teacher trainer's program described earlier must receive high priority. The registration of ECEC centers in both rural and urban areas must be accomplished following clear guidelines and regulations in order to improve overall program quality.

Neither the government nor local communities can shoulder the financial burdens of building construction, teacher payment, and teacher training alone. Continued effort must be made to find complementary ways of accomplishing these tasks, taking advantage when possible of the assistance offered by non-governmental organizations and other international sources of assistance (e.g., UNICEF).

During the next ten years (1991 to 2000) the national government plans to consolidate the activities of the ECEC system with the goal of developing one of the best early childhood education and care systems in the world.

REFERENCES

Bull, Theodore. (1967). *Rhodesian Perspective*. London: Michael Joseph.

(1976). *The Child and His Development from Birth to Six Years Old*. Paris: UNESCO. November.

Children's Protection and Adoption Regulations. (1972). Second Schedule, Section 21, Government Printers.

(1974). *The Children's Protection and Adoption Act*. Harare: Government Printers.

Elkind, David. (1976). *Child Development and Education: A Piagetian Perspective*. New York: Oxford University Press.

Gelfand, Michael. (1979). *Growing Up in Shona Society: From Birth to Marriage*. Harare: Mambo Press.

(1982). *Government Agricultural and Economic Review*. Harare.

(1981). Government of Zimbabwe (GOZ). *Growth with Equity: An Economic Policy Statement*. Harare: Government Printers.

(1981). Government of Zimbabwe. *An Inquiry Into Preschool Activities in Zimbabwe*. Harare: Ministry of Education and Culture.

(1985). Government of Zimbabwe and UNICEF. *Children and Women in Zimbabwe: A Situation Analysis*. Harare. July.

Heron, A. (1979). *Planning Early Childhood Care and Education in Developing Countries*. Paris: UNESCO.

(1976). International Commission of Jurists. *Racial Discrimination and Repression in Southern Rhodesia*. Geneva.

(1982). Ministry of Community Development and Women's Affairs (in cooperation with UNICEF). *Report on the Situation of Women in Zimbabwe*. Harare.

(1986). Ministry of Community Development and Women's Affairs. *Curriculum Handbook for the Child*. Harare: Government Printers.

(1986). Ministry of Community Development and Women's Affairs. *ECEC Trainers' Training Syllabus*. Harare.

(1988). Ministry of Community Development and Women's Affairs. *Field Work Training Guide*. Harare.

(1987). Ministry of Community Development and Women's Affairs. *The Zimbabwe Report on the United Nations Decade for Women*. Harare.

Muchena, O. (1988). *Taking Care of the Children: Organized Childcare in the Communal Areas of Zimbabwe*. Harare: Mambo Press. January.

(1973). *Nursery Schools Regulations*. Harare: Government Printers.

(1983). Prakasha, Veda. *Our Future Is in Our Children: The Case for Early Childhood Care and Education*. Paris, UNESCO/UNICEF Digest, No. I, July.

(1987). R. G. Mugabe, Prime Minister. Speech delivered at the Official Opening Ceremony of the Commonwealth Ministers' Response for Women's Affairs Meeting. Harare International Conference Center, 3 August.

(1965). *The Nursery School Movement in Rhodesia: A Memorandum*. Salisbury: Government Printers. July.

(1912). *The Rhodesia Herald*. Harare.

(1965). *The Rhodesia Herald*. Harare.

(1977). *The Royal Bank of Canada Monthly Letter*. Volume 58, Number 10, October.

(1985). *Situation Analysis of Women and Children in Zimbabwe*. UNICEF Report. Harare.

(1984). *VOICE, The Role of the Family: Particularly the Mother in Early Childhood Care and Education in Zimbabwe*. Harare. October 15.

(1989). The World Bank Report. *Education in Sub-Sahara Africa: Zimbabwe Journal of Education Research*. Volume I, Number I, March.

31

PUBLIC CHILD CARE, CULTURE, AND SOCIETY: CROSSCUTTING THEMES

Moncrieff Cochran

This is an exciting time in which to be engaged in crossnational comparison. Here in the United States *Newsweek* magazine has proclaimed the past ten years the "decade of democracy." All signs point to continuation of political transformation during the 1990s, although perhaps not always in more democratic directions. The recent changes affecting countries represented in this handbook have been highly visible and dramatic in some cases (the united Germany, Hungary, Nicaragua, the Philippines, Poland, South Africa, the new Commonwealth of Independent States), and in other instances they are less obvious, although perhaps equally significant (Canada, China, Colombia, Vietnam, Zimbabwe, the consolidation of the European Community). In all cases the political changes have been both reflected in and to some extent stimulated by institutions charged with rearing the young: the family, and community-based child care programs.

My challenge in writing this chapter has been to find a way of presenting patterns that cut across and unify these 29 chapters without losing the dynamic quality of the change that is documented in so many of them. Any attempt to generalize involves the risk that the results will be both static and unrepresentative. Three strategies are employed in an attempt to reduce this risk. I begin by offering the reader a framework, constructed from the case study data, for use in identifying the causes of policy and program development in the public child care arena, and understanding why similar causes can produce different policies or programs. Although this framework is made up of what appear to be separate components, in fact they interact and co-mingle to produce 29 distinct combinations. Each of these combinations is both less and more than the representation presented in Figure 31.1: less because no society contains every element shown, and more be-

Figure 31.1

A Framework Linking Macro-level Causes and Mediating Influences with Policy
and Program Outcomes

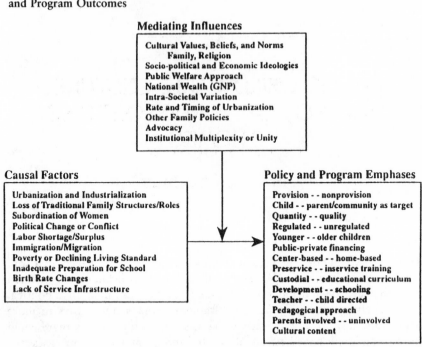

Mediating Influences

Cultural Values, Beliefs, and Norms
Family, Religion
Socio-political and Economic Ideologies
Public Welfare Approach
National Wealth (GNP)
Intra-Societal Variation
Rate and Timing of Urbanization
Other Family Policies
Advocacy
Institutional Multiplexity or Unity

Causal Factors

Urbanization and Industrialization
Loss of Traditional Family Structures/Roles
Subordination of Women
Political Change or Conflict
Labor Shortage/Surplus
Immigration/Migration
Poverty or Declining Living Standard
Inadequate Preparation for School
Birth Rate Changes
Lack of Service Infrastructure

Policy and Program Emphases

Provision - - nonprovision
Child - - parent/community as target
Quantity - - quality
Regulated - - unregulated
Younger - - older children
Public-private financing
Center-based - - home-based
Preservice - - inservice training
Custodial - - educational curriculum
Development - - schooling
Teacher - - child directed
Pedagogical approach
Parents involved - - uninvolved
Cultural content

cause each society combines elements in a manner that cannot be captured
by a single schematic representation and involves changes over time that
are also not portrayed.

AN INTERPRETIVE FRAMEWORK

The schematic representation shown in Figure 31.1 was first introduced
to the reader at the end of Chapter 1. There its purpose was to provide a
means of thinking about child care policies and programs that might serve
as an aid to understanding the rich diversity of case material that followed.
Now it is the framework itself that is the subject of scrutiny, in order that
the reader might assess its usefulness as an analytic tool.

The processes represented in the figure involve a number of demographic,
economic, cultural, and social factors in some combination that cause a
society to institute public child care policies, which in turn are manifested
in particular child care programs. Differences in both the meaning and the
form of these programs are not only the result of different causal factors
or combinations of factors, but also of different mediating influences. For

instance, a public child care system that in some societies may be a policy response to labor shortage and birthrate decline (Sweden, France), is in other cases an effort to better prepare children for school and to transmit to them the values of a politically transformed society (Kenya, Nicaragua).

But even when the factors stimulating policy and the policy objectives are similar, the program outcomes will differ if the economic, political, cultural, and social contexts surrounding those objectives are dissimilar. This means, for example, that the leadership in Venezuela, Vietnam, and the Philippines can all decide that public child care programs are an appropriate response to birthrates well above replacement and relatively high levels of poverty, and yet the resulting programs will differ markedly because their development was mediated by different political ideologies and cultural beliefs about the appropriate role of the family, the church, the larger community, and the state in the child-rearing process. These mediating influences are shown in Figure 31.1 as operating between causal factors and policy/program outcomes because they operate as filters, screening out policy and program alternatives that are incompatible with them.

The framework is intended to be comprehensive in a crossnational context. Analysis included all 29 national case studies, and I have tried to include in the framework all those causes and mediating influences that were identified in two or more cases.

Most of the chapter is devoted to elaborating the various elements listed under the component headings of the framework (factors, influences, emphases). However, before drawing attention to individual elements I want to reiterate the fact that the policies and programs of each society represented in this handbook have evolved as a result of a unique combination of these factors and influences. This uniqueness results from a "combination of combinations." That is, each society presents a combination of causal factors and mediating influences that also occur in some combination.[1] Moreover, these sets of causes and mediating influences combine in ways that are never quite the same from one society to the next, resulting in the 29 singular examples provided in this handbook.

Thus it is always inaccurate to claim that policies or programs arise from a single cause or are shaped by just one mediating source. By the same token, the framework shown in Figure 31.1 provides much more information than is needed to "explain" the policies and programs in any particular country. Use of the framework should permit the reader to identify from the array of possibilities provided there that particular set of causes and mediators that combine in a given society to result in policies and programs of the particular type found there. By presenting such a framework I am also suggesting that the number of possible causes and mediating influences is not infinite: a limited set of factors and influences is sufficient for an understanding of why the public policies and child care programs in a given country serve the functions and take the forms they do. At the same time this framework is undoubtedly incomplete, as the data from which it has been constructed are drawn from a limited sample of societies.

CAUSAL FACTORS

These factors, shown in the left most box of the framework, are presented in clusters where several causes are interrelated. I begin with those causes that occurred earlier in historical time in some or all of the handbook countries. The processes of industrialization and urbanization were major factors contributing to loss of traditional family roles and structures. Women had occupied positions clearly subordinate to men in virtually every society. Public child care has and continues to play a crucial part in efforts to redress that power differential. Where major political shifts in the direction of more egalitarian relations have taken place, child care has often been a key implementing policy. Labor supply and immigration/migration are linked because in some countries immigration is seen as a labor force alternative to supporting the efforts of mothers to participate in the labor market. Poverty and school preparation are coupled because it is typically those children living in low-income families who do not have access to those activities that prepare them for the schooling experience.

Urbanization and Industrialization

Jeanine Anderson has documented the difficulties that Peruvian families with customs developed for rural environments have adapting those practices to the different demands of urban settings. Industry requires the concentration of goods and services that produces the urban environment. Industrial work prevents parents from simultaneous supervision of their children (as also does large-scale or mechanized agriculture). In general, urbanization and industrialization reduce the child-caring capacity of the extended family and village.[2] The contemporaneous impacts of these shifts on traditional, agrarian-based families are especially well developed in the chapters on Brazil and Mexico.

Loss of Traditional Family Structures and Roles

Traditionally the non-parental resources available for child care included the child's grandparents and older siblings (especially sisters), and certain other members of the extended family. Such child care obligations may also have extended beyond kinship into the neighborhood or village. The authors of the chapters on India, Mexico, Peru, the Philippines, and Zimbabwe describe in some detail the loss to their societies of these resources largely as a result of industrialization and urbanization. In several of the case studies there is mention of attempts to retain or interest in recreating certain of these caring traditions (China, the Philippines).

The prevalence of the one-parent family (and within that family type that headed by a teenager) is reported by a number of the handbook authors to be on the increase in their countries. This structural form extends the more general shift from extended to nuclear family one step further in reduction of the child care resources available inside the family. If they are to provide economic support for their families through participation in the labor market, these solo parents must have public child care services, and those services must be subsidized in a way that makes them accessible to parents with relatively low incomes.

With the loss of traditional family structures has come diminished means for the transmission of cultural values and beliefs. Rosely Chada explains how the Zimbabwean ECEC is conceived in part to transmit cultural traditions in the manner (through stories, puzzles, proverbs, taboos, and songs) previously used by the grandparents and other elders. A somewhat analogous process is apparent in Ingerid Bø's description of culturally relevant preschool program activities in the Norwegian context. In the Zimbabwean case concern for transmission of cultural traditions provided one reason for initial program development; other societies have realized the potential for such transmission after programs had come into existence for other reasons. In still other instances (e.g., Vietnam) communal child care was part of an intentional effort to shift society away from traditional views of the family (women's subordinate roles) and toward alternative beliefs and practices.

Subordination of Women

The effort by women to gain greater power and control over their lives, both within the family and in the larger society, is a root cause of interest in public child care in all of the case studies. The extent to which it becomes visible in the various chapters depends on how subordinated women have been in the various cultures and what other causal factors are operating in a given society. In some cases women have formed social and political movements that have influenced policy (e.g., Brazil, Israel, Sweden, Italy, United States), while in others prevailing political ideology included the liberation of women from subordinate positions inside the family and in the society as a whole (Marxism, socialism, social democracy).

Political Change or Conflict

The impacts on child care policy of major shifts in the political system of a society are seen in a number of our case studies, including Russia after the Russian Revolution, Poland and Hungary with the imposition of communism after World War II, Italy also following World War II, Kenya and Zimbabwe after independence, Vietnam during and after the war of liberation, Nicaragua after Somoza, and South Africa with the imposition of apartheid. More subtle but still significant are the effects of shifts in political party control in Australia and Canada, and in Nicaragua after the loss of Sandinista control. The South African case provides a vivid illustration of how political tension and conflict can result in parallel policies and programs. In the United States political tension between the legislative and executive branches of federal government resulted in 20 years of stalemate in the development of national child care policy.

Political and economic interests are often closely intertwined. Venezuela provides a good example of the how the effects of fluctuating economic fortunes (based in this instance on the world oil market) can have political consequences that affect child care policy. The possible impacts of participation in the new European Community are noted by most of the Scandinavian authors and also by Bronwen Cohen (U.K.) and Josette Combes (France). Rudolf Pettinger (Germany) raises the question of what impacts will be felt from the merging of a nation heavily invested in public child care programs (the German Democratic Republic) with one far less committed to such policies (the Federal Republic of Germany).

Labor Shortage/Surplus

Our case studies indicate that a number of factors interact to determine whether such shortages bring more mothers of young children into the labor force: (1) cultural beliefs regarding the appropriateness of such a role shift, (2) the economic pressures experienced by families without any or with only one adult wage earner, (3) the amount of policy-making influence held by national women's groups, and (4) the relative cost to the employer of importing foreign labor. Seven of the ten European countries included in this handbook (the exceptions being the United Kingdom, Germany, and Italy) have expanded day care services at least in part because of labor shortages.

However, our case studies demonstrate that day care services can also be a policy response to high rates of unemployment. In countries as diverse as Australia, Colombia, Mexico, Peru, and the United States the establishment of day care programs is justified in part because of the jobs created by those programs.

Immigration and Migration

In addition to its effects on labor supply, immigration has major consequences related to a society's concern for social integration and acculturation. The French case is one illustration of day care as a policy response to this concern; others are found in Scandinavia and Israel.

The migration described in our case studies is most often movement from rural to urban areas in search of paid work, stimulated by the processes of industrialization and modernization. The impacts of such dislocations on traditional child care arrangements are most vividly portrayed in the chapters on Hungary, Kenya, Mexico, Peru, South Africa, Venezuela, and Zimbabwe. The Hungarian and South African cases illustrate the brutal violation of family stability that results from migration caused by the imposition of authoritarian political ideology.

Poverty or Declining Living Standard

Concern over the fact that large numbers of children live under the conditions resulting from family poverty is a current stimulus for public child care policies in societies as different as Brazil, India, the United States, Venezuela, and Vietnam. There is also an indication that a perception of decline in living standard among parents with incomes well above poverty level may stimulate increased labor market involvement, and so heighten the demand for day care services.

Inadequate Preparation for School

This is typically the result of poverty, but it may also occur with children in families with adequate incomes as a result of discrimination. This particular definition of the problem, either by the state or by parents, has led in some cases (e.g., Head Start in the United States) to heavy curricular emphasis on activities to promote cognitive development and "school readiness." Other examples are provided by Brazil, Hungary (the Gypsies), India, Israel (the children of immigrants), Kenya, and Venezuela.

Changes in Number of Births

Public child care policies are stimulated both by birthrates below replacement and rate increases or persistently high rates that result in numbers of children greater than families and communities can support successfully.[3] The stimulus of low birthrates is referenced by the authors of the chapters on Canada, Colombia, Denmark, Finland, France, Hungary, Japan, Poland, Sweden, the United Kingdom, and the Commonwealth of Independent States. High birthrates are a factor in Kenya, the Philippines, and Vietnam.[4]

Lack of Service Infrastructure

In some cases (Zimbabwe, Vietnam, China, India) national support for a public child care approach has resulted in part from the perceived need for an infrastructure for delivering other services (health care, nutritious meals) to families not currently receiving them. This need may result from the absence of a national health delivery system, as with the health component of the U.S. Head Start program, or because poverty, isolation, or lack of knowledge prevents parents from providing enough nutrition to their children.

MEDIATING INFLUENCES

The cultural and socio-political dimensions are discussed first because of my impression that they play especially powerful mediating roles in the development of public child care programs. However, this should not serve to diminish the other mediators discussed, each of which has well-documented effects on the shape of child care policies and programs. The reader is reminded to consult the index for comprehensive listings of national examples.

Cultural Values, Beliefs, and Norms

Two institutions through which these values and beliefs have traditionally been expressed are the family (via gender-based family practices and kinship relations) and religion. This data set as a whole makes a powerful statement about the ways that changing beliefs about the role of mothers and other family members continue to shape public child care policies and programs. On the one hand, there is overwhelming evidence of decline in the child-caring role of extended family members and even of siblings, caused by several of the factors discussed earlier. On the other hand, most of the handbook authors document ways that the policies of their countries reaffirm the role of the family as the institution with primary responsibility for childrearing. Even in societies where that belief was challenged by revolutionary political ideology (China, Hungary, Israel, Poland, the former U.S.S.R., Vietnam), there is evidence of shifts back toward the family. (See also family-state as value tension, below.) At the same time, traditional views of the woman's role within and outside the family continue to hamper the policy response to consumer needs for public child care services. These views are especially well described by Bronwen Cohen in Chapter 26.

The influence of religion on beliefs about the family and role divisions within the family comes through most powerfully in the chapter on Italy but is also a significant feature of the Philippine experience. The power of the church to define public child care as a charitable response to the inadequacy of families unable to support themselves in the traditional form (father employed and married to mother, mother caring for the children) has continued to be felt in Brazil and in the United States.

Socio-Political and Economic Ideologies

These ideologies, while often congruent with the dominant cultural beliefs shaping a society, are also differentiated by their more direct application in public policy. Thus, for instance, a shortage of labor (cause) leads to different policies in a socialist society (free, center-based, universally available care to native-born citizens) than in a free market, profit-oriented context (import cheap labor, centers operated as profit-making enterprises). Another example involves the use of public child care as a response to poverty, which is likely to be different in those countries where the "First Lady" is expected to take an active policy-making role (Mexico, Peru, Venezuela) than in those taking a more institutional approach (Kenya, Vietnam, Zimbabwe).

Political ideologies may operate as much to define how *not* to proceed as they do to guide policy making. It is clear that negative experiences under colonial rule taught the leaders of countries that gained their independence (India, Kenya, Vietnam, Zimbabwe) what kinds of social and educational institutions they wanted to avoid. One can expect those same kinds of reactions to discredited ideologies to influence future policy and program development in Eastern Europe, the Commonwealth of Independent States, the Baltic countries, and South Africa after apartheid. Japan provides an interesting example of the confluence of cultural values related to women's roles with a liberal view of market involvement in social welfare activities.

Public Welfare Approach

Ole Langsted and Dion Sommer in Chapter 8 distinguish the institutional welfare state, in which the state is responsible for the social needs of individuals and families, from the residual welfare state, which "is built on the assumption of the sovereignty of the market and in which the public sector plays only a minimal role." The Scandinavian societies are included in the first category, and the second contains those countries dominated by Anglo-Saxon traditions (Australia, Canada, the United Kingdom, the United States), as well as a number of the more recently industrialized countries in Asia and South America. Until recently the Eastern European models would have been described as still more dominated than Scandinavia by the public sector, as would China and Vietnam. Several countries in Africa and South America (Kenya, Zimbabwe, Colombia) are attempting to expand public sector involvement in care for children and families within the constraints of very limited national resources.

National Wealth (GNP)

The authors of the Latin American chapters do an especially good job of documenting how weaknesses in national economies affect the strategies employed for the provision of public child care. For instance, family day care models are especially attractive to policy makers in Venezuela and Colombia not only because they are congruent with cultural traditions regarding child care in home settings, but also because they are believed to be less expensive than center-based care. In some of those less wealthy countries where the center is receiving policy emphasis (Kenya, Mexico, Nicaragua, Zimbabwe) ways have been found for reducing costs to the state and municipalities by involving fathers and other men in the building of facilities and mothers and other women in the community in helping to staff the programs. Vietnam is an interesting example of a transition from a relatively expensive Soviet-style exclusively center-based model to increased development of family day care alternatives, partly to save money. The tension between cost and quality is discussed in some detail in the chapter on Brazil.

Intrasocietal Variation

This is a strong influence mediating program form and content, and my reading of the national case studies as a whole is that its significance will continue to increase as policy makers become aware of local differences and service consumers become more involved in local program development. Rural-urban variation has already been touched upon; it cuts across all our case studies. A number of the countries included in this handbook are multicultural societies (see especially Brazil, Canada, China, the Commonwealth of Independent States, France, India, Israel, Kenya, South Africa, the United Kingdom, and the United States). Some have tried harder and been more successful than others in finding approaches to public child care that can be adapted to these and other local and regional differences. Even in the relatively homogeneous Scandinavian countries, immigration of families from abroad has forced those responsible for child care systems to confront issues like second language learning and differences in belief about relationships between teachers and parents.

In her chapter on Kenya Lea Kipkorir describes the "localized curriculum" approach, developed during the past five years because of recognition "that the centralized curriculum cannot adequately serve all the cultural patterns represented in Kenya." She points out that as a result of this process, which emphasizes the initiatives of local teachers and parents, books of stories, poems, and riddles had been published in 21 different languages by 1990.

Deborah Brennan tells of the inability of the Australian child care system to adapt to the needs of the aboriginal people in that country, a story with powerful parallels in both Canada and the United States. Another source of variation in those three countries results from their relatively decentralized political systems, in which a great deal of policy-making authority is given by the national government to the states or provinces. This means that program quality varies considerably from state to state because of varied regulations regarding the training required of caregivers, group size limits, and caregiver-to-child ratios. Polly Spedding reports that staff-child ratios for U.S. infants range from one to three in the most restrictive to one to eight in the least restrictive states, except that one state has no requirement at all.

Rate and Timing of Urbanization/Industrialization

The mediating factor here is not the urbanizing and industrializing processes themselves, which have been taking place in all the case study countries, but the rate at which those processes have occurred and whether public child care approaches were introduced relatively early or much later in those processes. In countries where urbanization and industrialization took place over a relatively long period (50 years or more), there was an opportunity for an infrastructure to evolve and adjust to changing conditions. Policy planners in societies experiencing very rapid urbanization (see especially the African and Latin American countries) must cope with the deprivation of those living in the densely populated areas that came into being prior to any infrastructure development.

Other Family Policies

Other policies are directly related to child care, such as parental or maternity leave from employment immediately after the child's birth, and the Finnish home care allowance (called child care allowance in Hungary) that pays one parent (usually the mother) to stay out of the labor force and look after the child at home. Lars Gunnarsson describes how the extension of parental leave to 12 months has nearly eliminated the need for public infant care in Sweden. The absence of any mandated parental leave in the United States places a heavy burden on public child care provision, which sometimes must include service to children in the first month of life. In the Hungarian case, Mária Neményi attributes the decline in the percentage of newborn to three-year-old children attending day care centers in part to the use of the child care assistance alternative and the more recently introduced child care allowance.

Advocacy

Advocacy, especially by women's groups, has played an important facilitating role in the development of public child care systems under a wide range of cultural, ideological, and political circumstances. In Italy women organized to free themselves from a patriarchy powerfully reinforced by the Catholic church. In Brazil, also a Catholic country, mobilization began as resistance to dictatorship. Women's organizations in China and Vietnam have played an important part in pushing communist and socialist regimes to deliver on promises of the child care programs needed to free women for participation in education, employment, and government service on an equal basis with men. In Kenya women's organizations have both sponsored and run early childhood programs. Advocacy has also been very important in the United States, where it has been organized both by those concerned with the effects of poverty (e.g., The Children's Defense Fund), and those interested in improving the quality and expanding the amount of day care available to families with young children.

Institutional Multi-plexity or Unity

This refers to how fragmented or streamlined the lines of authority for various aspects of the child care system are in a given society. Many of the chapter authors describe systems in which from three to six different national ministries, departments, or agencies have authority over different aspects of child care provision, or the authorities responsible for services to newborn to three year olds are different from those directing provision to older children. This complexity reaches the height of absurdity in South Africa, where apartheid requires different systems for each of the official racial designations, and non-state services must be created to counter the effects of the state provision. The consensus of the handbook authors is that streamlining would result in less confusion and a higher quality of service provision at the local level. However, centralization and concentration of all decision-making authority at the top, regardless of how streamlined, is very likely to lead to dense bureaucracy and institutional rigidity. Mária Neményi uses historical analysis to document the results of such rigidity in the Hungarian case. Fulvia Rosemberg describes the cost to day care in São Paolo, Brazil, of extremely large and complex administrative mechanisms.

Regarding the question of what control should be exercised at the national level, and what should take place in localities or regions, there is general support in this handbook for national regulations to address issues like caregiver qualifications, staff-child ratios, and group size, which are consistent across program types and insure at least adequate levels of child development. However, there is also growing sentiment in favor of decisions about program content made at the local level, with significant input from parents, in order that programs be responsive to local beliefs, traditions, and practices.

POLICY AND PROGRAM EMPHASES

In the discussion that follows I have divided the features shown in the right-hand box of the framework in Figure 31.1 into policy-level and program-level emphases. Although admittedly crude, this differentiation is used to distinguish issues of general national intent from those dimensions that define the actual shape and content of programs operating in local communities.

Twelve of these 14 dimensions can be thought of as continua along which each country varies. In order to assign a particular country to a given point on such a continuum, one often must gloss over great variation *within* the nation; in some cases the within-country variation is as great as that between societies. In presenting examples I generalize in order to articulate what appear to be real overall crossnational differences, while at the same time recognizing underlying regional and local variations.

Policy Level

Provision–Non-provision. All of the handbook countries are found in the "provision" half of this spectrum, as provision was a condition for inclusion. Many other countries provide little or no public child care. The absence of child care policy is usually explained not by the lack of causes (as shown on the left side of the framework), but rather because of mediating cultural influences (e.g., religious beliefs, family values) that keep women in the home and child care within the family. For instance, religious beliefs continue to act powerfully in Moslem countries to maintain women in traditional roles and so mitigate against policy interest in public child care arrangements.

Although the policies of all the handbook countries support public child care provision to some extent, there is still considerable variation in the extent of that public commitment. National policies range from those in Scandinavia promising all preschool children whose parents are employed or studying a place in public child care, to the reluctant involvement of the United States government (where national policy has been aimed primarily at four year olds in low income families), and the emphasis in India and the Philippines on protecting children from labor exploitation and social neglect. Many handbook authors also point out the large discrepancy between what is promised in government policy and what is actually delivered to families.

Child–parent/community as targets. The push-pull between child and parents as policy targets is a tension of long standing. When public child care is seen primarily as a way of freeing women to go to school and enter the work force, or teaching mothers nutritional practices and birth control methods, the developmental needs of the child can become an issue of secondary concern. At the other extreme, policy emphasis on preparing children for school or integrating them into society may result in programs based on values in direct conflict with those expressed at home, especially if based on the assumption that professional teachers know better than parents what is best for their children. Both of these concerns are expressed repeatedly in the 29 national chapters. In general, policy direction is away from the extremes, toward greater concern for development in those societies that began primarily concerned with parents as "resources" and toward parent involvement and support where initial emphasis was primarily on the child. In addition, public child care has emerged in some African and Latin American countries as an entry point for community development, with particular emphasis on improvement of sanitary conditions, the health care infrastructure, and the nutritional status of children.

Quantity–Quality. The distinction here involves one of relative emphasis. In virtually every case there is a simultaneous desire both for increased service coverage and improved quality of the services already being provided, but the relative emphasis at the policy level depends largely on the stage of development the day care system is in at the time this handbook was under preparation. Societies further along in policy and program development, with a longer public child care tradition, are now focused more on quality. Societies recently entering the field (last 20 years) are still more preoccupied with coverage. In countries like Brazil, Israel, and the United States, where relatively large public child care systems have developed with relatively little emphasis on preparation of a highly trained cadre of caregivers, increasing concern is being expressed over the low quality of the care provided to many of the children in full-time, extra-familial care.

Regulated–Unregulated. Governments regulate public child care for various reasons. The most common goal identified by the handbook authors is to monitor the quality of care. This is done with stipulations involving caregiver training and qualifications, adult-child ratios, group sizes, and characteristics of the care environments. Another goal has been to control the curricular content of children's experiences. Both Yekatarina Foteyeva in the former Soviet Union and Mária Neményi in Hungary refer to the basic programs required in the "socialist kindergartens" during the 1950s, which have since been reshaped to reflect changes in political ideology. Centrally determined program content has not been limited to socialist states: in France the central government provided centralized guidelines for program functioning as recently as the early 1980s.

Regulations that serve to improve the quality of public child care also increase the cost of that care. The need to reduce costs pushes governments away from program standards that require greater expenditures in personnel or facilities. This pressure can result from the need to hold down the expenditure of public funds, or from market forces governed by parental ability to pay and the desire of private programs to make a profit. In general, those countries where a significant amount of public child care operates within the private sector of the economy (e.g., Japan, the United States, the United Kingdom, Australia, Canada, Mexico) emphasize voluntary compliance with state guidelines regarding teacher qualifications and curricular activities, while those countries in which extra-familial child care is reserved for the public sector (e.g., Scandinavia, Eastern Europe, France) apply and enforce regulations more systematically and thoroughly.

Younger–older children. All of the handbook countries provide group care and early education experiences for children over the age of three. Full-time center-based care for newborn to three-year-old children, while existing in many countries, is much less commonly found in most of them. In some cases (Germany, Japan) this has been due to the belief that mother and child should be together during the first three years of life. In other instances, where the policy emphasis has been on school preparation, the conviction has been that children are not ready for such activities until they are three years old. Other family policies have also played a significant role. For instance, 12 months of paid parental leave in Sweden has largely eliminated the need for the care of newborn to 12-month-old infants in extra-familial settings, and in Finland and Hungary parents can choose to remain at home with their children up to the age of three while receiving a home care allowance.

In general, there is a tendency to emphasize family day care homes for newborn to three year olds because they are perceived as having a more "home-like," personal, intimate atmosphere (see Finland and the United States).

Public–Private financing. At the broadest level, the extent to which public child care is financed in the public sector (through tax revenues) is defined by the economic system employed in a given country. Public revenues have been the primary source of funding in those countries where all or much of the national economy has been planned and run by the state (China, Hungary, Poland, the former Soviet Union, Vietnam). Some shift in the financing of care toward more use of parent fees is occurring in a number of those countries as the economic system shifts away from complete state control. The social democracies have made large public sector investments in their child care systems and have discouraged the use of profit as an incentive for the development of more programs, but they have expected parents to contribute on a sliding scale according to family income and in some cases (Finland, Norway) permitted private companies to develop child care facilities for their employees with some state subsidy. In countries with largely market economies the private-public mix of funds is still greater, and the direct fee burden on the parent is generally greater. The profit motive is permitted, and in at least one case (the United States of America) this has led to fully private companies that operate large networks of day care centers on a franchise basis. Polly Spedding describes in some detail the wide array of financing combinations at work in the United States.

Program Level

Center-based–Home-based care. Some countries (Colombia, Venezuela, United States, Germany) have day care systems dominated by family day care, while others (Kenya, Hungary, Sweden) emphasize center-based care. These differences are to some degree a reflection of differing political ideologies, cultural values, and national wealth. For instance, in Sweden influential policy advocates and others viewed family day care as reinforcement of traditional female roles and encouraged the use of the day care center to disassociate care from that tradition. Sweden was also able to afford the higher cost associated with a large-scale center approach. Family day care has been popular in the United States, Venezuela, Colombia, and for some families in other countries precisely because it did not break too sharply with traditional child-rearing patterns. It is also a "small business" approach, which is appealing in the context of a private-sector, market economy. Another appeal of family day care has been its lower cost to the state, although there is some indication that center-based and family day care approaches *of equal quality* do not differ greatly in overall cost. I mentioned earlier a general emphasis on homes for infant/toddler care, either via parental leave or in family day care settings.

Pre-service–In-service training strategy. The continuum here runs from the heavy emphasis on college-based, pre-service preparation for center caregivers and teachers found in Europe (especially in Scandinavia) to the almost exclusive reliance on in-service training found in southern Africa. National wealth appears to be a primary determining factor, but another major determinant involves the extent to which a nation is willing to embrace its child care system as a positive force in family support deserving high priority. The United States is an example of a wealthy country that relies heavily on in-service training for center caregivers, in part because both the status of preschool personnel and the salaries are low, and so there is little incentive for college-educated adults to enter the preschool field. The in-service approach is not necessarily undertaken on an informal basis; Kenya provides an example where a very formal, structured system of regional and local in-service training personnel has been established. In general, the training of family day care mothers is carried out with in-service methodologies, primarily because the provision of family day care is often a time-limited occupation rather than a career, so those providing care are very unlikely to prepare themselves in advance.

Custodial–educational curriculum. This continuum extends from the simple guarantee of a place for children to be and to survive while their parents are away to heavy emphasis on a highly stimulating educational environment. Again, much depends on the financial resources that a country can commit to preschool environments, but equally important is the extent to which public child care and early education are an explicit, proactive policy on the part of the national government, or a reaction to growing numbers of young children whose parents are unable to care for them while providing economic support to the family at the same time. For instance, the national strategies employed in Kenya and Zimbabwe contrast rather sharply with the more residual, survival-oriented approach found in India. A similar contrast can be found among the wealthier handbook countries between Scandinavia and the United States (except for Head Start) or the United Kingdom. There is strong sentiment among child care advocates in all the handbook countries in favor of shifting to a more educational approach, but actual movement is much more advanced in some countries than in others. To some extent the cost factor interacts with the need to expand coverage as quickly as possible, rather than stressing a more expensive educational curriculum in existing programs.

It is also important to note that there is great within-country variation along the custodial–educational continuum. Fulvia Rosemberg underscores this point in her chapter on Brazil, and it is a theme touched on by a number of the other authors.

Before moving on to the other five program dimensions characterizing the child care programs described by the handbook authors, it is important to note that countries tend to cluster at the same point on the three dimensions just discussed. That is, when center-based care is emphasized in a country, then it is likely also to take a pre-service approach to caregiver and teacher preparation, and to stress the importance of providing more than custodial care. While this pattern is not universal, it is the rule rather than the exception. New national models emerging in Africa and Latin America may result in different profiles on these three dimensions, depending on how willing those national governments are to make a serious investment in family-based care and in-service training strategies of high quality.

Development–Schooling. A different kind of resistance to an educational orientation in child care involves the schooling aspect of education. In this case the important distinction is made between the broader educational process and the more restrictive methods of teaching and learning in schools. In some countries (France, Kenya, the Philippines to some extent) there are strong pressures to emphasize schooling or preparation for school, while in others (Norway, Sweden, Zimbabwe) there is a strong commitment to stressing development and de-emphasizing schooling. In general, programs for very young children have a developmental focus (if they provide more than custodial care), and those serving three to six year olds may or may not begin to take on school-like characteristics.

Teacher–Child directed. There is a general trend on this dimension away from didactic, teacher dominated curricular approaches and toward those that allow the child to take the initiative in deciding what to investigate and how to engage with the environment. Ewa Korczak provides an especially detailed description of this shift as it has been occurring in Poland during the past five years, and Yekaterina Foteyeva refers to it in relation to Russia, suggesting that to some extent the shift may be part of a more general movement in highly centralized states away from the imposition of authority from above. But the fact that this theme is discussed by a number of the other authors indicates its more universal applicability to development in the preschool years.

Pedagogical approach. This is another way of characterizing the substance of interactions between caregiver and child. The influence of the pedagogy of play developed by Friedrich Froebel pervades the entire handbook, establishing him as far and away the most influential thinker in the preschool field. But the impact of others (e.g., Montessori, Erikson, Piaget, Freinet, Vygotski, Wallon, Bowlby, Ainsworth) is also very visible and more or less widespread. A broader range of pedagogies is influencing the national programs of more recent origin, indicating the more rapid transmission of knowledge and broader access to information that characterizes the end of the 20th century.

Parents Involved–Uninvolved. There is a global shift on this continuum in the direction of greater parent involvement. This shift is taking place for a number of different reasons. In countries with long histories of public child care and very centralized social welfare systems, the shift seems to signal a reaffirmation of parental rights and responsibilities and a desire to forge closer ties between the family and community. This change is part of the more general movement away from state control in Eastern Europe, and in Scandinavia it reflects a desire to improve the "fit" between life routines and practices in the center and those in the family.

Where public child care and early education are part of broader post-independence community development strategies aimed at nation building (Nicaragua, Kenya, Zimbabwe, Vietnam), parent involvement has a number of complementary goals: developing trust, meeting parental expectations, respecting local teaching and child-rearing traditions, and recruiting assistance in building and staffing child care centers. A similar approach could emerge in South Africa after the shift to majority control. Community development is also a goal in many of the other Latin American countries (Mexico, Colombia, Venezuela), partly as an employment opportunity for low-income parents and partly as one entry point in the process of empowering women to take more control of their lives. This empowerment approach receives special attention in Chapter 18 on Mexico. It is echoed in somewhat different form in Nicaragua, and may have something in common with Fulvia Rosemberg's description of neighborhood-level feminism in Brazil.

Parent education is a significant component of initiatives aimed at parents in China, India, the Philippines, and Vietnam. Although part of the educational goal involves child-rearing practices, it may also include heavy emphasis on family planning, preventive health care, and literacy.

Parent involvement may also be initiated by parents themselves, in reactions to dissatisfaction with the child care options available to them. Rudolf Pettinger describes parent initiatives undertaken for this reason in

Germany, and this is one element in the parent cooperative movements in France and Sweden.

Parent involvement in the United States contains elements of all the strategies and goals identified earlier. It is an explicit community development strategy in the national Head Start program, part of the governance mechanism in many not-for-profit programs, a source of labor for renovating space in buildings designed for other purposes, a means of reaching parents for parent education on a wide range of topics, and a vehicle for parent empowerment. At a deeper level the interest in parent involvement in the United States reflects the parental need to monitor the programs their children attend, partly because the diversity of values and norms in the United States results in a situation in which parents cannot assume that the values and expectations of the child care program are consonant with their own.

Cultural content. This final element is defined broadly to include social and emotional as well as intellectual subject matter. Examples of such culture-specific content described by the chapter authors range from the emphasis on cooperation in Sweden to aesthetic education in Poland, folklore in Kenya, and intellectual competence in Israel. Although authors were not asked to identify the ways that public child care programs reflect and reinforce themes unique to their particular cultures, the examples provided spontaneously suggest that this is a fruitful line of inquiry to pursue. Ingerid Bø provides an interesting analysis of "cultures" in the Norwegian context, distinguishing among children's cultures, local culture, and the cultural symbols and messages of the society as a whole.

I have referred to 12 of these policy and program dimensions as continua along which each of the 29 handbook countries can be distributed. By locating a country at a particular point on each of these 12 dimensions, and then connecting the points, it is possible to create a national profile. Such a profile offers a kind of "bird's eye view" of the more or less integrated system of child care policies and programs operating in a given country. Take Norway as an example. Provision is extensive, although demand exceeds supply. Policy focus is on development in a child-parent context, and policy targets are both the parent and the child. Although the pressure to serve more children has strained the capacity and willingness to invest in the resources that bring high quality (trained staff, low staff-child ratios, etc.), Norway gives much attention to qualitative issues when measured on the international scale. Regulations are clearly defined at the national level and systematically applied to local programs. Financing is a public-private mix, including government subsidies to private firms for establishing day programs limited to their own employees. The Norwegian system is closer to the center than the family-based end of that continuum, although it includes a substantial amount of family day care. The pedagogical approach is child centered, stressing development rather than schooling, and subject matter include uniquely Norwegian concerns for outdoor life and local culture. Caregiver training is highly organized and carried out primarily prior to becoming a service provider. Parents are encouraged to become involved in local programs, but such involvement is irregular and programs are designed to function without much parent participation.

The use of the dimensions for profile construction not only provides a systematic, internationally grounded means of characterizing the essence of policy and program in a given country, it also offers a structure for making crossnational policy and program comparisons. Such a method can be used to identify similarities and differences from one country to another, and commonalities within a particular continent (Africa, Asia) or region (Latin America, Scandinavia).

CROSSCUTTING VALUE TENSIONS

In some sense child care defines both the heart and the soul of a society, nurturing the next generation and transmitting the customs that constitute the core of the culture. By examining societies through their child-caring policies and practices we are observing a primary source of energy for their future functioning. Another way to understand the cultural imperatives that fuel policy development and program change is to examine how a particular society resolves value tensions that are to some degree universal, that is, that transcend particular cultures. As I have looked at these policies and practices across 29 countries, comparing them with each other, a number of such culturally grounded, value-based tensions have emerged.[5] Five of these tensions have been selected for brief elaboration because they received the most frequent attention (explicit or implicit) in the previous chapters and because they illustrate tensions at different levels in the integrative framework offered earlier: the levels of societal need, institutional structure, and program emphasis.[6]

The Importance of the Family Versus the State

This is really a tension between cultural ideology (family traditions) and political ideology. Located as they are at the intersection of family privacy and public affairs, child care policies and programs must respond to and reflect the society's current resolution of this ongoing tension. The 29 countries represented in this handbook have all found a balance that provides the state and the community with a role in child care; in that sense they stand apart from that smaller number of countries in which child care is provided exclusively within the family. But while none of the handbook nations is completely at the "family" end of the "family-state" responsibility continuum, they are still broadly distributed along that line. The United Kingdom occupies a policy position that illustrates a strong "family responsibility" emphasis. Bronwen Cohen states the government policy "that it is for parents who go out to work to decide best how to care for their children. If they want or need help in this task they should make the appropriate arrangements and meet the costs." Rudolf Pettinger describes an analogous belief in the German case, although restricted to younger children: "It is the commonly held view that during its first three years of life, a child's development is best furthered if its family provides an understanding and stimulating environment. It is hard to see how children of this age can experience more stimulation outside such a family." In the United States, another society heavily favoring family over state, the privacy of family life has been used by those owning centers in the private (profit-oriented) sector of the child care economy as one way to justify blocking the establishment of public laws (day care regulations) that would result in lower profit margins, implying that somehow collective care of children does not compete with a family orientation as long as profit is involved.

Beliefs much closer to the "state" end of this continuum are documented by Yekaterina Foteyeva for early post-revolutionary Russia: "This emphasis [on center-based rearing] emanated directly from the goals related to the socialization of a new generation: the need to rear members of a new socialist society, collectivist by nature, who would put public interests over personal ones, and would see the aim of life as working for the sake of the state."

The Danish case by Langsted and Sommer illustrates a position somewhat midway between the two extremes described above, a location occupied by the majority of these 29 societies: "Public day care institutions have the task, in cooperation with the parents, of creating a milieu for the children that can supplement the upbringing in the home. The aim should be that particular children develop as open and independent human beings with the willingness to cooperate, and try to employ their knowledge to improve their own and other people's living conditions." Here an attempt is made to resolve the tension by balancing private with public, independence with cooperation, and self with others. Another middle ground can justify state involvement on behalf of the family. Ewa Korczak documents the clear recognition of the family as the basic social unit in the constitution of the Polish Peoples Republic, in marked contrast with the Russian case, with that belief serving to justify state involvement in order to provide the family with legal protection and the child with specific rights.

It is critical to appreciate the dynamic nature of this tension, which can be seen in the policy shifts that many of the case study authors describe in their historical overviews. The Russian and Polish cases just referred to are cases in point. Foteyeva shows how the legitimacy of the family role in child rearing has reasserted itself over time in Russia. She describes a return to family values, and stresses that this is not a return to the closed family world of a generation ago, but a wish to give more emphasis to the family in combining professional and parental roles. In Poland one senses that socialist ideals were never fully accepted at the family level. Therefore the shift over time has been from greater to less discontinuity between the expectations of the political system and perceptions of the people regarding where responsibility for child rearing should lie, and what attitudes the preschool experience should foster in children. The general patterns of change seen in these 29 countries are toward a mid-range resolution of the family-state tension, with a "modernized" family reasserting itself in societies with a collective tradition (Eastern Europe, Vietnam, China) and a growing recognition in traditionally individualist societies (United States, United Kingdom, Australia, Canada) that the modern family can perform its child-rearing functions successfully only with the state in an actively supporting role. In some of the Latin American countries, where the development of public child care systems is relatively recent, the establishment of a Family Ministry (Venezuela) or National Institute of Family Welfare (Colombia, Peru) can be seen as reflecting the effort to find this middle ground; protection of the family is defined as a right of all citizens and therefore a duty of the state.

Centralized Versus Decentralized Authority

Here the question is the extent to which decisions about program standards and content are made at the national level or are either developed or adapted by region or local municipality. The tension is created by a recognized need, on the one hand, to have uniform standards of quality that protect children and support healthy development, and on the other hand to encourage the kinds of local involvement in program development and maintenance that activate parent and local staff involvement and result in program variations that respect cultural, ethnic, and family structural differences. Highly centralized systems benefit from unity of purpose and provide parents with the assurance that the services provided by different centers or family day care homes are equivalent. But a number of the handbook authors are very critical of highly centralized systems, especially when those systems represent dogmatic political philosophies. Neményi describes how an overly centralized system in Hungary has had difficulty responding to changing socio-economic pressures. Foteyeva describes the objectives of the standardized Soviet day care plan as "noble" but says that "in practice this program turned into a dogmatic interference with the initiative of the teacher." Part of the problem with extreme centralization is simply the magnitude of the resulting bureaucracy: Fulvia Rosemberg refers to the sheer cost in Brazil of maintaining what she describes as "perhaps the most complex administrative bureaucracy and staff in the world."

Where centralization has been relatively effective there have been clear lines of authority and a lack of competition among departments or ministries for control over goals and implementing strategies. A number of the authors portray the lack of direction that results from bureaucratic competition (e.g., China, Colombia, Peru, the Philippines, the United Kingdom, Israel). Zimbabwe provides a case in which the fragmented, contradictory approach of previous central authority (the colonial regime) provided the impetus for development of a much more community-based system, when change was made possible by independence in 1980.

The reader should not conclude from the strong critiques of rigidly centralized approaches that complete decentralization leads to optimal results. In the United States of America, the country in the handbook with the strongest ideological aversion to centralized authority, there is no consistent, nationally regulated definition of high quality child care. Polly Spedding points out that U.S. researchers have shown repeatedly that well-trained workers, developmentally appropriate activities, high ratios of adults to children, and small group sizes are crucial to quality care, but that because there are no federal guidelines "there is considerable variation in regulations from state to state and the regulation of family day care is far less rigorous than that of day care centers." Deborah Brennan indicates that in Australia, where there also is no national regulatory authority, "factors widely deemed to be crucial to determining the quality of services . . . all vary widely between States." Alan Pence provides excellent documentation of similar variations among the ten Canadian provinces.

The general trend, taking the handbook chapters as a whole, is in the direction of decentralization. It is important to note, however, that in most cases this movement is built on a well-developed existing infrastructure. France provides a good example of a country with highly centralized traditions in which the movement is to regionalization in an effort to better meet local needs. Josette Combes is concerned with the difficulties the French system has had adapting to the needs of families from minority groups, but at the same time she indicates that with regionalization has come great disparity "between regions and between municipalities within regions, in the coverage of child care needs, depending upon whether such needs are considered high priority." Ingerid Bø notes a similar concern in Norway, describing how the Norwegian national government has recently given final authority over space and teacher certification requirements for local programs to local authorities, in order to permit greater program flexibility and variety. But this local authority can lead to disparities from one municipality to the next. Bø documents the fear, "particularly among the pre-school teachers, that as the day care system moves toward full coverage, decisions about staffing and space will be driven more by economic considerations (keeping costs down) than by quality standards." Merja-Maaria Turunen expresses a similar concern in the Finnish instance, but there the less expensive alternative is an alternative family policy, the child home care allowance (see also Hungary). Turunen emphasizes that "this is one reason why it is so important that the day care laws require the municipalities to provide day care services."

Sukhdeep Gill recommends that in India service integration and comprehensive delivery be accomplished (funding, training, supervision, monitoring) through what she calls "intermediate level organizations," which are "voluntary agencies, district and municipal authorities, charitable trusts, and public sector undertakings." In this model authority for the actual running of programs rests with local organizations, and the national role is to provide an umbrella for overall policy development and coordination. Annabel Torres describes how zonal teams were formed by the Sandinista government in Nicaragua, each responsible for several neighborhoods, to "investigate and evaluate the needs and problems of their respective zones, and then plan, supervise, and evaluate projects designed to respond to local circumstances."

Child Development Versus Preparation for Schooling

The tension that involves these two potentially opposing purposes is actually still more faceted, including pressures for parent education and child survival (nutrition, health) dimensions in some countries. But the most embracing dialectic is between a holistic view of child care as involving the balanced development of all the child's capacities and the desire to prepare children for the cognitive and social challenges of the primary school.

Lea Kipkorir reports that Kenyan parents expect preschools to emphasize cognitive preparation because they see success in schooling as a channel of access to better occupations and higher life styles. In Vietnam child care is placed under the Ministry of Education, and special attention is attached to five year olds, in order to prepare them well for primary education. Combes points out that in France the increasing tendency to enroll two year olds in preschool settings has been stimulated by data indicating that the earlier the child enters group care, the better the chance of success at school. She reports that some French experts are concerned at the "increasingly marked tendency to introduce types of learning [to very young children] until now reserved for children at primary school." Wei Zhengao indicates that the development of pre-primary classes and programs in China was spurred in 1986 by the passage of a law mandating nine years of compulsory education.

At the same time, the dominant view in a number of the countries represented in the handbook emphasizes development of the whole child and explicitly rejects the idea of child care as preparation for school. In Russia progressive pre-revolutionary thinkers defined child rearing as a continuous process extending through the early years, and considerable weight has been given to Froebel's concept of play as the basis for the development of the child. While more emphasis on preparation for school infiltrated the kindergarten (for four to six year olds) with the introduction of compulsory primary education in the early 1930s, Foteyeva describes the underlying aim of the newest pedagogy as "humanization of the rearing process through orientation to a child's personality. Thus the main objective becomes to assist in the process of molding a child as an individual person." Froebel was also influential in Norway (as in Sweden, Finland, and in a number of other countries; see index), where the present day care programs are a blend of the "care" and "kindergarten" traditions that existed separately before World War II. Bø underscores the discomfort with the idea of schooling very young children, stressing that "when the Norwegian parliament in 1975 chose 'barnehage' [literally 'child garden'] as the official term to be used for all day care institutions, this can be said to be the official stance to protect this particular blend, which the majority felt would be endangered by the notion of school for young children." At the same time, she distinguishes between schooling and education, stressing that the Norwegian barnehage is an explicitly educational setting.

The emphasis in Zimbabwe as described by Chada is also on a holistic view of child development, "based on the belief that the needs of the young child are interdependent, and that therefore any measures for his/her advancement must be . . . implemented within the framework of an integrative structure . . . and take into account . . . the child's [entire] immediate environment."

In those countries where national child care policy is a relatively recent phenomenon, various models are emerging that blend developmentally appropriate caring with cognitive stimulation. The Philippines provides an illustration of child care services that began with a focus on socialization experiences and then built on nutrition with malnutrition caused by poverty of the 1970s. Luz Palattao-Corpus reports that this system is evolving in the direction of early education/stimulation and that there is a recent push to make preschool education a regular part of the educational ladder, in order to provide readiness for first grade. Another integrative model can be seen in the South African educare concept, an innovation that "bridges the gap . . . between custodial day care and educational nursery schools by integrating full-time care with a high quality education program." Peru provides an example of a society still undecided about how to reconcile the caring-schooling tension; Jeanine Anderson describes the view of day care as a strategy for moving primary school downward in age as just one of five contradictory perspectives on public child care.

Day care and more schooling-oriented nursery schools have developed on separate tracks in some of the handbook countries. These tracks have usually served different kinds of families. Rosemberg captures this difference clearly through the Brazilian lens: "day care services tend to be under the administration of welfare agencies, to offer a more custodial program, to accept younger children, and to operate full time. Preschools are more likely to be administered by the educational system, to function with more qualified personnel (professional teachers), to operate part time, and to serve children from more well-to-do families." Similar class-segregated patterns can be seen in the cases of the United Kingdom and the United States of America.

Somewhat related to the schooling versus development dialectic is the question of who should decide what activities the child is engaged in—the caregiver/teacher or the child. Several of the authors describe curricular reforms that involve a shift toward the child in this regard, and a number of others document pedagogical approaches that are already very child directed (often influenced by Froebel). Korczak reports on such a shift in Poland, saying "The children are not to be only the receivers of the outside world; they must participate in creating knowledge and think out for themselves 'methods' of gaining and constructing it.... The child himself organizes the surrounding environs for his own activity, and may be the initiator of various tasks and problem situations." She sees the introduction of systematic teaching into kindergartens as potentially interrupting this trend.[7]

Parent Versus Professional Control over Program Goals and Content

In her chapter on France, Combes provides a succinct summary of the parallel developments that have led to current reassessments of the professional-parent relationship in many of the handbook countries:

So the past half century has brought an increasingly scientific and professional approach to child care at the same time that communal care has shifted from a narrow focus on poor families to a much broader involvement with the majority of French families.... The significant point is that conceptions of the function and role of professionals with children are changing rapidly, both in terms of the needs and expectations of parents, and the organization of society.

In the past the professionalization of caregivers was often built on the idea that they would rescue children from the dangers of inadequate parents. As child care services have become available to the mainstream majority, rather than as charity to the poor, parents have begun to expect respect and collaborative support rather than "professional" distance from teachers and caregivers whose training may not have prepared them for such relationships. The French case illustrates one extreme: a history of great social and psychological distance between caregiver/educator and parents, which has led to tension as parents have become more assertive about their right to participate in day care affairs, and has stimulated a new and increasingly popular program model—the parental day care center. Abraham Sagi suggests that most day care in Israel reflects an analogous pattern: caregivers with established attitudes about what is good for children and parents who assume that the "system" is doing what is proper. "Many parents enroll their infants in day care centers without even visiting these settings prior to enrollment," he states. "Based on caregivers' reports, mothers often enquire whether their infants have eaten, or slept well, but very seldom raise questions concerning their infants' emotional adaptation and reaction to the center."

At the other extreme is a model, much more recent in origin, in which parents are the architects of local community-based child care programs, and paid caregivers—often local parents with apprenticeship and on-the-job caregiver training—work along side parents and other community volunteers. Kenya, Mexico, Nicaragua, and Zimbabwe provide center-oriented examples with this orientation, and home-based examples are described in the chapters on Colombia and Venezuela. These cases have in common as much emphasis on the activation of parents and the local community as on child development and preschool education. In her chapter on Kenya, Kipkorir captures very effectively the paradigmatic shift in thinking required in order to prepare professionals to perform in the consulting and facilitating roles with parents that this community development approach requires.

As coverage expands and caregiver training becomes more comprehensive in those countries with recently developed child care systems, there will undoubtedly be shifts in the balance of power between lay and professional participants. In some cases this shift is likely to be in the direction of the "experts." Where countries have a longer history of professional child care provision, the general shift appears to be in the other direction—toward greater concern about parent involvement and parental choice. In the Finnish chapter Turunen and Huttunen emphasize that "parents are in the best position to know their own children and family situations, so their views must be taken into consideration in the planning and developing of day care activities." They stress that in order to keep the child from facing contradictory messages, it is important that the day care staff and parents be aware of each other's educational aims. This issue of differing responses to the child at home and in day care is referred to as "dual socialization" by Langsted and Sommer, and conceptualized and elaborated in some detail by them in the chapter on Denmark. They report that a parent council is a part of most Danish centers, which works with center staff to make decisions on pedagogical matters, as well as on economic and practical issues. Parent councils are also attached to each Norwegian center and represented on the board governing the internal structure and functioning of the center. But Bø notes that in spite of these councils and a number of more informal opportunities for cooperation, "by and large there is a rather superficial cooperation between staff and parents." In Sweden the past decade has brought noticeably greater emphasis on parent involvement, which has been translated in typically Swedish fashion into structured opportunities for parents ranging from an adjustment period in the center with the child to individual conferences, group meetings, field trips, and "work days." Most in-depth involvement comes from participation in a parent cooperative center, which usually includes two weeks of work a year at the center. Gunnarsson, like Bø, points out that most parents have limited time and energy, which in turn limit the extent to which they can participate in day care related activities. Foteyeva even reports movement in the former Soviet Union away from the standardized "state" center and toward a variety of alternative arrangements better suited to parents with differing needs and wishes.

Child care advocates in the United States have tended to be more concerned with parent involvement than have their counterparts in many other Western, industrialized countries. Several features of the U.S. context intersect to stimulate and reinforce this concern. One is the absence of national quality standards, which places the responsibility for determining quality largely on the shoulders of parents. Another factor is the great ethnic, cultural, and racial diversity of the U.S. population, increasing the likelihood that children will be looked after by caregivers operating with attitudes and expectations for behavior different from those of their parents and other family members. A third factor involves an explicit policy goal: to provide parents with opportunities for involvement in program activities that will help them develop family- and work-related skills that will be useful in their own development. The potential in this policy is captured nicely by the authors of the chapter on Mexico, in their discussion of social sector day care:

> To the extent that social sector day care is primarily run by women, employs women, and allows women time for schooling, income generation and meaningful association with other working women, then community-based day care could be a powerful took for development. The concept of "empowerment," which seems to be associated with the positive effects of female education on fertility control, child survival, and household decision-making, may explain the similar benefits of community-based day care on women in the community, both for those mother/educators who provide and those mother/consumers who utilize its services. Unlike many "income generation" or "women in development" projects that may put women in competition with men for scarce jobs, or place women in conflict with cultural or family norms, child care projects tend to be compatible with women's roles and can be a more rapid, less divisive way to increase women's income, work experience, and status in the community, while providing role models and role changes that lead to the broader empowerment of women. However, one pitfall has been that child care as a profession is generally underappreciated and underpaid, and care should be taken that women who participate in day care as an income generation project are not further marginalized economically.

The juxtaposition of this quote with the discussion of day care in the United States illustrates nicely a new insight provided this author by analysis of these 29 case studies—that the factors driving day care provision in the United States, and the programs developed in response to those forces, have as much in common with Latin American and southern African contexts as they do with those of Western Europe.

Patterns of Change

It is easy to leave the impression that the public child care programs in a given society are a static resolution of these value tensions, when in fact historical analysis shows shifts over time in the ways that these pressures are addressed. Analysis of these historical changes across societies reveals what appear to be patterns that again transcend individual countries. This synthesis has emerged from one person's analysis of this case study material—an analyst with a different background and other biases might draw alternative conclusions.

The most powerful crosscutting trend in these chapters involves a shift in the direction of greater equality for women, both inside the family and in broader community affairs. At the same time, there is evidence of renewed appreciation for the capacities of families and family-like settings to rear healthy children. This is not a contradiction, for these are not the traditional, patriarchal families of the past. They have been reconfigured by modernization and changing gender roles into forms that are at the same time both more and less adaptable than before, and increasingly they are complemented (rather than supplanted) by a variety of stress-reducing community supports. A related shift is from unquestioned reliance on the professional as expert toward greater appreciation for parental perspectives and parent involvement in program activities. Another change involves an altered perspective of the child as learner—from passive recipient of didactic instruction to active organizer of learning experience.

There is also a trend, long established in some societies and just emerging in others, away from a narrow focus on school preparation and toward development of the whole child. This "whole child" orientation provides more room for family and parents than did a more exclusive schooling emphasis. Another change is away from centrally controlled standardization of program form and content and toward more local control. This shift can also be seen as giving families more choices and adapting better to the needs of different regions and groups (rural-urban, cultures, ethnic groups, religious groups). This shift toward local adaptations is not a return to narrower, more categorical definitions of need (the poor, single parents, minority groups): it appears to be occurring within the context of the growing recognition that public child care has universal appeal and value.

The reader should not conclude from this summary of convergent patterns that these changes are occurring in a linear and conflict-free fashion. Reflected in these national chapters are a number of ongoing tensions—dialectics, if you will—between opposing values and modes of operation. Each society resolves these tensions differently, and those resolutions—as manifested in existing policies and programs—are themselves in a constant state of flux. The utility in understanding these value tensions lies in the insight they provide into the forces, both convergent and divergent, that are propelling a given society into the future.

I close this chapter—and the handbook—by returning to a policy tension that was identified as an ongoing struggle, in one form or another, by every chapter author: the tension between quantity and quality. In its simplest form this conflict is between investing limited resources in expanding coverage to serve more families and children, or in improving the quality of existing services by reducing the ratio of adults to children and upgrading the training of caregivers. A number of authors emphasized that when service shortages are combined with great need, it is very difficult to argue for investment in improved quality ahead of expanded service. Others stressed the harm done in the longer term—to the public perception of day care, perhaps to the children themselves—by providing a level of service that is recognized in the larger society to be substandard. But the most powerful consensus of the authors emerged from recognition that because public child care is perceived in every society as a women's issue, child care programs have been allocated relatively few resources in most of those nations. That recognition cast a different light on the tension between quantity and quality, uniting contributors in the conviction that in a larger sense the conflict involves a false choice. We concluded that the advocates of public child care in any society should devote their energies not to choosing between quantity and quality, but to increasing the investment of public resources to the point where all those families that need them have access to child care programs that provide parents with role alternatives while at the same time enhancing the growth and development of their children.

NOTES

1. While there are always multiple causes, our case study materials show that they often occur at different points in the history of policy development, and the relative influence of each fluctuates over time. This means that there is some prior causality in these sequences (e.g., labor shortage may lead to immigration, urbanization to loss of traditional child care resources, poverty to inadequate school preparation).

2. For especially effective descriptions of how the demands of urban environments and industrial employment have disrupted child care provision by the extended family, friends, and neighbors, see the chapters by Nsamenang and Serpell in Lamb et al., 1992.

3. An excellent source of birthrate and other child, family, and community data

related to early child development is the *Statistical Chart on Children: Early Child Development and Learning Achievement, 1990*, which contains information for more than 150 countries. Copies can be obtained from Mary Chamie, U.N. Development Program, 2 U.N. Plaza, Rm. 1586, New York, NY 10017.

4. Drops in infant mortality also contribute to increases in the number of young children needing care in a given society. Venezuela provides an example of a country in which reduction in the infant mortality rate has contributed to population growth that has continued despite several decades of birthrate decline.

5. Lamb and Sternberg (1992) have identified what they call "dimensions of cross-cultural variation," which are somewhat analogous to the value-based tensions I have discerned in our case studies. The first of their four dimensions, *equality between men and women*, I have referred to in the same way. Their second dimension, *public responsibility—private or individual concern*, has much in common with the value tension I label state-family, although our ICCPP data indicate shifts away from this simple dichotomy, including increasing emphasis on family-based expressions of public responsibility. *Social welfare versus educational programs*, their third dimension, applies to only a portion of our case studies. Somewhat related but more generalizable tensions in our sample are between custodial and educational care, between a focus on development of the whole child and on school readiness, and between categorical and universal provision. Their fourth dimension, involving basic conceptions of childhood and developmental practice, does not appear to distinguish clearly among our 29 societies. However, a number of the authors contributing to this handbook indicate that the belief in what Lamb and Sternberg call "the crucial importance of the early weeks, months, and years of life" (p.9) has been manifested only comparatively recently in their societies.

6. Other tensions found in our data include those between (1) urban and rural values, (2) universal and categorical assistance, (3) traditional and "modern" family forms, (4) women and men as caregivers, (5) children and parents as program targets, (6) religious and non-religious values, (7) profit-oriented and nonprofit-oriented values, (8) center- and family-based care, (9) teacher- and child-centered learning, (10) rigid and flexible regulatory beliefs, and (11) pre- and in-service training of caregivers.

7. One wonders whether this shift away from authoritarian teaching practice, in Poland and in other countries, reflects a more general shift away from highly authoritarian political structures.

REFERENCES

Cochran, M. (1982). "Profits and policy: Child care in America." In Ray C. Rist (Ed.), *Policy Studies Annals*, Vol. 6, pp. 537–549.

Cochran, M. (1988). "Parental empowerment in family matters: Lessons learned from a research program." In D. Powell (Ed.), *Parent Education and Support Programs: Consequences for Children and Families*. New York: Ablex Publishing Corporation.

Cochran, M. (1991). "Child care and the empowerment process." *Empowerment and Family Support*, 2, 1, pp. 1–3.

Cochran, M. (1992). "A theoretical framework for parent empowerment." *Family Science Review*, Special Issue to be published in 1993.

Cochran, M., Larner, M., Riley, D., Gunnarsson, L. and Henderson, C., Jr. (1990). *Extending Families: The Social Networks of Parents and Their Children.* Cambridge, Eng./New York: Cambridge University Press.

Cochran, M. and Robinson, J. (1983). "Day care, family circumstances, and sex differences in children." In S. Kilmer (Ed.), *Advances in Early Education and Child Care.* Vol. 3, pp. 47–67. Greenwich, Conn.: J.A.I.

Haskins, R. and Adams, D. (Eds.). (1983). *Parent Education and Public Policy.* Norwood, N.J.: Ablex Publishing Corporation.

Kamerman, S. and Kahn, A. (1981). *Child Care, Family Benefits, and Working Parents.* New York: Columbia University Press.

Lamb, M., Sternberg, K., Hwang, C. P. and Broberg, A. (Eds.). (1992). *Child Care in Context: Cross-Cultural Perspectives.* Hillsdale, N.J.: Lawrence Erlbaum.

Olmstead, P. and Weikart, D. (1989). *How Nations Serve Young Children: Profiles of Child Care and Education in Fourteen Countries.* Ypsilanti, Mich.: High/Scope Press.

Appendix 1

MATERNAL AND PARENTAL
LEAVE POLICIES

Australia	52 weeks of unpaid leave, available to either mother or father, with former position guaranteed. In addition, the right to work part time until the child is aged two, with pro-rated reduction in salary. Women are also entitled to unpaid maternity leave commencing six weeks prior to expected confinement.
Brazil	120 days of paid maternity leave for all registered working women, with job protection for five months after birth. Paternity leave for five days.
Canada	Typical provision is maternity leave without pay for 17 weeks, with reinstatement to same or comparable position. Some provinces slightly more generous. Child care leave of up to 24 weeks is also provided by the Labour Code, available to either parent. There is also unemployment insurance for 15 weeks in period surrounding birth, for 10 weeks as a parental benefit, and for 15 weeks of sickness. A maximum of 30 weeks can be taken as a combination of these benefits.
China	90 days, including 15 days before childbirth. 15 additional days in case of difficult childbirth, and an additional 15 days for each additional child in the case of multiple births.
Colombia	90 days of maternity leave.
Commonwealth of Independent States	Maternity leave 70 days before and 56 days after childbirth, with additional two weeks for complicated birth. Partially paid leave for either parent until child is 18 months old. Unpaid leave for additional 18 months, with job protection.
Denmark	Paid leave for 4 weeks before and 24 weeks after childbirth, with 10 of the 24 weeks available to the father. In addition, the father can take "paternal leave" for two weeks following the birth, while the mother is recovering. Compensation ranges from 50% to 100% of salary. Job protected "in principle," although many exceptions occur.

Finland	275 work days of employment leave, with full salary for the first 105 work days (maternity leave) and normally 80% of salary for remaining 170 work days (parental leave, with father eligible for 6.5 months). Fathers also get 6-12 days additional paid leave at time of child's birth. Child care leave is then available until the child reaches age 3, and shorter work days until the child enters primary school, supported by partial home care allowance.
France	Paid maternity leave (90% of salary) for 6 weeks prior to and 10 weeks after the birth, with 2 weeks additional for multiple birth and 8 weeks additional if third or more child. Unpaid parental leave with job protection for an additional 33 months.
Germany	Partially paid, job protected parental leave for 36 months; fixed payment for first 6 months; level based on family income thereafter until the child is two years old.
Hungary	Job-protected maternity leave with full salary for 5 months. Job-protected parental leave at 75% of salary until child is 18 months old. Fixed amount of child care assistance to parent at home until child is 3 years old.
India	Maternity leave in organized employment sector (10% of working women) admissible for 180 days with full pay and job protection. Implementation varies from state to state.
Israel	84 days paid leave for mothers employed at least six continuous months before delivery. Job protected during pregnancy and leave.
Italy	Job-protected maternity leave for 12 weeks at 70% earnings, plus additional 6 months at 30% earnings. Can include pregnancy period.
Japan	Up to 12 months of parental leave. Employer establishes compensation of worker during leave period, and job placement and wages after return. Companies employing less than 30 people exempt from law.
Kenya	Maternity leave for 60 days with pay, but with forfeiture of vacation for that year. Only available to that small proportion of employed women working in the formal sector.

Mexico

Female workers in the formal employment sector entitled to 90 days of maternity leave, 45 days prior to and 45 days after the birth, with full pay. Government workers may take additional 6 month unpaid leave without loss of position or seniority. Most women work in jobs outside the formal sector, and so have no benefit.

Nicaragua

Not known.

Norway

Job-protected parental leave for 150 work days with full pay or 190 work days with 80% pay. A maximum of 60 days may be taken before delivery. A minimum of 30 days is to be taken by the mother. Additional 10-15 days leave for each child beyond one (twins, etc.).

Peru

90 days of paid maternity leave, 45 before and 45 after the child's birth. Limited to women employed in the formal sector.

The Philippines

Maternity leave for married women in the private sector for two weeks before delivery and one month after birth, with modest compensation. In the public sector the total is 60 days. Policy applies only to first 4 deliveries, live or stillbirth.

Poland

Maternity leave at full pay for 16 weeks after childbirth, or 18 weeks if second child or more. Educational leave may be taken for 24 months after the maternity leave (36 months if single mother), with payment only if the income for one family member is less than 25% of the average annual income in the state economy.

South Africa

Not known.

Sweden

12 months job-protected parental leave with 90% of salary. Fathers also receive 10 days paid leave at time of birth, to provide support to the mother and care for other children in the family.

United Kingdom

Statutory right for women to stop work 11 weeks before the birth and return to existing employment up to 29 weeks following birth. Payment 90% of earnings for 6 weeks, then low flat rate payment for additional 12 weeks.

USA

No national guarantee. Some states legislate unpaid maternity leave (maximum 12 weeks), and some insurance plans provide partial wage replacement.

Venezuela	Job protection during pregnancy and for one year after the birth. Full-salary maternity leave for 6 weeks before and 12 weeks after the birth.
Vietnam	Six months of maternity leave for women employed in the public sector, with job protection and full pay.
Zimbabwe	Maternity leave for 90 days with guarantee of the job, at 75% of salary.

Note: In this appendix parental leave always refers to time away from work for which either the father or the mother is eligible.

———— Appendix 2 ————

COMPARATIVE DEMOGRAPHIC DATA

Country	No. children under 5 (thousands) 1990-92	infant mortality rate (per 1000)	total fertility rate (per woman)	% urban/rural (children)	% women in work force w/ young children
Australia	1,234	8	1.9	83/17	45
Brazil	18,963	63	3.5	69/31	50
Canada	1,822	7	1.7	78/22	60
China	112,328	32	2.5	27/73	47
Colombia	5,139	40	3.1	70/30	NK
C.I.S.	17,222	24	2.4	65/36	NK
Denmark	297	8	1.6	95/05	95
Finland	308	6	1.7	NK	80
France	3,799	8	1.8	73/27	58
Germany	4,303	9	1.5	48/52(FRG)	35(FRG)
Hungary	603	20	1.8	60/40	74
India	114,364	99	4.3	22/78	NK
Israel	491	12	3.0	90/10	52
Italy	2,789	11	1.3	NK	NK
Japan	6,842	5	1.7	NK	NK
Kenya	4,675	72	7.0	NK	NK

Mexico	11,588	43	3.6	62/37	33
Nicaragua	690	62	5.5	NK	NK
Norway	275	7	1.9	75/25	72
Peru	2,851	88	4.0	70/30	NK
Philippines	9,192	45	4.3	41/59	49
Poland	3,036	18	2.2	58/42	41
South Africa	4,873	72	4.5	NK	NK
Sweden	542	6	2.1	81/19	86
United Kingdom	3,836	9	1.8	NK	46
U.S.A.	18,310	10	1.8	74/26	56
Venezuela	2,739	36	3.8	81/19	18
Vietnam	9,320	37	4.0	16/84	NK
Zimbabwe	1,714	66	5.8	NK	NK

Note: NK means not known

Sources: Statistical Chart on Children 1990, Statistical Office, United Nations Department of International Economic and Social Affairs, United Nations, New York, NY 10017, and the Handbook contributors.

SELECTED BIBLIOGRAPHY

Anderson, Jeanine. (1989). "Women's Community Service and Child Welfare in Urban Peru." In Leslie, Joanne and Michael Paolisso (Eds.), *Women, Work, and Child Welfare in the Third World*, pp. 237–253. Boulder, Colo.: Westview Press.

Andersson, B. E. (1992). "Effects of Day Care on Cognitive and Socio-emotional Competence in Thirteen-year-old Swedish School Children." *Child Development, 63,* 20–36.

Andersson, B. E. (1989). "Effects of Public Day-Care: A Longitudinal Study." *Child Development, 60,* 857–866.

Arango, Marta. (1982). "Implementing Alternative Programs for the Healthy Development of Young Children: A Challenge for Social and Economic Development." CINDE, Medellín.

Belsky, J. (1990). "Parental and Non-parental Child Care and Children's Socio-emotional Development: A Decade in Review." *Journal of Marriage and the Family, 51,* 885–903.

Belsky, Jay. (1984). "Two Waves of Day Care Research: Developmental Effects and Conditions of Quality." In R. Ainslie (Ed.), *The Child and the Day Care Setting.* New York: Praeger.

Boocock, S. S. (1991). "The Japanese Preschool System." In E. R. Beauchamp (Ed.), *Windows on Japanese Education.* Westport, Conn.: Greenwood Press.

Borchorst, A. and Siim, B. (1987). "Women and the Advanced Welfare State: A New Kind of Patriarchal Power?" In Sassoon, A. S. (Ed.), *Women and the State: The Shifting Boundaries of Public and Private.* London: Hutchinson.

Brennan, Deborah and O'Donnell, Carol. (1986). *Caring for Australia's Children: Political and Industrial Issues in Child Care.* Sydney: Allen and Unwin.

Broberg, A. (1989). *Child Care and Early Development.* Department of Psychology, University of Göteborg, Sweden.

Cochran, M. (1982). "Profits and Policy: Child Care in America." In R. Rist (Ed.), *Policy Studies Annals,* Vol. 6, pp. 537–549.

Corsaro, W., and Emiliani, F. (1992). "Child Care, Early Education, and Children's Peer Culture in Italy." In M. Lamb and K. Sternberg (Eds.), *The Cultural Context of Nonparental Care Arrangements*. Hillsdale, N.J.: Lawrence Erlbaum.

Cox, Eva (1983). " 'Pater-patria': Child-rearing and the State." In Cora V. Baldock and Bettina Cass (Eds.), *Women, Social Welfare and the State*, pp. 188–200. Sydney: George Allen and Unwin.

Dencik, L., Langsted, O. and Sommer, D. (1989). "Modern Childhood in the Nordic Countries: Material, Social and Cultural Aspects." In B. Elgaard, O. Langsted, and D. Sommer (Eds.), *Research on Socialization of Young Children in the Nordic Countries—An Annotated and Selected Bibliography*. Århus: Aarhus University Press.

Dunn, J. and Scarr, S. (1987). *Mother Care/Other Care*. London: Basic Books.

Fein, G. and Fox, N. (1988). "Infant Day-Care: A Societal Issue." *Early Childhood Research Quarterly, 3*, 227–234.

Kahn, A. and Kamerman, S. (1987). *Child Care: Facing the Hard Choices*. Dover, Mass.: Auburn House.

Kamerman, S. and Kahn, A. (1981). *Child Care, Family Benefits, and Working Parents*. New York: Columbia University Press.

Kiporir, L. I. and Mwaura, L.P.K. (1988). "Partnership in Development: Experiences in Early Childhood Education in Kenya." In *Towards a Brighter Future*, p. 77. Bernard van Leer Foundation, The Hague.

Lamb, M. E., Hwang, C., Bookstein, F. L., Broberg, A., Hult, G., and Frodi, M. (1988). "Determinants of Competence in Swedish Preschoolers." *Developmental Psychology, 24*, 58–70.

Lamb, M., Sternberg, K., Hwang, C. P., Broberg, A. (Eds.) (1992). *Child Care in Context: Cross-Cultural Perspectives*. Hillsdale, N.J.: Lawrence Erlbaum.

Leira, A. (1987). *Day Care for Children in Denmark, Norway and Sweden*. Institute for Social Research, Report nr. 5, Oslo.

Leira, A. (1989). *Models of Motherhood. Welfare State Policies and Everyday Practices: The Scandinavian Experience*. Oslo: Institute for Social Research.

LeVine, R. and White, M. (1986). *Human Conditions: The Cultural Basis of Educational Development*. New York: Routledge and Kegan Paul.

Mitchell, A., Seligson, M. and Marx, F. (1989). *Early Childhood Programs: Between Promise and Practice*. Dover, Mass.: Auburn, House.

Myers, Robert G. (To be published in 1993). "The Twelve Who Survive." Paris: UNESCO, and New York: The Consultative Group on Early Childhood Care and Development.

New, R. (1989). "The Family Context of Italian Infant Care." *Early Child Development and Care, 50*, 99–108.

Okin, S. M. (1989). *Justice, Gender, and the Family*. New York: Basic Books.

Olmstead, P. and Weikart, D. (1989). *How Nations Serve Young Children: Profiles of Child Care and Education in Fourteen Countries*. Ypsilanti, Mich.: High/Scope Press.

Pence, A. R. (1989). "In the Shadow of Mother-Care: Contexts for an Understanding of Child Day Care in Canada." *Canadian Psychology, 30*(2), 140–147.

Phillips, D. (Ed.). (1987). *Quality in Child Care: What Does the Research Tell Us?*

Washington, D.C.: National Association for the Education of Young Children.

Powell, D. (1989). *Families and Early Childhood Programs*. Washington, D.C.: National Association for the Education of Young Children.

Richardson, G., and Marx, E. (1989). *A Welcome for Every Child: How France Achieves Quality in Child Care*. Report of the child care study panel of the French-American Foundation. New York: The French-American Foundation.

Rosemberg, F. (Ed.). (1989). *Creche.* (Day Care.) São Paulo: Cortez.

Sagi, A., Lamb, M. E., Lewkowicz, K. S., Shoham, R., Dvir, R., and Estes, D. (1985). "Security of Infant-Mother, -Father, and -Metapelet Attachments among Kibbutz-Reared Israeli Children." In I. Bretherton and E. Waters, (Eds.), *Growing Points in Attachment Theory and Research. Monographs of the Society for Research in Child Development, 50,* (1–2, Serial No. 209), 257–275.

Swaminathan, M. (1985). *Who Cares: A Study of Child Care Facilities for Low Income Working Women in India.* New Delhi: Indraprastha Press.

van den Berg, O. and Vergnani, T. (1986). *Providing Services for Preschool Children in South Africa.* Bellville, S.A.: The University of the Western Cape.

van den Berg, O. and Vergnani, T. (Eds.). (1987). *Door to the Future: The Preschool Child in South Africa.* Bellville, S.A.: The University of the Western Cape.

Whitebook, M., Howes, C. and Phillips, D. (Principal Investigators). (1989). *Who Cares? Child Care Teachers and The Quality of Care in America.* Oakland, Calif.: Child Care Employee Project.

Zigler, E. F. and Goodman, J. (1982). "The Battle for Day Care in America: A View from the Trenches." In E. F. Zigler and E. W. Gordon (Eds.), *Day Care: Scientific and Social Policy Issues.* Boston: Auburn House.

INDEX

Employer-supported care, 25–27, 42–
44, 237, 255–56, 257–60, 340, 358,
384, 395–96, 420, 423, 444, 457,
501, 525, 526, 540, 588, 594;
advantages of, 25, 396, 594;
disadvantages of, 26–27, 256, 264–
65, 396; union involvement, 18, 25,
42

Employment: informal/unorganized
work sector, 252, 334, 336, 354,
416, 421, 436–37, 473; part-time,
14–15, 129, 146, 168, 216, 282,
318, 355, 497–98, 518; women and,
14–17, 36, 62, 69, 121, 127, 128–
29, 145–46, 167–69, 187, 190,
215–16, 232–33, 234, 251–53, 269,
271, 273, 294, 298, 313, 317–20,
335–36, 354, 355, 357, 392, 416–
17, 435, 436–37, 456, 497–98, 509,
518, 537–38, 562, 565, 585, 609–
10

Empowerment, 112, 114–15, 117,
118, 203–5, 338–39, 346, 348–49,
362, 366–72, 441, 617, 623, 624,
644, 654

Equity, 113, 276, 321, 327, 337, 395–
96, 400, 406, 454, 456, 469–88,
499, 510, 610; and employment,
168–69, 318, 610; gender, 168–69,
235–36, 610, 655, 657. *See also*
Ideologies; Policy purposes

Erikson, E., 501

Europe, 642, 655

Europe, Eastern, 635, 641, 644, 648

European Economic Community
(EEC), impact on child care policies,
169, 206, 515, 522, 525, 532, 627,
632

Exploitation. *See* Discrimination

Family day care, 137–38, 158–59,
176–77, 196, 198, 200, 207, 216–
18, 220–21, 261, 360, 384–85, 396,
397, 398–99, 425–26, 428, 474,
478, 481–82, 492, 510, 521, 525–
26, 541, 574, 576–79, 590, 595–96,
641–42; advantages of, 137, 159,
177, 207, 218, 221, 285, 372, 426,

510, 578, 596, 636, 641, 642; costs
of, 22, 114, 137, 198–200, 399,
541, 636; disadvantages of, 207,
220, 426–27, 578, 579–80, 596;
incentives for, 198, 399, 526; as
national strategy, 110–11, 114–15,
372, 595, 642; working conditions,
27–28, 399, 526. *See also* Quality of
care; Regulation; Training

Family patterns: alternatives to
traditional, 62, 86, 88, 126, 137–38,
147, 233, 242, 251, 257, 291, 298–
302, 305, 315–16, 317, 335, 356,
400, 455, 473–74, 498, 519, 537,
567, 584–86, 607–10, 631, 634;
effects of industrialization and
urbanization, 35, 119, 232, 315,
356, 473, 567, 630; impacts on
public child care, 62, 225, 356, 634;
traditional, 64, 119, 189, 212–14,
225, 250–51, 292, 295, 353, 357,
394, 417, 431–34, 472, 498, 519,
537, 566–72, 583–84, 605–7, 634;
and transfer of cultural values, 242,
341, 474, 609, 631

Family planning, 87–88, 190, 233,
234, 299, 334, 433, 440, 563, 585,
588–89, 597–98

Family policies, 151–53, 170–72, 233–
36; impacts on child care, 93–94,
129–30, 150, 221–22, 238, 299,
637. *See also* Child allowance; Child
care allowance; Parental leave

Fathers, 146, 152, 177, 221, 393,
410–11, 497–98, 518

Female-headed households. *See* Single
parent families

Feminism, 49–52, 298–301, 644. *See
also* Liberation; Women

Ferry, J., 190, 209

Financing, 28–29, 43–44, 77, 112,
114, 118–19, 132, 137, 152, 198–
200, 225, 275–76, 323–24, 339,
358, 359, 360, 366, 367, 368, 370,
382–83, 384, 395, 408–9, 422–23,
443, 458, 460, 465, 478–80, 488,
504, 512, 526, 532, 539, 551, 593–
94, 619, 622, 625, 636, 641

ABOUT THE EDITOR AND CONTRIBUTORS

JEANINE ANDERSON is Project Director, Working Group on Urban Services and Low-Income Women, in Lima, Peru.

MARTA ARANGO is Director of the International Center for Education and Human Development, which is located in Ft. Lauderdale, Florida, U.S.A. and serves as a base for her work with many governmental and nongovernmental agencies and organizations in Colombia and elsewhere in the world.

JOSEFINA FIERRO DE ASCANIO is Associate Professor of Psychology and Coordinator of the Graduate Program in Human Development at the Central University of Venezuela in Caracas.

INGERID BØ is a Senior Lecturer in Early Childhood Education and Child Care at the School of Education in Stavanger, Norway. Her research interests include the ecology of childhood, child care, and parent-caregiver relations.

DEBORAH BRENNAN is a Lecturer on Social Policy in the Department of Government and Social Administration at the University of Sidney, in Australia.

ROSELY N. E. CHADA is National Coordinator of the Early Childhood Education and Care Program, in the Ministry of Education and Culture, Harare, Zimbabwe.

GUADALUPE CHAPELA is a research assistant with the Population Council Office in Mexico City, Mexico.

PHAM MAI CHI is Deputy Director, Institute for Early Childhood Studies,

Ministry of Education and Training, Hanoi, Vietnam. Her research is in the areas of child nutrition and child development.

MONCRIEFF COCHRAN is a Professor of Human Development and Family Studies in the College of Human Ecology at Cornell University, Ithaca, New York, U.S.A. His research interests include child care, social networks, and the empowerment process.

BRONWEN COHEN is Director of the Scottish Child and Family Alliance, Scotland's national agency for statutory and voluntary organizations and professionals working with children and their families.

JOSETTE COMBES is Coordinator of the Association of Child-Parent Collectives, a non-governmental body in France that provides technical support to parents and professionals for the creation of parental day care centers.

YEKATERINA V. FOTEEVA is a senior researcher at the Institute of Sociology, C.I.S. Academy of Sciences, Moscow, engaged in research in family sociology and family policy.

SUKHDEEP GILL is an Associate Professor in the Department of Child Development, College of Home Science, at Pujab Agricultural University in Ludhiana, India, with research interest in child rearing, families, and public child care.

LARS GUNNARSSON is an Associate Professor at the Department of Education and Educational Research, Gothenburg University, Mölndal, Sweden. His research interests include child care, social networks, and the ecology of human development.

EEVA HUTTUNEN is a Professor in the Faculty of Education at the University of Joensuu, in Joensuu, Finland. Her research interests include home-day care collaboration and the ecology of child care.

LEA I. KIPKORIR is Director of the Kenya Institute of Education in Nairobi. Her special interests are in the design, development, and preparation of curricular materials and in the training of early childhood personnel.

ROBERT KLEIN was director of the Program on Child Health and Adolescent Fertility at the Population Council Office in Mexico City, Mexico.

EWA KORCZAK is a Senior Lecturer in the Department of Education and Psychology at the University of Silesia in Katowice, Poland.

NINA KOREN-KARIE is on the faculty of the Department of Psychology at the University of Haifa, Israel.

OLE LANGSTED is an Associate Professor at the National Danish School of Social Work in Aarhus, Denmark. His research involves the Danish day care system and the life conditions and everyday experiences of young children in Denmark and the other Nordic countries.

EDITH LASSEGARD is a graduate student in the Department of Human Service Studies, College of Human Ecology, Cornell University. She worked for several years in early childhood education settings in Japan.

DOROTEO MENDOZA is a research assistant at the Population Council Office in Mexico City, Mexico.

MILDRED MKHULISI is Principal of Zandile Primary School, in Umlazi, Natal Province, South Africa.

MÁRIA NEMÉNYI is a Senior Researcher at the Institute of Sociology of the Hungarian Academy of Sciences in Budapest. Her focus is on family sociology, including the social representation of the family, and social policy related to families with children.

REBECCA S. NEW is an Associate Professor in the Department of Education at the University of New Hampshire, Durham, New Hampshire. Her research involves crosscultural comparisons of child-rearing practices, with particular interest in Italy and day care in the U.S. context.

MARÍA ROSA FRIAS DE ORANTES teaches human development at the School of Psychology and conducts research at the Institute of Psychology, Central University of Venezuela in Caracas.

LUZ G. PALATTAO-CORPUS is Executive Director, Institute of Child-Youth Development and Family Life Research, Children's Medical Center, Manila, the Philippines.

ALAN R. PENCE is a Professor in the School of Child and Youth Care at the University of Victoria, Victoria, B.C., Canada. He is Co-Director of the Canadian National Child Care Study and is currently co-editing an international volume on family day care.

RUDOLF PETTINGER is head of the Department of Family Research and Family Policy at the German Youth Institute in Munich, Germany. His publications are in the fields of family development, the living conditions of young families, day care, and family policy.

DAO VAN PHU has been Deputy Director at the Research Center for Teacher Training and In-Service Training, Ministry of Education and Training, Hanoi, Vietnam. He is a senior teacher and administrator with important contributions to pedagogy, teacher training, and preschool education.

AURORA RÀBAGO is on the staff of the Reproductive Health Section at the Mexican Institute for Social Security, in Mexico City, Mexico.

ILEANA RECAGNO-PUENTE is Associate Professor of Psychology and

Head of the Applied Psychology Department at the Central University of Venezuela in Caracas. Her research interests include patterns of upbringing, quality of life, and development in middle- and lower-class children.

FULVIA ROSEMBERG is a Professor in Psychology at the University of São Paulo and a senior researcher at the Carlos Chagas Institute in São Paulo, Brazil. Her research interests include the life of Brazilian black families and their children, day care curriculum and evaluation, and women and development.

ABRAHAM SAGI is a professor in the Department of Psychology at the University of Haifa, in Israel. Topics in his research program have included attachment, fatherhood, and crosscultural studies.

ELIZABETH SHRADER is a private consultant living in Mexico and working in the areas of women's health and development. Her recent research has focused on women's work and nonmaternal child care strategies.

DION SOMMER is a Senior Research Fellow at the Institute of Psychology, Aarhus, Denmark. His research interests have included children's play, fathers and infants, and the living conditions of young children in Denmark and the other Nordic countries.

POLLY SPEDDING is a Senior Extension Associate in the Department of Human Development and Family Studies, College of Human Ecology, Cornell University, Ithaca, New York, U.S.A., where she specializes in child care, day care, and early childhood education.

KATHRYN TOLBERT is Director of the Regional Program on Reproductive and Child Health of the Population Council's Regional Office for Latin America and the Caribbean, in Mexico City, Mexico.

ANNABEL TORRES is a staff member with the Centro de Education y Communicacion (CANTERA) in Managua, Nicaragua.

TRAN THI TRONG is Director of the Institute for Early Childhood Studies, Ministry of Education and Training, Hanoi, Vietnam. She is a coordinator of the Parent Education Program being supported by UNICEF and UNFPA, with considerable experience in preschool education and methodology and preschool education reform.

MERJA-MAARIA TURUNEN is a senior researcher in the Planning Department at the National Social and Health Ministry in Helsinki, Finland.

WEI ZHENGAO headed the Division of Early Childhood Education of the Department of Primary Education in the Chinese Ministry of Education from 1983 until her retirement in 1988. She served as a member of the Experts' Committee of the China Children's Development Center between 1984 and 1987 and has lectured on early childhood education in 15 Chinese provinces and municipalities.